Lecture Notes of the Institute for Computer Sciences, Social Informatics and Telecommunications Engineering 585

AF148049

The LNICST series publishes ICST's conferences, symposia and workshops.
LNICST reports state-of-the-art results in areas related to the scope of the Institute.
The type of material published includes

- Proceedings (published in time for the respective event)
- Other edited monographs (such as project reports or invited volumes)

LNICST topics span the following areas:

- General Computer Science
- E-Economy
- E-Medicine
- Knowledge Management
- Multimedia
- Operations, Management and Policy
- Social Informatics
- Systems

Xiang Chen · Xijun Wang · Shangjing Lin ·
Jing Liu
Editors

IoT as a Service

9th EAI International Conference, IoTaaS 2023
Nanjing, China, October 27–29, 2023
Proceedings

 Springer

Editors
Xiang Chen
Sun Yat-sen University
Guangzhou, China

Xijun Wang
Sun Yat-sen University
Guangzhou, China

Shangjing Lin
Beijing University of Posts
and Telecommunications
Beijing, China

Jing Liu
Jinling Institute of Technology
Nanjing, China

ISSN 1867-8211   ISSN 1867-822X (electronic)
Lecture Notes of the Institute for Computer Sciences, Social Informatics
and Telecommunications Engineering
ISBN 978-3-031-70506-9   ISBN 978-3-031-70507-6 (eBook)
https://doi.org/10.1007/978-3-031-70507-6

This Springer imprint is published by the registered company Springer Nature Switzerland AG
The registered company address is: Gewerbestrasse 11, 6330 Cham, Switzerland

If disposing of this product, please recycle the paper.

Preface

We are delighted to introduce the proceedings of EAI IoTaaS 2023 - the 9th International Conference on Intelligent IoT. This conference, Making Civilized Life Gorgeous, aimed to bring together researchers and industry experts to present state-of-the-art research work on the challenges and developments related to IoT systems. This conference provided a domestic and international exchange and docking platform in the field of IoT, which plays an important role in absorbing the essence of the latest research achievements. At the same time, the conference promoted the integration of overseas talents and domestic scientific and technological forces, advanced high-level cooperative research and academic exchanges, and accelerated the rapid development of technology in IoT and communications.

The technical program of IoTaaS 2023 consisted of 33 full papers in oral presentation sessions. The conference tracks were: Track 1-Main Track; Track 2-Late Track. Aside from the high-quality technical paper presentations, the technical program also featured two keynote speeches and three technical workshops. The two keynote speeches were by Huaglory Tianfield from Glasgow Caledonian University, UK and Chong-Yung Chi from National Tsing Hua University, Taiwan.The three workshops organized were the 4th International EAI Workshop on Edge Intelligence and Computing for IoT Communications and Applications, the EAI International Workshop on Satellite Internet Network (SatNet 2023) and Transmission, Access and Route Technology for Internet of Vehicle.

Coordination with the steering chairs Bo Li, Huaglory Tianfield, Ren Ping Liu and Hui Tian was essential for the success of the conference. We sincerely appreciate their constant support and guidance. It was also a great pleasure to work with such an excellent organizing committee team for their hard work in organizing and supporting the conference, in particular, the Technical Program Committee, led by our TPC Co-Chairs, Xiang Chen, Changle Li and Zhongjiang Yan, completed the peer-review process of technical papers and made a high-quality technical program. We are also grateful to the Conference Manager, Jin Tian, for his support, and to all the authors who submitted their papers to the IoTaaS 2023 conference and workshops.

We strongly believe that EAI IoTaaS provides a good forum for all researchers, developers and practitioners to discuss all science and technology aspects that are relevant to Intelligent IoT systems. We also expect that future EAI IoTaaS conferences will be as successful and stimulating, as indicated by the contributions presented in this volume.

Jin Tian

Xiang Chen

Mao Yang

Changle Li

Zhongjiang Yan

Xijun Wang

Shangjing Lin

Jing Liu

Organization

Steering Committee

Bo Li	Northwestern Polytechnical University, China
Huaglory Tianfield	Glasgow Caledonian University, UK
Ren Ping Liu	University of Technology Sydney, Australia
Hui Tian	Beijing University of Posts and Telecommunications, China

Organizing Committee

General Chair

Jin Tian	Jinling Institute of Technology, China

General Co-chairs

Liang Xia	Xiamen University, China
Bo Li	Northwestern Polytechnical University, China

TPC Chair and Co-chairs

Xiang Chen	Sun Yat-sen University, China
Changle Li	Xidian University, China
Zhongjiang Yan	Northwestern Polytechnical University, China
Mao Yang	Northwestern Polytechnical University, China

Sponsorship and Exhibit Chair

Ji Ma	Jinling Institute of Technology, China

Local Chair

Qiong Yang   Jinling Institute of Technology, China

Workshops Chair

Xijun Wang   Sun Yat-sen University, China

Publicity and Social Media Chair

Jing Liu   Jinling Institute of Technology, China

Publications Chair

Shangjing Lin   Beijing University of Posts and
                                      Telecommunications, China
Xijun Wang   Sun Yat-sen University, China

Web Chair

Jing Liu   Jinling Institute of Technology, China

Technical Program Committee

Xiang Chen   Sun Yat-sen University, China
Changle Li   Xidian University, China
Zhongjiang Yan   Northwestern Polytechnical University, China
Xu Jing   Xi'an Jiaotong University, China
Jie Gong   Sun Yat-sen University, China
Xinghua Sun   Sun Yat-sen University, China
Zhijian Lin   Fuzhou University, China
Xiang Chen   Sun Yat-sen University, China
Yan Zhang   Beijing Institute of Technology, China
Shihui Zheng   Tsinghua University, China
Xijun Wang   Sun Yat-sen University, China
Ruxin Zhi   Beijing Information Science & Technology
                                      University, China

Fasheng Zhou   Guangzhou University, China
Yanzhao Hou   Beijing Information Science & Technology
                            University, China
Kai Liang   Xidian University, China
Sheng Zhou   Tsinghua University, China

Contents

Main Track

Optimal Access Point Selection Approach for User-Centric Cell-Free Massive MIMO Systems

Weifeng Ma[1], Xinghua Sun[1(✉)], Xijun Wang[2], and Wen Zhan[1]

[1] School of Electronics and Communication Engineering, Sun Yat-sen University, Shenzhen 518107, China
mawf3@mail2.sysu.edu.cn, {sunxinghua,zhanw6}@mail.sysu.edu.cn
[2] School of Electronics and Information Technology, Sun Yat-sen University, Guangzhou 510006, China
wangxijun@mail.sysu.edu.cn

Abstract. Recently, the Cell-Free Massive Multiple-Input Multiple-Out-put (MIMO) architecture has emerged as a promising solution for future wireless communication systems, where a substantial number of distributed wireless Access Points (APs) concurrently serve a significantly smaller count of User Equipment (UE). In this paper, we study the AP selection problem in user-centric cell-free massive MIMO, where each user is served by a restricted number of APs. To address this problem, we propose a Branch-And-Bound (BAB)-based AP selection algorithm to achieve maximum channel capacity, which is designed to efficiently obtain the optimal subset of APs for each user. Our simulation results show that the proposed algorithm outperforms other baseline methods in terms of channel capacity at the expense of some complexity. Meanwhile, our complexity is much lower than the exhaustive search, which also yields optimal results.

Keywords: Cell-Free Massive MIMO · User-Centric · AP selection

1 Introduction

Cell-Free Massive Multiple-Input Multiple-Output (MIMO) has emerged as a promising alternative network topology, attracting considerable interest due to its potential to mitigate inter-cell interference under the conventional cellular structure [1]. In cell-free massive MIMO networks, a multitude of geographically dispersed wireless Access Points (APs) are linked to a Central Processing Unit (CPU) through optical fibers, cooperatively serving all users by conjugate beamforming [2]. However, under this architecture, every user is simultaneously served by all available APs, leading to an elevated workload for each AP and a substantial increase in backhaul overhead [3]. To facilitate practical implementation [4], a user-centric framework is gaining increasing momentum, wherein each user is served exclusively by a restricted number of APs [5].

© ICST Institute for Computer Sciences, Social Informatics and Telecommunications Engineering 2025
Published by Springer Nature Switzerland AG 2025. All Rights Reserved
X. Chen et al. (Eds.): IoTaaS 2023, LNICST 585, pp. 3–15, 2025.
https://doi.org/10.1007/978-3-031-70507-6_1

In a User-Centric Cell-Free Massive MIMO system, every user is surrounded by neighboring serving APs, thereby forming a virtual cell [6]. This provides the following benefits: initially, each AP serves a subset of users, efficiently reducing the burden and power consumption. Furthermore, the data transmission from the AP to the CPU is minimized, resulting in a significant reduction in backhaul overhead. A proper AP selection scheme then becomes crucial since otherwise users can not obtain a good Quality of Service (QoS) [5] or high energy efficiency [7].

Several studies have been performed to obtain user-centric virtual cells by AP selection in cell-free massive MIMO networks [8–15]. One approach involves the user selecting a predetermined number of APs based on the optimal channel quality or minimal distance criteria [8–11]. Alternatively, each user can select the APs that collectively contribute a specified percentage to the overall channel gain [12,13]. In addition, the work [14] proposed a method named Average Channel Gain Based (ACGB) selection, i.e., each AP computes the average specification of the estimated channels of all User Equipment (UE), subsequently serving those UE whose channel specification is greater than the average. The work [15] investigated the problem from a game-theoretic perspective and formulated the creation of user-centric AP service clusters as a localized altruistic game. However, none of the above schemes can reach the upper limit of channel capacity for an individual user.

In this paper, we address the problem of selecting an appropriate subset of APs in the context of user-centric cell-free massive MIMO. Specifically, we derive the channel capacity in this scenario as our objective, followed by constructing a new objective function. This function applies to the Branch-And-Bound [16] (BAB) algorithm, which is commonly used to solve integer programming problems. Finally, a BAB-based AP selection algorithm is proposed to efficiently obtain an optimal solution to maximize the channel capacity. By comparing our approach with other baseline approaches, we find that the proposed method achieves better performance with an acceptable increase in computational complexity. To the best of our knowledge, this is the first research on AP selection schemes for individual users in cell-free massive MIMO systems, aiming at channel capacity optimization.

The remainder of the paper is structured as follows. In Sect. 2, we present the channel model of cell-free massive MIMO and derives the channel capacity expression. Section 3 describes the principle and detailed implementation of the BAB-based AP selection algorithm. Numerical results and discussions are provided in Sect. 4. Finally, we conclude the paper in Sect. 5.

2   System Model

Consider a user-centric cell-free massive MIMO network containing one UE and N access points. Within this cell-free network, a total of N geographically dispersed APs are all interconnected to a CPU through optical fibers, collectively providing service to the UEs. As Fig. 1 illustrates, each AP equips one single antenna and scatters randomly around the UE, whereas the UE is equipped with $M \geq 1$ antennas. We assume a flat fading channel, and it is presumed that the channel state information from all APs to the UE is accessible. Note that the analysis within this work focuses on the downlink scenario, the analysis can be extended to the uplink scenario due to the channel's symmetry.

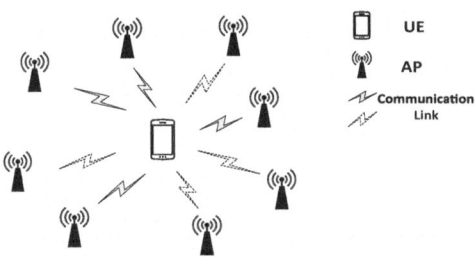

Fig. 1. A graphical illustration of the user-centric cell-free massive MIMO scenario containing one UE and N randomly-located APs, where the antennas at the UE are omitted for simplicity.

2.1   Channel Model

In the proposed network, the received signal at the UE through the channel fading, denoted as $\mathbf{r}$, is given by

$$\mathbf{r} = \mathbf{H}\mathbf{s} + \mathbf{n}, \tag{1}$$

where $\mathbf{s}$ denotes the $(N \times 1)$ transmitted signal. Here, $\mathbf{n}$ represents additive Gaussian noise with a zero mean and a variance of σ_n^2. Specifically, $\mathbf{H}$ represents an $M \times N$ channel matrix, within which each h_{mk} signifies the fading coefficient between the mth antenna at the user and the kth access point, where $m \in \{1, 2, \cdots, M\}$ and $k \in \{1, 2, \cdots, N\}$. These coefficients are related to the distance vector $d = [d_1, d_2, ..., d_N]^T$, where d_k signifies the distance between the user and the kth AP. Hence, the channel matrix $\mathbf{H}$ can be written as

$$\mathbf{H} = [\mathbf{h}_1(d_1), \mathbf{h}_2(d_2), ..., \mathbf{h}_N(d_N)], \tag{2}$$

where $\mathbf{h}_k(d_k) = [h_{1k}(d_k), h_{2k}(d_k), ..., h_{Mk}(d_k)]^T$.

Moreover, this study has taken into account a comprehensive compound channel model that encompasses the cumulative impact of path loss, shadow fading, and small-scale fading. The path loss is determined according to the fading with an exponent denoted by α, while the shadow fading is modeled using a normal distribution. Additionally, the small-scale fading follows a Rayleigh fading distribution. Let $s_k(d_k)$ refers to the average mean power of the shadow fading, then its logarithmic form s_{dB} satisfies the following distribution

$$s_{dB} = 10 \lg(s_k(d_k)) \sim \mathcal{N}(u_{dB}, \sigma_{dB}^2), \tag{3}$$

where σ_{dB} is the standard variance of $10\lg(s_k(d_k))$, μ_{dB} represents the logarithmic mean of $s_k(d_k)$ measured in dB, and $\mathcal{N}(\mu_{dB}, \sigma_{dB}^2)$ denotes Gaussian distribution with mean μ_{dB} and variance σ_{dB}^2. Furthermore, u_{dB} is determined by the path loss and can be obtained from

$$u_{dB} = 10\lg(P_T/N) - \alpha \times 10 \times \lg(d_i), \tag{4}$$

where P_T represents the total transmitted power from all the N APs and α represents the exponent of path loss.

Combining Eqs. (3) and (4), the fading coefficient between the mth antenna at the user and the kth access point with a distance d_k, denoted as $h_{mk}(d_k)$, can be obtained as

$$h_{mk}(d_k) = \mathcal{N}(0, \sqrt{\frac{s_k(d_k)}{2}}) + j\mathcal{N}(0, \sqrt{\frac{s_k(d_k)}{2}}). \tag{5}$$

2.2 Channel Capacity

In this paper, we assume perfect Channel State Information (CSI) is available at the transmitter, and the channel is considered to be independent and identically distributed (i.i.d). Supposing that the total transmitted power is set at a unit magnitude and the water-filling power allocation is applied, which is confirmed to be optimal. The transmission power of the kth AP when applying the water-filling method, denoted as P_k is given by

$$P_k = max\left(\left(u - \frac{\sigma^2}{\|\mathbf{h}_k\|}\right), 0\right), \tag{6}$$

where $\mathbf{h}_k$ is the kth column of $\mathbf{H}$, $k \in \{1, 2, \cdots, N\}$. Here u is a global constant and should be properly chosen to guarantee

$$P_{total} = \sum_{k=1}^{N} P_k = 1. \tag{7}$$

Referring to the channel analysis of distributed MIMO in [17] and combining Eqs. (6) and (7), we can derive the channel capacity of the MIMO system C as follows:

$$C = \log_2 \det[\mathbf{I}_M + \frac{1}{\sigma_n^2}\mathbf{HQH}^H], \tag{8}$$

where $\mathbf{Q} = \text{diag}(P_1, P_2, ..., P_N)$ represents the power allocation matrix at the transmitter, subject to the constraint $\text{tr}(\mathbf{Q}) = P_T$, and $\mathbf{I}_M$ is an M-dimensional identity matrix, while σ_n^2 corresponds to the variance of additive Gaussian noise and the operator $(\cdot)^H$ denotes conjugate transpose.

3   Bab-Based Selection Algorithm

In the previous sections, we have characterized the channel matrix $\mathbf{H}$ as well as the channel capacity C in the proposed user-centric cell-free massive MIMO scenario. Intuitively, as the number of available APs arises, better communication service quality guarantees to the UE. To optimize energy utilization and conserve total transmit power, a fixed number of APs are selected and connected to the UE. Hence, in this section, we focus on the optimization of the channel capacity C considering the constraint that the maximum amount of the optional APs, denoted as L and $0 < L \leq N$, for the UE to access each time is restricted.

The above AP selection problem could be further formulated as a mathematical matrix subset selection problem, which exhibits striking similarities to the problems of antenna selection and beam selection and numerous algorithms have been employed to address this type of problem. Among all the existing algorithms, the Branch-And-Bound (BAB) algorithm exhibits significant potential in attaining the global optimal solution while reducing complexity, compared with the exhaustive search [18]. The fundamental concept of the BAB algorithm revolves around constructing a search tree while incorporating pruning operations.

Specifically, the objective of the AP selection problem addressed in this paper is to derive the optimal L-amount subset out of N available APs considering the channel condition from each AP, in order to obtain the maximum channel capacity in the restricted situation. To tackle this problem, the BAB algorithm will be applied as the proposed solution methodology.

Note that performing a water-filling algorithm for each potential selection outcome can impose a significant computational burden. Hence we simplify the problem by initially assuming an average power distribution during the AP selection process and employing the water-filling method on the selected result to obtain the optimal power allocation scheme.

Let $\mathbf{H}_{opt}$ denotes the optimal channel matrix after selecting the optimal L-amount AP subset in the proposed network, which could be derived as

$$\mathbf{H}_{opt} = \arg \max_{\mathbf{H}_{sub} \subseteq \mathbf{H}} \left[\log_2 \det \left(\mathbf{I}_M + \frac{1}{N \times \sigma^2} \mathbf{H}_{sub} \mathbf{H}_{sub}^H \right) \right], \tag{9}$$

where $\mathbf{H}_{sub}$ denotes the channel matrix from any L-amount AP subset.

Define $\mathbf{H}_\tau$ as the matrix obtained by choosing τ columns from $\mathbf{H}$ after τth selection. Additionally, C_τ denotes the corresponding channel capacity, where $C_\tau = \log_2 \det(\mathbf{I}_M + \bar{\rho}\mathbf{H}_\tau \mathbf{H}_\tau^H)$ and $\tau = 0, 1, ..., L - 1$.(Note that $C_0 = 0$)

Assuming that in the $(\tau + 1)$th selection step, the k-th column of matrix $\mathbf{H}$, denoted as $\mathbf{h}_k$, will be chosen from the remaining candidate set. The resulting $(\tau + 1) \times M$ submatrix is denoted as $\mathbf{H}_{\tau+1} = [\mathbf{H}_\tau \ \mathbf{h}_k]$.

Accordingly, the channel capacity after τth selection could be obtained as

$$
\begin{aligned}
C_{\tau+1} &= \log_2 \det(\mathbf{I}_M + \bar{\rho}\mathbf{H}_{\tau+1}\mathbf{H}_{\tau+1}^H) \\
&= \log_2 \det(\mathbf{I}_M + \bar{\rho}\mathbf{H}_\tau\mathbf{H}_\tau^H + \bar{\rho}\mathbf{h}_k\mathbf{h}_k^H) \\
&= C_\tau + \log_2 \det(\mathbf{I}_M + \bar{\rho}(\mathbf{I}_M + \bar{\rho}\mathbf{H}_\tau\mathbf{H}_\tau^H)^{-1}\mathbf{h}_k\mathbf{h}_k^H) \\
&\overset{(a)}{=} C_\tau + \underbrace{\log_2\left(1 + \bar{\rho}\mathbf{h}_k^H\mathbf{G}_\tau\mathbf{h}_k\right)}_{\Delta_{k,\tau}},
\end{aligned}
\tag{10}
$$

Algorithm 1. The BAB-based AP Selection Algorithm with Selection Size Constraint

---

1: **INPUT** : original channel matrix $\mathbf{H}$, number of APs to be selected L, SNR$\bar{\rho}$
2: **OUTPUT** : final selected AP index vector $\bar{\mathbf{s}}$
3: Initialization: $\mathbf{G} = \mathbf{I}_M, B = -\infty, \widetilde{C} = M, \tau = 0, J = 0, \mathbf{s} = \mathbf{0}_L, \mathcal{K} = \{1, 2, \cdots, N\},$
$\quad \mathcal{L} = \{0, 1, \cdots, L-1\}, \Delta_0 = \log_2(1 + \bar{\rho}\mathbf{H}^H\mathbf{H})$
4: $\quad \mathcal{I}_\tau = \{\tau+1, \tau+2, ..., (N-L+\tau+1)\} \qquad \forall \tau \in \mathcal{L}$
5: $\quad \mathcal{I}_{\tau,K_\tau} = \{K_\tau+1, K_\tau+2, ..., (N-L+\tau+1)\} \;\; \forall \tau \in \mathcal{L}, \; K_\tau \in \mathcal{I}_{\tau-1}$
6: $\quad v_k = ||\mathbf{h}_k||^2 \qquad \forall k \in \mathcal{K}$
7: $\quad \zeta_m = \max_{k \in \mathcal{I}_m} v_k, \;\; Z_m = \log_2(1 + \bar{\rho}\zeta_m) \;\; \forall m \in \mathcal{K}$
8: $\quad c_k = \widetilde{C} + \Delta_k - Z_\tau \;\; \forall k \in \mathcal{I}_{\tau,K}$
9: **if** $\tau = L - 1$ **then**
10: $\quad$ **if** $\max_{m \in \mathcal{I}_{L-1}} c_m > B$ **then**
11: $\qquad$ update: $[\mathbf{s}]_L = \arg\max_{m \in \mathcal{I}_{L-1}} c_m, \;\; B = \max_{m \in \mathcal{I}_{L-1}} c_m, \;\; \bar{\mathbf{s}} = \mathbf{s}$
12: $\quad$ **end if**
13: **else**
14: $\quad$ sort c_k in descending order and obtain the ordered index vector $\mathbf{k}$.
15: $\quad \mathbf{G}_{tmp} = \mathbf{G}, \mathbf{v}_{tmp,j} = \mathbf{v}_k$
16: $\quad$ **for** $i = 1 : |\mathcal{I}_{\tau,K}|$ **do**
17: $\qquad K = [\mathbf{k}]_i$
18: $\qquad$ **if** $c_K > B$ **then**
19: $\qquad\quad \mathcal{K} = K + 1 : N$
20: $\qquad\quad$ update the index vector $[\mathbf{s}]_{\tau+1} = K$
21: $\qquad\quad \mathbf{g} = \frac{1}{\sqrt{\bar{\rho}^{-1} + v_{tmp,K}}}\mathbf{G}\mathbf{h}_K, \; \mathbf{G} = \mathbf{G}_{tmp} - \mathbf{g}\mathbf{g}^H, \; \widetilde{C} = c_K$
22: $\qquad\quad$ **for** $\forall m \in \mathcal{K}$:
23: $\qquad\qquad \xi_m = \mathbf{h}_m^H\mathbf{g}, \; v_m = v_{tmp,m} - |\xi_m|^2, \; \Delta_m = \log_2(1 + \bar{\rho}v_m)$
24: $\qquad\qquad \tau = \tau + 1$, return to line 8
25: $\qquad$ **else**
26: $\qquad\quad$ break this loop
27: $\qquad$ **end if**
28: $\quad$ **end for**
29: **end if**

---

where $\bar{\rho} = \frac{1}{N \times \sigma^2}$ represents the Signal-to-Noise Ratio(SNR), Step (a) is established using Sylvester's determinant identity and $G_\tau = (\mathbf{I}_M + \bar{\rho}\mathbf{H}_\tau\mathbf{H}_\tau^H)^{-1}$. It is obvious that G_τ is positive definite. As a result, the incremental value $\Delta_{k,\tau}$ presented in Eq. (10) is strictly positive when $\mathbf{h}_k \neq 0$, which implies that the channel capacity C_τ monotonically increases as the number of iteration τ enlarges.

Nevertheless, for efficient pruning, the BAB algorithm is only suitable for the monotonically decreasing functions with the determined maximum or the monotonically increasing functions with the determined minimum. Hence, to derive the maximum channel capacity, we have to reorganize a monotonically-decreasing objective function that accommodates the BAB algorithm, since C_τ in Eq. (10) has been proved to be monotonically increasing. Similar to [16], let

$$\tilde{C}_\tau = C_\tau - \sum_{m=0}^{\tau-1} Z_m, \tag{11}$$

where $Z_m = log_2(1 + \overline{\rho}\zeta_m^2)$ and $\zeta_m = \max_{k\in\mathcal{I}_m} \|\mathbf{h}_k\|_{\mathrm{F}}$. The index set $\mathcal{I}_m$ comprises all the AP indices to be chosen in the mth selection step. The equation in Eq. (11) has a key property presented as follows:

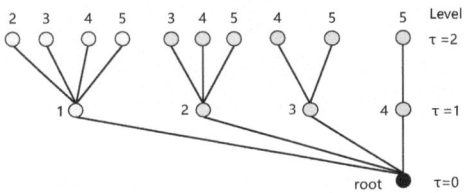

Fig. 2. Example of BAB algorithm: selecting 2 out of 5 APs.

Lemma 1. *The object function $\tilde{C}_\tau$ in Eq. (11) monotonically decreases with τ.*

Proof. See Appendix A.

Based on the property mentioned in Lemma 1, since the offset $\sum_{m=0}^{\tau-1} Z_m$ is solely determined by the channel realization and independent of the selected AP subset, the optimal solution achieved by employing the BAB algorithm for the new objective function is equivalent to the optimal solution for the original objective function. Therefore, we propose the algorithm to derive the maximum channel capacity in the user-centric cell-free massive MIMO networks with the L-amount optional APs constraint, as presented in Algorithm 1. Here we use $\mathcal{I}_{\tau,K_\tau}$ to represent the set of child nodes in the $(\tau+1)$th layer derived from the parent node K_τ in the τth layer. The candidate set, encompassing all candidates in the $(\tau+1)$th level, is denoted as $\mathcal{I}_\tau = \bigcup_{K_\tau\in\mathcal{I}_{\tau-1}} \mathcal{I}_{\tau,K_\tau}$.

Figure 2 demonstrates the fundamental searching and pruning procedure in the BAB algorithm. By constructing a L-layer multi-branch search tree, we enumerate all the possible L-amount APs selection schemes. During the search operation, we maintain a global variable B (e. g., $-\infty$) and compare it with each tree-node's value, which can be calculated by Eq. (11). If any of the tree node's value is lower than B, according to Lemma 1, it is evident that the values of all child nodes of that node will also be less than B and therefore subsequent computations at that node can be skipped or "pruned". It should be noted that the variable B is updated only at the leaf nodes at which their values are greater than B and have no child nodes. By iteratively performing the above steps, the optimal solution of the objective function, denoted as $\bar{s}$, can be obtained upon traversing the entire tree.

Table 1. Simulation parameters

Parameters	Value
UE's antennas M	4
Total APs N	18
APs to be selected L	4
Side length $R(m)$	1500
Path loss α	1
Shadow fading σ_{dB}	1
Simulation times T	2000

4   Simulation Results

In this section, we present simulation results to illustrate the performance of the BAB-based AP Selection Algorithm in user-centric cell-free massive MIMO networks. Specifically, we consider a cell-free networking where one user with M antennas and N single-antenna APs are randomly distributed within a square of side length R. We perform our algorithm to select L APs out of N available ones to serve the user. The detailed parameters of simulations are shown in Table 1.

We compare the proposed algorithm with the optimal algorithm (i.e., exhaustive search) and the other two strategies: Su's algorithm [19] and Jung's algorithm [20]. Su's algorithm calculates the Euclidean norms of the channel matrix and selects the first L APs based on the magnitudes of their corresponding norms, arranged in descending order from largest to smallest. Jung's algorithm, on the other hand, simplifies Eq. (8) under high SNR conditions and derives a new selection criterion as follows: During the initial step, we choose the column of the channel matrix with the highest power. In the nth step ($n \geq 2$), the column that produces the maximum product of the channel gain and the sum of the squared uncorrelated values with the previously selected columns is selected.

Figure 3 presents the correlation between SNR and channel capacity when the AP locations are fixed and the user is randomly distributed. It can be founded that at low SNR levels, the performance differences among all algorithms are marginal. However, as the SNR increases, the distinction between the optimal

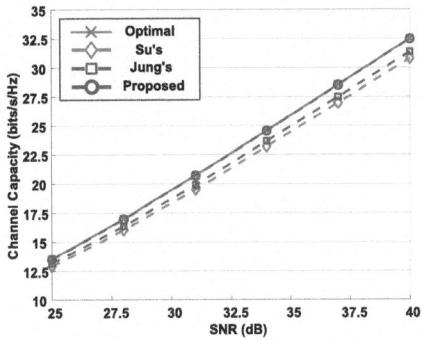
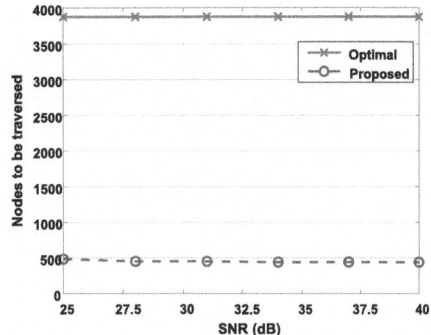

Fig. 3. Channel capacity obtained by different algorithms versus SNR.

Fig. 4. Nodes to be traversed by exhaustive search and proposed algorithm versus SNR.

Table 2. Complexity comparison

Algorithms	Order of complexity
Optimal	C_N^L
Su's	$O(N)$
Jung's	$O(M \cdot N \cdot L)$
Proposed	$O(M \cdot N \cdot N_{node})$

algorithm and another two algorithms (Su's and Jung's) gradually widens. Simultaneously, the gap between Jung's and Su's algorithms also increases. In contrast, our proposed algorithm (depicted by the blue dotted line with circles) consistently aligns with the optimal curve, demonstrating its ability to achieve a similar optimal performance as exhaustive search.

Table 2 shows the complexity comparison of the above four algorithms, where N_{node} denotes the number of nodes visited during the tree search, depending on the channel realizations. Since N_{node} is usually larger than L, the complexity of our proposed algorithm is slightly higher. Thus, although our algorithm outperforms two baseline algorithms, it sacrifices some complexity.

Figure 4 illustrates the computational complexity of both the exhaustive search and our proposed algorithm by comparing the number of nodes to be traversed. It is evident from the figure that although both algorithms can find the optimal solution, our algorithm traverses only approximately twelve percent of the nodes compared to the exhaustive algorithm, indicating a reduction of more than eighty percent in computational complexity.

Figure 5 demonstrates the channel capacity achieved by exhaustive search and our proposed algorithm, and the gap between the two approaches when the AP locations are fixed and the user is positioned at various locations within the area. Each bulge in the surface map indicates a high likelihood of the existence of

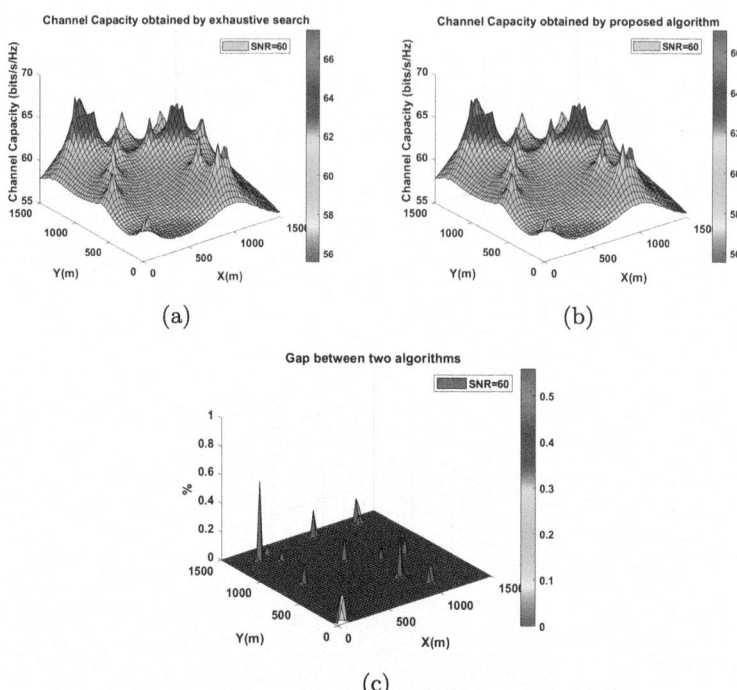

Fig. 5. Channel capacity achieved by (a) exhaustive search, (b) proposed algorithm, and (c) the performance gap between the proposed algorithm and exhaustive search. $M = 4$, $N = 18$, $L = 3$, $R = 1500\,\text{m}$, $\alpha = 1$, $\sigma_{dB} = 1$ and SNR $= 60\,\text{dB}$.

an individual AP. It can be observed from Fig. 5(c) that the proposed algorithm can effectively attain a similar optimal solution at almost every location within the region.

5   Conclusion

This paper focuses on AP selection problems in user-centric cell-free massive MIMO, where only a portion of the APs are dedicated to serving the user. To optimize the channel capacity while adhering to a selection size constraint, we formulate the AP selection problem as a mathematical matrix subset selection problem and propose a Branch-and-Bound (BAB)-based algorithm. Through constructing a multi-branch search tree and fast pruning, our proposed algorithm can efficiently find the optimal AP subset quickly. Simulation results demonstrate that the algorithm we propose is much closer to the optimal solution than the two baselines. Additionally, our algorithm achieves a noteworthy reduction in complexity. Looking forward, we are interested in exploring multi-user scenarios that consider Interference-plus-Noise Ratio(SINR), which aligns more closely with practical wireless communication systems.

Funding. The work was supported in part by National Key R&D Program of China 2022YFB2902004, in part by Guangdong Basic and Applied Basic Research Foundation under Grant 2024A1515012015, in part by The Shenzhen Science and Technology Program (No. RCBS20210706092408010), in part by National Natural Science Foundation of China under Grant 62001524, and in part by the Fundamental Research Funds for the Central Universities, Sun Yat-sen University, under Grant 24pnpy20.

A Proof of Lemma 1

Based on Eqs. (10) and (11), the recursive formulation of $\widetilde{C}_n$ is

$$\widetilde{C}_{\tau+1} = \widetilde{C}_\tau + \Delta_{k,\tau} - Z_\tau, \tau = 0, 1, ..., L-1. \tag{12}$$

It is evident that if $\Delta_{k,\tau} \leq Z_\tau$ holds for any τ, the function $\widetilde{C}_{\tau+1}$ monotonically decreases. Before that, we get $\mathbf{G}_{\tau+1}$ from Eq. (10) as:

$$
\begin{aligned}
\mathbf{G}_{\tau+1} &= \left(\mathbf{I}_M + \bar{\rho}\mathbf{H}_{\tau+1}^H \mathbf{H}_{\tau+1}\right)^{-1} \\
&= \left(\mathbf{I}_M + \bar{\rho}\mathbf{H}_\tau^H \mathbf{H}_\tau + \bar{\rho}\mathbf{h}_{J_\tau} \mathbf{h}_{J_\tau}^H\right)^{-1} \\
&= \mathbf{G}_\tau - \mathbf{g}_{\tau+1}\mathbf{g}_{\tau+1}^H, \tau = 0, 1, \cdots, L-1,
\end{aligned}
\tag{13}
$$

where $\mathbf{g}_{\tau+1} = \dfrac{\mathbf{G}_\tau \mathbf{h}_{K_\tau}}{\sqrt{\bar{\rho}^{-1} + \mathbf{h}_{K_\tau}^H \mathbf{G}_\tau \mathbf{h}_{K_\tau}}}$, K_τ is the AP index found in the τth step. Thus, we have

$$
\mathbf{G}_\tau = \begin{cases}
\mathbf{I}_M, & \tau = 0, \\
\mathbf{I}_M - \displaystyle\sum_{m=1}^{\tau} \mathbf{g}_m \mathbf{g}_m^H, & \tau = 1, 2, \cdots, L-1.
\end{cases}
\tag{14}
$$

Next we proceed to prove that $\Delta_{k,\tau} \leq Z_n$ holds for any τ, which could be discussed by the following parts:

1. For $\tau = 0$, we have

$$
\begin{aligned}
\Delta_{k,0} &= \log_2\left(1 + \bar{\rho}\mathbf{h}_k^H \mathbf{h}_k\right) \\
&\overset{(b)}{\leq} \log_2\left(1 + \bar{\rho}\zeta_0^2\right) = Z_0,
\end{aligned}
\tag{15}
$$

where the inequality (b) holds in the 0th selection step for candidate AP index $k \in \mathcal{I}_0$.
2. For $\tau = 1, 2, ..., L-1$. We define $\bar{\mathbf{G}}_\tau = \sum_{m=1}^{\tau} \mathbf{g}_m \mathbf{g}_m^H$. As the Gram matrix $\mathbf{g}_m \mathbf{g}_m^H$ is positive semi-definite, the summation of positive semi-definite matrices, denoted as $\bar{\mathbf{G}}_\tau$, also constitutes a positive semi-definite matrix. Then it can be inferred that:

$$\mathbf{h}_k^H \mathbf{G}_\tau \mathbf{h}_k - \mathbf{h}_k^H \mathbf{h}_k = -\mathbf{h}_k^H \bar{\mathbf{G}}_\tau \mathbf{h}_k \leq 0. \tag{16}$$

Thus, we have

$$
\begin{aligned}
\Delta_{k,\tau} &= \log_2\left(1 + \bar{\rho}\mathbf{h}_k^H \mathbf{G}_\tau \mathbf{h}_k\right) \\
&\leq \log_2\left(1 + \bar{\rho}\mathbf{h}_k^H \mathbf{h}_k\right) \\
&\overset{(c)}{\leq} \log_2\left(1 + \bar{\rho}\zeta_\tau^2\right) = Z_\tau,
\end{aligned}
\tag{17}
$$

where the inequality (c) holds in the τth selection step for candidate AP index $k \in \mathcal{I}_\tau$.

In conclusion, the new object function $\widetilde{C}_\tau$ in Eq. (11) monotonically decreases with τ.

References

1. Wang, J., Dai, L., Yang, L., Bai, B.: Clustered cell-free networking: a graph partitioning approach. IEEE Trans. Wirel. Commun. **22**(8), 5349–5364 (2023)
2. Du, M., Sun, X., Zhang, Y., Wang, J., Liu, P.: Joint cooperation clustering and downlink power control for cell-free massive MIMO with deep reinforcement learning. In: Proceedings of IEEE ICCT (2023)
3. Zhang, H., Su, R., Zhu, Y., Long, K., Karagiannidis, G.K.: User-centric cell-free massive MIMO system for indoor industrial networks. IEEE Trans. Commun. **70**(11), 7644–7655 (2022)
4. Wei, C., et al.: User-centric access point selection in cell-free massive MIMO systems: a game-theoretic approach. IEEE Commun. Lett. **26**(9), 2225–2229 (2022)
5. Buzzi, S., D'Andrea, C.: Cell-free massive MIMO: user-centric approach. IEEE Wirel. Commun. Lett. **6**(6), 706–709 (2017)
6. Ammar, H.A., Adve, R., Shahbazpanahi, S., Boudreau, G., Srinivas, K.V.: User-centric cell-free massive MIMO networks: a survey of opportunities, challenges and solutions. IEEE Commun. Surv. Tutor. **24**(1), 611–652 (2021)
7. Ngo, H.Q., Tran, L.-N., Duong, T.Q., Matthaiou, M., Larsson, E.G.: On the total energy efficiency of cell-free massive MIMO. IEEE Trans. Green Commun. Netw. **2**(1), 25–39 (2018)
8. Dai, L.: An uplink capacity analysis of the distributed antenna system (DAS): from cellular DAS to DAS with virtual cells. IEEE Trans. Wirel. Commun. **13**(5), 2717–2731 (2014)
9. Wang, J., Dai, L.: Downlink rate analysis for virtual-cell based large-scale distributed antenna systems. IEEE Trans. Wirel. Commun. **15**(3), 1998–2011 (2016)
10. Mai, T.C., Ngo, H.Q., Egan, M., Duong, T.Q.: Pilot power control for cell-free massive MIMO. IEEE Trans. Veh. Technol. **67**(11), 11264–11268 (2018)
11. Attarifar, M., Abbasfar, A., Lozano, A.: Subset MMSE receivers for cell-free networks. IEEE Trans. Wirel. Commun. **19**(6), 4183–4194 (2020)
12. Interdonato, G., Karlsson, M., Björnson, E., Larsson, E.G.: Local partial zero-forcing precoding for cell-free massive MIMO. IEEE Trans. Wirel. Commun. **19**(7), 4758–4774 (2020)
13. Liu, H., Zhang, J., Jin, S., Ai, B.: Graph coloring based pilot assignment for cell-free massive MIMO systems. IEEE Trans. Veh. Technol. **69**(8), 9180–9184 (2020)
14. Buzzi, S., D'Andrea, C., Zappone, A., D'Elia, C.: User-centric 5G cellular networks: resource allocation and comparison with the cell-free massive MIMO approach. IEEE Trans. Wirel. Commun. **19**(2), 1250–1264 (2020)

15. Wei, C., et al.: User-centric access point selection in cell-free massive MIMO systems: a game-theoretic approach. IEEE Commun. Lett. **26**(9), 2225–2229 (2022)

16. Gao, Y., Vinck, H., Kaiser, T.: Massive MIMO antenna selection: switching architectures, capacity bounds, and optimal antenna selection algorithms. IEEE Trans. Signal Process. **66**(5), 1346–1360 (2018)

17. Gong, Y., Wang, X.: Channel capacity analysis and simulations of distributed MIMO system. In: Proceedings of IEEE WiCOM (2009)

18. Gao, Y., Khaliel, M., Zheng, F., Kaiser, T.: Rotman lens based hybrid analog-digital beamforming in massive MIMO systems: array architectures, beam selection algorithms and experiments. IEEE Trans. Veh. Technol. **66**(10), 9134–9148 (2017)

19. Su, Y., Feng, G.: A novel fast antenna selection algorithm in distributed MIMO systems. In: Proceedings of IEEE ICCT (2010)

20. Jung, S.-Y., Kim, B.W.: Near-optimal low-complexity antenna selection scheme for energy-efficient correlated distributed MIMO systems. Int. J. Electron. Commun. **69**(7), 1039–1046 (2015)

Research on the Lip-Print Recognition Based on Multi-scale Feature

Hongcheng Zhou[✉]

School of Electronic and Information Engineering, Jinling Institute of Technology,
Nanjing, China
945516882@qq.com

Abstract. To address the problems of difficult feature extraction, small differences between texture information and recognition accuracy to be improved in lip-print recognition tasks, a lip-print recognition algorithm based on grouped multi-scale feature fusion is proposed. The ablation experimental results show that the improved recognition model achieves 98.56% recognition accuracy on the test set, and the model has strong generalization ability and feature refinement expression ability, which can provide support for the application of lip-print recognition technology in the field of identity verification.

Keywords: Lip-print recognition · Deep learning · Multi-scale feature fusion · Attention mechanism

1 Introduction

In recent years, more and more domestic and foreign scholars have paid attention to the field of lip pattern recognition and proposed different lip pattern recognition algorithms. Sandhya et al. [1] compared and analyzed lip pattern recognition methods based on machine learning algorithms, using classification algorithms such as support vector machine (SVM), K nearest neighbor (KNN), ensemble classifier, and artificial neural network (ANN) to classify the extracted features. Doroz et al. [2] proposed a lip pattern recognition algorithm that integrates complex image processing techniques, machine learning, and statistical methods. The proposed method can process partially damaged or incomplete lip patterns, identify and effectively eliminate low-quality areas in the 2 image. Chen Zongyang et al. [3] proposed a method for identifying coating surface defects based on the MobileNetV2 network. Wang Huanxin et al. [4] introduced an efficient channel attention and attention feature fusion module to establish an efficient crop leaf disease recognition model based on improved MobileNetV2. Li Zimao et al. [5] proposed a small sample recognition method for tea diseases. Zhang Dong et al. [6] proposed a counting method based on improved MobileNetV2, which adds volumes and attention modules to the original network to improve the refinement ability of fea-tures. However, its algorithm recognition accuracy still needs to be improved.

X. Chen et al. (Eds.): IoTaaS 2023, LNICST 585, pp. 16–21, 2025.
https://doi.org/10.1007/978-3-031-70507-6_2

2 Data and Preprocessing

2.1 Acquire Image

The collection of lip print images mainly includes contact and non-contact meth-ods. Therefore, combining the characteristics of deep learning algorithms and the ad-vantages of non-contact acquisition methods, a network camera is used to obtain lip print images. To obtain lip print images from different angles, video recording is used. The dataset captured 60 volunteers and ultimately obtained video recordings of each volunteer.

2.2 Data Enhancement

The final dataset consists of 60 people and 18000 images, including images from multiple angles and different noises. The dataset is divided into training, validation, and testing sets in a 7:2:1 ratio. The detailed information is shown in Table 1.

Table 1. Dataset Partitioning Information

Data Set	Training	Validation	Test Set/	Total/
	Set/Sheet	Set/Sheet	Sheet	Sheet
Original data set	2520	720	360	3600
Expanded dataset	12600	3600	1800	18000

3 Lip Pattern Recognition Model

3.1 MobileNetV2 Network

MobileNet is a lightweight convolutional neural network proposed by Google in 2017, which is committed to migrating the deep convolutional neural network model to mobile terminals and embedded devices. The deep separable convolutional structure is shown in Fig. 1. Adjust the data dimensions of input and output, and integrate fea-ture maps generated by different channels [7].

3.2 Improved MobileNetV2 Model

3.2.1 Embedded Attention Mechanism Module

The convolutional block attention module (CBAM) is a hybrid attention mecha-nism that includes channel attention submodules and spatial attention submodules, which are serially connected [8]. The calculation process of the channel attention sub-module is shown in Eq. 1.

$$M_c(F) = (MLP(AvgPool(F)) + MLP(MaxPool(F))) \qquad (1)$$

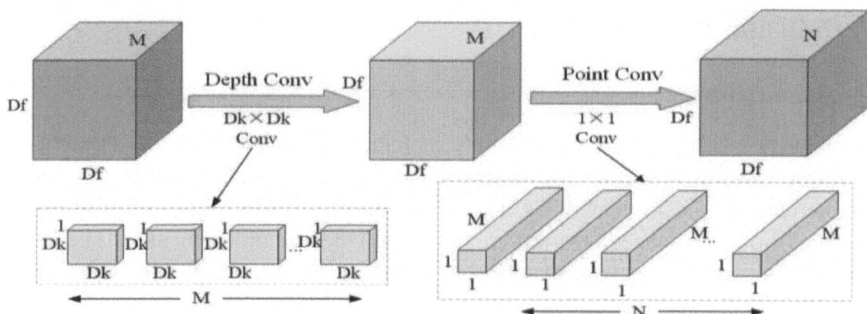

Fig. 1. Deep Separable Convolutional Structure

The calculation process of the spatial attention submodule is shown in Eq. 2. Firstly, this submodule performs an average pooling operation on the output of the channel attention submodule, and then concatenates the pooled feature maps on the channel dimension. This submodule can enable the model to better capture spatial in-formation and improve model performance.

$$M_s(F) = (f_{77}(AvgPool(F), \ MaxPool(F))) \tag{2}$$

3.2.2 Design of Grouped Multiscale Feature Fusion Module

In order to enable the network to fuse multi-scale feature information extraction, it can effectively utilize low dimensional features and adapt to input images of different resolutions [10]. And then uses 3 3, 5 5, 7 7, 9 9 to perform convolution operations on the input feature maps of each group using four different sizes of convolutions to generate feature subgraphs f_1, f_2, f_3, f_4 corresponding to each channel.

$$F = Concat(f, \ f_1, \ f_3, \ f_4) \tag{3}$$

Finally, perform channel blending on the feature maps generated from the four sets of channels to increase the exchange and fusion of feature information between different channels, and then perform feature stitching on the four different feature sub-graphs as shown in Eq. 3.

4 Experiment

4.1 Model Evaluation Indicators

All experiments used accuracy, precision, and specificity as indicators to evaluate network performance. Accuracy is a simple and intuitive evaluation indicator in image classification problems, which is the ratio of the sample size correctly predicted by the model to the total sample size. Precision refers to the proportion of positive samples predicted by the model to the positive samples predicted. Specificity refers to the ratio of the predicted negative sample size to the actual negative sample size. The specific calculation process is shown in the following equation.

$$\text{Accuracy} = \frac{TP + TN}{TP + TN + FP + FN} \tag{4}$$

$$Precision = \frac{TP}{TP + FP} \tag{5}$$

$$Specificity = \frac{TN}{TN + FP} \tag{6}$$

4.2 Experimental Results and Analysis

4.2.1 Experiments Introducing Different Attention Mechanisms

In recent years, the attention modules designed by convolutional neural network include squeeze and excitation (SE), efficient channel attention (ECA), bottleneck at-tention module (BAM), convolutional block attention module (CBAM) and coordinate attention (CA). The results are shown in Table 2.

Table 2. The recognition effect of MobileNetV2 combined with different attention mechanisms

Network	Parameter Quantity /M	Accuracy/%	Average Accuracy /%	Average Specificity/%
mbV2	2.30	96.91	96.97	99.95
mbV2_SE	2.86	95.72	95.78	99.90
mbV2_ECA	2.38	95.5	96.52	99.91
mbV2_BAM	3.67	95.11	95.79	99.91
mbV2_CA	2.75	96.56	96.72	99.93
mbV2_CBAM	3.14	97.39	97.61	99.95

From Table 2, it can be seen that the recognition accuracy of the network has changed to some extent after embedding the attention mechanism. Adding an attention module with convolutional layers will inevitably increase the number of network parameters.

4.2.2 Experiments to Reduce the Number of Network Parameters

Introducing the convolutional attention mechanism module will increase the num-ber of network parameters. The experimental results were analyzed and the value of parameter a in the improved net-work was determined. The experimental results are shown in Table 3.

Compared with the model without introducing parameter a, the recognition accuracy has improved by 0.44%. Although fewer parameters were obtained in other experimental

Table 3. Recognition Effects of Different Parameter Quantity Models

Network	Parameter Quantity/M	Model Size/MB	Accuracy /%	Average Accuracy/%
MobileNetV2	2.30	8.63	96.91	96.97
MobileNetV2_cbam	3.14	11.94	97.39	97.61
MobileNetV2_1234	2.12	8.12	96.36	96.72
MobileNetV2_4567	3.0	11.76	96.72	96.86
MobileNetV2_1357	2.42	9.21	97.83	98.17
MobileNetV2_1246	2.62	10.10	96.42	96.87

groups, priority must be given to the recognition accuracy of the network model. Through the analysis of the ablation experiment results, it was ultimately determined that the bottleneck modules 1, 3, 5, 7 in the improved network were constructed by introducing the true value of parameter a.

5 Summary

We conducted relevant model training and ablation experiments on the lip print dataset, and the experimental results showed that the improved network has better gen-eralization ability and higher recognition rate. The recognition accuracy and average accuracy have been improved by 1.65% and 1.73% respectively on the test set. From the attention heatmap of the network model before and after improvement, it can be concluded that the improved recognition model has better feature refinement and ex-traction capabilities.

Acknowledgment. This work was supported by Cooperative Project of Jiangsu Province production, teaching and research (No. BY2021381), Jin Ling Institute of Technology Ph.D. Startup Fund (jit-b-202314).

References

1. Sandhya, S., Fernandes, R., Sapna, S., et al.: Comparative analysis of machine learning algorithms for Lip print based person identification. Evolut. Intell. **15**, 743–757 (2021)
2. Doroz, R., Wrobel, K., Orczyk, T., et al.: Multidimensional nearest neighbors classification based system for incomplete lip print identification. Expert Syst. Appl. **202**, 117–137 (2022)
3. Zongyang, C.H.E.N., Hui, Z.H.A.O., Yongsheng, L.Y.U., et al.: A recognition method of coating sur-face defects based on the improved MobileNetV2 network. J. Harbin Eng. Univ. **43**(4), 572–579 (2022)
4. Huanxin, W.A.N.G., Zhihao, S.H.E.N., Quan, L.I.U., et al.: Identification of crop leaf diseases based on improved mobileNetV2 model. J. Henan Agric. Sci. **52**(04), 143–151 (2023)
5. Li Zimao, X., Jie, Z.L., et al.: Small sample recognition method of tea disease based on improved DenseNet. Trans. Chin. Soc. Agric. Eng. **38**(10), 182–190 (2022)

6. Zhang, D., Jiang, Y.: Drill pipe counting method based on improved Mo-bileNetV2. J. Mine Autom. **48**(10), 69–75 (2022)
7. Jinhui, L., Di, W., Xiaopan, S.: Research progress on visual image detection based on convolutional neural network. Chinese J. Sci. Instr. **41**(4), 167–182 (2020)
8. Lin, T.Y., Goyal, P., Girshick, R., et al.: Focal loss for dense object detection. IEEE Trans. Patt. Anal. Mach. Intell. **42**(2), 318–327 (2020)
9. Ma, L., Zheng, S.Y., Niu, B.: Action recognition method on regional association adaptive graph convolution. J. Front. Comput. Sci. Technol. **16**(4), 898–908 (2022)
10. Meng, L., Guo, X.Y., Du, J.J., et al.: A lightweight CNN model for image recognition of crop diseases. Jiangsu J. Agricult. Sci. **37**(5), 1143–1150 (2021)
11. Xu, Y.J., Li, C.: Light weight object detection network optimized based on YOLO family computer. Science **48**(11), 265–269 (2021)
12. Selvaraju, R.R., Cogswell, M., Das, A., et al.: Grad-CAM: visual explanations from deep net-works via gradient-based localization. Int. J. Comput. Vis. **128**(2), 336–359 (2020)
13. Lin, T.Y., Goyal, P., Girshick, R., et al.: Focal loss for dense object detection. IEEE Trans. Pattern Anal. Mach. Intell. **42**(2), 318–327 (2020)

Highway Obstacle Recognition Based on Improved YOLOv7 and Defogging Algorithm

Mingliang Fan, Jing Liu[✉], and Jiaming Yu

Engineering School of Networks and Telecommunications, Jinling Institute of Technology, Nanjing 211169, China
liuj608@jit.edu.cn

Abstract. This study explores a haze removal algorithm based on an enhanced Laplacian operator and guided filtering to enhance image visibility and quality. This algorithm is applicable not only to images taken in hazy weather conditions but also incorporates intelligent transportation systems by employing YOLOv7 object recognition technology. This enables accurate detection and identification of traffic objects within the images. By integrating the improved Laplacian operator into the traditional guided filtering framework, this approach effectively mitigates issues of image blurring and decreased contrast caused by haze, thereby enhancing image transparency. Simultaneously, the Integration of YOLOv7 into the system allows for rapid and precise detection of traffic objects, providing accurate data support for intelligent transportation systems. As a result, this study not only explores novel haze removal techniques in the field of image processing but also brings forth new technological applications for the advancement of intelligent transportation systems.

Keywords: highway · obstacle detection · YOLOv7 · deep learning

1 Introduction

With the continuous development and progress of human science and technology, computers have been widely used in various industries. At the same time, computer vision technology and its supporting equipment are also updated in parallel with the rapid development of computer technology. Image recognition technology [1], image super-resolution technology [2], video surveillance equipment [3], aerial photography drones [4] and so on have penetrated into every aspect of people's lives. Highway is an important part of modern transportation, which has the characteristics of fast driving speed and high passage efficiency, providing convenience for people's travel and logistics. However, highways also have some safety hazards, such as traffic accidents, congestion, intruding obstacles, etc. These problems not only affect the efficiency of transportation, but also threaten the safety of people's lives and properties. Therefore, how to effectively monitor and manage highways and improve the safety and intelligence of highways is an important topic in the current intelligent transportation field [5].

© ICST Institute for Computer Sciences, Social Informatics and Telecommunications Engineering 2025
Published by Springer Nature Switzerland AG 2025. All Rights Reserved
X. Chen et al. (Eds.): IoTaaS 2023, LNICST 585, pp. 22–34, 2025.
https://doi.org/10.1007/978-3-031-70507-6_3

Obstacle detection is a core task of highway monitoring and management and automatic driving, which detects obstacles on the road, such as vehicles, pedestrians, animals, etc., in real time by analyzing and processing images or videos of highway scenes, and outputs their categories and location information. Highway road surface temperature during the day, large temperature difference between day and night, very easy to form a dense haze, prompting a sharp decrease in local visibility, seriously affecting the normal imaging of computer vision acquisition equipment, reducing the clarity and contrast of the image, increasing the noise and interference in the image, resulting in a decrease in the accuracy and robustness of the target detection of obstacles, vehicles, and other objects, which affects the subsequent work of target classification and recognition.

However, the current target detection algorithms are not accurate in recognizing various types of target markers on highways under foggy weather, and the false detection rate and misdetection rate are high. Therefore, accurate and fast recognition of highway targets under foggy conditions has important research and application value. Based on the above problems, this paper combines the image de-fogging algorithm and the target detection algorithm to propose a novel highway obstacle detection method under foggy weather. The contributions of this paper are as follows:

(1) Combining the dark channel defogging [6] with the YOLOv7 [7] framework, the fog is successfully removed to avoid the interference of foggy weather on the recognition accuracy, which ensures the timeliness and at the same time, it can realize efficient and accurate obstacle and vehicle detection under different weather conditions.
(2) An image segmentation method based on Laplace operator [8] is proposed to divide the image into foreground and background parts, calculate their transmittance separately, and optimize the fused transmittance by guided filtering [9], so as to improve the accuracy and stability of the transmittance.
(3) The WIoU loss function is used to replace the original loss function of YOLOv7 to improve the generalization ability and convergence speed of the network to detect obstacles.
(4) A highway scene dataset is constructed, which contains highway images and videos under different weather conditions, as well as the corresponding obstacle labeling information, providing data support for the research of highway obstacle detection.

2 Related Work

According to the different processing methods, image defogging algorithms can be divided into three categories [10]: image enhancement, physical model defogging and deep learning model defogging. As shown in Fig. 1.

Image enhancement is a foggy image clarity means used in the early days, which is not based on the principle of image fogging recovery, only purely to improve the local or global contrast to alleviate the blurring of the image, so its recovery quality is general, and the effect on the real image is often not satisfactory; the physical model of defogging to the intrinsic principle of image degradation as a theoretical basis, through the tapped into the a priori knowledge or the use of the imaging model for the constraint processing to estimate the corresponding imaging parameters. Then, the estimated parameters are substituted into the model to recover a clear fog-free scene inversely. This type of method

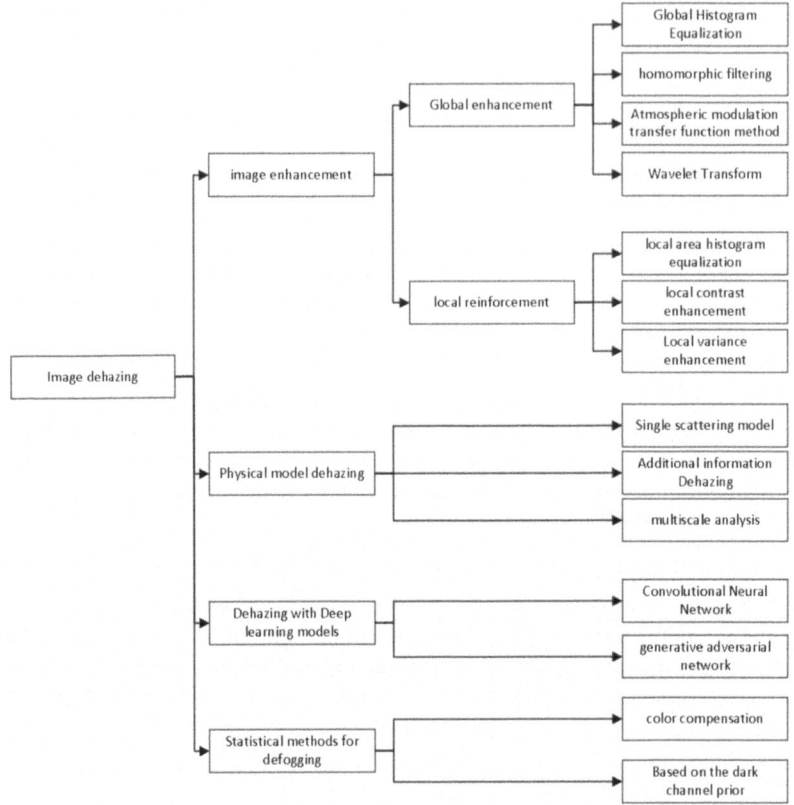

Fig. 1. Image defogging algorith

can obtain realistic defogging results for most images; deep learning model defogging benefits from the booming development of deep learning theory, and many scholars have designed a large number of deep learning model defogging methods in a data-driven manner.

Currently, the mainstream method is to calculate the atmospheric illumination and transmittance, and establish a physical model of atmospheric scattering for defogging. Chinese researchers He et al. proposed the dark channel prior principle in 2009 [6]. This method proposed the concept of dark channel for the first time, and compared with some complex image defogging algorithms, dark channel a priori principal defogging is easier to calculate. However, this type of method cannot deal with multi-scale or complex scenes, Luo Huilan et al. proposed an image defogging method based on multi-scale Retinex algorithm, by combining multi-scale Retinex and color recovery, this method can better deal with the details and color information in the image, so as to achieve a more accurate and natural image defogging effect. In 2013, He et al. introduced the concept of guided filter concept in combination with defogging processing to further enhance the defogging effect. These methods have the advantages of simplicity and real-time, but have limited effect on complex scenes and detail recovery in images, and such methods have insufficient edge protection may lead to blurring or distortion of edge information when performing smoothing operations. In 2011, ESL Gastal et al. proposed a domain transform-based method for realizing edge-aware image and video processing, which is more effective than the traditional bootstrap filtering method, this method can better preserve and enhance the edge information of the image. In 2011, Yu Jing et al. proposed a fast physical model-based defogging method. This algorithm performs haze removal by modeling the scattering model in the image using parameters such as transmittance and atmospheric light. This method can more accurately reproduce the real scene and has better results for complex images. However, this type of method has difficulties in calculating accurate transmittance. With the rise of deep learning, many researchers have started to apply it in haze removal algorithms. In 2019, Hodges C proposed about single image haze removal method using deep neural networks, which achieved better results, but there are limitations in coping with a wide range of haze types and the problem of haze removal under different environmental conditions.

Although the above dehaze algorithms can achieve good results in specific areas, when used in highway scenarios, there is a large deviation in the transmittance estimation, and the dehaze effect is poor, with obvious distortions, which needs to be further improved.

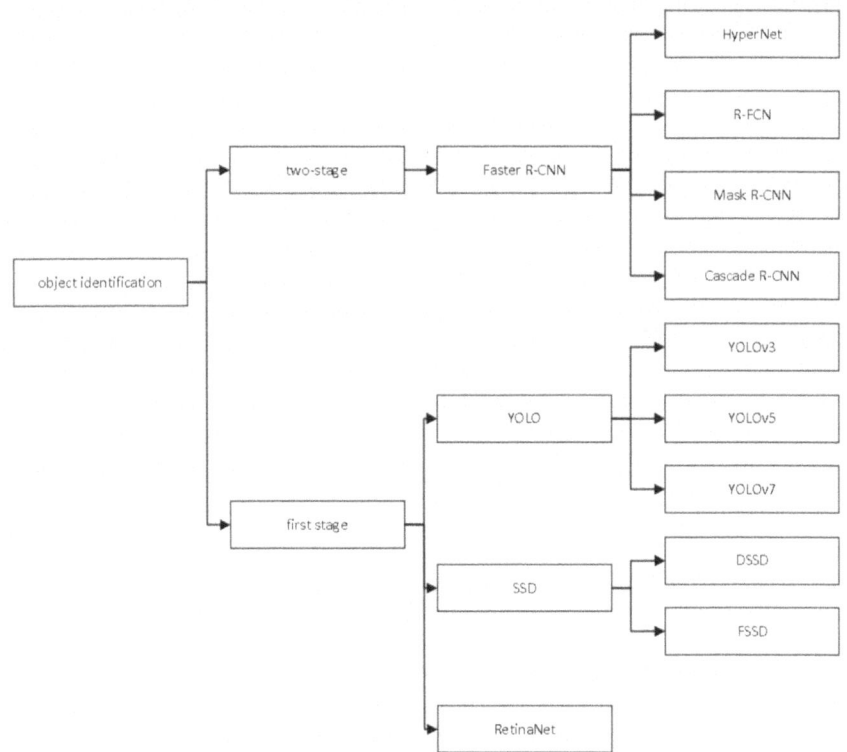

Fig. 2. Classification of target detection

According to the different detection processes, target detection algorithms can be divided into two categories: one-stage detection algorithms and two-stage detection algorithms. As shown in Fig. 2.

One-stage detection algorithm is to predict the category and location of the target directly on the image, without the generation of candidate regions, its advantage is fast, the disadvantage is low accuracy, especially for the detection of small targets. Representative algorithms include YOLO, SSD, etc. The two-stage detection algorithm is to generate candidate regions on the image first, and then classify and regress each candidate region, the advantage of which is high accuracy, the disadvantage of which is slow, especially for the processing of a large number of candidate regions. Representative algorithms include Faster R-CNN, Mask R-CNN, and so on.

In the past, scholars tended to improve only the deep learning methods or only the de-fogging algorithms, but did not consider combining the two algorithms closely. So the detection effect still cannot meet the demand when facing especially extreme weather.

3 Methods

3.1 General Flow of the Algorithm

In this paper, the defogging algorithm and the target detection algorithm are combined for obstacle detection. The detection flow is shown in Fig. 3.

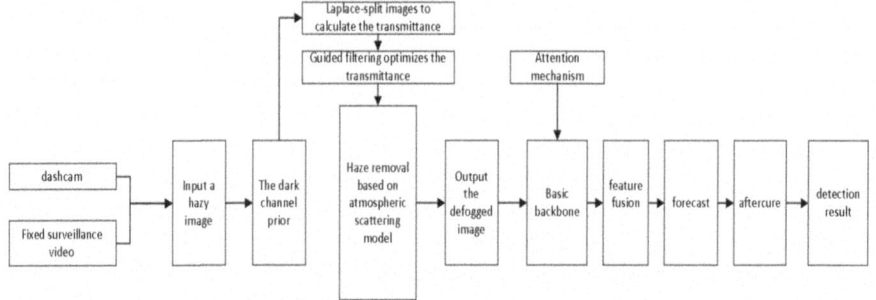

Fig. 3. General flowchart of the algorithm

As shown in the figure, the images captured by the camera on the highway will be transmitted to the computer for preprocessing followed by de-fogging, then advanced image features are extracted using deep neural networks, and finally, the detected obstacles can be visualized.

In this paper, highway obstacles are detected by de-fogging preprocessing combined with YOLOv7. The transmittance and atmospheric illumination are estimated by the dark channel a priori algorithm [10]. However, due to the special characteristics of the highway, most of the upper part of the image is the sky region, and the dark-channel a priori algorithm tends to distort the transmittance when facing the sky region. The use of Laplace operator to separate the sky and non-sky regions, respectively, calculate the transmittance of the two, and finally take the fusion of the two transmittances, to achieve a moderate transmittance, to achieve a more realistic de-fogging effect.

3.2 Image Preprocessing

For the transmittance of the sky region, because the brightness of the sky region is much larger than the brightness of the road surface, and the distribution of brightness is positively correlated with the depth of the scene, so we use the luminance intensity to estimate the transmittance, based on the luminance intensity model of the transmittance representation:

$$t_L(x) = \exp[-\beta L(x)] \tag{1}$$

$$L(x) = \frac{l(x)}{l^*} \times D \tag{2}$$

$l(x)$ is the brightness of the input image, l^* is the range of brightness in the current environment. D is the real scene depth range.

For non-sky regions: since the brightness of the road surface is much smaller than the area of the sky region, the transmittance can be estimated by the dark channel a priori algorithm.

$$t_{nosky}{}'(x) = 1 - \omega \min_{y \in \Omega(x)} \left[\min_c \frac{I^c(y)}{A^c} \right] \tag{3}$$

Assume that the overall luminance average of the input map is defined as L_1, the luminance average of the sky region is L_2, and the area of the number of pixels in the input map that are smaller than L_1 is S_1, and the area of the number of pixels that are smaller than L_2 is S_2. Fusion coefficient ρ and fusion transmittance $t(x)$ are defined as follows:

$$\rho = \frac{S_1}{S_2} \tag{4}$$

$$t(x) = \rho t_L(x) + (1 - \rho)t_{nosky}{}'(x) \tag{5}$$

When optimizing the transmittance map by using a fogged image as the guiding map and applying guiding filters, it results in the transmittance map containing a large amount of detailed information, although it is able to adequately capture the details of the changes in the guiding map. The transmittance represents the atmospheric scattering coefficient, which is usually considered constant over a localized region. Therefore, the transmittance is largely dependent on the depth of field of the scene. And in most cases, the depth of field is smooth, i.e., it has a similar and smooth depth of field in small localized areas that do not contain depth of field jumps. Therefore, the ideal transmittance should be similar and smooth in regions having the same depth of field, not containing detail information, and varying more in regions where the depth of field jumps or is discontinuous, i.e., retaining significant variations at object edge features. It can be seen that although the use of a grayscale map of a fogged image as a guiding map preserves clear edge features, it also results in too much detail and not enough smoothing in regions with the same depth of field. Therefore, this kind of guiding map still needs further improvement.

In this paper, the accuracy of transmittance can be improved by the guiding map with the following characteristics:

(1) Having the characteristics of foggy images at the edges.
(2) Smoothing at similar depth of field.
(3) As close as possible to the guided filter input.

The transmittance of foggy images is optimized using guided filtering by calculating the guided map based on the atmospheric light curtain model.

First, the RGB channel of the foggy image is minimized to obtain the image W. Then the local mean image T is obtained by applying bilateral filtering to W, so that T maintains the smoothness and retains the edge features. Calculate the local standard difference image between the image and the local mean image, perform bilateral filtering on this difference image and then differ from image T to obtain the quadratic difference image G. Use image G to obtain the atmospheric light curtain image, and finally derive the guiding map I_{guide}, the specific steps are as follows:

$$T(x, y) = Bilateral(W(x, y)) \tag{6}$$

$$G(x, y) = T(x, y) - Bilateral(|W - T(x, y)|) \tag{7}$$

$$I_{guide} = 1 - \frac{max(min(G, W), 0)}{A} \tag{8}$$

Secondly, using I_{guide} as the guiding map, the optimization of the transmittance $t(x)$ by using the guiding filter can make the optimized transmittance maintain the edge characteristics of the foggy image and tend to be smooth at the similar depth of field. The guiding filter is a local linear model between the guiding map I_{guide} and the filtered output $t_1(x)$, which can be considered as a linear transformation of all pixels in a window of size w_k centered at pixel k, as follows.

$$t_1(x) = a_k I_{guide} + b_k, \forall i \in w_k \tag{9}$$

(a_k, b_k) are linear transformation coefficients that are constant within the window w_k. Due to $\nabla t_2 = a_k \nabla I_{guide}$, which ensures that $t_1(x)$ has the same gradient information as I_{guide}. . The linear coefficients (a_k, b_k) are determined by minimizing the cost function that minimizes the difference between the output image of the guided filter and the input image. The cost function is given in the following equation.

$$E(a_k, b_k) = \sum \left(a_k [I_{guide}] + b_k - [t(x)]_i^2 + \varepsilon a_k^2 \right) \tag{10}$$

After defogging preprocessing as described above, the defogged image is subjected to target recognition by YOLOv7.

3.3   Image Classification and Recognition

The yolov7 network consists of four distinct components, input, backbone, neck and head.

The input module performs a series of preprocessing operations including resizing the input image to a standard size and augmenting the input data; the backbone module consists of several BConv modules, Extended ELAN (E-ELAN) module, and MPConv module, where the BConv module consists of convolutional layers, batch normalization (BN), and SiLU activation functions for extracting image features at different scales. The E -ELAN module guides the learning of different features through different computational blocks by operations such as expanding, shuffling, and merging bases without changing the original gradient paths. The MPConv layer enhances the generalization performance of the network by adding a Maxpool layer on top of the BConv layer; and between the head and the neck, there is a SPPCSPC module. In the SPPCSPC module, the inputs are split into multiple branches and undergo a MaxPool operation, and then merged by a cat operation to prevent image distortion; the Neck module employs the Path Aggregation Feature Pyramid Network (PAFPN) architecture, which is characterized by the efficient integration of multilevel semantic graphs using a pyramid-based framework. Finally, the Head module passes the REP structure and outputs predictions through subsequent convolutional operations.

The loss function is the most important aspect in the field of deep learning as it quantifies the difference between the predicted and actual outputs of the model and improves the performance of the model by optimizing the model parameters to effectively reduce this error. The precise selection and configuration of the loss function has a significant impact on the learning efficiency and overall results of the model.

The loss function of the YOLOv7 model consists of three distinct components: localization loss, confidence loss, and classification loss. These three losses are harmoniously integrated to form the total loss, which is obtained by weighted summation of the above components. The binary cross-entropy loss function is used to calculate the confidence loss and classification loss. Meanwhile, the localization loss is calculated utilizing the CIoU loss function.

$$LOSS = \alpha_{box} \times L_{box} + \alpha_{cls} \times L_{cls} + \alpha_{obj} \times L_{obj} \qquad (11)$$

where the weight values of the three loss functions are respectively. $\alpha_{\{box\}}$

4 Experimental Setup

4.1 Introduction to the Dataset

At this stage, datasets for highway target detection are not comprehensive and specific, so in this paper, we use our own labeled road camera dataset to test the performance of the algorithm. We have collected a large number of road camera datasets and used software to label different targets. Our labeled dataset includes six types of labels, i.e., cars, trucks, buses, motorcycles, pedestrians, and obstacles. The specific data categories and tag numbers are shown in Table 1.

Table 1. Dataset introduction

Form	Data volume
enclosed carriage	12800
trucks	5880
tourist bus	3220
motorcycle	3350
pedestrians	3150
obstacle	1600

4.2 Assessment Metrics

Transmittance describes the degree of light attenuation in a hazy environment. It reflects the degree of influence of haze on the propagation of light, and areas with higher transmittance indicate less light attenuation and relatively clearer images, while areas with lower transmittance indicate greater light attenuation and blurrier images.

Peak Signal-to-Noise Ratio (PSNR) [11] and Structural Similarity Index (SSIM) [12] are used to evaluate the image processing algorithms as well as to assess the effectiveness of image compression, noise reduction and restoration techniques.

Mean Average Precision (mAP) is used to evaluate the overall performance of the target detection algorithm.

Precision (Precision) refers to the proportion of detected positive samples that are true positive samples. That is, the ratio of correctly detected targets to all detected targets.

Recall (Recall): recall is the proportion of true positive samples that are correctly detected. That is, the ratio between detected targets and all true targets.

Transmittance is generally used as a judgment metric for estimating fog concentrations. In the case of different degrees of fog warning, the transmittance estimation value can be different according to the actual situation and the method used. In general, the higher the transmittance estimate, the lighter the degree of fog in the image and the clearer the target objects in the image. A high transmittance (close to 1) indicates that the haze in the image is very slight or almost absent, and the details and colors of the target objects can be clearly observed; a medium transmittance (between 0.3 and 0.7) indicates that there is a certain degree of haze in the image, but it can still be recognized and observed, which is equivalent to an orange fog warning; and a low transmittance (close to 0) indicates that the details and colors of the target objects are very dense. When the details and colors of the target object have low transmittance (close to 0), it means that the haze in the image is very thick, and the details and colors of the target object are almost unobservable, and the whole image shows a fuzzy and grey effect, which is equivalent to the fog red warning.

4.3 Hardware Environment

In order to in order to validate the effectiveness of the proposed model, we conducted the training and evaluation of the neural network on the basis of computer hardware and software configurations, and used specific model hyperparameters. The specific configurations and hyperparameters are shown in Tables 2 and 3.

Table 2. Hardware configuration and environment

Software	Matrix
CPU	12th Gen Intel(R) Core i9-13900K 3.0 GHz
GPU	NVIDIA GeForce RTX4090 (24G)
Operating System	Windows11
CUDA	11.7
Python	3.10.9
Torch	1.13.1

Table 3. Experimental parameters

Parameter name	Parameters
Momentum	0.937
Weight decay	0.0005
Batch size	32
Learning rate	0.01
Image size	640×640
Epochs	300

4.4 Experiments and Results

The objective of the algorithm in this paper is to explore and determine the best combination of de-fogging detection algorithms and to demonstrate the facilitation of the de-fogging algorithm proposed in this paper on the task of de-fogging detection, hence the experiments are carried out using the control variable approach.

Preprocessing Module:

In this paper, the effect of defogging is analyzed by comparing the difference in transmittance as well as PSNR and SSIM values under different defogging algorithms.

The comparison of the transmittance of fogged and fogged pictures by different defogging algorithms is shown in Fig. 4.

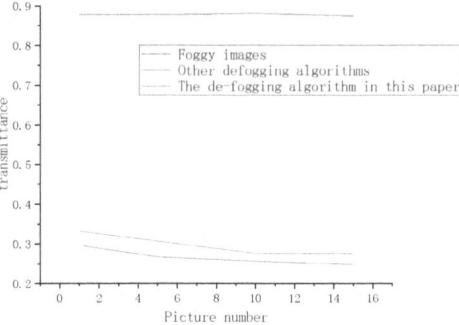

Fig. 4. Transmissivity values

The PSNR and SSIM values under different defogging algorithms are shown in Figs. 5 and 6:

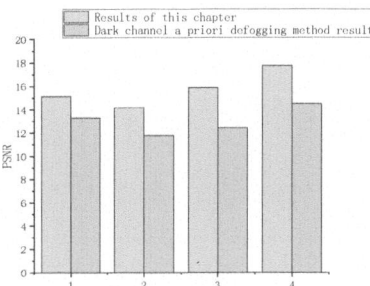

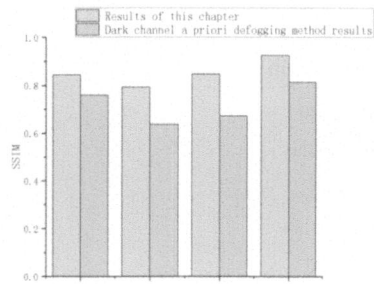

Fig. 5. PSNR values under different defog   **Fig. 6.** SSIM values under different defogg

It can be seen that the de-fogging algorithm improved in this paper has better de-fogging effect than other de-fogging algorithms.

The de-fogging method proposed in this chapter is used for target recognition of highway video pictures, and the original picture, the picture before de-fogging, and the picture after de-fogging are compared, and the comparison experiments are shown in Figs. 7, 8, and 9. The data in the table is obtained on a test set of 1000 samples. The images after performing the defogging process are compared to the images before defogging, where the accuracy P after defogging is improved by 9.859% compared to the accuracy P before defogging, and the recall R after defogging is improved by 9.5238% compared to the recall R before defogging, Average AP after defogging is 12.008% higher compared to average AP before defogging.

As shown in Figs. 7, 8 and 9. In fogged images, the accuracy, recall and average AP value are lower than the values of the three data compared to the de-fogged images for target recognition after going through the de-fogging method in this chapter, compared to the fogged images, the de-fogging algorithm in this chapter has a good effect on target recognition.

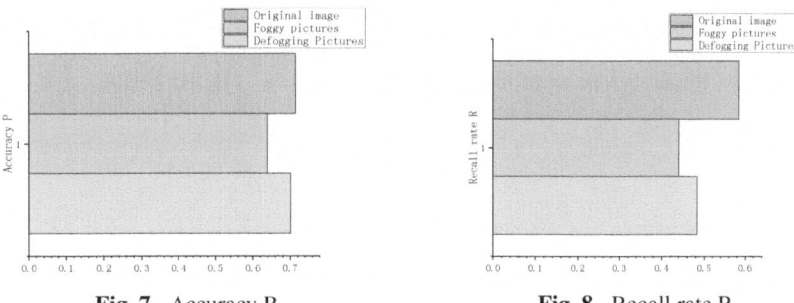

Fig. 7. Accuracy P   **Fig. 8.** Recall rate R

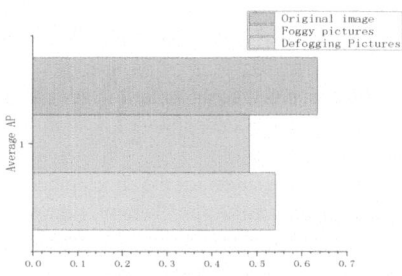

Fig. 9. Average AP

5 Conclusion

In this paper, we take foggy highway images as the object, and conduct in-depth research on the problems of inaccurate transmittance calculation, inaccurate target recognition, and low universality, which are commonly found in the current image defogging algorithms. In order to improve these problems, in the de-fogging algorithm, the method of dividing the image to calculate the transmittance and fusion respectively, and the method of optimizing the transmittance by guided filtering are proposed. In the target detection algorithm, it is proposed to use Wiou loss function to replace the loss function of YOLOv7 itself. After several experiments, the data processed by defogging using the method of this paper are closer to the expected data than those processed by other defogging algorithms. It fully demonstrates that the method in this paper is efficient and superior, and can be adapted to the needs of intelligent transportation.

Although the method based on deep learning and atmospheric scattering model proposed in this paper can obtain ideal results in most situations, the de-fogging effect for complex scenes and strong haze still needs to be improved, which is due to the insufficiently rich dataset. In the future, richer datasets will be collected and trained. In addition, the algorithm in this paper only de-fogs a single foggy image, while in modern smart city applications, real-time de-fogging is often required, and the future will study how to realize real-time video de-fogging.

Acknowledgement. This work was supported in part by the 2023 Jiangsu Province College Student Innovation Training Program (202313573086Y), and in part by the Natural Science Foundation of Higher Education of Jiangsu Province (Grant No. 17KJB510020).

References

1. Krizhevsky, A., Sutskever, I., Hinton, G.: ImageNet classification with deep convolutional neural networks. Adv. Neural Inform. Process. Syst. **25**, 2 (2012)
2. Huang, J.B., Singh, A., Ahuja, N.: Single image super-resolution from transformed self-exemplars. IEEE IEEE (2015)
3. Alomari, A.H., Lebdeh, E.A.: Smart real-time vehicle detection and tracking system using road surveillance cameras. J. Transp. Eng. Part A Syst. (2022). https://doi.org/10.1061/JTE PBS.0000728
4. Kotaro, et al.: Advantages of unmanned aerial vehicle (UAV) photogrammetry for landscape analysis compared with satellite data: A case study of postmining sites in Indonesia. Cogent Geoscience (2018)
5. Cui, C.A.I.: Status analysis and Suggestions for the development of intelligent transportation in China. Highway Transp. Sci. Technol. Appl. Technol. Edn. **9**(6), 4 (2013)
6. He, K., Sun, J., Tang, X.: Single image haze removal using dark channel prior. IEEE Trans. Pattern Anal. Mach. Intell. **33**(12), 2341–2353 (2010)
7. Redmon, J., et al.: You only look once: unified, real-time object detection. Comput. Vis. Patt. Recogn. IEEE (2016)
8. Wang, B., Yang, S.: Edge detection of gray image based on gauss-laplace operator. Comput. Eng. Appl. **39**(26), 3 (2003)
9. Chen, S., Ren, Z., Lian, Q.: Single image dehazing algorithm based on improved dark channel and guided filtering. Acta Automat. ICA Sin. **42**(3), 11 (2016)
10. Zhang, D., Ju, M., Qian, W.: Research status and Prospect of Image Dehazing algorithms. J. Nanjing Univ. Posts Telecommun. Natl. Sci. (2020)
11. Huang, H.F., Qing-Xin, C., JianKang, X.: Design of power supply noise and radiation free power—Ground plane for modern system in package. In: 2008 Asia- Pacific Symposium on Electromagnetic Compatibility and 19th International Zurich Symposium on Electromagnetic Compatibility. IEEE, 2008
12. Wang, Z., et al.: Image quality assessment: from error visibility to structural similarity. IEEE Trans. Image Process. **13**(4), 600–612 (2004)

4th Edge Intelligence and Computing for IoT Communications and Applications

Cloud Gaming Resource Management Platform Based on Edge Intelligence

Hu Yang$^{(\boxtimes)}$, Xie Yunsong, Li Jiaye, Su Xunjie, Wang Maoyu, Li Guanlin, and Lin Shangjing

School of Electronic Engineering, Beijing University of Posts and Telecommunications, Beijing, China
{hu.yang,xie.yunsong,li.jiaye,su.xunjie,wang.maoyu,li.guanlin,
lin.shangjing}@bupt.edu.cn

Abstract. This study thoroughly explores the rapid development of edge intelligence, emphasizing the synergy between cloud computing and edge computing to significantly enhance data processing efficiency. It highlights the advantages of edge intelligence-based cloud gaming platforms over traditional cloud gaming platforms. Traditional resource pooling techniques perform poorly and incur high costs during fluctuating user demands. To address this, we introduce edge intelligence to cloud computing and, employing the LSTM algorithm, construct a predictive model for resource pooling, demonstrating its efficiency and adaptability. The innovation of this paper lies in proposing a wireless communication traffic prediction model based on federated learning within a distributed architecture. Individual grid traffic prediction models are trained synchronously, and the central cloud server uses Jensen-Shannon (JS) divergence to select grid traffic models with similar distribution. It utilizes a federated averaging algorithm to merge parameters of grid traffic models with comparable distribution, aiming to enhance model generalization while accurately characterizing local traffic patterns. Additionally, the paper elaborates on optimizing resource caching through PID automatic control algorithms in the context of pooling strategies, addressing sudden spikes and drops in traffic.

Keywords: Edge Intelligence · Federated Learning · Pooling Techniques · PID

1 Introduction

With the advent of the 5G era, cloud gaming has undergone rapid development and maturation. Fundamentally, cloud gaming is an interactive online video stream, where games run on the server-side, and the rendered media is compressed and sent to users. Cloud gaming distinguishes itself from traditional

Supported by Research Innovation Fund for College Students of Beijing University of Posts and Telecommunications

X. Chen et al. (Eds.): IoTaaS 2023, LNICST 585, pp. 37–57, 2025.
https://doi.org/10.1007/978-3-031-70507-6_4

games by reducing user costs, enhancing content experience, ensuring cross-platform play, and countering piracy and cheats.

However, traditional cloud computing (centralized cloud model) faces challenges in terms of bandwidth, latency, connection quality, resource allocation, security, and more. To address the dilemmas posed by applications and scenarios that traditional cloud infrastructure may not adequately meet, the concept of edge computing has emerged. Edge computing involves shifting some of the capabilities of cloud computing from centralized data centers to the network edge. This creates a high-performance, low-latency, and high-bandwidth service environment, accelerating the response speed of various content, services, and applications in the network, providing consumers with uninterrupted high-quality network experiences.

Additionally, a key technology in cloud gaming is resource pooling. The pooling process involves two steps: first, predicting game traffic, and second, allocating cloud gaming cache resources based on these predictions. Traditional techniques, whether presetting queue lengths or dynamically adjusting them, fail to meet the demands of fluctuating traffic. Therefore, based on the edge intelligent time series prediction model, this paper introduces the PID algorithm to achieve real-time resource allocation. Compared to existing models, the newly constructed model in this paper exhibits higher adaptability. It demonstrates greater generalization in scenarios where game datasets frequently switch, improving pooling hit rates and game launch speeds, enhancing user experience, and reducing wastage.

The main contributions of this paper are:

1. This article utilized a real dataset provided by a collaborative industry-academic project to implement time series forecasting of game traffic using the LSTM algorithm. To enhance collaborative model training with data from multiple regions, this paper introduces a wireless communication traffic prediction model based on federated learning within a distributed architecture. Merging model parameters trained in different regions onto a central server aims to improve predictive performance. Experimental results indicate that the aggregated model outperforms individual models prior to federation.
2. Due to the inherent time-delay characteristics of time series forecasting based on historical data, there is a potential for slow responsiveness to sudden surges or drops in traffic, which may fail to meet user experience requirements or result in resource waste. Therefore, the paper proposes a resource pooling allocation model based on the PID automatic control algorithm. Simultaneously, to achieve the goal of enhancing user experience while reducing enterprise costs, the paper establishes a comprehensive evaluation metric to assess the resource pooling allocation model.

2   Related Research

2.1   Cloud Gaming

Cloud gaming is a novel gaming approach based on cloud computing. Under the cloud gaming operational mode, all games run on the server side, which compresses the rendered game scenes and sends them to the users over the network. Client devices do not require any high-end processors or graphics cards; basic video decompression capability suffices for a smooth gaming experience [1]. The concept of cloud gaming was first introduced by the Finnish company G-cluster and is also known as game-on-demand, a technology rooted in cloud computing [2].

Cloud gaming operates the game on the server side. When game updates are required, only a single upgrade on the server side is needed, eliminating waiting times on the client side and thereby enhancing the user experience. The process of users connecting to the cloud gaming service is as follows: firstly, the game client connects to the designated port server, which then processes the user's connection request [3]. Physical machines select an appropriate cloud gaming server based on an algorithm. Subsequently, the interface server provides the client with the IP address of the cloud gaming machine and a dynamic key [4]. Lastly, upon receiving the video streams, the client decompresses it and plays the game video on the cloud gaming client.

2.2   Mobile Edge Computing

Mobile Edge Computing (MEC) offers IT services and cloud computing capabilities close to users by leveraging wireless access networks, creating a telecommunication-grade service environment characterized by high performance, low latency, and high bandwidth [5]. It can reduce client waiting times through caching and place detachable computing tasks on edge nodes to alleviate network stress and computational loads on data centers [6].

Another significant application of Mobile Edge Computing involves utilizing MEC servers at the edge to process computing tasks, thereby offloading computational tasks from data centers. For user data uploaded under base station coverage, the MEC servers can filter and pre-aggregate this data, mitigating the computational pressure on data centers [7]. Within the design framework of edge computing, apart from the conventional content caching distribution and offloading of computational tasks from data centers, each base station's MEC server also supports a generic IT platform capable of interacting with software. Software service providers can deploy or withdraw edge computing services based on this platform to optimize their software service quality and performance [8].

2.3   Resources Pooling Technology

In the cloud gaming environment, resource pooling technology significantly influences the processing and scheduling of server-side cloud resources, thereby impacting game response latency and user experience. To address this issue, researchers proposed a cloud gaming resource allocation method based on predicting game duration. By predicting game duration using users' historical game data, resources are pre-pooled, speeding up response times and reducing latency [9]. Subsequently, researchers approached the problem from a different perspective and proposed a novel cloud gaming resource allocation strategy. Based on game attribute tags, they constructed game content feature vectors, computed recommendation indices, and performed dynamic corrections. This approach determined the initial deployment scale for cloud game content, pre-pooling resources to ensure the overall business load of the cloud game server remains balanced and stable during peak times, thereby improving key business metrics [10].

However, the dynamic nature of the cloud gaming system's load means that a one-size-fits-all resource allocation method is elusive. Keeping this challenge in mind, researchers introduced a cloud gaming adaptive resource allocation method based on reinforcement learning. By utilizing the Q-learning model in reinforcement learning, it can adaptively implement resource allocation, making optimal resource pooling decisions and reducing response latency [11].

2.4   Traffic Forecasting Models

In the digital age, traffic forecasting models play a crucial role in predicting traffic changes and optimizing resource planning. Time series analysis is a common method, exemplified by a model known for capturing data trends and patterns and widely utilized. Some researchers applied this model to forecast enterprises' free cash flow, obtaining a relatively accurate forecast value to gauge enterprise value.

Nevertheless, traditional time series models encounter limitations, requiring substantial historical data and exhibiting suboptimal performance when confronted with anomalies or irregular fluctuations. To address this challenge, machine learning methods are frequently employed in traffic forecasting. For instance, a group of researchers proposed a network traffic forecasting method based on a combined model. By integrating traditional time series analysis with machine learning, they developed a hybrid model enhancing prediction accuracy. Similarly, researchers utilized techniques based on technology for network traffic intrusion detection. Leveraging the features of technology, they extracted data characteristics, achieving higher accuracy rates in network traffic intrusion detection. Additionally, some researchers introduced a traffic forecasting method, enhancing a particle swarm algorithm to optimize neural networks. Capitalizing on the self-similarity and predictability of network traffic, they devised a superior neural network forecasting model.

3   Analysis of Traffic Characteristics

This article uses all cloud game data of a certain company in a certain month to provide the access time of different games under different service operators in Internet Data Center (IDC) computer rooms in different regions.

3.1   Data Processing

This article processes the original data to facilitate subsequent cache prediction. First, clean the data, complete the missing time series data, and delete spaces and illegal characters in the data to ensure the tidiness and effectiveness of the data. Next, time slicing and integration are performed to resample and integrate the data of the same region, the same computer room, and the same game at a 5-min granularity to obtain the number of user visits for every 5 consecutive minutes. The 24-h user access traffic under different IDCs is plotted as shown in Fig. 1. It can be found from the figure that the traffic data at noon and evening is relatively large, while the traffic data in the morning and afternoon is relatively small, which is related to people's work and rest. It shows that traffic data is highly correlated with time.

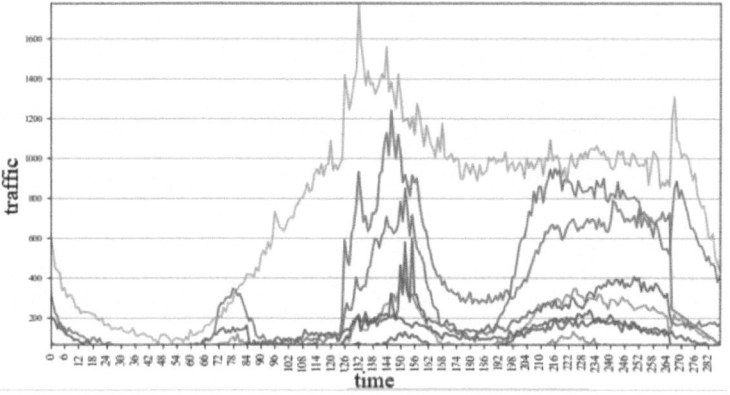

Fig. 1. Traffic changes every 5 min in different IDCs on a certain day

In order to accurately predict the cache pooling of cloud game resources below, this section conducts data analysis on game traffic for different IDC computer rooms, different games and different service operators. From the figure, it can be found that the traffic of different IDC computer rooms The difference is still quite large, and need to conduct a more detailed analysis.

3.2   Analysis of Data Traffic in Different IDC Computer Rooms

First, in order to explore whether there is a certain correlation in the data under different IDC computer rooms, the total number of single-day user visits under 10 different IDCs (from different provinces) was averaged, and the correlation coefficient matrix was made and visualized to obtain the average traffic of different IDCs. The correlation between them is shown in Fig. 2, in which the horizontal and vertical coordinates respectively represent 10 IDC computer rooms in various places.

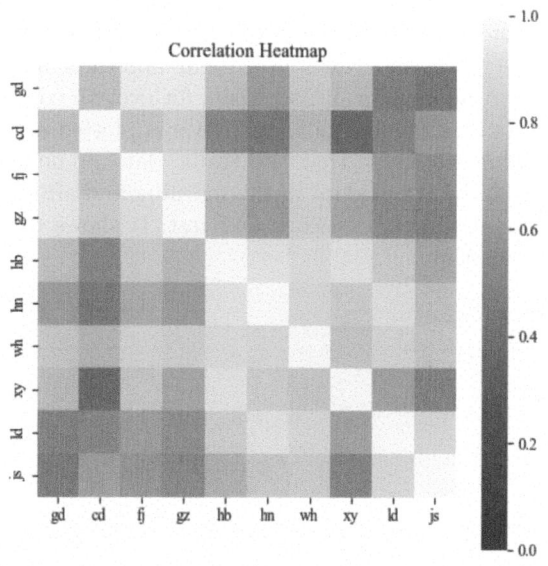

Fig. 2. Correlation between 24-h average traffic changes of different IDCs within a day

As can be seen from Fig. 2, the correlation between IDC traffic changes in different provinces within a single day is very high, and most of the correlation coefficients are above 0.8. Based on actual analysis, under the unified time system, the work and rest of users in each province are basically the same, so the data correlation is high, and the subtle differences will be more prominent under large time scale changes. The high correlation between traffic data is the prerequisite for applying transfer learning to the model.

Secondly, select the data of the same service operator under the base stations of two different provinces, and depict the traffic characteristics between them, as shown in Fig. 3: as can be seen from the box plot in Fig. 3, the overlap of the same service operator under different IDCs is small, the traffic difference is large, and the correlation is low.

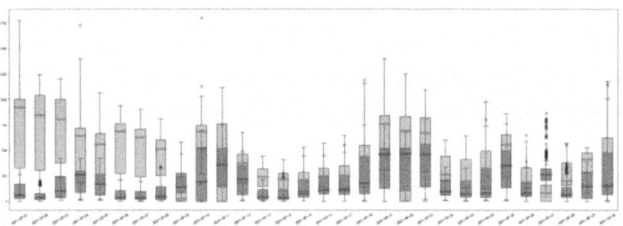

Fig. 3. Traffic characteristics of Region 1 and Region 2 under the same service operator

3.3   Traffic Data Analysis of Different Games

Analyzing the traffic data of different games, Fig. 5 shows the total traffic changes of different games within 30 days.

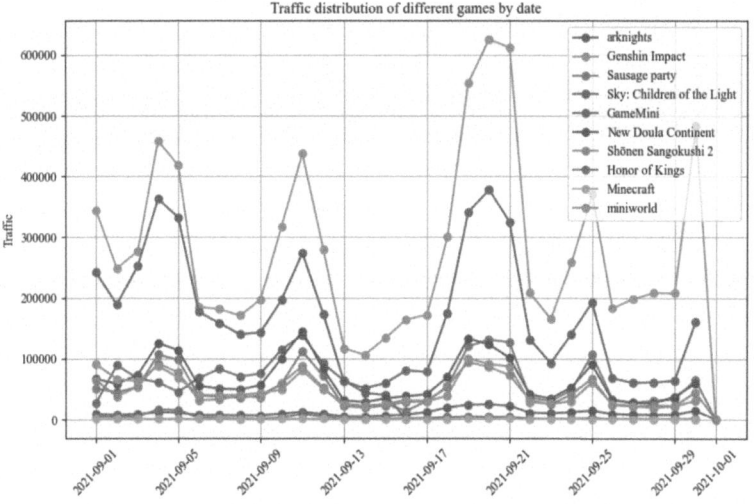

Fig. 4. Single-day total traffic characteristics of Top10 games

In Fig. 4, the games 'Genshin Impact' and 'Light Encounter' have the largest total traffic, and both reached their peak traffic of the month from the 19th to the 21st. The traffic change trends of different games within 30 days are generally similar. There will be a significant increase in traffic during holidays, while traffic is at a low point on weekdays. Special events and activities in the game will lead to sudden increases and decreases in game traffic. The traffic data of different games show a certain degree of correlation and high volatility in the time dimension.

3.4   Data Traffic Analysis of Different Service Operators

Analyzing the traffic data of different service operators, Fig. 6 shows the traffic changes of the top 10 service operators in total traffic within 30 days. The traffic change trend is similar to Fig. 5. The traffic changes of different service operators show high correlation and high volatility.

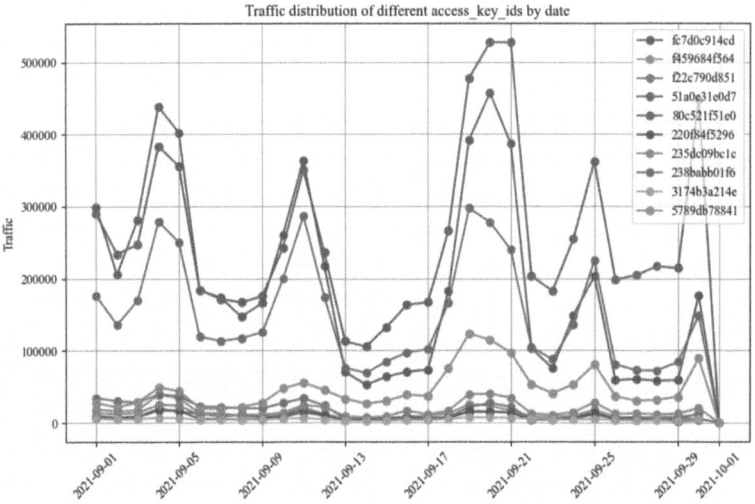

Fig. 5. Traffic characteristics among the top 10 service operators by day

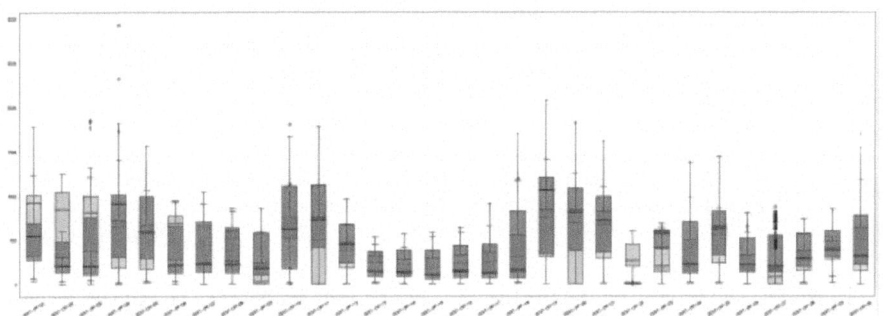

Fig. 6. Traffic characteristics of Top1 & Top2 IDC service operators

Further, select the service operators with Top1 & Top2 traffic in an IDC computer room within the top 10 total traffic. The traffic relationship characteristics between the two are shown in Fig. 6: It can be seen from the box plot that the traffic overlap of the two service operators in this area is relatively large, and the overall traffic is basically similar, with a certain statistical correlation. In addition, the traffic of both service operators shows significantly higher peaks during holidays compared with weekdays.

4   Cloud Gaming Demand Prediction Model

4.1   Federated Learning Within a Distributed Architecture

Training deep learning models using traffic data from multiple enterprises in different IDC (Internet Data Center) facilities across various regions enables the model to learn more relevant features of the traffic data, thereby further improving the predictive accuracy of the model. However, in practical applications, due to concerns about data privacy, it is not feasible for traffic data between different enterprises to be openly shared for model training. Therefore, in this section, this article employ federated learning algorithms. Models trained in different IDC facilities are uploaded to a central server for collaborative training. The trained identical model is then distributed back to each IDC facility for local training, achieving an enhancement in the predictive performance of the model.

Federated learning adopts a decentralized approach to handle collaborative learning tasks. In this framework, a central server is responsible for coordinating learning objectives and aggregating models, while multiple client nodes use their local datasets to train local models. This method combines accuracy and efficiency while satisfying user privacy requirements. Assuming there is a dataset with N local nodes $D_1,...,D_i,...,D_N$, and $D_i := |D_i|$ represents the number of data samples each node possesses, the federated learning algorithm aims to minimize the expression:

$$\min F(W) := \sum_{i=1}^{N} \Psi_i F_i(W) \tag{1}$$

where W represents the global model weights, and $\psi_i = D_i/\sum_{i=1}^{N} D_i$ is the weight of the model during federated learning aggregation. The local objective function $F_i(W)$ is employed instead of the global objective function $F(W)$. The following describes the role of the local objective function $F_i(W)$. $F_i(W)$ typically assesses the local empirical risk $p^{(i)}$ that may arise due to different data distributions on nodes. $F_i(W)$ is defined using cross-entropy:

$$\min F_i(W) = -\sum_{j=1}^{C} p^{(i)}(y = j) E_{x[y=j]} [\log f_j(x, w)] \tag{2}$$

where $f_j(x, w)$ represents the probability of data sample being classified as the jth class by the specified model w, and $p^{(i)}(y = j)$ represents the data classification on node i for class $j \notin [C]$.

In a typical federated learning setup, participating nodes use the same configuration for local training. In each update round, a subset of the total node set, denoted as $S_t (|S_t| = K \ll N)$, is selected, and the global model $W(t - 1)$

from the previous iteration is sent to the selected nodes. Each node involved in federated learning performs stochastic gradient descent (SGD) to optimize its respective local objective function $F_i(W)$:

$$w_i(t) = w(t-1) - \eta \nabla F_i(w(t-1)) \tag{3}$$

where η represents the learning rate and the gradient at node i. The equation provides the general principles of SGD optimization, where $w_i(t)$ can be the result of one or multiple local updates of SGD. In the scenario below, SGD is applied to a small dataset of size B, and thus the local dataset is updated $\tau = \frac{D_i}{B} \times E$ times, where D_i and E are the number of samples trained on the node and the number of local training rounds, respectively.

Afterwards, these nodes update the models trained locally to the central server, which aggregates this data and updates the global model.

$$\Delta(t) = \sum_{i=1}^{|S_i|} \psi_i \Delta_i(t) \tag{4}$$

$$W(t) = W(t-1) + \Delta(t) \tag{5}$$

4.2   Transfer Learning

Due to the asynchronous construction of IDC (Internet Data Center) facilities in different regions, when a new IDC facility needs to be established in a new location, training a traffic prediction model for that IDC facility requires collecting a substantial dataset. This is often impractical for recently commissioned IDC facilities. The lack of effective traffic prediction methods for IDC facilities can lead to resource wastage or network congestion. Therefore, employing transfer learning techniques to migrate pre-trained model parameters from IDC facilities in other regions to the newly deployed IDC facility's traffic prediction model can significantly reduce training time and save costs.

Transfer learning is a form of machine learning in which a well-trained machine learning model A is obtained by training on a known dataset. The parameters of this model A are saved, and when developing another machine learning model B, there is no need to start training from scratch. Instead, model B is trained based on the foundation of model A, simplifying the training process and reducing training costs. The prerequisite for successful transfer learning is that there should be some similarity between the datasets and the training models of both models. It is through this similarity that a bridge is constructed from old knowledge to new knowledge, allowing for faster and more effective learning of new knowledge.

5   Pooling Resource Allocation Model

5.1   Construction of Comprehensive Evaluation Metrics

After achieving accurate predictions of cloud gaming traffic data, it is essential to proactively manage the pooling resource allocation on the servers of cloud gaming service providers to meet the configuration demands of gamers. This paper considers the performance and rapid fitting capability of different prediction mechanisms.

On the server-side, within each 5-min interval, resource pooling is carried out based on the results of the prediction function. Assuming time slots in 5-min increments, let represent a specific time slot (where t denotes the t-th 5-min interval). Within time slot t, the relative pooling error rate $(PRER_t)$ can be calculated as $PRER_t = (Pool_t - Real_t)/Real_t$, where $Pool_t$ represents the total pooled resources on the server and $Real_t$ signifies the total number of requests from all covered users $N = \{1, 2, ..., N\}$ during that time slot.

To quantify the pooling effect, this paper employs a comprehensive pooling algorithm metric, denoted as δ_t to measure the pooling efficiency. Within specific pooling scenarios, the primary trade-off lies between user experience and corporate costs. Companies aim to provide a superior user experience to enhance user satisfaction, but they must also control costs to maintain profitability. In order to determine the optimal allocation strategy that strikes a balance between providing an excellent user experience and sustaining reasonable costs, this paper utilizes a 'multi-index comprehensive scoring method' to decompose δ_t into weighted sums of user experience indicators denoted as UXI_t and cost indicators denoted as CI_t .This decomposition is specifically defined as follows:

$$\delta_t = 0.4 * UXI_t + 0.6 * CI_t \tag{6}$$

Subsequently, through prior investigations into user experience perception and corporate cost assessments under varying pooling quantities, this paper individually plots curves for the user experience indicator (UXI_t) and the cost indicator (CI_t) concerning the relative pooling error rate $(PRER_t)$. These curves are fitted using an exponential modeling approach to closely capture the trends and characteristics of the original data. Consequently, expressions for UXI_t and CI_t as functions of $PRER_t$ are derived, and fitting curves are generated:

$$UXI_t = 1 - 0.5e^{-PRER_t} \tag{7}$$

$$CI_t = 1 - e^{PRER_t - 1.5} \tag{8}$$

When $PRER_t$ is equal to 0.2, meaning that the total pooling count is 1.2 times the total number of requests, the user experience indicator (UXI_t) reaches its maximum value of 1. This occurs because, under cost constraints, the total pooling count $(Pool_t)$ should slightly exceed the number of requests $(Real_t)$ for users to have a better experience. When pr is greater than 0, the cost indicator (CI_t) sharply decreases because unnecessary pooling waste leads to a meaningless increase in costs.

The main variables and their meanings in this study are summarized in Table 1. Representation of the Comprehensive evaluation metric (δ_t) in Terms of the Relative Pooling Error Rate $(PRER_t)$, along with the corresponding figure:

$$\delta_t = 1 - 0.2e^{-PRER_t} - 0.6e^{PRER_t - 1.5} \tag{9}$$

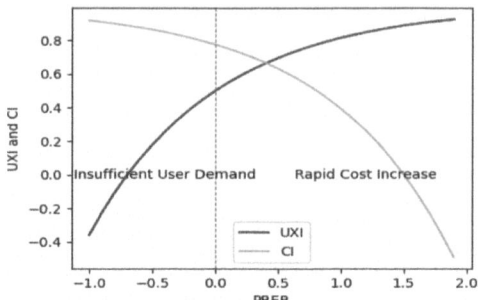

Fig. 7. Traffic characteristics among the top 10 service operators by day

Table 1. System Parameters

parameters	meaning
$PRER_t$	Relative pooling error rate in time slot
$Pool_t$	Total pooling in time slot
$Peal_t$	Actual number of user requests in time slot
$Pred_t$	Predicted number of user requests by servers in time slot
UXI_t	User experience indicator in time slot
CI_t	Cost indicator in time slot
δ_t	Comprehensive evaluation metric in time slot

From Fig. 8, it is evident that increasing the total pooling count $(Pool_t)$ enhances user experience, but it also leads to a higher number of idle processes, increasing server load and operational costs. Conversely, reducing the total pooling count $(Pool_t)$ decreases costs and server load but results in longer user wait times, diminishing the gaming experience. When the relative pooling error rate deviates from the optimal value, the comprehensive evaluation metric (δ_t) rapidly decreases. Therefore, the choice of the total pooling count ($Pool_t$) should strike a balance between user experience and enterprise costs.

In time slot, to minimize server-side pooling resource waste while ensuring an optimal user experience, the following constraints must be met: 1) Sufficient network link bandwidth for all users; 2) Available pooling resources on the server when user requests arrive; 3) Minimal server-side pooling quantity in the absence of user requests. Fulfilling constraints 1) and 2) is essential to guarantee a satisfactory user experience. Failure to meet constraint 3) may result in the server maintaining a high pooling quantity continuously, leading to resource wastage. Both the user experience indicator (UXI_t) and the cost indicator (CI_t) have been positively oriented. Consequently, the optimization goal of this paper is equivalent to finding the maximum value of the comprehensive evaluation metric (δ_t).

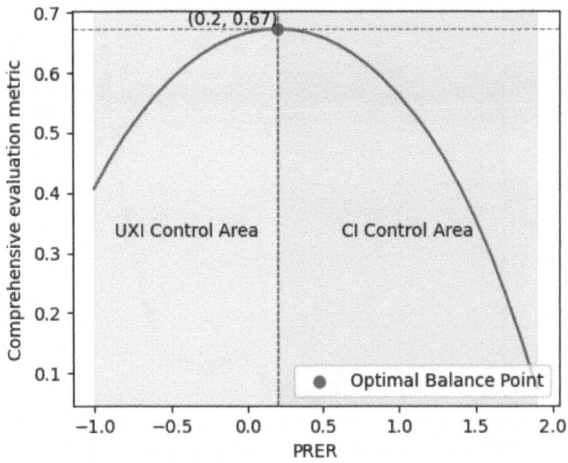

Fig. 8. Traffic characteristics among the top 10 service operators by day

5.2   PID-Based Delay Compensation Pooling Algorithm

When a cloud gaming player submits a web request, it typically corresponds to the initiation of a game. Consequently, this article correlate the access traffic of cloud games with the game pooling quantity, setting the pooling number every five minutes as a function related to the traffic prediction value. If this function represents a straightforward one-dimensional linear equation:

$$Pool_t = a \times Pred_t + b \tag{10}$$

Where both coefficients are to be optimized. Utilizing the comprehensive evaluation metric described earlier, this article can identify the coefficient values that yield the best user experience while maintaining cost-effectiveness. However, algorithms such as LSTM, ARIMA, and CATBOOST base their future predictions on historical data and inherently exhibit time-delay characteristics. This suggests their potential insensitivity in rapidly responding to sudden surges or drops in traffic. The following figure further elucidates this:

From the aforementioned figure, this article observe that at a specific time instance, the pooling value curve lags significantly behind the actual value. This observation suggests potential limitations of the linear pooling strategy in addressing sudden surges in user traffic. To reflect traffic trends in real-time and optimize our comprehensive algorithm metric, this study introduces a PID-based delay compensation strategy.

The PID algorithm is a widely-used feedback control strategy, adjusting the control output in real-time based on the error (the difference between the actual and desired outputs). In the context of this research, the PID strategy continuously monitors the discrepancy between the pooling value and the actual traffic value at the previous time instance, thereby adjusting the pooling strategy

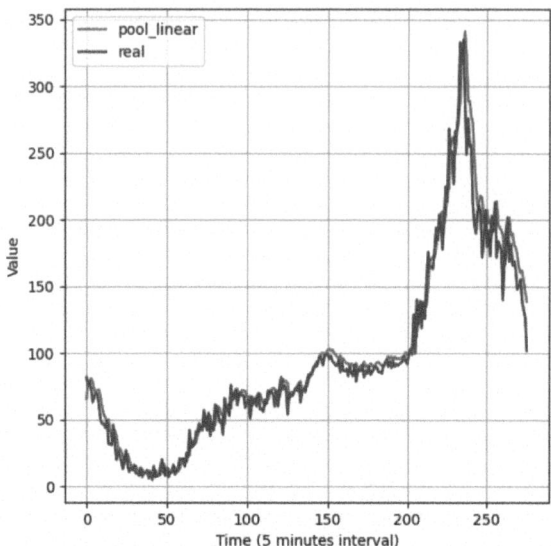

Fig. 9. Traffic characteristics among the top 10 service operators by day

for the next moment in real-time. If a significant deviation is detected between the pooling strategy and the real traffic value at the previous moment, PID will quickly recalibrate to ensure that subsequent pooling closely aligns with the true traffic trend.

The pooling function incorporating PID control is given by:

$$Pool_t = [a_t + P(Real_{t-1} - Pool_{t-1}) + D\nabla(Real_{t-1} - Pool_{t-1})] \times Pred_t + b_t \quad (11)$$

6   Performance Analysis

6.1   Analysis of Prediction Model

The fitting evaluation metrics used in this article are as follows:

1. Root Mean Square Error (RMSE):

$$RMSE = \sqrt{\frac{1}{n}\sum_{i=1}^{n}(\hat{y}_i - y_i)^2} \quad (12)$$

RMSE is the square root of the mean squared error between the predicted values and the actual values. A smaller RMSE indicates a better fit of the data.

2. Mean Absolute Error (MAE):

$$MAE = \frac{1}{n} \sum_{i=1}^{n} |\hat{y}_i - y_i| \tag{13}$$

MAE is the mean of the absolute differences between the predicted values and the actual values. A smaller MAE indicates a better fit of the data.

3. Coefficient of Determination: R-squared (R2):

$$R2 = 1 - \frac{\sum_{i=1}^{n}(\hat{y}_i - y_i)^2}{\sum_{i=1}^{n}(\bar{y}_i - y_i)^2} \tag{14}$$

The numerator is the sum of squared differences between the actual values and the predicted values, and the denominator represents the sum of squared differences between the actual values and the mean value. R-squared values range from $[0, 1]$, with values closer to 1 indicating a higher degree of fit.

The article describes the process of training models using a divided training dataset, introducing a validation set to monitor loss convergence, and utilizing the trained models to make predictions on a test dataset. The results for two different algorithms, ARIMA and LSTM, are presented for predicting traffic data for three games: 'Genshin Impact',using access_key_id 51a0e31e0d7.

The results are visualized in Figs. 10 and 11, with explanations for each figure:

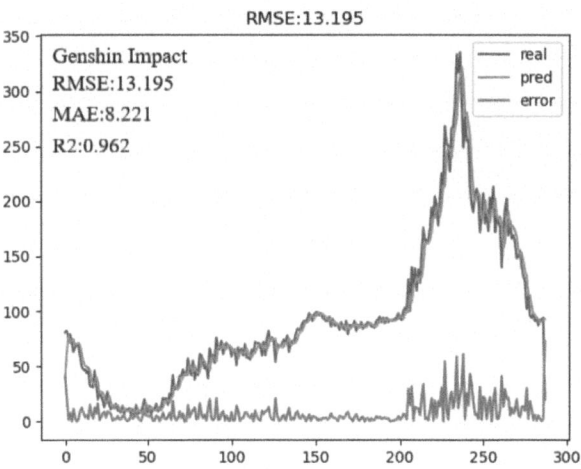

Fig. 10. ARIMA Predictive Results

In Fig. 10, the 'real' line represents the actual traffic data for the entire day on October 31st, while the 'pred' line represents the predictions made by the

ARIMA model after training on the traffic time series. The 'error' line shows the absolute differences between the actual and predicted values, providing an intuitive indication of prediction performance. Based on three evaluation metrics, it can be observed that the ARIMA algorithm can achieve reasonably accurate predictions for the high-traffic 'Genshin Impact' game.

Using the LSTM algorithm to predict traffic for the 'Genshin Impact' game with access_key_id 51a0e31e0d7 yields the results shown in Fig. 11.

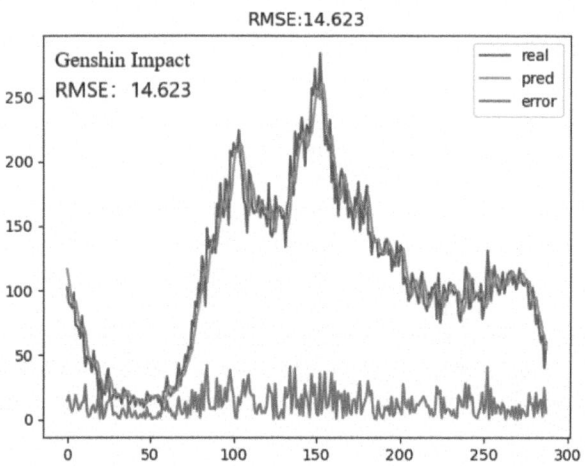

Fig. 11. LSTM Predictive Results

The 'pred' line represents the predictions made by the LSTM model after training on the traffic time series. The 'real' and 'error' lines serve the same purpose as in Fig. 11.

The text highlights that LSTM outperforms ARIMA in terms of accuracy, as indicated by a lower error (RMSE) for all three games: 'Genshin Impact' .

In summary, both ARIMA and LSTM algorithms are used for traffic data prediction, with LSTM demonstrating superior predictive accuracy compared to ARIMA, as indicated by lower error values. The results are presented graphically to provide a clear visual understanding of the models' performance.

To compare the predictive performance of the three algorithms, the article mentions using 'Genshin Impact' as an example and plotting the predictive results of the three algorithm models against the actual values in a single graph (Fig. 12). The evaluation metrics for each algorithm, namely RMSE, MAE, and R2, are also provided in Table 1 for this specific access_key_id and game.

From Fig. 12, it can be observed that the predictive results of the various algorithms closely match the actual values, indicating their capability to perform accurate predictions of game traffic. To assess the relative performance of these algorithms, evaluation metrics are necessary. Using 'Genshin Impact' as an

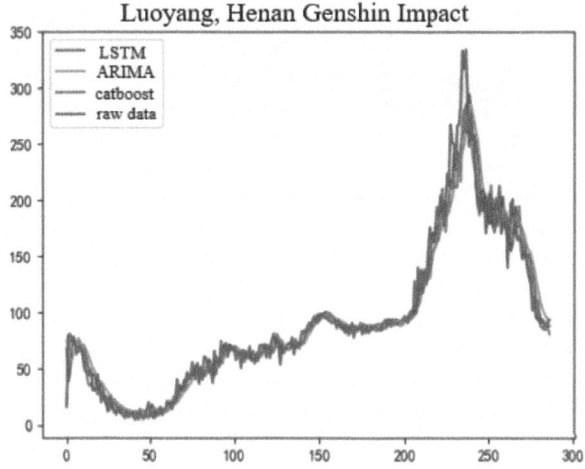

Fig. 12. Predictive Results for "Genshin Impact" Using Three Algorithms

illustrative example for this access_key_id, the RMSE, MAE, and R2 metrics for each algorithm are provided in Table 2.

Table 2. Three Algorithm Evaluation Metrics Comparison

	ARIMA	LSTM	Catboost
RMSE	13.195	12.474	13.148
MAE	8.221	8.137	8.049
R2	0.962	0.965	0.962

From the results, it is evident that the deep learning-based LSTM algorithm outperforms the traditional time series forecasting method ARIMA in terms of accuracy, as indicated by the significantly lower RMSE. The Catboost algorithm, based on machine learning, shows predictive performance similar to that of ARIMA. This suggests that LSTM, with its unique mechanisms like cell states and forget gates, has a significant advantage in cloud gaming traffic data prediction.

In summary, while all three algorithms provide reasonably good predictions for 'Genshin Impact' LSTM demonstrates superior accuracy compared to ARIMA and Catboost, with lower RMSE values.

6.2   Analysis of Resource Pooling Algorithms Model

Using the LSTM prediction strategy as an example and given different coefficients, the performance of the comprehensive evaluation metric $\delta(t)$ is illustrated by the contour lines in Fig. 13.

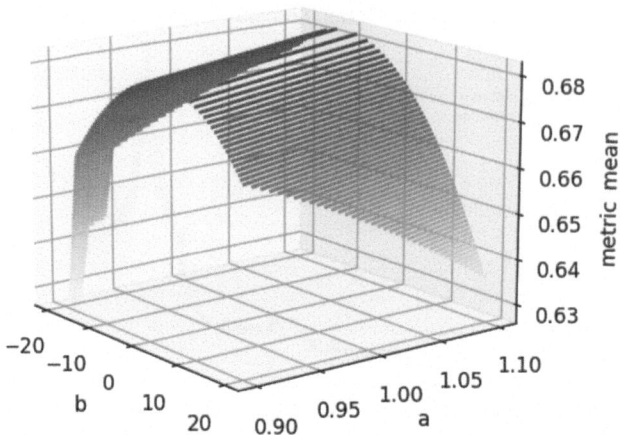

Fig. 13. Evaluation Metrics of Parameters a and b in the First Half-hour

In Fig. 13, the x-axis represents the range of possible values for parameter a, spanning from 0.9 to 1.1; the y-axis signifies the range for parameter b, ranging from −20 to 20; the z-axis showcases the average evaluation metric derived from various combinations of parameters a and b. A full day consists of 288 five-minute intervals. For a more precise analysis, these intervals are broken down into 48 half-hour segments. For each 5-min interval, user experience and cost metrics are computed using the provided formula, leading to a comprehensive pooling algorithm evaluation for that interval. By averaging the evaluation values across 30 consecutive 5-min segments, this paper obtain the average comprehensive metric for that particular half-hour. Based on this data, this article identified the a and b parameter values that maximize the average comprehensive evaluation metric.

Through such an analysis, this article determined an optimal set of a and b values for each half-hour segment. Subsequently, this article employed the PID algorithm to approximate these optimal a, b values, allowing for automatic adjustments of parameters a and b every half-hour in practical applications, aiming to further enhance the overall comprehensive evaluation metric.

After comprehensively considering user experience and cost metrics, this paper adjusted the predicted traffic value to arrive at what we term the 'optimal pooling value', represented by the red line in the figure. However, in real-time prediction, there is no prior knowledge of the actual traffic value. We can only adjust based on the previous moment's pooling situation and optimize parameters a and b using the PID algorithm. The goal is to make the actual pooling value align as closely as possible with the optimal pooling value. This adjusted pooling value is represented by the green line in the figure. Observations from the chart indicate that the revised PID approach allows the green line to fit the red line closely. Compared to the actual values, this significantly rectifies the

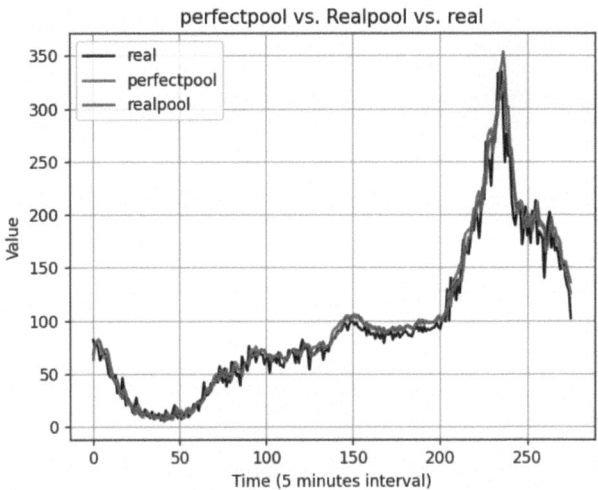

Fig. 14. Optimal Pooling Value, Actual Pooling Value, and Real Traffic Value

deviation caused by the delay between the pooling value and the actual traffic value.

This study primarily discusses the delay compensation method based on PID. Another effective solution is the 'accumulation' delay compensation method, which addresses the issue of pooling latency. The central idea behind this method is to set a higher pooling value at specific moments and then accumulate the excess pooling value to the subsequent intervals. This continuous accumulation ensures that when there's a sudden surge in traffic, the original pooling value augmented with the accumulated portion can meet the users' traffic needs, mitigating issues caused by the inherent delay.

Next, this paper will compare the PID-based delay compensation method with the 'accumulation' delay compensation approach, presenting a comparison of comprehensive evaluation metrics for each interval and an overall accumulated comprehensive evaluation comparison.

As illustrated in Fig. 15, the comprehensive evaluation metrics derived using the accumulation algorithm exhibited significant fluctuations, even reaching negative values at certain intervals. In contrast, the metrics calculated using the PID algorithm demonstrate much higher stability.

From Fig. 16, it is evident that the implementation of either the accumulation or PID algorithm has significantly enhanced the cumulative comprehensive evaluation metrics throughout the day, thereby achieving a better balance between user experience and enterprise costs. Notably, the PID algorithm outperforms the accumulation algorithm in terms of performance. This observation further confirms that, in the context of resource pooling allocation, the PID algorithm can more consistently and stably strike a balance between user experience and enterprise costs.

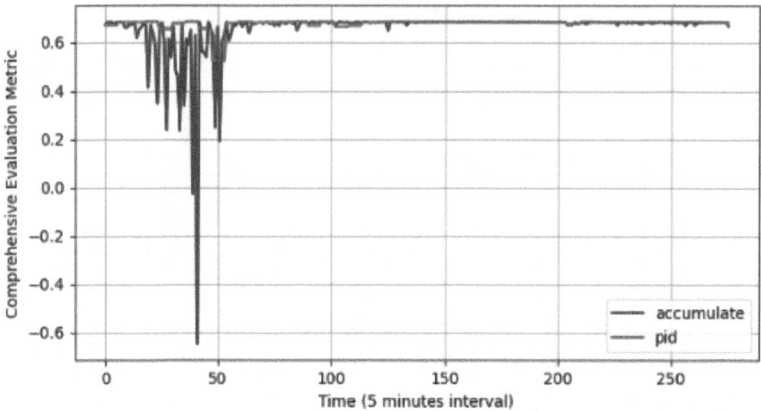

Fig. 15. Comparative Figure of Comprehensive Evaluation Metrics

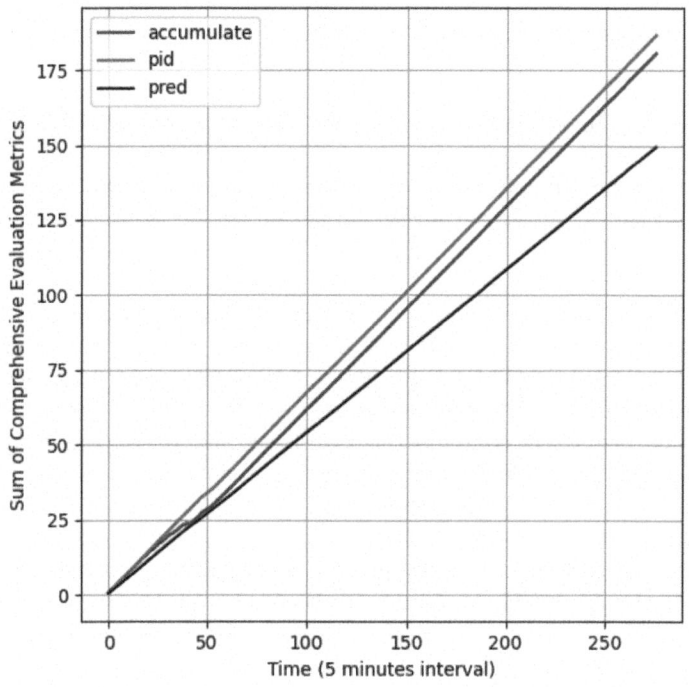

Fig. 16. Cumulative Comprehensive Evaluation Comparison

7   Conclusion

In the present era, marked by the rapid advancement of information technology, a new content distribution paradigm based on cloud gaming is diverging from the traditional modes of download-installation and interest recommendation, steadily expanding its market reach. While the current phase of cloud gaming predominantly focuses on cloud adaptations of already popular games, the continuous growth in cloud gaming users indicates a shift. It's anticipated that native cloud games will soon be embraced within the creative scope of major game developers. Thanks to the unique advantages of cloud gaming, it holds the potential to further attract not only avid gamers but also those previously uninterested, establishing a positive feedback loop for its continued evolution. This underscores the pressing need for more efficient traffic prediction algorithms and resource pooling management techniques.

Simultaneously, with a constant rise in the number of internet data centers nationwide, IDC's traffic throughput witnesses consistent year-on-year growth. Accurate and timely predictions of internet data center traffic can foster real-time optimization of network resource allocations. This not only avoids potential network congestion but also significantly elevates the service stability of these data centers, ultimately leading to reduced operational and maintenance costs. Thus, research focused on traffic prediction for internet data centers harbors a vast horizon of application potentials.

References

1. Guan, P.: Analysis of the convergence development of cloud computing and animation/game industries in Fujian Province. Res. Fine Arts Educ. **17**, 110–111 (2013)
2. Liu, K., Lin, G.: Discussion on cloud game technology in 5G era. Wirel. Connect. Technol. **19**(06), 104–105 (2022)
3. Tang, F., Liu, X.: Research on a novel cloud gaming resource allocation model. Guangdong Commun. Technol. **41**(12), 2–5 (2021)
4. Han, Z.: Cloud gaming: a new industry based on cloud computing platform. China Comput. Commun. **17**, 47–51 (2017)
5. Tang, J., Xu, F., Pu, Q.: Research on the core network architecture for Guangxi Unicom's Internet of Things in the 5G era. Guangxi Commun. Technol. **131**(02), 23–27 (2018)
6. Hou, J., Zhang, Y., Xu, H., Zhu, X., Xing, K.: Research on mobile edge computing unloading based on deep reinforcement learning. J. Jinling Inst. Technol.
7. Shen, H., Wang, L.: Task offloading based on mobile edge computing and its privacy-preserving issues: a survey. **69**(02), 258–269 (2023)
8. Ismail, B., Goortani, E., Karim, M.: Evaluation of docker as edge computing platform. In: 2015 IEEE Conference on Open Systems (ICOS). IEEE (2015)
9. Wei, B., Wei, D.: Resource allocation for cloud gaming based on game-session-length prediction. Comput. Eng. Des.
10. Tang, Y., Liu, X.: Research on a Novel Cloud Gaming Resource Allocation Model
11. Liu, H.: Research of Adaptive Resource Allocation in Cloud Gaming
12. Xu, L., Zhao, W.: Prediction of Free Cash Flow of Enterprises Based on ARIMA Model
13. Cao, Q., Chen, X., Liu, H.: Network Traffic Forecasting Method Based on SARIMA-LSTM Hybrid Model
14. Shi, L., Zhang, J., Gao, F.: Intrusion Detection in Network Traffic Using Transformer and BiLSTM-Based Technology
15. Shen, Y., Li, L.:The Realization of Traffic Prediction by Improving Particle Swarm Optimization and Optimizing BP Network

Hardware-Efficient Polar Decoder for 5G Internet of Things Communication

Jing Guo$^{(\boxtimes)}$ and Congduan Li

School of Electronics and Communication Engineering, Sun Yat-sen University,
Shenzhen, China
guoj233@mail2.sysu.edu.cn, licongd@mail.sysu.edu.cn

Abstract. Polar codes have aroused extensive attention due to their capacity-achieving property and low encoding and decoding complexity. With the increasing demand for real-time and high-quality applications, achieving low-latency communication in resource-constrained scenarios such as on Internet of Things (IoT) devices has become essential. This paper proposes a modified semi-parallel decoder for 5G IoT communication, with low decoding latency and high efficiency of hardware resources. 4-bit decoding algorithm and look-ahead approach are used in this work to reduce latency caused by conventional semi-parallel architecture. For a code length of N = 2^{10}, the proposed decoder improves latency by 48.64% and 75.19% than the conventional semi-parallel decoder and 2-bit decoder, separately. The significant improvement in hardware utilization rate of processing elements by 68.42% and 119.35% leads to high efficiency of hardware resources.

Keywords: Internet of things · Polar codes · Wireless communication · Hardware architecture · Field programmable gate array

1 Introduction

The evolving of fifth generation (5G) networks is becoming more readily available as a major driver of the growth of Internet of things (IoT) applications. The challenges for Emerging 5G-IoT Scenarios, such as reliability performance, latency and throughput, cost-efficiency, remain significant [1]. Polar code [2], proposed by Arıkan, is the first forward error-correcting code that achieves the channel capacity of binary-input discrete memoryless channels (B-DMCs). In the 5G enhanced mobile broadband (eMBB) scenarios[3], the polar codes are adopted as the coding scheme for the control channel. Since the encoding and decoding complexity of polar codes are relatively low, low-latency and hardware-efficient polar decoder is suitable for 5G-IoT communication.

Successive cancellation (SC) decoding [2], one of main types of polar codes decoding algorithm, achieves low complexity of O(NlogN). Derived from SC

© ICST Institute for Computer Sciences, Social Informatics and Telecommunications Engineering 2025
Published by Springer Nature Switzerland AG 2025. All Rights Reserved
X. Chen et al. (Eds.): IoTaaS 2023, LNICST 585, pp. 58–68, 2025.
https://doi.org/10.1007/978-3-031-70507-6_5

decoding, successive cancellation list (SCL) decoding [4] and successive cancellation flip (SCF) decoding [5], have been broadly studied for better error-correction
performance but with higher complexity. Belief propagation (BP) decoding [6]
takes the advantage of low latency as well as high throughput, at the cost of high
computation complexity, which is not suitable for resource-constrained applications.

In terms of hardware implementation, SC decoding architectures such as line
architecture and tree architecture were proposed in [7]. In [8], a semi-parallel
architecture was proposed to reduce processing complexity, which consumed less
hardware resources than the prior ones. However, less throughput is performed
by semi-parallel architecture than other architectures owing to its increased
latency. A partial-sum unit with shift register was proposed in [9], which reduces
delay in critical path and improve the frequency of the previous partial-sum
unit used in [10]. A look-ahead technique was proposed to accelerate SC decoding in [11] by calculating all the possible outcome of the bits that have not been
decoded yet ahead of time, and choosing the appropriate one once the corresponding bit is computed. Multi-bit decoding algorithm and architectures were
proposed to decode more than one bit in [12,13]. However, the relative increase
in hardware resources consumption is more than the relative decline in latency.

In this work, a novel semi-parallel architecture of polar decoder is introduced.
The proposed architecture uses 4-bit decoding algorithm and look-ahead approach to reduce latency and improve the efficiency of hardware resource, which
is suitable for resource-constrained devices. The main contributions of our work
can be summarized as follows: Our design extends the semi-parallel architecture in [10] to remain high efficiency of hardware resource and reduce latency
punishment. The proposed decoder reduces hardware resources by yielding better hardware utilization of processing elements with better latency performance
compared to [10,14,15].

The remainder of this paper is organized as follows: Sect. 2 provides an
introduction to polar codes and SC decoding algorithm. In Sect. 3, the proposed
architecture is presented. Then, the performance and comparisons are discussed
in Sect. 4. Section 5 concludes the work.

2   Background

2.1   Polar Codes

Polar codes are operated based on channel combination and polarization theory.
Consider an (N,K) polar codeword, where K represents the length of information
and $N=2^n$ denotes the length of codeword. The information vector (u_0, u_1, u_2,
u_3,..., u_{K-1}) is to be encoded and the rest of $N-K$ bits are defined as frozen bits.
K information bits are assigned at the most reliable positions and $N-K$ frozen
bits, usually set as '0', are assigned at the rest positions. Then, the encoded
vector $X_0^{N-1} = (X_0,X_1,X_2,X_3, ..., X_{N-1})$ can be derived from the information
vector u_0^{K-1} by the generator matrix G_N as

$$X_0^{N-1} = u_0^{K-1}G_N, \tag{1}$$

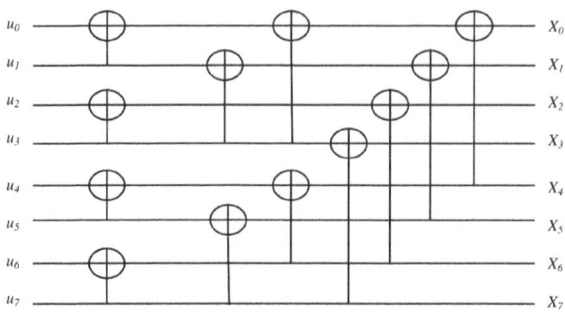

Fig. 1. Encoding graph of polar codes for N=8.

where the generator matrix can be obtained by n times kronecker power of following matrix

$$F = \begin{bmatrix} 1 & 0 \\ 1 & 1 \end{bmatrix}. \tag{2}$$

The encoding graph of polar codes for N=8 is shown as Fig. 1.

2.2   Successive Cancellation Decoding Algorithm

SC algorithm decodes the information vector from the log-likelihood ratios (LLRs) $L_{n,i}$. The bit u_i is estimated successively according to the previously decoded bits and LLR values. The process of decoding is illustrated in Fig. 2.

Function f and g can be calculated by the min-sum functions

$$f(L_a, L_b) \approx \text{sign}(L_a)\,\text{sign}(L_b)\,\min(|L_a|, |L_b|), \tag{3}$$

$$g(\hat{s}, L_a, L_b) = L_a(-1)^{\hat{s}} + L_b. \tag{4}$$

Consider $N = 2^n$ is the polar codes length and let $L_{l,i}$ be the LLRs at each stage. During the decoding process, the decoded vector can be calculated by

$$u_i = \begin{cases} 0 & \text{if } i \epsilon A_c \\ 1 & \text{if } L_{0,i} \geq 0 \\ 0 & \text{otherwise}, \end{cases} \tag{5}$$

where u_i is the decoded bit and $L_{0,i}$ is the LLR of corresponding bit u_i .

3   Proposed Semi-parallel Decoder Architecture

3.1   Over Architecture

The computation part of the proposed decoder mainly consists of processing elements (PEs), which perform g function or f function mentioned before. Due

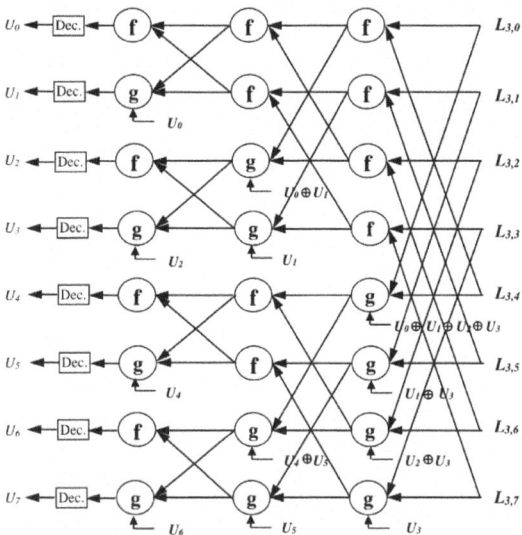

Fig. 2. SC decoding of polar codes for N = 8.

to the sequential nature of SC decoding, some of the PEs are set in idle state during the later stages of decoding, resulting in low utilization of the PEs. The most imperfection that all previous structures confronted is their utilization rate of PEs declines as the code length increases. [10] proposed a semi-parallel architecture to reduce the number of PEs implemented, resulting in higher resource utilization. However, as multiple cycles are required for node updates of LLR values, this leads to increased latency. Complicated multiplexing logic results in complicated control modules between PEs and the rest of the parts, which also increases latency.

In this work, we proposed a novel SC polar decoder with semi-parallel architecture using 4-bit decoding, as shown in Fig. 3. In order to make use of hardware resources, a larger codeword is decoder by PEs lesser than N/2.

The mechanism of the proposed decoder can be summarized as follows. Firstly, the LLRs received from the channel are loaded into the random access memory (RAM), which can store and output data simultaneously, to be further processed. The f node and g node of PEs receive LLRs respectively. Then, The PEs output intermediate LLR values such as minimum, added and subtracted LLRs. Then, these LLRs are put into the corresponding RAMs by multiplexers (MUXs). In the decoding process, f node LLRs and channel LLRs are preserved in one RAM. The rest two RAMs are utilized to preserved added and subtracted LLR values of g node respectively. The LLRs produced by the last but one stage are processed by 4-bit PEs and the output of these PEs are sent to decision unit to output decoded bits. Then, Partial-sum units (PUs) receive decoded bits to output partial sums required for the PEs of g node.

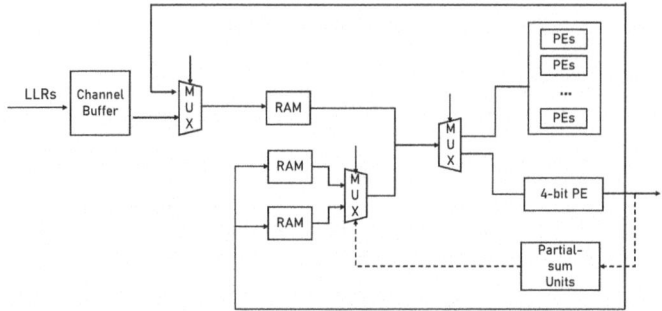

Fig. 3. Overall Architecture of Proposed Decoder.

3.2 Proposed 4-Bit Processing Element

According to Eqs. 3 and 4, 4-input functions can be calculated to be as follows

$$ff\left(L_0, L_1, L_2, L_3\right) \approx \mathrm{sgn}\left(L_0\right)\mathrm{sgn}\left(L_1\right)\mathrm{sgn}\left(L_2\right)\mathrm{sgn}\left(L_3\right)$$
$$\cdot \min\left\{|L_0|, |L_1|, |L_2|, |L_3|\right\}, \tag{6}$$

$$fg\left(L_0, L_1, L_2, L_3, \hat{s}_{00}\right) \approx \mathrm{sgn}\left(L_1\right)\mathrm{sgn}\left(L_3\right) \cdot \min\left\{|L_1|, |L_3|\right\}$$
$$+(-1)^{\hat{s}_{00}} \mathrm{sgn}\left(L_0\right)\mathrm{sgn}\left(L_2\right) \cdot \min\left\{|L_0|, |L_2|\right\}, \tag{7}$$

$$gf\left(L_0, L_1, L_2, L_3, \hat{s}_{01}, \hat{s}_{11}\right) \approx \mathrm{sgn}\left(L_0(-1)^{\hat{s}_{01}} + L_2\right)$$
$$\cdot \mathrm{sgn}\left(L_1(-1)^{\hat{s}_{11}} + L_3\right)$$
$$\cdot \min\left\{\left|\mathrm{sgn}\left(L_0(-1)^{\hat{s}_{01}} + L_2\right)\right|, \left|L_1(-1)^{\hat{s}_{11}} + L_3\right|\right\}, \tag{8}$$

$$gg\left(L_0, L_1, L_2, L_3, \hat{s}_{10}, \hat{s}_{01}, \hat{s}_{11}\right) = (-1)^{\hat{s}_{10}+\hat{s}_{01}} L_0$$
$$+(-1)^{\hat{s}_{11}} L_1 + (-1)^{\hat{s}_{10}} L_2 + L_3, \tag{9}$$

where s_{ij} is the ith partial sum located in the jth decoding level.

To reduce the decoding latency, 4-bit PEs are used in the last stage to decode 4 bits simultaneously. The corresponding hardware architecture of 4-bit PEs is illustrated in Fig. 4.

The intermediate nodes can be processed until the computations of corresponding partial sums are done, which is a bottleneck of decoding latency. The partial sum with look-ahead can accelerate the decoding process to compute intermediate nodes before the partial sums are available. This is achieved by calculating all possibilities and choosing the right value at the time the partial sums are produced. The idle PUs can be used for these processes, since not all PUs are occupied during decoding stage. The PU with look-ahead contributes to latency decrease at cost of a little more computation.

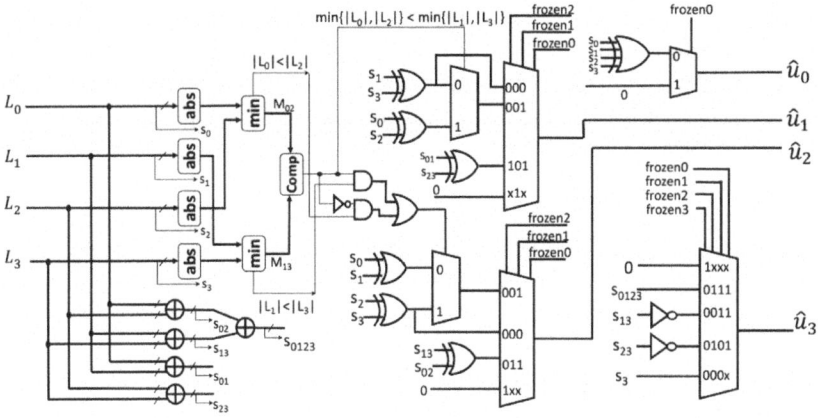

Fig. 4. Architecture of 4-bit PE.

3.3 Pipelined Partial-Sum Unit

Owing to its recursive nature, PU of code length 2^n, as depicted in Fig. 5, consists of 2^{n-1} PUs with extra filp flops (FFs), multiplexers (MUXs) and XOR gates.

Two XOR gates take the critical path of PU, since a XOR is processed 4 bits acquired from 4-bit PE , and the resultant is XOR with previous value $u_0 + u_1$ to generate a partial sum of $u_0 + u_1 + u_2 + u_3$.

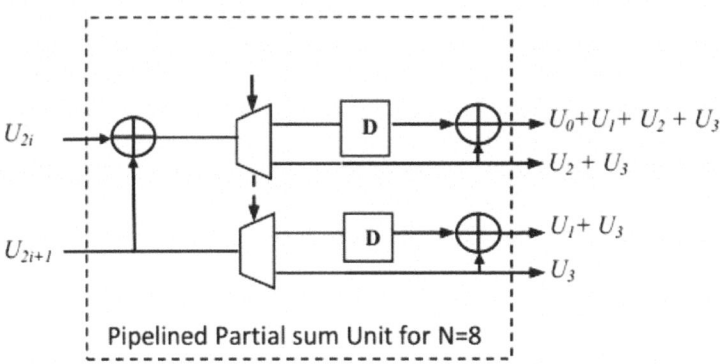

Fig. 5. Partial-sum Unit for N=8.

3.4 Channel Buffer and RAM

Due to limited processing elements used in the proposed architecture, it isn't viable to process all the channel data at the same time for polar codes with greater length. Thus, the channel LLRs in a gather of P are fed in the RAM, where P is settled as 64 in this work. For a code length of N = 1024, 16 clock cycles are need to load these LLRs into the channel buffer. The RAM is utilized to write the new LLRs and output LLRs to channel buffer at the same time.

3.5   Scheduling Principle

The most imperfection that all previous structures confronted is their utilization rate declines when the code length increases. The utilization rate is defined as the ratio of the whole number of node updates to the product of latency and hardware complexity.

In this work, the utilization rate of PEs can be increased by decreasing the number of PEs. Reduced PEs results in more node updates in each stage and more time to compute intermediate LLRs, resulting in the increase in latency. With the proposed approach, the PEs of last stage are replaced by 4-bit PEs, which decode 4 bits in a single time. Let P be the number of PEs, where P $= 2^p$. Within the stages l where $2^l < P$, the clock cycles is diminished by half, while the rest stages are not influenced. With look-ahead technique applied in partial-sum unit, all the possible values of 4-bit PEs are computed ahead of time. The last stage updated 2^{n-l-3} times when n >3 in a single clock cycle, and the corresponding values are chosen by MUX.

4   Experimental Results

4.1   FER Performance

Error correction performance of the proposed decoder is shown in Fig. 6 for different quantization bits. It is inferred frame error rate (FER) performance is degraded by only 0.25 dB for 5 bit quantization compared to floating point decoder.

The equivalent quantization bits of Q = 5 for the received LLR are given along with necessary inputs to the decoder and the estimated bits are compared with the message vectors for the error correction performance.

4.2   Latency Performance

The decoding latency L of the proposed decoder can be calculated by

$$L = \sum_{l=0} 2^{n-l-2} + \sum_{l=0} 2^{n-l-3} + \sum_{l=1}^{p} 2^{n-l-2} + \sum_{l=p+1}^{n-1} 2^{n-l-2} 2^{l-p}$$
$$= \frac{1}{2}N + \frac{N}{4P}(\log_2 \frac{N}{4P} - 1). \tag{10}$$

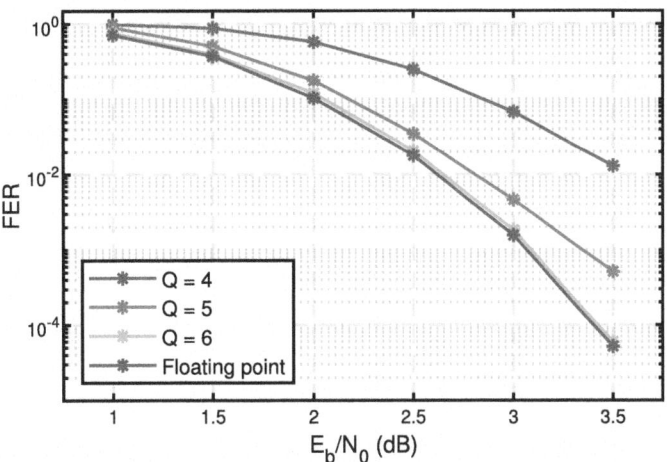

Fig. 6. Effect on FER performance of polar codes.

Figures 7 and 8 present the performance of the proposed decoder and existing SC polar decoders. The conventional semi-parallel SC decoder can be obtained from [10]. [14] presented a scalable SC decoder and [15] presented a 2-bit SC decoder.

According to Fig. 7, it is obvious that our proposed decoder costs much less clock cycles compared to previous decoders. For the length $N = 1024$, the latency of the proposed decoder is reduced by 48.64% and 75.19% than 2-bit SC decoder and conventional semi-parallel decoder, respectively.

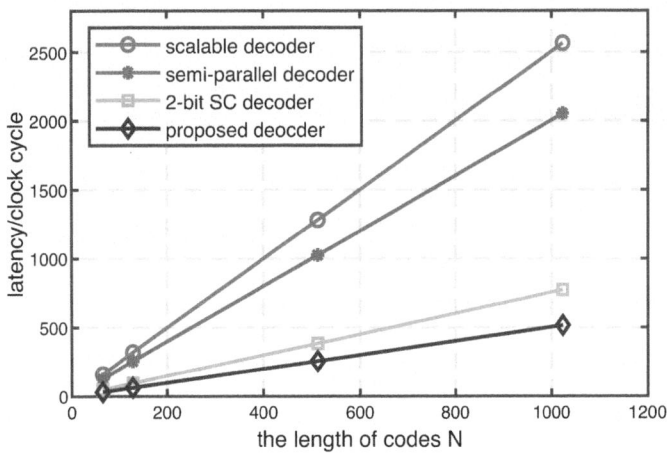

Fig. 7. Latency performance of proposed decoder and existing decoders.

4.3 Hardware Resources Consumption

The computation part of decoder mainly consists of processing elements (PEs). Thus, the efficiency of hardware resources depends on the utilization rate of PEs.

The utilization rate α [10] is defined as the ratio of the whole number of node updates to the product of computation time and computational resource complexity as

$$\alpha \triangleq \frac{\text{total number of node updates}}{\text{computational resource complexity} \times \text{computation time}}. \tag{11}$$

The utilization rate of PEs in this work can be calculated as

$$\alpha = \frac{N \log_2 N}{2P \left(\frac{1}{2}N + \frac{N}{4P}(\log_2 \frac{N}{4P} - 1)\right)} = \frac{2 \log_2 N}{2P + \log_2 \frac{N}{4P} - 1}. \tag{12}$$

Figure 8 indicates that our proposed decoder significantly contributes to the improvement in efficiency of hardware resources. The utilization rate of our decoder increased by 68.42% than semi-parallel decoder and 119.35% than scalable decoder. The utilization rate of 2-bit SC decoder declines with the increase of the length of codes, since the tree architecture used in 2-bit SC decoder and other conventional decoders require more PEs for computation. While semi-parallel and scalable architecture utilize relatively fixed PEs.

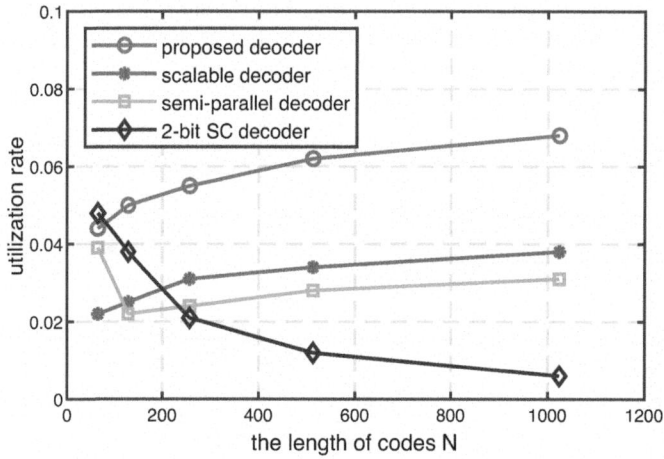

Fig. 8. Utilization rate of the proposed decoder and existing decoders.

All these four polar decoders for a code length of N=1024 with 5-bit quantization are implemented using Xilinx Kintex-7 FPGA. Table 1 shows the hardware resource consumption of conventional semi-parallel decoder, scalable decoder, 2-bit SC decoder and the proposed decoder. LUT refers to Look-up table and

FF denotes flip flop, which are the fundamental resources of FPGA. It can be concluded that the proposed decoder utilizes less hardware resources like LUTs and FFs than existing decoders. While its RAM consumption is higher than previous semi-parallel decoder and 2-bit SC decoder because of extra storage required by look-ahead partial-sum units.

Table 1. The hardware resource consumption of decoders.

Decoder	LUT	FF	RAM(bits)
Conventional semi-parallel decoder	4,130	1,691	15,104
Scalable decoder	2,866	1,304	41,648
2-bit SC decoder	7,432	972	14,324
Proposed decoder	2,544	830	31,104

5   Conclusion

In this paper, we have introduced a hardware-efficient architecture for polar decoder by modifying semi-parallel architecture. With reduced PEs, its hardware utilization rate is improved significantly. The proposed architecture utilizes 4-bit decoding and look-ahead technique to reduces latency. The results show a higher efficiency of hardware resources and lower latency than previous decoders. For a code length of $N = 2^{10}$, the proposed decoder improves latency by 48.64% and 75.19% than the conventional semi-parallel decoder and 2-bit decoder, separately. The significant improvement in hardware utilization rate of processing elements by 68.42% and 119.35% leads to high efficiency of hardware resources.

Acknowledgement. This work was supported by the National Science Foundation of China (NSFC) with grant no. 62271514 and the Science, Technology and Innovation Commission of Shenzhen Municipality with grant no. JCYJ20210324120002007, and ZDSYS20210623091807023.

References

1. Shafique, K., Khawaja, B.A., Sabir, F., Qazi, S., Mustaqim, M.: Internet of things (IoT) for next-generation smart systems: a review of current challenges, future trends and prospects for emerging 5G-IoT scenarios. IEEE Access **8**, 23022–23040 (2020)
2. Arikan, E., Telatar, E.: On the rate of channel polarization. In: 2009 IEEE International Symposium on Information Theory, pp. 1493–1495. IEEE (2009)
3. Notes, C.: 3GPP TSG ran WG1 meeting no. 87, chairmans notes of agenda item 7.1. 5 channel coding and modulation (2016)
4. Tal, I., Vardy, A.: List decoding of polar codes. IEEE Trans. Inf. Theory **61**(5), 2213–2226 (2015)

5. Dai, B., Gao, C., Yan, Z., Liu, R.: Parity check aided SC-flip decoding algorithms for polar codes. IEEE Trans. Veh. Technol. **70**(10), 10359–10368 (2021)
6. Arıkan, E.: Polar codes: a pipelined implementation. In: Proceedings of 4th ISBC vol. 2010, pp. 11–14 (2010)
7. Leroux, C., Tal, I., Vardy, A., Gross, W.J.: Hardware architectures for successive cancellation decoding of polar codes. In: 2011 IEEE International Conference on Acoustics, Speech and Signal Processing (ICASSP), pp. 1665–1668. IEEE (2011)
8. Pamuk, A.: An FPGA implementation architecture for decoding of polar codes. In: 2011 8th International Symposium on Wireless Communication Systems, pp. 437–441. IEEE (2011)
9. Berhault, G., Leroux, C., Jego, C., Dallet, D.: Partial sums generation architecture for successive cancellation decoding of polar codes. In: SiPS 2013 Proceedings, pp. 407–412. IEEE (2013)
10. Leroux, C., Raymond, A.J., Sarkis, G., Gross, W.J.: A semi-parallel successive-cancellation decoder for polar codes. IEEE Trans. Signal Process. **61**(2), 289–299 (2012)
11. Zhang, C., Yuan, B., Parhi, K.K.: Reduced-latency SC polar decoder architectures. In: 2012 IEEE International Conference on Communications (ICC), pp. 3471–3475. IEEE (2012)
12. Hassan, H.G., Hussien, A.M., Fahmy, H.A.: A simplified radix-4 successive cancellation decoder with partial sum lookahead. AEU-Int. J. Electron. Commun. **96**, 267–272 (2018)
13. Yuan, B., Parhi, K.K.: Low-latency successive-cancellation polar decoder architectures using 2-bit decoding. IEEE Trans. Circuits Syst. I Regul. Pap. **61**(4), 1241–1254 (2013)
14. Raymond, A.J., Gross, W.J.: A scalable successive-cancellation decoder for polar codes. IEEE Trans. Signal Process. **62**(20), 5339–5347 (2014)
15. Babu, G.S., Madala, L.R., Gopalakrishnan, L., Sellathurai, M.: Low-complex processing element architecture for successive cancellation decoder. Integration **66**, 80–87 (2019)

Design and Optimization of a Solar-Powered IRS and Relay Assisted MEC System

Kai Xu$^{(\boxtimes)}$, Xuwei Huang, and Gaofei Huang

Guangzhou University, Guangzhou 510006, China
2112130004@e.gzhu.edu.cn

Abstract. This paper studies a mobile edge computing system where two solar-powered nodes (i.e., a relay and an intelligent reflecting surface (IRS)) assist a user node in task offloading to an access point. To save the long-term energy consumption at the user, a novel protocol is first proposed so that the system can adaptively select the operating modes. Then, based on this protocol, the optimization problem of the system is formulated to minimize the energy consumption of task offloading and computing at the user by optimizing the system operation modes and the resource allocation in each mode, subject to the battery energy states of the IRS and the relay with the energy causality constraints. The problem is solved using the Lyapunov optimization framework and an alternating optimization algorithm. Simulation results show that the proposed system optimization scheme can save 70%-95% of energy consumption as compared to the baseline schemes.

Keywords: MEC · IRS · Cooperative Computing · Energy Harvesting · Stochastic Optimization

1 Introduction

With the rapid growth of the Internet of Things (IoT), an increasing number of IoT smart sensor relays need to perform computationally intensive tasks that typically have strict latency requirements. However, it is often costly to perform these computational tasks locally on these relays due to computational resource constraints. As one of the emerging technologies in IoT, Mobile Edge Computing (MEC) provides an effective solution to the above problems. By offloading computational tasks from IoT relays to servers with sufficient computational resources for execution, MEC is expected to alleviate these challenges [1, 2].

However, considering the complexity of the propagation environment and the deterioration of the propagation link due to the high mobility of the users, Intelligent Reflecting Surface (IRS) have received much attention in wireless transmission enhancement to improve the communication quality in MEC systems [5]. IRS is a technique that has been proposed in recent years to achieve high spectral efficiency in wireless communication systems. It is clear that IRS requires power supply for its operation, and

© ICST Institute for Computer Sciences, Social Informatics and Telecommunications Engineering 2025
Published by Springer Nature Switzerland AG 2025. All Rights Reserved
X. Chen et al. (Eds.): IoTaaS 2023, LNICST 585, pp. 69–81, 2025.
https://doi.org/10.1007/978-3-031-70507-6_6

to ensure the high efficiency of MEC systems over a long period of time, energy harvesting (EH) technologies have attracted attention [3].Meanwhile, in 5G networks, it is expected that there will be a large number of wireless devices with certain computational and communication resources that can act as cooperative nodes by making their computational resources available to users who need to perform urgent tasks, and this paradigm is known as cooperative computing. But the assumption in [4] that borrowable computational resources can be obtained in advance is unreasonable.

There have been many existing research works on EH-MEC systems, such as [2] and [6], but the existing works, in order to simplify the analyses, adopt the harvest-then-use (HTU) strategy for energy scheduling. Due to energy unpredictability and limited battery storage capacity, efficient use of limited energy from relay and IRS as well as energy harvesting techniques in fading channels is essential. There are two dominant approaches in the existing optimization of MEC systems to deal with the dynamic computational offloading problems: one is to transform the problem into a series of individual time-slot problems using the Lyapunov optimization framework [7, 8]. The other is to use Markov Decision Processes (MDPs), but in MDPs the high-dimensional state and action space lead to prohibitive computational complexity.

Based on the above analysis, in this paper, we consider a solar-powered IRS and relay jointly assisted time-slot system for edge computing, and our goal is to achieve the minimization of the long-term average energy consumption of users in a dynamic environment. A task offloading and cooperative computing protocol that can fully utilize the computational and communication resources of the system is first designed. Specifically, the Relay-assist MEC system under the new protocol considers the assist time allocation of the IRS on each time slot, so the paper proposes four modes. They are denoted as Mode I to Mode IV, respectively. Due to the stochastic nature of the wireless channel and task arrivals, and the fact that the system operating modes and resource allocation decisions for individual time slots are interrelated, the resulting problem is difficult to solve directly. To solve this problem, we first use the Lyapunov optimization framework to transform the described problem into a series of single time-slot optimization problems. The solution of the single time slot optimization problem is then achieved by convex optimization theory and alternating optimization (AO) algorithm.

2   System Model and New Protocol

2.1   Network Model

As shown in Fig. 1, in this paper we consider a solar-powered IRS and relay jointly assisted single user task offloading MEC system, which consists of an AP (A) base station with a MEC server, a user (U), a relay (cooperative node, N) an IRS (R), and two solar-powered power supplies used to power the relay and the IRS, respectively. This work investigates the long-term time (duration of $K * T$, where the number of time slots is K and the duration of each time slot is T. At the beginning of each time slot $k \in \mathcal{K} = \{1, ..., K\}$, there are new computational tasks $A(k)$ arriving at the user in bits with the maximum delay constraint T. At the same time, the relay itself also has $L(k)$ tasks (in bits) to perform in each time slot k in bits, and the maximum delay constraint is also T.

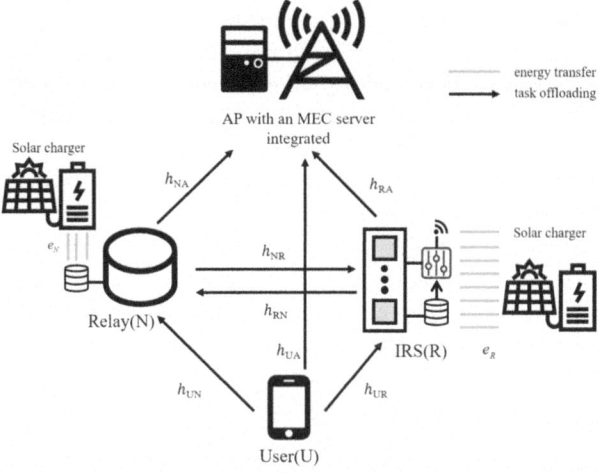

Fig. 1. Network model

2.2 New Protocol Design

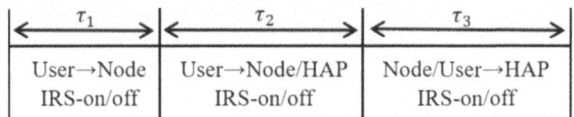

Fig. 2. The structure of one time slot in the newly designed protocol

Both the user and the relay will process their own tasks locally throughout the time slot as $\ell(k)$ and $L(k)$ respectively. In Fig. 2, a time slot is divided into three phases, $s \in \{1, 2, 3\}$. We define the IRS as assisting only the first phase, which we call mode I; assisting only the second phase, which we call mode II; assisting only the third phase, which we call mode **III**; and assisting the full phase, which we call mode IV. Denote the set of the above four operating modes of the MEC system as $\mathbb{M} \triangleq \{I, ..., IV\}$. Let $\phi_m(k) \in \{0, 1\}$ be the operating mode indicator, where $m \in \mathbb{M}, k \in \mathcal{K}$. If $\phi_m(k) = 1$, the MEC system is operating in mode m in time slot k. In a time slot, the system can choose only one operating mode, so $\sum_{m \in \mathbb{M}} \phi_m(k) = 1$. The delay constraint for the user's task is:

$$\tau_1(k) + \tau_2(k) + \tau_3(k) = T \tag{1}$$

As considered in most of the MEC literatures, we also ignore the time for remote execution and result download [7].

2.3 Channel Model

In this paper it is assumed that all channels follow block fading, i.e., the channel remains constant within the current time slot but changes at the boundary of each time slot. In each time slot k, the NLos channel gain from the user to the AP is denoted by $h_{UA}(k)$, which is modelled as Rayleigh fading. The NLos channel gain expression from the user to the relay and the relay to AP are both similar to $h_{UA}(k)$.

The channel gain from the user to the IRS $\mathbf{h}_{UR}(k) \in \mathbb{C}^{N \times 1}$ follows the Rician distribution. Let $\mathbf{h}_{RA}(k)$, $\mathbf{h}_{RN}(k)$, $\mathbf{h}_{NR}(k)$ denote the channels gains from the IRS to AP and the relay, and the relay to the IRS respectively, which follow Rician distribution. Their specific expressions are similar to $\mathbf{h}_{UR}(k)$.

IRS can be controlled independently in each phase s divided by time slot k. Let the diagonal matrix $\Theta_s(k) = diag(\beta_s^1(k)e^{j\theta_s^1(k)}, \beta_s^2(k)e^{j\theta_s^2(k)}, ..., \beta_s^N(k)e^{j\theta_s^N(k)})$, where $\theta_s^n(k) \in [0, 2\pi), \beta_s^n(k) \in [0, 1]$ represent the phase shift and amplitude reflection coefficients, respectively, of the n-th reflective element of the IRS during the s-th phase in the time slot k. $\forall n \in \{1, \cdots, N\}, s \in \{1, 2, 3\}$. In each time slot k, the combined channel gain from the user to the AP is: $\left|\hat{h}_{UA}(k, s)\right|^2 = \left|\mathbf{h}_{RA}^H(k)\Theta_s(k)\mathbf{h}_{UR}(k) + h_{UA}(k)\right|^2$, $s \in \{2, 3\}$. The combined channel gains $\hat{h}_{UN}(k, s)$ and $\hat{h}_{NA}(k)$ from the user to the relay and from the relay to the AP are both similar to $\hat{h}_{UA}(k, s)$.

2.4 Task Offloading and Energy Consumption Model

Let $\{p_{U,1}(k), p_{U,2}(k), p_{U,3}(k), p_N(k)\}$ denotes the transmit power of the user and the relay at different phases of each mode in the time slot k. At time slot k, in the first phase of each operating mode, the maximum achievable transmission rate from the user to the relay can be expressed as: $R_{UN\text{-}irs\,on}(p_{U,1}(k), 1) = B\log_2\left(1 + \dfrac{p_{U,1}(k)\left|\hat{h}_{UN}(k,1)\right|^2}{\sigma^2}\right)$

and $R_{UN\text{-}irs\,off}(p_{U,1}(k)) = B\log_2\left(1 + \dfrac{p_{U,1}(k)|h_{UN}(k)|^2}{\sigma^2}\right)$ correspond to the two cases of whether or not the IRS is involved in the assistance, where B is the system bandwidth and σ^2 is the additive white Gaussian noise power in the system.

Similarly, in the second phase, the maximum achievable transmission rate from the user to the relay are $R_{UN\text{-}irs\,on}(p_{U,2}(k), 2)$ and $R_{UN\text{-}irs\,off}(p_{U,2}(k))$. The maximum achievable transmission rate from the user to AP are $R_{UA\text{-}irs\,on}(p_{U,2}(k))$ and $R_{UA\text{-}irs\,off}(p_{U,2}(k))$.

Note that in the third phase, the user and the relay send the task data information to the AP simultaneously using the rateless code (RC) technique, where the maximum achievable transmission rate at the AP are: $R_{UNA\text{-}irs\,on}(p_N(k), p_{U,3}(k))$ are $R_{UNA\text{-}irs\,off}(p_N(k), p_{U,3}(k))$.

1) Task Offloading to Relay: The amount of data and energy consumed by the user offloaded to the relay to assist in the computation in the first phase of each operating mode in time slot k are expressed as follows:

$$d_N(k) \leq \tau_1(k)\left(\sum_{m\in\{I,IV\}} \phi_m(k)R_{UN\text{-}irs\,on}(p_{U,1}(k), 1)\right)$$

$$+ \sum_{m \in \{\text{II,III}\}} \phi_m(k) R_{\text{UN - irs off}}(p_{\text{U},1}(k))\Bigg) \tag{2}$$

$$E_{\text{off}}^{(m-1)}(k) = \tau_1(k) p_{\text{U},1}(k), \quad \forall m \in \{\text{I}, ..., \text{IV}\} \tag{3}$$

In the second phase, the amount of data and energy consumed by the user offloaded to the relay for assistance forwarding has the following expression:

$$d_{\text{A},1}(k) = \tau_2(k) \Bigg(\sum_{m \in \{\text{II,IV}\}} \phi_m(k) R_{\text{UN - irs on}}(p_{\text{U},2}(k), 2)$$

$$+ \sum_{m \in \{\text{I,III}\}} \phi_m(k) R_{\text{UN - irs off}}(p_{\text{U},2}(k)) \Bigg) \tag{4}$$

$$E_{\text{off}}^{(m-2)}(k) = \tau_2(k) p_{\text{U},2}(k), \quad \forall m \in \{\text{I}, ..., \text{IV}\} \tag{5}$$

2) Task Offloading to AP: In the second phase, at time slot k, when the user offloads the assist forwarded data to the relay, the AP also receives part of this date and hence the following expression:

$$d_{\text{A},2}(k) = \tau_2(k) \Bigg(\sum_{m \in \{\text{II,IV}\}} \phi_m(k) R_{\text{UA - irs on}}(p_{\text{U},2}(k), 2)$$

$$+ \sum_{m \in \{\text{I,III}\}} \phi_m(k) R_{\text{UA - irs off}}(p_{\text{U},2}(k)) \Bigg) \tag{6}$$

In the third phase, the user and the relay send the task data information to the AP at the same time using the RC technique, at which time the received task data at the AP is :

$$d_{\text{A},3}(k) = \tau_3(k) \Bigg(\sum_{m \in \{\text{III,VI}\}} \phi_m(k) R_{\text{UNA - irs on}}(p_{\text{N}}(k), p_{\text{U},3}(k))$$

$$+ \sum_{m \in \{\text{I,II}\}} \phi_m(k) R_{\text{UNA - irs off}}(p_{\text{N}}(k), p_{\text{U},3}(k)) \Bigg) \tag{7}$$

In this phase, the offloading energy consumption of the user and the relay are respectively:

$$E_{\text{off}}^{(m-3)}(k) = \tau_3(k) p_{\text{U},3}(k), \quad \forall m \in \{\text{I}, ..., \text{IV}\} \tag{8}$$

$$E_{\text{off}}^{\text{N}}(k) = \tau_3(k) p_{\text{N}}(k) \tag{9}$$

To summarize, in the first seven modes, the data received at the AP for the computation task in time slot k is as follows:

$$d_{\text{A}}(k) \leq \min(d_{\text{A},1}(k), d_{\text{A},2}(k) + d_{\text{A},3}(k)) \tag{10}$$

2.5 Task Computing and Energy Consumption Model

1) Local Computing at User: Definition $C_U \geq 0$ denotes the number of CPU cycles required by the user to perform one-bit computation task. The DVFS technique [7] is applied, where the user performs local computation in each time slot using a constant CPU frequency $f_U(k)$, and $f_{U,max}$ is the maximum CPU frequency of the user, and in this case the energy consumption of the user for local computation at time slot $k \in \mathcal{K}$ is denoted as:

$$E^U_{com}(k) = C_U \ell(k) \zeta_U (f_U(k))^2 = \zeta_U C_U^3 \ell^3(k)/T^2 \tag{11}$$

where $\zeta_U > 0$ denotes the effective capacitance coefficient of the user.

2) Cooperative Computing at Relay: We assume that the relay has two independent processors for processing its own task $L(k)$ and the user's offloaded task $d_N(k)$. $f_{N,max}$ is the maximum CPU frequency of the two independent processors of the relay. C_N denotes the number of CPU cycles required by the relay to perform one-bit computation task. Similarly, the task execution energy consumption of relay is:

$$E^N_{com}(k) = \zeta_N C_N^3 L^3(k)/T^2 + \zeta_N C_N^3 d_N^3(k)/(T - \tau_1(k))^2 \tag{12}$$

where $\zeta_N > 0$ denotes the effective capacitance coefficient of the relay.

Based on the above analysis, the total energy consumption of the user in time slot k can be expressed as:

$$E^U_{total}(k) = E^U_{com}(k) + E^{(m-1)}_{off}(k) + E^{(m-2)}_{off}(k) + E^{(m-3)}_{off}(k) \tag{13}$$

Similarly, the total energy consumption of the relay in time slot k can be expressed as:

$$E^N_{total}(k) = E^N_{com}(k) + E^N_{off}(k) \tag{14}$$

2.6 Energy Harvesting Model

$e_N(k)$ and $e_R(k)$ denotes the energy obtained by the relay and IRS by harvesting solar energy in time slot k, where $e_N(k) = TP^N_H(k)$, $e_R(k) = TP^R_H(k)$, $P^N_H(k)$ and $P^R_H(k)$ denote the energy harvesting power of the relay and the IRS, respectively, in time slot k. P^N_{Hmax} and $P^R_{H\,max}$ are the maximum energy harvesting power of the relay and the IRS, respectively. We denote the relay's battery energy state as $B_N(k) \geq 0$ at the beginning of time slot k, so the energy state in each battery $B_N(k)$ evolves over time as follows:

$$B_N(k+1) = \min\left\{B_N(k) - E^N_{total}(k) + e_N(k), B_N^{max}\right\} \tag{15}$$

where B_N^{max} indicates the maximum energy can be stored in the relay's battery. It also follows from the causality of energy:

$$E^N_{total}(k) \leq B_N(k) \tag{16}$$

Also denote by $t_R(k)$ the assistance duration of the IRS in time slot k. The energy consumption of the IRS in time slot k is as follows:

$$E_R(k) = \mu N t_R(k) \tag{17}$$

where μ denote the power consumption of a single reflective element.

Similarly to the relay case, for the IRS we have:

$$B_R(k+1) = \min\{B_R(k) - E_R(k) + e_R(k), B_R^{max}\} \tag{18}$$

where B_R^{max} indicates the maximum energy can be stored in the relay's battery.

$$E_R(k) \le B_R(k) \tag{19}$$

3 Solution to the Proposed Problem

3.1 Problem Statement

In this paper, we focus on a MEC system in which solar-powered IRS and relay jointly assist a single user in task offloading by jointly optimizing the mode selection $\phi(k)$, task allocation $\mathbf{D}(k)$, time allocation $\mathbf{t}(k)$, IRS reflection coefficient matrix $\Theta(k)$, and user and relay transmit power allocations $\mathbf{p}(k)$ at each time slot, where $\Psi(k) = \{\phi(k), \mathbf{D}(k), \mathbf{t}(k), \Theta(k), \mathbf{p}(k)\}, \phi(k) = \{\phi_I(k), \phi_{II}(k), \phi_{III}(k), \phi_{IV}(k)\}, \mathbf{D}(k) = \{\ell(k), d_N(k), d_A(k)\}, \mathbf{t}(k) = \{\tau_1(k), \tau_2(k), \tau_3(k)\}, \Theta(k) = \{\Theta_1(k), \Theta_2(k), \Theta_3(k), \Theta_R(k)\}, \mathbf{p}(k) = \{p_{U,1}(k), p_{U,2}(k), p_{U,3}(k), p_N(k)\}$ to achieve the minimization of the user's long-term average energy consumption E_{avg}. Thus, the optimization problem of the MEC system studied in this paper can be expressed as follows:

$$(P1) \quad \min_{\Psi(k)} \mathbb{E}_{avg} = \lim_{K\to\infty} \frac{1}{K} E\left\{\sum_{k=0}^{K-1}\left(E_{total}^U(k)\right)\right\} \tag{20a}$$

s.t. (1), (2), (10), (16), (19) and

$$\phi_m(k) \in \{0, 1\}, \sum_{m\in\mathbb{M}} \phi_m(k) = 1 \tag{20b}$$

$$\left|\Theta_s^{n,n}(k)\right| \le 1, \forall n, \forall s \in \{1, 2, 3\} \tag{20c}$$

$$0 \le \tau_i(k) \le T, \forall i = \{1, 2, 3\} \tag{20d}$$

$$\ell(k) + d_A(k) + d_N(k) = A(k) \tag{20e}$$

$$d_A(k) \ge 0, \ell(k) \ge 0, d_N(k) \ge 0 \tag{20f}$$

$$\frac{C_U \ell(k)}{T} \le f_{U,MAX}, \frac{C_N d_N(k)}{T - \tau_1(k)} \le f_{N,MAX} \tag{20g}$$

$$0 \leq p_{U,1}(k) \leq p_{U,max}, \forall i = \{1, 2, 3\}, \ 0 \leq p_N(k) \leq p_{N,max} \tag{20h}$$

where $p_{U,max}$ and $p_{N,max}$ denote the maximum transmit power of the user and the relay, respectively. In problem (P1), (20b) and (20c) are the mode selection constraints and the IRS reflection coefficient constraints, (16) and (19) are the energy causality constraints for the relay and the IRS, respectively, (1) and (20d) are the time allocation constraints, (20e), (20f), (20g), (2) and (10) are the task allocation constraints, (20h), (2), (10) are the user and relay transmission power constraints.

Problem (P1) is a classical dynamic optimization problem that is difficult to solve directly, and the Lyapunov optimization framework is considered as an effective solution. Therefore, in this paper, the original problem is first simplified based on the Lyapunov optimization method, and then the simplified problem is solved by convex optimization theory and AO algorithm, so as to propose an efficient algorithm with low complexity.

3.2 Problem Transformation

To solve the problem (P1) using the Lyapunov optimization method, first, define two virtual queues for the energy states $B_N(k)$ and $B_R(k)$, respectively, as $X(k) = B_N(k) - G_1$, $Y(k) = B_R(k) - G_2$, where G_1 and G_2 are time independent constants, in this paper $G_1 = B_N^{max}$, $G_2 = B_R^{max}$. The problem (P1) can then be rewritten as:

$$\text{(P2)} \ \min_{\Psi(k)} VE_{total}^U(k) + X(k)\left(e_N(k) - E_{total}^N(k)\right) + vY(k)(e_R(k) - E_R(k)) \tag{21}$$

$$\text{s.t. (1), (2), (10), (16), (19) and (20b−h)}$$

where v is a non-negative constant, and V is a non-negative weighting factor.

Unlike problem (P1), problem (P2) only requires solving the optimization variables for one time slot, making it a relatively simple problem to solve.

3.3 Solving Single Time-Slot Optimization Problem

To solve problem (P2), note that the system operation mode indicator $\phi(k)$ is a binary optimization variable, but since there are only four system operation modes, the optimal solution to problem (P2) can be obtained by solving the corresponding optimization problems under each of the four system operation modes separately, and then determining the optimal system operation mode.

Combined with the protocol design in the previous section, an in-depth analysis of problem (P2) shows that for the four modes of the system, there is no difference in the structure of the optimization problems corresponding to them. Therefore, in the following section, only the steps for solving the optimization problem when the system is in the first mode are given. The details are as follows:

when $\phi_I(k) = 1$, the system works in the first mode, let $\Psi^1(k) = \{\phi(k), \mathbf{D}(k), \mathbf{t}(k), \mathbf{p}(k)\}$ and the problem (P2) can be shorten as follows:

$$\text{(P2.1)} \ Y_I(k) = \min_{\Psi^I(k)} VE_{total}^U(k) + X(k)\left(e_N(k) - E_{total}^N(k)\right)$$

$$+ vY(k)(e_R(k) - \mu N\tau_1(k))s.t.\ (1),(16),(20c-h)\text{and} \tag{22a}$$

$$\left|\Theta_s^{n,n}(k)\right| \leq 1, \forall n, \forall s \in \{1\} \tag{22b}$$

$$\mu N\tau_1(k) \leq B_R(k) \tag{22c}$$

$$d_N(k) \leq \tau_1(k)R_{\text{UN - irs on}}\big(p_{U,1}(k), 1\big) \tag{22d}$$

$$d_A(k) \leq \tau_2(k)R_{\text{UN - irs off}}\big(p_{U,2}(k)\big) \tag{22e}$$

$$d_A(k) \leq \tau_2(k)R_{\text{UA - irs off}}\big(p_{U,2}(k)\big) + \tau_3(k)R_{\text{UNA - irs off}}\big(p_N(k), p_{U,3}(k)\big) \tag{22f}$$

To solve the problem (P2.1), we introduce an auxiliary variable vector $E(k) = \{E_{U,1}(k), E_{U,2}(k), E_{U,3}(k), E_N(k)\}$ with $E_{U,i}(k) = \tau_i(k)p_{U,i}(k), \forall i \in \{1, 2, 3\}, E_N(k) = \tau_3(k)p_N(k)$. The same applies to $E_N(k)$. So the problem (P2.1) can be rewritten as:

$$(\text{P3.1}) \min_{D(k),t(k),\Theta(k),E(k)} V\left(E_{\text{com}}^U(k) + \sum_{i=1}^{3} E_{U,i}(k)\right) + X(k)\cdot$$

$$\left(e_N(k) - E_{\text{com}}^N(k) - E_N(k)\right) + vY(k)(e_R(k) - \mu N\tau_1(k)) \tag{23a}$$

subject to (1),(16),(20d-20g), (22b-22c) and

$$0 \leq E_{U,i}(k) \leq \tau_i(k)p_{U,max}, \forall i = \{1, 2, 3\} \tag{23b}$$

$$0 \leq E_N(k) \leq \tau_3(k)p_{N,max} \tag{23c}$$

$$d_N(k) \leq \tau_1(k)R_{\text{UN - irs on}}\left(\frac{E_{U,1}(k)}{\tau_1(k)}, 1\right) \tag{23d}$$

$$d_A(k) \leq \tau_2(k)R_{\text{UN - irs off}}\left(\frac{E_{U,2}(k)}{\tau_2(k)}\right) \tag{23e}$$

$$d_A(k) \leq \tau_2(k)R_{\text{UA - irs off}}\left(\frac{E_{U,2}(k)}{\tau_2(k)}\right) + \tau_3(k)R_{\text{UNA - irs off}}\left(\frac{E_N(k)}{\tau_3(k)}, \frac{E_{U,3}(k)}{\tau_3(k)}\right) \tag{23f}$$

The problem (P3.1) remains intractable because the optimization variables are coupled. To make it manageable, the AO technique [6] is proposed to solve the problem, where the problem (P3.1) is divided into two phases to be solved.

1.1) Phase 1: Jointly Optimizing $\{D(k), t(k), E(k)\}$.

When $\Theta(k)$ is fixed, the (P3.1) can be rewritten as:

$$(P3.1.1) \quad \min_{\mathbf{D}(k),\mathbf{t}(k),\mathbf{E}(k)} V\left(\frac{\zeta_U C_U^3 \ell^3(k)}{T^2} + \sum_{i=1}^{3} E_{U,i}(k)\right)$$

$$+X(k)\left(e_N(k) - \frac{\zeta_N C_N^3 L(k)^3}{T^2} - \frac{\zeta_N C_N^3 d_N(k)^3}{(T-\tau_1)^2} - E_N(k)\right) \quad (24a)$$

$$+vY(k)(e_R(k) - \mu N \tau_1(k))$$

$$s.t. \quad (1), (16), (20d-20g), (22c) \, and \, (23b-f)$$

It can be shown that problem (P3.1.1) is a convex optimization problem, and the optimal solution can be obtained efficiently using convex optimization solvers such as CVX.

1.2) Phase 2: Optimizing IRS Reflection Coefficients.

Based on the results of the first phase, (P3.1) turns out to be a feasibility problem with only the optimization variable $\Theta(k)$, i.e.:

$$(P3.1.2) \quad \text{Find } \Theta(k)$$

$$s.t. \quad (22b) \, and \, (22d) \quad (25)$$

To deal with the non-convex constraints (22d), we have: $s\Theta_1(k)\mathbf{h}_{UN}(k) + h_{UN}(k))$, $Z_{UN}^{(1)}(k) = \text{Im}\left(\mathbf{h}_{RN}^H(k)\Theta_1(k)\mathbf{h}_{UN}(k) + h_{UN}(k)\right)$ are the introduced slack variables, where $\text{Re}(W), \text{Im}(W)$ are the real and imaginary parts of W, respectively. We then use the successive convex approximation (SCA) technique. Specifically, at the r-th iteration, given the initial point $\left(X_{UN}^{(1),(r)}(k), Z_{UN}^{(1),(r)}(k)\right)$ there has:

$$\left(X_{UN}^{(i)}(k)\right)^2 + \left(Z_{UN}^{(i)}(k)\right)^2 3\left(X_{UN}^{(1),(r)}(k)\right)^2 + \left(Z_{UN}^{(1),(r)}(k)\right)^2$$

$$+ 2X_{UN}^{(1),(r)}(k)\left(X_{UN}^{(1)}(k) - X_{UN}^{(1),(r)}(k)\right)$$

$$+ 2Z_{UN}^{(1),(r)}(k)\left(Z_{UN}^{(1)}(k) - Z_{UN}^{(1),(r)}(k)\right) = R_{UN}^{(1),lb}$$

herefore, at the r-th iteration, the convex optimization problem for solving problem (P3.1.2) can be expressed as:

$$(P3.1.2.1) \quad \text{Find } \Theta(k)$$

$$s.t \quad (22b) \, and \quad (26a)$$

$$d_N(k) \le \tau_1(k) B \log_2\left(1 + \frac{p_{U,1}(k) R_{UN}^{(1),lb}}{\sigma^2}\right) \quad (26b)$$

which can be solved using the interior point method.

Finally, after obtaining the optimal solutions of the corresponding optimization problems for each of the four system operation modes, the value of $Y_m(k), \forall m \in \mathbb{M}$ can be determined, and thus the optimal system operation mode for the k-th time slot can be determined by:

$$m^*(k) = \arg\min_{m\in\mathbb{M}} Y_m(k).$$

4 Simulation Results

In this section, the performance of the design scheme of the solar-powered IRS and intelligent relay joint-assisted MEC system proposed in this paper is verified by simulation. In the simulation, it is assumed that AP, IRS, relay and user are located in a two-dimensional coordinate system, and their positions are set to $(x_A, y_A) = (20, 0), (x_R, y_R) = (1, -1)$, $(x_N, y_N) = (10, 2)$ and $(x_U, y_U) = (0, 10)$, respectively. The path-loss exponent for UR, UN, NR, NA and RA links are set to $\alpha_{UR} = \alpha_{UN} = \alpha_{NR} = \alpha_{NA} = \alpha_{RA} = 2$. And since the UA link is assumed to have obstacles, the path-loss exponent of the UA link is set to $\alpha_{UA} = 4$. The bandwidth of the system is $B = 1$ MHz. The variances of AWGN are set as $\sigma^2 = -80$ dBm. We set the time slot duration $T = 0.08$ s. Furthermore, we set $P^N_{Hmax} = 8$ mW, $P^R_{Hmax} = 0.2$ msW, $B^{max}_N = 20\, TP^N_{Hmax}$ J, $B^{max}_R = 20TP^R_{Hmax}$ J, $N = 20$, $v = 2 * 10^3$, $V = 0.5626$.

Besides, the computation parameters of the user and relay in the considered MEC system are set as $C_U = C_N = 1000$ cycle/bit, $f_{U,max} = 2$ GHz, $f_{N,max} = 3$ GHz, $\zeta_U = 10^{-27}, \zeta_N = 3 \times 10^{-28}$. The maximum transmission power is set to $p_{U,max} = 2W$ and $p_{N,max} = 3$ W for the user and the relay respectively. All of the above parameters are used in the following simulations unless otherwise stated.

In the simulation, the design scheme of this paper will be compared with the following two other baseline schemes: 1) Unactive optimization of IRS energy consumption scheme: The optimization problem corresponding to this scheme differs from problem (P2) in that its objective function does not include the IRS term and the IRS tends to assist the three phases. 2) Unactive optimization of the relay energy consumption scheme: The optimization problem corresponding to this scheme differs from problem (P2) in that it excludes the IRS term and the relay term from its objective function and assumes that each time slot the IRS tends to assist the three phases.

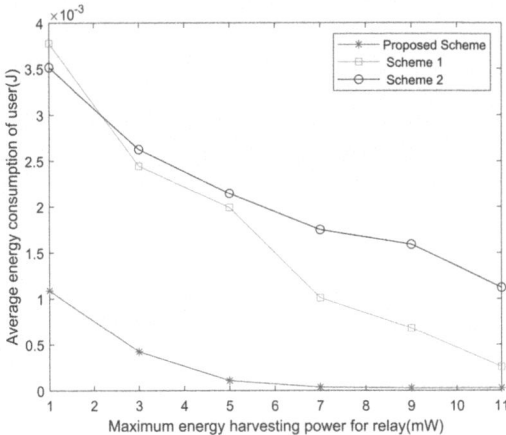

Fig. 3. User's average energy consumption versus the maximum energy harvesting power for relay

Figure 3 plots the variation of the user's average energy performance of the proposed scheme in this paper and the two baseline schemes when the maximum energy harvesting power (i.e., P_{Hmax}^N) varies in the relay. Here, the system operates with a number of time slots of 600, i.e., $K = 600$. As can be seen from Fig. 3, the average energy consumption of the proposed scheme in this paper is the lowest compared to the two baseline schemes. Specifically, the average energy consumption of the system of the proposed scheme in this paper is only 5–30% of the average energy consumption compared to scheme 1, and the savings are more compared to scheme 2. Therefore, by using the new protocol and the system optimization algorithm proposed in this paper, the energy consumption at the user side can be saved significantly. In addition, it can be seen that when P_{Hmax}^N is large (e.g., $P_{Hmax}^N = 11$ mW), the average energy consumption of scheme 1 and scheme 2 is also significantly reduced, and the gap between their energy performance and that of the scheme proposed in this paper is further narrowed, which is due to the fact that in this case, the energy collected by the relay at each time slot k is already more sufficient, and the long-term benefits of the system's active optimization of its energy consumption are reduced. However, when $P_{Hmax}^N = 7$ mW, the average energy consumption of the proposed scheme in this paper is much lower than that of schemes 1 and 2, thus illustrating the need for the system to proactively optimize the energy consumption of the relay.

Figure 4 plots the effect of changing the relay location on the average energy performance of the different schemes. From Fig. 4, it can be seen that for the scheme proposed in this paper, scheme 1 and scheme 2, the average energy performance of the scheme proposed in this paper is significantly better than the performance of the two baseline schemes, regardless of the changes in relay location. Our proposed scheme exploits energy conservation based on the relay and IRS battery energy states and opportunistic transmission based on channel conditions to minimize the user's long-term average energy consumption. Unlike our scheme, the alternative schemes do not jointly dynamically optimize the user, relay and IRS as a whole, and/ or focus only on minimizing user energy consumption in the current time slot.

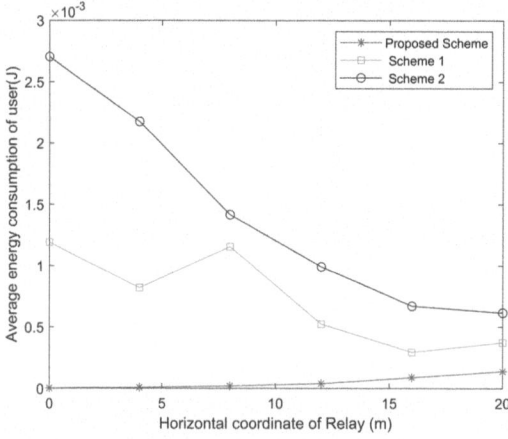

Fig. 4. Performance comparisons under varying relay horizontal coordinates

5 Conclusion

This paper investigated the design and optimization of a solar-powered IRS and relay (cooperative node), jointly assisted MEC system. Minimizing user's long-term average energy consumption by jointly optimizing mode selection, task allocation, time allocation, IRS reflection coefficient matrix, user and relay transmit power allocation for each time slot, an efficient algorithm was developed to achieve superior performance in the system. Simulation results showed that the energy performance of this algorithm in MEC systems is significantly better than the baseline schemes studied.

References

1. Guo, K., Gao, R., Xia, W., et al.: Online learning based computation offloading in MEC systems with communication and computation dynamics. IEEE Trans. Commun. **69**(2), 1147 (2020)
2. Wang, F., Xu, J., Cui, S.: Optimal energy allocation and task offloading policy for wireless powered mobile edge computing systems. IEEE Trans. Wireless Commun. **19**(4), 2443–2459 (2020)
3. Blasco, P., Gunduz, D., Dohler, M.: A learning theoretic approach to energy harvesting communication system optimization. IEEE Trans. Wirel. Commun. **12**(4), 1872–1882 (2013)
4. Cao, X., Wang, F., Xu, J., et al.: Joint Computation and Communication Cooperation for Energy-Efficient Mobile Edge Computing. IEEE Int. Things J. **3**, 4188 (2019)
5. Wu, Q., Zhang, R.: Intelligent reflecting surface enhanced wireless network via joint active and passive beamforming. IEEE Trans. Wirel. Commun. **18**(11), 5394–5409 (2019)
6. Mao, S., et al.: Computation rate maximization for intelligent reflecting surface enhanced wireless powered mobile edge computing networks. IEEE Trans. Veh. Technol. **70**(10), 10820–10831 (2021)
7. Dong, M., Li, W., Amirnavaei, F.: Online joint power control for two-hop wireless relay networks with energy harvesting. IEEE Trans. Signal Process. **66**(2), 463–478 (2018). https://doi.org/10.1109/TSP.2017.2768040
8. Sun, M., Xu, X., Huang, Y., Wu, Q., Tao, X., Zhang, P.: Resource management for computation offloading in D2D-aided wireless powered mobile-edge computing networks. IEEE Internet Things J. **8**(10), 8005–8020 (2021). https://doi.org/10.1109/JIOT.2020.3041673

Highway Image Enhancement Method Based on Jade

Yang Li, Jing Liu[✉], Shengxiang Wang, and Jin Tian

Engineering School of Networks and Telecommunications, Jinling Institute of Technology,
Nanjing 211169, China
liuj608@jit.edu.cn

Abstract. This article elaborates on an innovative high-speed highway image enhancement approach that relies on the Joint Approximate Diagonalization of Eigenmatrices (JADE) algorithm. This technique is highly efficient at segregating statistically independent source signals of the image, subsequently enhancing their visibility. By doing so, it significantly elevates the performance of highway monitoring systems and assures the safety of motorists. Experimental findings demonstrated that this methodology outperforms conventional image enhancement techniques in effectiveness and efficiency. Consequently, given its substantial application potential and developmental prospects, this technique is expected to witness extensive utilization in practical settings.

Keywords: blind signal separation (BSS) · noise interference suppression · joint approximate diagonalization of eigenmatrices (JADE)

1 Introduction

Highway image denoising has wide application and important significance in many fields. For automatic driving, road image denoising can enhance the perception ability of driving assistance system, reduce the misjudgment caused by image noise, and improve driving safety. In highway inspection, clear road images can more accurately identify the damage of the road surface, which is convenient for repair and maintenance. At the same time, in traffic flow monitoring and traffic accident analysis, de-noised images can improve the rate and accuracy of vehicle identification, so as to provide more accurate data support and optimize traffic management. Using Jade can help improve the contrast and brightness of the image, thus improving the visual quality of the image, facilitating applications such as obstacle detection and vehicle identification [1].

In recent years, the research on the high-speed highway image enhancement method based on Jade has received extensive attention from domestic and foreign researchers, and many related research results have been published [2]. Here are some research results of domestic and foreign scholars in this field: Xu Jie and others published an article in "Computer Application Research", introducing a method for restoring motion blurred images of high-speed highway vehicles based on Jade. The results show that the method

X. Chen et al. (Eds.): IoTaaS 2023, LNICST 585, pp. 82–90, 2025.
https://doi.org/10.1007/978-3-031-70507-6_7

has high image restoration accuracy and noise resistance [3]. Liu Li et al. published a paper in "Intelligent Computers and Applications", exploring an image enhancement algorithm for high-speed highway traffic videos based on Jade. The study shows that the method can effectively improve the clarity and contrast of the video[4].

In foreign countries, researchers at the University of Michigan in the United States proposed a method for detecting highway lane lines using the Jade algorithm, effectively solving the difficulties and complexity problems in lane line detection.[5].

In summary, the high-speed highway image enhancement method based on Jade has received extensive research and applications in the domestic and foreign research fields. Relevant research results are also increasingly attracting attention from academia and industry [6].

The rest of the paper is organized as follows. In the second section, how to convert image signals into matrices for JADE algorithm recognition is presented. The third section describes in detail the denoising of image matrix by dark channel prior technology and JADE algorithm. Finally, the proposed image enhancement technique based on JADE algorithm is verified by simulation experiments [7].

2 Image Remodeling and Initial Noise Reduction

2.1 Image Preprocessing

First read the image, denoted as img. It is then converted to a double precision data type and normalized, which makes the data easier to work with and compare.

Then the image is preprocessed, where the median filter is used for initial noise reduction of the image. The advantages of this are:

Effective removal of salt and pepper noise, due to the appearance of black and white pixels, salt and pepper noise will lead to image distortion. The median filter can effectively remove the salt-and-pepper noise and restore the clarity of the image by selecting the middle of the surrounding pixel to smooth the image. Median filtering can better preserve the details of the image. Median filtering performs well in handling outlier pixels. Outlier pixels refer to pixels that are significantly different from surrounding pixels, which may be abnormal points caused by sensor errors, environmental interference, and other reasons. By processing group pixels by taking the median of the surrounding pixels, they can be accurately eliminated, making the image smoother. It is important to note that median filtering also has some limitations and may not be suitable for certain types of noise, such as Gaussian noise, or specific image details, such as texture details.

Here we use the median filter to denoise the color image, which needs to be processed separately for each color channel. This is because a color image consists of three color channels, red, green, and blue, each of which contains different color information about the image. Therefore, when applying the median filter, the filter needs to be applied to each color channel separately to ensure that the noise of each channel can be effectively reduced. Then the processed three channels are re-synthesized into color images, so that the color image results after noise reduction can be obtained.

2.2 Dark Channel Prior Technology

Dark channel prior is a technique for image de-fogging and image enhancement. It is based on an observed image in a natural scene having a channel caused by atmospheric light that has a lower brightness value in most places. By using this observation, the scattered and atmospheric light components in the image can be inferred and used to remove haze or improve image quality.

First define the de-fog function, the variable I represents the input image (img) and the variable J usually represents the output image

$$J = \text{dehaze}(I) \tag{1}$$

Setting the global atmospheric light to 1 means that there is no obvious atmosphere in the image

$$A = 1 \tag{2}$$

Secondly, the transmission rate of the image is estimated, which represents the degree of light attenuation caused by haze. According to the dark channel prior principle, the transmission rate is estimated by calculating the ratio of the brightness value of each pixel to the atmospheric light, and then multiplying by a weight coefficient. Here the weight coefficient ω is set to 0.95.

$$t = 1 - \omega * \min\left(\frac{I}{A}\right) \tag{3}$$

Then a guide filter is used to refine the estimated transmission rate. The guide filter uses image I as the guide image and filters the transmission rate image t to refine the transmission rate estimation. Where GuidedFilter is the function of the guide filter, I is the original image, t is the original estimated transmission rate, r is the radius of the guide filter (set to 15), ϵ is the constant of the guide filter (set to 0.001).

$$t' = \text{GuidedFilter}(I, \ t, \ r, \ \varepsilon) \tag{4}$$

Finally, restore scene lighting. This is achieved by subtracting atmospheric light from the original image I, then dividing by the refined transmission rate, and adding atmospheric light. A minimum transmission rate $t0$ (set to 0.1) is also set to prevent pixel values from being too bright at very low transmission rates. Where t' is the optimized transmission rate, I is the brightness of the image, and A is the atmospheric illumination.

$$J = (I - A)/\max(t', \ t_0) + A \tag{5}$$

3 Denoising Algorithm

3.1 JADE Algorithm Description

Call the jade function to process this matrix

$$\text{function } [A, S] = \text{jade}(J, m) \tag{6}$$

J is the image matrix obtained after the fog removal processing mentioned above. m is an optional parameter that indicates the number of source signals. They are two input parameters of Jade. The outputs of the function are A and S, where A is an estimated mixed matrix of n x m and S is an estimate of the source signal of m x T.

The received image signal can be represented as matrix J. The whitening process of mixed matrix can be expressed as $Y = WJ$ where W is Whitening matrix. Whitening processing is to reduce the correlation between eigenvalues in the observation data, so as to improve the separation performance of the algorithm. The covariance matrix R of the J can be expressed as

$$R = E\left[JJ^H\right] \tag{7}$$

The covariance matrix R is decomposed by eigenvalue decomposition to get top K larger eigenvalues, where K is the number of sources signal. The top K larger eigenvalues constitute the matrix P, and the corresponding eigenvector is recorded as D, so the whitening matrix W is

$$W = \left(PD^{-\frac{1}{2}}\right)^H \tag{8}$$

The whitened signal Y can be expressed as

$$Y = WJ \tag{9}$$

where U is the unitary matrix obtained after whitening. Obviously, to get J, it is necessary to estimate the unitary matrix U, which is obtained by calculating the fourth-order cumulant of the mixed matrix after whitening.

First, define the cumulative function

$$um\left(x_i, x_k^*, x_1, x_m^*\right) = E\left\{x_i x_k^* x_1 x_m^*\right\} - E\left\{x_i x_k^*\right\}E\left\{x_1 x_m^*\right\}$$
$$- E\{x_i x_1\}E\left\{x_k^* x_m^*\right\} - E\left\{x_i x_m^*\right\}E\left\{x_k^* x_1\right\} \tag{10}$$

According to the definition of cumulant, the mixed signal after whitening can be used to calculate the cumulant matrix. The element of the matrix (i, j) is

$$Q_{k,l}(i, j) = cum\left(y_k, y_l^*, y_i, y_j^*\right) 1 \leq k, l, i, j \leq K \tag{11}$$

Feature decomposition of $Q_{k,l} = \hat{U} \sum \hat{U}^H$, the estimation $\hat{U}$ of unitary matrix is obtained, where Σ is a diagonal matrix.

Separate the mixed matrix using the whitening matrix W and the estimation unitary matrix $\hat{U}$, Get the source signal S

$$S = \hat{U}WJ = \hat{U}Y \tag{12}$$

3.2 Post-processing and Image Restoration

We then restore the processed S to a single channel image I and normalize it, mapping its pixel values to the range of [0,1]

$$I = \frac{S - \min(S)}{\max(S) - \min(S)} \tag{13}$$

Next, we use the imadjust function to increase the contrast of the image

$$I' = \text{imadjust}(I, \text{stretchlim}(I, [0.01, 0.99]), []) \tag{14}$$

Finally, we post-process each channel, including smoothing the image with a Gaussian filter (standard deviation 0.5), and sharpening the image

$$I'' = \text{imgaussfilt}(I', 0.5) \tag{15}$$

$$I''' = \text{imsharpen}(I'') \tag{16}$$

The image processed by ICA is mixed with the original image in a certain proportion, get the final image IMG

$$IMG = 0.5I''' + 0.5 \, \text{img} \tag{17}$$

Displays the blended color image IMG.

The general flow chart of the combination of Jade algorithm and dark channel prior technology is shown as follows.

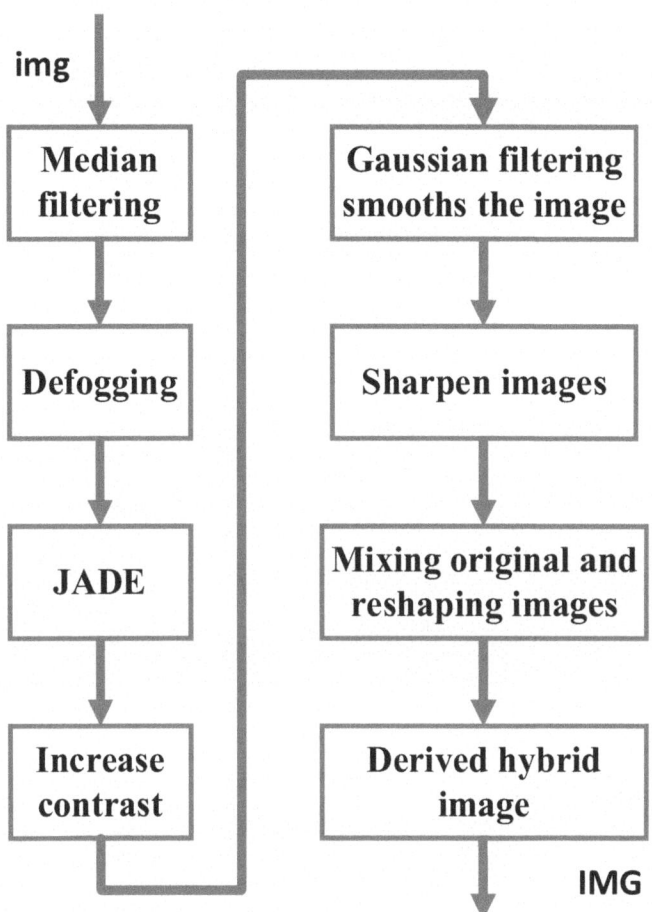

4   Experiments and Results

4.1   Experimental Environment

To commence, the captured highway surveillance footage is processed via software, wherein each frame is extracted and subsequently subjected to a filtering mechanism that discriminates against any image devoid of significant obstacle features, while expunging the irrelevant ones.

To alleviate the limitations imposed by hardware operations, the original image was downscaled to a 640 × 640 RGB three-channel image using a bilinear interpolation method [32] prior to the experiments. It is worth noting that the use of bilinear interpolation for image scaling may result in information loss in the case of significantly larger scaling ranges. Therefore, multiple bilinear interpolation techniques are used in this study. If half of the image has a dimension greater than 640, it is linearly interpolated once to halve its original size. If half of the image dimension is less than 640, bilinear interpolation is applied so that its dimension is 640.

To validate the efficacy of the proposed model, we conducted training and evaluation of the neural network with the utilization of computer hardware and software configurations, along with specific model hyperparameters, as documented in Table 1.

Table 1. Experimental environment Configuration.

Parameter	Configuration
CPU	12th Gen Intel(R) Core i9-13900K 3.0 GHz
GPU	NVIDIA GeForce RTX4090 (24G)
Operating System	Windows11
CUDA	11.7
Momentum	0.937
Weight decay	0.0005
Batch size	32
Learning rate	0.01
Image size	640 × 640
Epochs	300
Matlab	2021

4.2 Experiment Results

Fig. 1. .

As shown in Figs. 1 and 3 the original image without any processing, and Figs. 2 and 4 represents the processed image after applying the Jade algorithm. Compared with the original image, the details of the processed image are clearer, which is helpful to observe and analyze the details in the image. The colors are sharper; the visual quality of the image is improved, which is more conducive to the application of machine learning algorithm.

Fig. 2. .

Fig. 3. .

Fig. 4. .

5 Conclusion

The Jade-based highway image enhancement method effectively improves the clarity and contrast of the image through the analysis and processing of image features, making the image more visually pleasing and easier to perceive. The main advantage of this method is its ability to process different types of images quickly with low latency. In addition, this method has high robustness and can deal with some abnormal situations in image processing. We combined Jade algorithm with dark channel prior technology for image enhancement and denoising. This method has a better effect on image detail processing under bad weather (such as fog and other obstructed vision) than only using a single method.

It is worth noting that the application of this method in the field of highway image enhancement has been widely verified and applied, and it has practical value and promotional value. However, there is still room for improvement in the scalability and accuracy of this method, which needs to be further explored and perfected in practical applications. Overall, the Jade-based highway image enhancement method is currently one of the relatively outstanding and reliable image enhancement techniques, which can provide strong support and help for practical applications in related fields.

Acknowledgment. This work was supported in part by the 2023 Jiangsu Province College Student Innovation Training Program (202313573086Y), and in part by the Natural Science Foundation of Higher Education of Jiangsu Province (Grant No.17KJB510020).

References

1. He, H., Yan, Z., Geng, Z., Liu, X.: Research on pedestrian tracking algorithm based on deep learning. In: *Proceedings of International Conference on Computer Information Science and Artificial Intelligence (CISAI)*, pp. 487–490 (2021)
2. Ahmed, Z., Iniyavan, R., M.M.P.: Enhanced vulnerable pedestrian detection using deep learning. In: *Proceedings of International Conference on Communication and Signal Processing (ICCSP)*, pp. 0971–0974 (2019)
3. Song, H., Choi, I.K., Ko, M.S., Bae, J., Kwak, S., Yoo, J.: Vulnerable pedestrian detection and tracking using deep learning. In: *Proceeding of International Conference on Electronics, Information, and Communication (ICEIC)*, pp. 1–2 (2018)s
4. Hou, C.B., Liu, G.W., Tian, Q., Zhou, Z.C., Hua, L.J., Lin, Y.: Multi-signal modulation classification using sliding window detection and complex convolutional network in frequency domain. IEEE Int. Things J. **9**(19), 19438–19449 (2022)
5. Zhang, X.-X., Adebisi, B., Gacanin, H., Adachi, F.: NAS-AMR: neural architecture search based automatic modulation recognition method for integrating sensing and communication system. IEEE Trans. Cognit. Commun. Netw. **8**(3), 1374–1386 (2022)
6. Girshick, R., Donahue, J., Darrell, T., Malik, J.: Rich feature hierarchies for accurate object detection and semantic segmentation. In: *Proceedings of IEEE Conference on Computer Vision and Pattern Recognition*, pp. 580–587 (2014)
7. Ren, S., He, K., Girshick, R., Zhang, X., Sun, J.: Object detection networks on convolutional feature maps. IEEE Trans. Pattern Anal. Mach. Intell. **39**(7), 1476–1481 (2017)

Method and Practice of Borehole Group Detection in Borehole Drilling Based on Six-Axis Sensing

Jiang Yuhang[1](✉), Yu Jiming[1](✉), Wang Wenfeng[2], Chen Miao[1], Zhang Mingming[1], and Qu Wentao[1]

[1] School of Software Engineering, Jinling University of Science and Technology, Nanjing 211169, China
320763536@qq.com, yujm@jit.edu.cn
[2] Mining Branch of Nanjing Baodi Meishan Industrial City Development Co. Ltd., Nanjing 210041, China

Abstract. This article proposes a method for detecting the diameter of underground rock drilling holes based on intelligent spatial 3D motion sensors. The three-dimensional motion sensors are used to accurately measure the acceleration and angular velocity information of underground rock drilling tools. Combined with algorithm analysis and image processing technology, the length and direction of underground rock drilling hole groups are accurately detected, and algorithms are designed to predict the diameter slices and blasting effects of multiple planes. This method can assist in evaluating the effectiveness of rock drilling construction, provide guidance for rock drilling remedial construction, and reduce construction costs.

Keywords: underground rock drilling · aperture detection · spatial three-dimensional motion sensor · aperture group slicing

1 Introduction

As an important underground engineering technology, underground rock drilling has been widely applied in fields such as mining, geological exploration, and underground construction [1–3]. During the process of rock drilling, the accurate detection of pore size has always been a focus of attention in the engineering field, and the application of guidance and positioning technology has also been widely applied in underground rock drilling. By using high-precision measurement equipment such as laser ranging, total station, and GPS, real-time position and attitude information of underground operations can be obtained, thereby accurately controlling the operation and guidance of rock drilling equipment. The application of this technology can improve accuracy, reduce waste, and improve drilling effectiveness. Traditional aperture detection methods have some limitations, such as low accuracy and poor real-time performance. To address these issues, this paper proposes a method for detecting the borehole diameter of underground drilling based on spatial three-dimensional motion sensors.

© ICST Institute for Computer Sciences, Social Informatics and Telecommunications Engineering 2025
Published by Springer Nature Switzerland AG 2025. All Rights Reserved
X. Chen et al. (Eds.): IoTaaS 2023, LNICST 585, pp. 91–100, 2025.
https://doi.org/10.1007/978-3-031-70507-6_8

This method mainly measures the position and posture information of the rock drilling tool in the hole in real-time by installing a spatial three-dimensional motion sensor on the rock drilling tool. The spatial three-dimensional motion sensor can simultaneously measure the acceleration and angular velocity of the tool in three directions. Through data processing and algorithm analysis, the displacement and angle changes of the tool during rock drilling can be obtained. By monitoring displacement and angle changes, the pore size formed by rock drilling tools can be accurately calculated.

2   Overall Design of Exploratory Holes

The entire system consists of a computer processor, RS485 communication interface, spatial three-dimensional motion sensor WT61PC485, perception detection module, visual transmission module, control transmission module, and probe hole sensing device. The overall structure of the system is shown in Fig. 1.

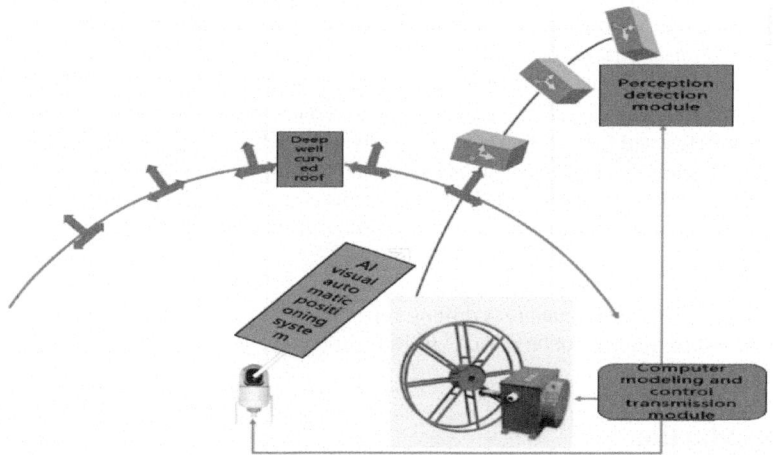

Fig. 1. Overall Design

As shown in Fig. 1, the hole position is determined through a camera assisted by AI vision technology, and the spatial 3D motion perception detection module is installed on the drilling device. During the drilling process, the spatial three-dimensional motion sensor collects real-time acceleration and angular velocity information of the drilling device, and transmits it back to the computer for calculation and processing. It deduces the trajectory and posture of the drill bit in the rock, calculates the orientation, inclination angle, and depth of the drilling hole, displays the changes in angle and attitude during this exploration process, and generates a visual model of the aperture.

2.1 Perception Detection Module and Computer Control Transmission Module

The main modules for trajectory calculation and formation are the perception detection module and the computer control transmission module. The modules are connected by RS485 bus, which is a serial communication protocol and physical interface standard suitable for long-distance data transmission and multi-point communication. Adopting differential transmission method, it has good anti-interference ability and reliability. The computer controlled transmission module is installed on the operating platform of the drilling machine, while the sensor is installed in the extended pipeline of the drilling machine. The sensor contains modules that integrate high-precision gyroscopes and accelerometers, which have the characteristics of convenient connection, long transmission distance, strong anti-interference ability, and stable transmission, as shown in Fig. 2.

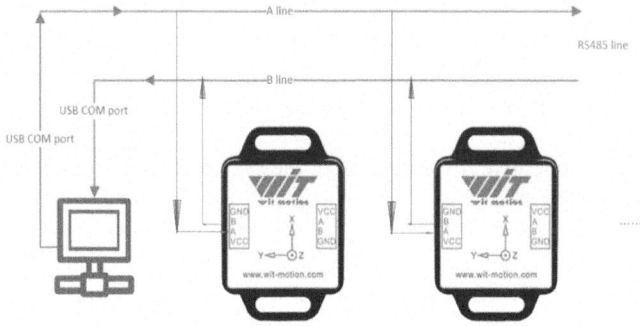

Fig. 2. Computer Control Transmission Module and Detection Module

After the computer control transmission module sends instructions to collect information such as acceleration and angular velocity, the command transmission is transmitted to each sensor through the A-line. After the sensor collects data, the data is returned to the computer control transmission module through the B-line for processing [4–6].

3 Calculation of Exploratory Hole Trajectory

According to kinematics, the trajectory of an object's motion can be drawn by double integrating its acceleration [7–10]. During the process of object movement, the accelerations of the three axes in the three-dimensional space of the object, X, Y, and Z, are continuously collected at high frequencies. At the same time, the three axes are integrated simultaneously to obtain the instantaneous velocity and position of the object. The position is ultimately accumulated into a trajectory, as shown in Fig. 3. The horizontal axis is the time axis t, and the vertical axis is the velocity v. The slope of the tangent at any point in the graph is the instantaneous acceleration a at that time point.

Starting from a certain moment for sampling, according to the principle of mathematical integration, the relationship between displacement s (t), velocity v (t), and

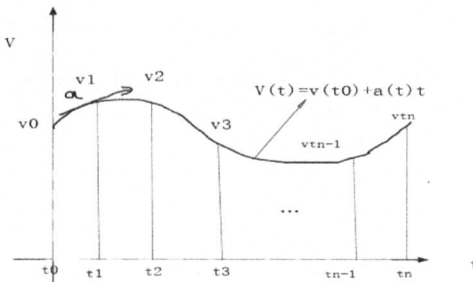

Fig. 3. Speed and Time Curve

acceleration a (t) during this continuous period from a certain moment t0 to time t is shown in Eqs. 1 and 2:

$$s(t) = \int_{t_0}^{t} v(t)dt + s(t_0) \tag{1}$$

$$v(t) = \int_{t_0}^{t} a(t)dt + v(t_0) \tag{2}$$

where $s(t_0)$ is the cumulative displacement of the system from 0 to t_0 time, and $v(t_0)$ is the instantaneous velocity of the system at time.

When the sensor is collecting at high frequency, when it is small enough, the velocity time curve can be approximated as a straight line, which can be subdivided into several right angle trapezoids. The displacement and route of the object become an integral of each trapezoid.

When the initial state $s(t_0) = 0$, then:

$$s(t) = \int_{t_0}^{t} v(t)dt = \frac{v(t_0) + v(t_1)}{2}(t_1 - t_0)... + \frac{v(t_{n-1}) + v(t_n)}{2}(t_n - t_{n-1}) \tag{3}$$

Among them, $\Delta t = t_1 - t_0 = t_2 - t_1 = ... = t_n - t_{n-1}$, Δt is the interval between each period of time. Where $n > 1$.

$$s(t) = \sum_{k=1}^{n} \frac{v(t_{k-1}) + v(t_k)}{2} \Delta t \tag{4}$$

Because acceleration is a discrete set of data, the above equation can be rewritten as:

$$s(n) = \sum_{k=1}^{n} \frac{v(k-1) + v(k)}{2} \Delta t \tag{5}$$

In the discrete domain, when n > 1:

$$s(n) = \sum_{k=1}^{n} \frac{v(k-1) + v(k)}{2} \Delta t = \frac{1}{2}[v(0) + v(n)] \cdot \Delta t + [v(1) + v(2) \ldots + v(n-1)] \cdot \Delta t \qquad (6)$$

$$v(n) = \sum_{k=1}^{n} \frac{a(k-1) + a(k)}{2} \Delta t = v(0) + \frac{1}{2}[a(0) + a(n)] \cdot \Delta t + [a(1) + a(2) \ldots + a(n-1)] \cdot \Delta t \qquad (7)$$

Therefore, the travel distance of a single axis at time n is:

$$s(n) = n \cdot v(0) \cdot \Delta t + [(n-1) \cdot a(1) + (n-2) \cdot a(2) + \ldots + v(n-1)] \cdot \Delta t^2 + \frac{1}{4}[a(0) + a(n)] \cdot \Delta t^2 \qquad (8)$$

From the above equation, it can be seen that only by knowing v (0) and the acceleration of the acceleration sensor, the motion path of the object can be determined. However, the above formula requires multiple repeated operations, which are cumbersome and time-consuming, so iterative algorithms can be used instead:

Because there are:

$$v(n) - v(n-1) = \frac{a(n) + a(n-1)}{2} \cdot \Delta t \qquad (9)$$

$$s(n) - s(n-1) = \frac{v(n) + v(n-1)}{2} \Delta t = v(n-1) \cdot \Delta t + \frac{1}{4}[a(n-1) + a(n)] \cdot \Delta t^2 \qquad (10)$$

Therefore, as long as the velocity v (n-1) and acceleration a (n-1) in the n-1 state are obtained, the velocity v (n) and displacement s (n) in the n state can be calculated.

The above are all calculations in one-dimensional state. Now, the conclusion can be extrapolated to three-dimensional space. As long as the acceleration and initial velocity of the X, Y, and Z axes are known separately, the displacement trajectory of the three axes can also be calculated. X. The instantaneous accelerations of the Y and Z axes are as follows:

$$\vec{v}_x(t) = \vec{v}_x(t - \Delta t) + \frac{\vec{a}_x(t) + \vec{a}_x(t - \Delta t)}{2} \Delta t \qquad (11)$$

$$\vec{v}_y(t) = \vec{v}_y(t - \Delta t) + \frac{\vec{a}_y(t) + \vec{a}_y(t - \Delta t)}{2} \Delta t \qquad (12)$$

$$\vec{v}_z(t) = \vec{v}_z(t - \Delta t) + \frac{\vec{a}_z(t) + \vec{a}_z(t - \Delta t)}{2} \Delta t \qquad (13)$$

At time t, by adding the vectors of the three axis velocities, the instantaneous acceleration in space is:

$$\vec{v}(t) = \vec{v}_x(t) + \vec{v}_y(t) + \vec{v}_z(t) \qquad (14)$$

Therefore, at time t, the three axis X, Y, and Z motion displacements are:

$$s_x(t) = s_x(t - \Delta t) + v_x(t - \Delta t)\Delta t + \frac{1}{4}[a_x(t - \Delta t) + a_x(t)] \cdot \Delta t^2 \qquad (15)$$

$$s_y(t) = s_y(t - \Delta t) + v_y(t - \Delta t)\Delta t + \frac{1}{4}\left[a_y(t - \Delta t) + a_y(t)\right] \cdot \Delta t^2 \qquad (16)$$

$$s_z(t) = s_z(t - \Delta t) + v_z(t - \Delta t)\Delta t + \frac{1}{4}\left[a_z(t - \Delta t) + a_z(t)\right] \cdot \Delta t^2 \qquad (17)$$

At time t, the spatial coordinates of the object are $(s_x(t),\ s_y(t),\ s_z(t))$, and after connecting these points in sequence, the spatial movement trajectory of the object is formed.

4   Calculation Results of Exploratory Hole Trajectory

Tables 1, 2, and 3 respectively show the acceleration, angle, and angular acceleration collected during the drilling process. When the probe hole generates a downward and forward motion state, the acceleration in the X-axis direction remains basically unchanged, while the Y-axis generates a forward negative acceleration, and the Z-axis generates an overweight acceleration with a vertical downward direction, as shown in Table 1.

Table 1. Acceleration Data

Collecting Acceleration Data from Spatial 3D Motion Sensors		
X (m/s^2)	Y (m/s^2)	Z (m/s^2)
0.0806	−0.0498	1.0068
0.0835	−0.0825	0.9868
0.0830	−0.0625	0.9888
0.0737	−0.0498	1.0063
0.0957	−0.0693	0.9795
0.0815	−0.0845	0.9731
0.0703	−0.1133	0.9468
0.0894	−0.1104	0.9795
0.0933	−0.0005	1.0396
0.1201	−0.0498	1.0732
0.1025	−0.0342	0.9834
0.0522	−0.0752	0.9800
0.0903	−0.0649	0.9795
0.1660	−0.0454	0.9727

Due to the fixed attitude of the probe during its movement, there is no significant change in angle and angular velocity during the movement, only slight changes in pitch angle, as shown in Tables 2 and 3.

Table 2. Angle Data

Collecting Angle Data from Spatial 3D Motion Sensors		
X(°)	Y(°)	Z(°)
−3.5330	−4.8070	125.1910
−3.5760	−4.8850	125.1840
−3.6130	−4.8470	125.1990
−3.5190	−4.8710	125.1950
−3.5120	−4.8980	125.1940
−3.5010	−5.0230	125.1810
−3.6090	−5.0090	125.1990
−3.6170	−5.0660	125.1830
−3.0840	−5.1060	125.1680
−2.2360	−5.2800	125.1320
−1.7580	−5.3890	125.2230
−2.0840	−5.3030	125.2160
−2.1980	−5.2580	125.2460
−2.2320	−5.5680	125.2230

The acceleration data in the accelerometer sensor can be converted into the coordinates of the probe hole space points through integral iteration to simulate the spatial trajectory of motion. The data of the probe hole space movement acceleration is shown in Fig. 4. After processing the acceleration using the above algorithm, the aperture detection calculation result shown in Fig. 4 can be obtained, which can reflect the motion trajectory of the probe hole.

According to the data in Table 4, it can be seen that the probe hole first receives an upward force on the Z-axis, generating a positive acceleration in the direction, and then continuously receives a downward force, generating a negative acceleration in the Z-axis direction. Due to the change in acceleration direction, the velocity of the probe hole at this point is zero, as shown in Fig. 4. The highest point position is always subjected to a forward force on the Y-axis, and the acceleration direction remains unchanged. Therefore, a forward trajectory is generated on the y-axis. The final trajectory of the exploratory hole is the trajectory that continues downward after reaching the highest point upwards, as shown in Fig. 4.

Table 3. Angular velocity data

Collecting angular velocity data using spatial 3D motion sensors		
X (°/S)	Y (°/S)	Z (°/S)
0.3052	−0.6104	0.0610
0.0000	−0.4272	0.1831
0.6714	−0.6104	−0.1221
0.7935	−0.9766	0.2441
0.4883	−1.1597	−0.4883
1.5869	−0.8545	0.3662
3.9063	−1.0986	0.1831
8.4839	−1.2207	−0.7324
10.0708	−1.7090	−0.2441
4.8828	−1.0376	−0.1221
−1.0376	−0.5493	0.6104
−0.4272	−08545	1.2207
0.7324	−2.0752	0.1221
1.5869	−1.3428	−0.8545

Table 4. Acceleration data during motion

Acceleration data during motion		
X(m/s^2)	Y(m/s^2)	Z(m/s^2)
−0.0845	−0.0361	0.9287
−0.0715	−0.1597	−0.8369
0.1318	−0.2188	−0.7964
0.0723	−0.1567	−0.6958
−0.0347	−0.1563	−0.6787
−0.0391	−0.0425	−0.6411
0.0713	−0.0405	−0.7520
0.0723	−0.0479	−0.7280
−0.1133	−0.1001	−0.7559

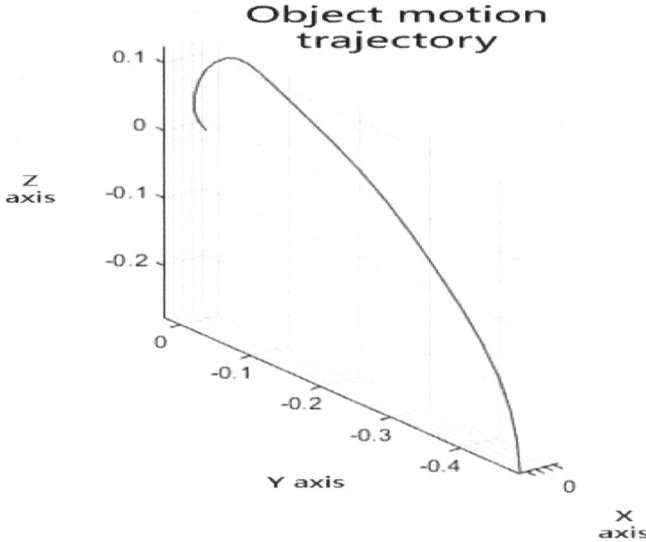

Fig. 4. Test result

5 Summary

Based on the above experiments, it can be concluded that according to the working principle of spatial three-dimensional motion sensors, the collection and verification of angles, accelerations, and angular accelerations have been completed. Then, mathematical algorithms are used to obtain the calculation results of aperture detection based on the collected accelerations, and the trajectory is simulated through the calculation results. To provide a more accurate and detailed description of the path and state of the probe hole in its working state, it is necessary to add the attitude angle of the three-axis gyroscope and slice and analyze the aperture to make the trajectory more accurate.

The application prospects of this project are broad, and the practical operation is simple. It can not only reduce the development cost of underground rock drilling in future engineering, but also improve the safety of underground operations. In the actual mining of the future underground, more other measuring equipment will be applied.

References

1. Huang, K., Su, J., Zhang, Y.: Research progress on autonomous operation methods for underground rock drilling robots. Min. Mach. (2013)
2. Guo, X., Li, Y.: Current situation and thinking of drilling and rock drilling machinery used in coal mines. Min. Mach. (2008)
3. Li, X.: Research on safe autonomous navigation of underground hydraulic drilling trolley. Central South Univ. (2014)
4. Shi, H., You, J., Wang, L., et al.: Design and simulation research of a calibration platform for six dimensional acceleration sensors. Sens. Microsyst. (2023)

5. Li, Y.: Research on human posture recognition based on acceleration sensors. Electron. Compon. Inform. Technol. (2022)
6. Chen, H., Zhou, F.: Application of three-axis acceleration sensors in intelligent vehicle path recognition. Sens. Microsyst. (2010)
7. Yuan, X., Wang, X.: A balanced vehicle attitude detection and control scheme based on MPU6050 spatial 3D motion sensor. Inform. Comput. (Theoret. Edn.) (2018)
8. Zhan, H., Zou, L., Ouyang, Y.: Design of a balanced car based on MPU6050 spatial 3D motion sensor. Electron. Testing (2017)
9. Chengquan, H., Kai, W., Lili, H., et al.: Upper limb motion recognition system based on MEMS spatial 3D motion sensors. J. Dalian Univ. Technol. **12288**, 183 (2017)
10. Li, X., Guo, L., Wang, J.: Design of gait analysis system based on spatial 3D motion sensors. Sens. Microsyst. **33**, 89–91 (2014)

Satellite Internet Network (SatNet 2023)

Deep Reinforcement Learning-Based Channel and Power Allocation in Multibeam LEO Satellite Systems

Junrong Li, Fuzhou Peng, Xijun Wang, and Xiang Chen[✉]

School of Electronics and Information Engineering, Sun Yat-Sen University,
Guangzhou, China
{lijr75,pengfzh}@mail2.sysu.edu.cn,
{wangxijun,chenxiang}@mail.sysu.edu.cn

Abstract. With the continuous growth in communication demand, improving the efficiency of resource allocation becomes crucial. Furthermore, flexible resource allocation for meeting the non-uniform and time-varying traffic demand has emerged as an important task in multi-beam satellite systems. To improve power utilization and meet dynamic traffic demand, this paper formulates an optimization objective that minimizes the trade-off between the unmet traffic demand and power consumption. This is realized by optimizing the allocation of channel and their power, while considering the impact of co-channel interference(CCI). We propose the deep reinforcement learning (DRL) technique to optimize resource allocation. Simulation comparisons between our proposed algorithm and benchmark schemes show its effectiveness in achieving a balance between power allocation and traffic demands. Notably, our algorithm outperforms others in terms of power consumption and meeting traffic demand.

Keywords: Multibeam satellite system · Dynamic resource allocation · Deep reinforcement learning

1 Introduction

Satellite communication is crucial in aviation, maritime, and rescue fields due to its extensive coverage and powerful communication capabilities [1]. With the continuous growth of traffic demand, some challenges, such as spectrum congestion and power limitations [2], have exacerbated. Therefore, optimizing resources allocation to improve resource efficiency are crucial. Furthermore, flexible resource allocation adapting to the distribution of traffic demand has become necessary for the future multibeam satellite systems [3]. Fortunately, the application of flexible payloads and multibeam provides opportunities for

This work was supported by the Key-Area Research and Development Program of Guangdong Province under Grant 2019B010158001.

X. Chen et al. (Eds.): IoTaaS 2023, LNICST 585, pp. 103–116, 2025.
https://doi.org/10.1007/978-3-031-70507-6_9

advanced resource allocation strategies [4]. These technology enables the flexibility of resource allocation and promote the efficiency of satellite communication systems. Therefore, numerous studies have focused on how to improve flexible and efficiency of resource allocation in satellite communication systems.

Many works have studied flexible resource allocation strategies to meet non-uniform traffic among beam in satellite systems. These strategies can be mainly divided into three types: bandwidth allocation [5], power allocation [6], and joint allocation of both bandwidth and power [7–9]. The authors [7] introduced a joint power and channel resource allocation scheme to match the asymmetric traffic demand among beam. The work [8] proposed a noval objective function that aims to closely match the non-uniform traffic demand and consider fairness among the beams. However, these studies mainly focus on meeting traffic demands alone, ignoring minimize the power usage. Considering that power consumption impacts satellite lifetime, minimization of power consumption becomes critical in satellite systems [10].

Some work [11–13] attempted to meet the traffic demand while minimizing the power consumption. More precisely, the authors in their work [11] proposed a multi-objective approach that not only achieved the satisfaction of traffic demand but also considered minimizing power consumption. To achieve this, a two-stage heuristic algorithm was employed to solve it. The work [12]shared the same optimization objective, but it applied a successive convex approximation algorithm. The work [13] focused on minimizing utilized power and bandwidth conditioned on satisfying the traffic demand, and it used a successive convex approximation approach to solve the non-convex problem. These iterative algorithms have a specific convergence time and overlook the correlation information among time-varying traffic, which might be not suitable for dynamic traffic. Compared with traditional static strategies, DRL can adapt to dynamic environments. Some DRL methods have been applied [14–16], effectively leveraging the inherent time and spatial correlations of the dynamic traffic demand. In their work [14], the authors optimized the allocation policy aimed to minimize both power consumption and unmet system demand. However, their approach simply allocated power for each beam, with only one channel for each beam, thereby overlooking the critical issue of CCI. The work [15] dynamically adjusted bandwidth allocation strategy adapting to time-varying traffic demand. The authors in the work [16] combined DRL and Simulated Annealing (SA) to adapt to uncertain and dynamic demand. However, their approach assumed equal power allocation for channel within the same beam and does not consider minimizing power consumption during the optimization process.

In this paper, we investigate the flexible and efficient resource allocation strategy for multibeam satellite system. In order to meet the time-varying and heterogeneous traffic demand while reducing power consumption, we formulate an optimization objective that aims to minimize both the unmet traffic demand and power consumption. This is realized by optimizing the allocation of channel and their power, while considering the impact of CCI. To solve this problem, we formulate it as a Markov decision process (MDP) and apply a model-free

DRL method specifically proximal strategy optimization (PPO) algorithm. In the simulation, we evaluate the proposed method and two baseline schemes within dynamic traffic demand. Our method shows its effectiveness in achieving the balance between power consumption and traffic demand.

The rest of the paper is structured as follows. Section 2 describes the system model and formulates the optimization problem. Section 3 formulates the problem as a Markov decision process. In Sect. 4, we present PPO based resource allocation. Section 5 presents the simulation results. Finally, Sect. 6 concludes the paper.

2 System Model and Problem Formulation

2.1 System Model

We focus on the downlink of a multibeam Low Earth Orbit (LEO) satellite system which consists of N_b beams ($\mathcal{N} = \{i|i = 1, 2, \ldots, N_b\}$) and K channel ($\mathcal{K} = \{k|k = 1, 2, \ldots, K\}$). The total available bandwidth is denoted as B_{tot} and each channel bandwidth is B_{sc}, where $B_{sc} = B_{tot}/K$. The total bandwidth is reused by all the beams, i.e. the frequency reuse factor is 1. The system model is illustrated in Fig. 1. Assuming the LEO satellite uses earth fixed cells scenario [17], the area covered by the satellite beam remains fixed. Furthermore, we assume that there is a single super user in the center of each beam, which represents the aggregation of the overall beam demand. The dynamic time-varying requested traffic of all the beams is expressed as $D_i(t) = \{D_1(t), D_2(t), \ldots, D_{N_b}(t)\}$.

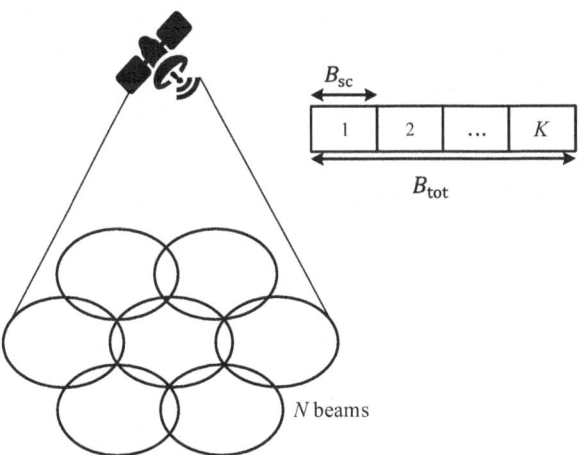

Fig. 1. An illustration of system model.

The channel coefficient from satellite to the user within the coverage of beam i is defined as:

$$h_i = \frac{a_i\sqrt{G_i G_r}}{4\pi f_n d_i / c}, \tag{1}$$

where G_i is the transmission antenna gain from satellite feed towards the beam i, G_i is calculated by $G_i = G_{\mathrm{MAX}} - \frac{12 G_{\mathrm{MAX}}}{\eta}\left(\frac{\theta_i}{70\pi}\right)^2$, and θ_i is the angle between the antenna axis of beam i and user. In addition, G_r is the receiver antenna gain of user, a_i is the small-scale fading model with Rician distribution, c and f_n are the light speed and the frequency of channel respectively, d_i is the distance between satellite and ground user within the beam i.

Considering the channel interference of different beams, the Signal-to-Interference plus Noise Ratio (SINR) of beam i on the channel k is given by

$$SINR_{i,k} = \frac{g_i \cdot x_{i,k} \cdot p_{i,k}}{\sum_{j=1, j\neq i}^{N_b} g_j \cdot x_{j,k} \cdot p_{j,k} + N_0 B_{sc}}, \tag{2}$$

where g_i is the channel gain, i.e., $g_i = |h_i|^2$. $x_{j,k}$ is a binary variable that indicates whether the channel k in the beam j is occupied or not, $x_{i,k} = 1$ indicates the channel is occupied. In addition, $p_{j,k}$ denotes the transmit power allocated to channel k in the beam j and N_0 is the noise power density.

According to Shannon's formula, the capacity of the channel k in the beam i is calculated as follows

$$C_{i,k} = B_{sc} \log_2 \left(1 + SINR_{i,k}\right). \tag{3}$$

The offered capacity of the beam i thus is given by:

$$C_i = \sum_{k=1}^{K} C_{i,k}. \tag{4}$$

2.2   Problem Formulation

In the multibeam satellite system, power and channel are dynamically allocated to meet dynamic demand. The objective of this paper is to satisfy time-varying and non-uniform traffic demand while optimizing power consumption. To evaluate the level of traffic satisfaction, the unmet system capacity (USC) [8] is adopted as a metric, which is the capacity not satisfied in the satellite system, defined by

$$USC = \sum_{i=1}^{N_b} \max\left(D_i - C_i, 0\right), \tag{5}$$

where D_i and C_i is the traffic demand and offered capacity of the beam i respectively. The proposed optimization problem is formulated as follows:

$$\min \quad \sum_{t=1}^{T} \left[\sum_{i=1}^{N_b} \max\left(D_i - C_i, 0\right) + w \sum_{i=1}^{N_b} \sum_{k=1}^{K} p_{i,k} \right]$$

$$\text{s.t.} \quad \text{C1: } x_{i,k} \in \{0,1\}, \forall i \in \mathcal{N}, \forall k \in \mathcal{K}, \forall t \in \{1,\ldots,T\},$$

$$\text{C2: } 0 \le p_{i,k} \le x_{i,k} P_{max}, \forall i \in \mathcal{N}, \forall k \in \mathcal{K}, \forall t \in \{1,\ldots,T\}. \tag{6}$$

In problem (6), the optimization goal is formulated to minimize both the USC and the total power consumption, and the predefined weighted factor w represents the importance of the total power consumption compared to the USC. In constraint C1, $x_{i,k}$ is a binary variable that indicates whether a channel is occupied or not, with $x_{i,k} = 1$ indicating the channel is occupied, and $x_{i,k} = 0$ otherwise. Constraint C2 represents that the power is allocated to channel k only if the channel is occupied ($x_{i,k} = 1$), and the power allocated to each channel should be less than the maximum power limit P_{max}.

3 MDP Formulation

In this work, we consider the LEO satellite as the agent and formulate the resource allocation problem (6) as a Markov Decision Process (MDP). An MDP consists of states, actions, rewards, state transition probabilities. However, due to the difficulty in modeling the state transition probabilities, we adopt a model-free reinforcement learning algorithm. This type of algorithm learns directly from the interaction with the environment without requiring an explicit model of environment. Following is the MDP.

3.1 State

The state at time slot t is defined as

$$S_t = \{D_t, P_{t-1}, B_{t-1}\}. \tag{7}$$

Here, D_t represents the traffic demand requested by each beam at the current time t and is denoted as $D_t = \{D_i(t)\}_{i \in \mathcal{N}}$. The second component, P_{t-1}, is the power allocated to each channel at the previous time slot $t-1$. It is expressed as $P_{t-1} = \{p_{i,k}(t-1)\}_{i \in \mathcal{N}, k \in \mathcal{K}}$. The final component of the state, B_{t-1}, denotes the satisfaction of traffic demand for each beam at the previous time slot $t-1$. This is given by $B_{t-1} = \{B_i(t-1)\}_{i \in \mathcal{N}}$, where $B_i(t-1)$ is computed as the ratio $C_i(t-1)/D_i(t-1)$.

3.2 Action

The agent needs to determine the allocation of channel and power at time slot t based on the current state. We can use the single variable $p_{i,k}(t)$ to indicate the allocation of channel and power at time slot t. More specifically, when $p_{i,k}(t) = 0$, it indicates that channel k is not allocated to beam i,i.e., $x_{i,k} = 0$. Conversely, when $p_{i,k}(t) \neq 0$, it indicates that channel k is allocated to beam i, and the value of $p_{i,k}(t)$ determines the power allocated to that channel. Thus, the action taken by the agent at time slot t is defined as

$$A_t = \{p_{i,k}(t)\}_{i\in\mathcal{N},k\in\mathcal{K}}. \tag{8}$$

It should be noted that power values are within the range of 0 to P_{max}, and they are continuous.

3.3   Rewards

The reward function takes into account both the USC and power consumption. The reward received by the agent in time slot t is formulated as

$$R_t = \sum_{i=1}^{N_b} \max\left(D_i(t) - C_i(t), 0\right) + w \sum_{i=1}^{N_b}\sum_{k=1}^{K} \frac{p_{i,k}(t)}{P_{\max}}, \tag{9}$$

where $P_{\max}$ is the maximum power limit of each beam, and w controls the trade-off between the USC and power consumption. A higher value of w would place more emphasis on reducing the power consumption, while a lower value of w would prioritize reducing the USC.

4   PPO Based Resource Allocation

Algorithm 1. PPO based Resource Allocation

1: Initialize the value network $V_\omega(s)$, policy network π_θ with θ. Initialize $\lambda, \gamma, \epsilon$, total episode E, epoch N, time slot T
2: **for** episode $= 1, 2, \cdots, E$ **do**
3:    **for** time slot $= 1, 2, \cdots, T$ **do**
4:        Run old policy $\pi_{\theta_{old}}$ in environment
5:        Save the trajectory (s_t, a_t, r_t, s_{t+1})
6:    **end for**
7:    Estimate advantage $\hat{A}_t = \sum_{t'\geq t}(\lambda\gamma)^{t'-t}\delta_t$
8:    **for** epoch $= 1, 2, \cdots, N$ **do**
9:        Compute $L^{\text{critic}} = \frac{1}{2}\left(r_t + \gamma V_\omega(s_{t+1}) - V_\omega(s_t)\right)^2$
10:       Compute L^{clip} according to (10)
11:       Update ω by $\nabla_\omega L^{\text{critic}}$
12:       Update θ by $\nabla_\theta L^{\text{clip}}$
13:    **end for**
14:    $\theta_{old} \leftarrow \theta$
15: **end for**

In this section, we will use the PPO algorithm to optimize the channel and power allocation of the system based on the MDP model developed. PPO is a policy gradient-based reinforcement learning algorithm, which includes the policy network and the state-value network.

The policy network aims to learn the optimal policy to maximize long-term cumulative rewards. The objective function of policy network proposed by OpenAI [18] is shown as

$$L^{\text{clip}}(\theta) = \mathbb{E}_t \left[\min \left(p_t(\theta) \hat{A}_t, \text{clip} \left(p_t(\theta), 1 - \epsilon, 1 + \epsilon \right) \hat{A}_t \right) \right], \tag{10}$$

where $p_t(\theta)$) is the policy probability ratio between the new policy and the old policy, which is defined as

$$p_t(\theta) = \frac{\pi_\theta(a_t \mid s_t)}{\pi_{\theta_{old}}(a_t \mid s_t)}. \tag{11}$$

The clip $(p_t(\theta), 1 - \epsilon, 1 + \epsilon)$ is used to limit the range of $p_t(\theta)$ to $(1 - \epsilon, 1 + \epsilon)$, where ϵ is a hyperparameter to control the clipping range.

The symbol $\hat{A}_t$ denotes an estimator of the advantage function at time slot t, which is calculated using a technique called Generalized Advantage Estimation (GAE) [19]. The estimator is written as

$$\hat{A}_t = \sum_{t' \geq t} (\lambda\gamma)^{t'-t} \delta_t. \tag{12}$$

where $\delta_t = r_t + \gamma V_\omega(s_{t+1}) - V_\omega(s_t)$ and $V_\omega(s_t)$ is a state-value function of policy at time slot t.

The objective of state-value network is defined as follows

$$L^{\text{critic}} = \frac{1}{2} \left(r_t + \gamma V_\omega(s_{t+1}) - V_\omega(s_t) \right)^2, \tag{13}$$

where $\delta_t = r_t + \gamma V_\omega(s_{t+1}) - V_\omega(s_t)$ and $V_\omega(s_t)$ is a state-value function of policy at time slot t, and γ is the discount factor.

Table 1. Simulation Parameters

Parameters	Values
Satellite altitude	1200km
Frequency band f_n	12GHz
Number of beams N_b	19
Beam radius	100km
Number of channels K	4
System Bandwidth B_{tot}	1000M
channel bandwidth B_{sc}	125M
Maximum power per channelP_{max}	8W
Noise power spectral density N_0	-174dBW/Hz
User antenna gain G_r	37.7dBi
Maximum satellite beam antenna gain	36.7dBi

PPO based resource allocation is presented in Algorithm 1. The algorithm consists of two stages: initialization and training. During the initialization stage, the parameters of the network and the parameters of the satellite resource allocation scenario are initialized. In each round of the training stage, the algorithm interacts with the environment for T time slots using the old policy and store the trajectory (s_t, a_t, r_t, s_{t+1}). Subsequently, the advantage function is estimated by the GAE method. Next, we calculates the loss functions of the policy network and the critic network, and updates the policy network and the critic network for N epochs using gradient-based methods. After multiple rounds of episode updates, the algorithm has converged, and we save the resource allocation policy for decision-making.

5   Simulation and Discussion

5.1   Simulation Setup

The simulation parameters [20] and training hyperparameter are shown in Table 1 and 2, respectively. The requested traffic demand is dynamically changing with time and space. The dynamic traffic model over time is based on the analysis and modeling of internet traffic in the Milan area. The average traffic demand of beams follows a sin curve with a period of 24 h [21]. In terms of spatial variability, the traffic demand among different beams is uneven at any given moment. Traffic demand in each beam follows a Gaussian distribution with a mean equal to the current average rate demand and a standard deviation is 0.2 times the the current average rate.

Table 2. Training Hyperparameters

Parameters	Values
Discount factor γ	0.9
Learning rate of actor	1e-4
Learning rate of critic	5e-3
Number of time slots per episode T	1024
Number of epochs per episode N	30
clip range ϵ	0.2
λ	0.9
Optimizer	Adam
Network Hidden sizes	[128,128]

5.2   Performance Evaluation Metrics

In order to evaluate the performance of the proposed resource allocation algorithm in the multi-beam satellite system, the following evaluation metrics have been defined:

1) USC: the total unsatisfied capacity across all beams, is defined by Eq.(5).
2) Due to the limited power resources of the satellite system, the total power consumption of the system is used as a metric, which is formulated as

$$PC = \sum_{i=1}^{N_b} \sum_{k=1}^{K} p_{i,k}. \tag{14}$$

To validate the performance of the proposed algorithm, this paper compares it with the following two algorithms:

1) Uniform power: a method that assigns equal power to all the channels with a frequency reuse factor of 1, i.e. $p_{i,k} = P_{\max}$.
2) SA: using SA algorithm for power allocation with the objective of minimizing the USC, with the same power allocation used as the starting point [8].

5.3 Performance Comparison

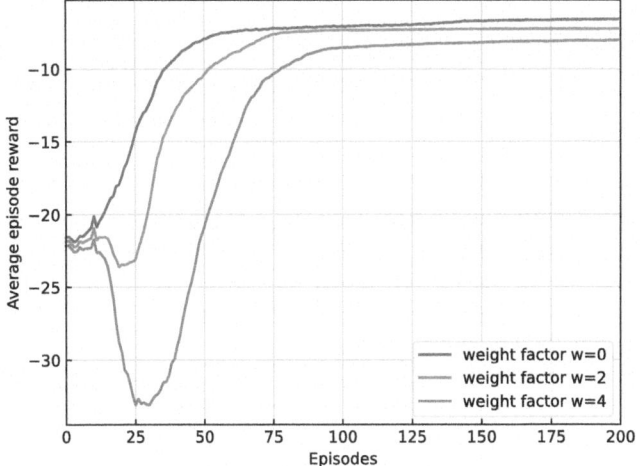

Fig. 2. The average reward with training process.

For the offline training of the DRL algorithm, the algorithm was trained for 200 episodes. Besides, each episode consisted of 1024 time slots, which were sampled from the traffic demand during a day. Figure 2 illustrates the change of the reward function during the training process of the algorithm with weight factor w set to $0, 2, 4$. Different w values adjust the weight of the power consumption and USC. For example, when w is set to 0, representing the case of minimizing USC. After 100 episodes of training, the algorithm has essentially converged. In the ideal scenario, the maximum value of the reward function is 0 with $w = 0$. However,

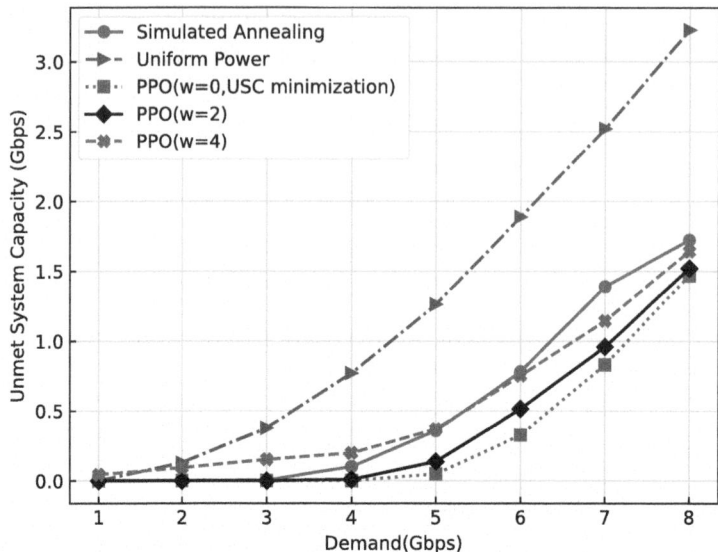

Fig. 3. USC versus traffic demand.

due to the existence of an upper limit on the maximum system capacity, not all traffic demand can be met. Therefore, when the algorithm converges, the reward is only a number close to 0.

After training the DRL agent, its performance was tested using dynamical traffic demands. Figure 3 and Fig. 4 show the USC and total power consumption of the proposed algorithm ($w = 0, 2, 4$), uniform power and SA algorithms at various total traffic demand level. The results from Fig. 3 indicate that when the total traffic demand is low (1, 2, 3 Gbps), the performance of SA and PPO algorithms ($w = 0, 2, 4$) is comparable, with USC tending towards 0, indicating that all traffic demand can be met. As the traffic demand increases, the PPO algorithm ($w = 0$, USC minimization) achieves the lowest USC. In comparison to $w = 0$, the power consumption decreases by approximately 10% with $w = 2$, while the increase in USC is minimal. This suggests that the PPO algorithm ($w = 2$) effectively balances USC and power consumption. The decrease in power consumption is due to considering the power consumption in the optimization objective. Meanwhile, the slight increase in USC can be explained by the Eq. (2), indicating that increasing the power beyond a threshold does not result in a significant improvement in SINR. Overall, the PPO algorithm with w of 0 and 2 outperforms the SA algorithm in both USC and power consumption. As for the uniform power, although it uses all the power, the power allocation cannot adapt to different channel conditions and traffic demand between beams, resulting in the higher USC.

Figure 5 illustrates the offered capacity per beam for different schemes under the total traffic demand of 6 Gbps. The uniform power scheme is unable to meet

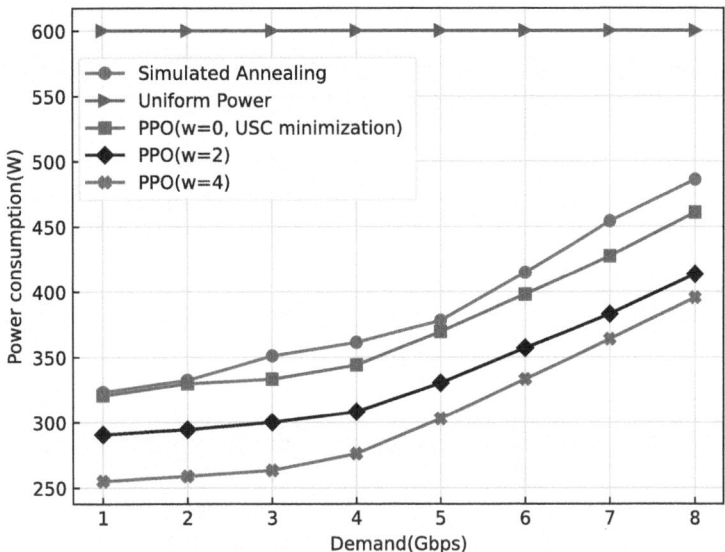

Fig. 4. power consumption versus traffic demand.

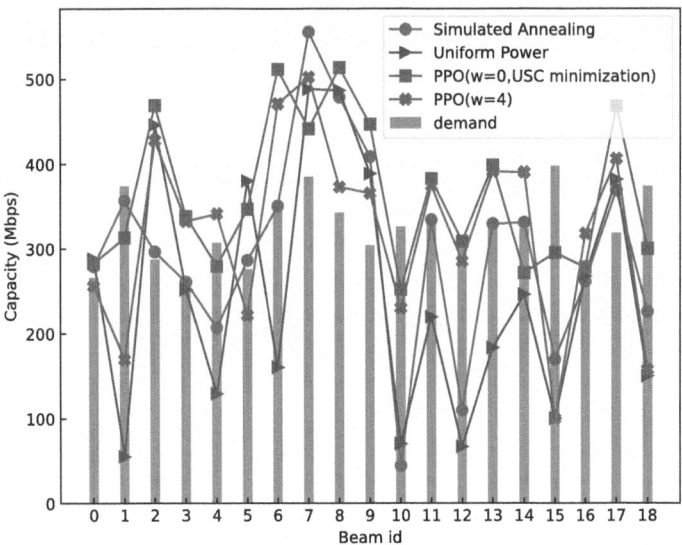

Fig. 5. The capacity provided by different schemes for each beam.

the traffic demand of each beam, while the PPO and SA algorithm can meet the demand of each beam as much as possible. Specifically, the PPO algorithm ($w = 0$) performs the best, while the SA and PPO ($w = 4$) algorithms show similar performance.

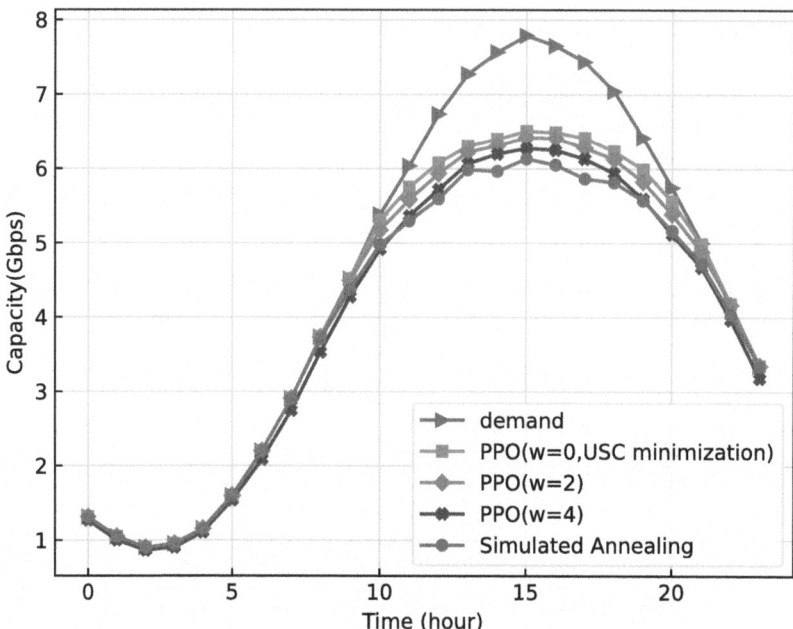

Fig. 6. System demand and provided capacity during a day.

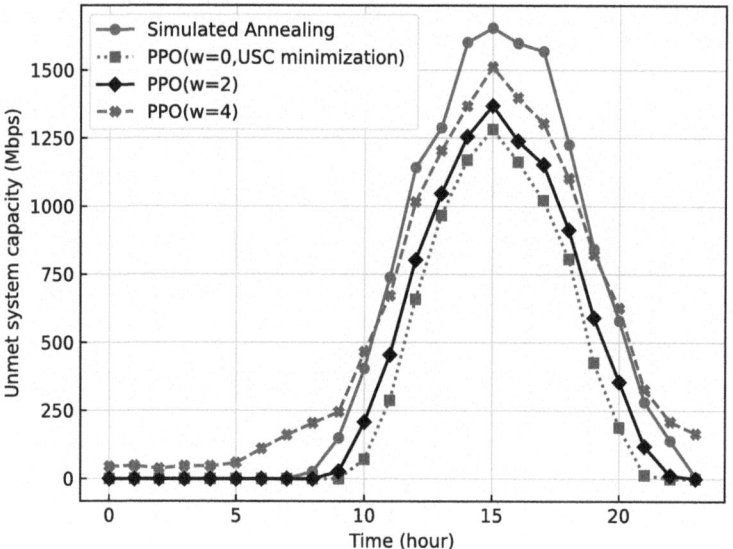

Fig. 7. Unmet system demand during a day.

To evaluate the performance of the proposed algorithm in response to time-varying traffic demands, Fig. 6 and Fig. 7 show the satisfied demand and USC during a day, respectively. In Fig. 6, we observe that the proposed algorithm can dynamically adjust the capacity to meet changing demand. However, when the demand exceeds 5Gbps, some demand cannot be fully met because there is an upper limit for the capacity of system. From the Fig. 7, it can be seen that the USC of system is smaller when using the PPO algorithm with $w = 0$ and $w = 2$.

6 Conclusion

In this paper, we studied dynamic resource allocation in the multibeam LEO satellite system. In order to meet the dynamic traffic demand and reduce power consumption, we formulated an optimization objective aimed at minimizing both unmet traffic demand and power consumption. Subsequently, we applied PPO based algorithm to optimize resource allocation, which can learn dynamic characteristics of traffic and developing effective strategies. In the simulations, we employed different weight factors to adjust the trade-off between power consumption and unmet traffic demand in our proposed algorithm, resulting in diverse resource allocation schemes. Comparing these schemes with other benchmarks, our algorithm effectively can balance power consumption and unmet traffic demand and outperform the benchmarks in both power consumption and unmet system capacity.

References

1. Al-Hraishawi, H., Chougrani, H., Kisseleff, S., Lagunas, E., Chatzinotas, S.: A survey on nongeostationary satellite systems: the communication perspective. IEEE Commun. Surv. Tutor. **25**(1), 101–132 (2023). https://doi.org/10.1109/COMST. 2022.3197695
2. Guan, Y., Geng, F., Saleh, J.H.: Review of high throughput satellites: Market disruptions, affordability-throughput map, and the cost per bit/second decision tree. IEEE Aerosp. Electron. Syst. Mag. **34**(5), 64–80 (2019). https://doi.org/10. 1109/MAES.2019.2916506
3. Kisseleff, S., Lagunas, E., Abdu, T.S., Chatzinotas, S., Ottersten, B.: Radio resource management techniques for multibeam satellite systems. IEEE Commun. Lett. **25**(8), 2448–2452 (2021). https://doi.org/10.1109/LCOMM.2020.3033357
4. Kodheli, O., Lagunas, E., Maturo, N., Sharma, S.K., Shankar, B., Montoya, J.F.M., Duncan, J.C.M., Spano, D., Chatzinotas, S., Kisseleff, S., et al.: Satellite communications in the new space era: a survey and future challenges. IEEE Commun. Surv. Tutor. **23**(1), 70–109 (2020)
5. Hu, X., Liao, X., Liu, Z., Liu, S., Ding, X., Helaoui, M., Wang, W., Ghannouchi, F.M.: Multi-agent deep reinforcement learning-based flexible satellite payload for mobile terminals. IEEE Trans. Veh. Technol. **69**(9), 9849–9865 (2020). https:// doi.org/10.1109/TVT.2020.3002983
6. Destounis, A., Panagopoulos, A.D.: Dynamic power allocation for broadband multi-beam satellite communication networks. IEEE Commun. Lett. **15**(4), 380–382 (2011). https://doi.org/10.1109/LCOMM.2011.020111.102201
7. Lei, J., Vazquez-Castro, M.A.: Joint power and carrier allocation for the multibeam satellite downlink with individual sinr constraints. In: 2010 IEEE International Conference on Communications. pp. 1–5. IEEE (2010)

8. Cocco, G., de Cola, T., Angelone, M., Katona, Z., Erl, S.: Radio resource management optimization of flexible satellite payloads for dvb-s2 systems. IEEE Trans. Broadcast. **64**(2), 266–280 (2018). https://doi.org/10.1109/TBC.2017.2755263

9. Zhao, D., Qin, H., Xin, N., Song, B.: Flexible resource management in high-throughput satellite communication systems: a two-stage machine learning framework. IEEE Trans. Commun. **71**(5), 2724–2739 (2023). https://doi.org/10.1109/TCOMM.2023.3255239

10. Gerard Maral, Michel Bousquet, Z.S.: Satellite Communications Systems: Systems, Techniques and Technology. Hoboken, NJ, USA: Wiley (2009)

11. Aravanis, A.I., Arapoglou, P.D., Danoy, G., Cottis, P.G., Ottersten, B.: Power allocation in multibeam satellite systems: a two-stage multi-objective optimization. IEEE Trans. Wirel. Commun. **14**(6), 3171–3182 (2015)

12. Efrem, C.N., Panagopoulos, A.D.: Dynamic energy-efficient power allocation in multibeam satellite systems. IEEE Wirel. Commun. Lett. **9**(2), 228–231 (2019)

13. Abdu, T.S., Kisseleff, S., Lagunas, E., Chatzinotas, S.: Flexible resource optimization for geo multibeam satellite communication system. IEEE Trans. Wireless Commun. **20**(12), 7888–7902 (2021)

14. Luis, J.J.G., Pachler, N., Guerster, M., del Portillo, I., Crawley, E., Cameron, B.: Artificial intelligence algorithms for power allocation in high throughput satellites: a comparison. In: 2020 IEEE aerospace conference. pp. 1–15. IEEE (2020)

15. Ma, S., Hu, X., Liao, X., Wang, W.: Deep reinforcement learning for dynamic bandwidth allocation in multi-beam satellite systems. In: 2021 IEEE 6th International Conference on Computer and Communication Systems (ICCCS). pp. 955–959 (2021). https://doi.org/10.1109/ICCCS52626.2021.9449160

16. Hu, X., Wang, Y., Liu, Z., Du, X., Wang, W., Ghannouchi, F.M.: Dynamic power allocation in high throughput satellite communications: a two-stage advanced heuristic learning approach. IEEE Trans. Veh. Technol. **72**(3), 3502–3516 (2023). https://doi.org/10.1109/TVT.2022.3218565

17. 3GPP: Solutions for nr to support non-terrestrial networks (ntn) v1.0.0 (release 16). Tech. Rep. TR 38.821, 3rd Generation Partnership Project (3GPP) (December 2019)

18. Schulman, J., Wolski, F., Dhariwal, P., Radford, A., Klimov, O.: Proximal policy optimization algorithms. arXiv preprint arXiv:1707.06347 (2017)

19. Schulman, J., Moritz, P., Levine, S., Jordan, M., Abbeel, P.: High-dimensional continuous control using generalized advantage estimation. arXiv preprint arXiv:1506.02438 (2015)

20. del Portillo, I., Cameron, B.G., Crawley, E.F.: A technical comparison of three low earth orbit satellite constellation systems to provide global broadband. Acta Astronaut. **159**, 123–135 (2019)

21. Andrew Fager: Analysis and modeling of internet usage (2017). https://www.kaggle.com/code/andrewfager/analysis-and-modeling-of-internet-usage/notebook

Transmission, Access and Route Technology for Internet of Vehicle

CSI-Based Signal Reconstruction for WiFi Localization

Yunbing Hu[1,2]([✉]) [iD], Ao Peng[1], and Shenghong Li[3]

[1] The School of Informatics, Xiamen University, China, Xiamen 361001, China
`yunbinghu@stu.xmu.edu.cn`
[2] Chongqing College of Electronic Engineering, Chongqing 401331, China
[3] Commonwealth Scientific and Industrial Research Organisation Marsfield,
Canberra, NSW 2122, Australia
`shenghong.li@csiro.au`

Abstract. With the advent of the 5G era, the demand for high-precision wireless positioning continues to grow. However, traditional ranging-based positioning systems are highly susceptible to interferences caused by multipath and none-line-of-sight (LOS) propagation, which can significantly degrade the accuracy of the estimated time-of-arrival (TOA) values. To address this challenge, this paper proposes a Deep neural networks (DNN)-based approach for accurate TOA estimation in indoor environments. Using a complex-values neural network model, the proposed method predicts TOA directly from the frequency domain channel state information (CSI) of wideband WiFi receivers. We also propose an input normalization method based on peak search in the channel impulse response, which improves both the accuracy of TOA estimation and the efficiency of model training. The proposed method was verified experimentally both in an outdoor area of 900 m^2 with 6 anchors and an indoor area of 700 m^2. It is shown that the proposed approach significantly outperforms conventional methods, with 77% of the positioning errors within 0.5 m in the outdoor test and 95% within 1 m. In the indoor test, about 64% of the positioning errors were within 0.5 m, and approximately 80% were within 1 m.

Keywords: Channel state information · IEEE 802.11 signals ·
Complex value deep neural network

Supported by the National Key Research and Development Project of China (2020YFB1711000), the National Scientific Research Foundation of Chongqing (cstc2019jcyj-msxmX0509), and the Social Scientific Research Foundation of China (19VSZ084), and the National Scientific Research Foundation of Chongqing Municipal Education Commission (KJQN201803110, KJZD-K201903101), and the Social Scientific Research Foundation of Chongqing Municipal Education Commission (20SKGH313), and the National Scientific Research Foundation of Hunan Province Education Commission (18B367), and the Youth Innovation talent Program of Guangxi(AD19245156), and the Teaching Reform Project of Guangxi Normal University(2019XJGZ08).

X. Chen et al. (Eds.): IoTaaS 2023, LNICST 585, pp. 119–128, 2025.
https://doi.org/10.1007/978-3-031-70507-6_10

1   Introduction

Wireless localization is an important research focus because it compensates for the unavailability or inaccuracy of satellite-based positioning systems due to environmental constraints. Applications for wireless indoor and outdoor positioning include underground mining, factory automation, and hospitals. The harsh propagation environment limits the coverage and accuracy of satellite-based localization systems.

In recent years, accurate, reliable and ubiquitous indoor and outdoor localization solutions have been extensively studied based on a range of wireless signals, such as WiFi [1], Bluetooth [2], radar [3], horus [4],Radio Frequency Identification (RFID) [5] , ultra-wideband (UWB) [6], infrared [7], visible light [8], sound [9] , geomagnetic field [10], and so on. However, among these technologies, due to the mass popularity of WiFi systems, the cost of hardware investment is very low, and WiFi based positioning is probably the most popular. Existing wifi devices can be located in a Wifi-based communication system with a firmware upgrade.

The indoor fingerprint recognition system based on CSI has better performance. For example, Liu *et al.* [15] performed CSI amplitude-based localization fingerprint through Cluster-Mapping, which is an adaptive pre-processing system and showed improvement in localization with 98% accuracy with 2-meter localization error. In [16], the authors used only the amplitude of CSI with a deep learning approach and showed 80% localization accuracy with a 2-meter error. In [17], the authors created the collected CSI data as an image and used a deep convolutional neural network to realize localization. The advantage of fingerprint positioning is that while the positioning accuracy is relatively high, it requires laborious survey and measurement of the environment in advance. Once changed, the environment of the position area needs to be measured again, which adversely impacts the commercial versatility of the equipment.

This paper proposes a peak search algorithm based on CSI, which is more accurate than the celebrated MUSIC and ESPRIT algorithms. In practical application, it achieves high positioning accuracy. The main contributions of this work are as follows:

1. We propose a complex neural network model which predicts TOA directly from the frequency domain CSI of wideband WiFi receivers.
2. We propose an input normalization method based on peak search in the channel impulse response, which improves both the accuracy of TOA estimation and the efficiency of model training.
3. The proposed algorithm was experimentally verified on an outdoor positioning system with 6 anchor points covering 900 m^2. The results show that the proposed algorithm has high precision and broad application prospect.

The rest of this article is organized as follows. Section 2 gives the system model, including the structure system and signal structure. Section 3 introduces the data preparation after peak search, and Sect. 4 introduces the neural network structure. Section 5 introduces the evaluation, analysis and experimental verification of the simulation results, and Sect. 5 summarizes the characteristics of the proposed method.

2   System Model

In this paper, we use the wireless ad hoc system for positioning (WASP) [18] developed by the Commonwealth Scientific and Industrial Research Organization (CSIRO) of Australia. The WASP platform features a low-cost, off-the-shelf hardware design that utilizes a bandwidth of 125 MHz for TOA based distance measurement. At the same time, the system has achieved commercial application, and continues to undergo extensive testing and commercial applications in athlete tracking and underground mining.

2.1   System Structure

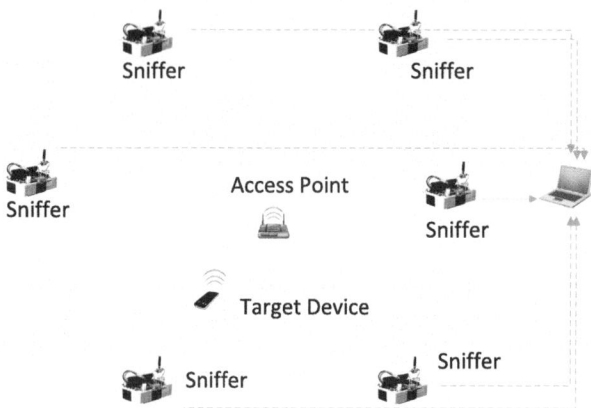

Fig. 1. structure of beacon transmissions in the WASP system.

The localization structure of Fig. 1 is based on a passive WiFi system based on TDOA. The system is composed of 6 custom WiFi sniffers deployed at known locations, a WiFi router, and a laptop computer. The sniffer is used to monitor WiFi network communications, the laptop is used to estimate the target's location from the time stamps collected, and the timestamp monitored by the sniffer is used to calibrate the system hardware delay and provide system clock synchronization.

2.2   Signal Structure

The WASP system adopts WiFi communication technology. WiFi technology based on 802.11a/g/n protocol adopts OFDM system [19]. It includes multiple transmitting antenna at an Access Point (AP) and receiving network card multiple receiving antennas.

Figure 2 shows the architecture of OFDM system, and the architecture of channel estimation and signal detection based on deep learning. At the sending end, the parallel transmission data is converted to serial data. The real and imaginary parts are then converted to the analog domain using a digital-to-analog converter and transmitted out.

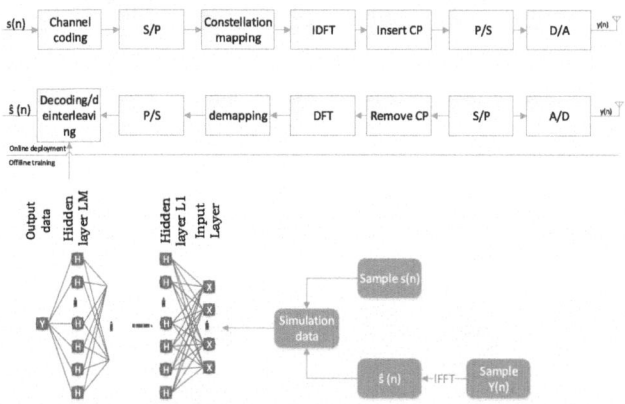

Fig. 2. The system structure of TOA estimation using neural network based on OFDM.

Receiving is the opposite of sending. OFDM enables several subcarriers that are very close to each other to carry the transmitted data to improve the transmission data rate. Each subcarrier transmits data synchronously at the beginning of a frame. Therefore, on the receiving side, using an IEEE 802.11a/g/n compatible wireless network card, a set of CSI can be obtained from each received packet.

3   Deep Learning-Based ToA Estimation

This section presents a method where deep learning is exploited to estimate the received CIR for ToA Estimation. The complex neural network model is trained based on sampling data offline from the WASP system.

3.1   Normalization

Normalization can accelerate the learning speed in the deep network training.

Convertion from Frequency Domain CSI to CIR In practical application, CSI can be characterized by CFR or CIR, and the raw CSI received by the WASP system is CFR in the frequency domain, but the TOA required for positioning is acquired in the time domain. Since CIR is the inverse Fourier transform of CFR [20], it can be expressed as:

$$CIR = IFFT(CSI * W) \tag{1}$$

where W indicates the sampling bandwidth. To do this effectively, the broadband channel is first filled to 1280 samples. Then calculate the IFFT of 1024 points. This improves the sampling accuracy to some extent, making the sampling interval of the impulse response 2.5ns.

Find the Index of the First Significant Peak in the CIR The shape of the leading edge is extracted from the impulse response. The leading edge is resampled to use 25 sample points with a spacing of 1.875ns, such that the peak occurs at sample 25. If the impulse response has multiple peaks, then several leading edges may be extracted. Due to noise and multipath propagation, identifying the leading edge of the impulse response is somewhat involved. Three conditions are used to identify when a peak in the impulse response is due to a received signal, as opposed to being due to noise: (1) The peak must have an amplitude greater than the amplitude of the previous two peaks in the impulse response. (2) The peak must have an amplitude greater than a fixed fraction of the biggest peak amplitude. (3) The peak must have an amplitude greater than the noise floor, which is determined as a multiple of the maximum value of the impulse response in the first 256 samples of the 1024 sample impulse response.

Phase and Amplitude Normalization Phase and amplitude normalization is a linear transformation, which can accelerate the neural network's learning and training speed and improve classification accuracy. Shift the CIR so that the first peak is located at the index center. Figure 3 shows the Phase and amplitude normalization in the CIR. and , the amplitude normalization is adopt to divide by the Amplitude peak value in CIR. this is applied as a normalization step in the machine learning algorithm. It is written as

$$CIR\_norm[N] = CIR[N]/\max(CIR[N]) \tag{2}$$

where $CIR\_norm[N]$ is saved as the normalization of CIR, N represent the number of CIR.

3.2   Training Data Generation

To get good performance from the DL methods, we use the Saleh-Valenzuela channel model to generate 1 million simulated samples of data. The model adopts the time constant of 5ns and 300ns within and between clusters, respectively. The complex amplitude of each path can be expressed as

$$h_k = N(0, \sigma^2) + jN(0, \sigma^2) \tag{3}$$

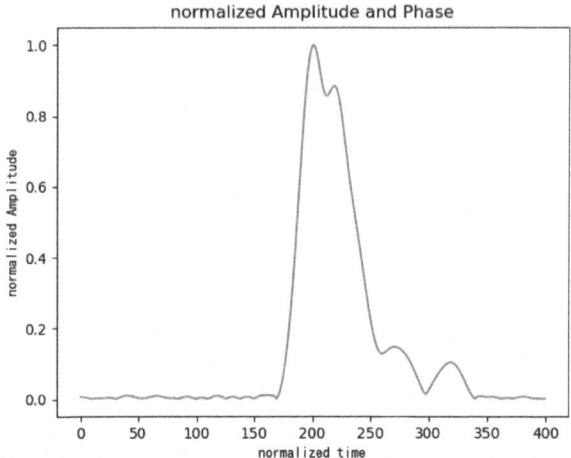

Fig. 3. shift the cir so that the first peak is located at index center.

where $N(\mu, \sigma^2)$ indicates a value drawn from the normal distribution with mean μ and variance σ^2. Equation (3) creates Raleigh amplitude fading. The variance σ^2 undergoes exponential decay both within a cluster and between clusters according to

$$\sigma^2 = e^{-T_l/\Gamma} e^{-\tau_{kl}/\gamma} \tag{4}$$

where T_l is the delay of the l th cluster and $\tau_k l$ is the delay of the k-th path in the l-th cluster. In our simulation, we set $\Gamma = 60$ ns and $\gamma = 20$ ns. We also add noises to give an SNR of 30 dB.

4   Interpretation of the Network

The WASP system based on 802.11a/g/n protocol adopts OFDM system, and the CSI complex H(n) that we can obtain through the WASP system is the n−th subcarrier from Target and Sniffer to AP. So given a CSI complex-valued vector $h = x + iy$ [22] , it is represented as

$$h = \begin{bmatrix} x \\ y \end{bmatrix} \tag{5}$$

where is a real component x and a virtual component y. For performing forward propagation of an equivalent traditional real-valued two-dimensional DNN fully connected network, through vector h we construct DNN hidden layer complex filter matrix $W = A + iB$, where the A and B are real matrix, we obtain

$$W * h = (A * x - B * y) + i(Bx + Ay) \tag{6}$$

If we use matrix represent real and imaginary parts of the CSI, we have

$$\begin{bmatrix} \Re(\boldsymbol{W} * \boldsymbol{h}) \\ \Im(\boldsymbol{W} * \boldsymbol{h}) \end{bmatrix} = \begin{bmatrix} \boldsymbol{A} & -\boldsymbol{B} \\ \boldsymbol{B} & \boldsymbol{A} \end{bmatrix} * \begin{bmatrix} \boldsymbol{x} \\ \boldsymbol{y} \end{bmatrix} \tag{7}$$

To improve the cvDNN fitting ability, we construct a complex bias value $b = m + in$ for cvDNN, where b dimension are the same as and h. Therefore, the linear relationship learned between the output and input of the n-th cvDNN neuron z can be expressed as

$$z = \begin{bmatrix} \boldsymbol{A} & -\boldsymbol{B} \\ \boldsymbol{B} & \boldsymbol{A} \end{bmatrix} * \begin{bmatrix} \boldsymbol{x} \\ \boldsymbol{y} \end{bmatrix} + \begin{bmatrix} \boldsymbol{m} \\ \boldsymbol{n} \end{bmatrix} \tag{8}$$

A fully connected feed forward cvDNN consist of an input layer, a complex layer, two real hidden layers (from first to third, each 256 neurons), and an output layer in Fig. 4. The CReLU is used as the activation function of the complex hidden layers, and Parametric Rectified Linear Unit(PReLU) [27] is used as the activation function of the real hidden layers.

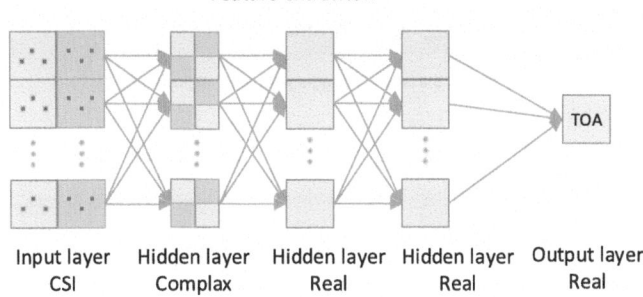

Fig. 4. A diagram illustrating the implementation of a fully connected cvDNN.

Both the complex hidden and the real layer adopted the real Mean Square Error(MSE) loss function. The network is trained in a supervised manner with the MSE loss function, with 0.001 learn rate, 10000 train batch size and 10000 iterations of backpropagation.

5   Experimental Validation

The system was tested under outdoor line-of-sight (LOS) conditions, evaluate its performance. We deployed 6 sniffers around a WiFi network with one access point and one WiFi dongle. A laptop with a WiFi USB dongle was used as the target devices. The topology of the system is shown in Fig. 5.

The laptop communicates with the WiFi router periodically, and the CSI data that the sniffer can sample is used as a reference for hardware delay calibration.

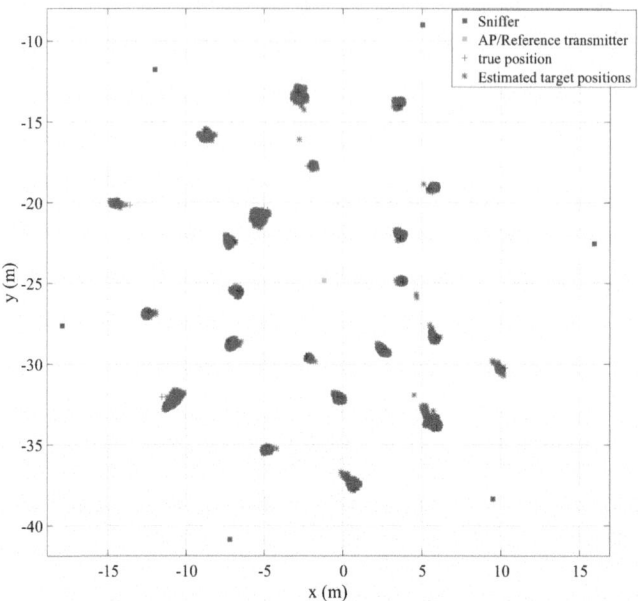

Fig. 5. Positioning effect in outdoor LOS environments.

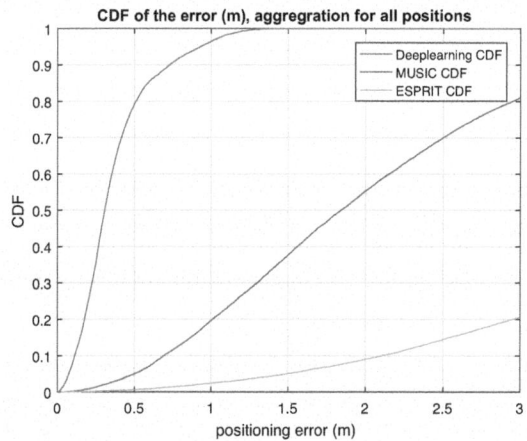

Fig. 6. Comparison of cumulative distribution function of positioning error in outdoor LOS test.

Figure 6 shows that the TOA estimated by our cvDNN algorithm is better than the positioning accuracy of MUSIC and ESPRIT algorithms. About 80 % of the positioning errors are within the range of 0.5 m.

CONCLUSION

We propose a method to find the CIR peak to obtain the first peak, and then obtain the CIR phase normalization, thereby improving the performance of neural network regression, and propose a cvDNN method suitable for CSI. The experimental verification was carried out on an outdoor positioning system covering an area of 900 square meters and 22 nodes. The results show that the proposed algorithm has higher localization accuracy, and it has greater market application potential than fingerprint legal bit because it does not need to collect data in the experiment site in advance.

References

1. Yang, C., Shao, H.-R.: WiFi-based indoor positioning. IEEE Commun. Mag. **53**(3), 150–157 (2015)
2. Kriz, P., Maly, F., Kozel, T.: Improving indoor localization using Bluetooth low energy beacons. Mobile Inf. Syst. **2016**, 2083094 (2016)
3. Bahl, P., Padmanabhan, V.N.: Radar: an in-building RF-based user location and tracking system. In Proc, pp. 775–784. Tel Aviv, Israel, (2000), IEEE INFOCOM
4. Youssef, M., Agrawala, A.: The Horus WLAN location determination system. In: Proceeding Seattle, WA, USA ACM MobiSys. pp. 205–218 (2005)
5. Zhou, Z., Shangguan, L., Zheng, X., Yang, L., Liu, Y.: Design and implementation of an RFID-based customer shopping behavior mining system. IEEE/ACM Trans. Netw. **25**(4), 2405–2418 (2017)
6. B. Kempke, P. Pannuto, B. Campbell, and P. Dutta, "SurePoint: Exploiting ultra wideband flooding and diversity to provide robust, scalable, high-fidelity indoor localization. In: Proceedings 14th ACM Conference Embedded Network Sensor Syst. (CD-ROM), pp. 137-149 (2016)
7. Hauschildt, D., Kirchhof, N.: Advances in thermal infrared localization: challenges and solutions. In: Proceedings IEEE International Conference Indoor Positioning Indoor Navigation. (IPIN). pp. 1–8 (2010)
8. Pathak, P.H., Feng, X., Hu, P., Mohapatra, P.: Visible light communication, networking, and sensing: a survey, potential and challenges. IEEE Commun. Surveys Tuts. **17**(4), 2047–2077 (2015)
9. Moutinho, J.N., Araújo, R.E., Freitas, D.: Indoor localization with audible sound-Towards practical implementation. Pervas. Mobile Comput. **29**, 1–16 (2016)
10. Shu, Y., Bo, C., Shen, G., Zhao, C., Li, L., Zhao, F.: Magicol: Indoor localization using pervasive magnetic field and opportunistic WiFi sensing. IEEE J. Sel. Areas Commun. **33**(7), 1443–1457 (2015)
11. Yang, Z., Zhou, Z., Liu, Y.: From RSSI to CSI: indoor localization via channel response. ACM Comput. Surv. **46**(2), 25–32 (2013)
12. Bahl, P., Padmanabhan, V.N.: RADAR: An in-building RF-based user location and tracking system[C]// INFOCOM 2000. Nineteenth Annual Joint Conference of the IEEE Computer and Communications Societies. Proceedings. IEEE. IEEE (2000)
13. Gu, Yang, et al.: Semi-supervised deep extreme learning machine for WiFi based localization. Neurocomputing **166**(7), 282–293 (2015)

14. Halperin, D., Hu, W., Sheth, A., Wetherall, D.: Tool release: Gathering 802.11n traces with channel state information. ACM SIGCOMM Comput. Commun. Rev. **41**(1), 53–53 (2011)
15. Liu, Wen, et al.: C-Map: hyper-resolution adaptive preprocessing system for csi amplitude-based fingerprint localization. IEEE Access **99**, 1–10 (2019)
16. Wang, Xuyu, et al.: CSI-based fingerprinting for indoor localization: a deep learning approach. IEEE Trans. Vehi. Technol. **66**(1), 763–776 (2016)
17. Wang, Xuyu, Wang, X., Mao, S.: Deep convolutional neural networks for indoor localization with CSI images. IEEE Trans. Netw. Sci. Eng. **7**(1), 316 (2018)
18. Li, Shenghong, Hedley, M., Collings, I.B.: New efficient indoor cooperative localization algorithm with empirical ranging error model. IEEE J. Select. Areas Commun. **33**(7), 1407–1417 (2015)
19. Cheng, Peng, et al.: Sparse blind carrier-frequency offset estimation for OFDMA uplink. IEEE Trans. Commun. **64**(12), 5254–5265 (2016)
20. Zhou, Z., Wu, C., Yang, Z., Liu, Y.: Sensorless sensing with WiFi. Tsinghua Sci. Technol. **20**(1), 1–6 (2015)
21. K. Pahlavan, A. Levesque, "Wireless information network s", 2^{nd}ed. chapter 6, Wiley 2005
22. Trabelsi, Chiheb, et al. Deep Complex Networks. (2017)
23. Li, Shenghong, et al. TDOA-based passive localization of standard WiFi devices. Ubiquitous Positioning, Indoor Navigation and Location-Based Services 0
24. Bao, Qiao, et al.: Research on single frequency component based MUSIC algorithm for impact localization." International Conference on Noise & Fluctuations IEEE, (2015)
25. Li, Shenghong, et al.: TDOA-based passive localization of standard WiFi devices. 2018 Ubiquitous Positioning, Indoor Navigation and Location-Based Services (UPINLBS) (2018)
26. Li, Shenghong, et al.: TDOA-based localization for semi-static targets in NLOS environments. IEEE Wirel. Commun. Lett. **4**(5), 1–1 (2015)
27. He, K. , et al.: Delving Deep into Rectifiers: surpassing human-level performance on imagenet classification. CVPR IEEE Computer Society (2015)
28. Shang, W., et al.: Understanding and improving convolutional neural networks via concatenated rectified linear units. JMLR (2016)

An Indoor Navigation Algorithm Using Multi-dimensional Euclidean Distance and the Adaptive Particle Filter

Yunbing Hu[1,2] ⓘ, Ao Peng[1(✉)], and Shenghong Li[3]

[1] The School of Informatics, Xiamen University, China Xiamen 361001, China
yunbinghu@stu.xmu.edu.cn
[2] Chongqing College of Electronic Engineering, Chongqing 401331, China
[3] Commonwealth Scientific and Industrial Research Organisation Marsfield,
Marsfield, NSW 2122, Australia
shenghong.li@csiro.au

Abstract. The inertial navigation systems exhibit excellent short-term positioning accuracy, yet they are susceptible to cumulative errors over time. WiFi fingerprint localization avoids cumulative errors, but it is prone to mismatching issues. Therefore, a commonly used technique is the integration of an inertial navigation system and WiFi fingerprint matching. The particle filter employs dead reckoning (DR) for the state transfer equation, while utilizing the disparity between inertial navigation and WiFi fingerprint matching as the observation equation. Floor map information is introduced to detect whether particles cross the wall and if so, the weight is set to zero. For the particles that do not cross the wall, considering the distance between the current particles and the historical particles, an adaptive particle filter is proposed. The adaptive factor increases the weight of highly trusted particles and reduces the weight of untrusted particles. Another innovation is the introduction of a multidimensional Euclidean distance algorithm to reduce inconsistencies in WiFi fingerprint matching. The experimental results show that the proposed algorithm achieves high positioning accuracy.

Keywords: The inertial navigation system · WiFi fingerprint mathcing · The adaptive particle filter · Multi-dimensional Euclidean distance

Supported by the National Key Research and Development Project of China (2020YFB1711000), the National Scientific Research Foundation of Chongqing (cstc2019jcyj-msxmX0509), and the Social Scientific Research Foundation of China (19VSZ084), and the National Scientific Research Foundation of Chongqing Municipal Education Commission (KJQN201803110, KJZD-K201903101), and the Social Scientific Research Foundation of Chongqing Municipal Education Commission (20SKGH313), and the National Scientific Research Foundation of Hunan Province Education Commission (18B367), and the Youth Innovation talent Program of Guangxi(AD19245156), and the Teaching Reform Project of Guangxi Normal University(2019XJGZ08).

1   Introduction

A high level of positioning accuracy is currently achievable in open outdoor spaces through global satellite navigation systems. Examples include Baidu Maps and Google Maps, both of which offer navigation and location services for pedestrians and vehicles. In the indoor, tunnel, and other areas, due to the transmission of obstacle occlusion signal, the wireless signal attenuates greatly, so the scheme which using satellite navigation can not provide reliable positioning accuracy. Therefore, the study of indoor navigation solutions has aroused greater interest among researchers [1,2]. Smart phones have the advantages of high penetration and easy portability, Therefore, scholars have conducted extensive studies on indoor navigation utilizing smartphone platforms.

The inertial navigation system (INS) is an autonomous navigation system that operates independently without relying on external information or emitting energy externally. It can provide carrier position, attitude and speed information continuously and in real time. The main disadvantage of inertial navigation systems is the cumulative effect of positional errors. That is, as the elapsed time increases, the errors get bigger. The citation [3] indicates that the accumulated positional error in a two-dimensional plane is proportional to the cube of time. Aiming at the problem of cumulative error, many researchers have carried out in-depth research.The HDR and HDE algorithms [4,5] have been successful in mitigating cumulative errors during pedestrian movement in standard corridors. By incorporating map information, the study presented in references [6,7] employs a map-aided algorithm to mitigate the directional drift observed in inertial navigation. Another approach involves introducing the magnetic field and utilizing its north-pointing characteristic to correct the direction of the inertial navigation system (INS).

The utilization of WiFi wireless signals for positioning is widespread, with two typical indoor WiFi positioning technologies being the signal attenuation model and fingerprint matching model. The signal attenuation model requires prior knowledge of the anchor point's location, and based on the received channel state information[8], estimate the time to reach the direct or reach the Angle, and use the arrival time difference positioning method to estimate the user's position. The WiFi signal state fluctuates with time, and complex indoor environments, such as pedestrians walking or changes in the position of obstacles, are easy to affect the propagation model, resulting in deviations in parameter estimation and a decline in positioning accuracy.The WiFi fingerprint matching model typically consists of two stages: offline training and online positioning. In the off-line training stage, the received channel state information and the corresponding calibration coordinates are saved in the database, and the model is obtained after training. In the online positioning stage, the collected channel state information is used as the fingerprint and then matched with the state information in the database after the model estimation. Usually, the location marked by the fingerprint that is most similar to the fingerprint database is used as the pedestrian location. Because the channel state information of WiFi is easily polluted by environmental noise, it will inevitably cause the mismatch of fingerprints. Therefore, the reference [9] proposed a magnetic fingerprint matching method, which can reduce the location estimation error caused by the WiFi fingerprint mismatch phenomenon. Therefore, considering the complementary characteristics of the positioning errors of these two signal sources, an adaptive particle filter combining INS and WiFi is proposed. The main innovations of this paper are as follows

- To address the challenge of fingerprint mismatching, the multi-dimensional WiFi fingerprint is used instead of the traditional one-dimensional fingerprint, and the multi-dimensional Euclidean distance algorithm is proposed to compute the multi-dimensional WiFi fingerprint distance.
- To address the challenge of traditional particle filter weight updating, the improved particle filter uses adaptive factors to improve the high trusted particle weight and reduce the low trusted particle weight.
- Two cellularphone are used to carry out navigation experiments in two navigation areas, and the Observational results show that the average positioning accuracy is 1.84 m.

2   Framework Description

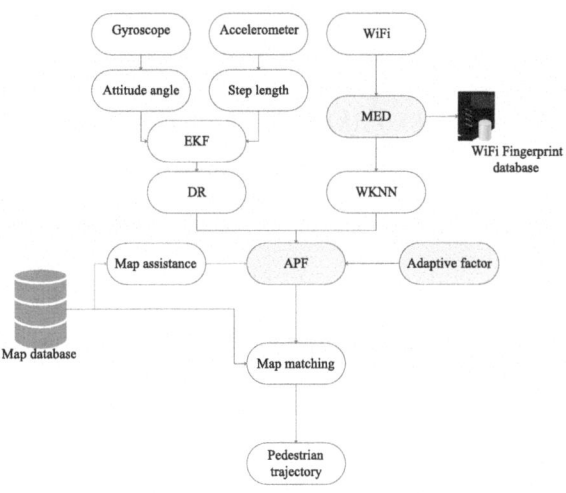

Fig. 1. Algorithm framework of MED and APF.

The smartphone's gyroscope and accelerometer are used to obtain the values of the smartphone's angular velocity and acceleration sensors in real time. Then the integration technology is used to obtain the attitude angle, and the gait technology is used to obtain the pedestrian's step length, so as to estimate the pedestrian's position based on the attitude angle and step length DR. The positioning process using the WiFi fingerprint positioning method can be divided into an offline channel state information fingerprint database construction stage and an online channel state information fingerprint matching stage. The reference point of the positioning area is calibrated through pre-placed anchor points, and then the fingerprint information of the reference point area is collected. The fingerprint data of two collection points are generated through interpolation technology, and a fingerprint database of the area is constructed. At the online stage, the distance between the MED to calculate the online collection of WIFI fingerprints and the fingerprints saved in the database.The weighted K-Nearest neighbor (WKNN) algorithm is used to further improve position performance by selecting the Kwifi matching results.The DR model is used as a state transmission equation for a particle filter. The difference between the distance result of the WiFi fingerprint and the inertial navigation result is used as an observation equation.A adaptive factor is proposed to increase the weight of high trust particles.Finally, MAP matching is used to further reduce estimated pedestrian position errors.The algorithm framework of the MED and APFs is shown in Figure 1.

2.1   DR module

EKF for Attitude Angle. When a pedestrian is moving, its vertical speed should be zero when its feet touch the ground. Therefore, an EKF filter is constructed to remove walking noise. The system model is as follows

$$X(k) = [Z(k), V_z(k), \text{Roll}(k), \text{Pitch}(k), \text{Yaw}(k)] \tag{1}$$

where $Z(k)$ and $V_z(k)$ represent vertical displacement and vertical velocity, respectively; $\text{Roll}(k), \text{Pitch}(k), \text{Yaw}(k)$ represent the attitude angle.

The vertical velocity and vertical displacement of the transition model is as follows

$$\begin{bmatrix} Z(k+1) \\ V_z(k+1) \end{bmatrix} = \begin{bmatrix} 1 & T_s \\ 0 & 1 \end{bmatrix} \otimes \begin{bmatrix} Z(k+1) \\ V_z(k) \end{bmatrix} + \begin{bmatrix} 0 & 0 & \frac{T_s^2}{2} \\ 0 & 0 & T_s \end{bmatrix} \otimes \begin{bmatrix} a_x \\ a_y \\ a_z \end{bmatrix} \tag{2}$$

where T_s represents the sampling interval, a_z, a_y, a_z represent tri-axis acceleration, respectively.

While the time moves to the moment where zero vertical velocity is detected by ZUPT, EKF is triggered. The vertical velocity is updated to zero. The algorithm flow chart for EKF is shown in Algorithm 1.

Attitude Angle. When the angular velocity is collected by the gyroscope, the increment of the three-axis angular velocity $[\Delta\theta_k^x, \Delta\theta_k^y, \Delta\theta_k^z]$ is calculated as follows [25]

$$\begin{aligned} \Delta\theta_k^x &= \omega_k^x * T_s \\ \Delta\theta_k^y &= \omega_k^y * T_s \\ \Delta\theta_k^z &= \omega_k^z * T_s \end{aligned} \tag{3}$$

Algorithm 1. The EKF module

Input: Accelerometers and gyroscopes collect acceleration and angular velocity
1. Extract the vertical acceleration from acceleration.
2. Estimate Zero Velocity Point using Vertical acceleration.
3. Compensate for acceleration and angular velocity errors.
4. Use acceleration to calculate the quaternion.
5. Obtain the attitude angle from the quaternion.
6. Filter noise using EKF.

where $[\omega_k^x, \omega_k^y, \omega_k^z]$ represents the angular velocity of the three axes respectively. T_s represents the sampling interval.

According to the reference [26], the quaternion vector is updated as follows

$$\mathbf{q}_{k+1} = \left[\mathbf{I} \cos \frac{\Delta\theta_k}{2} + \Delta\Theta \frac{\sin \frac{\Delta\theta_k}{2}}{\Delta\theta_k} \right] \mathbf{q}_k \tag{4}$$

where $\mathbf{I}$ denotes a $3 * 3$ identity matrix. $\Delta\Theta$ is calculated as follows

$$\Delta\Theta = \begin{bmatrix} 0 & \Delta\theta_k^z & -\Delta\theta_k^y & \Delta\theta_k^x \\ -\Delta\theta_k^z & 0 & \Delta\theta_k^x & \Delta\theta_k^y \\ \Delta\theta_k^y & -\Delta\theta_k^x & 0 & \Delta\theta_k^z \\ -\Delta\theta_k^x & -\Delta\theta_k^y & -\Delta\theta_k^z & 0 \end{bmatrix} \tag{5}$$

After the quaternion are updated, the direction cosine matrix is calculated as follows

$$C_b^n = \begin{bmatrix} q_1^2 - q_2^2 - q_3^2 + q_4^2 & 2q_1q_2 - 2q_3q_4 & 2q_1q_3 + 2q_2q_4 \\ 2q_1q_2 + 2q_3q_4 & -q_1^2 + q_2^2 - q_3^2 + q_4^2 & 2q_2q_3 - 2q_1q_4 \\ 2q_1q_3 - 2q_2q_4 & 2q_2q_3 + 2q_1q_4 & -q_1^2 - q_2^2 + q_3^2 + q_4^2 \end{bmatrix} \tag{6}$$

After the direction cosine matrix are updated, the attitude angle is calculated as follows [25]

$$\vartheta = \tan^{-1} \frac{-C_b^n(3,1)}{\sqrt{(C_b^n(3,2))^2 + (C_b^n(3,3))^2}}$$

$$\phi = \tan^{-1} \frac{C_b^n(3,2)}{C_b^n(3,3)} \tag{7}$$

$$\psi = \tan^{-1} \frac{C_b^n(2,1)}{C_b^n(1,1)}$$

where ϑ, ϕ, ψ are called pitch, roll and yaw, respectively.

Step Length. Gait-based step length estimation has been successfully applied to low-end inertial sensors [27]. In the process of pedestrian walking, the vertical displacement is periodic, as shown in Figure 2.

The vertical displacement of pedestrians during walking is calculated as follows [28]

$$h(k) = -\int_{t1}^{t2} V_z(k) \tag{8}$$

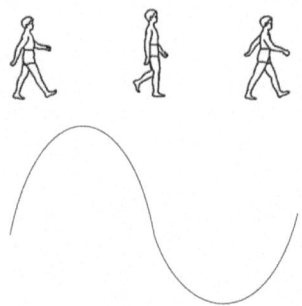

Fig. 2. Pedestrian walking posture.

where $h(k)$ and $V_z(k)$ denotes the vertical displacement and the vertical speed at the kth time.

According to the literature [28], the step length is calculated as follows

$$SL(k) = 2\sqrt{-2L \int_{t1}^{t2} V_z(k) - \left(\int_{t1}^{t2} V_z(k) \right)^2} \tag{9}$$

where L represents the leg length.

DR. Based on the step length, direction, and the position at the kth time, the pedestrian position at the $(k + 1)th$ time is calculated as follows

$$\begin{bmatrix} x(k+1) \\ y(k+1) \end{bmatrix} = \begin{bmatrix} x(k) \\ y(k) \end{bmatrix} + SL(k+1) \times \begin{bmatrix} \sin(\psi(k+1)) \\ \cos(\psi(k+1)) \end{bmatrix} \tag{10}$$

where $x(k)$ and $y(k)$ denote the position at the kth time.

2.2   MED for WiFi Matching

WiFi fingerprint matching is commonly used as a single point fingerprint matching [29]. Because WIFI fluctuates greatly, there is a "jump point" problem in single point matching. As shown in Figure 3, there is a "jump point" when estimating pedestrian position. Once the WiFi fingerprint is matched, use a triangle to mark the matching location. Obviously, the fourth triangle is far away from the other three triangles. The WiFi matching location of the fourth triangle is not reliable.

We propose a multi-dimensional fingerprint recognition algorithm to solve the jump point problem. In order to improve the algorithm matching stability, we add historical fingerprint information to reduce the impact of single fingerprint matching. n indicates the number of WiFi access points collected at the same time. The square represents the RSS of the access point. k indicates the kth time for collecting WiFi fingerprints, as shown in Figure 4.

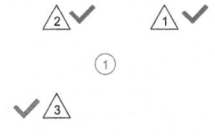

Fig. 3. A "jump point" for WiFi fingerprint matching.

Fig. 4. The multi-dimensional WiFi fingerprint matching.

The traditional Euclidean distance is only suitable for one-dimensional WiFi fingerprints, so it is necessary to modify the traditional Euclidean distance, that is, MED. MED is calculated as follows

$$d = \sum_{i=k-3}^{k} \left[\sum_{j=1}^{n} (RSS(j) - RSS_{db}(j)) \right] \tag{11}$$

where $RSS(j)$ denotes the jth access point value in the online stage. $RSS_{db}(j)$ denotes the jth access point value in the offline stage. After calculating the fingerprint distance, WKNN is used to estimate the WiFi fingerprint matching position. For the detailed process, please refer to reference [19].

2.3 APF for Pedestrian Localization

System Equation for APF. Compared with Kalman filtering, particle filtering provides a different technique for nonlinear system state estimation[30]. Particle filtering is widely used in a variety of nonlinear and non-Gaussian system models because it is independent of the system model. The state equation and observation equation of particle filter are defined as follows

$$\mathbf{X}_k = f(\mathbf{X}_{k-1}) + \boldsymbol{\omega} \tag{12}$$

$$\mathbf{Z}_k = h(\mathbf{X}_k) + \boldsymbol{\nu} \tag{13}$$

where $f(\cdot)$ and $h(\cdot)$ represent known processes and observation equations, respectively; $\mathbf{X}_k$ and $\mathbf{Z}_k$ represent the process state and the observed state at the kth time, respectively; $\boldsymbol{\omega}$ and $\boldsymbol{\nu}$ represent process noise and observation noise, respectively.

The DR-based particle filtering process takes into account the errors of step size, direction and estimated position, and assumes that their noise follows Gaussian distribution and the mean is zero.

$$\mathbf{X}_k = f(\mathbf{X}_{k-1}) + \boldsymbol{\omega}$$

$$= \begin{bmatrix} L_{k-1} \\ \theta_{k-1} \\ x_{k-1} \\ y_{k-1} \end{bmatrix} + \begin{bmatrix} \Delta L \\ \Delta \theta \\ L_k \cos(\theta_k) \\ L_k \sin(\theta_k) \end{bmatrix} + \boldsymbol{\omega} \tag{14}$$

where L_{k-1} and θ_{k-1} represent the step length and direction at $(k-1)th$ time. (x_{k-1}, y_{k-1}) represents the estimated position of pedestrians at $(k-1)th$ time; ΔL and $\Delta \theta$ represent pedestrian step length and direction change, respectively.

In the process of pedestrian walking, WiFi positioning system can provide positioning results. Combined with DR, the observation equation is defined as follows

$$\mathbf{Z}_k = h(\mathbf{X}_k) + \boldsymbol{\nu} = \begin{bmatrix} x_{DR} \\ y_{DR} \end{bmatrix} - \begin{bmatrix} x_{WIFI} \\ y_{WIFI} \end{bmatrix} + \boldsymbol{\nu} \tag{15}$$

where $[x_{DR}, y_{DR}]^T$ represents the positioning result of DR. $[x_{WIFI}, y_{WIFI}]^T$ represents the positioning result of WiFi fingerprint matching.

Particle Weight Technique. In order to deal with the difficulty of solving the posterior distribution of particle filter for nonlinear systems, it is more feasible to replace the analytical solution with the approximate solution. In order to solve the sampling problem of a posterior distribution, resampling technique can be adopted[31].

$$q(\mathbf{X}_{0:k} \mid \mathbf{Z}_{1:k}) = q(\mathbf{X}_{0:k-1} \mid \mathbf{Z}_{1:k-1}) q(\mathbf{X}_k \mid \mathbf{X}_{0:k-1}, \mathbf{Z}_{1:k}) \tag{16}$$

The recursive formula for calculating the importance weight from each generation of particles is

$$\begin{aligned} \omega 1_k^i &= \frac{p(\mathbf{X}_{0:k} \mid \mathbf{Z}_{1:k})}{q(\mathbf{X}_{0:k} \mid \mathbf{Z}_{1:k})} \\ &\propto \omega 1_{k-1}^i \frac{p(\mathbf{Z}_k \mid \mathbf{X}_k) p(\mathbf{X}_k \mid \mathbf{X}_{k-1})}{q(\mathbf{X}_k \mid \mathbf{X}_{0:k-1}, \mathbf{Z}_{1:k})} \\ &\sim \frac{1}{(2\pi)^{m/2} |R|^{1/2}} \exp\left(\frac{-\left[\mathbf{Z}^* - h\left(\mathbf{X}_{k,i}^-\right) \right]^T R^{-1} \left[\mathbf{Z}^* - h\left(\mathbf{X}_{k,i}^-\right) \right]}{2} \right) \end{aligned} \tag{17}$$

where $\mathbf{Z}^*$ represents the estimated observation; $\mathbf{X}_{k,i}^-$ represents the priori estimated state vector; m represents the vector dimension; R represents the observation noise.

During a move, the position of the next point in time is limited by the position of the previous point in time, as shown in Figure 5. Assume that the pedestrian is in the center of a circular area at time $(k-1)th$. Considering the limited step length of the pedestrian, the position of the pedestrian inside the circle at kth is more reliable, while the position outside the circle is less reliable. The particle weight is not only related to the WiFi fingerprint matching results, but also to the step size, so an adaptive factor is introduced to calculate the particle weight.

$$dist = \begin{bmatrix} x_{est} \\ y_{est} \end{bmatrix}_k - \begin{bmatrix} x_{est} \\ y_{est} \end{bmatrix}_{k-1} \tag{18}$$

$$\omega 2_k^i = \frac{1}{1 + e^{-dist}} \tag{19}$$

where $\begin{bmatrix} x_{est} \\ y_{est} \end{bmatrix}_k$ represents the estimated position at the kth time.

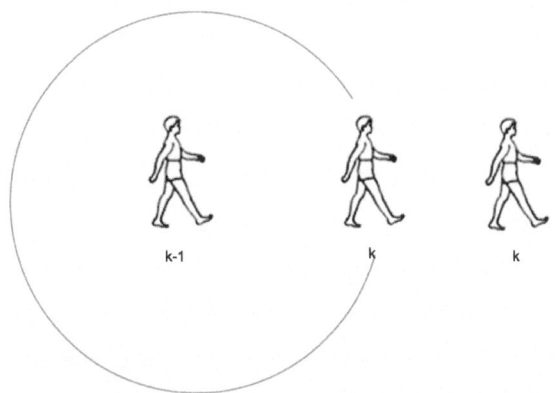

Fig. 5. Pedestrian walking position.

Combining the two-particle weight calculation methods, the new particle weight is calculated as follows

$$\omega = \omega 1 * \omega 2 \tag{20}$$

Map Assistance. In the offline phase, the floor structure map information is stored in the map database in advance. The online phase requires verification of the validity of the newly generated particles. If the particle passes through the wall, the weight is set to 0; If the particle does not pass through the wall, the original weight is used. The map-assisted algorithm can be referred to [21].

3   Experimental Results

3.1   Experimental Scene

In this experiment, we carried out the actual walking experiment in the office building. Participants walked from start to finish at a normal walking pace, holding a smartphone and measuring their true position with the help of a laser rangefinder. In the offline phase, the tester once again held a smartphone to walk from start to finish, using the smartphone's WiFi chip to collect the RSS value of the AP. Using the laser rangefinder and the corner of the building's hallway, we set up a WiFi fingerprint database. In order to conduct the experiment in the online phase, we asked pedestrians to collect the RSS values of AP in two office buildings at normal walking speed with smartphones in hand. The two office buildings are 123 metres and 138 metres walking distance respectively. We can download it from url https://github.com/Localization-IMU smartphones to collect data.

3.2 Acceleration and Gyroscope Data

The figure 6 is acceleration and angular velocity collected in the office building. The acceleration is approximately periodic. The stride size of the pedestrian is obtained by gait simulation. At the inflection point, the angular velocity increases significantly.

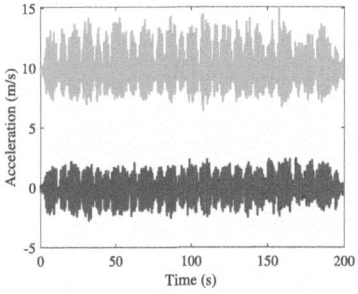

Fig. 6. Acceleration in the office building.

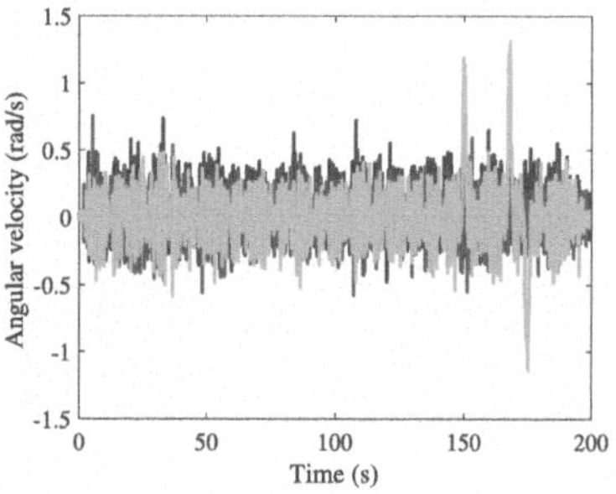

Fig. 7. Angular velocity in the office building .

3.3 The Office Building

The pedestrian was holding a cell phone, walk along a pre-set path in the office building. Figures 8 and 9 show the positioning locus and cumulative distribution function (CDF) of DR, WiFi, particle filter (PF) and MED + APF respectively. According to the data of table 1, the average deviations of DR, WiFi, PF and MED + APF are 8.03m, 1.98m, 3.45m and 1.51m respectively. The corresponding root-mean-square errors were 10.02 m, 2.43 m, 4.82m and 1.92m, respectively. In the initial stage, the positioning trajectory is on the Y-axis, and the positioning accuracy is high. With the passage of time, the track of walking location obviously deviates to the right, which leads to the increase of location error. We can observe that inertial navigation positioning (DR) has a cumulative error, and the longer the pedestrian walking time, the greater the error. In contrast, WiFi fingerprint matching does not have cumulative errors, but there may be fingerprint mismatch. Therefore, we use particle filtering (PF) to integrate DR

And WiFi technology to reduce positioning errors. In order to solve the problem of WiFi fingerprint mismatch and particle poverty, an algorithm called MED and an improved particle filter are introduced in this study. MED algorithm improves the accuracy of WiFi fingerprint matching by increasing the redundancy of fingerprint information. The improved particle filter increases the weight of reliable particles and reduces the weight of unreliable particles by considering the spatial position of pedestrians. The combined effect of these two algorithms significantly improves the accuracy of pedestrian location.

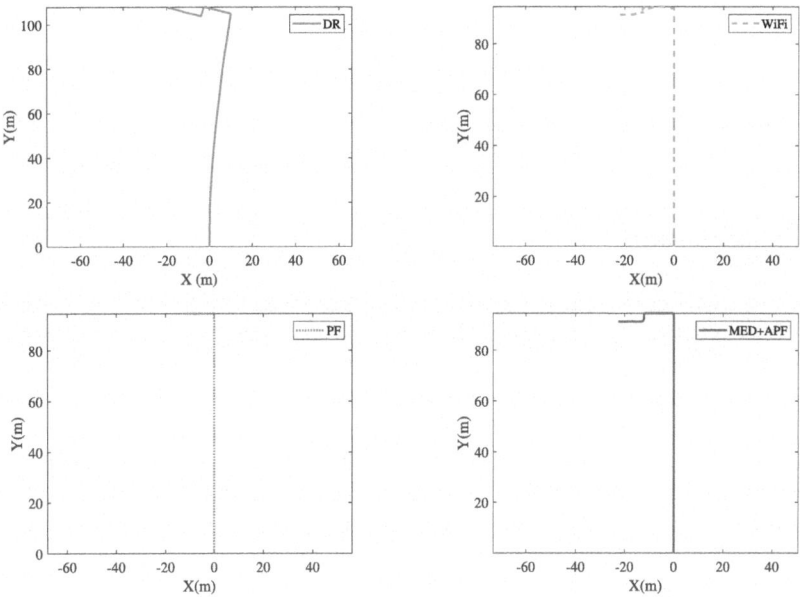

Fig. 8. Positioning trajectories with different strategies.

Table 1. Position errors of DR, WiFi, PF, and MED+APF.

Position error	Average error	Root mean square error
DR	8.03	10.02
WiFi	1.98	2.43
AVPF	3.45	4.82
MDE+APF	1.51	1.92

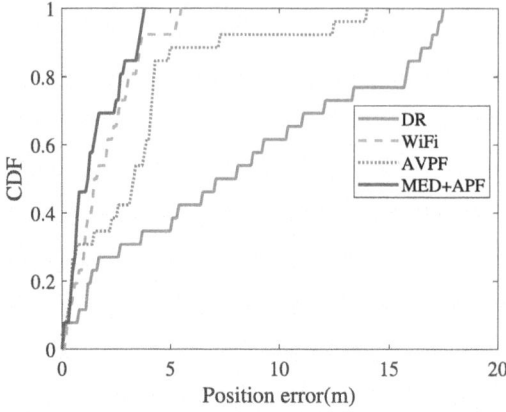

Fig. 9. CDF of errors.

4   Conclusions

Inertial navigation system is less affected by external interference and has high short-term positioning accuracy. However, its DR Error will accumulate over time, resulting in a large long-term positioning error. Unlike the WiFi fingerprint matching method, there is no cumulative error, but there may be problems with fingerprint mismatch. Under this background, this paper presents a MED method and an APF method. MED uses multi-dimensional WiFi fingerprint to reduce the occurrence of fingerprint mismatch. APF uses adaptive factors to increase the weight of high confidence particles and decrease the weight of low confidence particles. These two methods effectively reduce the indoor positioning error.

References

1. Martinez del Horno, M., García-Varea, I., Orozco Barbosa, L.: Calibration of Wi-Fi-based indoor tracking systems for Android-based smartphones. Remote Sens. **11**(9), 1072 (2019)
2. Sánchez-Rodríguez, D., Quintana-Suárez, M.A., Alonso-González, I., Ley-Bosch, C., Sánchez-Medina, J.J.: Fusion of channel state information and received signal strength for indoor localization using a single access point. Remote Sens. **2020**, 12 (1995)
3. Ali, A., El-Sheimy, N.: Low-cost MEMS-based pedestrian navigation technique for GPS-denied areas. J. Sensors **2013**, 1–11 (2013)
4. Borenstein, J., Ojeda, L., Kwanmuang, S.: Heuristic reduction of gyro drift. J. Navigation **62**, 41–58 (2009)
5. Borenstein, J., Ojeda, L.: Heuristic drift elimination for personnel tracking systems. J. Navigation **63**, 591–606 (2010)

6. Pinchin, J., Hide, C., Moore, T.: A particle filter approach to indoor navigation using a foot mounted inertial navigation system and heuristic heading information. In: 2012 International Conference on Indoor Positioning and Indoor Navigation (IPIN) (pp. 1-10). IEEE (2012)

7. Zhao, W., Gao, J., Li, Z., Yao, Y.: An indoor positioning system based on map-aided KF-PF module. Geomat. Inf. Sci. Wuhan Univ. **43**, 806–812 (2018)

8. Zhuang, Y., Li, Y., Lan, H., Syed, Z., El-Sheimy, N.: Wireless access point localization using nonlinear least squares and multi-level quality control. IEEE Wirel. Commun. Le. **4**, 693–696 (2015)

9. Li, Y., Zhuang, Y., Lan, H., Zhang, P., Niu, X., El-Sheimy, N.: WiFi-aided magnetic matching for indoor navigation with consumer portable devices. Micromachines **6**, 747–764 (2015)

10. Zhang, L., Liu, Y., Sun, J.: A hybrid framework for mitigating heading drift for a wearable pedestrian navigation system through adaptive fusion of inertial and magnetic measurements. Appl. Sci. **2021**, 11 (1902)

11. Shi, S., Gao, T., Gao, D., Ding, Z., Zhang, Z.: Inertial navigation aid indoor navigation based on the establishment of accurate magnetic reference map. In: Journal of Physics: Conference Series (Vol. 1802, No. 4, p. 042022). IOP Publishing (2021)

12. Qin, F., Zuo, T., Wang, X.: CCpos: WiFi fingerprint indoor positioning system based on CDAE-CNN. Sensors **21**, 1114 (2021)

13. Karkar, A.G., Al-Maadeed, S., Kunhoth, J., Bouridane, A.: CamNav: a computer-vision indoor navigation system. J. Supercomput. **77**, 7737–7756 (2021)

14. Bao, H., Wong, W.-C.: A novel map-based dead-reckoning algorithm for indoor localization. J. Sens. Actuator Netw. **3**, 44–63 (2014)

15. Yu, C., El-Sheimy, N., Lan, H., Liu, Z.: Map-based indoor pedestrian navigation using an auxiliary particle filter. Micromachines **8**, 225 (2017)

16. Tian, Q., Salcic, Z., Wang, K.I.K., Pan, Y.: A hybrid indoor localization and navigation system with map matching for pedestrians using smartphones. Sensors **15**, 30759–30783 (2015)

17. Qian, J., Ma, J., Ying, R., Liu, P., Pei, L.: An improved indoor localization method using smartphone inertial sensors. In: International Conference on Indoor Positioning and Indoor Navigation (pp. 1-7). IEEE (2013).

18. Chen, P., Kuang, Y., Chen, X.: A UWB/improved PDR integration algorithm applied to dynamic indoor positioning for pedestrians. Sensors **17**, 2065 (2017)

19. Kang, W., Han, Y.: SmartPDR: smartphone-based pedestrian dead reckoning for indoor localization. IEEE Sens. J. **15**(5), 2906–2916 (2014)

20. Li, Y., Zhuang, Y., Lan, H., Zhang, P., Niu, X., El-Sheimy, N.: Self-contained indoor pedestrian navigation using smartphone sensors and magnetic features. IEEE Sens. J. **16**, 7173–7182 (2016)

21. Wang, J., Hu, A., Li, X., Wang, Y.: An improved PDR/magnetometer/floor map integration algorithm for ubiquitous positioning using the adaptive unscented Kalman filter. ISPRS Int. J. Geo-Inf. **4**, 2638–2659 (2015)

22. Li, Z., Liu, C., Gao, J., Li, X.: An improved WiFi/PDR integrated system using an adaptive and robust filter for indoor localization. ISPRS Int. J. Geo-Inf. **5**, 224 (2017)

23. Zhuang, Y., El-Sheimy, N.: Tightly-coupled integration of WiFi and MEMS sensors on handheld devices for indoor pedestrian navigation. IEEE Sens. J. **16**, 224–234 (2015)

24. Li, Z., Zhao, L., Qin, C., Wang, Y.: WiFi/PDR integrated navigation with robustly constrained Kalman filter. Meas. Sci. Technol. **31**, 084002 (2020)

25. Chen, J., Ou, G., Peng, A., Zheng, L., Shi, J.: An INS/floor-plan indoor localization system using the firefly particle filter. ISPRS Int. J. GEO-INF. **7**, 324 (2018)
26. Li, Y., Zhuang, Y., Lan, H., Niu, X., El-Sheimy, N.: A profile-matching method for wireless positioning. IEEE Commun. Lett. **20**, 2514–2517 (2016)
27. Yu, C., Lan, H., Gu, F., Yu, F., El-Sheimy, N.: A map/INS/Wi-Fi integrated system for indoor location-based service applications. Sensors **17**, 1272 (2017)
28. Chen, J., Ou, G., Peng, A., Zheng, L., Shi, J.: An INS/WiFi indoor localization system based on the Weighted Least Squares. Sensors **18**, 1458 (2018)
29. Deng, Z.A., Wang, G.F., Hu, Y., Wu, D.: Heading estimation for indoor pedestrian navigation using a smartphone in the pocket. Sensors **15**, 21518–21536 (2015)
30. Brajdic, A., Harle, R.: Walk detection and step counting on unconstrained smartphones. In: Proceedings of the 2013 ACM international joint conference on Pervasive and ubiquitous computing (pp. 225-234) (2013)
31. Zheng, L., Wu, Z., Zhou, W., Weng, S., Zheng, H.: A smartphone based hand-held indoor positioning system, pp. 639–650. Singapore, In Frontier Computing (2016)
32. Moghaddasi, S.S., Faraji, N.: A hybrid algorithm based on particle filter and genetic algorithm for target tracking. Expert Syst. Appl. **147**, 113188 (2020)
33. Chen, J., Ou, G., Peng, A., Zheng, L., Shi, J.: An INS/floor-plan indoor localization system using the firefly particle filter. ISPRS Int. J. GEO-INF. **7**, 324 (2018)

Research on the PID Controllers Algorithm of the Quad Rotor

Zhou Hongcheng[⊠] and Fang Yuzhuo

School of Electronic and Information Engineering, Jinling Institute of Technology,
Nanjing 211169, China
945516882@qq.com

Abstract. In particular affine nonlinear controllers designed using geometric non-linear control methods, integral backstepping control and backstepping based nonlinear PID controllers have been designed for quad rotor aircraft. A nonlinear simulator was designed to help validate the flight dynamics, aerodynamics models, and controllers developed for quad rotor aircraft. The rotation and translation performance of different nonlinear controllers designed for quad rotor aircraft can be easily verified using simulators in various configurations and subject to interference.

Keywords: Nonlinear control · PID · Flight dynamics · Aerodynamic model · Quad rotor

1 Introduction

Linear controllers offer several advantages for quadrotor aircraft in terms of design information and the availability of control design tools, particularly in relation to robot applications [1]. However, as performance continues to improve and operability becomes a priority, complex control systems are required due to factors such as unpredictable environmental changes, stronger dynamic coupling, and nonlinearity [2]. To address these challenges, there is a need for more sophisticated control systems.

To address the tracking and stability issues of quadcopter aircraft, a nonlinear controller was designed. Additionally, a 3D graphic animation was implemented in the simulator to visualize the behavior of the quad rotor, as shown in Fig. 1. The response of a quad rotor in terms of attitude, position, and altitude can be obtained along the 3D path of the quad rotor.

© ICST Institute for Computer Sciences, Social Informatics and Telecommunications Engineering 2025
Published by Springer Nature Switzerland AG 2025. All Rights Reserved
X. Chen et al. (Eds.): IoTaaS 2023, LNICST 585, pp. 143–151, 2025.
https://doi.org/10.1007/978-3-031-70507-6_12

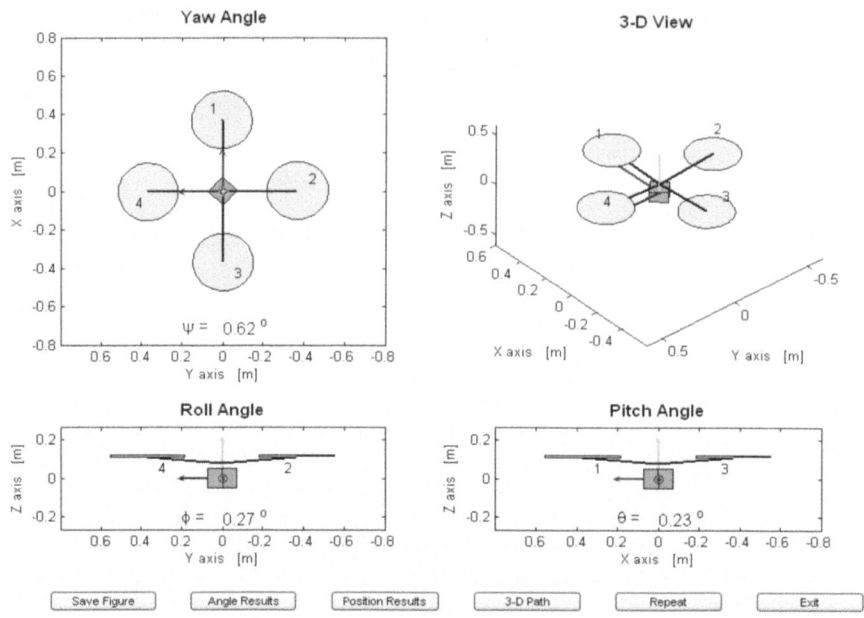

Fig. 1. Quad rotor simulator.

We recall derived nonlinear model for translational and rotational quad rotor aircraft,

$$
f(x, u)_{translational} = \begin{pmatrix} \dot{x} \\ \dfrac{(\cos\phi\sin\theta\cos\psi + \sin\phi\sin\psi)}{m}u_1 \\ \dot{y} \\ \dfrac{(\cos\phi\sin\theta\sin\psi - \sin\phi\cos\psi)}{m}u_1 \\ \dot{z} \\ -g + \dfrac{(\cos\phi\cos\theta)}{m}u_1 \end{pmatrix} \tag{1}
$$

$$
f(x, u)_{rotational} = \begin{pmatrix} \dot{\phi} \\ \dot{\theta}\dot{\psi}\left(\dfrac{J_y - J_z}{J_x}\right) + \dfrac{l}{J_x}u_2 \\ \dot{\theta} \\ \dot{\phi}\dot{\psi}\left(\dfrac{J_z - J_x}{J_y}\right) + \dfrac{l}{J_y}u_3 \\ \dot{\psi} \\ \dot{\phi}\dot{\theta}\left(\dfrac{J_x - J_y}{J_z}\right) + \dfrac{1}{J_z}u_4 \end{pmatrix} \tag{2}
$$

where x represents the states and u the inputs to the quad rotor aircraft. The inputs to quad rotor are defined as, vertical force input u_1, roll actuator input u_2, pitch actuator input u_3 and yaw moment input u_4 given by [3],

$$\left. \begin{aligned} u_1 &= b(\Omega_1^2 + \Omega_2^2 + \Omega_3^2 + \Omega_4^2) \\ u_2 &= b(\Omega_4^2 - \Omega_2^2) \\ u_3 &= b(\Omega_3^2 - \Omega_1^2) \\ u_4 &= d(\Omega_2^2 + \Omega_4^2 - \Omega_1^2 - \Omega_3^2) \end{aligned} \right\} \tag{3}$$

The coefficients of thrust b and resistance d are respectively represented in the equation. The control strategy used to stabilize the quadcopter aircraft uses priority rules to sequentially adjust each state [4]. The height of the quad rotor is controlled by vertical force input u_1, and the required roll and pitch angles for the quadcopter are extracted from the translation subsystem. The rotation controller controls the input u_2, u_3, u_4 and stabilizes the quad rotor.

2 Rotational Control

If there is a nonlinear feedback control law that converts the system into an adjoint form of coordinate transformation and eliminates nonlinear dynamics, then the nonlinear control system (4) is feedback linearizable, simplifying the original system into a linearly controllable system [5].

The dimension vector field $f_1(x), f_2(x), \ldots, f_k(x)$ defined on the open subset D_0. A mapping which is each point x of D_0 is assigned a dimension vector.

Definition 1 The dimensional distribution on D_0 is a mapping that assigns a dimensional subspace $\Delta(x)$ to each D_0, such that there exists a satisfying $k-$ dimensional vector field $f_1(x), f_2(x), \ldots, f_k(x)$,

Let $[f_i, f_j]$ denote the Lie bracket,

$$[f_i, f_j] = ad_{f_i}f_j \overset{\Delta}{=} \frac{\partial f_j}{\partial x}f_i - \frac{\partial f_i}{\partial x}f_j \tag{4}$$

$$ad_{f_i}^k f_j = ad_{f_i}ad_{f_i}^{k-1}f_j \ ad_{f_i}^0 f_j = f_j \tag{5}$$

$$f(x) = \left[x_2 \ (x_4 x_6)\left(\frac{J_y - J_z}{J_x}\right) \ x_4 \ (x_2 x_6)\left(\frac{J_z - J_x}{J_y}\right) \ x_6 \ (x_2 x_4)\left(\frac{J_x - J_y}{J_z}\right) \right]^T \tag{6}$$

$$g_1(x) = \left[0 \ \tfrac{1}{J_x} \ 0 \ 0 \ 0 \ 0 \right]^T \tag{7}$$

$$g_2(x) = \left[0 \ 0 \ 0 \ \tfrac{1}{J_y} \ 0 \ 0 \right]^T \tag{8}$$

$$g_3(x) = \left[0 \ 0 \ 0 \ 0 \ 0 \ \tfrac{1}{J_z} \right]^T \tag{9}$$

$$y = \begin{bmatrix} x_1 & x_3 & x_5 \end{bmatrix}^T \tag{10}$$

Let us check the distribution $\Delta(x)$ for involutivity.

$$\Delta_0(x) = span\{g_1(x), g_2(x), g_3(x)\} = span \left\{ \begin{bmatrix} 0 \\ 1/J_x \\ 0 \\ 0 \\ 0 \\ 0 \end{bmatrix}, \begin{bmatrix} 0 \\ 0 \\ 0 \\ 1/J_y \\ 0 \\ 0 \end{bmatrix}, \begin{bmatrix} 0 \\ 0 \\ 0 \\ 0 \\ 0 \\ 1/J_z \end{bmatrix} \right\} \tag{11}$$

$$\Delta_1(x) = span\{g_1(x), g_2(x), g_3(x), ad_f g_1(x), ad_f g_2(x), ad_f g_3(x)\} \tag{12}$$

$$ad_f g_1(x) = -\left[1/J_x \ 0 \ 0 \ \tfrac{x_6 l}{J_x}\left[\tfrac{J_z - J_x}{J_y}\right] 0 \ \tfrac{x_4 l}{J_x}\left[\tfrac{J_x - J_y}{J_z}\right] \right]^T \tag{13}$$

$$ad_f g_2(x) = -\left[0 \ \tfrac{x_6 l}{J_y}\left[\tfrac{J_y - J_z}{J_x}\right] 1/J_y \ 0 \ 0 \ \tfrac{x_2 l}{J_y}\left[\tfrac{J_x - J_y}{J_z}\right] \right]^T \tag{14}$$

$$ad_f g_3(x) = -\left[0 \ \tfrac{x_4}{J_z}\left[\tfrac{J_y - J_z}{J_x}\right] 0 \ \tfrac{x_6}{J_z}\left[\tfrac{J_z - J_x}{J_y}\right] 1/J_z \ 0 \right]^T \tag{15}$$

Since the matrices in expressions (12) and (13) have equal rank values, the new vector field obtained by performing a lie bracket operation on two arbitrary vector fields from the original vector field k (i.e. evaluating the derivative of one vector field k along another vector field) is not linearly independent, but linearly related to the previous vector field. In other words, the new vector field remains in the original span space of the vector field and does not form a new direction [8].

The vector field $ad_f g_1$ along g_1 was obtained. The rank of the augmented matrix remains equal to the rank of the original matrix. Therefore, $\Delta_o(x)$ is involutive. All conditions are met, and the affine nonlinear system is feedback linearized. Furthermore, the sum of the two vector fields f and g in the parentheses indicates that the quad rotor of the rotating subsystem is completely controllable.

Secondly, the relative degree of the rotating subsystem was studied. Two conditions were found to be met. For the nonlinear system (10), we take into account the nonlinear coordinate transformation. Nonlinear coordinate transformation can be described as,

$$Z = \Phi(x) \tag{16}$$

where Z and X were vectors of equal dimensions, Φ was nonlinear vector functions,

$$\begin{aligned} Z_1 &= \phi_1(x_1, x_2, \cdots, x_n) \\ Z_2 &= \phi_2(x_1, x_2, \cdots, x_n) \\ &\vdots \\ Z_n &= \phi_n(x_1, x_2, \cdots, x_n) \end{aligned} \tag{17}$$

The first condition for nonlinear coordinate transformation is that its inverse transformation exists and is single valued,

$$X = \Phi^{-1}(Z) \tag{18}$$

The second condition is that both $\Phi(X)$ and $\Phi^{-1}(Z)$ are smooth vector fields, that is, the functions of both Φ and Φ^{-1} have continuous partial derivatives of any order. In short, the first condition is reversible, and the second condition is differentiable [9].

The diffeomorphism $\zeta = (\zeta_1, \zeta_2, \zeta_3, \zeta_4, \zeta_5, \zeta_6) = \varsigma_F(x)$ that transforms (10) to a linear controllable system can be obtained by solving the partial differential equations,

$$L_{g_1}h_1(x) = 0, L_{g_2}h_2(x) = 0, L_{g_3}h_3(x) = 0$$

For $\Delta_o(x)$, due to its involution, the Frobenius theorem guarantees the existence of solutions.

$$\begin{aligned}
\zeta_1 &= h_1(x) = x_1, \ \zeta_2 = L_f h_1(x) = x_2 \\
\zeta_3 &= h_2(x) = x_3, \ \zeta_4 = L_f h_2(x) = x_4 \\
\zeta_5 &= h_3(x) = x_5, \ \zeta_6 = L_f h_3(x) = x_6
\end{aligned} \tag{19}$$

Therefore, differential homeomorphism $\zeta = \varsigma_F(x) = (x_1, x_2, x_3, x_4, x_5, x_6)$ is globally defined in $D_0 \to \Re^6$. Then $w = \begin{pmatrix} w_1 \ w_2 \ w_3 \end{pmatrix}^T$ can be transformed into Brunovsky form by definition,

$$w_i^{(r_i)} = L_f^{r_i} h_i + \sum_{j=1}^{m} L_{g_j} L_f^{r_i-1} h_i u_j \tag{20}$$

In our case, $i = (1, 2, 3)$ and $m = (1, 2, 3)$ with $L_{g_j} L_f^{r_i-1} h_i(x) \neq 0$ for at least one j. A routine calculation shows that,

$$w_1 = \left[x_4 x_6 \left(\frac{J_y - J_z}{J_x} \right) + \frac{l}{J_x} u_1 \right] \tag{21}$$

$$w_2 = \left[x_2 x_6 \left(\frac{J_z - J_x}{J_y} \right) + \frac{l}{J_y} u_2 \right] \tag{22}$$

$$w_3 = \left[x_2 x_4 \left(\frac{J_x - J_y}{J_z} \right) + \frac{1}{J_z} u_3 \right] \tag{23}$$

From (21), (22) and (23),

$$\begin{bmatrix} w_1 \\ w_2 \\ w_3 \end{bmatrix} = \begin{bmatrix} x_4 x_6 \left(\frac{J_y - J_z}{J_x} \right) \\ x_2 x_6 \left(\frac{J_z - J_x}{J_y} \right) \\ x_2 x_4 \left(\frac{J_x - J_y}{J_z} \right) \end{bmatrix} + E \begin{bmatrix} u_1 \\ u_2 \\ u_3 \end{bmatrix} \tag{24}$$

or,

$$
\begin{bmatrix} u_1 \\ u_2 \\ u_3 \end{bmatrix} = E^{-1} \left(\begin{bmatrix} w_1 \\ w_2 \\ w_3 \end{bmatrix} - \begin{bmatrix} x_4 x_6 \left(\dfrac{J_y - J_z}{J_x} \right) \\ x_2 x_6 \left(\dfrac{J_z - J_x}{J_y} \right) \\ x_2 x_4 \left(\dfrac{J_x - J_y}{J_z} \right) \end{bmatrix} \right)
\tag{25}
$$

where E is a decoupling square matrix defined obviously.

Therefore, using differential equations $\zeta = \varsigma_F(x)$ substituting (25) into (10) to obtain the form,

$$
\dot{\zeta} = \begin{bmatrix} 1 & 0 & 0 & 0 & 0 & 0 \\ 0 & 0 & 0 & 0 & 0 & 0 \\ 0 & 0 & 1 & 0 & 0 & 0 \\ 0 & 0 & 0 & 0 & 0 & 0 \\ 0 & 0 & 0 & 0 & 1 & 0 \\ 0 & 0 & 0 & 0 & 0 & 0 \end{bmatrix} \zeta + \begin{bmatrix} 1 & 0 & 0 \\ 0 & 0 & 0 \\ 0 & 1 & 0 \\ 0 & 0 & 0 \\ 0 & 0 & 1 \\ 0 & 0 & 0 \end{bmatrix} \begin{bmatrix} w_1 \\ w_2 \\ w_3 \end{bmatrix}
\tag{26}
$$

Any stable linear control law (26) can be used to stabilize the original system (10) by performing inverse $x = \varsigma_F^{-1}(\zeta)$ and control transformations given in (26). The control law (25) with a linear controller asymptotically stabilizes the attitude angles of the quad rotor aircraft. In addition, stability is global on D because $x = \varsigma_F^{-1}(\zeta)$ is a differential homeomorphism on D, and the control law (25) is well defined on D [10].

3   Nonlinear Simulation Results

The angle and its time derivative of the rotating subsystem are not dependent on the translation component, as can be clearly seen from the 6-DOF equation of a quad rotor aircraft. However, the conversion depends on the angle. Ideally, it can be imagined as two subsystems, angular rotation and linear translation. Due to the complete independence of the angular rotation subsystem from other subsystems, adjustments have been made to it [13].

The rotation control maintains the 3D direction of the quadcopter at the desired value. The roll and pitch angles are usually forced to zero, allowing hovering flight. The task of the rotation controller is to compensate for initial errors, stabilize roll angle, pitch angle, and yaw angle, and maintain them at zero. This is achieved using a nonlinear control law u_2, u_3 and u_4.

Let's use a nonlinear controller to simulate a closed-loop system. We summarize the different system parameters of quad rotor used in nonlinear simulations in Table 1.

The initial conditions used are $\phi = \theta = 0.5$ rad, $\dot{\phi} = \dot{\theta} = 0.5$ rad/sec, $Z = 1$ meters. For the controller, the reference inputs are $Z_d = 1$, $\dot{x}_d = \dot{y}_d = 0$, $\psi_d = 0$.

Since the prototype system has some delays because of RS232 communications and actuators dynamics and actuator saturation problem. As a solution to address the

Table 1. Physical parameters of quad rotor

Parameter	Value	Unit
l	0.3	m
J_x	0.0154	$kg \cdot m^2$
J_y	0.0154	$kg \cdot m^2$
J_z	0.0309	$kg \cdot m^2$
m	0.6	kg

delays caused by RS232 communications and actuator dynamics, two Simulink discrete step delay blocks were implemented in the feedback loop and actuator. Furthermore, considering the maximum angular speed of the motor, which is 650 rad/sec, a saturation block was strategically positioned between the controller and the delay block. Altitude data is provided at 20Hz (as on the SFR sensor). Angles data and angular rates are provided at 100Hz max. Simulation is also done at 100Hz. The added noise and delay are reasonably close to the reality.

It shows the response of the attitude nonlinear controller to a stable quad aircraft in Fig. 2. The simulation results in Fig. 2 were obtained using the dynamic model of the actuator. From the attitude response of the quad rotor, it can be seen that the controller effectively stabilized the roll angle, pitch angle, and yaw angle in less than 6 s.

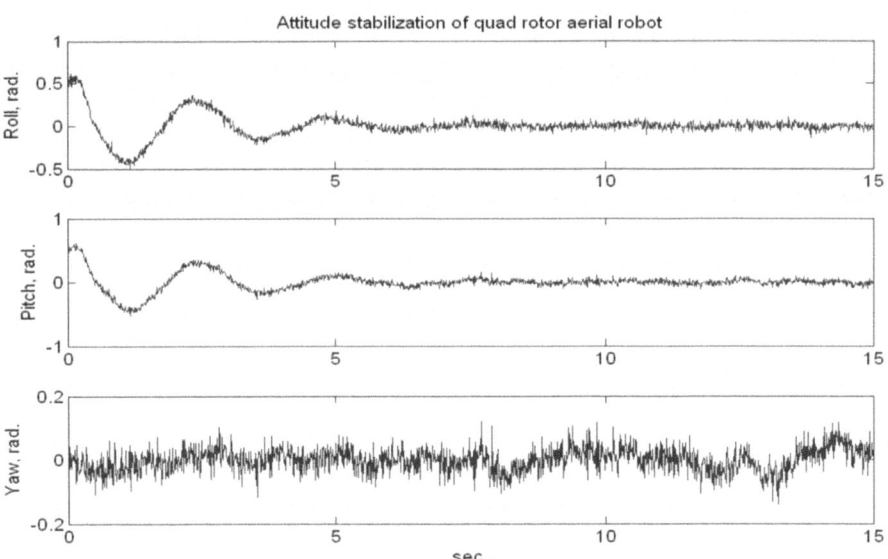

Fig. 2. Attitude response of quad rotor

Figure 3 presents the altitude and position response of a quad rotor aircraft. The results depicted in Fig. 3 demonstrate the effectiveness of the position controller in successfully maintaining the quad's attitude at a specified point.

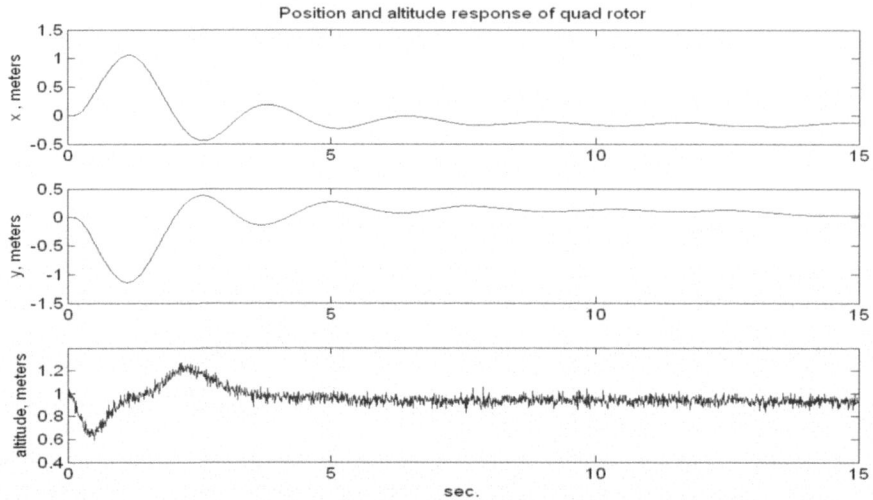

Fig. 3. Position and altitude response of quad rotor

The nonlinear simulation results provide evidence of the effective control achieved by the nonlinear controller for the quad rotor aircraft. In contrast to traditional Jacobian linearization, the feedback linearization employed in this study utilizes an accurate feedback linearization of the rotating subsystems rather than a Taylor series extension. This approach involves transforming the nonlinear dynamics into a linearized form through the application of state feedback and input state linearization techniques. However, it is important to note that feedback linearization does have certain limitations. The presence of parameter uncertainty or unmodeled dynamics can compromise its robustness. This is due to the unavailability of an exact model of the nonlinear system during the feedback linearization process.

4 Conclusion

Three different nonlinear control strategies for full control of quad rotor aircraft are presented. The first technique employed in this study utilizes affine nonlinear control methods, incorporating geometric approaches to nonlinear control. The stabilization and tracking performance with affine nonlinear controller is presented which seems to be quite good. Global asymptotic stability of the designed nonlinear controller is proved. However, it is important to note that the presence of parameter uncertainty or unmodeled dynamics poses a challenge to ensuring robustness. This limitation arises from the unavailability of an exact model of the nonlinear system during the process of feedback linearization.

Acknowledgment. This work was supported by Cooperative Project of Jiangsu Province production, teaching and research (No. BY2021381), Jin Ling Institute of Technology Ph. D. Startup Fund(jit-b-202314).

References

1. Ma, L., Zhu, F., Zhang, J., Zhao, X.: Leader-follower asymptotic consensus control of multi-agent systems: an observer-based disturbance reconstruction approach. IEEE Trans. Cybern. **53**, 1311 (2021)
2. Wu, G., Chen, G., Zhang, H., Huang, C.: Fully distributed event-triggered vehicular platooning with actuator uncertainties. IEEE Trans. Veh. Technol. **70**(7), 6601–6612 (2021)
3. Tang, Y., Zhang, D., Shi, P., Zhang, W., Qian, F.: Event-based formation control for nonlinear multiagent systems under dos attacks. IEEE Trans. Autom. Control **66**(1), 452–459 (2021)
4. Zhao, G., Hua, C.: Leader-following consensus of multiagent systems via asynchronous sampled-data control: a hybrid system approach. IEEE Trans. Autom. Control **67**(5), 2568–2575 (2022)
5. Wei, C., Gui, M., Zhang, C., Liao, Y., Dai, M.Z., Luo, B.: Adaptive appointed-time consensus control of networked euler lagrange systems with connectivity preservation. IEEE Trans. Cybern. **52**(11), 12379 (2021)
6. Zhao, L., Chen, X., Yu, J., Shi, P.: Output feedback-based neural adaptive finitetime containment control of non-strict feedback nonlinear multi-agent systems, IEEE Trans. Circuits Syst. I Regul. Pap. **69**(2), 847–858 (2022)
7. Jiang, D., Wen, G., Peng, Z., Huang, T., Rahmani, A.: Fully distributed dual-terminal event-triggered bipartite output containment control of heterogeneous systems under actuator faults. IEEE Trans. Syst. Man Cybern. Syst. **52**, 5518 (2021)
8. Cheng, F., Liang, H., Wang, H., Zong, G., Xu, N.: Adaptive neural self-triggered bipartite fault-tolerant control for nonlinear mass with dead-zone constraints. IEEE Trans. Autom. Sci. Eng. **20**(3), 1663 (2022)
9. Zhang, H., Zhao, X., Zong, G., Xu, N.: Fully distributed consensus of switched heterogeneous nonlinear multi-agent systems with hysteresis input. IEEE Trans. Netw. Sci. Eng. **9**(6), 4198–4208 (2022)
10. Yan, C., Zhang, W., Su, H., Li, X.: Adaptive bipartite time-varying output formation control for multiagent systems on signed directed graphs. IEEE Trans. Cybern. **9**, 1–14 (2021)
11. Cai, Y., Zhang, H., Wang, Y., Gao, Z., He, Q.: Adaptive bipartite fixed-time varying output formation-containment tracking of heterogeneous linear multiagent systems. IEEE Trans. Neural Networks Learn. Syst. **9**, 1–11 (2021)
12. Luo, Y., Zhu, W., Cao, J., Rutkowski, L.: Event-triggered finite-time guaranteed cost h-infinity consensus for nonlinear uncertain multi-agent systems. IEEE Trans. Network Sci. Eng. **9**(3), 1527–1539 (2022)
13. Yu, J., Dong, X., Li, Q., Ren, L.J.Z.: Fully adaptive practical time-varying output formation tracking for high-order nonlinear stochastic multiagent system with multiple leaders. IEEE Trans. Cybern. **51**(4), 2265–2277 (2021)

Based on the Nonlinear State Equations
of 6-DOF Robot with Application
to Autonomous Flight

Zhou Hongcheng[✉] and Fang Yuzhuo

School of Electronic and Information Engineering, Jinling Institute of Technology,
Nanjing 211169, China
945516882@qq.com

Abstract. The paper provides a linearized model of the quad rotor aircraft. Linearization is carried out around each state to optimize the system for larger flight envelopes. Each coupling term is represented by fixing and changing each time one state. Non-fragile optimal controller realization for the quad rotor aircraft is obtained by considering two different approaches for computation of controller fragility, stability radii comparison and weighted eigenvalue sensitivity calculation. A numerical method for reduction of controller fragility is presented. The simulation results show that the time delay compensation effect is well realized.

Keywords: Linearization · Non-fragile optimal · Controller · Nyquist · Circle criterion

1 Introduction

The derived nonlinear translational and rotational model, quad rotor aircraft needs to be simplified for control design [1]. The drag and rolling moment caused by speed are ignored, and the thrust and drag coefficients are assumed to be constant,

$$T_i = b\Omega_i^2$$
$$Q_i = d\Omega_i^2 \tag{1}$$

In this context, b and d represent the thrust factor and resistance factor, respectively, for a quad rotor aircraft system. The system's inputs consist of a vertical force input denoted as u_1, roll actuator input as u_2, pitch actuator input as u_3, and yaw moment input as u_4, given by [2],

The inputs for a quad rotor aircraft system can be represented as follows: the vertical force input is designated as u_1, the roll input as u_2, the pitch input as u_3, and the yaw

X. Chen et al. (Eds.): IoTaaS 2023, LNICST 585, pp. 152–162, 2025.
https://doi.org/10.1007/978-3-031-70507-6_13

input as u_4. These particular inputs are defined by the equation provided below:

$$\left.\begin{aligned}
u_1 &= b(\Omega_1^2 + \Omega_2^2 + \Omega_3^2 + \Omega_4^2) \\
u_2 &= b(\Omega_4^2 - \Omega_2^2) \\
u_3 &= b(\Omega_3^2 - \Omega_1^2) \\
u_4 &= d(\Omega_2^2 + \Omega_4^2 - \Omega_1^2 - \Omega_3^2)
\end{aligned}\right\} \tag{2}$$

Therefore, the 6-DOF nonlinear equation for controlling a quad rotor aircraft can be formulated in state space representation. $\dot{\mathbf{X}} = f(\mathbf{X}, \mathbf{u})$ using input vectors $\mathbf{u}$ and state vectors $\mathbf{X}$. The state is defined as [3],

$$\left.\begin{aligned}
x_1 &= x & x_2 &= \dot{x} \\
x_3 &= y & x_4 &= \dot{y} \\
x_5 &= z & x_6 &= \dot{z} \\
x_7 &= \phi & x_8 &= \dot{\phi} \\
x_9 &= \theta & x_1 &= \dot{\theta} \\
x_{11} &= \psi & x_1 &= \dot{\psi}
\end{aligned}\right\} \tag{3}$$

The state vector X is represented by,

$$\mathbf{X} = \begin{bmatrix} x & \dot{x} & y & \dot{y} & z & \dot{z} & \phi & \dot{\phi} & \theta & \dot{\theta} & \psi & \dot{\psi} \end{bmatrix} \tag{4}$$

The transformation matrix between the rate of change in orientation angles $(\dot{\phi}, \dot{\theta}, \dot{\psi})$ and the angular velocity (p, q, r) of an object can be considered as [4]. Simulation results have shown that this assumption is valid. Thus,

$$(\dot{\phi}, \dot{\theta}, \dot{\psi}) \approx (p, q, r) \tag{5}$$

Provided a translation model for a quad rotor aircraft that meets the real-time constraints of the embedded control loops, is given by [5],

$$f(\mathbf{X}, \mathbf{u})_{translational} = \begin{pmatrix} \dot{x} \frac{(\cos\phi \sin\theta \cos\psi + \sin\phi \sin\psi)}{m} u_1 \\ \dot{y} \frac{(\cos\phi \sin\theta \sin\psi - \sin\phi \cos\psi)}{m} u_1 \\ \dot{z} - g + \frac{(\cos\phi \cos\theta)}{m} u_1 \end{pmatrix} \tag{6}$$

2 Linearization of Nonlinear State Equations

Equations (6) are nonlinear and must be linearized in order to design linear controllers [6]. The linear state space is represented as,

$$
\mathbf{A} =
\begin{bmatrix}
0 & 1 & 0 & 0 & 0 & 0 & 0 & 0 & 0 & 0 & 0 & 0 \\
0 & 0 & 0 & 0 & 0 & 0 & 0 & 0 & 0 & 0 & 0 & 0 \\
0 & 0 & 0 & 1 & 0 & 0 & 0 & 0 & 0 & 0 & 0 & 0 \\
0 & 0 & 0 & 0 & 0 & 0 & 0 & 0 & 0 & 0 & 0 & 0 \\
0 & 0 & 0 & 0 & 0 & 1 & 0 & 0 & 0 & 0 & 0 & 0 \\
0 & 0 & 0 & 0 & 0 & 0 & 0 & 0 & 0 & 0 & 0 & 0 \\
0 & 0 & 0 & 0 & 0 & 0 & 0 & 1 & 0 & 0 & 0 & 0 \\
0 & 0 & 0 & 0 & 0 & 0 & 0 & 0 & 0 & \dot\psi_e\left(\frac{J_y-J_z}{J_x}\right) & 0 & \dot\theta_e\left(\frac{J_y-J_z}{J_x}\right) \\
0 & 0 & 0 & 0 & 0 & 0 & 0 & 0 & 0 & 0 & 1 & 0 \\
0 & 0 & 0 & 0 & 0 & 0 & 0 & \dot\psi_e\left(\frac{J_z-J_x}{J_y}\right) & 0 & 0 & 0 & \dot\varphi_e\left(\frac{J_z-J_x}{J_y}\right) \\
0 & 0 & 0 & 0 & 0 & 0 & 0 & 0 & 0 & 0 & 0 & 1 \\
0 & 0 & 0 & 0 & 0 & 0 & 0 & \dot\theta_e\left(\frac{J_x-J_y}{J_z}\right) & 0 & \dot\varphi_e\left(\frac{J_x-J_y}{J_z}\right) & 0 & 0
\end{bmatrix}
\begin{bmatrix}
x \\ \dot x \\ y \\ \dot y \\ z \\ \dot z \\ \phi \\ \dot\varphi \\ \theta \\ \dot\theta \\ \psi \\ \dot\psi
\end{bmatrix}
\tag{7}
$$

$$
\mathbf{B} =
\begin{bmatrix}
0 & 0 & 0 & 0 \\
\frac{\cos\phi \sin\theta \cos\psi + \sin\phi \sin\psi}{m} & 0 & 0 & 0 \\
0 & 0 & 0 & 0 \\
\frac{\cos\phi \sin\theta \cos\psi - \sin\phi \sin\psi}{m} & 0 & 0 & 0 \\
0 & 0 & 0 & 0 \\
\frac{\cos\phi \cos\theta}{m} & 0 & 0 & 0 \\
0 & 0 & 0 & 0 \\
0 & \frac{l}{J_x} & 0 & 0 \\
0 & 0 & 0 & 0 \\
0 & 0 & \frac{l}{J_y} & 0 \\
0 & 0 & 0 & 0 \\
0 & 0 & 0 & \frac{1}{J_z}
\end{bmatrix}
\begin{bmatrix}
u_1 \\ u_2 \\ u_3 \\ u_4
\end{bmatrix}
\tag{8}
$$

3 Controllability and Observability

The non-controllable and non-observable states of the state-space model, which are not connected to any input or output, are eliminated [7]. The resulting state space model is structurally minimal. After eliminating non-minimum state dynamics, we only have left the rotating subsystem, given by

$$
\mathbf{A\dot{X} + BU} =
\begin{bmatrix}
0 & 1 & 0 & 0 & 0 & 0 \\
0 & 0 & 0 & \dot{\psi}_e\left(\frac{J_y-J_z}{J_x}\right) & 0 & \dot{\theta}_e\left(\frac{J_y-J_z}{J_x}\right) \\
0 & 0 & 0 & 1 & 0 & 0 \\
0 & \dot{\psi}_e\left(\frac{J_z-J_x}{J_y}\right) & 0 & 0 & 0 & \dot{\varphi}_e\left(\frac{J_z-J_x}{J_y}\right) \\
0 & 0 & 0 & 0 & 0 & 1 \\
0 & \dot{\theta}_e\left(\frac{J_x-J_y}{J_z}\right) & 0 & \dot{\varphi}_e\left(\frac{J_x-J_y}{J_z}\right) & 0 & 0
\end{bmatrix}
\begin{bmatrix}
\phi \\ \dot{\varphi} \\ \theta \\ \dot{\theta} \\ \psi \\ \dot{\psi}
\end{bmatrix}
+
\begin{bmatrix}
0 & 0 & 0 & 0 \\
0 & \frac{1}{J_x} & 0 & 0 \\
0 & 0 & 0 & 0 \\
0 & 0 & \frac{1}{J_y} & 0 \\
0 & 0 & 0 & 0 \\
0 & 0 & 0 & \frac{1}{J_z}
\end{bmatrix}
\begin{bmatrix}
u_1 \\ u_2 \\ u_3 \\ u_4
\end{bmatrix}
\tag{9}
$$

To account for the lack of direct coupling between the input and output of the system, the direct conversion matrix, denoted as D, is assigned a value of zero. This indicates that there is no direct correlation or interaction between the input variables and the output variables within the system [8].

3.1 System Implementation

Let the transfer function be expressed as,

$$
G(\theta) = \frac{b(\theta)}{a(\theta)} = \frac{\sum_{i=0}^{n_b} b_i \overline{\theta}^i}{\sum_{i=0}^{n_a} a_i \overline{\theta}^i}
\tag{10}
$$

where, n_b and n_a are the numerator and denominator respectively, such that $n_a > n_b$ [9].

Where, n_b and n_a represent the numerator and denominator respectively, with the constraint that $n_a > n_b$ [9].

Let controller (proper) be defined as,

$$
H(\theta) = \frac{q(\theta)}{p(\theta)} = \frac{\sum_{i=0}^{n_q} q_i \overline{\theta}^i}{\sum_{i=0}^{n_p-1} p_i \overline{\theta}^i + \overline{\theta}^{n_p}}
\tag{11}
$$

where, n_q and n_p represent the numerator and denominator of the controller respectively, such that $n_p \geq n_q$.

3.2 Stability Radius & Weighted Eigenvalue Sensitivity

Radius of stability ball can be considered as one of the measures for fragility. If the parameterization **X** undergoes perturbation, the measure of stability radius r_s is determined by,

$$
r_s := \{\inf[\|\Delta\|] : closed\ loop\ system\ is\ in\ stability\}
\tag{12}
$$

Another measure for fragility is weighted eigenvalue sensitivity Ψ_{total} defined as,

$$
\Psi_{total} = \sum_{k=1}^{N} w_k \Psi_k
\tag{13}
$$

where N represents the number of closed-loop eigenvalues, w_k is a non-negative real weighting factor, and Ψ_k denotes the weighted sum of the 2-norm sensitivity of an individual closed-loop system eigenvalue to perturbations in the controller parameters. This is calculated using the following equation [10]

$$\Psi_k = \sum_{i=1}^{n_x} \left(\frac{\partial \lambda_k}{\partial x_i}\right)^2 \tag{14}$$

4 Application to 3-DOF Rotorcraft

The optimal (non-fragile) controller realization method is applied to a standard control problem, i.e., longitudinal pitch hold controller of a 3-DOF UH-60 rotorcraft. Consider the longitudinal dynamics of a hovering UH-60 rotorcraft. At hover, the vertical and longitudinal dynamics are decoupled. In Fig. 1, the standard block diagram correctly describes the rotorcraft.

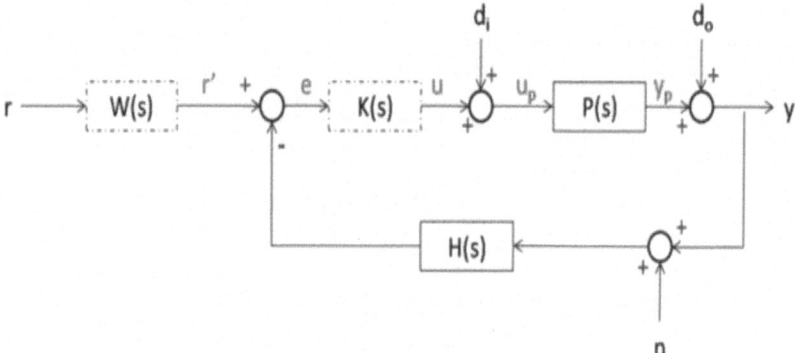

Fig. 1. Block Diagram of the rotor aircraft system

The dynamics of the aircraft in the longitudinal direction around the hover state are influenced by factors such as horizontal velocity, pitch attitude, and periodic pitch control. In particular, the horizontal velocity is characterized by the model described in [11],

$$\frac{\dot{x}}{B_{lc}} = X_{Blc}\left[\frac{s^2 - M_q s - \frac{gM_{Blc}}{X_{Blc}}}{s^3 - (X_u + M_q)s^2 + M_q X_u s + gM_u}\right] \tag{15}$$

The pitch attitude of the aircraft is influenced by various factors such as horizontal speed denoted by $\dot{x}$ in $ft/$ sec, and periodic pitch control denoted by B_{lc} in degrees. The pitch attitude can be described as follows:

$$\frac{\theta}{B_{lc}} = M_{Blc}\left[\frac{s + \left(\frac{X_{Blc}M_u}{M_{Blc}} - X_u\right)}{s^3 + (X_u + M_q)s^2 + M_q X_u s + gM_u}\right] \tag{16}$$

where θ is the pitch attitude in *deg*.

Figure 2 shows the block diagram for this controller [12].

$$B_{lc} = \frac{[K_\theta]}{s}\left(\theta_c - \left[\frac{50^2(s+b)^2}{(s+50)^2 b^2}\right]\theta\right) \tag{17}$$

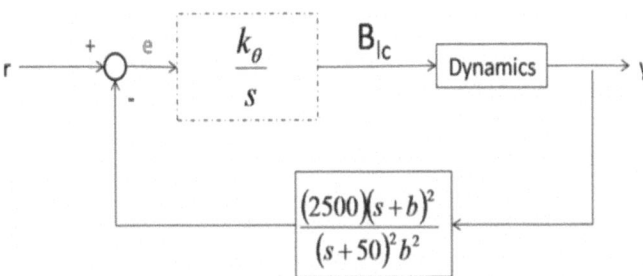

Fig. 2. U-60 rotorcraft Longitudinal Pitch-Hold

The pitch attitude of the aircraft is influenced by several variables: θ represents the true pitch attitude in radians, θ_c represents the commanded pitch in radians, b represents the control design parameter, and $k_\theta \leq 0$ represents the proportional gain constant for the pitch attitude. After the step command, the desirable low-frequency pitch attitude command is represented by $b = 2.0$ and $k_\theta = -1$.

Therefore, using a transfer function form controller, the calculated weighted eigen-values 1.6011×10^{10} have extremely high sensitivity, while the actual stability radius is 1.000×10^{-3}. In the normalized form of modal state space, the controller is characterized by the weighted eigenvalue sensitivity denoted as 2.3021×10^3 and the real stability radius denoted as 42.23×10^{-3}. The optimal weighted eigenvalue sensitivity is represented by 214.3169, while the actual stable radius is denoted as 59.18×10^{-3}. Hence, for this particular application, the weighted closed-loop eigenvalue sensitivity serves as a reasonable measure of controller vulnerability.

4.1 Open Loop Controller Performance

The implementation of the controller was simulated in an open loop using a discrete time controller. Different canonical forms, namely adjoint form, modal form, optimal form, and equilibrium form, were obtained. The response of the open-loop controller was compared with the response of the Simulink discrete time state space block under the same conditions. To excite the controller in the open loop, a Chirp signal with a frequency range of 0.1 Hz–10 Hz was used. Random signal inputs were also utilized to confirm the results obtained from the Chirp signal.

From Fig. 3, Upon analysis, it is evident that among open loop systems, the optimal non-fragile form demonstrates the most favorable outcomes. Following this, the balanced implementation and modal form exhibit relatively lower performance, respectively.

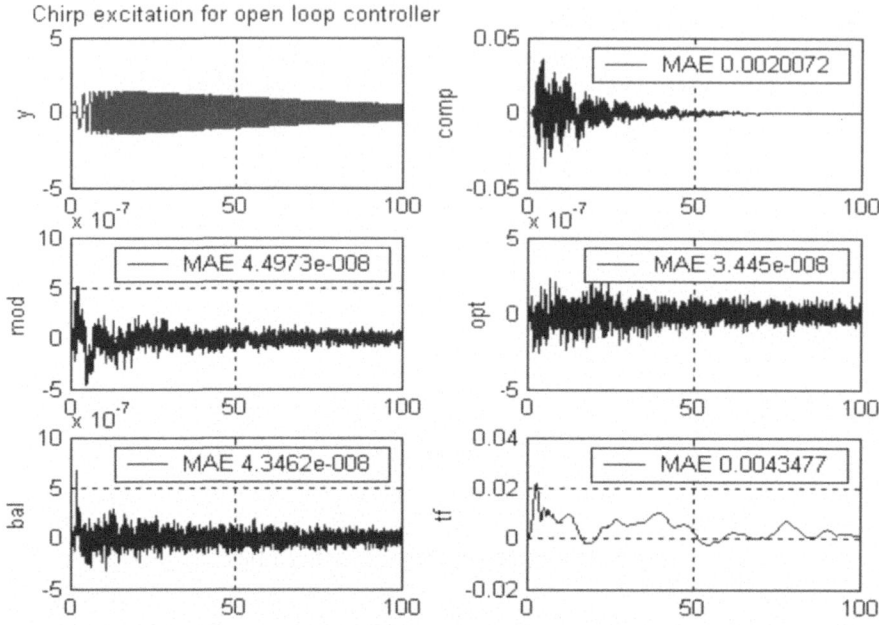

Fig. 3. The output response in different normative forms

4.2 Closed Loop Performance

The comparison results are presented in Fig. 4. The obtained results clearly demonstrate that the optimal form of the closed-loop system yields the most optimal outcome, followed by the balanced implementation and modal form.

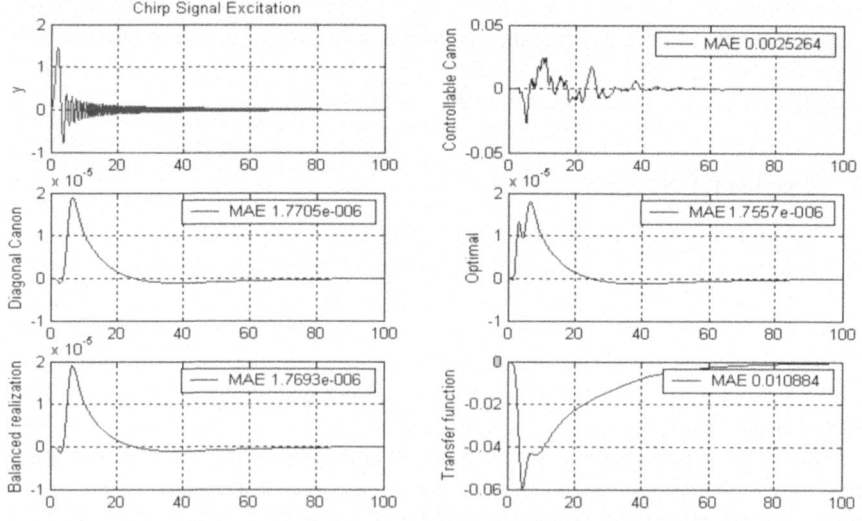

Fig. 4. The output response in different normative forms

An effective method for reducing controller vulnerability has been derived. This method applies complex Schur decomposition and QR decomposition to obtain suboptimal solutions. The method is applied to longitudinal pitch attitude controller of a UH-60 rotorcraft reducing its fragility by a large margin.

4.3 Non-fragile Optimal Control Design

When designing a control system, always choose the control vector **u** to minimize the system's performance indicators. For the design of linear quadratic regulators, the performance index J is given by the following equation:

$$J = \int_0^\infty \left(x'Qx + u'Ru \right) dt \tag{18}$$

In the given context, Q represents a positive definite matrix that can be either Hermite or real symmetric, while R represents a positive definite Hermite symmetric matrix. The variable u is unconstrained. The minimum performance index J of a state space system is defined using the minimum principle as follows,

$$\min_{u(t)} J = x(t_f)' S(t_f) x(t_f) + \frac{1}{2} \int_{t_0}^{t_f} \left(x'Qx + u'Ru \right) dt \tag{19}$$

And assuming that $S(t_f) \geq 0, Q \geq 0, R \geq 0$. To determine the minimum value, the Hamiltonian function is formulated as follows:

$$H = \frac{1}{2} \left(x'Qx + u'Ru \right) + \lambda'(Ax + Bu) \tag{20}$$

And the following optimal conditions must be met:

$$\left[\frac{\partial H}{\partial u} \right]' = 0 \quad and \quad \left[\frac{\partial H}{\partial x} \right]' = -\dot{\lambda}(t) \tag{21}$$

Equation (21) gives, $u(t) = -R^{-1}B^T \lambda(t)$, the optimal control is

$$\dot{\lambda} = -\left(Qx(t) + A'\lambda(t) \right) \tag{22}$$

The optimal control (22) is substituted into the state space system model to derive the resulting expression.

$$\begin{bmatrix} \dot{x} \\ \dot{\lambda} \end{bmatrix} = \begin{bmatrix} A & -BR^{-1}B' \\ -Q & -A' \end{bmatrix} \begin{bmatrix} x \\ \lambda \end{bmatrix} \triangleq H \begin{bmatrix} x \\ \lambda \end{bmatrix} \tag{23}$$

Equation (23) can be substituted,

$$\lambda = Px \tag{24}$$

Regarding the differential Eq. (24), we have

$$\frac{d\lambda}{dt} = \frac{dP}{dt}x + P\frac{dx}{dt} \tag{25}$$

Since $\dot{x} = dx/dt$ and $\dot{\lambda} = d\lambda/dt$, from the equation of state, we obtain

$$P\frac{dx}{dt} = PAx - PBR^{-1}B'Px$$
$$\frac{d\lambda}{dt} = -Qx - A'Px \tag{26}$$

By substituting (25) in (26), we achieved the following differential equation,

$$-\frac{dP}{dt} = A'P + PA + Q - PBR^{-1}B'P \tag{27}$$

The state feedback gain matrix K is utilized to revise the control signal u,

$$u = -Kx, \ K = R^{-1}B'P \tag{28}$$

In order to get the state feedback gain matrix K, $dP/dt \rightarrow 0$, and the positive definite solution of the algebraic Riccati equation (ARE), an asymptotically stable closed-loop system was obtained. Then we write the state space equation of the quad rotor aircraft as,

To obtain the state feedback gain matrix K, $dP/dt \rightarrow 0$ as well as the positive definite solution of the algebraic Riccati equation (ARE), an asymptotically stable closed-loop system is established. This involves writing the state space equation for the quadrotor aircraft as follows:

$$\dot{x} = (A - BK)x + Bu$$
$$y = Cx \tag{29}$$

Figure 5 illustrates the closed-loop diagram for the system using LQR state feedback gain A.

In order to ensure a meaningful optimization problem, it is required that Q be symmetric positive semidefinite and R be symmetric positive definite. Specifically, Q must be symmetric positive semidefinite to meet this requirement. Similarly, for meaningful optimization problems, R must be symmetric positive definite.

The parameters used for the simulation are,$l = 0.3\,m$,$J_x = 0.0158$ kg $\cdot$ m^2,$J_y = 0.0154$ kg $\cdot$ m^2, $J_z = 0.0309$ kg $\cdot$ m^2 and $m = 0.6$kg. The initial conditions used are $\varphi = \theta = \psi = 0.5$ rad, $\dot{\varphi} = \dot{\theta} = \dot{\psi} = 0.5$ rad/sec.

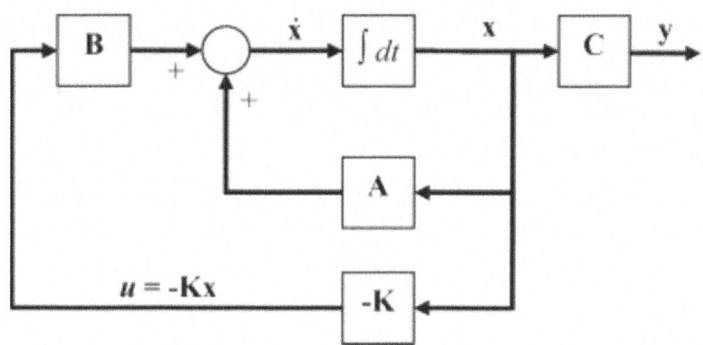

Fig. 5. Closed loop block diagram

5 Conclusions

An improved and efficient controller vulnerability reduction method was designed and implemented for a quad rotor craft that significantly reduces controller vulnerability. This method combines ordered complex Schur decomposition and QR decomposition to converge to suboptimal solutions. Various implementations of controllers for rotor craft were obtained and compared, including open-loop and closed-loop controllers. The Simulink state space block was utilized for this comparison, and the calculation of overall error was based on the Mean Absolute Error (MAE) parameter. The stability analysis of the non-fragile MIMO control system was conducted using extended Nyquist and Circle methods.

Acknowledgment. This work was supported by Cooperative Project of Jiangsu Province production, teaching and research (No. BY2021381), Jin Ling Institute of Technology Ph. D. Startup Fund(jit-b-202314).

References

1. Karahan, O., Karci, H.: Swarm intelligence based nonlinear friction and dynamic parameters identification for a 6-DOF robotic manipulator. J. Int. Robot. Syst. **108**(2), 19 (2023)
2. Sancak, K.V., Bayraktaroglu, Z.Y.: Nonlinear Computed Torque Control of 6-DoF Parallel Manipulators. Int. J. Control Automat. Syst. **20**(7), 2297–2311 (2022)
3. Cruz, G.L., Alazki, H., Cortes-Vega, D., et al.: Application of robust discontinuous control algorithm for a 5-DOF industrial robotic manipulator in real-time. J. Intell. Rob. Syst. **101**(4), 1–17 (2021)
4. Wang, H., Li, X., Liu, X., et al.: Fuzzy sliding mode active disturbance rejection control of an autonomous underwater vehicle-manipulator system. J. Ocean Univ. China **19**(5), 1081–1093 (2020)
5. Khankalantary, S., Badri, P., Mohammadkhani, H.: Designing a hierarchical model-predictive controller for tracking an unknown ground moving target using a 6-DOF quad-rotor. Int. J. Dyn. Control **9**, 985–999 (2021)

6. Sai, H., Xu, Z., Li, Y., et al.: Adaptive nonsingular fast terminal sliding mode impedance control for uncertainty robotic manipulators. Int. J. Precis. Eng. Manuf. **22**(12), 1947–1961 (2021)
7. Li, C., Ren, C., Ding, Y., et al.: Non-singular terminal sliding mode control of an omnidirectional mobile manipulator based on extended state observer. Int. J. Int. Robot. Appl. **5**(2), 219–234 (2021)
8. Loucif, F., Kechida, S., Sebbagh, A.: Whale optimizer algorithm to tune PID controller for the trajectory tracking control of robot manipulator. J. Braz. Soc. Mech. Sci. Eng. **42**(1), 1–11 (2020)
9. Kumar, J., Kumar, V., Rana, K.P.S.: Fractional-order self-tuned fuzzy PID controller for three-link robotic manipulator system. Neural Comput. Appl. **32**(11), 7235–7257 (2020)
10. Liu, A., Zhao, H., Song, T., et al.: Adaptive control of manipulator based on neural network. Neural Comput. Appl. **33**(9), 4077–4085 (2021)
11. Tran, D.T., Truong, H.V.A., Ahn, K.K.: Adaptive nonsingular fast terminal sliding mode control of robotic manipulator based neural network approach. Int. J. Precis. Eng. Manuf. **22**(3), 417–429 (2021)
12. Ma, F., Li, J., et al.: Tensor product based polytopic LPV system design of a 6-DoF multistrut platform. Int. J. Control. Autom. Syst.Autom. Syst. **20**(1), 137–146 (2022)

A Study on Collaborative Lane Change Decision Making of Multi-automated Vehicles Based on Deep Graph Reinforcement Learning

Xiang Li[1(✉)], Jianxun Cui[1,2], and Haozhe Ji[3]

[1] Harbin Institute of Technology, Harbin City 150000, Heilongjiang Province, China
`23s132082@stu.hit.edu.cn`
[2] Chongqing Research Institute of HIT, 618 Liangjiang Avenue,
Longxing Town, Yubei District,Chongqing, China
[3] Jiamusi University, Jiamusi City 154000, Heilongjiang Province, China

Abstract. The lane change decision making module plays a crucial role in autonomous driving systems, facing the challenge of balancing collaborative traffic operation. Modeling complex interactions among multiple autonomous vehicles in coexisting environments poses significant challenges. This study focuses on collaborative lane change decision making for multiple autonomous vehicles by employing deep graph convolutional neural networks. These networks effectively model the interaction and collaboration among vehicles, while reinforcement learning facilitates the iterative evolution of decision-making. To evaluate the performance of the proposed Graph Reinforcement Learning (GRL) method, an interactive driving scenario with two ramps on a highway was developed. Simulation experiments were conducted on the SUMO platform to compare different GRL methods. Results were analyzed from multiple perspectives and dimensions to compare the characteristics of different GRL methods in the scenario of highway merging traffic. The findings demonstrate that the utilization of deep graph convolutional neural network can effectively model the complex interactions among vehicles and the combination of graph convolution and reinforcement learning can significantly improve the performance of lane-changing behaviors in terms of both efficiency and safety.

Keywords: Autonomous Driving · Collaborative Decision Making · Deep Graph Reinforcement Learning

1 Introduction

Due to economic development and improved quality of life, traffic frequency has significantly increased,resulting in more severe issues related to traffic safety and

X. Chen et al. (Eds.): IoTaaS 2023, LNICST 585, pp. 163–182, 2025.
https://doi.org/10.1007/978-3-031-70507-6_14

congestion. Global road traffic fatalities reach 1.35 million annually since 2000, with injuries totaling 5,000. Additionally, economic losses surpass $500 billion each year. According to a 2015 report by the U.S. Department of Transportation, 94% of traffic accidents were caused by driver errors, including recognition errors (41%) and decision-making errors (33%)[1].

In the field of intelligent networked vehicles research, driving behaviors including lane keeping, merging into traffic, lane changing, and overtaking play a crucial role in ensuring driving safety. Making reasonable decisions based on different traffic environments is especially important, particularly in high-complexity and high-dynamics traffic scenarios, where irrational decision-making behaviors can lead to serious consequences. These traffic environments are characterized by high dynamics and uncertainty, making behavioral decision-making a challenging task in self-driving vehicle research. The problem of behavioral decision-making in intelligent networked vehicles is a high-dimensional and continuous sequential decision-making problem. Traditional dynamic planning methods and rule-based traffic models are insufficient to meet the requirements of dynamic decision-making in complex environments. Recently, reinforcement learning methods have gained attention as a research hotspot in the field of autonomous driving. By utilizing reinforcement learning, more accurate decision-making of single automated vehicle can be achieved, effectively avoiding traffic accidents and reducing economic losses. Furthermore, studying multi-vehicle automatic cooperative lane-changing control for intelligent networked vehicles in mixed traffic flow can enhance lane-changing efficiency, particularly in complex environments (e.g. highway on/off ramping scenarios). But how to effectively capture the complex interactions among the decisions made by different automated vehicles and finally improve the overall driving efficiency and safety of this multi-vehicle system is essentially very challenging. In this research, we try to use deep graph convolutional neural network combined with reinforcement learning, i.e. GCN-DRL, to model the information sharing and collaborative decision making among multiple automated vehicles.

2   Literature Review

Current research on lane changing decision making for intelligent networked vehicles mainly focuses on the following aspects: controlling vehicles for decision making by setting up scenarios and rules in advance, lane changing decision making based on deep reinforcement learning, and applying Vehicle-to-Vehicle (V2V) communication technology for multi-vehicle collaboration.

2.1   Rule-Based Decision Modeling for Lane Changes

In 1986, Gipps proposed a model that takes into account the necessity, propensity, and safety aspects of lane-changing behavior, and this approach prioritizes different influences on lane-changing choices, but does not take into account subsequent differences in driver behavioral characteristics [2]. Yang et al. improved the flexibility of the model by considering lane change probability [3]. Ahmed designed a probabilistic model by stepwise decomposition of lane changing behavior, mainly based on utility selection theory [4].Toledo et al. continued Ahmed et al.'s work on probabilistic models of utility selection and designed a model that can integrate forced and active lane changing, but the model, although very theoretically rigorous, is overly complex and extremely difficult to calibrate the parameters [5]. In 2007, Kesting et al. proposed the MOBIL model [6]. In a paper published in 2014, Jakob Erdmann proposed the LC2013 model applied to the open-source simulation platform SUMO, which sets up four lane-changing scenarios, and decides whether to change lanes or not by calculating whether a threshold is reached in each scenario through a formula that facilitates the successful execution of the desired lane-changing maneuver [7] .

2.2 Deep Reinforcement Learning Based Lane Change Decision Making

In addition to rule-based lane changing methods, the most mainstream application of deep reinforcement learning for decision making is currently available. In 2017, Sallab et al. applied DQN for the learning of lane-merging strategies, focusing on vehicle ramp merging [8] . In this strategy, Sallab et al. took into account both the short-term goal of successful merging and the long-term goal of smoothing the merging trajectory. To ensure that the learned strategy balances safety and strategy, the state perception of the surrounding environment is sensed through a long and short-term memory network. For the same ramp merging scenario, Huegle et al. of the University of Freiburg, in 2019, analyzed the performance of existing classical perception methods utilized during reinforcement learning strategy optimization, and tested a comparison of ramp merging scenarios via the DQN algorithm [9] . Although deep reinforcement learning has more advantages, it also has certain problems, mainly including the problem of slow learning rate due to frequent interaction with the environment for data collection. To address these problems, Ye et al. proposed a lane-changing strategy based on the optimization of the proximal policy, which effectively solves the problem of slow learning efficiency of reinforcement learning without destroying the more stable performance of lane-changing [10]. After that, Mukadam et al. proposed a Q-masking technique to improve the learning rate again . Mukadam et al. proposed a Q-masking technique to improve the learning rate again [11]. Mukadam et al. Most of the above studies are single-vehicle automated driving, in order to improve the efficiency of the passage, multi-vehicle collaboration is a direction that must be considered, but this involves the balance between the overall efficiency and the individual efficiency, so multi-intelligent body reinforcement learning is applied in the lane changing process [12] . For example, Dong et al. had collected data from surrounding vehicles through sensors for cooperative strategy training [13] .

3   Methodology

The objective of this paper is to generate cooperative lane change decisions for self-driving cars in an interactive traffic scenario. To achieve this goal, a framework (named as GCN-DRL) is proposed (see Fig. 1), which consists of three key components: an interactive traffic scene, a GCN algorithm and several DRL algorithms, and a simulation platform. The vehicles in the scenario are modeled as a graph, where nodes represent different vehicles and edges represent interactions between every two vehicles. The graph is then processed into node features, adjacency matrices and RL filters, which will be used to get the state description of the whole vehicle system and will be detailed in Sects. 3.1-3.2 separately. The GCN-DRL algorithm is developed to train lane changing strategies, which takes the graphical representation as an input and generates the Q-values for different lane changing actions. The simulation part takes the Q-values as input and generates the lane change decision of each vehicle to update the interactive traffic scene for continuous training of the GCN-DRL network.

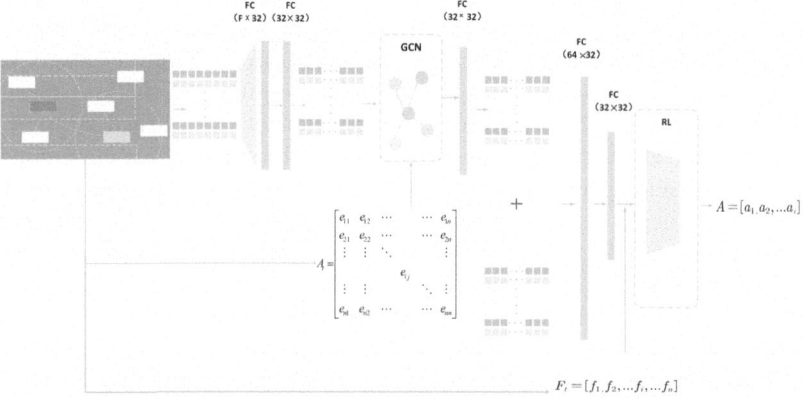

Fig. 1. Collaborative control decision model based on graph neural network and deep reinforcement learning

The scenario studied in this paper is based on a mixed traffic flow scenario on a freeway. The scenario consists of a 3-lane freeway with two ramp exits. In this scenario, two types of vehicles operate: human-driven vehicles and self-driven vehicles. Different vehicles have different driving tasks and need to cooperate in order to accomplish the intended driving tasks more efficiently. White vehicles represent HVs, entering from the left side of the freeway and exiting from the right side. Colored vehicles represent AVs entering from the left side of the freeway, specifically yellow vehicles exiting from Ramp 1 and blue vehicles exiting from Ramp 2 (Fig. 2).

Fig. 2. Collaborative control decision model based on graph neural network and deep reinforcement learning

The self-driving vehicle interacts with the traffic environment by taking lane changing actions in discrete time steps in a constructed traffic scenario. After the action is taken, a state of the traffic environment changes and the self-driving vehicle receives a reward. Moreover, the environment information is fully observable within the observation range of the self-driving vehicle.

The scene is modeled as an undirected graph. Each car in the scene is considered as a node of the graph, and the interactions between cars are considered as edges of the graph. More precisely, the constructed graph is described as $G = \{N, E\}$, where $N = \{n_i, i \in \{1, 2, ...N\}\}$ is a set of node attributes and $E = \{e_{ij}, i, j \in \{1, 2, ...N\}\}$ is a set of edge attributes. Specifically, n denotes the number of nodes in the constructed graph, which is equal to the total number of vehicles. The properties and interactions of the vehicles are then modeled using the graph representation. The state space is discrete and can be described as follows:

$$S_t = [N_t, A_t, F_t] \tag{1}$$

where:N_t denotes the node feature matrix, A_t denotes the adjacency matrix, and F_t denotes the RL filter matrix. Together, the above three matrices form the state space matrix, which is the initial input to the entire model.

Node Characterization Matrix. The node feature matrix represents the features of the constructed scene. It consists of a feature matrix for each vehicle and can be described as follows:

$$N_t = \begin{bmatrix} [V_1 & X_1 & L_1 & I_1] \\ [V_2 & X_2 & L_2 & I_2] \\ & \cdots & \\ [V_i & X_i & L_i & I_i] \\ & \cdots & \\ [V_n & X_n & L_n & I_n] \end{bmatrix} \tag{2}$$

where $[V_i, X_i, L_i, I_i]$ denotes the normalized state matrix of each vehicle. Specifically, in the lane changing task, $V_i = V_{ipractice} \setminus V_{max}$ denotes the normalized longitudinal velocity of the vehicle with respect to the maximum longitudinal velocity; $X_i = X_{ivertical} \setminus L_{highway}$ denotes the normalized longitudinal coordinates of the vehicle with respect to the length of the roadway; L_i denotes a one-heat-code matrix of the current channel representing the vehicle's position (left lane, right lane, and middle lane); and Ii is a one-heat-code matrix denoting the vehicle's current intention (change to left lane, change to right lane, and straight ahead) of a one-heat code matrix.

Adjacency Matrix. The adjacency matrix represents the interactions between vehicles and reflects the information sharing between vehicles in the constructed scenario. The adjacency matrix is computed based on the following assumptions:

- All vehicles can share information with themselves.
- All AVs can share information.
- All AVs can get information from HVs, which are within the sensing range of the AVs.

The adjacency matrix is derived as follows:

$$A_t = \begin{bmatrix} e_{11} & e_{12} & \cdots\cdots & e_{1n} \\ e_{21} & e_{22} & \cdots\cdots & e_{2n} \\ \vdots & \vdots & \ddots & \vdots \\ & & e_{ij} & \\ \vdots & \vdots & & \ddots \\ e_{n1} & e_{n2} & \cdots\cdots & e_{nn} \end{bmatrix} \tag{3}$$

where e_{ij} indicates whether or not $vehicle_i$ and $vehicle_j$ are within their respective observation ranges. When $vehicle_i$ and $vehicle_j$ share information, i.e., can be observed or information can be transferred, $e_{ij} = 1$; while when $vehicle_i$ and $vehicle_j$ are not in the observation range or cannot transfer information $e_{ij} = 0$.

RL Filtering Matrix. The RL filtering matrix is constructed to filter out the corresponding terms of the HVs used for the output of the algorithm.The RL filtering matrix is derived as follows (Fig. 3):

$$F_t = \begin{bmatrix} f_1, f_2, \cdots f_i, \cdots f_n \end{bmatrix} \tag{4}$$

where $f_i = 0$ or 1, and $f_i = 1$ if $vehicle_i$ belongs to an artificial vehicle controlled by the GCN-DRL algorithm; otherwise $f_i = 0$.

3.1   Graph Convolutional Neural Network Module

Autonomous vehicles can transmit information to each other through the vehicular network, but artificial vehicles cannot transmit information to each other. And each self-driving vehicle can only observe the information of artificial vehicles within a certain range of itself, therefore, the communication function of self-driving vehicles can be utilized to share the information of each self-driving vehicle through the vehicular network, so that the self-driving vehicles within the road section have a more comprehensive control of the information in the road section, in order to realize the function of information aggregation, we designed the graph neural network module, i.e. GNN module.

The GNN module consists of a fully connected layer and a graph convolutional network,where the fully connected network is two layers and the GCN network is one layer.

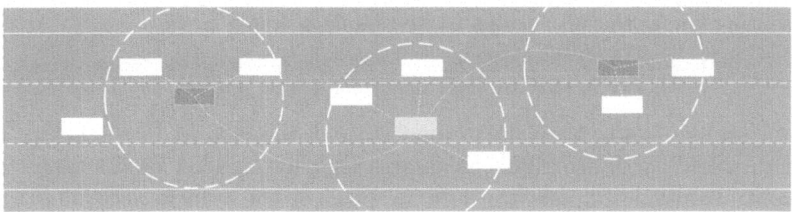

Fig. 3. Schematic diagram of graphical neural network information aggregation

Before implementing the graph convolution process, the node feature matrix Nt is first input into the fully connected layer to map the node features into the sample labeling space as described below:

$$N_{FC} = \phi_{FC}(N_t) \tag{5}$$

Where: N_{FC} denotes the node feature matrix output from the fully connected layer; ϕ_{FC} denotes the neural network with full connectivity. Then, N_{FC} and the adjacency matrix A_t are firstly input into the GCN to generate graph convolution features; and the graph convolution process can be expressed as the following equation:

$$G_t = \phi_{GCN}(N_{FC}, A_t) = \sigma(D_t^{1/2} A_t D^{-1/2} N_{FC} W_t + b) \tag{6}$$

Where: g_t denotes the graph convolution feature starting from GCN; ϕ^{GCN} denotes the graph convolution operator; matrix D_t is calculated based on A_t ; W_t denotes the layer-specific trainable weight matrix; b denotes the offset and b=0 is defined in this study; σ denotes the activation function and ReLU is chosen in this study. The output of the graph neural network module is fed into the DRL module and then filtered through the RL filter matrix to generate the Q-value of the AV's lane changing maneuver, the Q-value is derived as follows:

$$Q(s,a) = F_t - \left[\phi^{DRL}(G_t)\right] \tag{7}$$

where $Q(s,a)$ denotes the Q-value of the AVs' lane-changing action; and ϕ^{DRL} denotes the policy neural network.

3.2 Deep Reinforcement Learning Module for Lane Change Decision Making Problems

The deep reinforcement learning module for the lane change decision problem selects DQN , Double DQN , Dueling DQN , Dueling Double DQN (D3QN) for the comparison, and the state space is the information of the self-driving vehicle that has been processed by the graph neural network module. This section defines the behavior space and reward function of the self-driving vehicle in the reinforcement learning module.

Behavioral Space. For each time step, each CAV has a discrete action space representing the potential actions to be taken, as follows:

$$a_i = \{turn \quad left, straight, turn \quad right\} \tag{8}$$

Where: "straight" is to keep the current state of the vehicle. In the lateral decision, "turn left" or "turn right" generates the lane number of the target lane. The control module adjusts the lateral speed of the vehicle according to the target lane number. The overall action space of the deep reinforcement learning module is a combinatorial space that aggregates all possible combinations of a single CAV: $A = \{a_i\}_{i=1}^n$, i is the number of CAVs at the current time step. It is important to note that the simulation process restricts vehicles from leaving the simulated path, but does not prevent them from colliding during lane changes.

Reward Function. The reward function consists of: 2 reward types and 2 penalty types. They are intentional reward, speed reward, lane change penalty and collision penalty (Table 1). The intent reward is to ensure that all CAVs merge out of the prescribed ramp. Speed rewards encourage actions that improve system efficiency. Specifically, to balance with other reward sources and encourage cooperation, we define "soft and smooth" intentional rewards at each time step, rather than rewarding vehicles immediately upon successful divergence. We denote CAVs exiting the first ramp as "$merge\_1$" CAVs and CAVs merging from the second ramp as "$merge\_2$" CAVs. Intentional rewards are computed only on the first 2 segments: seg_1 and seg_2, where p_{ij} and r_{ij} are the penalties and rewards for vehicles exiting from different ramps on two different segments, and x_{ij} is the perpendicular distance of a vehicle exiting from a different ramp from the baseline defining the different segments, and thus reverts to 0 when the vehicle enters a new segment (Fig. 4).

Table 1. Reward and Penalize

Sections	Norm	Define	Calculation
Seg_1	p_{11}	Penalty for "$merge\_1$" CAV in the top lane increases as approaching Ramp 1.	$p_{11} = \frac{x_{11}}{L_1}$
	r_{11}	Reward for "$merge\_1$" CAV in the bottom lane, increased from approach to ramp 1.	$r_{11} = 1 + \frac{x_{11}}{L_1}$
	p_{21}	Penalty for "$merge\_2$" CAV in the top lane, increase on approach to ramp 1.	$p_{21} = \frac{x_{21}}{L_1}$
Seg_2	p_{22}	Penalty for the "$merge\_2$" CAV in the top lane increases as you approach ramp 2.	$p_{22} = \frac{x_{22}}{L_2}$
	r_{11}	The bottom lane on the "$merge\_2$" CAV is rewarded with an increase from approaching ramp 2.	$r_{22} = 1 + \frac{x_{22}}{L_2}$

The total intent reward is defined as the individual reward or penalty for each CAV on different sections of the road:

$$R_i = \sum_{k=1}^n \sum_{i,j} (r_{ij} - p_{ij})\delta_{ij}^n \tag{9}$$

Among them: δ_{ij}^n is used to determine whether a vehicle has entered the area where it can get penalties and rewards, p_{ij} and r_{ij} are the penalties and rewards

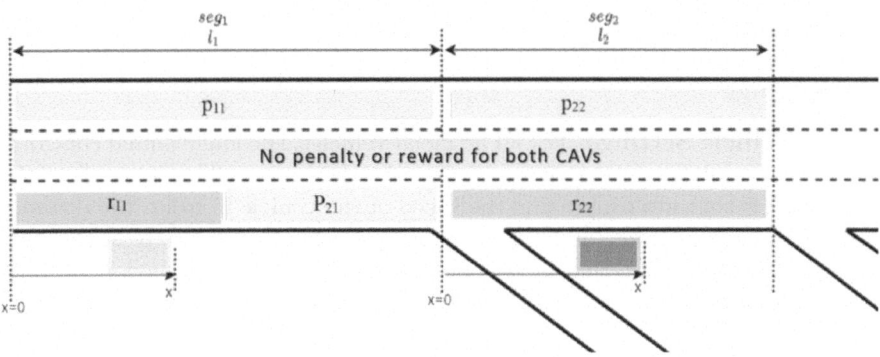

Fig. 4. Schematic diagram of penalties and rewards

for different types of vehicles in different segments, and we have set a "soft" reward to encourage "$merge\_2$".

CAVs yield the bottom lane to "$merge\_1$" CAVs before the first on-ramp and merge into the bottom lane as soon as they enter the second segment. In addition, the absolute value of the reward and penalty is a function of vehicle position to encourage CAVs to make early lane changing decisions.

In addition to the intent bonus, other performance metrics were considered, including efficiency, safety, and comfort, which were expressed using the speed bonus, collision penalty, and lane change penalty. Speed bonus is defined as R_V:

$$R_V = 1/n \sum_{i=1}^{n} \frac{v_{cav}^i}{v_{max}} \tag{10}$$

Where: v_{cav}^i denotes the speed of the ith CAV on the road; v_{max} is the maximum speed limit of the vehicle on the roadway. The collision penalty P_c is a fixed large positive value used to constrain behaviors that may produce collisions. Lane Change Penalty P_{LC} is defined as a constant penalty added to each lane change decision and is used to encourage CAVs to stay in their lanes instead of changing lanes frequently.

The overall reward function is defined as:

$$R_{total} = \omega_1 R_l + \omega_2 R_V + \omega_3 P_C + \omega_4 P_{LC} \tag{11}$$

Where: $\omega_1 \ldots \omega_4$ are weights that can be adjusted according to the model, it should be noted that the ratios between "Intent Satisfaction", "Driving Speed", "Safety", and It should be noted that when ω_1 and ω_2 are dominant compared to ω_3 and ω_4. This setting will encourage vehicles to change lanes to meet intentions and travel fast to reach their destinations, but there is a risk that decision-making will be error-prone and overly aggressive. On the other hand, making ω_3 and ω_4 larger than ω_1 and ω_2 means higher penalties for unsafe and frequent lane changing behavior. In this case, the model learns to adopt very conservative and safety-conscious behaviors even at the risk of failing to achieve the merger intent.

4   Experiments

4.1   Settings

Barrier Vehicle Settings. For all artificial vehicles, the longitudinal control is done using an intelligent driver model, i.e., the IDM model.The principle of the IDM model is that after inputting the speed of the vehicle in front, the distance from the vehicle in front, and the speed of the self vehicle variables, the final output is an acceleration that is used for the vehicle to perform the longitudinal control, and the equations of acceleration are obtained as follows:

$$\dot{v} = a \left[1 - \left(\frac{v}{v_0} \right)^{\delta} - \left(\frac{s^*(v, \Delta v)}{s} \right)^2 \right] \tag{12}$$

Where: a is the maximum acceleration of the modeled vehicle; v is the current speed of the modeled vehicle; v_0 is the desired speed of the modeled vehicle; Δv is the relative speed between the modeled vehicle and the vehicle in front of it; δ is the acceleration index, with the increase of δ, the acceleration and deceleration process of the vehicle will be more intense; s is the distance between the modeled vehicle and the vehicle in front of it; $s^*(v, \Delta v)$ is the desired following distance of the modeled vehicle. $\left(\frac{v}{v_0} \right)^{\delta}$ is used to measure the difference between the current speed and the desired speed to promote vehicle acceleration. $\left(\frac{s^*(v, \Delta v)}{s} \right)^2$ is used to measure the difference between the current distance and the desired distance to facilitate vehicle braking.The desired vehicle spacing is obtained from the following equation:

$$s^*(v, \Delta v) = s_0 + vT + \frac{v\Delta v}{2\sqrt{ab}} \tag{13}$$

Where:b for the comfortable deceleration;s_0 for the vehicle minimum distance, this parameter is related to the assumption of the IDM model, even if the vehicle is at a standstill, the minimum distance to be maintained, if the distance between the two workshops is less than s_0 , it can be assumed that a collision of the two vehicles;T for the safety of the headway when the distance.The expectation distance equation contains a balancing term $s_0 + vT$, and a power term $\frac{v\Delta v}{2\sqrt{ab}}$ to realize an intelligent braking strategy. The settings of the model parameters for the IDM model in this experiment are shown in the table below:

Table 2. IDM model parameters

Parameters	Value	Unit
maximum acceleration	6	m/s^2
Maximum (comfortable) deceleration	-5	m/s^2
Desired speed of the vehiclev_0	30	m/s^2
acceleration index (math.)δ	4	–
Minimum distance between cars s_0	2	s
For safe headway T_0	1	s

The experimental vehicle lateral control algorithms all use SUMO's built-in rule-based LC2013 algorithm.LC2013 calculates the vehicle's decision to change lanes in a single simulation step, based on the vehicle's travel route and the current and historical traffic conditions around the vehicle. In addition, it calculates the vehicle's own and the obstacle vehicle's speed change to facilitate the successful execution of the desired lane change maneuver.The LC2013 model explicitly distinguishes between four different motivations for changing lanes: Strategic change, Cooperative change, Tactical change, and Obligatory change. Each of the four motivations is calculated independently, and a lane change is triggered when the value of a certain motivation reaches a certain threshold.LC2013 has one drawback, namely, it considers that a lane change occurs instantaneously and does not take into account factors such as the angle of deflection of the vehicle during the lane change, as shown in Fig. 5:

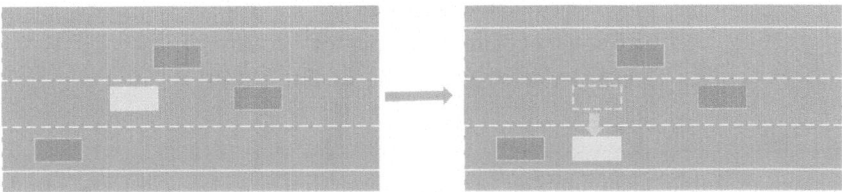

Fig. 5. Schematic diagram of LC2013 lane change model

Experimental Scenarios and Parameter Settings. This experiment uses the SUMO platform to design a 500m long highway. The highway is a three-lane road with exit ramps at 200m and 400m from the entrance. The vehicles involved in the experiment include artificial vehicles and self-driving vehicles. The artificial vehicles are white and their longitudinal control algorithm is selected from the IDM model. Their transverse algorithms are based on the built-in LC2013 model in SUMO. The self-driving vehicles are categorized into two types based on the exit ramps. Vehicles exiting from the first ramp are yellow, while vehicles exiting from the second ramp are blue. The longitudinal control algorithm of the self-driving vehicles is the same as that of the manual vehicles. However, the transverse control algorithm (i.e., lane changing process) adopts the GCN-DRL model proposed in this paper. The self-driving vehicle fuses the information from both the manually driven vehicle and the self-driving vehicle through the GCN algorithm. The fused information is used as input to the deep reinforcement learning module, which in turn outputs the lane changing behavior of each self-driving vehicle. In this paper, different deep reinforcement learning algorithms are selected for training for three times, and each training is set to 200 rounds.

After training, each algorithm is tested three times with each test set to 20 rounds. The following table shows the parameters of the experimental settings. The following table shows the parameters of the experimental settings.

Table 3. Parameter settings for simulation experiments

Parameters	Value
Number of training rounds	200
Followed by exploration phase step	20000
Number of small batches processed	32
Experience pool capacity	50000
Discount factor γ	0.9
Adam Learning Rate	10^{-4}
randomized action probability	0.3
Frequency of online web updates	10
Frequency of target network updates	1000

As shown in Table 3, the number of manually driven vehicles is 20. The number of self-driving vehicles from the first ramp is 10, and the number of self-driving vehicles from the second ramp is 10. The traffic flow of various vehicles will be changed according to the purpose of the experiment. The maximum speed of the manual vehicles is 30 m/s, and the maximum speed of the self-driving vehicles is 25 m/s. The units of speed are all m/s, which is consistent with the default units of speed in SUMO. The observation radius of the self-driving vehicle is set to 25m, which can be changed according to the specific experimental objectives. A Warmup session was performed for the first 2000 steps, i.e., a smaller learning rate was used for about 15 rounds to prevent overlearning in the early stages when the simulation data and vehicle behavior were poor, resulting in the need for more training rounds in the later stages in order to correct the training results. In reinforcement learning, the intelligence is trained through each state transfer process. In general simulation, after learning a state transfer process, this state transfer process is discarded, which results in a large amount of wasted experience. Therefore, this paper adopts the method of experience playback: set up an experience pool which can store 50000 processes. When the experience pool is full, for each step of simulation, one old data in the experience pool is eliminated, and then an updated state transfer process is deposited. In order to improve the efficiency, we set the minimum batch as 32, when the experience pool data is larger than 32 that is, we adopt the minimum batch method and randomly select 32 data in the experience pool for training. In addition, in order to increase the chance of exploration, a simple greedy strategy with a random action probability of 0.3 is set in the training process.

Table 4. Parameters of the training process

Parameters	Value
umber of manual vehicles	20
Number of self-driving vehicles	20
Number of self-driving vehicles exiting the first ramp	20
Number of self-driving vehicles exiting the second ramp	10
Length of highways	500
First ramp location	200
Second ramp location	400
Maximum speed for manual vehicles	$30m/s$
Maximum speed of self-driving vehicles	$25m/s$
Traffic flow of manual vehicles	$0.1 - 0.5vel/s$
Volume of Autonomous Vehicles Exiting Ramp 1	$0.1 - 0.5vel/s$
Traffic flow of self-driving vehicles exiting the second ramp	$0.1 - 0.5vel/s$
Radius of observation for self-driving vehicles	$25m$

Test Task Setting and Evaluation Indicators. In order to obtain more generalized and accurate results, we set up a variety of scenarios during the testing process:

- The reward loss etc. obtained during training is analyzed for the rule-based approach as well as for four different deep reinforcement learning algorithms.
- Changing the proportions of the components of the reward function in the deep reinforcement learning module makes the vehicle more efficiency-focused or more robust as it travels to its destination.
- Changing the traffic flow of manual and self-driving vehicles and comparing the difference between the metrics of different deep reinforcement learning algorithms and rule-based methods, respectively.
  In order to better judge the experimental results, the following evaluation indexes are selected in this paper:
- The final total reward value of each round. The reward value is one of the important indexes for evaluating the effect of reinforcement learning module, which directly reflects the effect of lane changing, and because the speed, the number of lane changing, and the intention to change lanes have been taken into account when setting the reward function, the reward is also an index with comprehensive evaluation, which is of great significance.
- Loss per round in training. The speed of loss decrease reflects the efficiency of the training process.
- Average speed of the self-driving vehicle. Although this paper designs only the lane changing decision model, the lane changing behavior of the self-driving vehicle still affects the longitudinal following behavior. Therefore the lane changing decision model should not only realize the task of driving out of the ramp through the lane changing behavior, but also need to be beneficial to

enhance the vehicle speed and improve the driving efficiency. So the average speed is also an important evaluation index.

4.2   Experiments Results

Experimental Results of Different Reinforcement Learning Lane-changing Strategies. The longitudinal control algorithms of the vehicles all use the IDM model, and the lateral control method of the manual vehicle uses LC201.The lateral control of the self-driving vehicle uses five methods, namely LC2013, DQN, DoubleDQN, Dueling DQN, and D3QN, respectively. It should be noted that when performing the per-round reward statistics, the reward function calculation is also performed when the self-driving vehicle uses LC2013, a rule-based lane-changing model, and the reward function calculation method is the same as that of the four reinforcement learning algorithms. However, no training in terms of reinforcement learning is performed on the vehicle. This is the explanation for setting the Rule-based curve in the reward image. In the simulation process, it can be found that in the early stage of training, due to the setting of collision penalties, the vehicle's lane changing is very frequent, and even shows oscillation phenomenon. With the increase in the number of iterations and the constraint of frequent lane changing penalty, the vehicle can gradually avoid unnecessary lane changing behavior.

Below is a line graph of the reward values for each round in training for the five lane changing methods LC2013, DQN, DoubleDQN, Dueling DQN, and D3QN. Three training sessions were conducted for each method in training, and the results of the three tests were eventually averaged.

As shown in Fig. 6 The total reward value of the four reinforcement learning algorithms is much higher than the rule-based LC2013 method. It proves that GCN can well fuse the information between individual vehicles and allow vehicles to interact. And the use of various types of reinforcement learning algorithms in combination with GCN can improve the performance of lane changing behavior generation. In the Warmup phase, the reward value is low and volatile due to the use of a smaller learning rate and the random generation of the behavior of the self-driving vehicle. After the Warmup phase, the reward value increases rapidly and the fluctuation becomes smaller. However, the reward curves of these four types of reinforcement learning do not show significant differences. From the table, it can be concluded that the average reward of Double DQN is higher than that of DQN; the average rewards of Dueling DQN and D3QN are much higher than that of DQN.This is because the establishment of Dueling Network can better optimize the generation of behavioral decisions of AV.

As shown in Fig. 7 The loss of the four algorithms during the training process decreases as the number of training times increases and converges to a stable value.DQN and Double DQN do not have significant differences in the loss convergence process, but are significantly higher than Dueling DQN. and the convergence speed is relatively slow. After the loss convergence process, the loss curves of the four algorithms are not significantly different. From the table, it can be seen that Dueling DQN has the lowest average loss and there is no significant difference in the average loss between DQN and Double DQN. This result can prove that using Dueling Network optimization strategy can effectively reduce the loss during the training process.

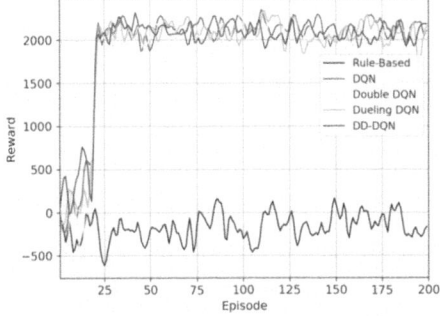

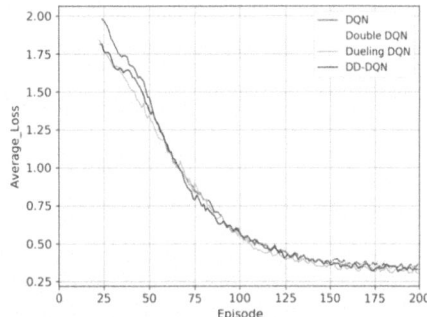

Fig. 6. Reward for five lane changing methods

Fig. 7. Losses for four lane changing methods

Table 5. Average loss for different channelization methods

Loss	Value
DQN	0.712
Double DQN	0.707
Dueling DQN	0.694
Double Dueling DQN	0.692

As can be seen in Fig. 8, the average Q-value increases as the number of trainings increases. However, the four algorithms have different trends in the average Q. The curve of DQN is higher in the later stages, but the average return is relatively low, which is due to the overestimation problem caused by the maximal operator in calculating the target Q. The relatively smooth change of the curve of D3QN suggests that the implementation of Double and Dueling operations can effectively stabilize the Q evaluation. The average Q of the Dueling DQN is is lower than that of DQN, but higher than that of Double DQN and D3QN, indicating that the establishment of Dueling network is also favorable for Q-value evaluation.

After training, we conducted twenty tests of the four GRL algorithms with the same experimental parameter settings. In the simulation process, even in the first round, the test process did not have the same phenomenon of frequent lane changing of vehicles as in rounds 1 and 2 of the training, which proves that the frequent lane changing penalty set in the reward effectively curbed the unnecessary lane changing behavior.

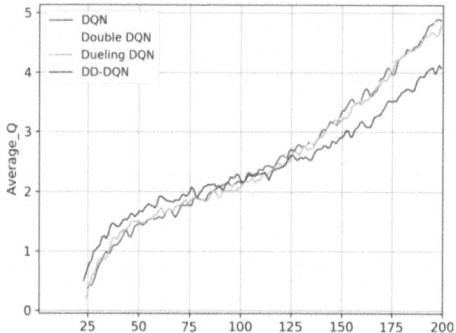

Fig. 8. Average Q of different channelization methods

Table 6. Test reward

Reward	Value
DQN	2053.4779
Double DQN	2055.7757
Dueling DQN	2102.6616
Double Dueling DQN	2165.0412

During the test, the average reward was calculated and the results are shown in Table 6 and the rewards for each round are shown in Fig. 9.

In Table 6, the average test rewards of the four GRL algorithms are the highest for D3QN, and the improved D3QN method gives better results in the constructed traffic scenarios. During the test, the average speed was calculated and the results are shown in the Table and Figure (Fig. 10).

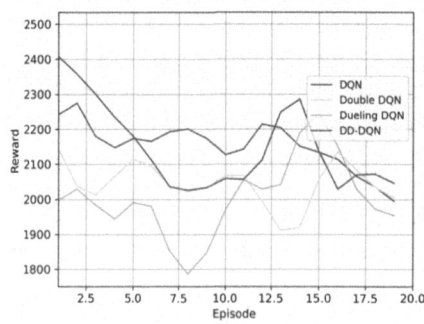

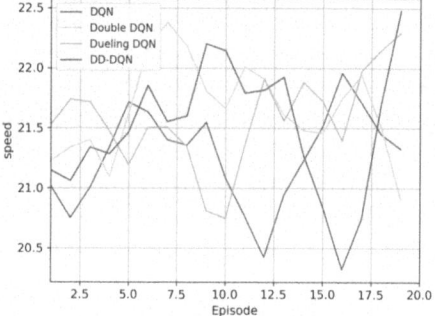

Fig. 9. Testing Reward

Fig. 10. Testing Speed

Table 7. Testing Speed

Speed	Value
DQN	21.2783
Double DQN	21.6193
Dueling DQN	21.5666
Double Dueling DQN	21.5114

In Table 7, Double DQN is the fastest, Dueling DQN and Double Dueling DQN are the next fastest, and DQN is the worst realized, but no gap is created in the average speed of the four GRL algorithms.

Test Results for Different Reward Function Weights. The reward function in this paper (see Equation 17), contains four components: 2 reward types and 2 penalty types. These are intent reward, speed reward, lane change penalty and collision penalty, where:$\omega_1...\omega_4$ are weights that can be adjusted according to the model.When ω_1 and ω_2 dominate compared to ω_3 and ω_4. This setting will encourage vehicles to change lanes to meet the intent, but carries the risk of error-prone and overly aggressive decision making. When ω_3 and ω_4 are greater than ω_1 and ω_2, this means higher penalties for unsafe and frequent lane changing behavior. The model will adopt very conservative and safety-conscious behavior. In order to explore the impact of two different reward function weights, this paper sets up two experiments using DQN as the lane changing decision algorithm, the data of the two experiments are shown in the table, and the experimental results are shown in Figs. 11 and 12

Table 8. First experiment weights

Parameters	First experiment		Second experiment	
	Weights	Value	Weights	Value
R_I	ω_1	3	ω_1	8
R_V	ω_2	0.8	ω_2	3
P_C	ω_3	0.05	ω_3	0.05
P_{LC}	ω_4	0.8	ω_4	0.8

In order to facilitate the comparison of the size of the weights and change, the weights of the two experiments are not normalized, and the size of the reward function of each part of the order of magnitude is not the same, so after changing the weights, the significance of the rewards, losses, and Q-value invalidated, but the average speed of the vehicle and the number of collisions during the training process is still valid and important indicators.

The results exhibited in Figs. 11 and 12 coincide with those previously conjectured.

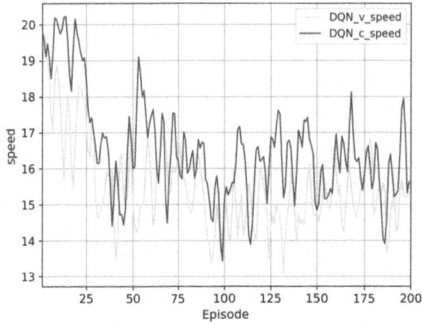

Fig. 11. Velocity of two experiments

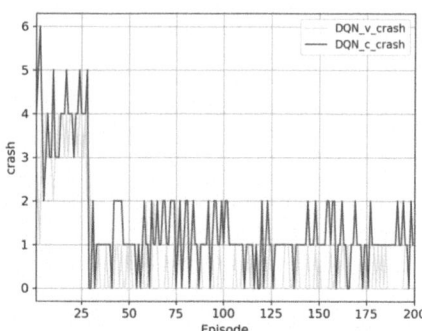

Fig. 12. Number of collisions in two experiments

Different Manual Traffic Flow Test Results. The combined model using GCN and DQN was tested in mixed traffic with different traffic densities. The training in the previous section was performed at a density of $0.3veh/s$ for manual vehicles , $0.2veh/s$ for self-driving vehicles. In this section, the model is tested with different flow rates, with the flow rate of manual vehicles set to $0.1veh/s$, $0.2veh/s$, $0.3veh/s$, $0.4veh/s$, $0.5veh/s$, for a total of 200 rounds of training, and the rest of the settings are the same as in the previous section. Finally, the respective reward values as well as the average speeds for different flows were counted as follows.

Table 9 shows the reward values for different flow rates, and the reward values basically show a climb as the manual vehicle flow rate increases. After the artificial traffic flow changes from $0.3veh/s$ to $0.4veh/s$, there is a relatively large increase in the reward value, presumably because of the fixed number of artificial vehicles set, if the artificial driving vehicle traffic is too large, it will all drive out when the self-driving vehicles are not all present in the environment, resulting in only self-driving vehicles in the later simulation phase. Due to fewer vehicles, there is an increase in speed, which in turn increases the speed bonus, while the collision penalty is almost zero.The average speed gradually increases as the flow rate of manual vehicles increases.

Table 9. First experiment weights

Reward	Value	Speed	Value
DQN_Reward_01	1763.8816	DQN_speed_01	21.4422
DQN_Reward_02	1819.7418	DQN_speed_02	22.0929
DQN_Reward_03	1819.3983	DQN_speed_03	22.1618
DQN_Reward_04	1943.0998	DQN_speed_04	22.6169
DQN_Reward_05	1954.3864	DQN_speed_05	22.6594

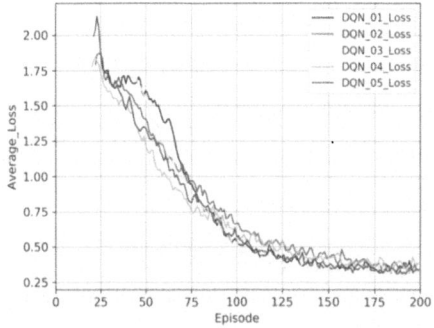

Fig. 13. Average loss

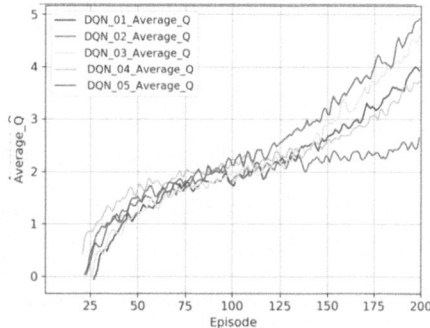

Fig. 14. Average Q

5   Conclusion

In this research, collaborative lane change decision making of multiple automated vehicles in a complex, mixed and highly interactive traffic scene is studied by deep graph neural network combined with reinforcement learning, i.e. GRL. An innovative modular framework, named as GCN-DRL, is proposed which supports different types of combinations of GNN and DRL methods and can be validated in various types of interactive traffic scenarios. Besides, this research proposes a new fusion method based on graph convolutional neural network, which solves the dynamic input size problem by aggregating information from multiple sources with graphical representations. A centralized multi-intelligence body controller is then constructed based on the fused information to make collaborative lane change decisions for a dynamic number of CAVs in a CAV network. Subsequently, the proposed framework is programmed in Ubuntu 20.04 system using python and simulated through SUMO platform to verify the functionality of the proposed framework. Through a series of experiments, the differences between the four different deep reinforcement learning networks were compared by validating them one by one and counting the information of their respective reward value, loss value and Q value. The final results show that the decision-making effect of the method using graph neural network with reinforcement learning is much better than the rule-based LC2013 model, and among the four kinds of reinforcement learning, the best comprehensive effect is Dueling Double DQN,and the worst one is DQN, but the difference between the four is not big.

References

1. Singh, S.: Critical reasons for crashes investigated in the national motor vehicle crash causationsurvey (2019)
2. Gipps, P.G.: A model for the structure of lane-changing decisions. Trans. Res. Part B: Method. **20**(5), 403–414 (1986)
3. Yang, Q.I., Koutsopoulos, H.N.: A microscopic traffic simulator for evaluation of dynamic traffic management systems. Trans. Res. Part C: Emerging Technol. **4**(3), 113–130 (1996)
4. Ahmed, K.I.: Modeling drivers' acceleration and lane changing behavior. Massachusetts Institute of Technology, Cambridge (1999)
5. Toledo, T., Koutsopoulos, H.N., Ben-Akiva, M.: Integrated driving behavior modeling. Trans. Res. Part C Emerging Technol. **15**(2), 96–112 (2007)
6. Schubert, R., Schulze, K., Wanielik, G.: (2010) Situation assessment for automatic lane-change maneuvers. IEEE Trans. Int. Trans. Syst. **11**(3), 607–616 (2010)
7. Erdmann, J.: Lane-changing model in SUMO, Proceedings of the SUMO2014 modeling mobility with open data, **24**, 77-88 (2014)
8. Sallab, A.E., Abdou, M., Perot, E., et al.: Deep reinforcement learning framework for autonomousdriving. Electron. Imaging **26**(19), 70–76 (2017)
9. Huegle,M., Kalweit,G., Mirchevska,B., et al.: Dynamic input for deep reinforcement learningin autonomous driving, In: 32nd IEEE/RSJ International Conference on Intelligent Robotsand Systems (IROS),pp. 7566-7573.IEEE (2019)
10. Ye ,F., Cheng,X., Wang, P., et al.: Automated lane change strategy using proximal policy104 optimization-based deep reinforcement learning, In: 31st IEEE Intelligent Vehicles Sym-posium (IV),pp. 1746-1752. IEEE (2020)
11. Mukadam ,M., Cosgun, A. ,Nakhaei, A., et al.: Tactical decision making for lane changing withdeep reinforcement learning . In:6th International Conference on Learning Representations,(2017)
12. Wang, G., Hu, J., Li, Z., et al.: Harmonious lane changing via deep reinforcement learning. IEEE Trans. Int. Trans. Syst. **23**(5), 4642–4650 (2022)
13. Dong, J., Chen, S., Li, Y., et al.: Space-weighted information fusion using deep reinforcementlearning: the context of tactical control of lane-changing autonomous vehicles and connec-tivity range assessment. Trans. Res. Part C: Emerging Technol. **128**, 103192 (2021)

A Short Term Traffic Prediction Model Based on Deep Capture of Temporal Periodic Drift

Yong Liu[1], Jianxun Cui[1,2]([✉]), and Zhaohua Long[3]

[1] School of Transportation Science and Engineering, Harbin Institute of Technology,
Harbin, China
`cuijianxun@hit.edu.cn`
[2] Chongqing Research Institute of HIT, 618 Liangjiang Avenue, Longxing Town,
Yubei District, Chongqing, China
[3] Chongqing Hualian Zhongzhi Technology Co., Ltd., No.21-1-205, Zhuoyue Road,
Longxing Town, Yubei District, Chongqing, China

Abstract. Accurate prediction of short-term traffic flow is crucial for the control and guidance of urban traffic. This paper proposes a new deep learning traffic flow prediction model, Spatial-Temporal fusion model based on Deformable Convolution (DConv-ST), which deeply captures the spatiotemporal correlations present in the sequences. The model divides the raw data into three types of sequences containing information about recent, daily, and weekly periods. A deformable convolutional module is constructed to solve the problem of temporal periodic drift in the sequence, and graph attention network and multi-head attention mechanism are used to capture local and global spatial correlations. A gated mechanism is used to fuse the results of each component module for output. Experiments including model performance analysis, important component analysis, and ablation analysis were conducted on the publicly available transportation network datasets PeMS04 and PeMS08. The experimental results all demonstrate the superior performance of the proposed model.

Keywords: Short-term traffic flow prediction · Temporal periodic drift · Attention mechanism

1 Introduction

Short-term traffic flow prediction involves forecasting upcoming traffic conditions within a brief time period. This prediction is based on historical traffic data and relevant external factors like weather and events. It covers the short-term prediction of traffic state indicators including speed, flow, density, and congestion status. This field of research tackles fundamental and essential scientific challenges that underlie intelligent transportation applications like regional traffic coordination, route guidance, travel information dissemination, formulation of emergency traffic management strategies, and more.

© ICST Institute for Computer Sciences, Social Informatics and Telecommunications Engineering 2025
Published by Springer Nature Switzerland AG 2025. All Rights Reserved
X. Chen et al. (Eds.): IoTaaS 2023, LNICST 585, pp. 183–199, 2025.
https://doi.org/10.1007/978-3-031-70507-6_15

Despite the impressive predictive performance achieved by deep learning-based short-term traffic flow prediction, only a few studies have taken into consideration the fluctuations inherent in the periodic variations of historical traffic flows, referred to as the temporal periodic drift phenomenon. As an illustration, with the arrival of winter, the timing of evening rush hours gradually shifts earlier, and the peak hours on different days may not align consistently, exhibiting variations across 1-2 time intervals. Failing to comprehensively address this temporal periodic drift phenomenon hinders the potential for further enhancing the predictive performance of deep learning in short-term traffic flow prediction. Conversely, the majority of current research emphasizes capturing spatial correlations within traffic flows predominantly through the adjacency matrix defined by the road network topology. This approach involves the fusion of spatial node features. However, due to the nonlinear and intricate propagation characteristics of urban traffic flows, relying solely on the spatial correlations derived from the existing adjacency relationships defined by road network topology falls short in thoroughly characterizing the diverse and underlying associations among spatial nodes.

To address this, we propose a novel short term traffic prediction model: Spatial-Temporal fusion model based on Deformable Convolution (DConv-ST), driven by the following primary objectives:

- Our approach involved dividing the original data into three distinct sequences, each containing different temporal features. We developed deformable convolution module specifically designed for sequences with daily-periodic and weekly-periodic sequences that display temporal periodic drift. These modules consist of data deformation, linear interpolation, multiple convolutions, and gated outputs, effectively capturing the temporal periodic drift phenomenon inherent in historical traffic flows. This leads to a more robust temporal correlation between predicted and known historical traffic flow sequences.
- Concerning spatial fusion, our strategy aimed to facilitate feature fusion between non-adjacent nodes. Building upon the foundation of graph attention network, which capture local spatial correlations using the road network's adjacency matrix. We also introduced multi-head attention mechanism to capture global spatial correlations. We then integrated a gated mechanism to produce the fused output from both local and global approaches.
- A comprehensive set of experiments were conducted on actual highway traffic datasets, affirming that our model surpasses existing baselines in predictive performance. We performed experiments utilizing diverse variant models and offered in-depth explanations regarding their performance and underlying design principles.

2   Related Works

Constrained by three key factors: the depth of problem understanding, the scale of sample data, and the modeling capacity of forecasting methodologies, the initial phase of short-term traffic state prediction commenced with time series models [9, 16]. These encompassed autoregressive models, moving average models, Autoregressive Moving Average models (ARMA), historical average models, and others. As comprehension grew, the recognition of non-stationarity and non-linearity in traffic flow sequences led to the adoption of techniques like Autoregressive Integrated Moving Average (ARIMA [20]), Generalized Autoregressive Conditional Heteroskedasticity (GARCH), and Kalman Filtering [15] for prediction.

During the 1980s and 1990s, machine learning theory witnessed significant advancement and widespread commercial applications [10]. Pertinent theories like Support Vector Machines (SVM [4]) and Support Vector Regression (SVR [17]) were also applied to road traffic prediction. Additionally, Bayesian methods, K-Nearest Neighbors (KNN [13]), shallow neural networks, and other strategies found application in road traffic prediction.

In the contemporary context, thanks to the availability of abundant traffic big data and the maturity of deep learning theory, the utilization of deep neural networks as the foundational methodology for short-term traffic state prediction has emerged as a prominent and mainstream research pursuit. Models have widely integrated auto-encoders, diverse Convolutional Neural Networks (CNN) [6, 23, 25] (such as 1D causal convolutions, 2D image convolutions, 3D image convolutions), Recurrent Neural Networks (RNN) [3] (like LSTM [8, 14, 27], GRU [1]), hybrid convolutional and recurrent networks [24] (ConvLSTM, PredRNN), and Graph Neural Networks (GNN, including GCN [11], Diffusion Convolution [12], GAT [19]). When combined with deformable convolution networks [2], these models possess the ability to dynamically and flexibly modify the shape of convolutional kernels to accommodate deformation characteristics. Additionally, concepts from the field of neural networks, such as spatiotemporal attention mechanisms [5] and transformers [21, 22], have found extensive application in the study of short-term traffic state prediction.

Current traffic flow models based on spatiotemporal fusion extract temporal and spatial features separately using graph neural networks and temporal models. Yu et al. [25] introduced a method named Spatiotemporal Graph Convolution Model (STGCN), utilizing Temporal-Spatial-Temporal (TST) triple convolution units to simultaneously capture the spatiotemporal features of road networks. The model exhibits excellent performance. Guo et al. [7] proposed ST-3DNet, incorporating 3D convolutions to capture temporal and spatial similarities in traffic data, considering short-term and long-term temporal attributes. Attention mechanisms are also integrated in several models. Zhao et al. [26] introduced STCGAT, primarily composed of node adaptive learning, graph convolutions, and local and global causal temporal convolution modules to collectively learn local and global spatiotemporal dependencies. Guo et al. [5] proposed ASTGCN, which employs three identical components to extract spatiotemporal correlations from input data spanning three distinct historical periods. The final outcomes are obtained through weighted fusion. These components consist of spatiotemporal attention mechanisms, one-dimensional convolutions, and graph convolutions.

3 Methodology

3.1 Problem Definition

Sensors within the road network can be depicted as a graph denoted by $G = (V, E, A)$, in which $V = \{v_1, v_2, \cdots, v_N\}$ signifies the node set and $|V| = N$ denotes the count of nodes; E signifies the set of edges connecting nodes; $A \in \mathbb{R}^{N \times N}$ stands as the adjacency matrix for the graph G. The traffic flow features observed on the graph G at time t are indicated as $\boldsymbol{x}^t \in \mathbb{R}^{N \times C}$, with C being the number of features per node. Assuming historical data from T time periods is utilized to predict data for the future T_p time periods, the objective is to learn a function $f(\cdot)$ to achieve

$$\left[\boldsymbol{x}^{t-T+1}, \boldsymbol{x}^{t-T}, \ldots, \boldsymbol{x}^t; G\right] \xrightarrow{f(\cdot)} \left[\boldsymbol{x}^{t+1}, \boldsymbol{x}^{t+2}, \ldots, \boldsymbol{x}^{t+T_p}\right] \tag{1}$$

3.2 Model Architecture and Data Organization

Fig. 1 presents the overall framework of the DConv-ST model proposed in this paper. The model is comprised of three primary modules. The raw data must be structured into three distinct sequence types: the recent sequence, the daily-periodic sequence, and the weekly-periodic sequence. The model will then individually handle the modeling of these three sequence types.

Given a sampling frequency of q times per day, the current time interval is denoted as t_0, and the historical time periods for the three sequences are labeled as T_r, T_d, and T_w, respectively. The latter two satisfy the conditions $T_d = N_d \cdot (T_p + 2T_{drift})$ and $T_w = N_w \cdot (T_p + 2T_{drift})$, where N_d and N_w correspond to the number of historical days for the daily-periodic sequence and the number of historical weeks for the weekly-periodic sequence, respectively. T_{drift} signifies the length of indirectly related time period data introduced to address the temporal periodic drift issue. The specific formats of these three time sequences are as delineated below:

(1)The recent sequence: $\boldsymbol{\mathcal{X}}_r = \left(\mathbf{X}^1, \mathbf{X}^2, \ldots, \mathbf{X}^N\right) \in \mathbb{R}^{N \times T_r}$, where $\mathbf{X}^n = \left(x_{t_0-T_r+1}^n, x_{t_0-T_r+2}^n, \ldots, x_{t_0}^n\right) \in \mathbb{R}^{T_r}$.

(2)The daily-periodic sequence: $\boldsymbol{\mathcal{X}}_d = \left(\mathbf{X}_d^1, \mathbf{X}_d^2, \ldots, \mathbf{X}_d^N\right)$ $\in \mathbb{R}^{N \times N_d \times (T_p + 2T_{drift})}$, where $\mathbf{X}_d^n = \left(\mathbf{X}_{N_d}^n, \mathbf{X}_{N_d-1}^n, \ldots, \mathbf{X}_1^n\right) =$ $((x_{t_0-N_d \cdot q-T_{drift}+1}^n, \ldots, x_{t_0-N_d \cdot q}^n, x_{t_0-N_d \cdot q+1}^n, \ldots, x_{t_0-N_d \cdot q+T_p}^n, x_{t_0-N_d \cdot q+T_p+1}^n, \ldots, x_{t_0-N_d \cdot q+T_p+T_{drift}}^n), (x_{t_0-(N_d-1) \cdot q-T_{drift}+1}^n, \ldots, x_{t_0-(N_d-1) \cdot q+1}^n, \ldots, x_{t_0-(N_d-1) \cdot q+T_p}^n, x_{t_0-(N_d-1)}, \ldots, x_{t_0-(N_d-1) \cdot q+T_p+T_{drift}}^n), \ldots, (x_{t_0-q-T_{drift}+1}^n, \ldots, x_{t_0-q}^n, x_{t_0-q+1}^n, \ldots, x_{t_0-q+T_p}^n, x_{t_0-q+T_p+1}^n, \ldots, x_{t_0-q+T_p+T_{drift}}^n))$ $\in \mathbb{R}^{N_d \times (T_p + 2T_{drift})}$. $\mathbf{X}_{N_d}^n$ denotes the data of node n from N_d days ago. The subscripts span from $(t_0 - N_d \cdot q - T_{drift} + 1)$ to $(t_0 - N_d \cdot q)$ and from $(t_0 - N_d \cdot q + T_p + 1)$ to $(t_0 - N_d \cdot q + T_p + T_{drift})$, representing indirectly related time period data at both ends with a length of T_{drift}. The subscripts from $(t_0 - N_d \cdot q + 1)$ to $(t_0 - N_d \cdot q + T_p)$ correspond to directly related time period

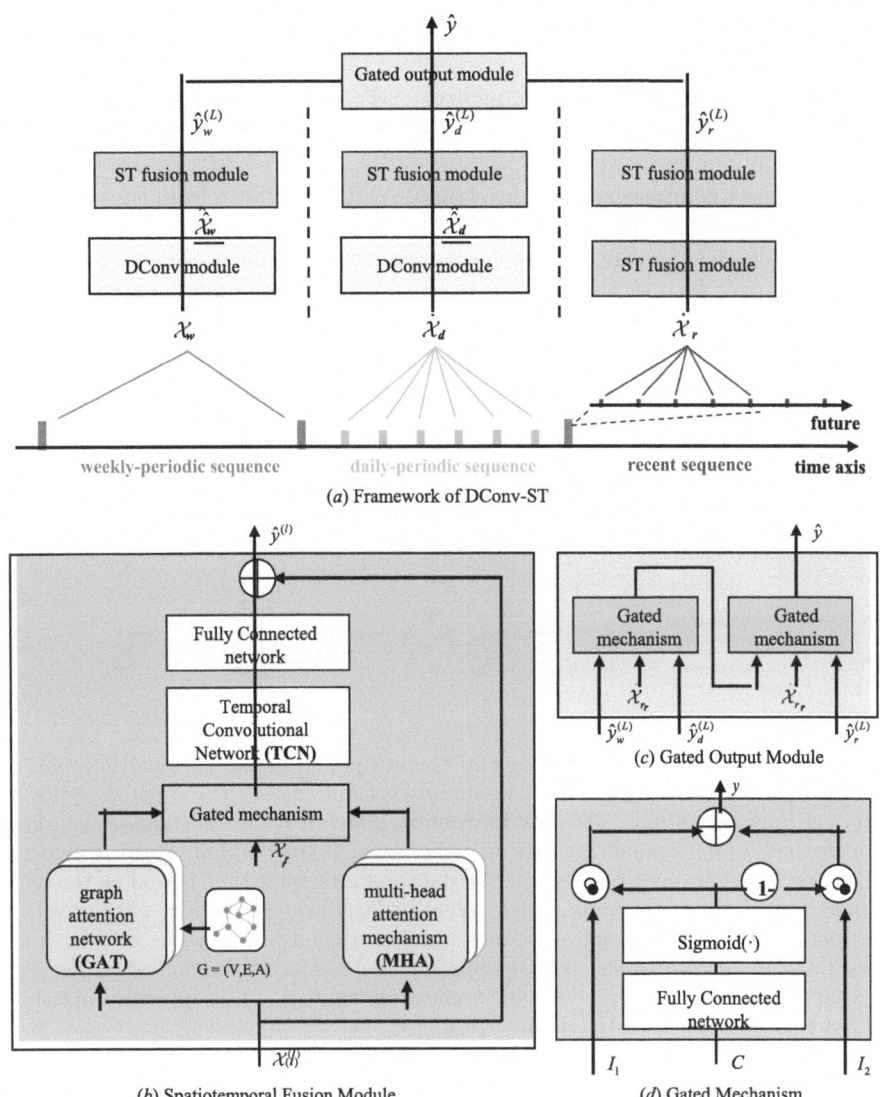

Fig. 1. The overall framework and main modules of DConv-ST. (a) The framework of DConv-ST. The three main modules are: the spatiotemporal fusion module (ST fusion module), the deformable convolution module (DConv module), and the Gated output module. (b) Spatiotemporal fusion module, including spatial fusion and temporal fusion. (c) Gated output module, which fuses the results of three sequences. (d) Gated Mechanism, used to implement gated output module.

data with a length of T_p. The representation of data for other historical days follows a similar pattern.

(3)The weekly-periodic sequence: $\boldsymbol{\mathcal{X}}_w = (\mathbf{X}_w^1, \mathbf{X}_w^2, \ldots, \mathbf{X}_w^N)$ $\in \mathbb{R}^{N \times N_w \times (T_p + 2T_{drift})}$, where $\mathbf{X}_w^n = (\mathrm{X}_{N_w}^n, \mathrm{X}_{N_w-1}^n, \ldots, \mathrm{X}_1^n)$. Its form is similar to the daily-periodic sequence.

It's crucial to emphasize that the structured data deviates from the depiction in Eq.1 in two distinct manners: firstly, there's a reversal in the order of dimensions between the number of time periods and the number of nodes; secondly, the dimension of feature number C is fixed at 1, signifying that the model learns and predicts only one feature (flow, speed, density) at a time, necessitating the establishment of distinct models for different features. Fig. 2 visually illustrates the process of organizing raw data into a set of data.

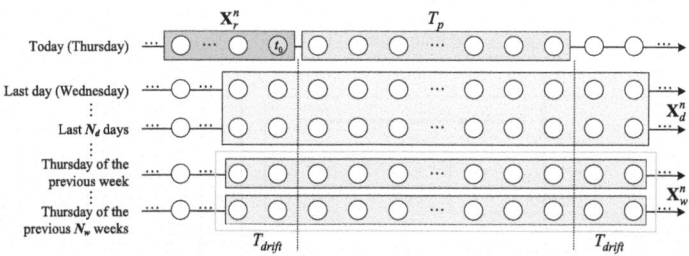

Fig. 2. In each data set, the subsequent T_p data points of the current time period are taken as the prediction target. The input data consists of three different types of historical time period data: **Recent Sequence**, which involves the time period data from the last T_r data points leading up to the current time period. **Daily-Periodic Sequence**, which involves the time period data from the same time period on the days ranging from 1 day ago to N_d days ago. **Weekly-Periodic Sequence**, which involves the time period data from the same day and time period in the weeks ranging from 1 week ago to N_w weeks ago. Furthermore, on both sides of the daily-periodic and weekly-periodic sequence, an additional segment of length T_{drift} is appended, which is utilized to address temporal periodic drift issues.

3.3   Deformable Convolution Module

The role of the deformable convolution module serves a dual purpose. Firstly, it tackles the challenge of temporal periodic drift within the sequences by modifying the dimensions and structures of the daily-periodic and the weekly-periodic sequence, ensuring their smooth incorporation through the spatiotemporal fusion module. Secondly, this module can capture the spatiotemporal traits intrinsic to these two sequences, setting them apart from the recent sequence. For instance, it has the ability to capture the periodic patterns existing between distinct days and weeks.

Taking the deformable convolution process of the daily-periodic sequence as an example (as shown in Fig. 3). First, the input sequence undergoes a deformation process. Let's use the data of one node as an illustration:

$$\mathbf{X}_{d,p}^{n(deform)} = \sum_{p_n \in \mathcal{R}} h\left(p_n, T_{drift} \cdot \sigma_t\left(M_{d,p}\right)\right) \cdot \mathbf{X}_{d,p+T_{drift}+p_n}^{n} \tag{2}$$

where $\mathcal{R} = \{-T_{drift}, -(T_{drift} - 1), \ldots, -1, 0, 1, \ldots, T_{drift} - 1, T_{drift}\}$, $d = 1, 2,$ $\ldots, N_d$, and $p = 1, 2, \ldots, T_p$. The matrix $M \in \mathbb{R}^{N_d \times T_p}$ serves as the offset matrix. Initially, all its elements are initialized to 0, and they are subsequently updated during model learning, constituting the parameters that the model must acquire. Denoted as $\sigma_t(\cdot)$, the activation function is chosen as the hyperbolic tangent function $\tanh(\cdot)$, generating outputs within the range of -1 to 1. $h(\cdot, \cdot)$ stands for the linear interpolation function, defined as $h(a, b) = \max(0, 1 - |a - b|)$.

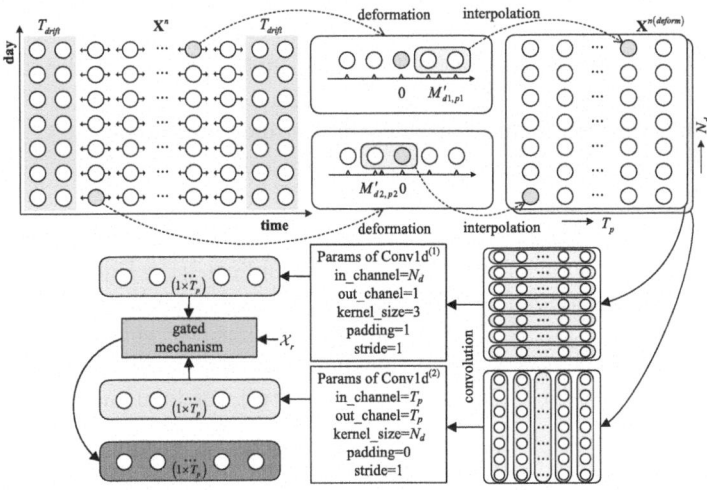

Fig. 3. An example diagram of the deformable convolution process for the daily-periodic sequence. It mainly includes four operations: deformation, interpolation, convolution, and gated output.

The process mentioned above is depicted in the upper section of Fig. 3, where $M'_{d,p} = T_{drift} \cdot \sigma_t(M_{d,p})$, and each $M'_{d,p}$ is confined within the range of $(-T_{drift}, T_{drift})$. By interpolating the data corresponding to the positions resulting from rounding this value both upwards and downwards, the modified result is obtained. Through the process of deformation and interpolation, the dimensions of the input data transform from $\mathbf{X}^n \in \mathbb{R}^{N_d \times (T_p + 2T_{drift})}$ to $\mathbf{X}^{n(deform)} \in \mathbb{R}^{N_d \times T_p}$, incorporating the relevant segment of indirectly related time period data into the directly related time period data. This procedure contributes to mitigating the temporal periodic drift issue inherently present in the sequence, to some extent.

The deformed sequence yields a two-dimensional array denoted as $\mathbf{X}^{n(deform)}$. Along its dimension of length T_p, it represents traffic feature data from historical days that correspond to the same time intervals as the prediction period, after addressing the temporal periodic drift issue. Hence, one-dimensional convolution is employed to capture the changing characteristics of the time sequence. Along its dimension of length N_d, it represents traffic data for the same time intervals across different days. Recognizing that traffic flow characteristics between distinct days can exhibit fluctuations and divergent relevance levels to the features of the target period, one-dimensional convolution is employed to attribute distinct weights to different days. The process of implementation is outlined as follows:

$$\boldsymbol{\mathcal{X}}_d^{(d)} = \|_{n=1}^N \mathrm{Conv1d}^{(1)} \left(\|_{d=1}^{N_d} \mathbf{X}_{d,:}^{n(deform)} \right) \tag{3}$$

$$\boldsymbol{\mathcal{X}}_d^{(p)} = \|_{n=1}^N \mathrm{Conv1d}^{(2)} \left(\|_{p=1}^{T_p} \mathbf{X}_{:,p}^{n(deform)} \right) \tag{4}$$

where $\|$ signifies the concatenation of outputs. The chosen parameters for one-dimensional convolution and linear weighting must ensure that the dimensions of the results satisfy $\boldsymbol{\mathcal{X}}_d^{(d)}, \boldsymbol{\mathcal{X}}_d^{(p)} \in \mathbb{R}^{N \times T_p}$. Ultimately, the integration of the two results occurs through a gated mechanism, outlined as follows:

$$G\left(C, I_1, I_2\right) = I_1 \odot \sigma_s(C \cdot W_g + b_g) + I_2 \odot (1 - \sigma_s(C \cdot W_g + b_g)) \tag{5}$$

where I_1 and I_2 denote the inputs, representing the two sets of data to be fused, while C is the control parameter. The symbol $\odot$ indicates the Hadamard product. The activation function $\sigma_s(\cdot)$ is chosen to be the sigmoid function. The matrices $W_g \in \mathbb{R}^{T_r \times T_p}$ and $b_g \in \mathbb{R}^{N \times T_p}$ are utilized for linearly weighting the control parameter. These matrices are dynamically adjusted through model learning to regulate the two input sets. Utilizing $\boldsymbol{\mathcal{X}}_r$ for control, the final output after gating is as follows:

$$\hat{\boldsymbol{\mathcal{X}}}_d = G\left(\boldsymbol{\mathcal{X}}_r, \boldsymbol{\mathcal{X}}_d^{(d)}, \boldsymbol{\mathcal{X}}_d^{(p)}\right) \tag{6}$$

3.4   Spatiotemporal Fusion Module

The spatiotemporal fusion module consists of two main components: spatial fusion and temporal fusion. Let the input for the l-th spatiotemporal fusion module be denoted as $\boldsymbol{\mathcal{X}}^{(l)} \in \mathbb{R}^{N \times T_{in}^{(l)}}$, and its output as $\hat{\boldsymbol{y}}^{(l)} \in \mathbb{R}^{N \times T_{out}^{(l)}}$. This implies that $\boldsymbol{\mathcal{X}}^{(l+1)} = \hat{\boldsymbol{y}}^{(l)}$ and $T_{in}^{(l+1)} = T_{out}^{(l)}$. The three sets of sequences passing through the spatiotemporal fusion modules share the same structure. Specifically, the inputs entering the first spatiotemporal fusion module are $\boldsymbol{\mathcal{X}}_r^{(1)} = \boldsymbol{\mathcal{X}}_r \in \mathbb{R}^{N \times T_r}$, $\boldsymbol{\mathcal{X}}_d^{(1)} = \hat{\boldsymbol{\mathcal{X}}}_d \in \mathbb{R}^{N \times T_p}$, and $\boldsymbol{\mathcal{X}}_w^{(1)} = \hat{\boldsymbol{\mathcal{X}}}_w \in \mathbb{R}^{N \times T_p}$.

In the l-th spatiotemporal fusion module, let the inputs and outputs of the spatial and temporal fusion modules be represented as $\boldsymbol{\mathcal{X}}^{s(l)}, \hat{\boldsymbol{y}}^{s(l)}, \boldsymbol{\mathcal{X}}^{t(l)}$, and $\hat{\boldsymbol{y}}^{t(l)}$ respectively. This leads to $\boldsymbol{\mathcal{X}}^{s(l)} = \boldsymbol{\mathcal{X}}^{(l)}$ and $\hat{\boldsymbol{y}}^{t(l)} = \hat{\boldsymbol{y}}^{(l)}$. Since the spatial and temporal fusion modules are directly linked, we have $\boldsymbol{\mathcal{X}}^{t(l)} = \hat{\boldsymbol{y}}^{s(l)}$, with its dimension set as $\mathbb{R}^{N \times T_{hid}^{(l)}}$.

Spatial Fusion Module Within the spatial fusion module, both graph attention network(GAT) and multi-head attention mechanism(MHA) are utilized to aggregate distinctively the local and the global spatial correlations of the graph.

Within the framework of GAT , node features are merged based on the adjacency matrix associated with each node, enabling the capture of immediate spatial correlations among nodes. The procedural execution is outlined as follows: For the node i in the graph, calculate the similarity coefficients $S_{i,j}$ and the attention coefficient matrix S' between it and its neighboring nodes $\mathcal{N}_i$ one by one:

$$S_{i,j} = [\boldsymbol{h}_i \| \boldsymbol{h}_j] \cdot a, j \in \mathcal{N}_i \tag{7}$$

$$S'_{i,j} = \begin{cases} \frac{\exp(\text{LeakyReLU}(S_{i,j}))}{\sum_{k \in \mathcal{N}_i} \exp(\text{LeakyReLU}(S_{i,k}))} & j \in \mathcal{N}_i \\ 0 & j \notin \mathcal{N}_i \end{cases} \tag{8}$$

where $\boldsymbol{h}$ denotes the input sequence following feature enhancement and $\boldsymbol{h} = \boldsymbol{\mathcal{X}}^{s(l)} W_a \in \mathbb{R}^{N \times T'}$. The operation $[\cdot \| \cdot]$ concatenates the features transformed from node i and node j. Subsequently, through the mapping a, a scalar is generated, representing the similarity coefficient between them. This coefficient is then employed to calculate the attention coefficient matrix $S' \in \mathbb{R}^{N \times N}$. Then, the outcome of feature fusion is achieved by weighting $\boldsymbol{h}$ using this matrix:

$$g\left(\boldsymbol{\mathcal{X}}^{s(l)}, \mathcal{N}\right) = \|_{i=1}^N \left(S'_{i,:} \cdot \boldsymbol{h} + b_a\right) \in \mathbb{R}^{N \times T'} \tag{9}$$

where $b_a \in \mathbb{R}^{1 \times T'}$. With the introduction of the Multi-Head concept, a spatial fusion module incorporates K graph attention networks, and the resulting outputs are as depicted:

$$\hat{\boldsymbol{y}}_{gat}^{(l)} = g\left(\|_{k=1}^K g_{(k)}\left(\boldsymbol{\mathcal{X}}^{s(l)}, \mathcal{N}\right), \mathcal{N}\right) \in \mathbb{R}^{N \times T_{hid}^{(l)}} \tag{10}$$

where $g_{(k)}(\cdot, \cdot)$ corresponds to the network at the k-th head. Each distinct head within the network undergoes training using separate parameter sets W_a and a. The concatenated outcomes from all these individual heads result in a dimensionality of $\mathbb{R}^{N \times KT'}$. This combined output is employed as input for an additional GAT, where T' is configured to match $T_{hid}^{(l)}$ within this specific network.

MHA dispenses with the necessity for a predefined adjacency matrix; it can dynamically learn a matrix for the purpose of fusion. It conducts fusion based on the pairwise similarity between each node and others, thereby capturing global and latent spatial correlations. The procedural sequence is outlined as follows: Given the input $\boldsymbol{\mathcal{X}}^{s(l)}$, three distinct subspaces are derived: the query subspace $Q \in \mathbb{R}^{N \times t_q}$, the key subspace $K \in \mathbb{R}^{N \times t_k}$, and the value subspace $V \in \mathbb{R}^{N \times t_v}$. The method to obtain them is elucidated as follows:

$$Q = \boldsymbol{\mathcal{X}}^{s(l)} W^Q, K = \boldsymbol{\mathcal{X}}^{s(l)} W^K, V = \boldsymbol{\mathcal{X}}^{s(l)} W^V \tag{11}$$

The output obtained through the calculation using Scaled Dot-Product Attention is as follows:

$$\text{Attention}(Q, K, V) = \text{softmax}\left(\frac{QK^T}{\sqrt{t_k}}\right) V \tag{12}$$

It's important to highlight that the dimensions of Q and K must fulfill the condition $t_q = t_k$. When incorporating the notion of multi-head, the resulting output from MHA is as follows:

$$\hat{\boldsymbol{y}}_{mha}^{(l)} = \left(\|_{h=1}^{H} \mathrm{head}_i\right) W^O \in \mathbb{R}^{N \times T_{hid}^{(l)}} \tag{13}$$

where each head, denoted as $\mathrm{head}_i = \mathrm{Attention}\,(Q_i, K_i, V_i)$, operates independently. Also, the matrix $W^O \in \mathbb{R}^{H \cdot t_v \times T_{hid}^{(l)}}$ is selected to ensure the output dimension matches that of GAT.

Finally, resembling the gated mechanism used in the deformable convolution module, the linearly weighted outcome $\boldsymbol{X}_r$ is utilized to regulate the fusion process between the outputs of GAT and MHA. This procedure is executed as outlined below:

$$\hat{\boldsymbol{y}}^{s(l)} = G_s \left(\boldsymbol{X}_r, \hat{\boldsymbol{y}}_{gat}^{(l)}, \hat{\boldsymbol{y}}_{mha}^{(l)}\right) \tag{14}$$

where the implementation of the gated mechanism $G_s\,(\cdot, \cdot, \cdot)$ is presented in Eq.5, with distinct parameters W_g and b_g that are not shared with other gated mechanisms.

Temporal Fusion Module The temporal fusion module predominantly employs a Temporal Convolutional Network (TCN) for its execution. For a specific node data $\boldsymbol{X}_{n,:}^{t(l)} \in \mathbb{R}^{T_{hid}^{(l)}}$ within the input sequence of this module, and a set of filters $F = \{f_1, f_2, \ldots, f_K\}$, the dilated convolution with dilation factor d at position $\boldsymbol{X}_{n,\tau}^{t(l)}$ within the sequence $\boldsymbol{X}_{n,:}^{t(l)}$ is expressed as:

$$\left(F *_d \boldsymbol{X}_n^{t(l)}\right)(\tau) = \sum_{k=1}^{K} f_k \cdot \boldsymbol{X}_{n,\tau-d(K-k)}^{t(l)} \tag{15}$$

Each node's sequence is individually processed by a TCN, and then passed through two linear layers to more comprehensively incorporate historical temporal information.

3.5   Gated Output Module

After each of the three temporal sequences has passed through the spatiotemporal fusion module for all L layers, the outputs $\hat{\boldsymbol{y}}_r^{(L)}$, $\hat{\boldsymbol{y}}_d^{(L)}$, and $\hat{\boldsymbol{y}}_w^{(L)}$ undergo fusion via the gated mechanism. Since gating typically involves two data sets, the gating fusion process is initially applied to $\hat{\boldsymbol{y}}_d^{(L)}$ and $\hat{\boldsymbol{y}}_w^{(L)}$, owing to their shared characteristics - both having been subject to processing through the deformable convolution module and possessing historical cyclic features. Subsequently, the outcome of this fusion is further combined through gating with $\hat{\boldsymbol{y}}_r^{(L)}$. Similarly, the adjacent temporal sequences $\boldsymbol{X}_r$ are employed as control values for these two gating operations. The ultimate output of the entire model, denoted as $\hat{\boldsymbol{y}}$, is then derived as follows:

$$\hat{\boldsymbol{y}} = G_{o2} \left(\boldsymbol{X}_r, \hat{\boldsymbol{y}}_r^{(L)}, G_{o1} \left(\boldsymbol{X}_r, \hat{\boldsymbol{y}}_d^{(L)}, \hat{\boldsymbol{y}}_w^{(L)}\right)\right) \tag{16}$$

where the definitions of the gating functions $G_{o1}(\cdot,\cdot,\cdot)$ and $G_{o2}(\cdot,\cdot,\cdot)$ can be found in Eq.5. The linear weighting parameters, W_{o1} and W_{o2}, belong to the space $\mathbb{R}^{T_{out}^{(L)} \times T_p}$, while b_{o1} and b_{o2} belong to $\mathbb{R}^{N \times T_p}$.

4   Experiment

In order to assess the effectiveness of DConv-ST, a range of experiments were formulated. These encompassed evaluating the performance of the DConv-ST model itself, conducting experiments with variant models, and performing ablation analyses. These experiments were conducted on two highway traffic datasets, PeMS04 and PeMS08, both originating from California, USA.

4.1   Datasets

The data for PeMS04 is derived from 3,848 sensors situated along 29 roadways within the San Francisco Bay Area. This dataset covers the time span from January 1st to February 28th, 2018. The data for PeMS08, on the other hand, is collected from 1,979 sensors positioned along 8 roadways in San Bernardino, spanning from July 1st to August 31st, 2016. Following the elimination of redundant sensors, each dataset retains information from 307 and 170 sensors respectively. Additionally, these datasets incorporate adjacency details among the sensors. The original data is aggregated into 5-minute intervals, capturing three key attributes: total flow, average speed, and average occupancy.

4.2   Settings

When it comes to data processing, linear interpolation is employed to address missing data. The selected predictive feature is traffic flow. When structuring the data into the desired sequence format, the parameters are configured as follows: $T_r = 12$, $N_d = 7$, $N_w = 4$. The introduction of indirectly related time period data brings a length of $T_{drift} = 3$, while the prediction interval extends for $T_p = 12$, signifying the aim to forecast traffic flow for the upcoming hour. Following this organization, the PeMS04 dataset yields a total of 8914 data sets, and the PeMS08 dataset produces 9778 data sets. The dataset is partitioned into three segments, allocating 60% for training, 20% for validation, and 20% for testing. Standardization is implemented on the sequences $\mathcal{X}_r$, $\mathcal{X}_d$, and $\mathcal{X}_w$ within each subset using the formula $x' = (x - \text{mean}(x))/\text{std}(x)$.

The DConv-ST model is instantiated within the PyTorch framework. For this model, the layers in the spatiotemporal fusion module are configured as 2 for $\mathcal{X}_r$, 1 for $\mathcal{X}_d$, and 1 for $\mathcal{X}_w$ sub-models, respectively. In the last two sub-models, the deformable convolution module consists of a single layer. Throughout the model training process, the Mean Squared Error (MSE) serves as the loss function, and the backpropagation algorithm is applied to minimize the discrepancy between predicted and true values. During training, the batch size is 16, and the learning rate is 0.001.

4.3   Baselines

We compare DConv-ST with the following ten baselines:

- HA: Historical Average method.
- ARIMA : Autoregressive Integrated Moving Average method.
- VAR: Vector Autoregression model. It can capture relationships among all traffic flow sequences.
- LSTM [8]: Long Short-Term Memory network. It's a special type of gated RNN model.
- GRU [1]: Gated Recurrent Unit network. It incorporates learnable gate mechanisms and is a variation of LSTM.
- DCRNN [12]: Diffusion Convolutional Recurrent Neural Network. It simulates the information diffusion process using random walks on graphs and employs gated recurrent units to build a sequence-to-sequence model.
- STGCN [25]: Spatio-Temporal Graph Convolutional Network. It replaces RNN with 1D causal convolutions for temporal dependencies and employs spectral graph convolutions for spatial dependencies.
- STSGCN [18]: Spatio-Temporal Synchronous Graph Convolutional Network. It introduces a synchronous modeling mechanism to capture complex local spatio-temporal dependencies.
- MSTGCN, ASTGCN [5]: The latter is Attention-based Spatio-Temporal Graph Convolutional Network. MSTGCN removes the spatio-temporal attention module from ASTGCN.

Root Mean Square Error (RMSE) and Mean Absolute Error (MAE) are chosen as evaluation metrics in the experiments.

4.4   Experimental Results

Performance Comparison The performance of DConv-ST was assessed against ten baselines using the PeMS04 and PeMS08 datasets. Table 1 showcases the RMSE and MAE outcomes for each model when forecasting traffic flow for the upcoming hour (12 time intervals, excluding HA). It is evident that the proposed DConv-ST model surpasses all other models across various evaluation metrics on both datasets. In comparison to traditional time series analysis methods, deep learning-based models exhibit superior overall performance and stronger feature capturing capabilities, making them more advantageous in handling highly nonlinear and complex traffic data. Particularly noteworthy are models that account for both spatial and temporal correlations, encompassing the last four baselines and the DConv-ST model introduced in this study. They consistently outperform traditional deep learning models such as LSTM and GRU. In contrast to ASTGCN, which also employs attention mechanisms, our model showcases reduced errors. This is partially attributed to the incorporation of deformable convolution modules, augmenting the model's precision in capturing spatiotemporal features.

Table 1. The performance of the 10 selected baselines and DConv-ST on the PeMS04 and PeMS08 datasets. DConv-ST model surpasses all other baselines across various evaluation metrics on both datasets.

Models	PeMS04		PeMS08	
	RMSE	**MAE**	**RMSE**	**MAE**
HA	54.14	36.76	44.03	29.52
ARIMA	68.13	32.11	43.30	24.04
VAR	51.73	33.76	31.21	21.41
LSTM	45.82	29.45	36.96	23.18
GRU	45.11	28.65	35.95	22.20
DCRNN	38.12	24.70	28.83	19.86
STGCN	35.55	22.70	27.87	18.88
STSGCN	33.65	21.19	26.80	17.13
MSTGCN	35.64	22.73	26.47	17.47
ASTGCN	32.82	21.80	25.27	16.63
DConv-ST (ours)	**31.59**	**19.78**	**24.49**	**15.71**

Component Analysis The performance of deformable convolution modules and spatial fusion methods was investigated on the PeMS04 dataset.

Influence of Deformable Convolution Module In order to investigate the influence of deformable convolution modules on model performance, three sets of control experiments were carried out. The outcomes are depicted in Table 2. The incorporation of deformable convolution module leads to a reduction in prediction errors. Specifically, for the $\mathcal{X}_d$ sub-model, the RMSE and MAE decreased by 4.64% and 4.47% respectively. In the case of the $\mathcal{X}_w$ sub-model, these two metrics experienced minimal decreases, amounting to 0.89% and 1.42% respectively. The substitution of deformable convolution modules within the DConv-ST model corroborates this finding, resulting in respective metric reductions of 1.77% and 2.75%. When comparing these outcomes to the predictions of AST-GCN in Table 1, the errors of the fusion model utilizing standard convolutions closely align. This observation partially suggests that relying solely on attention mechanisms and convolution operations isn't sufficient for achieving further reductions in model errors. The deformable convolution module we devised contribute to an improved precision in traffic flow prediction results.

Methods of Spatial Fusion An investigation was conducted into the spatial fusion methods using GAT and MHA, and the results are presented in Table 3. Observing the results from the sub-models, it becomes apparent that the global spatial fusion using MHA tends to yield superior performance in the majority of cases. In contrast to the local spatial fusion accomplished by GAT, the global fusion process entails the consideration of features from all nodes within the road network. However, when dealing with substantial amounts of data, this approach

Table 2. Experimental results on the impact of deformable convolution modules on model performance. The first four rows present outcomes derived solely from the $\mathcal{X}_d$ and $\mathcal{X}_w$ sub-models, whereas the last two rows exhibit results generated by the fusion model. The terms (conv) and (dconv) signify whether the model utilizes conventional convolution modules (one-dimensional convolutions) or deformable convolution modules.

Models	RMSE	MAE
$\mathcal{X}_d$(conv)	34.90	22.35
$\mathcal{X}_d$(dconv)	33.28	21.35
$\mathcal{X}_w$(conv)	33.80	21.74
$\mathcal{X}_w$(dconv)	33.50	21.43
$\mathcal{X}_r$ - $\mathcal{X}_d$ (conv) - $\mathcal{X}_w$(conv)	32.16	20.34
$\mathcal{X}_r$ - $\mathcal{X}_d$ **(dconv)** - $\mathcal{X}_w$**(dconv)** **(DConv-ST)**	**31.59**	**19.78**

might encounter difficulties in accurately capturing crucial information, potentially leading to comparatively diminished performance within the fusion model. Analyzing the experimental results of the fusion model reveals that simultaneous utilization of both spatial fusion methods leads to a reduction of 2.11% and 8.06% in RMSE compared to models that exclusively employ GAT or MHA for spatial fusion, respectively.

Ablation Study Additionally, the effectiveness of individual components within the DConv-ST model was verified through ablation experiments, and the resulting RMSE and MAE outcomes are visualized in Fig. 4. Models that exclusively utilize recent sequences, lacking daily-period and weekly-period information, demonstrate the weakest performance across all models. Their performance steeply declines as the prediction interval increases, reflecting the fact that the enhanced historical information is contained within daily-period and weekly-period sequences. The outcomes of the other three ablation experiments consistently exhibit improved short-term predictive capabilities. However, as the prediction interval extends, their stability diminishes. Notably, when the prediction interval reaches 60 minutes, their performance distinctly diverges from that of DConv-ST. Our DConv-ST model integrates recent, daily-period and weekly-period sequences. It addresses temporal periodic drift issues through deformable convolution modules, and captures both global and local spatial correlations among road network nodes. This holistic approach enhances the accuracy and resilience of prediction outcomes.

Table 3. Experimental results on the impact of spatial fusion methods on model performance. The terms (gat) and (mha) respectively denote models that solely utilize GAT local spatial fusion and MHA global spatial fusion, and (gat & mha) represents the model that simultaneously employs both spatial fusion methods.

	Models	RMSE	MAE
Sub-models	$\mathcal{X}_r$(gat)	39.96	26.11
	$\mathcal{X}_r$(mha)	38.17	24.60
	$\mathcal{X}_r$(**gat & mha**)	34.47	22.31
	$\mathcal{X}_d$(gat)	34.71	22.19
	$\mathcal{X}_d$(mha)	34.36	21.90
	$\mathcal{X}_d$(**gat & mha**)	33.28	21.35
	$\mathcal{X}_w$(gat)	32.22	20.22
	$\mathcal{X}_w$(mha)	33.12	20.90
	$\mathcal{X}_w$(**gat & mha**)	32.84	20.72
Fusion models	$\mathcal{X}_r$ - $\mathcal{X}_d$ - $\mathcal{X}_w$ (gat)	32.27	20.23
	$\mathcal{X}_r$ - $\mathcal{X}_d$ - $\mathcal{X}_w$ (mha)	34.36	21.90
	$\mathcal{X}_r$ - $\mathcal{X}_d$ - $\mathcal{X}_w$ (**gat & mha**) (**DConv-ST**)	**31.59**	**19.78**

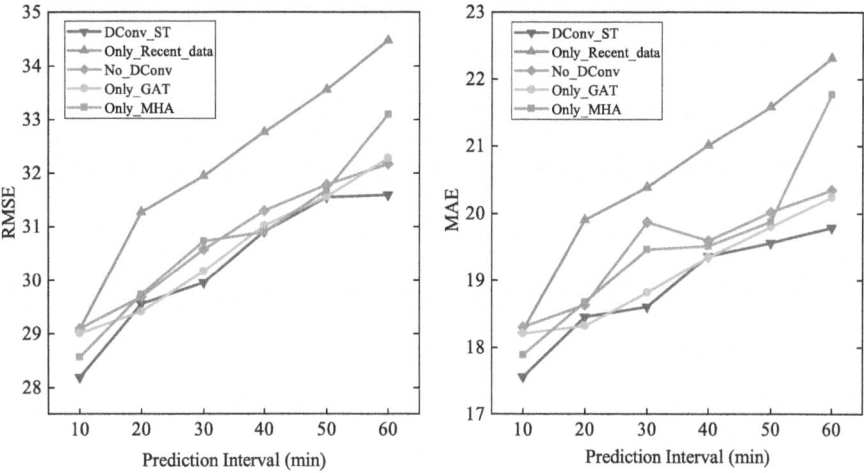

Fig. 4. The graph depicting RMSE and MAE results obtained from the ablation experiments. The experiments encompassed five scenarios: using only recent sequences (Only_Recent_data), omitting deformable convolution module (No_DConv), using only GAT for local spatial fusion (Only_GAT), using only MHA for global spatial fusion (Only_MHA), and using the complete DConv-ST model. Training and multi-step traffic flow prediction were executed using the PeMS04 dataset.

5   Conclusion

In this paper, we construct the DConv-ST short-term traffic flow prediction model. The model mainly consists of three modules: the deformable convolution module, the spatiotemporal fusion module, and the gated output module. Among them, the deformable convolution module is used to address the issue of temporal periodic drift in sequences. The spatiotemporal fusion module employs graph attention networks, multi-head attention mechanisms, and temporal convolutional networks to capture deep latent spatiotemporal correlations. The gated output module combines the results of the three types of sequences for fused output. Experimental results demonstrate that the DConv-ST model outperforms the baseline models, with the deformable convolution module and spatiotemporal fusion module playing crucial roles in enhancing model performance.

References

1. Chung, J., Gulcehre, C., Cho, K., Bengio, Y.: Empirical evaluation of gated recurrent neural networks on sequence modeling. arXiv preprint arXiv:1412.3555 (2014)
2. Dai, J., Qi, H. et al.: Deformable convolutional networks. In: Proceedings of the IEEE international conference on computer vision. pp. 764–773 (2017)
3. Elman, J.L.: Finding structure in time. Cogn. Sci. **14**(2), 179–211 (1990)
4. Evgeniou, T., Pontil, M., Poggio, T.: Regularization networks and support vector machines. Adv. Comput. Math. **13**, 1–50 (2000)
5. Guo, S., Lin, Y., Feng, N., Song, C., Wan, H.: Attention based spatial-temporal graph convolutional networks for traffic flow forecasting. Proc. AAAI Conf. Artif. Int. **33**, 922–929 (2019)
6. Guo, S., Lin, Y., Li, S., Chen, Z., Wan, H.: Deep spatial-temporal 3d convolutional neural networks for traffic data forecasting. IEEE Trans. Intell. Transp. Syst. **20**(10), 3913–3926 (2019)
7. Guo, S., Lin, Y., Li, S., Chen, Z., Wan, H.: Deep spatial-temporal 3d convolutional neural networks for traffic data forecasting. IEEE Trans. Intell. Transp. Syst. **20**(10), 3913–3926 (2019)
8. Hochreiter, S., Schmidhuber, J.: Long short-term memory. Neural Comput. **9**(8), 1735–1780 (1997)
9. Kamarianakis, Y., Prastacos, P.: Forecasting traffic flow conditions in an urban network: comparison of multivariate and univariate approaches. Transp. Res. Rec. **1857**(1), 74–84 (2003)
10. Karlaftis, M.G., Vlahogianni, E.I.: Statistical methods versus neural networks in transportation research: differences, similarities and some insights. Trans. Res. Part C: Emerging Technol. **19**(3), 387–399 (2011)
11. Kipf, T.N., Welling, M.: Semi-supervised classification with graph convolutional networks. arXiv preprint arXiv:1609.02907 (2016)
12. Li, Y., Yu, R., Shahabi, C., Liu, Y.: Diffusion convolutional recurrent neural network: Data-driven traffic forecasting. arXiv preprint arXiv:1707.01926 (2017)
13. Luo, X., Li, D., Yang, Y., Zhang, S., et al.: Spatiotemporal traffic flow prediction with KNN and ISTM. J. Adv. Trans. **2019**(1), 4145353 (2019)
14. Ma, X., Tao, Z., Wang, Y., Yu, H., Wang, Y.: Long short-term memory neural network for traffic speed prediction using remote microwave sensor data. Trans. Res. Part C: Emerging Technol. **54**, 187–197 (2015)

15. Mir, Z.H., Filali, F.: An adaptive kalman filter based traffic prediction algorithm for urban road network. In: 2016 12th International Conference on Innovations in Information Technology (IIT). pp. 1–6. IEEE (2016)
16. Rakha, H., Van Aerde, M.: Statistical analysis of day-to-day variations in real-time traffic flow data. Transportation research record pp. 26–34 (1995)
17. Smola, A.J., Schölkopf, B.: A tutorial on support vector regression. Stat. Comput. **14**, 199–222 (2004)
18. Song, C., Lin, Y., Guo, S., Wan, H.: Spatial-temporal synchronous graph convolutional networks: A new framework for spatial-temporal network data forecasting. In: Proceedings of the AAAI conference on artificial intelligence. **34**, 914–921 (2020)
19. Velickovic, P., Cucurull, G., Casanova, A., Romero, A., Lio, P., Bengio, Y., et al.: Stat. Graph attention networks **1050**(20), 10–48550 (2017)
20. Williams, B.M., Hoel, L.A.: Modeling and forecasting vehicular traffic flow as a seasonal Arima process: theoretical basis and empirical results. J. Transp. Eng. **129**(6), 664–672 (2003)
21. Xu, M., Dai, W., Liu, C., Gao, X., Lin, W., Qi, G.J., Xiong, H.: Spatial-temporal transformer networks for traffic flow forecasting. arXiv preprint arXiv:2001.02908 (2020)
22. Yan, H., Ma, X., Pu, Z.: Learning dynamic and hierarchical traffic spatiotemporal features with transformer. IEEE Trans. Intell. Transp. Syst. **23**(11), 22386–22399 (2021)
23. Yan, S., Xiong, Y., Lin, D.: Spatial temporal graph convolutional networks for skeleton-based action recognition. In: Proceedings of the AAAI conference on artificial intelligence. vol. 32 (2018)
24. Yao, H. et al.: Deep multi-view spatial-temporal network for taxi demand prediction. In: Proceedings of the AAAI conference on artificial intelligence. vol. 32 (2018)
25. Yu, B., Yin, H., Zhu, Z.: Spatio-temporal graph convolutional networks: A deep learning framework for traffic forecasting. arXiv preprint arXiv:1709.04875 (2017)
26. Zhao, W., Zhang, S., Zhou, B., Wang, B.: Stcgat: A spatio-temporal causal graph attention network for traffic flow prediction in intelligent transportation systems. arXiv preprint arXiv:2203.10749 (2022)
27. Zhao, Z., Chen, W., Wu, X., Chen, P.C., Liu, J.: LSTM network: a deep learning approach for short-term traffic forecast. IET Intel. Transport Syst. **11**(2), 68–75 (2017)

Multi-agent Reinforcement Learning for Cooperative On-Ramp Merging of Connected Automated Vehicles

Boyuan Zhao[1] and Jianxun Cui[1,2(✉)]

[1] School of Transportation Science and Engineering, Harbin Institute of Technology,
Harbin 150000, China
cuijianxun@hit.edu.cn

[2] Chongqing Research Institute of HIT, 618 Liangjiang Avenue, Longxing Town, Yubei District,
Chongqing, China

Abstract. Ramp merging areas on highways often serve as bottleneck areas, leading to frequent interactions and accidents between vehicles on the ramp and the arterial road. This results in severe congestion and reduced traffic performance. The emergence of Connected Autonomous Vehicles (CAVs) offers advanced solutions to address these issues and improve traffic operations at ramp merging areas. While previous studies have explored CAV decision-making approaches such as optimization control, model predictive control, and reinforcement learning, they face difficulties in accurately modeling the complex and dynamic scenarios of ramp merging. To overcome these challenges, this paper proposes a collaborative decision-making and control model based on Multi-agent Reinforcement Learning (MARL) for mixed vehicles (CAV-HDV) in multi-lane ramp merging scenarios on arterial roads. The paper introduces three novel MARL algorithms and conducts simulations in six different scenarios to evaluate traffic performance under various lane numbers and traffic densities. The results demonstrate the effectiveness of the proposed collaborative model for ramp merging vehicles. The proposed algorithms significantly reduce collision rates and improve traffic efficiency.

Keywords: Highway Ramp Merging · Multi Agent Reinforcement Learning · Connected Automatic Vehicle · Decision-making and Control

1 Introduction

The merging of ramp vehicles can cause chaos in the arterial road traffic flow, leading to a decrease in driving speed and an increase in delay, even more accidents. It can be seen that the center of merging on highway ramps involves that vehicles cooperate with each other to ensure traffic safety and efficiency, which is a practical research issue and a "strong interaction" problem.

For highway ramp merging, there have been traditional traffic flow level control methods in the past, such as ZONE [1] and ALINEA [2], which are both macro level

© ICST Institute for Computer Sciences, Social Informatics and Telecommunications Engineering 2025
Published by Springer Nature Switzerland AG 2025. All Rights Reserved
X. Chen et al. (Eds.): IoTaaS 2023, LNICST 585, pp. 200–221, 2025.
https://doi.org/10.1007/978-3-031-70507-6_16

controls. Although they have improved the traffic efficiency of ramp merging vehicles, insufficient considerations and limitations of technology at the time still cause short-comings, for example, less of accuracy and randomness. On the basis of the above, Connected Autonomous Vehicle (CAV) has become the best choice to solve the problem of highway ramp merging. Unlike traditional cars, CAVs are equipped with advanced sensors, controllers, integrating environmental awareness, intelligent decision-making, and collaborative control. CAV provides two characteristics: automatic driving control-lability and Vehicle-to-everything connectivity. Compared to traffic flow level control, CAV achieves more collaborative control, transitioning from traffic flow level control to individual level control, providing the possibility of further improving the safety and efficiency of ramp merging.

In recent years, optimization control [3], MPC [4] and Single-agent Reinforcement learning methods [5] are widely used in the research of CAV decision-making and control problems. By optimizing the decision-making and control performance of individual CAV, the overall traffic flow performance is improved to a certain extent. Despite the achievement, for freeway merging scenarios, there are complex, dynamic and nonlinear interactive decision-making among CAVs, resulting in difficulties for efficient decision-making and cooperation control.

The existing highway ramp merging control methods considering CAV are divided into two categories based on traffic flow composition conditions: complete CAV scenario and mixed scenario of CAV and Human Driving Vehicle (HDV). For the research in the complete CAV scenario, the high-level decisions of CAV mainly include the optimization of confluence gap [6, 7], the arrangement of merging sequence [8], and Game theory coordination decisions [9, 10]. However, there will be a long period of coexistence between CAVs and HDVs before all vehicles on the road become CAVs, where HDV is uncontrollable. Therefore, in the actual traffic scenario, the control of CAV needs to resist the interference generated by HDV. At present, the mainstream research methods in mixed scenarios mainly include trajectory optimization method [11–15], Game theory method [16, 17] and Reinforcement learning method [18–20]. Among many research methods, Reinforcement learning has great potential in the high-level decision-making learning of CAVs, which can significantly improve the traffic efficiency and safety of ramp merging, and has received extensive attentions from researchers in recent years. Despite the advantages, few researchers have combined low-level control of CAV with high-level decision-making to design a collaborative comprehensive system. At the same time, there is also insufficient consideration for the lane changing behavior of mixed vehicles in the scene of multi-lane ramp merging on the arterial road.

In view of this, this paper aims to conduct cooperative merging decision making mod-eling of CAVs based on MARL and constructs a comprehensive framework for vehicle merge decision and control, which realizes the coordination of low-level control and high-level decision-making. We take MAPPO as a baseline MARL algorithm and also improve algorithm performance and scene adaptability respectively from the perspective of group collaborative optimization, proposing 2 specified versions of MAPPO. Finally, the two mechanisms were combined to obtain the DDNRCC-MAPPO algorithm, which further improves the overall traffic flow operation efficiency and safety characteristics. At the same time, through extensive experiments on the Highway simulation platform in six scenarios with different number of lanes and vehicle density on the arterial road, 3 novel algorithms and 2 classic algorithms, were used for training and comparison. We systematically verified the efficiency and safety of the three novel algorithms from quantitative analysis of algorithm performance, traffic performance and training mechanism effectiveness.

2 Methods

The main content of this section is the collaborative decision-making modeling of highway ramp merging vehicles based on MARL. Firstly, we give the detail description of the problem we are addressing in this research, and a systematic framework for decision-making and control of merging vehicles on highway ramps is designed. Then, the control of HDV and the low-level control and high-level collaborative decision-making parts of CAV are elaborated separately. Next, we construct a Markov model for the collaborative decision-making problem of merging vehicles, in which the state space, action space, and reward function are presented. Finally, based on MARL, the algorithm and training mechanism of highway ramp merging vehicle collaborative decision-making are carried out.

2.1 Problem Statement

This research delves into the issue of ramp merging in a situation involving both CAV and HDV. The scene of ramp merging is presented in Fig. 1, showcasing a mix of CAV (depicted in red) and HDV (depicted in grey) in a composite driving environment. Cars traversing the secondary roadway amalgamate onto the arterial road via the ramp.

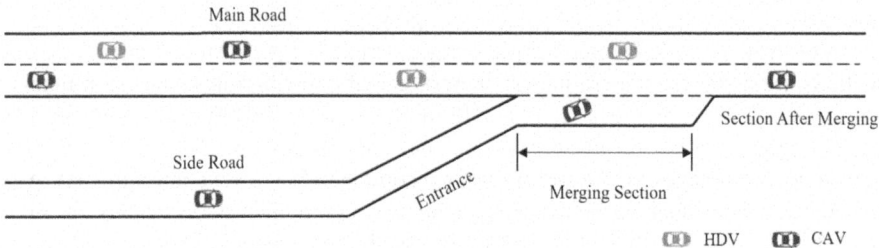

Fig. 1. A figure of highway ramp merging scenario.

In this context, CAVs are able to establish network communication. HDV is driven by the car following model IDM [21] and lane changing model MOBIL [22] for control. While MOBIL handles the lateral control, IDM manages the longitudinal control - with additional information on these coming up in the subsequent sections. A two-layer collaborative framework (see Fig. 2) consisting of low-level control and high-level decision-making is proposed for the collaborative decision-making control problem of CAVs. Therefore, the collaborative decision-making of CAV in the process of highway ramp merging is the primary research focus of this paper.

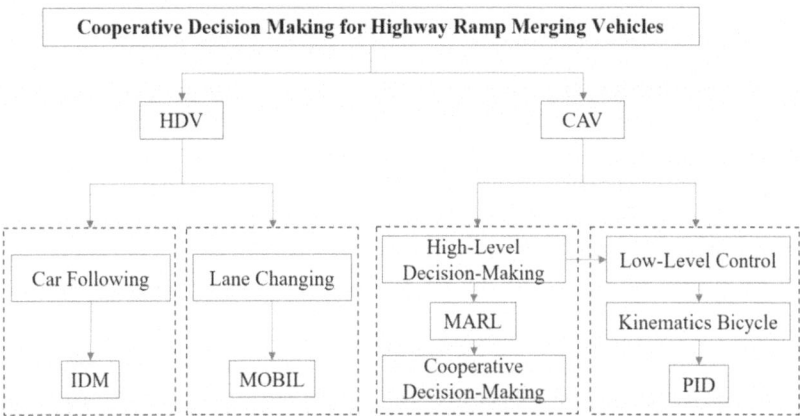

Fig. 2. Framework of vehicle decision-making and control method.

2.2 Decision Making and Control of HDV

Longitudinal Control (IDM). IDM Which is a rule-based car following model is employed to model longitudinal control of HDV. IDM was originally proposed in the field of adaptive cruise control (ACC) to generate appropriate acceleration for the ego vehicle based on its relative driving state with the leading on a single lane. the longitudinal control formulas described by IDM are shown in Eq. 1–2.

$$a = a_{max}(1 - \left(\frac{v}{v_d}\right)^{\delta} - (\frac{d^*(v, \Delta v)}{d})^2)$$ (1)

$$d^*(v, \Delta v) = d_{min} + vT + \frac{v\Delta v}{2\sqrt{ba_{max}}}$$ (2)

where, a is the instant accerlation of ego vehicle, which is needed to be determined in each decision step; a_{max} is the maximum acceleration of ego vehicle; v, v_d is the current and desired speed of ego vehicle; Δv is the speed difference between ego vehicle and its leading vehicle; d is the gap between ego vehicle and its leading vehicle; d_{min} is the minimum safety gap between ego vehicle and its leading vehicle; T is safe time headway; b is the desired acceleration of ego vehicle.

As is seen in the Eq. 1–2, original IDM model only restricted the acceleration of ego vehicle by maximum acceleration a_{max}, however the minimum deceleration is not indicated. So, a condition depicted by Eq. 3 is added by us to limit minimum deceleration of ego vehicle.

$$a = \left\{ \begin{array}{l} a, a \geq a_{min} \\ a_{min}, otherwise \end{array} \right\}$$ (3)

where, a_{min} is the minimum deceleration allowed.

In practice, the HDVs on each single lane execute the IDM longitudinal decision-making model respectively, and then generate their own acceleration decisions in each time interval. If there is no leading vehicle in front of an HDV, its Δv and d is set to 0 and d_{max} (maximum gap for empty lane).

Lateral control (MOBIL). MOBIL is a rule-based lane change model and is adopted to make lateral decision of HDV. MOBIL determines whether lane change is safe and accessible according to the relative acceleration between the ego vehicle and the vehicles on the adjacent lanes. MOBIL's control process is divided into two steps: First, according to the limit of safety standards, the deceleration of new following vehicles should not be too low when lane changing occurs, which is described in Eq. 4.

$$\hat{a}_{new-follower} > b_{safe} \tag{4}$$

where, $\hat{a}_{new-follower}$ is the acceleration of new following vehicles after lane change of ego vehicle, which can be calculated by IDM; b_{safe} is the maximum safe deceleration. Second, if the first condition defined in Eq. 4 is met, MOBIL will check the second condition defined in Eq. 5 to make final decision about whether trigger a lane change of ego vehicle.

$$\hat{a}_{ego} - a_{ego} + p\left(\hat{a}_{new-follower} - a_{new-follower}\right) + q\left(\hat{a}_{old-follower} - a_{old-follower}\right) > a_{th} \tag{5}$$

where, $\hat{a}_{ego}, a_{ego}$ are the new acceleration of ego vehicle calculated by IDM after lane change and the old acceleration before lane change; $\hat{a}_{new-follower}, a_{new-follower}$ are the new and old accelerations respectively of the new follower vehicle when lane change of ego vehicle occurs. $\hat{a}_{old-follower}, a_{old-follower}$ Are the new and old accelerations respectively of the old follower vehicle when lane change of ego vehicle occurs; p and q are politeness factors respectively of the new and old following vehicles; a_{th} is a predefined threshold value.

2.3   Decision Making and Control of HDV

High-level Decision Making of CAV.   The collaborative decision-making problem of merging vehicles can be defined as a Decentralized Partial Observable Markov Decision Process (Dec-POMDP). Each agent can only observe nearby agents, meaning that CAVs can only perceive and communicate with nearby vehicles. In addition, this problem can be described using $\{\{S_i, A_i, R_i\}, T\}$, in which T represents the state transition function and S_i, A_i, R_i respectively represent the state, action, and reward of the i-th vehicle. In this section, we will give a detailed introduction to the design of these parts.

(1) **State space.** Effective state representation directly affects the performance of deep reinforcement learning algorithm. The state space is designed as a matrix $N \times F$, where N represents the number of vehicles observed by the ego vehicle and F represents the number of features of each vehicle's state. We assume that the ego vehicle can only observe adjacent vehicles, which are defined as the nearest N vehicles within the range of 75 m forward to 75 m backward in the longitudinal direction of it. Because this paper focus on the ramp merging scenario, we set $N \leq 5$. In addition, when $F = 5$, the 5 features of each vehicle state are designed as follows:

"Whether there are surrounding vehicles", the longitudinal and lateral relative distance between the observed vehicle and the ego vehicle, and the longitudinal and lateral relative speed of the observed vehicle and the ego vehicle. If the state of the i-th agent is defined as S_i, then the joint state of all agents is $S = S_1 \times S_2 \times \cdots \times S_N$.

(2) **Action space.** The action space of this article includes five discrete actions for vehicle speeds and lane changes in ramp merging scenarios: "Acceleration", "Deceleration", "Turn Left", "Keep Current Speed and Lane", and "Turn Right". Define the action of the i-th agent as A_i, and the joint action of all agents is $A = A_1 \times A_2 \times \cdots \times A_N$.

(3) **Reward space.** The design of rewards is crucial to the effectiveness of a reinforcement learning algorithm. In order to encourage safer and more efficient merging process, a multi-objective reward function is proposed from 4 perspectives: safety, stability, efficiency, and constraints, which are defined separately in Eq. 6–10.

$$r_1 = \begin{cases} 0 & no\ collision \\ -1 & otherwise \end{cases} \tag{6}$$

Stability-related reward:

$$r_2 = log\left(\frac{d}{t_h v_t}\right) \tag{7}$$

where, d is the headway of the vehicle, t_h is a predefined time threshold. If the time interval is less than t_h, the agent will be punished.

Efficiency-related reward:

$$r_3 = min\left(\frac{v_t - v_{min}}{v_{max} - v_{min}}, 1\right) \tag{8}$$

where, v_t, v_{min} and v_{max} respectively represent the current speed, minimum speed, and maximum speed.

Constraint-related reward:

$$r_4 = -\exp\left(-\frac{(x - L)^2}{10L}\right) \tag{9}$$

where, x is the distance traveled by the CAV on the ramp merging area, and L is the length of the ramp merging area. As the CAV approaches the merging end, the penalty increases to avoid deadlock (too long waiting time in the merging area).

In addition, due to the presence of multiple lanes on the arterial road in a multi-lane scenario, lane changing behavior can affect vehicle driving. Therefore, r_5 is designed to ensure driving comfort and reduce frequent lane changes. r_5 is recorded as -1 when the vehicle changes lanes, otherwise 0.

Total reward can be defined as follows:

$$r_{i,t} = w_1 r_1 + w_2 r_2 + w_3 r_3 + w_4 r_4 + w_5 r_5 \tag{10}$$

where, w_1, w_2, w_3, w_4 and w_5 are weight coefficients of different reward components, which can be adjusted to balance during training process.

Low-level Control of CAV

Kinematics Bicycle Model. Utilized in this study is a conventional vehicle kinematics model capable of tracking and describing vehicular motion [23]. The kinematics bicycle model accepts inputs like the steering wheel angle and acceleration output from the PID control algorithm to detail vehicle movements and forecast states such as lateral position, longitudinal position, speed, and yaw angle [24]. Given its capacity to genuinely represent vehicle characteristics, and its efficiency, the kinematics bicycle model stands out among other vehicle kinetics models. Hence, it serves to delineate the lower-level control of CAVs in This paper.

PID Control. The PID control algorithm consists of three control algorithms: proportional, integral, and derivative [25]. During the control process, they cooperate with each other to regulate the errors between input and output. The core formula of PID control algorithm is as follows (Eq. 11):

$$U(t) = K_p \text{err}(t) + K_i \int \text{err}(t)dt + K_d \frac{\text{derr}(t)}{dt} \tag{11}$$

where, K_p is the proportional coefficient, K_i is the integral coefficient, K_d is the differential coefficient, err(t) is the feedback error, $K_p \text{err}(t)$ represents proportional control, $K_i \int \text{err}(t)dt$ represents integral control and $K_d \frac{\text{derr}(t)}{dt}$ represents differential control. Based on this, the control flow of the PID control algorithm is shown below (see Fig. 3).

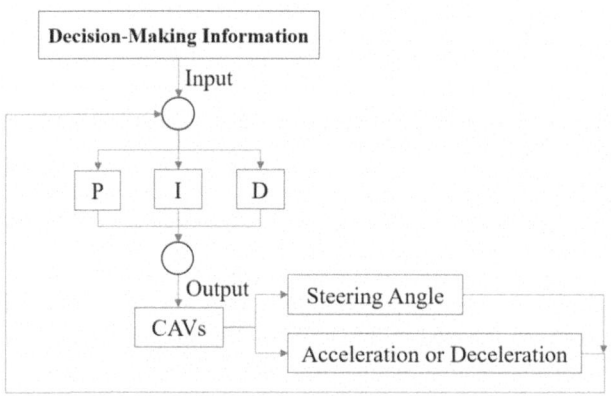

Fig. 3. PID Control-flow diagram.

2.4   Algorithm Design

In the collaborative decision-making of highway ramp merging that involves interactions among CAVs, this research develops an algorithm rooted in MARL for resolution. The training has two paradigms: centralized training and decentralized training. However, centralized training is difficult to consider the individual decision difference from agents, and decentralized training is less adept at managing environmental instability while achieving globally optimal decisions. Therefore, to progress the collaboration of CAVs on highway ramps, the framework proposed adopts a Centralized Training and Decentralized Execution (CTDE) strategy All agents can leverage information of other agents to learn the parameters of the decision network. Hence, this study improves upon the performance and scenario adaptation of the classic CTDE Multi Agent Proximal Policy Optimization (MAPPO), proposing novel algorithms in the process.

Algorithm Performance Improvement (DDNRC-MAPPO). For developing the algorithm performance, we introduce deep dense network (DDN) to improve the sampling efficiency of agents in the environment, and change the policy network objective function of the algorithm from clipping objective function to rollback clipping objective function to improve the stability of the algorithm.

Deep Dense Network (DDN). MAPPO uses multilayer perceptron (MLP), and both the actor and critic networks contain two fully connected layers, with 128 hidden layer neurons. When faced with high-dimensional state space problems such as highway ramp merging decision-making, this network is difficult to achieve ideal learning results. If more layers are just simply added to MLP, the performance of the agent will only deteriorate. Deep dense networks connect state action pairs to each hidden layer of the network (See Fig. 4), using deeper features to better optimize the network while meeting data processing inequality.

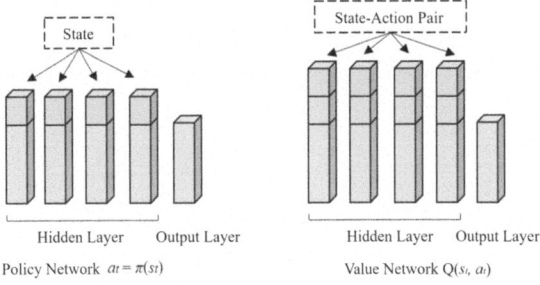

Fig. 4. Schematic diagram of Deep Dense Network.

Fallback Clipping Objective Function. MAPPO cannot strictly control the likelihood ratio as it attempts to do, so it still carries the risk of unstable performance. Therefore, we develop a new clipping function to support fallback operations, which adopts negative incentive measures to limit the differences between the new and old strategies.

Considering the original objective functions in MAPPO does not strictly limit the likelihood ratio within the pruning range, which may exceed $(1 - \varepsilon, 1 + \varepsilon)$. To address this issue, the improved fallback pruning objective function is proposed in the following form (see Fig. 5).

In DDNRC-MAPPO (see Fig. 6), the network of an individual agent has been modified by DDN. Firstly, the actor network interacts with the environment to obtain information. After training, the ratio of the new and old strategies is limited by a backtracking

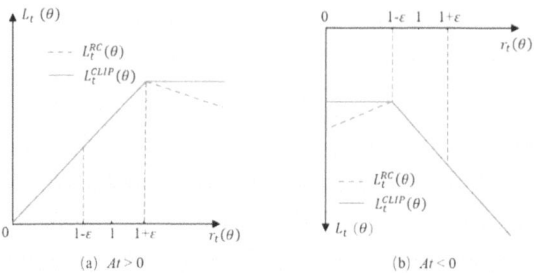

Fig. 5. A figure of improved clipping function.

pruning objective function. Finally, the critic network evaluates the actor network's strategy, which aims to implement strategy optimization.

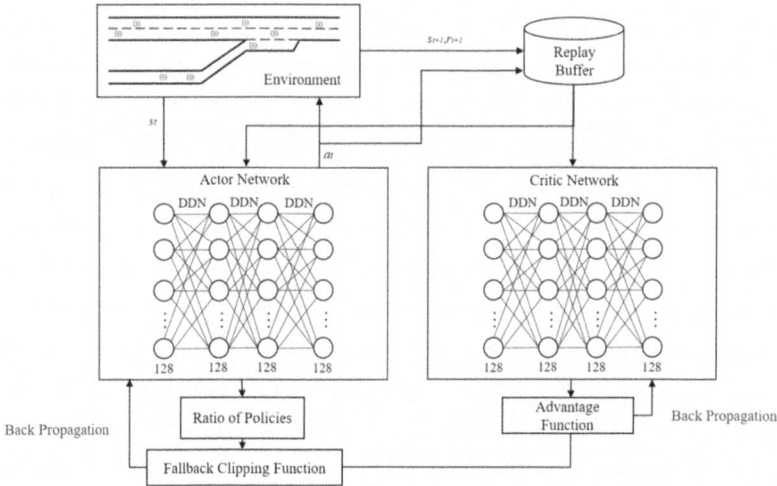

Fig. 6. A basic structure figure of DDNRC-MAPPO.

Scenario Adaptation Improvement (C-MAPPO). In Terms of adapting to ramp merging scenarios, this paper introduces the collision prediction optimization component to predict the driving trajectory of HDVs, which is compared with the trajectory of CAVs to optimize CAV actions. Based on this, a novel algorithm, C-MAPPO was proposed. The algorithm is divided into two operational steps: collision prediction and action optimization.

In the process of predicting a collision, if at any point at any time point $t(t = 1,2, ..., 8)$, the distance between two trajectories is less than the vehicle's width, it is determined that the vehicles are on a collision course. In light of this, optimizing the action selection is a necessity, which involves picking the best action from the available set to modify the present course. The rules for action change include the following two points: firstly, if the target vehicle takes actions, the component will select the action from the available action set that minimizes the headway between the target vehicle and the colliding vehicle; Secondly, if the target vehicle takes left or right turns when colliding, the component will select the action from the available action set that minimizes the distance along the lane between the target vehicle and the colliding vehicle.

Comprehensive Improvement (DDNRCC-MAPPO). Combining the above algorithms with the improvement of performance and scenario adaptability, integrating the advantages of improving algorithm sampling efficiency and stability, as well as reducing vehicle collision rate, a comprehensive algorithm DDNRCC-MAPPO is proposed to achieve the best optimization effect.

2.5   Reward Mechanism Improvement

In the training process of MARL, the design of reward mechanism is directly related to the training effect and the cooperative decision-making efficiency of agents. In order to improve algorithm performance deeply, we optimized the reward mechanism by introducing local reward and curriculum learning mechanism.

Local Reward Mechanism. When it comes to ramp merging, an issue that involves cooperative MARL, the primary training objective is to maximize the global reward - the cumulative rewards of all agents. even though the global reward captures the total system rewards, it does have limitations. for instance, it doesn't provide specific rewards for each individual agent.

To tackle these challenges, we implement a local reward strategy that considers only the proximal vehicles surrounding our vehicle. The closest n vehicles ($n \leq 5$) within a 75 m stretch in our agent's longitudinal direction can be identified and the local reward computed as the mean reward of these n vehicles.

Curriculum Learning Mechanism. When using reinforcement learning to train agents, the rewards in the environment are sparse in most cases. To address the issue of sparse rewards, we adopt curriculum learning (CL). The concept of curriculum learning was first proposed by Bengio [26] as a training strategy that mimics human learning processes, advocating for agents to start learning from easy samples and gradually advance to complex samples and knowledge (See Fig. 7).

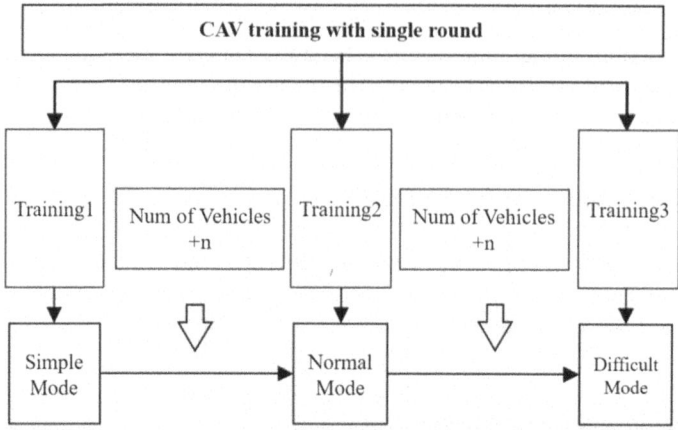

Fig. 7. Schematic diagram of Curriculum Learning.

2.6 Simulation Settings

In this section, simulation scenarios, control models, and algorithm hyper-parameters for highway ramp merging will be designed, and evaluation metrics for subsequent experimental results will be provided from multiple perspectives.

Parameters of HDV Model. In the simulation experiments, HDVs are driven by IDM and MOBIL for making longitudinal and lateral decision and control. The related parameters of IDM and MOBIL are set according to Table 1.

Table 1. Parameters setting of IDM and MOBIL.

Parameters	Value
IDM	
a_{max}	6 m/s^2
b_{min}	− 5 m/s^2
T_0	1.5 s
d_0	10 m
v_d	23–25 m/s
MOBIL	
p	0.1
b_s	2 m/s^2
Acceleration Gain	0.2 m/s^2

Hyper-Parameters of CAVs' High Level Decision-Making Model.   The parameter design of the CAV high-level decision-making algorithm is shown in the Table 2 Below.

Table 2. Parameter settings of MARL algorithm.

Parameters	MAACKTR	MAPPO	DDNRC-MAPPO	C-MAPPO	DDNRCC-MAPPO
Actor Learning Rate	0.0005				
Critic Learning Rate	0.0005				
Optimization and Learning Rate	RMSprop, 0.00001				
Account Factor	0.99				
Replay Buffer Size	10000				
Batch Size	100				
Clipping factor ε	/	0.2	0.2	0.2	0.2
Fallback Clipping Factor α	/	/	0.3	/	0.3

Scenario Design.   This Experiment was conducted on the Ubuntu 18.04, and all experiments are based on the highway ramp environment provided by highway env. In order to connect with the simulation software highway env, the experimental code is written in python, and the reinforcement learning framework uses PyTorch.

At the same time, we modify the density of traffic flow and set the number of lanes on the arterial road, completing the construction of the simulation scenario for the highway entrance ramp required for this experiment (Single-Lane & Low-Density, Single-Lane & Medium-Density, Single-Lane & High-Density, Double-Lane & Low-Density, Double-Lane & Medium-Density, and Double-Lane & High-Density).

Performance Evaluation Metrics.   To give a comprehensive evaluation of the ramp merging vehicle collaborative decision model, six key performance indicators encompassing algorithmic and traffic performance are chosen. This entails three metrics assessing the learning performance of the proposed model and three additional metrics measuring the model's safety and efficiency. They are defined as follows: for collaborative performance:

(1) **Average Episode Reward (AER)**: With each training set at 20000 rounds, AER is the mean reward every 200 rounds.

(2) **Total Average Reward (TAR)**: Evaluating the algorithm's overall performance, TAR is calculated as the sum of rewards garnered from the 20000 rounds of training, averaged by dividing by 20000.

(3) **Average Step (AS_t)**: Each training round comprises of 100 steps. A higher average step size aligns with superior task execution by the agent, and generally a more efficient task completion rate, reflecting the efficacy and duration of task execution.

For traffic performance:

(1) **Average Speed (AS_p)**: A total of 20000 rounds of training will be conducted, and the average speed of every 200 rounds will be taken as the average speed, making it easy to observe the trend of speed changes.

(2) **Total Average Speed (TAS)**: Accumulate the speed obtained from 20000 rounds of training and divide it by 20000 to obtain the total average speed, which can analyze the overall performance of the algorithm.

(3) **Average Collision Rate (ACR)**: Collision can be determined by the step size of the turn, and the collision rate is obtained by dividing the number of turns in collision by the total number of turns of 20000.

With this basis, MAACKTR, MAPPO, DDNRC-MAPPO, C-MAPPO, and DDNRCC-MAPPO were trained through six simulation scenarios. Experimental results were analyzed and evaluated from the standpoint of policy algorithmic performance and traffic performance.

3 Results

In this section, we show the results about performance evaluation of 5 algorithms in six simulation scenarios from policy algorithm performance and traffic performance, and finally a comprehensive comparison among the algorithms is shown.

3.1 Policy Algorithm Performance Evaluation

Firstly, we analyze and evaluate AER. The experimental results of the single lane (in the first line) and two-lanes (in the second line) scenario on the arterial road are shown below (see Fig. 8). And three columns from left to right represent density from low to high respectively. By analyzing the AER of the ramp merging experiment with the scenarios on the arterial road, we can summarize the results as follows.

(1) The comparison between DDNRC-MAPPO proposed in this article and the baseline algorithm MAPPO demonstrates that DDNRC-MAPPO can help agents learn quickly in simple scenarios and significantly improve exploration efficiency, while the improvement is not significant in complex scenarios.

(2) By comparing C-MAPPO proposed in this article with the baseline algorithm MAPPO, it is found that C-MAPPO can significantly improve the reward value, and it can also be said that collisions are a key factor affecting the reward value, which indirectly confirms the role of C-MAPPO in reducing collisions.

(3) In the six scenarios, AER of the agent trained by DDNRCC-MAPPO proposed in the paper is much higher than the baseline algorithm, indicating that DDNRCC-MAPPO has achieved the goal of improving training effectiveness and excellent performance. However, deep dense networks and fallback pruning objective functions can only improve algorithm performance to a certain extent in low density scenarios with two lanes on the arterial road.

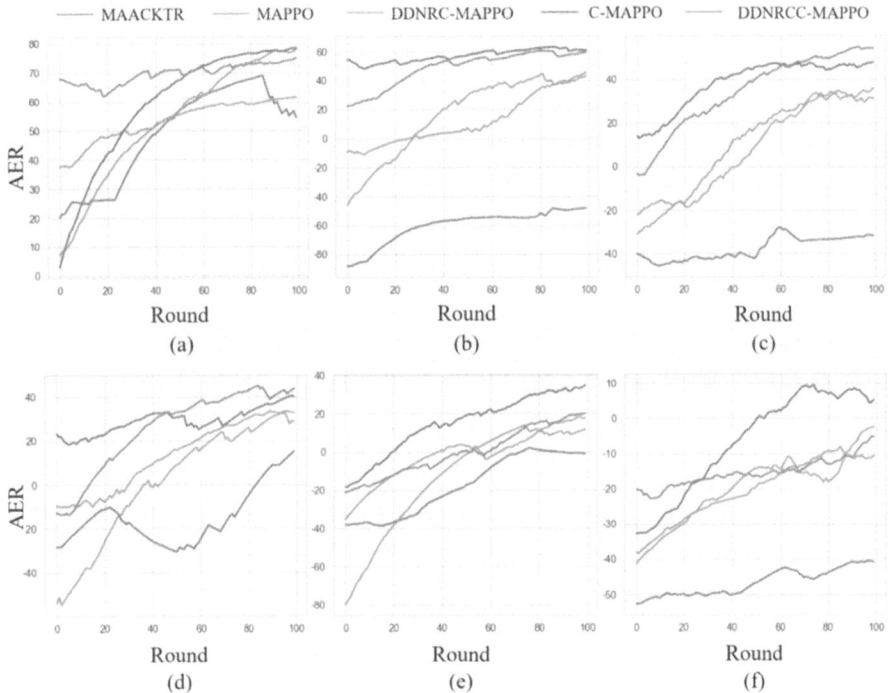

Fig. 8. Comparison of AER under Single Lane Arterial Road Scenarios.

The second policy performance evaluation indicator is AS_t. The relevant experimental results for the scenarios with single lane and two-lanes on the arterial road are shown in Fig. 9. The density from low to high is represented respectively in the 3 columns from left to right. The results can be described as follows.

(1) MAACKTR has little difference in training completion compared to other algorithms in simple scenarios, but in complex scenarios, its AS_t remains at a low value, making it difficult for agents to complete tasks successfully and resulting in poor training effectiveness.

(2) The performance difference between DDNRC-MAPPO and the baseline algorithm MAPPO in terms of training completion is not significant. In simple scenarios, agents can complete tasks smoothly, and in complex scenarios, agents can also achieve high task completion.

(3) AS_t of C-MAPPO and DDNRCC-MAPPO proposed in this paper is generally higher than the baseline algorithm during the training process, improving the task completion of the agent. In addition, the training effect of DDNRCC-MAPPO is slightly better.

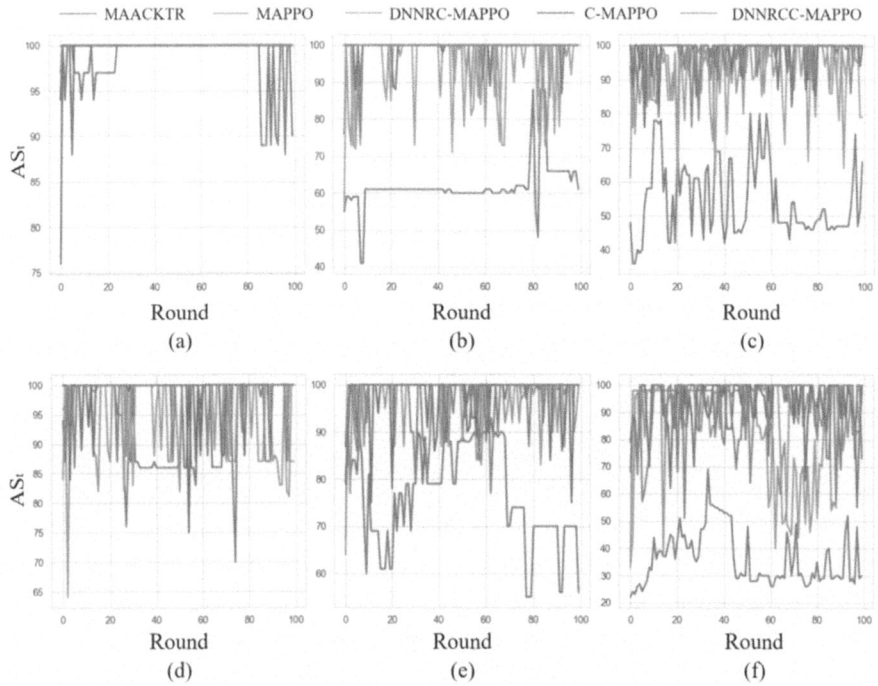

Fig. 9. Comparison of ASt under Single Lane Arterial Road Scenarios.

3.2 Traffic Performance Evaluation

In this section, we further validated algorithms' improvement in traffic performance, including the analysis and evaluation of ASp and ACR.

The experimental results of the single lane (in the first line) and two-lanes (in the second line) scenario on the arterial road are shown below (see Fig. 10). And three columns from left to right represent density from low to high respectively. Based on the analysis of ASp of the ramp merging experiments, the following conclusions can be drawn:

(1) MAACKTR algorithm trains agents with good ASp in low density scenarios, while in medium and high-density scenarios, low task completion results in low average speed reference value, indicating that the baseline algorithm is difficult to adapt to complex scenarios.

(2) The comparison between DDNRC-MAPPO and the baseline algorithm MAPPO shows that in low density scenarios, DDNRC-MAPPO significantly improves ASp of the agent. In medium and high-density scenarios, the training performance of the two algorithms is basically the same. It can be seen that DDNRC-MAPPO has a significant help in improving ASp performance in simple traffic scenarios.

(3) ASp of C-MAPPO and DDNRCC-MAPPO are basically the same in low and medium density scenarios, while in high-density scenarios, DDNRCC-MAPPO can help agents achieve higher ASp. We can see that among the five algorithms, DDNRCC-MAPPO has the best average speed performance.

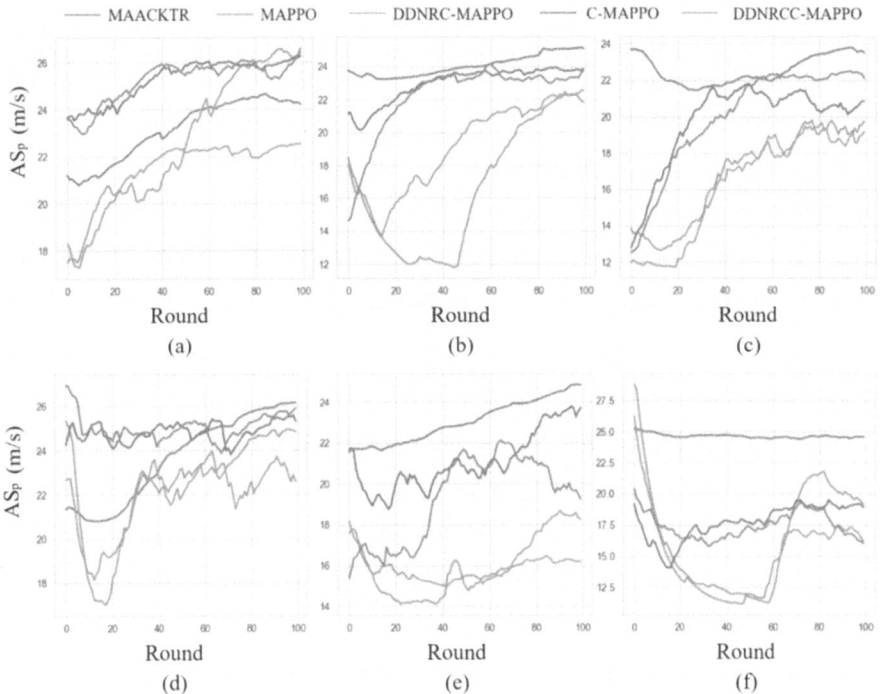

Fig. 10. Comparison of ASp under Single Lane Arterial Road Scenarios.

The ACR (Average Collision Rate) of various algorithms in six distinct scenarios is presented in Table 3. Upon analysis, it becomes evident that, with the exception of the two-lane medium density scenario, DDNRCC-MAPPO consistently exhibits the lowest ACR across all five scenarios. Following closely behind is C-MAPPO, with a slightly higher ACR compared to the former. DDNRC-MAPPO demonstrates the lowest ACR in the single lane low density and two-lane medium density scenarios, while slightly surpassing C-MAPPO and DDNRCC-MAPPO in other scenarios. Conversely, MAACKTR consistently yields the highest ACR in all six scenarios, resulting in poor performance.

Table 3. Comparison of ACR under different scenarios.

Algorithms/Scenarios	Single-Lane			Double-Lane		
	Low-Density	Medium-Density	High-Density	Low-Density	Medium-Density	High-Density
MAACKTR	0.06	0.69	0.92	0.15	0.58	0.98
MAPPO	0.01	0.09	0.24	0.07	0.08	0.39
DDNRC-MAPPO	0	0.09	0.20	0.11	0.05	0.37
C-MAPPO	0.01	0.03	0.08	0.04	0.07	0.19
DDNRCC-MAPPO	0	0.01	0.08	0.04	0.11	0.17

3.3   Comprehensive Performance Evaluation

This section comprehensively analyzes the performance of three improved algorithms and two baseline algorithms, and compares them from four aspects: safety, efficiency, robustness, and effectiveness (see Fig. 11).

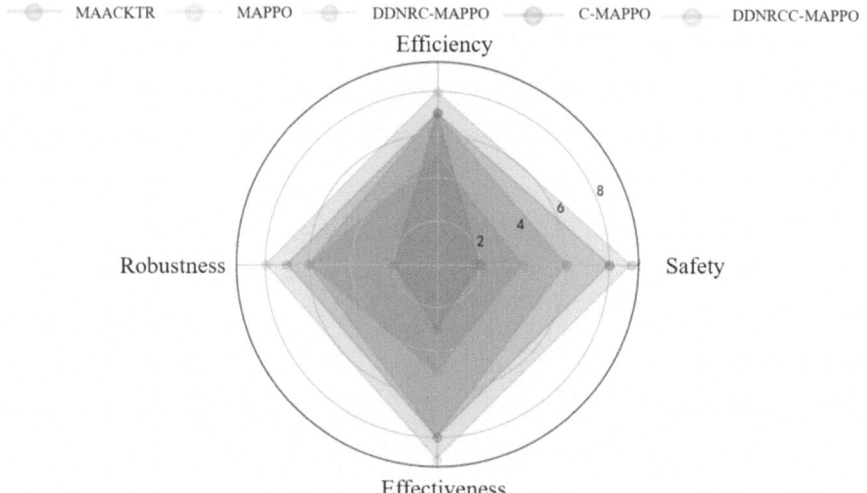

Fig. 11. Comprehensive comparison of algorithm performance.

From Fig. 11, we see that the three algorithms proposed in this paper have improved in terms of security, efficiency, robustness, and effectiveness compared to the baseline algorithms. Among them, DDNRCC-MAPPO has the highest score and the best performance in all four aspects.

4   Discussion

This section further discussed the performance of algorithms in typical scenarios based on the above experimental results and the improved reward mechanisms from 6 indicators.

For the two kinds of reward mechanisms, this experiment takes the improved algorithm DDNRCC-MAPPO as an example to train in a single lane medium density scenario. In this medium difficulty scenario, the impact of using the local reward mechanism and Curriculum Learning on training effectiveness is compared. The experimental results are shown in Fig. 12 and Table 4.

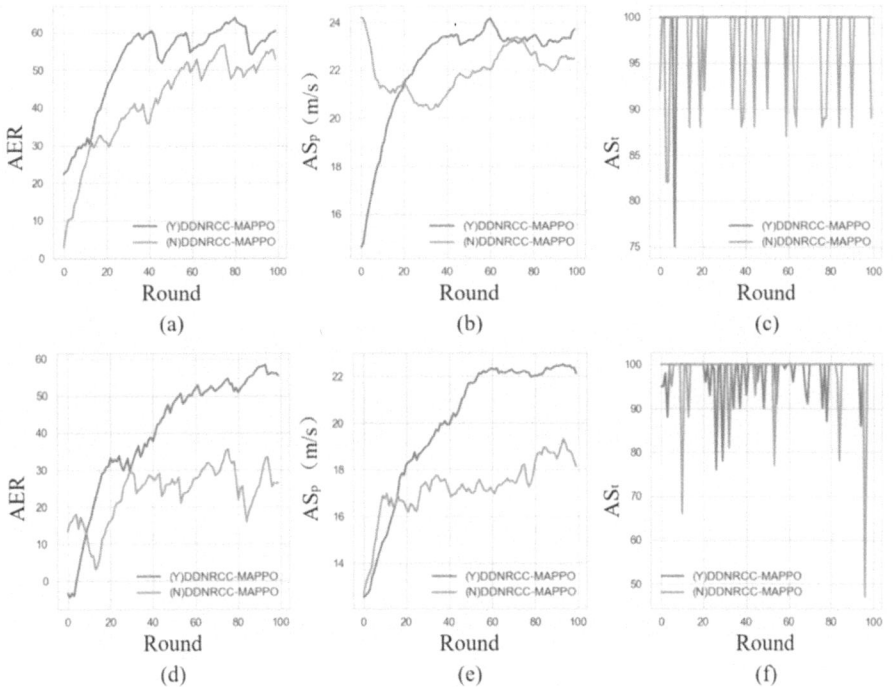

Fig. 12. Performance comparison of reward mechanisms before and after used.

In the 6 subgraphs of Fig. 12, the blue line represents the experimental results using the improved reward mechanisms, while the orange line represents the experimental results without using them. Except for whether using the reward mechanisms, all other settings are the same.

Figure 12 (a, d) show a comparison chart of AER, with the horizontal axis representing training rounds and the vertical axis representing AER. All curves of the two subgraphs show an upward trend, but the blue line is always higher than the orange line, indicating that the use of local reward mechanism and curriculum learning improves the exploration efficiency of the agent and can obtain higher AER.

Figure 12 (b, e) show1 a comparison chart of AS_p. In (b), the blue line in the figure shows an overall upward trend, with small fluctuations. In the later stage of training, it tends to converge and the AS_p is higher than the orange line. In (e), the orange line has a higher AS_p than the blue line in the first 20 rounds but shows a downward trend, then rises and tends to converge in the later training, However, its AS_p is always lower than the blue line, indicating that curriculum learning can help the agent improve speed faster.

Figure 12 (c, f) show a comparison of AS_t. In (c), the orange line has 19 rounds with an AS_t of less than 100, while the blue line has only 2 rounds with an AS_t of less than 100. It can be seen that using the local reward mechanism can improve the task completion of the agent. And AS_t of algorithms using curriculum learning fluctuates between 76 and 100, while those without curriculum learning fluctuate between 45 and 100. In view of this, it can be seen that the curriculum learning mechanism can make agents complete tasks as much as possible.

Table 4. Performance comparison table of reward mechanisms before and after used.

Whether Using Local Reward Mechanism	TAR	AS_p	ACR
(Y)DDNRCC-MAPPO	55.06	23.01	0.01
(N)DDNRCC-MAPPO	45.97	21.79	0.07
Whether Using Curriculum Learning	TAR	AS_p	ACR
(Y)DDNRCC-MAPPO	45.63	20.86	0.08
(N)DDNRCC-MAPPO	24.85	17.71	0.09

In Table 4, (Y) DDNRCC-MAPPO represents algorithms that use novel reward mechanisms, and (N) DDNRCC-MAPPO represents algorithms that do not use novel reward mechanisms. It can be observed that after using local reward mechanism, TAR of the agent increased from 45.97 to 55.06, TAS increased from 21.79 m/s to 23.01 m/s, and ACR decreased from 7% to 1%. And with curriculum learning, TAR of the agent increased from 24.85 to 45.63, TAS increased from 17.71 m/s to 20.86 m/s, and ACR decreased from 9% to 8%.

Based on the above experimental analysis, it can be found that after using the local reward mechanism and curriculum learning, all evaluation indicators have been improved to varying degrees, indicating that the improvement can effectively help agents explore the environment and improve training effectiveness.

5   Conclusions

The gradual popularization of Connected Autonomous Vehicles (CAV) provides a new solution to the problem of highway ramp confluence. In recent years, there are optimization control, MPC control, single agent Reinforcement learning and other methods for the decision control of CAV, which improves the traffic performance to a certain extent, but insufficient consideration is given to the interactive decision-making between multiple vehicles in complex scenes. For this reason, this paper proposes a MARL based collaborative Decision model and strategy for highway ramp merging vehicles. Based on the MAPPO algorithm, the algorithm performance and adaptation to ramp merging scenarios are improved respectively, and the training mechanism is optimized. Then, the strategy is tested and evaluated in a series of ramp merging scenarios with different number of lanes on the arterial road and vehicle density. The main research findings can be summarized as follows:

(1) A comprehensive framework was developed for decision-making and control of merging vehicles on highway ramps. This framework incorporates a decentralized partial observable Markov decision model, specifically designed to tackle the collaborative decision-making challenges faced by merging vehicles on highway ramps;
(2) Multiple enhanced versions of collaborative decision algorithms based on MAPPO were designed specifically for Connected Autonomous Vehicles (CAVs) during ramp merging;
(3) The use of local rewards and curriculum learning training mechanisms proved effective in training the proposed MARL models;
(4) Extensive simulation evaluations were carried out to assess the performance of collaborative decision-making strategies for merging vehicles on highway ramps.

For six simulation scenarios, namely Single-Lane & Low-Density, Single-Lane & Medium-Density, Single-Lane & High-Density, Double-Lane & Low-Density, Double-Lane & Medium-Density, and Double-Lane & High-Density, four indicators (AER, AS_t, AS_p and ACR) were used to assess both the algorithm performance and the traffic performance of the merging vehicle collaborative decision-making strategy. This was done from three aspects, and the results from employing baseline algorithms MAACKTR, MAPPO, and improved algorithms DDNRC-MAPPO, C-MAPPO, and DDNRCC-MAPPO were systematically compared. Such comparisons verified the efficiency of our proposed cooperative decision-making strategy, anchored on MARL for on-ramp merging.

References

1. Xin, W., Michalopoulos, P.G., Hourdakis, J., Lau, D.: Minnesota's new ramp control strategy: design overview and preliminary assessment [J]. Transp. Res. Rec. **1867**(1), 69–79 (2004)
2. Hadj-Salem, H., Blosseville, J.M., Papageorgiou, M.: ALINEA: a local feedback control law for on-ramp metering; a real-life study. In: Third International Conference on Road Traffic Control, 1990. (pp. 194-198). IET (1994)
3. He, X., Liu, H.X., Liu, X.: Optimal vehicle speed trajectory on a signalized arterial with consideration of queue. Trans. Res. Part C: Emerg. Technol. **61**, 106–120 (2015). https://doi.org/10.1016/j.trc.2015.11.001
4. Wen, J., Wang, S., Wu, C., Xiao, X., Lyu, N.: A longitudinal velocity CF-MPC model for connected and automated vehicle platooning. IEEE Trans. Int. Trans. Syst. **24**(6), 6463–6476 (2022)
5. Zhou, M., Yu, Y., Qu, X.: Development of an efficient driving strategy for connected and automated vehicles at signalized intersections: A reinforcement learning approach. IEEE Trans. Intell. Transp. Syst. **21**(1), 433–443 (2020)
6. Chen, J., Zhou, Y., Chung, E., Ozbay, K.: CAV-based active congestion resolving for improving mainline traffic flow efficiency of a freeway on-ramp merging section. In: 2022 IEEE 25th International Conference on Intelligent Transportation Systems (ITSC). IEEE

7. Zhu, J., Tasic, I., & Qu, X.: Improving freeway merging efficiency via flow-level coordination of connected and autonomous vehicles. *arXiv preprint* arXiv:2108.01875 (2021)

8. Zhu, J., Tasic, I.: Safety analysis of freeway on-ramp merging with the presence of autonomous vehicles. Accid. Anal. Prev. **152**, 105966 (2021)

9. Hu, Z., Huang, J., Yang, Z., Zhong, Z.: Embedding robust constraint-following control in cooperative on-ramp merging. IEEE Trans. Veh. Technol. **70**(1), 133–145 (2021). https://doi.org/10.1109/TVT.2021.3049866

10. Wang, M., Hoogendoorn, S.P., Daamen, W., van Arem, B., Happee, R.: Game theoretic approach for predictive lane-changing and car-following control. Trans. Res. Part C: Emerg. Technol. **58**(SEP.PT.A), 73–92 (2015). https://doi.org/10.1016/j.trc.2015.07.009

11. Sabouni, E., Cassandras, C.G.: Optimal merging control of an autonomous vehicle in mixed traffic: an optimal index policy. IFAC-PapersOnLine **56**(2), 2353–2358 (2023)

12. Zhou, Y.: Trajectory planning strategies of connected automated vehicles for cooperative on-ramp merging and mainline facilitating maneuvers. Queensland University of Technology (2019)

13. Sun, Z., Huang, T., Zhang, P.: Cooperative decision-making for mixed traffic: a ramp merging example. Trans Res. Part C: Emerg. Technol. **120**, 102764 (2020)

14. Huang, T., Sun, Z.: Cooperative ramp merging for mixed traffic with connected automated vehicles and human-operated vehicles. IFAC-PapersOnLine **52**(24), 76–81 (2019). https://doi.org/10.1016/j.ifacol.2019.12.384

15. Gao, Z., Zhizhou, W., Hao, W., Long, K., Byon, Y.-J., Long, K.: Optimal trajectory planning of connected and automated vehicles at on-ramp merging area. IEEE Trans. Int. Trans. Syst. **23**(8), 12675–12687 (2022). https://doi.org/10.1109/TITS.2021.3116666

16. Le, V.-A., Malikopoulos, A.A.: A cooperative optimal control framework for connected and automated vehicles in mixed traffic using social value orientation. In: 2022 IEEE 61st Conference on Decision and Control (CDC), Cancun, Mexico, pp. 6272–6277 (2022), https://doi.org/10.1109/CDC51059.2022.9993337

17. Liao, X., Zhao, X., Wang, Z.: Game theory-based ramp merging for mixed traffic with unity-SUMO co-simulation. IEEE Trans. Syst., Man, Cybernet.: Syst. **52**(9), 5746–5757 (2022). https://doi.org/10.1109/TSMC.2021.3131431

18. Zhou, S., Zhuang, W., Yin, G., Liu, H., Qiu, C.: Cooperative on-ramp merging control of connected and automated vehicles: distributed multi-agent deep reinforcement learning approach. In: 2022 IEEE 25th International Conference on Intelligent Transportation Systems (ITSC), Macau, China, (pp. 402–408) (2022) https://doi.org/10.1109/ITSC55140.2022.9922173

19. Li, M., Li, Z., Wang, S., Zheng, S.: Enhancing cooperation of vehicle merging control in heavy traffic using communication-based soft actor-critic algorithm. IEEE Trans. Intell. Transp. Syst. **24**(6), 6491–6506 (2023). https://doi.org/10.1109/TITS.2022.3221450

20. Wang, S., Fujii, H., Yoshimura, S.: Generating merging strategies for connected autonomous vehicles based on spatiotemporal information extraction module and deep reinforcement learning. Phys. A: Stat. Mech. Appl. **607**, 128172 (2022)

21. Treiber, M., Hennecke, A., Helbing, D.: Congested traffic states in empirical observations and microscopic simulations. Phys. Rev. E **62**(2), 1805–1824 (2000). https://doi.org/10.1103/PhysRevE.62.1805

22. Kesting, A., Treiber, M., Helbing, D.: General lane-changing model MOBIL for car-following models. Trans. Res. Rec.: J. Trans. Res. Board **1999**(1), 86–94 (2007). https://doi.org/10.3141/1999-10

23. Polack, P., Altché, F., d'Andréa-Novel, B., de La Fortelle, A.: The kinematic bicycle model: a consistent model for planning feasible trajectories for autonomous vehicles?. In: 2017 IEEE intelligent vehicles symposium (IV) (pp. 812-818). IEEE. (2017) https://doi.org/10.1109/IVS.2017.7995816

24. Park, F.C., Lynch, K.M.: Modern robotics: mechanics, planning, and control. Cambridge University Press, Cambridge, UK (2017)
25. Kiong, T.K., Qing-Guo, W., Chieh, H.C., Hägglund, T.J.: Advances in PID control. Springer London, London (1999)
26. Bengio, Y., Louradour, J., Collobert, R., Weston, J.: Curriculum learning. In: Proceedings of the 26th annual international conference on machine learning (pp. 41-48) (2009).

Late Track

SVM Multi-class Classification Method for Device Identification Using Eye Diagram Parameters

Jian Yuan[1,2(✉)] and Aiqun Hu[1]

[1] School of Cyber Science and Engineering, Southeast University, Nanjing, People's Republic of China
{yuanj,aqhu}@seu.edu.cn
[2] Research Center of Hengtong Information Security, Suzhou, People's Republic of China

Abstract. In this paper, we investigate the problem of identification of RS-485 devices. The proposed method utilizes their physical layer features in terms of time-domain overlapping traces. The first step is the acquisition of the physical layer waveform with an oscilloscope. The waveform is then preprocessed, a pulse shaping filter is applied, and the eye diagram is generated. These eye diagram parameters are estimated and stored as datasets. Then, the datasets are divided into two conventional categories. The first one is defined as the training set for deriving key parameters, the second one is used as the test set to verify the proposed algorithm. The eye diagram parameters of the test set are used for training, and the parameters of multi-class the supporting vector machine (SVM) are obtained. The data from the testing set is used to classify the devices. The results of the classification are used for device identification. Our experimental results show that classification accuracies of RS-485 devices can be higher than 88%, which indicate that our proposed method is practical and thus has a potential to be used in a number of applications including industrial Internet of Things (IoT) device identifications.

Keywords: device identification · eye diagram · supporting vector machine · physical layer security

1 Introduction

Identification and authentication are two important security functions. Identification is the capability to uniquely identify an entity (e.g., user, system or application) among other entities. Authentication is the capability to prove that an entity (e.g., user, system or application) is what it claims to be. Identification and authentication is extensively used in ensuring the security of Information and Communication Technologies (ICT) for the access and provision of services. For example, it is critical to distinguish between legitimate users (who are paying for a service) from other users (who may use the same services in an illegal way). Identification and authentication can be based on three

© ICST Institute for Computer Sciences, Social Informatics and Telecommunications Engineering 2025
Published by Springer Nature Switzerland AG 2025. All Rights Reserved
X. Chen et al. (Eds.): IoTaaS 2023, LNICST 585, pp. 225–238, 2025.
https://doi.org/10.1007/978-3-031-70507-6_17

main factors: information that an entity knows (such as a password), something that entity has (a smartcard) or something the entity is (biometric features). Identification and authentication can be based on each of these elements or a combination of these elements in the so-called multi-factor authentication, which is usually stronger than Identification /authentication based on a single element. Each of these elements has its own advantages/disadvantages as it is well known in literature [1].

There are three main physical layer-based device identification methods: measuring received signal strength, channel state information, and device characteristics [2].

The received signal strength is mainly affected by channel characteristics, physical media and other factors. Some possible causes may include the distance and channel conditions. The distance between the transmitter to the receiver varies from 10 m to 10 km. The channel distortion may be introduced by the hardware circuits, inter-symbol interference (ISI), and copper line materials [3].

If we only measure the strength of the received signal, the channel features can not be used to distinguish the devices, because the strength dynamic values are not adequately stable [4]. Channel State Information (CSI) can separate the multipath components, so it can provide a more fine-grained fingerprint based on the state of the medium. For example, in the case of Wi-Fi networks, the presence of multiple subcarriers makes CSI-based device identification more characteristic [5].

The third method of physical layer identification is to use device characteristics (such as hardware manufacturing defects) for identification. Such defects in hardware will cause offsets in transient or steady-state signals during signal transmission, thus generating device fingerprints [6]. The classification and identification of wireless devices using device fingerprints is mainly divided into three steps: (a) collect the signals emitted by the device to be identified; (b) extract appropriate signal characteristics; (c) use signal characteristics to create device fingerprints and classify device fingerprints. By extracting and analyzing these device fingerprints, the purpose of device classification can be achieved [7–9].

In general, the device fingerprint should have the following characteristics [10–12]. (a) Uniqueness: No two devices can have the same fingerprint. (b) Persistence: The device fingerprint obtained should remain unchanged for a long time. (c) Collectability: The signal emitted by the device to be identified can be captured by existing acquisition equipment. (d) Robustness: The characteristics should be unaffected by environmental factors and channel environment.

Eye diagram is a kind of graph which is presented by overlapping signals gradually accumulated on oscilloscope [13–15]. It contains rich damage information, which can completely reflect the performance characteristics of optical signal, qualitatively reflect the influence of various damage on signal quality, and then reflect the pros and cons of optical communication system [16]. From the eye diagram, we can not only obtain the modulation format information, but also estimate the signal quality indicators such as height, width and so on [11]. Therefore, eye diagrams have long been the core and first choice for signal integrity embodiment. In this paper, the eye diagram of the signal is used as the analysis object to extract the device features for training and identification of the device [17].

In order to quickly and effectively judge and evaluate the integrity of the time domain waveforms, some characteristics must be derived from the obtained eye diagram image, then the relevant parameters are defined according to several key positions of the eye diagram [18]. Through the judgment and estimation of these key parameters, the performance of the optical network system is effectively measured. There are many eye diagram parameters related to the system performance change, such as low level, high level, eye height, eye width, eye amplitude, extinction ratio, eye cross ratio, average power, Q factor, jitter, etc. These parameters can be used for feature extraction to identify different devices.

The organization of the rest of this paper is as follows. In Sect. 2, we discuss the standard RS-485 protocols and some common features of hardware devices. Next, in Sect. 3, the multiclass SVM theory is reviewed. Furthermore, the experimental findings and results are shown and explained in more detail in Sect. 4.

2   Analysis of an RS-485 Device's Eye Diagram

2.1   The RS-485 Bus Overview

The traditional RS-485 bus technology plays a crucial role in current industrial production due to its numerous advantages. Its key characteristics are as follows:

The RS-485 bus network utilizes differential signal technology at the physical layer. The voltage difference between twisted pair lines represents high-level signal logic, ranging from positive 2 V to positive 6 V, while the voltage difference representing low-level signal logic 0 ranges from negative 2 V to negative 6 V. The specified signal voltage by the RS-485 bus interface standard is relatively low, reducing the complexity in designing and producing bus driver chips. Moreover, the level specified by the RS-485 bus standard is compatible with TTL level, facilitating interconnection with TTL circuits (see Fig. 1).

Fig. 1. RS-485 Specified Minimum Bus Signal Levels

In the physical layer of the RS-485 bus, a balanced driver and differential receiver solution are employed. This means that when transmitting data using RS-485 bus technology, signals are modulated into symmetric signals sent through two lines (balanced transmission). If a single line is used for transmission (with a reference level), it is referred to as unbalanced transmission. On the receiving end of RS-485 bus technology, symmetric reception (balanced reception) is utilized; however, if asymmetric reception occurs (single-line reception corresponding to one reference level), it is considered unbalanced reception. The physical layer technology of RS-485 provides excellent resistance against common mode interference or external noise (see Fig. 2).

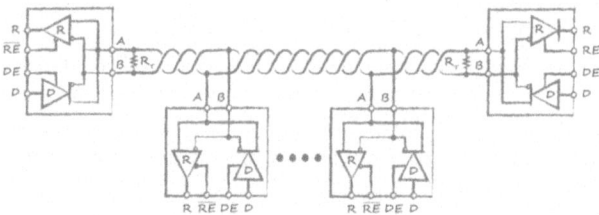

Fig. 2. Typical RS-485 network topology

2.2 Line Coding

The RS-485 bus utilizes digital data for signal transmission, employing direct encoding of binary digital data through the use of digital signals. The coding methods commonly employed include Non Return To Zero (NRZ) coding and Non Return to Zero Inverse (NRZI) coding. NRZ coding represents transmitted data using high and low signal levels, with high level representing data 1 and low level representing data 0. NRZI coding represents transmitted data based on whether there is a transition at the start of each bit; no transition indicates data 1, while a transition indicates data 0. Non-return-to-zero coding is often used in short-range communication due to its simplicity in implementation. However, it can result in DC drift due to an unequal distribution of zeros and ones when continuously transmitting either all zeros or all ones, thereby affecting stable signal transmission.

In our study, RS-485 Communication channel model is shown in Fig. 3. At the transmitter, binary data is encapsulated into an RS-485 protocol frame and subsequently encoded by hardware before being transmitted through the channel. Upon acquisition of the time-domain waveform on the channel, an eye diagram can be generated for further usage. At the receiver, decoding via hardware yields output in binary format.

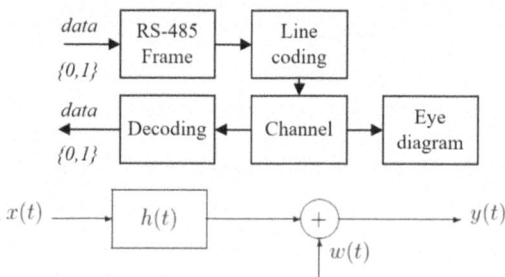

Fig. 3. RS-485 Communication channel model

2.3 Wireline Communication Model

When an electric signal is transmitted over a channel, it will be definitely contaminated. This may due to various signal transmission path imperfections. The reasons of signal distortion are now analyzed as follows. The received waveform is defined as

$$y(t) = x(t) * h(t) + w(t) \tag{1}$$

where $w(t)$ represents several linear or non-linear noise processes.

1) **Channel noises**

The simplest noise is the additive white Gaussian noise (AWGN). This can be used for mathematical modelling various physical transmission path. However, the RS-485 wireline channel may also introduce other types of noises, such as amplifier nonlinearities caused by hardware impairments.

2) **Linear Distortion**

We shall first consider linear time-invariant channels. Signal distortion can be caused over such a channel by nonideal characteristics of magnitude distortion, phase distortion, or both.

We can identify the effects these nonidealities will have on a pulse $h(t)$ transmitted through such a channel.

3) **Distortion Caused by Channel Nonlinearities**

The linear channel is applicable only to weak signals, while for strong signals, the significance of nonlinearity becomes more prominent. The nonlinear channel can be modeled as follows: we consider a memoryless simple scenario where both the input h and output y are governed by a set of nonlinear equations.

$$y = f(h) \tag{2}$$

After expansion, this equation can be express as

$$y(t) = a_o + a_1 h(t) + a_2 h^2 h^2 + \cdots \tag{3}$$

In a digital communication system, linear and nonlinear distortions have significantly different impacts on the signal. Linear distortion can cause interference between signals in the same frequency band, while nonlinear distortion can lead to interference between signals in different frequency bands.

2.4   Features of Eye Diagram

In order to efficiently and effectively assess the signal quality based on the shape characteristics of the generated eye image, relevant parameters are defined for key positions within the eye image. The performance is accurately evaluated by analyzing and estimating these key parameters. There exist numerous Eye diagram parameters that are associated with changes in system performance, including "Zero"/"One" Level, Eye Height, Eye Width, Eye Amplitude, among others (see Fig. 4).

The following key eye diagram parameter indicators are briefly introduced:

(1) "0" level and "1" level: In the eye diagram, these levels represent the logic 0 and logic 1 voltage of the received signal. The middle value of the eye diagram is selected as a reference point (20% of the signal peak value), and by projecting it vertically in the eye diagram, a histogram is obtained. The median value of this projection represents the "0" and "1" levels.

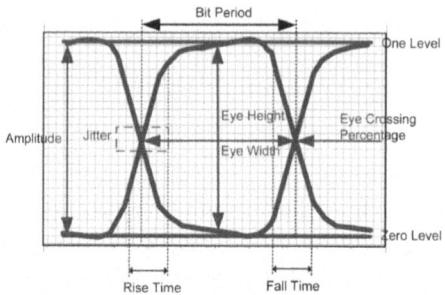

Fig. 4. Typical Eye Diagram Measurements

(2) Amplitude of eye: It signifies the difference between mean values of signal distribution represented by logic voltage "1" and logic voltage "0". Similar to determining the "0"/"1" level in an actual measurement, it involves calculating differences within a 20% distribution area near the middle position of an eye diagram.

(3) Height of eye: This indicates how open or closed an eye is in terms of vertical direction at its midpoint. While similar to measuring amplitude, it specifically focuses on capturing maximum differences within an eye diagram. The height reflects both noise-induced distortion in signals and serves as a measurement for signal-to-noise ratio.

These parameters can be used for feature extraction to identify different devices.

3   An Introduction to LS-SVM Algorithm

3.1   Introduction to Support Vector Machines

SVM is first proposed to distinguish binary classes. Then, it is applied to solve functional regression problem and multi-class classification problems. Although SVM algorithms are suitable for solving binary classification problems, a large number of multi-class classification problems in practical applications are also needed to solve by using extended SVM algorithms. At present, there are the following commonly used methods:

(1) One-to-many method. The idea is to treat the samples from one class as one class and the samples from the remaining classes as another class, making it a two-class classification problem. Then, the above steps are repeated for the remaining samples. This approach requires constructing K-SVM models, where K represents the amount of classes to be classified. However, this scheme usually needs a large number of training samples.

(2) One-to-one method. The multiclass classification problems involve considering only two classes at a time, resulting in the utilization of the SVM model for each pair of classes. Consequently, K(K-1)/2 SVM models are designed in total. Generally, this approach necessitates constructing multiple binary classifiers and subsequently comparing every pair of classes, thereby leading to a significant increase in computational complexity.

(3) Decision tree method. This method involves combining binary classification decisions to create a multi-class recognizer. However, one drawback of this approach is that if a classification error occurs at any node, it will propagate and impact the overall recognition accuracy.

3.2 Application of Support Vector Machine in Classification Problem

Firstly, let us consider the linearly separable case, and suppose there are linearly separable training samples:

$$(x_i y_i), x_i \in R^n, y_i \in \{+1, -1\}, i = 1, \ldots, l \tag{4}$$

The objective of the separation problem is to identify a hyperplane that can effectively and completely separate the two classes of samples. On one hand, the optimal separating hyperplane should accurately classify the samples into their respective classes, on the other hand, it should maximize the distance between the closest data points from each class and the hyperplane. This distance is referred to as the maximum classification margin.

Finally, the discriminant function is obtained as

$$f(x) = \text{sgn}\left(\sum_{i=1}^{l} \alpha_i y_i K(x_i, x) + b\right) \tag{5}$$

where $\alpha_i \geq 0, i = 1, \cdots, l$.

In general, the solution to the above-mentioned problem can be found, since most values of α_i will be zero. The samples corresponding to the non-zero a will be the Supporting Vector (SV).

3.3 Multiple Classification Algorithm

The one-class classification method under linear programming can be extended to the multiple classification case in the following. The proposed method involves the classification of each class of samples, followed by the derivation of the decision function $f(x)$ for binary classification. Then the sample to be tested is input into each decision function, and the class to which the point belongs is determined according to the maximum value of the decision function. The specific algorithm is described as follows:

Let the training samples be:

$$\{(x_1, y_1), \cdots, (x_i, y_i)\} \subset R^n \times R \tag{6}$$

where n is the dimension of the input sample, $y_i \in \{1, 2, \cdots, M\}$, and M is the number of categories. The samples are divided into M classes, and each class is written as follows.

$$\{(x_1^{(m)}, y_1^{(m)}), \cdots, (x_{l_m}^{(m)}, y_{l_m}^{(m)}), m = 1, \cdots, M\} \tag{7}$$

where $x_1^{(m)}$ and $y_1^{(m)}$ represents training samples of the m-th class, and $l_1 + \cdots + l_M = l$. Then we can formulate a linear programming problem as follows:

$$\min\left\{ C \sum_{m=1}^{M} \sum_{i=1}^{l} \xi_{mi} + \rho \right\} \tag{8}$$

The constraint here is

$$\sum_{j=1}^{l_m} \alpha_j^{(m)} k(x_j^{(m)}, x_i^{(m)}) \geq p - \xi_{mi}, i = 1, \cdots, l_m \tag{9}$$

$$\sum_{j=1}^{l_m} \alpha_j^{(m)} = 1, \tag{10}$$

$$\alpha_i^{(m)}, \xi_{mi} \geq 0, i = 1, \cdots, l_s \tag{11}$$

Solving this linear program, M decision functions can be obtained

$$f_m(x) = \sum_{j=1}^{l_m} \alpha_j^{(m)} k(x_j^{(m)}, x) \tag{12}$$

Given a sample z to be identified, calculate $\gamma_i = f_i(z), i = 1, \cdots, M$, by comparing their values, the largest γ_k can be obtained. This indicates that z classified as the k-th class.

4 Experimental Results

4.1 RS-485 Devices for Different Sensors

We assume that there are 5 sensors in the industrial site, each sensor collects different types of field data, and then data transmission is carried out through the RS-485 bus. At the same time, these devices use the same hardware scheme including chips, resistors, capacitors and inductors. However, the material and length of the copper cable connecting the device are different (see Fig. 5).

These types of sensors include temperature, humidity, illuminance, vibration, pressure, acceleration, distance, and gases (see Table 1).

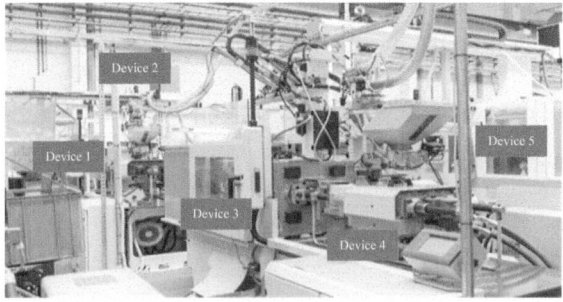

Fig. 5. RS-485 devices in a factory

Table 1. RS-485 devices of the same vendor.

Device Number	Sensor type
RS-485 Device 1	Temperature
RS-485 Device 2	Humidity
RS-485 Device 3	Illuminance
RS-485 Device 4	Vibration
RS-485 Device 5	Pressure

4.2   Overall Flow Diagram of RS-485 Device Classification

The overall process of device identification is shown in the following figure. The first step is the acquisition of the physical layer waveform with an oscilloscope. The waveform is then preprocessed, a pulse shaping filter is applied, and the eye diagram is generated. The eye diagram datasets are categorized into two groups, with 60% of the data allocated for training purposes and the remaining 40% designated as the test set. The eye diagram of the test set is used for training, and the parameters of the SVM are obtained. The data from the test set is used to classify the devices. The result of the classification is used for device fingerprint extraction (see Fig. 6).

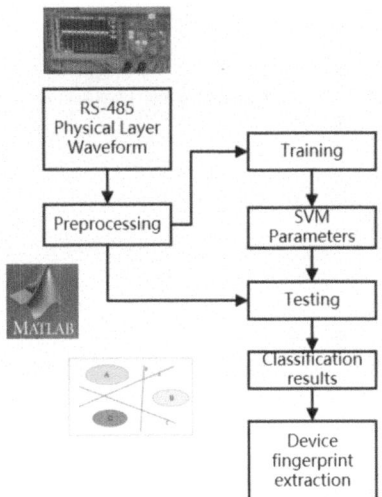

Fig. 6. RS-485 device fingerprint extraction

4.3   Physical Signal Acquisition by an Oscilloscope

Most of the oscilloscopes contain simple Math functions. Using this functionality, the second channel can be subtracted from the first channel.

The subtraction result must be inverted. After this result should look more correct. The noise level was decreased.

The RS-485 waveform can be saved as a *.csv file using USB portable disk, and then the raw datum in this file can be preprocessed by MATLAB.

4.4   Eye Diagram Generation Using MATLAB

(1) Raised Cosine Pulse

The Nyquist criterion states that an impulse response of a filter must satisfy certain conditions in order to eliminate ISI. In practical engineering, where the channel transmission inevitably introduces signal distortion, an equalizer can be employed at the receiver to mitigate ISI. This aspect will be elaborated further due to the uncontrollable nature of channel characteristics, whereby controlling both transmit and receive filters allows for manipulation of the overall impulse response of the transmission system. Consequently, the entire transfer function H(f) can be approximated as a product of transmitter and receiver filter functions. An efficient end-to-end transfer function, H(f), is typically achieved by employing filters with H(f) as their transfer functions at both ends. Such filters exhibit a frequency domain characteristic known as square-root raised cosine roll-off property; this property is demonstrated when cascading two square root raised cosine roll-off filters at both transmitter and receiver stages in the frequency domain (see Fig. 7).

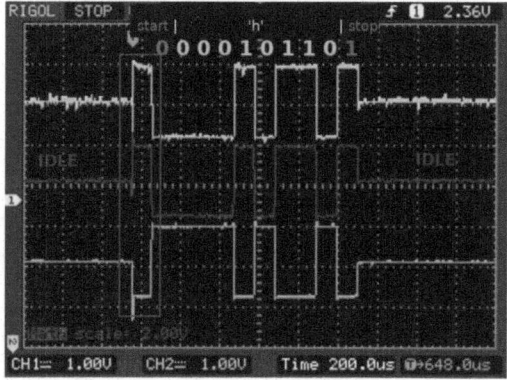

Fig. 7.   Encoder output driven by differential driver and reconstructed by receiver

(2) Eye Diagram of RS-485 Devices

In the present study, we conduct a time-domain eye diagram test on the 10 Mbps signal. The test is performed using an oscilloscope and a 100 m twisted pair cable. Here's the procedure for conducting the test: an instrument is connected to one end of the bus, and random data is transmitted through the bus. The random data is generated by an FPGA at a rate of 10 Mbps, with consecutive sequences of 0 s or 1 s not exceeding a length of 7. This process is repeated continuously. The other end of the bus is connected to an oscilloscope, which measures and analyzes the eye diagram of the bus signal. Matching resistors are configured at both ends of the bus, allowing us to assess signal quality by adjusting their values. Then the datum are stored in a USB disk. Finally, these datum are pre-processed in MATLAB (see Fig. 8).

4.5   Feature Extraction Using Eye Diagram Parameters

The eye diagram encompasses numerous parameters, among which we have adopted the transverse time parameter and the longitudinal amplitude parameter. Lateral time parameters include eye width, rise time, fall time, etc., while longitudinal amplitude parameters encompass "0" Level, "1" level, Mean Level, Eye amplitude, Eye Height, etc. (see Fig. 8).

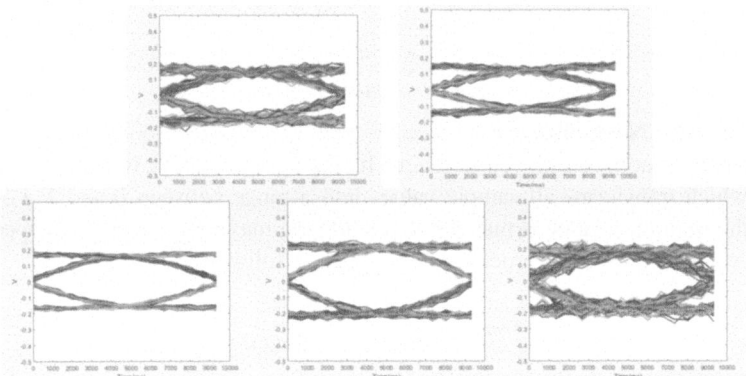

Fig. 8. Eye diagrams of RS-485 devices

The fundamental longitudinal eye diagram parameters are defined by the "0" level and the "1" level. Specifically speaking, in a complete eye diagram, data points located within the central 20% of the diagram are projected onto the vertical axis to form a histogram. The center values of this histogram represent levels "1" and "0", respectively.

Another crucial parameter in longitudinal eye plots is eye height. It signifies the vertical opening within an eye diagram and reflects interference from noise. A larger eye height indicates less distortion in signal quality with respect to amplitude.

Eye width denotes the horizontal opening inside an eye diagram. By dividing two adjacent intersections of the diagram into two sets and considering data points within these sets as Gaussian distributions as well.

Based on both eye width and eye amplitude measurements, one can calculate rise time and fall time accordingly. These times refer to transitions from a 10% amplitude to a 90% amplitude (see Table 2).

Table 2. Eye diagram parameter used for devices feature.

Device Feature 1	Device Feature 2	Device Feature 3	Device Feature 4	Device Feature 5	Device Feature 6
Zero Level	One Level	Eye Height	Eye Width	Eye Rise Time	Eye Fall Time

4.6 Data Preprocessing Using Python

(1) Standardisation

The purpose of normalization is to ensure that the mean is centered at zero and the standard deviation is scaled to one by resizing the data. The formula can be expressed as follows:

$$x_{std} = \frac{x - mean(x)}{std(x)} \tag{13}$$

(2) Max-Min Normalization

Another commonly employed technique for data preprocessing is max-min normalization, which transforms all sample values into a range between 0 and 1. For each feature, the minimum value is mapped to 0 while the maximum value is mapped to 1. The general formula for this process can be stated as follows:

$$x_{norm} = \frac{x - min(x)}{max(x) - min(x)} \tag{14}$$

4.7 Test Results

In this experiment, we collected a total of 250 samples, 50 samples for each device. We split these 250 samples into training and test sets. The training set is 60% and the test set is 30%. General data in the test set for cross-validation.

The classification accuracy can reach 90%, and the classification performance is good, which proves that the RS-485 device fingerprint extraction technology based on eye diagram parameters and support vector machine is feasible. The confusion matrix is shown in Table 3.

Table 3. Confusion matrix results.

Device 1	**0.90**	0.06	0.04	0.00	0.00
Device 2	0.00	**0.92**	0.03	0.05	0.00
Device 3	0.00	0.00	**0.95**	0.03	0.02
Device 4	0.00	0.06	0.04	**0.88**	0.02
Device 5	0.00	0.00	0.00	0.00	**0.93**
	RS-485 Device 1	RS-485 Device 2	RS-485 Device 3	RS-485 Device 4	RS-485 Device 5

5 Conclusions

In this paper, we study the problem of physical layer feature extraction for 485-bus devices. We first analyze the signal characteristics of 485 bus device, and find that its eye diagram parameters can be used to do feature extraction. Next, we introduce the algorithm of support vector machine. In the experiment section, we detail the steps of the 485-bus device physical signal acquisition, eye diagram generation method, feature extraction and data preprocessing. The experimental results indicate that the correct classification rate of most devices is more than 90%, which means that different devices can be recognized basically. In future work, we will further test more devices and plan to combine eye map features and sensor data features to further improve the accuracy.

References

1. Yener, A., Ulukus, S.: Wireless physical-layer security: Lessons learned from information theory. Proc. IEEE **103**(10), 1814–1825 (2015)
2. Pappu, R., Recht, B., Taylor, J., Gershenfeld, N.: Physical one-way functions. Science **297**(5589), 2026–2030 (2002)
3. Rührmair, U., Busch, H., Katzenbeisser, S.: Strong PUFs: models, constructions, and security proofs. Towards Hardware-Intrinsic Security: Foundations and Practice, 79-96 (2010)
4. Kori, B., Maubach, S., Kevenaar, T., Tuyls, P.: Information-theoretic analysis of capacitive physical unclonable functions. J. Appl. Phys. **100**(2), 024902–024911 (2006)
5. Baldini, G., Giuliani, R., Steri, G.: Physical layer authentication and identification of wireless devices using the synchro-squeezing transform. Appl. Sci. **8**(11), 2167 (2018)
6. Jiang, Y., Peng, L., Hu, A., Wang, S., Huang, Y., Zhang, L.: Physical layer identification of LoRa devices using constellation trace figure. EURASIP J. Wirel. Commun. Netw. **2019**(1), 273 (2019)
7. Peng, L., Zhang, J., Liu, M., Hu, A.: Deep learning based RF Fingerprint identification using differential constellation trace figure. IEEE Trans. Veh. Technol. **69**(1), 1091–1095 (2020)
8. Liu, M., Liao, G., Yang, Z., Song, H., Gong, F.: Electromagnetic signal classification based on deep sparse capsule networks. IEEE Access **2019**(7), 83974–83983 (2019)
9. J. Carbino T., A. Temple M., J. Bihl T.: Ethernet card discrimination using unintentional cable emissions and constellation-based Fingerprinting. In: International Conference on Computing, Networking and Communications (ICNC) 369–373 (2015)
10. Ometov, A., Bezzateev, S., Mäkitalo, N., Andreev, S., Mikkonen, T., Koucheryavy, Y.: Multi-factor authentication: A survey. Cryptography **2**(1), 1–4 (2018)
11. Masdari, M., Ahmadzadeh, S.: A survey and taxonomy of the authentication schemes in telecare medicine information systems. J. Netw. Comput. Appl. **87**, 1–19 (2017)
12. Mukherjee, A.: Physical-layer security in the internet of things: sensing and communication confidentiality under resource constraints. Proc. IEEE **103**(10), 1747–1761 (2015)
13. Chen, X., Li, J., Han, H., Ying, Y.: Improving the signal subtle feature extraction performance based on dual improved fractal box dimension eigenvectors. Royal Soc. Open Sci. **5**(5), 180087 (2018)
14. Li, J., Ying, Y., Lin, Y.: Verification and recognition of fractal characteristics of communication modulation signals. In: IEEE 2nd International Conference on Electronic Information and Communication Technology (ICEICT) (2019)
15. Tu, Y., Lin, Y., Wang, J., Kim, J.U.: Semi-supervised learning with generative adversarial networks on digital modulation classification. Comput. Mater. Cont. **55**(2), 243–254 (2018)

16. Han, H., Li, J., Chen, X.: The individual identification method of wireless device based on a robust dimensionality reduction model of hybrid feature information. Mob. Netw. Appl. **23**(4), 709–716 (2018)
17. Merchant, K., Revay, S., Stantchev, G., Nousain, B.: Deep learning for RF device Fingerprinting in cognitive communication networks. IEEE J. Select. Topics Signal Process. **12**(1), 160–167 (2018)
18. Yu, J., Hu, A., Li, G., Peng, L.: A robust RF Fingerprinting approach using multisampling convolutional neural network". IEEE Int. Things J. **6**(4), 6786–6799 (2019)

Users Collaborative Computing for Hierarchical Federated Learning Based on Incentive Mechanism

Bei Zhuang[1(✉)], Shangjing Lin[1], Yueying Li[1], Ji Ma[2], Jin Tian[2], Chunhong Zhang[3], and Zheng Hu[3]

[1] School of Electronic Engineering, Beijing University of Posts and Telecommunications, Beijing, China
{zhuangb,linshangjing,yyingli}@bupt.edu.cn
[2] School of Network and Communication Engineering, Jinling Institute of Technology, Nanjing, China
{Maji,jim.tian}@jit.edu.cn
[3] School of Information and Communication Engineering, Beijing University of Posts and Telecommunications, Beijing, China
zhangch.bupt.001@gmail.com, huzheng@bupt.edu.cn

Abstract. Nowadays, Federated Learning (FL) is widely applied in the Internet of Things (IoT). However, when a large number of devices participate in FL, they still face the challenge of low communication efficiency. In addition, how to reasonably allocate FL trained models to third parties (e.g. task publishers) is also a problem that needs to be solved. In this article, we propose a hierarchical FL (HFL) framework based on incentive mechanisms, where task publishers mobilize users for collaborative computing through edge servers. At the lower layer, evolutionary game is used to model the dynamic decision-making process of users with bounded rationality, and users select user groups (UGs) to participate in training by considering model accuracy and training costs. At the upper layer, an iterative double auction mechanism is adopted to allocate the model reasonably to multiple task publishers, maximizing the total social welfare. Finally, the effectiveness of the proposed scheme is verified through experiments.

Keywords: Federated Learning · Evolutionary Game · Double Auction · Internet of Things · Hierarchical

1 Introduction

In recent years, Artificial Intelligence (AI) based model training methods mainly use the traditional cloud-based centralized learning framework [1–3]. However, this method of transmitting training data to the cloud server for processing has a series of problems, including transmission quality, data privacy and high consumption. Therefore, edge computing [4] is proposed to improve these problems,

X. Chen et al. (Eds.): IoTaaS 2023, LNICST 585, pp. 239–254, 2025.
https://doi.org/10.1007/978-3-031-70507-6_18

and data processing and other tasks are placed on the edge server closer to the device. Federated Learning (FL) [5], as a distributed framework, promotes the development of edge computing. Users are allowed to save data locally, and only upload training model parameters to the edge server. At present, FL has been widely used in the Internet of Things (IoT), such as intelligent object detection [6], data sharing [7] and autonomous vehicle (AV) [8].

Service providers with cloud servers need to act as task publishers to mobilize users to participate in FL to jointly train an AI model, and provide users with services such as target recognition and content recommendation[9]. Due to distance limitations, task publishers are unable to directly mobilize users, so they need to collaborate with edge servers close to the user end for training. However, participants in FL are selfish and unwilling to contribute their private data and resources to participate in training. Paper [10] uses evolutionary game to consider data size and privacy costs to motivate users to participate and optimize resource allocation. However, in the case of a large number of users participating in FL, parameter interaction between users and edge servers can easily lead to communication congestion, and reducing the number of users can reduce the performance of the training model. How to balance model performance with communication load faces challenges. In addition, how to reasonably allocate the AI model trained on edge servers to numerous task publishers is also an urgent problem to be solved.

In response to the above issues, we propose a hierarchical federated learning (HFL) framework based on incentive mechanisms, which incentivizes users to efficiently collaborate and allocate AI models reasonably. Specifically, the contributions of this article can be summarized as follows: 1) An HFL framework based on incentive mechanism is proposed. In the lower layer, evolutionary game is used to model the process of users' autonomous selection of edge servers. The replicator dynamic depicts the dynamic nature and bounded rationality of user decisions, so as to achieve the goal of balancing the accuracy of the model and the cost of communication and computing, and further proves the uniqueness and stability of the evolutionary game to achieve equilibrium. 2) In the upper layer, we use the iterative double auction mechanism to reasonably allocate the model to the task publisher. Double auction achieves a many-to-many competitive situation and maximizes social welfare. 3) The experiment verifies the performance of evolutionary game in a large number of user scenarios and the effectiveness of iterative double auction mechanisms.

2   System Model

We consider an HFL architecture, which is composed of the task publisher (TP) layer, the edge layer and the user layer, as shown in Fig. 1. TPs may be individuals or enterprises. The set of TPs is denoted by $\mathcal{P} = \{1, ..., p, ..., P\}$.

The user layer is composed of U devices with certain computing power, represented by the set $\mathcal{U} = \{1, ..., u, ..., U\}$. Each device, as a user, can use private data to train the local model. The edge layer includes K edge servers, such as

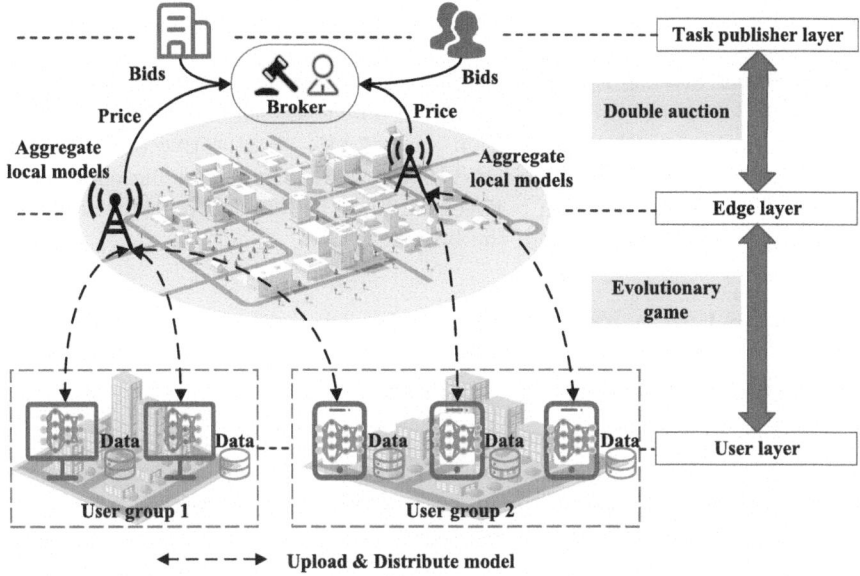

Fig. 1. Incentive mechanism based HFL framework for user collaborative computing

base stations, which receive and aggregate local models from the user layer, represented by the set $\mathcal{K} = \{1, ..., k, ..., K\}$. Users can choose to associate with any edge server and form a user group (UG) by selecting users from the same edge server. The edge server further distributes the aggregated model to each user of the corresponding UG.

Repeat the FL training process above until the maximum number of iterations T is reached. Assuming FL trains a classification model, the user updates the model parameters through the stochastic gradient descent (SGD) method, and uses the cross entropy loss function as follows:

$$F = -\frac{1}{H} \sum_{h=1}^{H} \sum_{m=1}^{M} y_{hm} \log(s_{hm}), \tag{1}$$

where H is the total number of training samples, M is the number of categories. y_{hm} is the true value, $y_{hm} \in 0, 1$, and when the true categories of sample h is m, $y_{hm} = 1$, otherwise $y_{hm} = 0$. s_{hm} is the prediction probability that sample h belongs to category m.

The lower layer is an evolutionary game process. In the user layer, users randomly select edge servers to form initial UGs. Edge servers need to mobilize more users to join their UGs collaborative training model to improve model accuracy. However, a large number of users choosing the same edge server can easily lead to communication congestion. In order to motivate users, balance model accuracy and communication and computing costs, we model the process of users' dynamic selection of UG to join as an evolutionary game. Users tend to join UG that can obtain higher returns. After each round of FL training, users adjust their strategies.

The upper layer is a double auction process. The lower layer provides the trained model for the upper level, and the TPs select the model based on their quality. Considering the competition among TPs, an iterative double auction mechanism is adopted, in which P TPs bid for K models of the edge servers. Facilitate iterative interaction between multiple buyers and multiple sellers and adjust bids and pricing through the broker.

3   Lower-Layer Evolutionary Game

3.1   Evolutionary Game Formulation

In this section, we model the dynamic process of users' selecting UG participating in training as the evolutionary game. Evolutionary game includes four basic elements: population, pay off function, dynamics and equilibrium.

Population. We consider modeling evolutionary game among individuals of a single population. All users sets $\mathcal{U}$ participating in FL training are participants in evolutionary game. We divide all users in the population into multiple UGs, and the UG set is expressed as $\mathcal{J} = \{1, ..., j, ..., J\}$, a total of J. Among them, the number of users in UG $j \in \mathcal{J}$ is $n^j = x^j U$, $x^j \in [0, 1]$ and $\sum_{j=1}^{J} x^j = 1$. x^j is the proportion of the users in UG j in the whole population. In other words, users of all UGs form a complete population.

Pay Off Function. The pay off function refers to the expected profit obtained by the users choosing to join a UG, that is, the fitness function. It is related to the UG selected by the users and the proportion distribution of current different UGs. We define the fitness function as the difference between the benefits of joining the UG and the communication and computing costs of participating in the training. Relevant contents are further discussed in Sect. 3.2

Dynamics. The learning and imitation process of users is dynamic, and the game is iterative. In each iteration, the user dynamically chooses to exit a UG and join other UGs or stay in the current UG to maximize its profit. The users' strategy is to select a certain UG to join.

Equilibrium. The result of evolutionary game is to reach a convergent stable state, that is, the UG proportion converges to a point, which is unique and stable. The final UGs state is expressed as vector $\mathbf{x}^* = \left[x^{1*}, ..., x^{j*}, ..., x^{J*}\right]$, and x^{j*} refers to the proportion of users who choose UG j.

3.2   Dynamic Process Modeling

In this section, the fitness function we defined will be described in detail.

The proportion of UG j in the whole population changes with the user adjustment strategy of each iteration, expressed as $x^j(t)$. The fitness of users after joining UG j and participating in FL training at time t is:

$$A^j\left(x^j(t)\right) = \mathcal{L}\left(R^j\left(x^j(t)\right) - E^j_{total}\left(x^j(t)\right)\right), \tag{2}$$

where we assume $\mathcal{L}(\cdot)$ to be a linear utility function. It is a function related to $x^j(t)$. $R^j\left(x^j(t)\right)$ is the accuracy function of FL training model, which is used to express the benefits obtained by users participating in UG j. $E^j_{total}\left(x^j(t)\right)$ is the communication and computing costs generated in training.

In the FL scenario of this article, the more users, the more data they contribute, and the higher the accuracy of the model. According to [11], the relationship between the number of users and accuracy can be expressed as follows:

$$R^j\left(x^j(t)\right) = p\log\left(Ux^j(t)\right) + q. \tag{3}$$

We use the total size of parameters that users in the UG j need to transmit to the edge server after each iteration as the communication cost to represent the communication congestion level of the UG j. The communication cost required for the t-th iteration of UG j is defined as follows:

$$C^j_{com}\left(x^j(t)\right) = |w|Ux^j(t), \tag{4}$$

where $|w|$ is the size of the model parameter. In the computation phase of FL, each user trains the local model on local data D_i. The computing energy consumption, i.e. the computing cost, for all users in the UG j is represented as

$$C^j_{cmp} = \sum_{i \in j} \xi_i D_i f_i^2. \tag{5}$$

The number of CPU cycles of the user i needed to execute one unit of data is denoted as ξ_i, and the CPU cycle frequency is denoted as f_i. Therefore, the total cost $E^j\left(x^j(t)\right)$ is defined as follows:

$$E^j_{total}\left(x^j(t)\right) = C^j_{com}\left(x^j(t)\right) + C^j_{cmp}. \tag{6}$$

Further, we can get the average fitness of all UGs for the t-th iteration as follows:

$$\overline{A}\left(x^j(t)\right) = \frac{1}{J}\sum_{j=1}^{J} A^j\left(x^j(t)\right). \tag{7}$$

In the game, users can exchange the fitness value that can be obtained by choosing different UGs, that is, the information of profit, so as to compare with the current UG. By comparison, users will be more inclined to join UG with higher profit. Due to the replicator dynamics being applicable to a large population of members with slow learning speeds for random selection in iterative games, we define replicator dynamics to capture and model the dynamic process of user's selecting UG, as follows:

$$\dot{x}^j(t) = f^j\left(\mathbf{x}(t)\right) = \alpha x^j(t)\left(A^j\left(x^j(t)\right) - \bar{A}\left(x^j(t)\right)\right), \tag{8}$$

where α is the positive learning rate of UG, which controls the speed of user adaptation strategy. When the population size is large, the user needs more time to transfer and obtain the status and information between UGs, and the learning speed is often slow.

Considering the reality, when users are large, they cannot learn global information in a short time (the number of every UG's users and the self conditions of other users, etc.). Therefore, the user is an individual with finite rationality, they play the game repeatedly with only limited information (its own conditions, the fitness of the current UG and the average fitness of all UGs). Specifically, when the fitness of the current UG is lower than the average fitness, the probability of users in the current UG joining other UGs will be increased. At a specific time t, $\dot{x}^j(t) = 0$, $\forall j \in \mathcal{J}$, and then it reaches evolutionary equilibrium, that is, all users get the same pay off, and there is no need to adjust the strategy.

The game among users will eventually evolve to a unique and stable equilibrium point. Stability refers to keeping $\dot{x}^j(t) = 0$ in all time periods after a specific time t. Uniqueness refers to the evolution from any initial proportion to the same equilibrium point. Due to the difference of users conditions and the uncertainty of adjusting strategy based on probability, $\dot{x}^j(t)$ will fluctuate in a small range around 0. Therefore, we define the threshold γ. When $\dot{x}^j(t)$ is less than γ, we consider that the evolutionary game reaches equilibrium.

3.3 Proof of Evolutionary Equilibrium

In this section, we prove the existence, uniqueness and stability of evolutionary equilibrium solution.

Existence. Firstly, we prove the boundedness of (8) in Lemma 1.

Lemma 1. *The first order derivatives of $f^j\left(\mathbf{x}(t)\right)$ with respect to $x^q(t)$ is bounded for $\forall q \in \mathcal{J}$.*

Proof. For ease of presentation, we omit the notations of t in the proof. The first order derivative of $f^j(\mathbf{x})$ with respect to x^q, $\forall q \in \mathcal{J}$, is given by

$$\frac{df^j(\mathbf{x})}{x^q} = \alpha\left[\frac{dx^j}{dx^q}\left(A^j - \bar{A}\right) + x^j\left(\frac{dA^j}{dx^q} - \frac{d\bar{A}}{dx^q}\right)\right]. \tag{9}$$

And then, the $\frac{dA^j}{dx^q}$ is as follows:

$$\frac{dA^j}{dx^q} = \frac{p}{Ux^j}\frac{dx^j}{dx^q} - |w|U\frac{dx^j}{dx^q}. \tag{10}$$

Obviously, $\frac{dA^j}{dx^q}$ and $\frac{d\bar{A}}{dx^q}$ are bounded $\forall q \in \mathcal{J}$, which represents that $|\frac{df^j(\mathbf{x})}{x^q}|$ is bounded. This proof also applies to all time periods.

Uniqueness. Secondly, we prove the uniqueness of (8) in Theorem 1.

Theorem 1. *For any initial condition* $\mathbf{x}(0)$, *there exists a unique evolutionary equilibrium to the dynamics defined in (8).*

Proof. According to Lemma 1, we have proven that the $f^j(\mathbf{x}(t))$ is bounded and continuously differentiable. Thus, the maximum absolute value of its partial derivative is a Lipschitz constant. According to the Mean Value Theorem, there exists a constant c between $x_1(t)$ and $x_2(t)$ such that $\frac{|f^j(x_1(t))-f^j(x_2(t))|}{(x_1(t)-x_2(t))} = \frac{df^j(c)}{dx^q}$. So that we can define the relation

$$|f^j(x_1(t)) - f^j(x_2(t))| \le \Gamma |x_1(t) - x_2(t)|, \tag{11}$$

where $\Gamma = max\left\{\frac{df^j(c)}{dx^q}\right\}$ and Any $x_1(t)$, $x_2(t)$ belongs to vector $\mathbf{x}$ for $\forall t$. Following the Lipschitz condition, it shows that for any initial value $\mathbf{x}(0)$, (8) has a unique solution x^{j*}.

Stability. Thirdly, we prove the stability of (8) in Theorem 2.

Theorem 2. *For any initial condition* $\mathbf{x}(0)$, *the evolutionary equilibrium to the dynamics in (8) is stable.*

Proof. We define the Lyapunov function

$$Q(\mathbf{x}(t)) = \left(\sum_{j=1}^{J} x^j(t)\right)^2, \tag{12}$$

which is positive definite since:

$$Q(\mathbf{x}(t)) \begin{cases} = 0, & \text{if } \mathbf{x}(t) = 0 \\ > 0, & \text{otherwise.} \end{cases} \tag{13}$$

Taking the first-order derivative with of $Q(\mathbf{x}(t))$ with respect to t,

$$\frac{dQ(\mathbf{x}(t))}{dt} = 2\left(\sum_{j=1}^{J} x^j(t)\right)\left(\sum_{j=1}^{J} \dot{x}^j(t)\right). \tag{14}$$

Because that at any point of time $\sum_{j=1}^{J} x^j(t) = 1$, the replicator dynamics have to equate to zero for this to make (14) equate to zero. Specifically,

$$\sum_{j=1}^{J} \dot{x}^j(t) = 0, \forall t. \tag{15}$$

$\frac{dQ(\mathbf{x}(t))}{dt} = 0$ satisfies the Lyapunov conditions required for stability, as defined in the Lyapunov's second method for stability [12].

From above, we prove the uniqueness and stability of evolutionary equilibrium. In Algorithm 1, we show the whole process of users selecting UGs to participate in FL training.

Algorithm 1. Users Dynamic Evolutionary Game

Require: Users and the UGs set $\mathcal{J} = \{1, ..., j, ..., J\}$;
Ensure: Evolutionary equilibrium solution $\mathbf{x}^*$;
1: Each user select a UG;
2: **for** $t = 1, 2, ..., T$ **do**
3:      Pay Off Computation
4:      **for** $j \in \mathcal{J}$ **do**
5:          Derive $A^j(x^j(t)) = R^j(x^j(t)) - E^j_{total}(x^j(t))$
6:      **end for**
7:      User Strategy Adjustment
8:      **for** $j \in \mathcal{J}$ **do**
9:          Derive $\dot{x}^j(t) = f^j(\mathbf{x}(t)) = \alpha x^j(t)(A^j(x^j(t)) - \bar{A}(t))$ and $x^j(t)$
10:     **end for**
11: **end for**
12: Derive $\mathbf{x}^* = \left[x^{1*}, ..., x^{j*}, ..., x^{J*} \right]$

---

4   Upper-Layer Double Auction

In the upper layer, a double auction mechanism is designed to encourage edge servers to actively response to the task publishers' requests and find out the balanced solution.

Specifically, the task requester, edge servers, and broker can be seen as an auction market, where the task requesters act as buyers who expect that the edge servers can contribute models with lower loss values. The model is provided by the lower layer, and the model loss value is calculated by (1). The loss that requester expects can be expressed as a loss vector $\boldsymbol{F_p} = \{F_{p,1}, F_{p,2}, ..., F_{p,K}\}$). The edge servers act as sellers who prefer to consume less resources to train models and the loss of models that the edge servers are willing to contribute can be represented as $F_k = \{F_{k,1}, F_{k,2}, ..., F_{k,P}\}$. We use a strictly concave and decreasing utility function $U_p(F_p)$ to measure the task publishers' received revenue with respect to its request loss F_p in (16).

$$U_p(F_p) = a \sum_{p=1}^{P} \log(b\frac{1}{F_{p,k}} + 1) \tag{16}$$

where log can catch the concave nature, and a indicates the level of the buyers' purchasing intention.

Similarly, a strictly convex utility function $C_k(F_k)$ is used to measure edge servers' total cost, which indicates the sum of communication and computation energy consumption required to achieve model loss F_k for all users under the edge servers.

The task publishers and edge servers cannot independently decide the request loss and accept loss to reach an agreement because of their contradictory intentions. There is a need for a broker to help determine the equilibrium solution. From a social perspective, the optimal solution is when trading maximizes social welfare. The Social Welfare Optimization (SWO) problem is expressed as (17):

$$\max_{F_p, F_k} \sum_{p=1}^{P} U_p(F_p) - \sum_{k=1}^{K} C_k(F_k) \tag{17}$$

$$s.t. 0 \le F_p \le F^{max} \forall p \in \mathcal{P} \tag{17a}$$

$$0 \le F_k \le F^{max}, \forall k \in \mathcal{K} \tag{17b}$$

$$F_p = F_k, \forall p \in \mathcal{P}, \forall k \in \mathcal{K} \tag{17c}$$

Constraints (17a) and (17b) indicate that the loss value has to satisfy the tolerate value. (17c) indicates the requested loss should equal to the accepted loss when the deal is completed.

However, the optimal solutions F_p^* and F_k^* of the SWO problem cannot be solved directly because the utility functions of the task publishers and edge servers are confidential. An iterative double auction mechanism is designed to tackle the asymmetric information problem. The broker manages them to iteratively interact and adjust their bidding strategy. Assume the bids of buyers are b_p and the bids of sellers are b_k, then the SWO problem can be converted to the form in (18) according to the BAP problem in paper [13]:

$$\max_{F_p, F_k} \sum_{p=1}^{P} \sum_{k=1}^{K} (b_p \log F_p - \frac{1}{2} b_k F_k^2) \tag{18}$$

$$s.t. 0 \le F_p \le F^{max} \forall p \in \mathcal{P} \tag{18a}$$

$$0 \le F_k \le F^{max}, \forall k \in \mathcal{K} \tag{18b}$$

$$F_p = F_k, \forall p \in \mathcal{P}, \forall k \in \mathcal{K} \tag{18c}$$

where constraints of (18) are the same as (17a)-(17c). The log F_p and F_k^2 are used to capture the concave nature of publishers' utility and convex nature of servers' utility.

According to (18), the relationship between the bids and the optimal loss solution can be obtained. If buyers and sellers can submit bids as above, the broker can get an optimal solution. The complete solution process is not described in detail here. We have referred to the classic iterative double auction paper [13].

5   Performance Evaluation

In this section, the performance of evolutionary game and double auction algorithms is mainly demonstrated. We assume that each user is assigned a computing task, and each user trains a CNN model on the local MNIST image dataset. In order to obtain the specific values of p and q in (3), we fitted the relationship between the number of users and model accuracy in the experimental scenario of this article. Each user is assigned 600 different images as a training set, and 1000 different images as a test set. The fitting process is shown in Fig. 2. The data for each point is the average obtained after 100 repeated experiments.

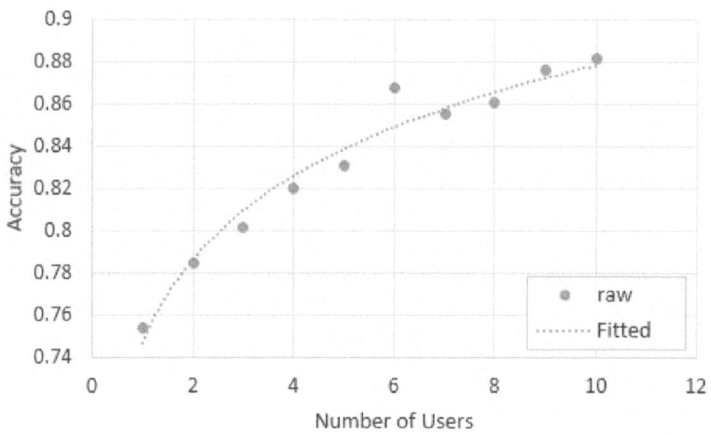

Fig. 2. Accuracy fitting

The fitting correlation coefficient $R^2 = 0.9153$, which is highly consistent. The relationship is as follows:

$$R^j \left(x^j(t) \right) = 0.0571 \log \left(U x^j(t) \right) + 0.7468. \tag{19}$$

Table 1. Simulation parameters

CPU Cycle (ξ_i)	5
Total number of users (U)	[50,75,100,125,150]
Parameters Size (w_i)	0.02 M
Local Data Size(D_i)	3.76 M
Threshold(γ)	0.001
Epoch	30
Batch Size (B)	128

All parameter settings in the experiment are shown in Table 1.

The comparison algorithm selects K-means[14] and spectral clustering algorithm [15]. Using the two clustering algorithms, users are divided into two groups based on their location, and their locations are randomly generated.

5.1 Performance of Evolutionary Game

The experiment sets all users to be divided into two UGs for dynamic evolutionary game, with strategy A selecting UG 1 and strategy B selecting UG 2.

Figure 3 shows the process of the evolution of strategy A proportion ultimately converging to the Nash equilibrium point under different initial strategy distributions. The initial proportion of selecting strategy B for a given population is 0.8, 0.7, and 0.8, respectively. The users in the population constantly change their own strategy choice, and eventually tend to be stable, and choose the strategy that is most beneficial to them. From the figure, it can be seen that under different initial ratios, the final convergence is $\mathbf{x}^* = [0.56, 0.44]$.

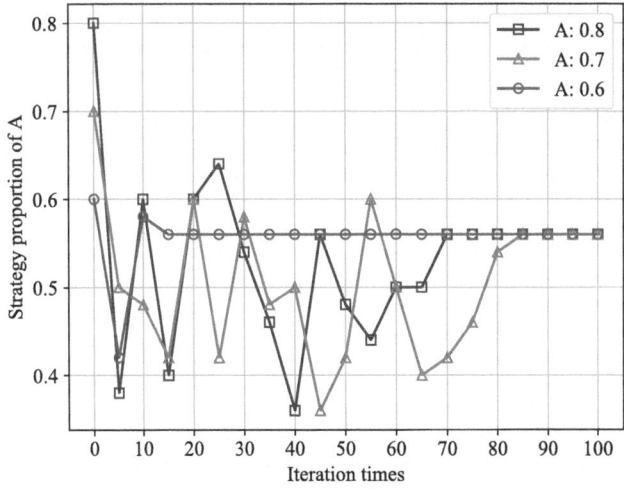

Fig. 3. Strategy proportion equilibrium with different initial proportion

Figure 4 analyzes the changes in strategy proportion under different user densities. Simulate scenarios with 50, 75, and 100 users at the same initial proportion. It can be seen that the more users involved, the slower the convergence speed. This is because the more users there are, the more time they need to adapt to the strategy. It can be seen that evolutionary games are suitable for a large number of user scenarios, and can reach stable states in different population sizes, and individuals can learn the optimal strategy.

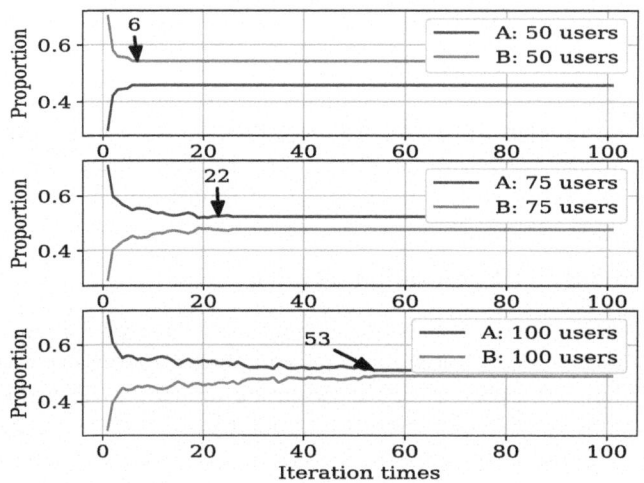

Fig. 4. Strategy proportion equilibrium with different number of users

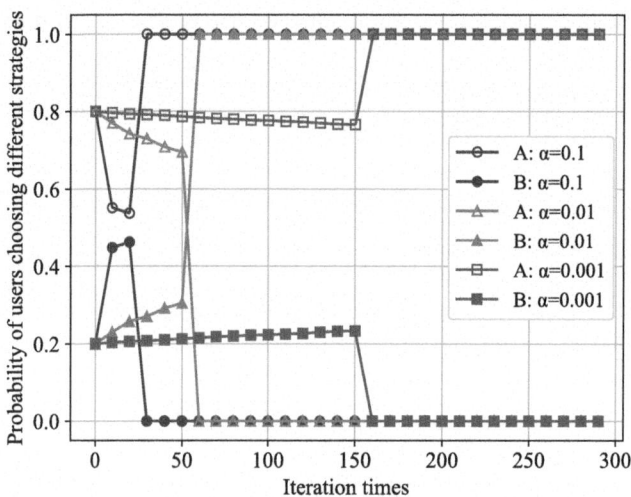

Fig. 5. Individual probability equilibrium with different learning rate

Figure 5 shows the probability changes of users choosing different strategies when different learning rate α are set under the same initial conditions. As can be seen, the larger α is, the faster the probability of choosing strategies A and B converges, that is, the faster the population adapts to the strategy, and the final convergence value is 0 or 1.

Figure 6 shows the changes in profit, accuracy, and cost corresponding to user choices A and B under different user densities. Among them, the profit is calculated by (2). It can be seen that as the number of users increases, both cost and accuracy are on the rise. The profit is gradually decreasing because as the number of users increases, the speed of accuracy increase is slower than the speed of cost increase. Therefore, in practical applications, the number of users participating in training should be selected based on the demand for accuracy and tolerance for cost.

Figure 7 shows a comparison of the total profits of different algorithms under different user numbers. Sum the benefits of different strategies to obtain the total population benefits. It can be seen that using the evolutionary game algorithm yields the highest total profits, and the more users there are, the more significant the effect, proving the effectiveness of the proposed evolutionary game algorithm. The K-means and spectral clustering algorithms can not balance the accuracy and cost when clustering, so as to maximize the interests of users and the whole.

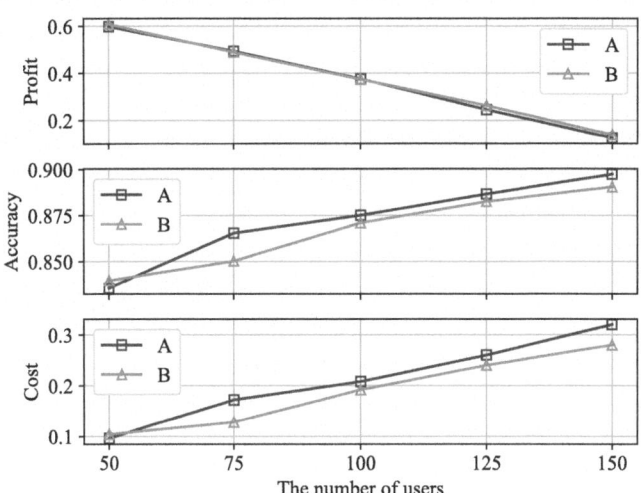

Fig. 6. Changes in profit, accuracy, and cost with different number of users

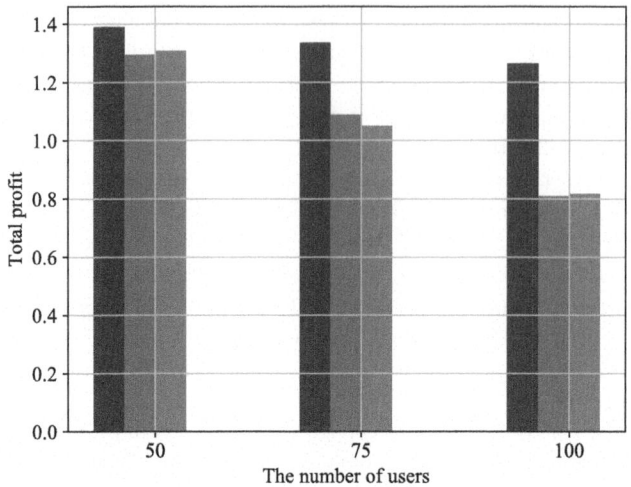

Fig. 7. Total profit

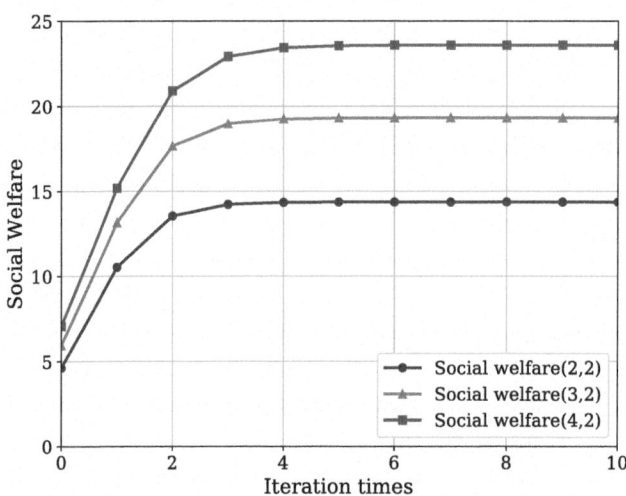

Fig. 8. Social welfare with different numbers of task publishers

5.2 Performance of Double Auction

In this part, we evaluate social welfare with the different numbers of buyer-seller matches (2 buyers-2 sellers, 3 buyers-2 sellers and 4 buyers-2 sellers). The buyers' purchasing intention factor a is set to 2. Fig. 8 shows that the total social welfare converges as the iteration number increases, and the welfare increases with the buyers increasing. This is because more members can contribute more external utility. The trend of the social welfare proves that the designed iterative double auction mechanism can effectively incentivize transactions between publishers and edge servers and converge total market utility to the maximum value.

6 Conclusion

In this paper, we propose an HFL framework based on incentive mechanism consisting of multiple TPs, edge servers and users. We use the evolutionary game to assist users to make decisions by balancing model accuracy and training cost, avoiding communication congestion. Design iterative double auction algorithm between TPs and edge servers, allocate models reasonably, and achieve maximum social welfare. The simulation demonstrates the effectiveness of the proposed framework. In the future, we will consider more factors that affect user choices in our algorithms.

References

1. Hagos, D., Engelstad, P.E., Yazidi, A., Kure, Ø.: General TCP state inference model from passive measurements using machine learning techniques. IEEE Access **6**, 28372–28387 (2018)
2. Afify, A. A., Mokhtar, B.: Machine Learning-based Services Provisioning for Intelligent Internet of Vehicles. In: 2021 IEEE 7th World Forum on Internet of Things (WF-IoT), pp. 51–54. IEEE (2021)
3. Tang, F., Mao, B., Kato, N., Gui, G.: Comprehensive survey on machine learning in vehicular network: technology, applications and challenges. IEEE Commun. Surv. Tutor. **23**(3), 2027–2057 (2021)
4. Shi, W., Cao, J., Zhang, Q., Li, Y., Xu, L.: Edge computing: vision and challenges. IEEE Int. Things J. **3**(5), 637–646 (2016)
5. McMahan, H. B., et al.: Communication-efficient learning of deep networks from decentralized data. In: the 20 th International Conference on Artificial Intel-ligence and Statistics (AISTATS), IEEE (2016)
6. Zhou, X., Liang, W., She, J., Yan, Z., Wang, K.I.-K.: Two-layer federated learning with heterogeneous model aggregation for 6G supported internet of vehicles. IEEE Trans. Veh. Technol. **70**(6), 5308–5317 (2021)
7. Lu, Y., Huang, X., Zhang, K., Maharjan, S., Zhang, Y.: Blockchain empowered asynchronous federated learning for secure data sharing in internet of vehicles. IEEE Trans. Veh. Technol. **69**(4), 4298–4311 (2020)
8. Zhao, N., Wu, H., Yu, F.R., Wang, L., Zhang, W., Leung, V.C.M.: Deep-reinforcement-learning-based latency minimization in edge intelligence over vehicular networks. IEEE Int. Things J. **9**(2), 1300–1312 (2022)
9. Hammoud, A., Otrok, H., Mourad, A., Dziong, Z.: On demand fog federations for horizontal federated learning in IoV. IEEE Trans. Netw. Serv. Manage. **19**(3), 3062–3075 (2022)
10. Ng, J.S., et al.: A hierarchical incentive design toward motivating participation in coded federated learning. IEEE J. Sel. Areas Commun. **40**(1), 359–375 (2022)
11. Zou, Y., Feng, S., Xu, J., Gong, S., Niyato, D., Cheng, W.: Dynamic Games in Federated Learning Training Service Market. In: 2019 IEEE Pacific Rim Conference on Communications, Computers and Signal Processing (PACRIM), pp. 1–6. IEEE (2019)

12. Tsuneo, Y.: Lyapunov Stability Theory. Analysis and Control. MIT Press, Foundations of Robotics (2003)
13. Li, Z., Yang, Z., Xie, S.: Computing resource trading for edge-cloud-assisted internet of things. IEEE Trans. Indust. Inf. **15**(6), 3661–3669 (2019)
14. Tanir, D., Nuriyeva, F.: On selecting the Initial Cluster Centers in the K-means Algorithm. In: 2017 IEEE 11th International Conference on Application of Information and Communication Technologies (AICT), pp. 1–5. IEEE (2017)
15. Lahmar, I., Zaier, A., Yahia, M. Bouallegue, R.: A New Self Adaptive Fuzzy Unsupervised Clustering Ensemble Based On Spectral Clustering. In: 2020 17th International Multi-Conference on Systems, Signals & Devices (SSD), pp. 1–5. IEEE (2020)

Spatio-Temporal Traffic Prediction of Wireless Communication Network Based on Multi-source Data

Yu Wang[1(✉)], Yangyang Sun[1], Yanlin Fan[1], Tao Jiang[1], Jiansheng Xiong[1], Ying Zhou[1], and Zhibo Han[2]

[1] Intelligent Network Innovation Center, China United Network Communications Corporation Limited, Beijing 100048, China
{wangyu216,sunyy204,fanyl51,jiangt30,xiongjs,zhouy36}@chinaunicom.cn
[2] Beijing Key Laboratory of Work Safety Intelligent Monitoring, Beijing University of Posts and Telecommunications, Beijing, China
Hzb123159@bupt.edu.cn

Abstract. Accurate prediction of wireless communication network traffic can assist operators in precise operation, improve communication network management, and reduce energy consumption. However, due to the highly complicated spatio-temporal dependence and the influence of multi-source cross domain data, the accurate prediction of cellular traffic is facing great challenges. In this work, we propose a Dense-convolutional-neural-network-based traffic prediction model for fusion of Multi-Source Data(MS-DCN). The model includes spatio-temporal module and external feature module. We leverage DenseUnit architecture to capture temporal characteristics with different degree of dependence and study spatial characteristics. In external feature module, the same DenseUnit architecture is employed to capture multi-soure factors. Spatiotemporal features and external features are effectively integrated to achieve accurate prediction of large-scale wireless communication traffic. In the experimental part, MS-DCN is proved to have higher prediction accuracy than the existing models on the actual cellular data set.

Keywords: Wireless Traffic Prediction · Spatio-Temporal Data · Multi-source Data

1 Introduction

With the rapid development of mobile internet and the continuous growth in the number of mobile devices, along with the widespread adoption of services like high-definition videos and file downloads, mobile data traffic has undergone explosive growth. In 4G and 5G networks, the spatial and temporal fluctuations within each cell have significantly increased. If traditional static design methods

Supported by organization x.

X. Chen et al. (Eds.): IoTaaS 2023, LNICST 585, pp. 255–267, 2025.
https://doi.org/10.1007/978-3-031-70507-6_19

continue to be employed, many base stations will remain in a low-load operational state for prolonged periods. Therefore, accurate modeling and prediction of wireless traffic will assist operators in optimizing their operations.

However, there are still many difficulties in effective prediction of cellular traffic. The essence of community traffic is the reflection of crowd activity. First, the spatio-temporal characteristics of crowd activities lead to the spatio-temporal dependence of community traffic. Nowadays, individuals in real world have dual identities–individuals in the social network and users with intelligent terminals in the communication network. Users' behavior (daytime activities, night rest) in the temporal dimension combined with their activities (commuting, shopping, entertainment, work) in the spatial dimension will infiltrate into the communication network through intelligent terminal carried by them, and further form the cell business flow in a specific time and space frame. In addition, with the popularity of modern means of transportation (subway, car), the range of users' activities in the spatial dimension is increasing, which leads to the global dependence of traffic between geographically distant communities. Therefore, how to capture the highly complex spatio-temporal dependence of cell traffic in a large area is an arduous task. Second, the crowd activity is affected by many external factors, which brings out traffic's multi-source cross-domain property. For instance, the deployment density of cellular base stations determines the upper limit of traffic in the area; User data on social network reflects the demand of mobile users for online services, and the weather and external environment will affect the activity of the crowd. As a result, how to efficiently integrate cross domain heterogeneous data (base station distribution, social network, weather, etc.) with spatio-temporal traffic data is also a problem to be solved. Moreover, once the above difficulties are solved and accurate traffic prediction is realized, how to realize the function of traffic prediction in a wider scope simultaneously (different regions in the same city, and even different countries) is a problem that needs to be considered.

Motivated by the aforementioned problems, this paper aims to solve. propose a deep learning based cross domain spatio-temporal data traffic prediction model MFMS-DenseNet. The contributions of this work can be summerized as follows:

- Firstly, this paper proposes the architecture of MS-DCN, which jointly learns the spatial-temporal correlation features and interdependence of multi-modality traffic data by multimodal deep learning architecture.
- Secondly, Extensive experiments are conducted using a realistic dataset of Beijing city, which demonstrates the efficiency of our proposed MS-DCN.

The remainder of the paper is organized as follows.

2   Related Work

With the development of mobile communication technology and Internet industry, the demand for wireless traffic prediction technology is increasing. Now the rise of artificial intelligence and machine learning has injected infinite vitality into the field of wireless traffic prediction. From the traditional time series model to the complex spatio-temporal traffic prediction model integrated with deep learning technology, many scholars at home and abroad have made large amounts of related research, which brings traffic prediction a more complete foundation.

In the traditional traffic prediction, the prediction objects are mostly single base station traffic, which can be regarded as time series without spatial characteristics. For instance, Sadek et al. [1] proposed a k-factor Geigenbauer Autoregressive Moving Average Model to predict high-speed network traffic time series with long-term dependence.

With the introduction of Convolutional Neural Network (CNN), an increasing number of researchers have taken advantage of its ability to capture spatial characteristics quickly and efficiently and applied it to traffic prediction models. The Residual Network(ResNet) can train a deep convolutional neural network model, which has been applied to a large number of traffic prediction research since it was first proposed in 2016. For instance, work [2] designed a simplified deep residual network model, which used the combination of two convolution layers and one residual units to learn the spatio-temporal characteristics of traffic.

In order to obtain more accurate prediction results, more researchers prefer to combine convolutional neural network and recurrent neural network to build traffic prediction model, which capture the spatial and temporal characteristics of traffic respectively. Gu et al.[3] established a traffic flow prediction model based on Spatio-temporal Convolution Recurrent Neural Network (STGCRNN), which uses graph convolution to obtain the spatial dependence of traffic flow data, and uses gated recurrent neural network to obtain the time dependence of traffic flow data. For instance, Zhang et al.[4] designed a Multi-Channel Sparse LSTM model, which can capture multi-source network traffic information while considering long-term and short-term dependence. Similarly, Wu et al. [5] proposed a cellular network traffic prediction model STA-LSTM based on improved Spatio-Temporal Multi-Level Attention Mechanism and LSTM, which tends to retain long-term dependent input data[6].

The above research has made some achievements in traffic prediction. Based on the previous research, this work establishes a cellular traffic prediction model for multi-source spatio-temporal data. The DenseNet convolution neural network is used to capture the spatio-temporal characteristics more completely. At the same time, the model combines the impact of multi-source cross domain data on cell traffic to extract other attribute characteristics of traffic. It can accurately predict the flow of large-scale cells.

3 Traffic Prediction Model

In this section, we first introduce our wireless communication network prediction model MFMS-DenseNet, including the design principle of the spatio-temporal module and the external feature module.

3.1   Model Framework

Figure 1 shows the architecture of MS-DCN, which is based on multi-source cross-domain data and dense connection network. The model is composed of two main components: spacio-temporal module and external feature module. The spatio-temporal module includes closeness layer, period layer, trend layer and parameter matrix fusion part. The external feature module learns the social attributes (weekdays and holidays) and weather attributes of traffic.

Based on the analysis of the closeness, period and trend of traffic in time dimension, we first extracts the data set by sliding window. Since the selected data set can be seen as the change of traffic distribution in two-dimensional space with time and has the characteristics of video stream, for the historical obser- vations which possess three kinds of temporal properties, we collect data with different timestamps, and then feed collected data into three same sub modules for training, so as to capture three kinds of time dependence: closeness, period and trend, respectively. The input data is normalized by Min-Max to improve the convergence speed of the model. After data entering the sub module, the spa- tial dependence is captured by convolutions in the DenseUnit which is mainly composed of stacked DenseLayers, and the learned features of sub modules are combined by parameter matrix fusion.

The influence of closeness, period and trend characteristics of wireless traf- fic on the final predicted output is different. We use the method of parameter matrix fusion to reflect the strength of different time characteristics with dif- ferent weights, and define the weights as W_{p1}, W_{p2}, W_c, and W_t respectively. During the training process, the learning parameters are transformed into ten- sors with the same form as the input features, so that the Hadamard product can be carried out, and then we get the output of matrix fusion, i.e. the output of spatio-temporal module. The output can be written as

$$X_T = W_{p1} \circ X_{p1}^7 + W_{p2} \circ X_{p2}^7 + W_c \circ X_c^7 + W_t \circ X_t^7 \tag{1}$$

where $\circ$ represents Hadamard product, the learning parameter matrix and the corresponding feature output matrix are multiplied respectively, and the period, closeness and trend are added to obtain the predicted feature output. Through the iterative training of neural network, the model calculate the gradient and update weight continuously, so as to accurately determine the degree of determi- nation of period, closeness and trend characteristics on wireless traffic prediction.

The external feature module uses the same DenseUnit as the spatio-temporal module to learn from the quantified data of working days, holidays and weather factors. The input is regarded as a three channel feature, and the two channel prediction results are output after convolution of the module, which is defined as X_{Ext}. Afterwards, the output of the spatio-temporal module is spliced with the

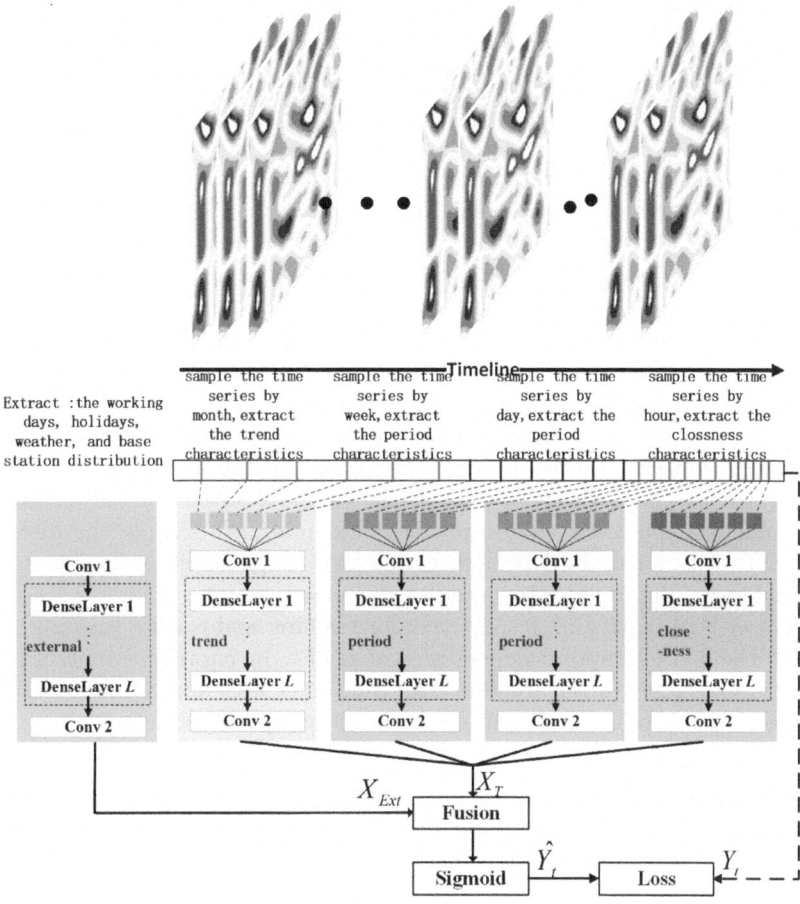

Fig. 1. MS-DCN Architecture

output matrix of the external feature before activation. We achieve the prediction output of model MFMS-DenseNet at time t, which can be written as:

$$\hat{Y}_t = \sigma(X_T \oplus X_{Ext}) \tag{2}$$

where $\oplus$ represents splicing operation, σ represents Sigmoid activation function.

Although we have used Min-Max normalization method to scall all input data into the range [0,1], the range of the output prediction data has changed after the complex operation of the model. However, the range of the real traffic label is [0,1]. In order to facilitate the error calculation between the prediction data and the real data, it is necessary to select the sigmoid activation function to map the prediction results to [0,1] one by one.

According to the predicted results and the real results, we use L2 norm (Mean Squared Error, MSE) to represent the loss function and update the parameters of the whole model during the training process:

$$L(\boldsymbol{W}) = ||Y_t - \hat{Y}_t||_2^2 \qquad (3)$$

where $\boldsymbol{W}$ refers to the set of parameters trained by the model to minimize the loss function, Y_t refers to true value. When the loss function is the smallest, the weights W_{p1}, W_{p2}, W_c, W_t and W_{Ext} also get the optimal value.

3.2   Spatio-Temporal Module

In the previous chapter, we proved that the cell traffic has temporal and spatial attributes, thus wen should set the spatio-temporal module first when building the traffic prediction model. This module includes the period layer (short period and long period layer), the closeness layer, the trend layer and the parameter matrix. Among them, the period layer, the closeness layer and the trend layer adopt independent dense connection network units. We sample the historical traffic data with a certain dependence, and then map sampled data into spatio-temporal data, put them into period layer, closeness layer and trend layer in the form of "video stream" respectively for training and feature learning, so as to mine the spatiotemporal dependence of traffic. In parameter matrix fusion part, we fuse the features learned in each time layer with appropriate weights to obtain the final prediction output of the spatio-temporal module.

Period Layer In order to get the final prediction output of the spatio-temporal module more accurately, we sample the time series in days and weeks respectively in the period layer to express the short period and long period.

Short Period Layer If $p1$ is set as the size of short periodic dependence, the historical traffic data of length l_{p1} is selected as the input of period layer. For instance, in order to predict the wireless traffic of a cell at 15:00 on January 5th, the $p1$ value is 3, then we need to take the traffic of the cell at 15:00 on January 2th, January 3th and January 4th as the input which is similar to a three-channel video. The input traffic is trained by DenseUnit, and the period layer model is shown in Figure 9 (a).

- **DenseUnit**
Denseunit contains a 3×3 convolution layer, DenseBlock framework and the last layer 1×1 convolution layer. We set the input traffic size to 20×20, $p1$ is 3. Because of the need to consider the input and output traffic, the initial input of DenseUnit in period layer should be regarded as a 6-channel input. The multi-channel input first passes through the 3×3 convolution layer. The depth of 3×3 convolution kernel is also 6. We set the number of output features of the first layer is 32, thus we need to use 32 $3 \times 3 \times 6$ convolution kernel to turn the 6-channel input of this layer into 32 feature outputs, which are defined as tensor X_{p1}^0. In addition, the zero filling operation is used to keep the output

feature size unchanged. The output of the first convolution layer passes through DenseBlock architecture, and then passes through the last convolution layer. The last convolution layer uses 1 × 1 kernel function to ensure output two flow feature graphs, i.e. two 20 × 20 3D prediction graph, which represents the uplink traffic and downlink traffic of the periodic layer respectively.

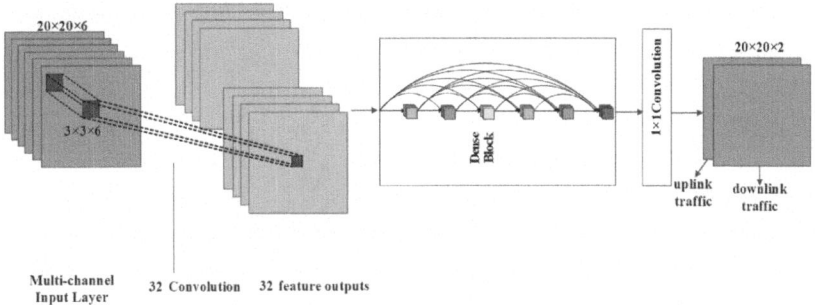

Fig. 2. DenseUnit

● **DenseBlock**

The 32 output features of the first convolution layer is taken as the initial input of DenseBlock. In this work, we define that DenseBlock contains six DenseLayers, and the dense full connection is used between each layer, namely the input of each layer is channel merging for the learned features of all previous layers. Assuming that the number of layers is i, and we define the number of output channels of each DenseLayer is 12, then the input of layer i is 32+12i and the output of the whole DenseBlock is 104.

● **DenseLayer**

The structure of one DenseaLayer in DenseBlock is shown in Fig. 10, including Batch Normalization(BN) + ReLU activation function + 1 × 1 convolution kernel, BN + ReLU + 3 × 3 convolution kernel. The combination of these six steps is defined as a composite nonlinear function $f_l(.)$, $l = 1, 2, \ldots, 6$. BN normalizes the input to avoid the input data offset to affect the training speed; ReLU function activates one part of neurons and makes the output of the other part of neurons to 0, which can alleviate the phenomenon of over-fitting; convolution kernel is used to extract features. The input features and convolution kernels are point multiplied and superimposed to get the corresponding features. The above nonlinear function BN-ReLU-Conv(1 × 1)-BN-ReLU-Conv(3 × 3) is the bottleneck structure, of which 1 × 1 convolution can be used to reduce the dimension of the picture, thus solving the problem of large number of channels caused by DenseNet full connection, greatly reducing the calculation amount.

The vector obtained after DenseBlock is denoted as:

$$X_{p1}^6 = f_l(X_{p1}^0 \oplus X_{p1}^1 \oplus X_{p1}^2 \oplus X_{p1}^3 \oplus X_{p1}^4 \oplus X_{p1}^5) \tag{4}$$

where $\oplus$ represents splicing operation, X_{p1}^{0} represents initial input and X_{p1}^{1} refers to the output vector of the first DenseLayer. The output of DenseBlock goes through the last 1×1 convolution kernel and a dual-channel output is obtained, which respectively represents the final prediction result of short period layer: incoming flow and outgoing flow. The result is written as X_{p1}^{7}.

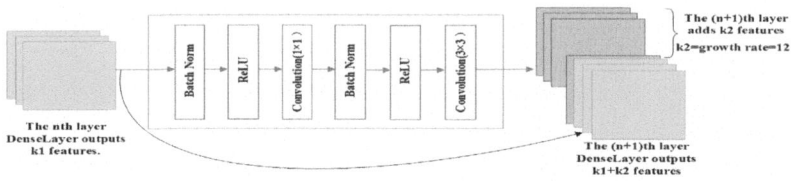

Fig. 3. One DenseLayer Architecture

Long Period Layer If $p2$ is set as the size of long period dependence, the historical traffic data of length l_{p2} is selected as the input of long period layer. For example, in order to predict the wireless traffic of a cell at 15:00 on January 5th, the $p2$ value is 2, then we need to take the traffic of the cell at 15:00 on December 22nd and December 29nd of the previous year as a dual-channel input. We still use DenseUnit to obtain the prediction output vector of the long period layer, which is written as X_{p2}^{7}.

Closeness Layer If c is set as the size of closeness dependence, the historical traffic data of length l_{c} is selected as the input of closeness layer. Assume we still predict the wireless traffic of a cell at 15:00 on January 5th, the c value is 3, then we need to take the traffic of the cell at 12:00, 13:00 and 14:00 on January 5th of the cell as a three-channel input. Closeness layer still use DenseUnit to obtain the prediction output vector, which is written as X_{c}^{7}.

Trend Layer If t is set as the size of trend dependence, the historical traffic data of length l_{t} is selected as the input of trend layer. Assume we still predict the wireless traffic of a cell at 15:00 on January 5th, the t value is 2, then we need to take the traffic of the cell at 15:00 on November 5th and December 5th of the previous year as a dual-channel input. Trend layer still use DenseUnit to obtain the prediction output vector, which is written as X_{t}^{7}.

3.3   External Feature Module

In addition to the most basic spatio-temporal attributes, the community traffic also has other attributes. We focus on the social attributes and weather attributes that have great impacts on traffic prediction. Social attributes include: working days and holidays; weather attributes include: weather conditions.

In the model MS-DCN, we propose an external feature module, and use the same DenseUnit to extract the working days, holidays and weather features of traffic. We first add labels on the data sets of working days, holidays and weather: add label 1 on working days/holidays, define non-working days/non-holidays as 0; add labels 1, 2 and 3 on sunny days, cloudy days and rainy days respectively. We extract their feature vectors respectively in hours, and then reshape each feature into 20×20 size. These three features are defined as X_D, X_H and X_W, which is regarded as a three-channel input. After going through DenseUnit, the dual-channel output is obtained, which is namely the prediction output of the whole external feature module X_{Ext}.

4   Experiment Results

In this section, we present the experiment results. Subsection 2 examines the performance of the proposed model from three aspects: traffic prediction performance, comparing methods, and comparing results between different functional regions.

4.1   Data Discription and Hyperparameter Setting

In this section, to evaluate the proposed model, we conduct experiments on the Beijing dataset. This paper utilizes the air interface total traffic data for August 2021 in Haidian, Beijing, and conducts analysis and processing on an hourly basis. The dataset is dividied into two segments: the training set encompasses hourly measurements spanning from August 1st, 2021, to August 25th, 2021, totaling 600 records, while the testing set comprises hourly measurements captured from August 26th, 2021, to August 31st, 2021, amounting to 144 records.The simulation parameters are set as Table 1.

The hardware configuration of the experimental environment includes an Intel(R) Core(TM) i9-10940X CPU @ 3.30GHz, an RTX 3090 GPU with 24GB of VRAM, and 128GB of CPU memory. The software configuration consists of Python 3.8, PyTorch 2.0.1 with CUDA 11.7 and cuDNN 8.2.4 support.

Table 1. SIMULATION PARAMETERS

Parameters	Values
Length of data	3
Learning rate	0.001
Batch size	32
Epoch size	300
close size	3
period size	3
Size with periodic dependence	3

4.2   Model Performance

Figure 4 represents traffic curves depicting actual and predicted values for a randomly selected region. The MS-DCN model proposed in this paper demonstrates strong performance on the multi-source dataset, with a high degree of curve fitting and accurate control over traffic peak occurrences.

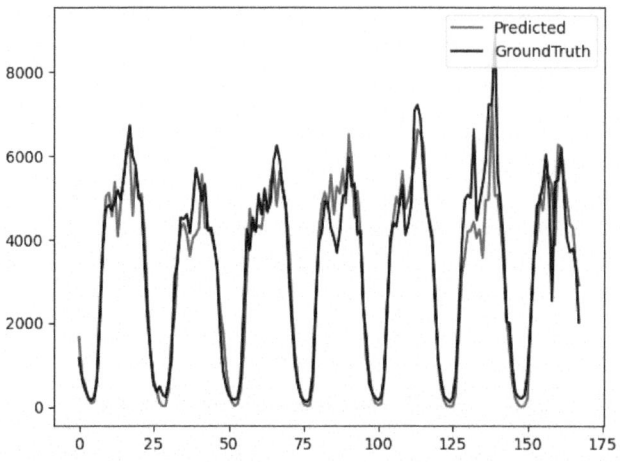

Fig. 4. Traffic volume predicted by MS-DCN

To furtherly verify the predictive performance of the proposed model in this paper, this paper compares the predictive errors of several models, including ARIMA[7], LSTM [8], XGBoost [9], DenseNet[10], and Holt-Winters [11], with the prediction error of the MS-DCN model proposed in this paper, using the same dataset as shown in Figure 5. In this experiment, the evaluation criterion

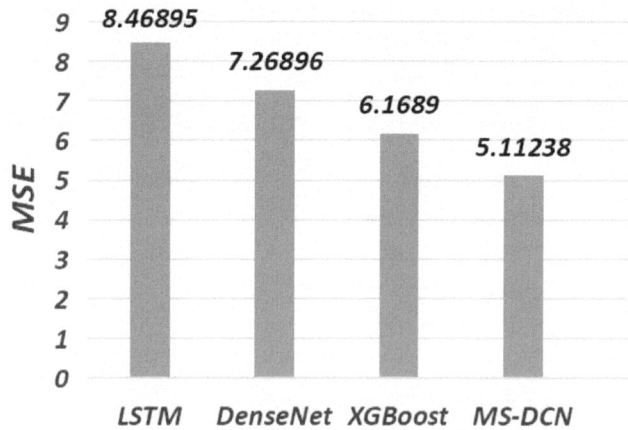

Fig. 5. Different Models' Traffic Prediction Errors

utilized was the Mean Squared Error (MSE). The LSTM and DenseNet models performed poorest, achieving MSE values of 8.46895 and 7.26896, respectively. On the other hand, the XGBoost and DenseNet models exhibited the most favorable results among the four considered models. Particularly, the MS-DCN excelled with the most optimal performance, achieving an MSE of 5.11238.

To validate the predictive accuracy of the proposed model across multiple source datasets, this paper selects two typical geographic functional areas in Beijing: University Region(UR) and Scenic Region(SR) for model prediction. In Figure 6 of the map of Beijing, the red region represents UR, and the black region SR. The predicted results by MS-DCN are shown in Figure 7.

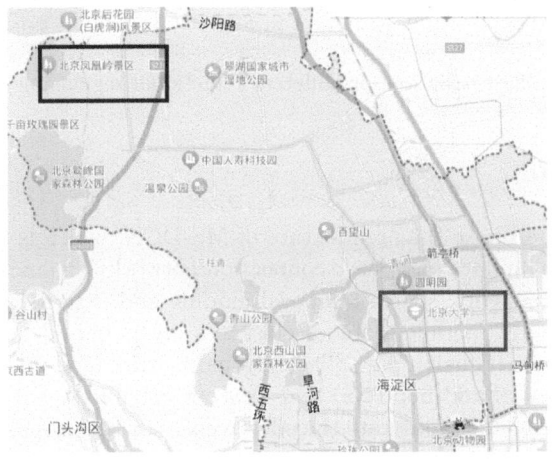

Fig. 6. Different functional regions in Haidian District, Beijing

From the Figure 7 (a) and (b), it is evident that MS-DCN performs well in terms of overall predictive performance. However, during periods of high network traffic, the model's predictions show some slight inconsistencies with the actual values. This may be attributed to certain challenges the model faces in handling data characteristics, complexity, or nonlinear dynamic changes during peak traffic hours, resulting in a slight fluctuation in prediction accuracy during these time periods.

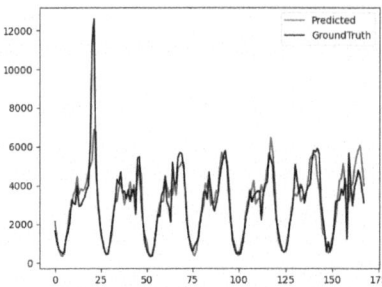 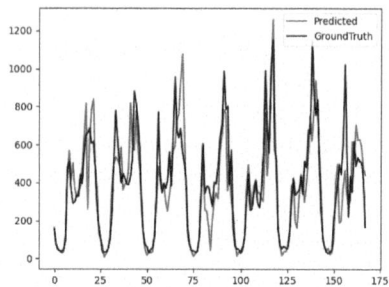

(a) Traffic volume predicted by MS-DCN (b) Traffic volume predicted by MS-DCN
in UR   in SR

Fig. 7. Traffic Prediction for Different Functional regions by MS-DCN

5   Conclusion

In this work, we propose the architecture of MS-DCN, which is based on multi-source cross-domain data and dense connection network. The model is composed of two main components: spacio-temporal module and external feature module. The spatio-temporal module includes closeness layer, period layer, trend layer and parameter matrix fusion part. The external feature module learns the social attributes (weekdays and holidays) and weather attributes of traffic.In conclusion, the experiments demonstrate the effectiveness of the proposed model's performance.

References

1. Sadek, N., Khotanzad, A.: Multi-scale high-speed network traffic prediction using k-factor gegenbauer arma model. In: 2004 IEEE International Conference on Communications (IEEE Cat. No.04CH37577), vol. 4, pp. 2148–2152 (2004)
2. Hu, X., Dai, G., Ge, Y., Ning, Z., Liu, Y.: A simplified deep residual network for citywide crowd flows prediction. In: 2018 14th International Conference on Semantics, Knowledge and Grids (SKG), pp. 60–67 (2018)
3. Cao, Y., Chen, Y.: Qoe-based node selection strategy for edge computing enabled internet-of-vehicles (ec-iov). In: IEEE Visual Communications and Image Processing (VCIP) **2017**, 1–4 (2017)
4. Zhao, L., Song, Y., Zhang, C., Liu, Y., Wang, P., Lin, T., Deng, M., Li, H.: T-gcn: a temporal graph convolutional network for traffic prediction. IEEE Trans. Intell. Transp. Syst. **21**(9), 3848–3858 (2020)
5. Xiaolong, L.I., Pan, G., Zhaohui, W.U., Guande, Q.I., Shijian, L.I., Zhang, D., Zhang, W., Wang, Z.: Prediction of urban human mobility using large-scale taxi traces and its applications. Front. Comp. Sci. **6**(001), 111–121 (2012)
6. Tian, Z.: Network traffic prediction method based on wavelet transform and multiple models fusion. Int. J. Commun. Syst. (2) (2020)

7. Wang, K., Ma, C., Qiao, Y., Lu, X., Dong, S.: A hybrid deep learning model with 1dcnn-lstm-attention networks for short-term traffic flow prediction. Physica A: Statistical Mechanics and its Applications. (12), 126293 (2021)

8. Wang, J., Tang, J., Xu, Z., Wang, Y., Xue, G., Zhang, X., Yang, D.: Spatiotemporal modeling and prediction in cellular networks: a big data enabled deep learning approach. In: IEEE INFOCOM 2017 - IEEE Conference on Computer Communications, pp. 1–9 (2017)

9. Zhang, C., Zhang, H., Qiao, J., Yuan, D., Zhang, M.: Deep transfer learning for intelligent cellular traffic prediction based on cross-domain big data. IEEE J. Sel. Areas Commun. **37**(6), 1389–1401 (2019)

10. Zhang, C., Zhang, H., Yuan, D., Zhang, M.: Citywide cellular traffic prediction based on densely connected convolutional neural networks. IEEE Commun. Lett. **22**(8), 1656–1659 (2018)

11. Zhao, Z., Chen, W., Wu, X., Chen, P.C.Y., Liu, J.: Lstm network: a deep learning approach for short-term traffic forecast. IET Intel. Transport Syst. **11**(2), 68–75 (2017)

Flying Ad-Hoc Network Routing Protocol Based on Backward Algorithm

Zheng Yu[✉] and Jianguo Yu

School of Electronic Engineering, Beijing University of Posts and Telecommunications,
Beijing 100876, China
h3104793106@163.com

Abstract. To cope with the challenge of nodes moving at high speed, we propose a flying ad hoc routing protocol based on backward algorithm (FANET-BA). When selecting a relay node, the neighboring node who has the maximum path value will be selected as relay node based on the backward algorithm. When a node encounters a routing void, we categorize this problem into two cases namely the half routing void and the whole routing void, then propose solutions for them respectively. Simulation results show that compared with greedy perimeter stateless routing protocol (GPSR), FANET-BA improves throughput by about 89.0% and successful packet delivery rate by about 55.9%.

Keywords: Flying Ad Hoc Network · Backward Algorithm · The Half Routing Void · The Whole Routing Void

1 Introduction

With the rapid growth of ad hoc, the application of flying ad hoc network (FANET) becomes more and more widespread. Traditional mobile ad hoc routing protocols including greedy perimeter stateless routing (GPSR), ad hoc on-demand distance vector routing (AODV), etc. perform well in low dynamic networks and hence they become a hot topic for researchers. However, their performance decreases drastically when the speed of nodes increases.

For the last few years, researchers conducted many researches around traditional routing protocols for ad hoc networks. In [1] and [2], the authors improved the AODV protocol to make it perform better in dynamic ad hoc. The authors of [3, 4] and [5] have studied the optimized link state routing (OLSR) protocol and made some improvements to its performance. However, it has been shown that GPSR has better performance in dynamic ad hoc networks compared with other traditional routing protocols [6][7].

Therefore, more and more researchers are focusing on GPSR protocol. The authors of [8] proposed an improved GPSR based on ant colony algorithm and improved the performance of the protocol by integrating parameters including energy, speed and deflection angle. In [9], the authors proposed a scheme designed specifically for flying ad hoc network and improved the relay node selection in the FANET environments. To obtain better

X. Chen et al. (Eds.): IoTaaS 2023, LNICST 585, pp. 268–275, 2025.
https://doi.org/10.1007/978-3-031-70507-6_20

latency performance, the authors of [10] proposed an improved GPSR (TD-GPSR) based on consideration of cross-layer factors, in which the suitable relay node was selected by considering time and space distance. In [11], the authors proposed a hybrid relay node selection strategy, in which the node would select two relay nodes. In addition, there are studies that combine GPSR and AODV routing protocol [12], the authors divided FANETs' routing process into two stages, which are the greedy routing stage and the flooding path-finding stage.

In summary, although there have been many studies on GPSR, they focused on the link quality from source node to its neighboring nodes and did not focus on the link quality after the neighboring nodes.

Therefore, we propose a flying ad hoc network routing protocol based on backward algorithm (FANET-BA). Compared with traditional ad hoc routing protocols, FANET-BA is more suitable than them for flying ad hoc networks such as UAV ad hoc and so on. Of course, it also has some limitations such as that UAV nodes must be able to know their position and speed at all times and they want more overhead to ensure that the nodes get information about their two-hop neighboring nodes. In this paper, we have two main contributions. First, when selecting a relay node, according to the backward algorithm, we consider the sum of link qualities from one-hop neighboring nodes to the two-hop neighboring nodes. Second, when encountering the routing void, we categorize this problem into two cases namely the half routing void and the whole routing void, then propose solutions for them respectively.

2   Relay Node Selection Based on Backward Algorithm

2.1   Backward Algorithm and Hello Package Format

First, in order to apply the backward algorithm to relay node selection, we need to add not only the node's own position and speed to the hello package, but also the corresponding information of one-hop neighboring nodes. Therefore, the new hello package is formatted as Table 1.

Table 1. Hello Package Format

ID	Position	Speed
I_o	P_o	V_o
I_n	P_n	V_n

As shown in Table 1, I_o, P_o and V_o are the node's own ID, location, and speed. I_n, P_n and V_n are those of one-hop neighboring nodes. Nodes periodically broadcast and receive hello packets. Based on this information, nodes can predict the location of their one-hop as well as two-hop neighboring nodes.

As shown in Fig. 1, D, E and F are the next states of A, B and C. The numbers are the weights of the paths. According to the backward algorithm, the total weights of A, B,

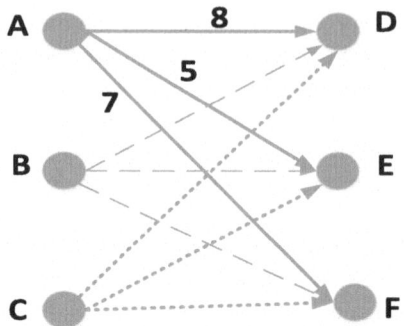

Fig. 1. The example of backward algorithm

C are the sum of weights of their paths to the next states. Then the state with the largest total weight is the optimal state. The weights of the paths are composed of state transfer probabilities and observation probabilities.

2.2 Relay Node Selection

In FANET, the next states correspond to the next hop nodes. A, B and C are one-hop neighboring nodes of source node, D, E and F are two-hop neighboring nodes. Then the state transfer probability P_{ist}, observation probability P_{iob} and the weight of path η_i are shown in (1).

$$
\begin{cases}
P_{ist} = \dfrac{1}{d_i} \\[2mm]
P_{iob} = \dfrac{1}{\left| \overrightarrow{V_o} - \overrightarrow{V_t} \right|} \\[2mm]
\eta_i = P_{ist} * P_{iob}
\end{cases}
\tag{1}
$$

where d_i is distance from two-hop neighboring nodes to the destination node, $\overrightarrow{V_o}$ and $\overrightarrow{V_t}$ are the speeds of one-hop neighboring nodes and two-hop neighboring nodes.

According to (1), we can get the total weight η of A, B or C, which is shown in (2).

$$
\eta = \sum_{i=1}^{m} \eta_i
\tag{2}
$$

where m is the number of two-hop neighboring nodes.

The node carrying data packets called source node will select the one-hop neighboring node with max$\{\eta\}$ as its relay node.

3 Solutions for Routing Voids

When a source node does not have any one-hop neighboring node who is closer to the destination node, it encounters a routing void. To solve the problem of routing voids, we subdivide it into two cases and propose corresponding solutions for them.

3.1 The Half Routing Void

When the source node has some two-hop neighboring nodes who are closer than source node to destination node, it encounters the half routing void.

In this case, we only need to calculate the path weights from the source node to these two-hop neighboring nodes. η_i of path from one-hop neighboring nodes to two-hop neighboring nodes is calculated in the same way as (1). So we can get η_{new}.

$$\eta_{new} = \sum_{i=1}^{k} \eta_i \tag{3}$$

where k is the number of these two-hop neighboring nodes who are closer than source node to destination node.

Then we need to calculate a new parameter ω_{new}, which is shown in (4).

$$\omega_{new} = \eta_{new} * \frac{\left|\vec{V_s}\right|}{\left|\vec{V_s} - \vec{V_o}\right|} \tag{4}$$

where $\vec{V_s}$ and $\vec{V_o}$ are the speeds of source node and one-hop neighboring nodes.

The source node carrying data packets will select the one-hop neighboring node with $\max\{\omega_{new}\}$ as its relay node.

3.2 The Whole Routing Void

When the source node has no two-hop neighboring node who is closer to destination node, it encounters a whole routing void. In this case, the source node will combine the number of two-hop neighboring nodes m and the relative speed of one-hop neighboring nodes to get a new parameter τ, which is shown in (5).

$$\tau = \frac{\left|\vec{V_s}\right|}{\left|\vec{V_s} - \vec{V_o}\right|} * m \tag{5}$$

Then the source node will select the one-hop neighboring node with $\max\{\tau\}$ as its relay node.

4 Simulation Tests

To verify the performance of FANET-BA, we compared it with GPSR protocol in terms of network throughput (THP) and packet loss rate (PLR).

4.1 Simulation Parameters

In our simulation, we randomly placed 50 and 100 UAV nodes. The range of network is 100 km * 100 km, the communication distance of nodes is 10 km and the broadcast period of Hello message is 60 s. The speed of nodes is 25 to 125 m/s. The parameters are shown in Table 2.

Table 2. The simulation parameters.

Parameters	Value
Number of nodes	50 and 100
Range of network	100 km*100 km
Communication distance	10 km
The speed of nodes	25–125 m/s
Broadcast period	60 s

4.2 Simulation Results

First, we randomly placed 50 nodes and their speeds are 25–125 m/s. The performance of two routing protocols is shown in Figs. 2 and 3.

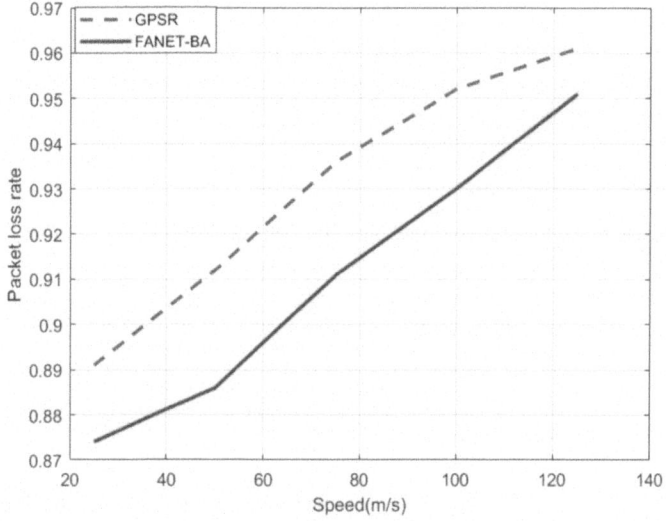

Fig. 2. The PLR of the two routing protocols

As shown in Fig. 2, the PLR of both routing protocols increases with increasing speed, but the PLR of FANET-BA is always lower than that of GPSR. In other words, compared with GPSR, the successful packet delivery rate (PDR) of FANET-BA increases by about 28.6%.

As shown in Fig. 3, the THP of both routing protocols decreases with increasing speed, but the THP of FANET-BA is higher than that of GPSR. Compared with GPSR, THP of FANET-BA increases by about 17.3%.

Then we randomly placed 100 nodes. Their speeds are also 25–125 m/s. The performance of two routing protocols is shown in Figs. 4 and 5.

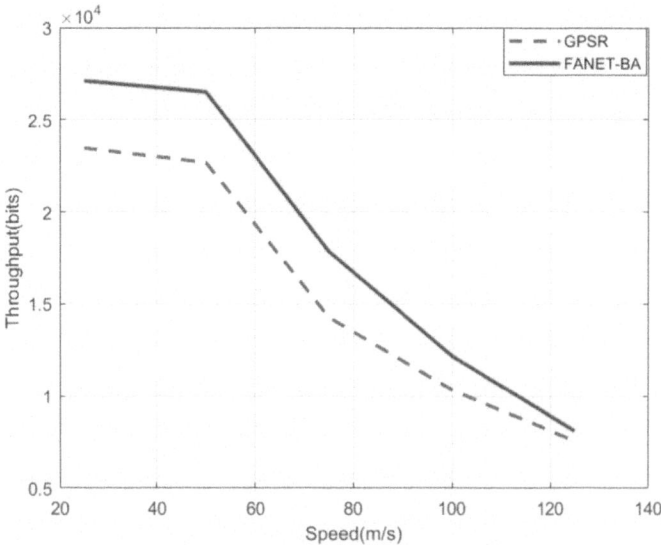

Fig. 3. The THP of the two routing protocols

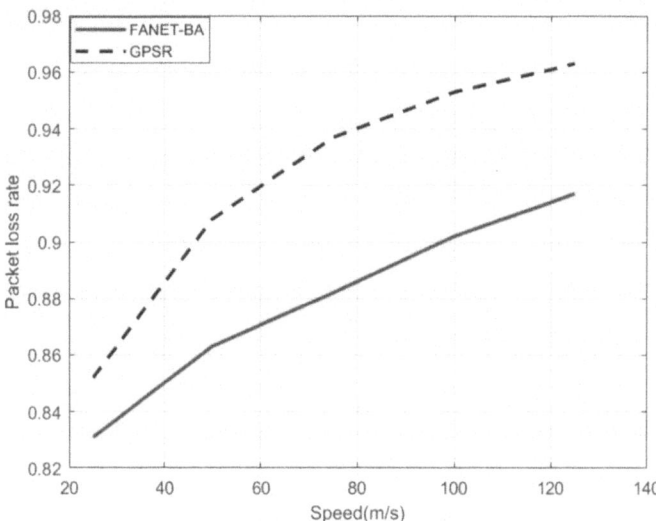

Fig. 4. The PLR of the two routing protocols

As shown in Fig. 4, the trend of PLR is similar to Fig. 2. Compared with GPSR, the PDR of FANET-BA increases by about 55.9%.

As shown in Fig. 5, the trend of THP is similar to Fig. 3. Compared with GPSR, the THP of FANET-BA increases by about 89.0%.

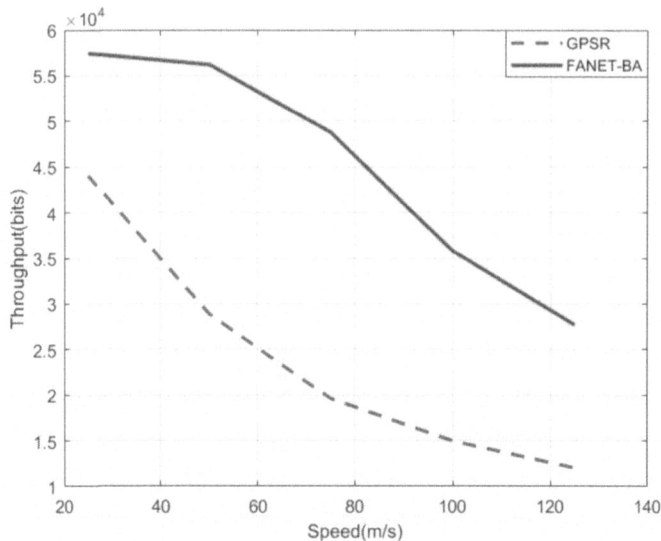

Fig. 5. The THP of the two routing protocols

5   Conclusion

Our simulation shows that compared with GPSR protocol, FANET-BA has lower packet loss rate and higher throughput in flying ad hoc networks. This shows that FANET-BA has better adaptability as well as development prospects in flying ad hoc networks.

References

1. Liu, H., Yang, L., Zhang, Y.: Improved AODV routing protocol based on restricted broadcasting by communication zones in large-scale VANET. Arab. J. Sci. Eng. **40**, 857–872 (2015). https://doi.org/10.1007/s13369-015-1585-1
2. Nurwarsito, H., Jefta, J.C.: Analysis of the AODV Protocol with Prediction Node Trend and Static Intersection Node on the Vehicular Ad-Hoc Network (VANET). In: 2021 2nd International Conference on ICT for Rural Development (IC-ICTRuDev) (pp. 1-6). IEEE (2021). https://doi.org/10.1109/IC-ICTRuDev50538.2021.9656524
3. Li, C., Zheng, L., Xie, W., Yang, P.: Ad hoc network routing protocol based on location and neighbor sensing. In: 2018 IEEE international conference on computer and communication engineering technology (CCET) (pp. 1-5). IEEE (2018). https://doi.org/10.1109/CCET.2018.8542225
4. Mostafaei, Y., Pashazadeh, S.: An improved OLSR routing protocol for reducing packet loss ratio in ad-hoc networks. In: 2016 Eighth international conference on information and knowledge technology (IKT) (pp. 12-17) IEEE (2016). https://doi.org/10.1109/IKT.2016.7777778
5. Amraoui, H., Habbani, A., Hajami, A.: Mobility quantification for MultiPoint Relays selection algorithm in Mobile Ad hoc Networks. In: 2016 5th International Conference on Multimedia Computing and Systems (ICMCS) (pp. 278-283). IEEE (2016). https://doi.org/10.1109/ICMCS.2016.7905672

6. Bala, R., Krishna, C.R.: Scenario based performance analysis of AODV and GPSR routing protocols in a VANET. In: 2015 IEEE International Conference on Computational Intelligence & Communication Technology (pp. 432-437). IEEE (2015).

7. Singh, K., Verma, A.K.: Experimental analysis of AODV DSDV and OLSR routing protocol for flying ad hoc networks (FANETs). In: *2015 IEEE International Conference on Electrical Computer and Communication Technologies (ICECCT)* (2015)

8. Jiang, Y., Xu, G., Dong, H., Fang, Z., Guan, Y., Zhang, Z.: Improved GPSR protocol and performance evaluation. In: 2020 IEEE Eurasia Conference on IOT, Communication and Engineering (ECICE) (pp. 234-238). IEEE (2020). https://doi.org/10.1109/ECICE50847.2020.9301937

9. Rodrigues, A., Reis, A.B., Sargento, S.: GPSR-PPU: Greedy perimeter stateless routing with position prediction and uncertainty for FANETs. In: *2020 IEEE International Conference on Pervasive Computing and Communications Workshops (PerCom Workshops)*, Austin, TX, USA, (pp. 1–6) (2020), https://doi.org/10.1109/PerComWorkshops48775.2020.9156255

10. Gao, Y., Fu, J., Lu, Y.: Improvement of GPSR Routing Protocol for TDMA-Based UAV Ad-Hoc Networks. In: *2021 World Conference on Computing and Communication Technologies (WCCCT)*, Dalian, China, (pp. 58–63) (2021), https://doi.org/10.1109/WCCCT52091.2021.00018

11. Liu, K., Niu, K.: A hybrid relay node selection strategy for VANET routing. In: *2017 IEEE/CIC International Conference on Communications in China (ICCC)*, Qingdao, China, (pp. 1–6) (2017), https://doi.org/10.1109/ICCChina.2017.8330400

12. Wang, F., Chen, Z., Zhang, J., Zhou, C., Yue, W.: Greedy forwarding and limited flooding based routing protocol for UAV flying Ad-Hoc networks. In: *2019 IEEE 9th International Conference on Electronics Information and Emergency Communication (ICEIEC)*, Beijing, China, 2019, pp. 1–4, https://doi.org/10.1109/ICEIEC.2019.8784505

A Novel HPSO-IGWO Algorithm for Rapidly Searching Optimal Fire Rescue Paths Based on IoT Architecture

Yifan Xu[1,2] , Xinpeng Wang[3] , Xiaode Chen[1,2], Jin Zheng[3], Xin Xiong[1,2] ,
and Xi Hu[1,2(✉)]

[1] School of Artificial Intelligence, Jianghan University, Wuhan 430056, China
huxi027@163.com
[2] Artificial Intelligence Institute, Jianghan University, Wuhan 430056, China
[3] School of Law, Jianghan University, Wuhan 430056, China
zhengjinsoci@jhun.edu.cn

Abstract. It is essential to choose the best fire rescue paths in the fire. By taking the advantage of both the Particle Swarm Optimization (PSO) algorithm and the Grey Wolf Optimizer (GWO) algorithm, a novel Hybrid PSO-Improved GWO (HPSO-IGWO) algorithm for rapidly searching fire rescue paths based on the IoT architecture. Firstly, hybrid particles based on the PSO algorithm and the GWO algorithm are proposed to make the process optimization of these two algorithms. Secondly, the hybrid particles are utilized to search for the optimal fire rescue paths. This not only provides a decision basis for choosing the optimal rescue path in the fire, but also provides theoretical support for the emergency rescue system, and greatly reduces the number of fire casualties. Finally, the experiment is executed for verifying the effectiveness of our proposed HPSO-GWO algorithm.

Keywords: Fire rescue paths · Particle Swarm Optimization (PSO) · Grey Wolf Optimizer (GWO)

1 Introduction

In recent years, with the acceleration of urbanization and the improvement of living standards, there has been a continuous increase in people's demand for entertainment and shopping. Currently , large shopping malls are the best choice due to their various offerings, combining entertainment, shopping, dining, and other functions. This trend has contributed to the annual growth in the number of large shopping malls. In order to attract customers more effectively, most of large shopping malls chose to locate in downtown areas or built near the city landmarks. However, this concentration of commercial structures in densely settled areas presents a significant fire hazard. In the event of a fire, it can lead to a chain reaction with serious accidents. Therefore, it is essential that people pay attention to fire safety in large shopping malls [1].

X. Chen et al. (Eds.): IoTaaS 2023, LNICST 585, pp. 276–290, 2025.
https://doi.org/10.1007/978-3-031-70507-6_21

This paper focuses on reducing fire casualties from the perspective of escape personnel. It evaluates escape personnel's individual competencies and the trade-offs between their competencies and the risk of explosion. Escape personnel aim to avoid areas with a high probability of explosions and maintain a certain escape distance from potential explosion sites. Responses of escape personnel are influenced by their physical condition: people in better physical condition can escape more quickly, but people in poorer physical condition face an increased risk of moving slowly during escape. This leads to easier death of people in poor physical condition. In this paper, A novel HPSO-IGWO algorithm is proposed, of which takes the advantage of both the Particle Swarm Optimization (PSO) algorithm and the Grey Wolf Optimizer (GWO) algorithm. It can rapidly search fire rescue paths based on the IoT architecture.

2 PSO Implementation Basis: Information Sharing

PSO algorithm is an evolutionary computation technique [2–6] for optimization which is inspired by the social behavior of individuals in groups in nature. The particle swarm algorithm applied to optimization problems is very simple [7]. In each iteration of PSO, every particle evaluates the fitness of its current position (solution) and compare it with the best solution they have arrived at. If the new best solution particle is better, it will replace the individual/group best solution. In the end of each iteration, the new best solution is compared with the previous best solution, if the fitness is better, the record of the best solution of population will be updated. The process will continue until the fitness requirement or the maximum number of iterations is reached. At this point, the final result can be outputted (Fig. 1, Tables 1, 2).

2.1. In the particle swarm optimization algorithm, each person in the fire is represented as a particle. This algorithm aims to find the best escape route for every escaped person. In the process of finding the best of escape routes, two types of behavior are exhibited as follows:

(1) Individual behaviors;
(2) Group behaviors.

Individual behaviors: the escaped person will update his/her position in the process of finding the best route.

Group behaviors: escaped people update their position as they search for the best route based on the direction of the group's escape.

Suppose there is a swarm of N particles at the fire site, each particle has a position vector.

$$X_{id} = \{x_{i1}, x_{i2}, x_{i3}, ..., x_{iN}\}, i = 1, 2, 3, ..., N, d = 1, 2, 3, ..., N \tag{1}$$

Each particle has the best route value called the individual historical optimum.

$$P_{bestid} = \{P_{besti1}, P_{besti2}, P_{besti3}, ..., P_{bestiN}\}, \; i = 1, 2, 3, ..., N, d = 1, 2, 3, ..., N \tag{2}$$

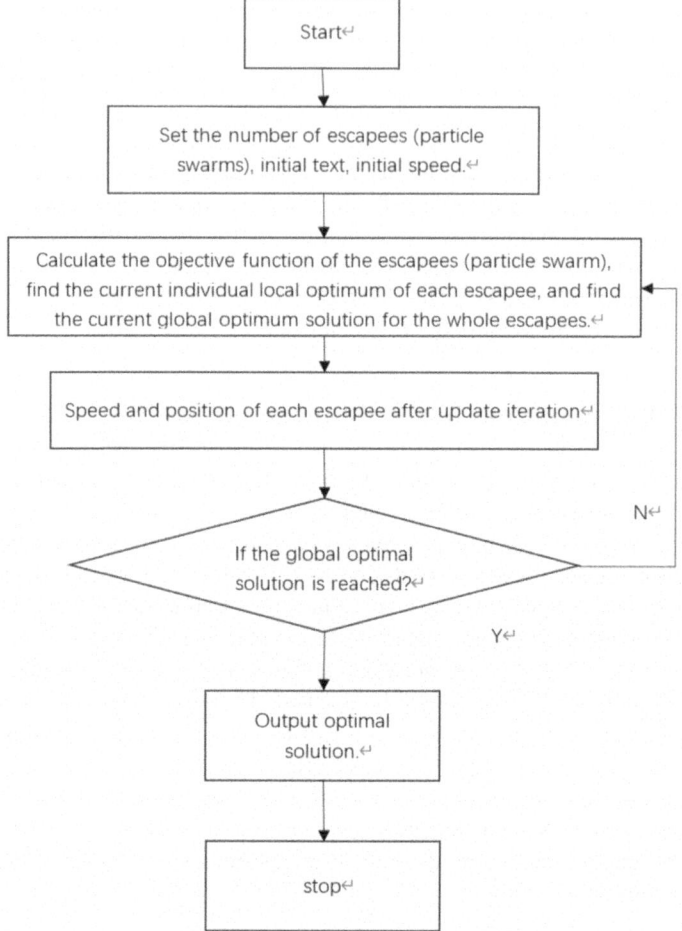

Fig. 1. Flowchart of the PSO algorithm

Table 1. Physical significance of the PSO algorithm

Escapees	PSO
human	particulate
fire area	solution space
circumstances of an injury	degree of adaptation
arrival location	individual solutions in space
The safest way to escape	global optimum solution

Table 2. Parameters that may be used in PSO-based scheduling algorithms for searching fire rescue path.

Parameter name	Connotation
D	solve the space dimension vector
N	particle swarm size
I	iteration number
i	current count
ω	inertia weight
c_1	Individual Learning Factor
c_2	Group Learning Factor
r1,r2	random number [0,1]
x_i	Position of the particle at the ith iteration
v_i	Velocity of the particle at the ith iteration
P_{best}	Optimal position of individual particles
G_{best}	optimal position of the population of particles
f_{best}	Optimal fitness of particle swarms

The best route location for the entire population of particles is denoted as the global optimum:

$$G_{bestid} = \{G_{besti1}, G_{besti2}, G_{besti3}, ..., G_{bestiN}\}, \quad i = 1, 2, 3, ..., N, d = 1, 2, 3, ..., N \tag{3}$$

The speed of each escaped person is inconsistent, and the flight speed of the ith escaped person is noted as:

$$V_{id} = \{V_{i1}, V_{i2}, V_{i3}, ..., V_{iN}\}, i = 1, 2, 3, ..., N, d = 1, 2, 3, ..., N \tag{4}$$

Speed of the ith escaped person after nth iteration:

$$V_{id}(t + 1) = +m_1 n_1 (P_{bestid}(t) - x_{id}(t)) + m_2 n_2 (G_{bestid} - x_{id}(t)), \quad i = 1,2,...,N, c = 1,2,...,N \tag{5}$$

Location Updates:

$$X_{id}(t + 1) = X_{id}(t) + V_{id}(t), i = 1, 2, 3, ..., N, d = 1, 2, 3, ..., N \tag{6}$$

3 The Flight Speed of the Escaped People (Particles) Mentioned Earlier Comprises Three Components

(1) **Inertial Component**: It consists of the previous velocity and own displacement of the escaped people (particles). It indicates the degree of dependence of the escaped people (particles) on their motion condition at the fire site.

(2) **Cognitive Component**: It consists of a learning factor, a random number and the positional difference between the current position and the best position previously reached by the escaped person. It indicates how much the escaped person thinks about and how much he trusts the result of his exploration.

(3) **Social Component**: It consists of a learning factor, a random number and the positional difference between the current position and the best position ever reached by the escaped group. It evaluates the degree of confidence in the results of group exploration according to their reflections on the results when the individuals try to escape.

The GWO algorithm was introduced to manage the phenomena related to dependency and self-learning in response to a fire and explosion incidence. It defines different hierarchies of identities present that exist at a fire and explosion incident. These identities include firefighter, able-bodied young people (male), able-bodied young people (female) and young or elderly persons (who are physically capable of independent mobility). These identities are "hunter-grey wolves", indicating that they play a specific role in responding to fire and explosion incidents, similar to the different levels and roles in a grey wolf pack (Table 3).

Table 3. Hierarchy of the GWO algorithm

identities	hierarchy
firefighter	α
able-bodied young people (male)	β
able-bodied young people (female)	δ
Young or elderly persons (who are physically capable of independent mobility)	ω

Grey wolf packs are divided into 4 hierarchies α, β, δ, ω (physical condition from the largest to the smallest) modelling leadership. Consider α as the individual fitness best solution, followed by β, the best solution as δ, the waiting solution as ω, and ω hunting following α, β, δ bootstrapping.

3.1 "Surrounding the prey"

In the course of the "hunt", the behaviors of the "grey wolf" in rounding up the "prey" is defined as follows:

Formula for distance between individual and casualty:

$$D = |C * X_p(t) - X(t)| \tag{7}$$

"Grey wolf" position update formula:

$$X(t+1) = X_p(t) - A \cdot D \tag{8}$$

coefficient vector:

$$A = 2a \cdot r1 - a \tag{9}$$

$$C = 2 \cdot r2 \tag{10}$$

where: t is the number of iterations, α is the convergence factor, r1 and r2 are random vectors. After the movement of the "grey wolf" group to α, the "grey wolf" identified the location of the injured, under the leadership of α, β, δ. In order to guide the "wolf pack" to rescue the injured surrounded people.

3.2 "Hunting"

In the model of an individual "grey wolf",tracking the location of its prey is described as follows:

(The "wolf pack" will search for "prey" by first identifying α, β, δ. As α, β, δ each approach the target point, their routes of movements are not the same. They have different speeds and directions. So the average position of the three is defined as follows.)

$$D_\alpha = |C_1 \cdot X_\alpha - X| \tag{11}$$

$$D_\beta = |C_2 \cdot X_\beta - X| \tag{12}$$

$$D_\delta = |C_3 \cdot X_\delta - X| \tag{13}$$

where: $D_\alpha, D_\beta, D_\delta$ represent the distance between α, β, δ and other injured individuals, respectively; $X_\alpha, X_\beta, X_\delta$ represent the current position of α, β, δ, respectively; C_1, C_2, C_3 is a random vector and X is the current position of the grey wolf.

$$X_1 = X_\alpha - A_1 \cdot D_\alpha \tag{14}$$

$$X_2 = X_\beta - A_2 \cdot D_\beta \tag{15}$$

$$X_3 = X_\delta - A_3 \cdot D_\delta \tag{16}$$

$$X_{t+1} = \frac{X_1 + X_2 + X_3}{3} \tag{17}$$

3.3   Improved GWO Algorithm Description

In the GWO algorithm, the improper initial selection of escaped people result in the objective function leading to slower convergence rates and failing to converge to the best solution. Ultimately, it increases the potential for casualties.

It can increase the diversity of the wolf pack in this new algorithm. And the nonlinear control parameter is used to balance the global search and local search ability of the algorithm and improve the convergence speed of the algorithm. At the same time, the idea of PSO is introduced, it utilize the best value of the individual and the best value of the wolf pack to update the position information of each grey wolf. This method preserves the best position information of the individual and avoids the algorithm falling into a local optimum [8]. The PSO algorithm is reintroduced into the process. In this framework, the PSO algorithm is utilized to sort the generated escape routes and assign routes length and routes nodes to variables α, β and δ, respectively. And the the GWO algorithm follows routes α, β and δ to escape or rescue.

It illustrates that the GWO algorithm updates the position of the "grey wolf" by considering the positions of wolves α, β and. However, it does not consider the problem of information exchange between the "grey wolves", which increases the possibility falling into a local optimum. To solve this problem, a dynamic weighting rule is introduced to maintain the leadership role of "gray wolf α.

Dynamic weighting rules:

$$C_1 = \frac{random(0,\, 1)}{2} \tag{18}$$

$$C_2 = \frac{1 - random(0,\, 1)}{2} \tag{19}$$

$$C_3 = 0.5 \tag{20}$$

$$W_{(t+1)} = C_3 W_1 + C_2 W_2 + C_1 W_3 \tag{21}$$

The dynamic weighting rule is designed to maintain the relative proportions of "grey wolves". And random inertia weights are introduced for β and δ. This rule facilitates the communication between the two sub-populations, it enables the exchange of information in the population and accelerates the transfer of information between different "wolves". Because α is experienced and gradually tends to find the best solution. It is regarded as the "grey wolf leader". By using different coefficients, communication between β and δ is enhanced to diversify the population dynamics. As a result, it reduces the sensitivity of the algorithm to local optimal solutions and accelerates the overall convergence to the global optimal solution.

4   A New HPSO-IGWO Algorithm

Many researchers have proposed hybridized variants of several heuristic variants. According to Talbi [9], two variants can be hybridized in low level or high level with relay or coevolutionary techniques as heterogeneous or homogeneous. We hybridize PSO with GWO algorithm using low-level coevolutionary mixed hybrid [10].

$$\vec{d_\alpha} = \left| \vec{c_1} \cdot \vec{x_\alpha} - \omega * \vec{x} \right| \tag{22}$$

$$\vec{d_\beta} = \left| \vec{c_2} \cdot \vec{x_\beta} - \omega * \vec{x} \right| \tag{23}$$

$$\vec{d_\delta} = \left| \vec{c_3} \cdot \vec{x_\delta} - \omega * \vec{x} \right| \tag{24}$$

The updated velocity and equation:

$$v_i^{k+1} = \omega * \left(v_i^k + c_1 r_1 \left(x_1 - x_i^k \right) + c_2 r_2 (x_2 - x_i^k) + c_3 r_3 \left(x_3 - x_i^k \right) \right) \tag{25}$$

$$x_i^{k+1} = x_i^k + v_i^{k+1} \tag{26}$$

4.1   Stop Scrambling Strategies and Greedy Mechanisms

The GWO is a new efficient population-based optimizer. The GWO algorithm can reveal an efficient performance compared to other well-established optimizers. However, because of the insufficient diversity of wolves in some cases, a problem of concern is that the GWO still is prone to stagnation at local optima. To solve the problem, an interruption perturbation strategy is introduced, drawing inspiration from Lévy flight. Lévy flights are a particular class of generalized random walk in which the step lengths during the walk are described by a 'heavy-tailed' probability distribution. They can describe all stochastic processes that are scale invariant [11–13]. In this paper, an improved modified GWO algorithm is proposed for solving both global and real-world optimization problems [11].

$$\sigma_u = \left[\frac{\Gamma(1 + \beta) \sin(\frac{\pi \beta}{2})}{\Gamma(\frac{1+\beta}{2}) \beta \times 2^{\frac{\beta-1}{2}}} \right] \tag{27}$$

$$\sigma_u = 1 \tag{28}$$

$$S = \frac{u}{|v|^{\frac{1}{\beta}}} \tag{29}$$

In the formula: s is a random step size, u and v are normally distributed parameters, Γ is a gamma function, and β is a random value chosen in the interval [0,2] at each iteration. In the strategy of Lévy's flight algorithm, it can generate many small and sudden long-distance jumps, which can help the "grey wolf" in the process of exploring the "prey" balance, and reach the global optimum as soon as possible.

4.2 Spoiler Strategy

$$W_i^{t+1} = W^* + randn \times Levy(W_i) + randn \times \left| W^* - W_i^t \right| \tag{30}$$

$$Levy(W_i) = ts(W^* - W_i^t) \tag{31}$$

In this formula, *randn* is the normal distribution of the random two; $t \in [-1, 1]$ is the scale factor; W^* is the global optimum, which may change with the number of iterations.

4.3 Analysis

Lévy flight has the ability to generate a large number of small jumps and the occasional sudden long jumps. These movements facilitate random position updates to prevent the 'grey wolf' from falling into local optimal solutions. However, Lévy flight cannot guarantee an improvement in fitness compared to the original solution [13].

Motivated by the above, the Lévy flight algorithm is seamlessly integrated with the First-Come-First-Served (FCFS) priority scheduling algorithm. FCFS is an effective way to minimize casualties by consistently prioritizing the process currently at the top of the rescue queue for execution.

5 At the Fire Blasting Site, the Previously Defined Identities are not the Sole Occupants; There Are also Specific Categorizations for Casualties

(1) Critical Injuries: These critically injured patients need immediate treatment. Timely intervention can provide a chance of survival.
(2) Stable Injuries: Patients with stable injuries are able to maintain a steady respiratory cycle despite being injured and unable to walk. The treatment of their injuries can wait a little while. It is not immediately life-threatening and does not cause muscle disability.
(3) Minor Injuries: These patients with minor injuries are still able to move on their own. They are assigned a lower priority for treatment and can assist rescuers with initial assistance.
(4) Non-responsive Injuries: Patients in this category have non-beating hearts and have ceased breathing due to severe injuries. These people are confirmed dead or near dead at the scene, and they are given the lowest priority for treatment (Table 4)

Each casualty has a priority, which is represented by the number of priorities.

If the priorities are different, the process with the highest priority is scheduled; if the priorities are the same, it is scheduled in FCFS order, and the casualty with the same priority who has waited the longest in the rescue queue is selected, to avoid the death of currently surviving casualties due to excessive waiting time.

Table 4. Priority of the scheduling algorithm

Classification of casualties	priority
Injuries are critical, and these are the types of patients who need immediate treatment for their injuries If treated in time they have a chance of survival	1
Patients with stable injuries, but who are unable to walk, have stable respiratory circulation, and have significant trauma.but can still wait briefly without endangering their lives or causing muscular disability	2
They are minor injuries and can move on their own, these patients are given a third order of treatment and even these patients can be used as a human resource to help the rescuers in first aid	3
Injured patients whose hearts are not beating and who are not breathing due to the severity of their injuries and who have been confirmed dead or dying at the scene are among the lowest priority patients	4

The rescuers are prioritized to rescue casualties with high priority, it reduces the number of deaths. Define the above classification of casualties as "prey" status in the GWO algorithm, and "hunter-grey wolf" ($\alpha,\beta,\delta,\omega$) play an important role in the collective rescue process by completing the following steps under the leadership of α during the rescue process:

① Finding and approaching the injured
② Judging the classification of casualties
③ Whether or not assistance is provided

5.1 Attacking "Prey"

When the rescuers stop moving, in order to stimulate the approaching casualties, the value of a will gradually decrease during the iterations and the value of A will stabilize, this ultimately determines whether or not the next casualty is rescued or selected. (n is the current number of iterations, N is the maximum number of iterations.)

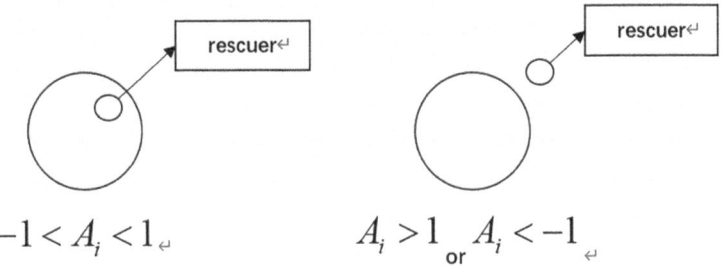

$$a = 2 - 2 \cdot n/N \tag{32}$$

$$A = rand(-a, a) \tag{33}$$

After patrolling the "prey", it is able to determine which of the above scenarios the casualty falls into (Priority 1 - Priority 4), setting the judgement value to S_i and storing the results of each iteration of the calculation into A_i when the priority is $-1 < A_i < 1$. The "wolves" attack the "prey" according to priority scheduling - this is a local optimum. When the priority is $A_i > 1$ or $A_i < -1$, the "grey wolf" stays away from the "prey" and explores the rest of the area (in order to find the global optimal solution and save as many people as possible). Judging the value of S_i at each iteration. If $1 < S_i < 3$, then conduct rescue; if $S_i > 4$, then give up and move on to the next casualty, in order to minimize the number of casualties and help more to survive. (The priorities of rescue is mentioned above and can be further divided, but we don't deep in here.)

6   The Ablation Experiment (PSO, GWO, HPSO-GWO)

At the beginning of the PSO algorithm experiment, it is assumed that each trapped person in the fire area could be regarded as a particle which could constantly update the position of the individual and the group during the iterative process. After the constant and random movement, the individual and the global optimums are eventually reached, with the final iteration converging to 1. The following images are based on the algorithm in the context of a fire scene (specify security fitness > 0.99 for convergence):

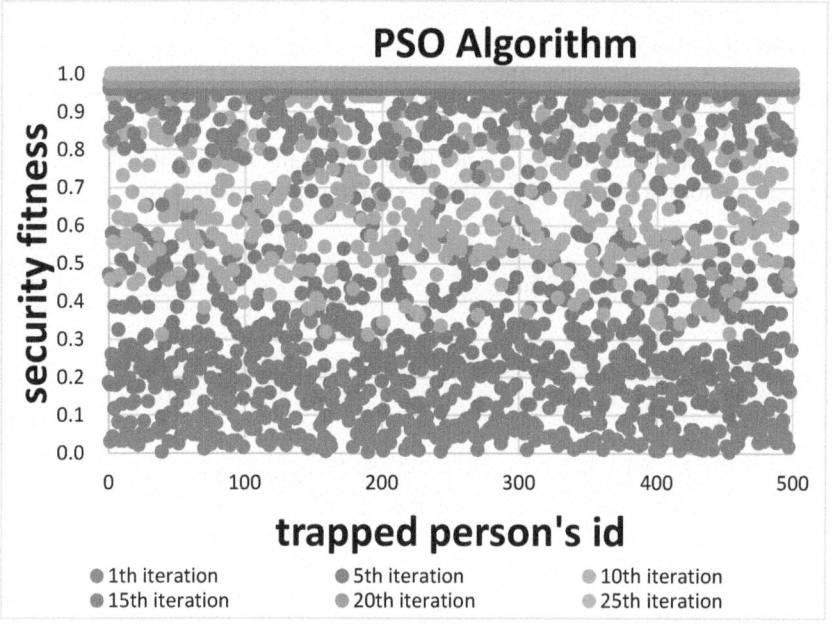

(a) obtained resulted after respective initialization, 1th, 5th, 10th, 15th, 20th, 25th. **(Marker: the algorithm stabilized after the 25th iteration with results converging to 1).**

It is then assumed that the fire area constitutes a population relationship similar to that of a wolf pack in nature. In this area, the "first level leader" who is responsible for leading the entire population, is the optimal solution of the algorithm; the "second level leader" who takes responsibility for assisting the "first level leader", is the suboptimal solution; the "third level leader" is under the direction of the "first level leader" as well as the "second level leader"; and the "fourth level leader" follows the above "leaders", leading the "wounded" in the fire area out of the danger zone according to the "hierarchical order", thereby obtaining the global optimal value. The following images are based on the GWO algorithm in the context of a fire scene (specify security fitness > 0.99 for convergence):

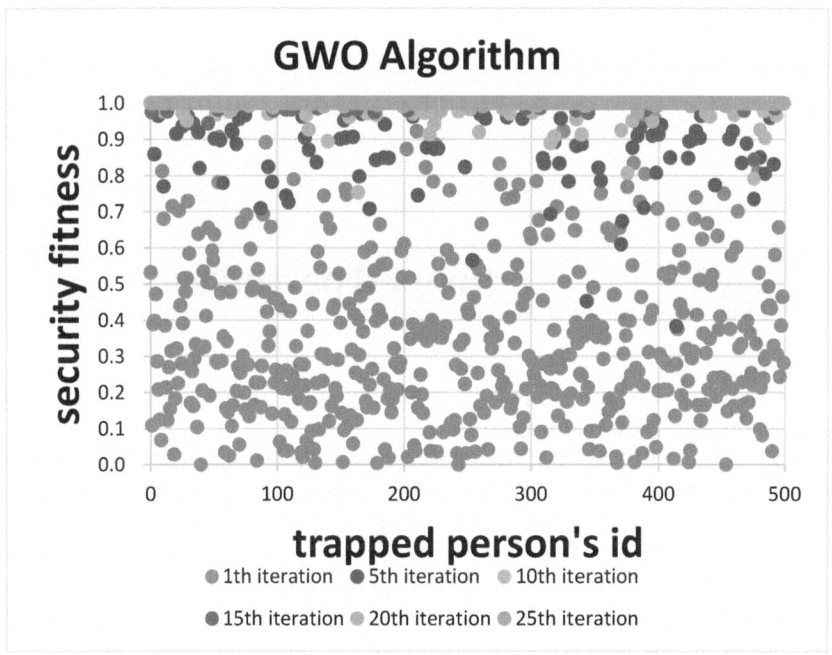

(b) obtained resulted after respective initialization,1th,5th,10th,15th,20th,25th. **(Marker: faster iteration results, but more jumps that is unstable).**

To optimize the two algorithms, a solution is needed to reduce the PSO algorithm to reduce the possibility of falling into local minima. In the proposed hybrid algorithm, the GWO algorithm is used to support the PSO algorithm to solve this problem. Therefore, mixing two algorithms to form the HPSO-GWO algorithm cloud help reduce the possibility of falling into a local optimum, for the reason that the GWO algorithm has the ability to explore the region. The following hybrid HPSO-GWO algorithm is based on the fireground context (specify security fitness > 0.99 for convergence):

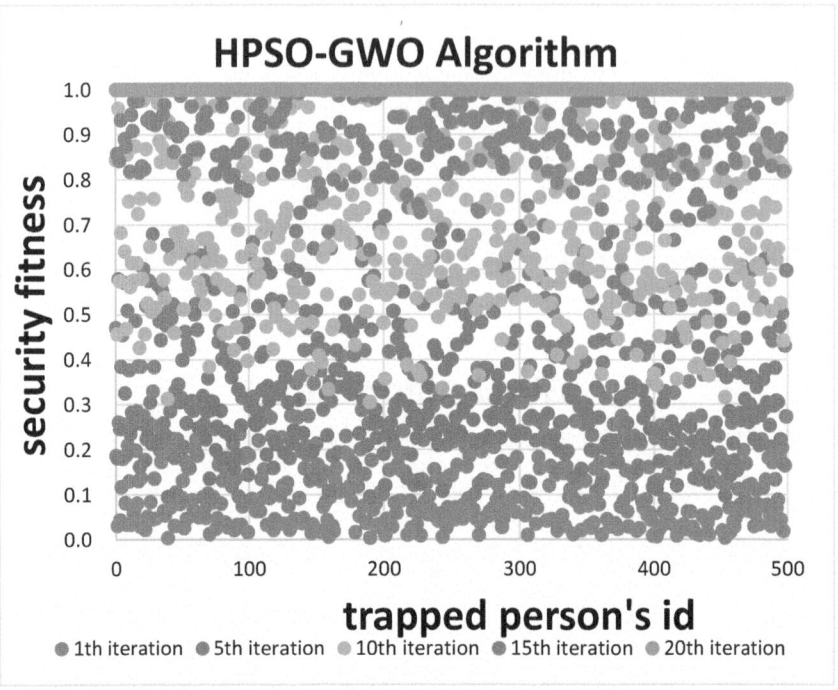

(a) obtained resulted after respective initialization,1th,5th,10th,15th,20th. (**Maker: faster and more stable iteration results**).

Specify security fitness > 0.99 for convergence, although the PSO algorithm shows outstanding performance in any practical problems that could obtain correct results, the PSO algorithm tends to fall into the local optimum rather than giving the integrate one during the iteration. Thus, the velocity of convergence is slow. The GWO algorithm has the capability of exploring, which could extend its move outward continually to find the global optimum. As mentioned above, the PSO algorithm has advantages for fast random guidance, and the GWO algorithm could explore convergence of the HPSO-GWO algorithm with the fastest and most stable speed. On the basis of these, under the circumstance of a fire scene, the faster and more precise path is needed to have more efficient rescue and minimize casualties, which is the most important thing in fire rescue.

6.1   The following is the Flowchart of this Hybrid Algorithm

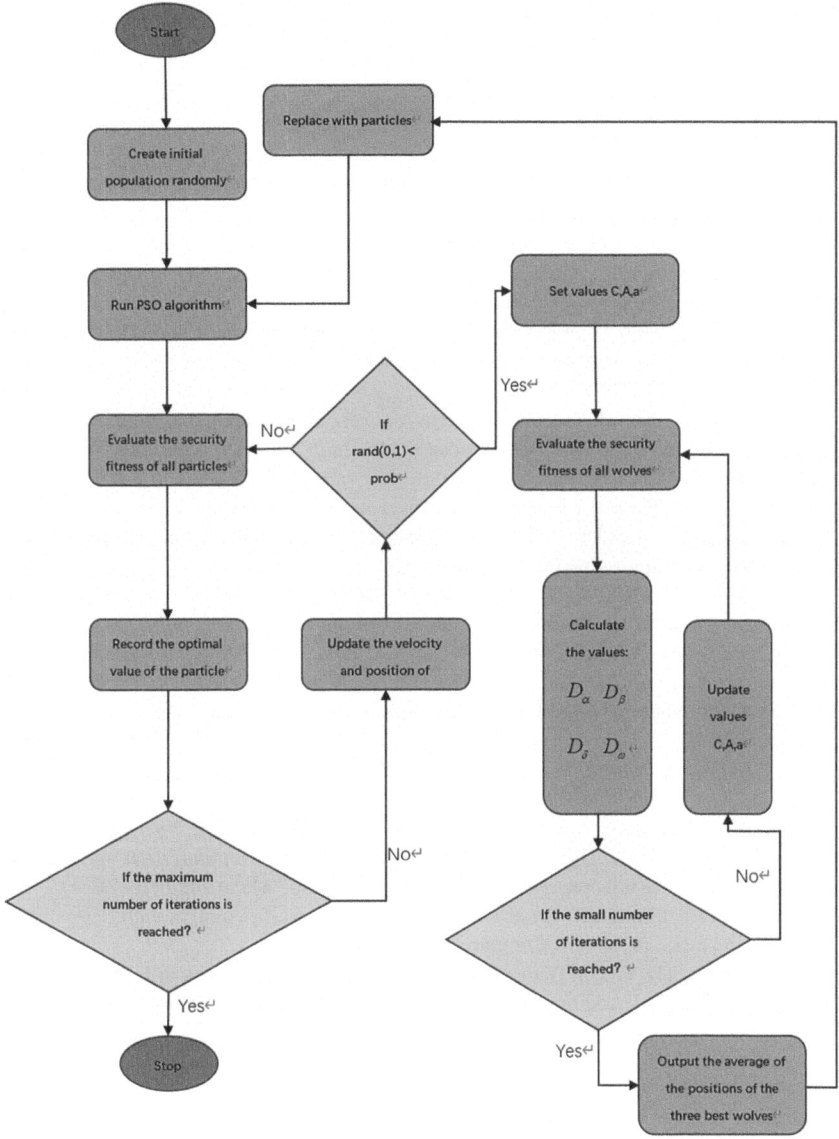

Acknowledgment. This work was supported in part by the National Natural Science Foundation of China under Grant 61901298, 71601085; in part by the Key Research and Development Project of Hubei Province, China under Grant 2020BCA084; in part by the State Key Laboratory of Precision Blasting, Jianghan University under Grant PBSKL2022303; in part by the Scientific Research Project of Education Department of Hubei Province under Grant B2022280; in part by the Young Talents Science and Technology Innovation Planning Program of Education Department of Hubei Province under Grant T2022045; in part by the Scientific Research Project of Tianjin Education Commission under Grant 2021KJ186; in part by the Scientific Research Foundation of Jianghan University under Grant 2023KJZX18; in part by the 2023 Student Research Key Project of Jianghan University under Grant 2023zd114.

References

1. Cheng, T. F.: Research on fire risk evaluation and evacuation of large shopping malls (Master's thesis, Shenyang University of Aeronautics and Astronautics) (2022). https://kns.cnki.net/KCMS/detail/detail.aspx?dbname=CMFDTEMP&filename=1023014644.nh
2. Fernández Martínez, J.L., García Gonzalo, E.: The generalized PSO: a new door to PSO evolution. J. Artif. Evol. Appl. 2008 (2008)
3. Xiong, X., Hu, X., Guo, H.: A hybrid optimized grey seasonal variation index model improved by whale optimization algorithm for forecasting the residential electricity consumption. Energy **234**, 121127 (2021)
4. Xiong, X., Hu, X., Tian, T., Guo, H., Liao, H.: A novel optimized initial condition and seasonal division based grey seasonal variation index model for hydropower generation. Appl. Energy **328**, 120180 (2022)
5. Li, Z.K., Hu, X., Guo, H., Xiong, X.: A novel weighted average weakening buffer operator based fractional order accumulation seasonal grouping grey model for predicting the hydropower generation. Energy **277**, 127568 (2023)
6. Hu, X., Xiong, X., Wu, Y., Shi, M.J., Wei, P., Ma, C.M.: A hybrid clustered SFLA-PSO algorithm for optimizing the timely and real-time rumor refutations in online social networks. Expert Syst. Appl. **212**, 118638 (2023)
7. Kennedy, J., Eberhart, R.: Particle swarm optimization. in Proceedings of the IEEE International Conference on Neural Networks (ICNN'95), vol. 4, pp. 1942–1948, Perth, WA, Australia (1995)
8. Teng, Z.J., Lv, J.L., Guo, L.W.: An improved hybrid grey wolf optimization algorithm. Soft. Comput. **23**, 6617–6631 (2019)
9. Talbi, E.-G.: A taxonomy of hybrid metaheuristics. J. Heuristics **8**(5), 541–564 (2002)
10. Singh, N., Singh, S.B.: Hybrid algorithm of particle swarm optimization and grey wolf optimizer for improving convergence performance. J. Appl. Math. 2017 (2017)
11. Heidari, A.A., Pahlavani, P.: An efficient modified grey wolf optimizer with Lévy flight for optimization tasks. Appl. Soft Comput. **60**, 115–134 (2017)
12. Mandelbrot, B.: The Fractal Geometry of Nature. Freeman, New York (1977)
13. Lévy, P.: Théorie de l'Addition des Variables Aléatoires. Gauthier-Villars, Paris (1954)

A Hybrid WOA-MTCNN Algorithm for Accurate Face Detection Based on IoT Architecture

Xi Hu[1,2,3] (iD), Hang Ruan[2,3] (iD), Xin Xiong[1,2,3] (iD), Siqi Zhang[2,3,4(✉)] (iD), Ning Huang[1] (iD), and Jun Wang[2,3] (iD)

[1] State Key Laboratory of Precision Blasting, Jianghan University, Wuhan 430056, China
[2] School of Artificial Intelligence, Jianghan University, Wuhan 430056, China
sinkia0723@gmail.com
[3] Artificial Intelligence Institute, Jianghan University, Wuhan 430056, China
[4] Dongfeng Motor Corportation Technical Center, Wuhan 430058, China

Abstract. To further improve the detection accuracy in face detection based on IoT architecture, this paper designs and implements a hybrid face detection system based on the MTCNN model, and optimize the MTCNN model by combining Whale Optimization Algorithm (WOA). Firstly, we select and train the loss function weights and batch_size of MTCNN to estimate the model. Secondly, we utilize the WOA algorithm to further optimize the weights and batch_size parameters. Thirdly, we train and simulate the prediction by applying the obtained optimal parameters. Finally, we design and implement a face detection software based on the MTCNN model to test the practical application capabilities of the model.

Keywords: Convolutional Neural Network (CNN) · Deep learning · Face detection · Image pyramid · Whale Optimization Algorithm (WOA)

1 Introduction

With the rapid increase in video and image database, there is an incredible requirement of face detection for automatic target detection of face information based IoT (Internet of Things) architecture, which has a wide range of uses to greatly improve the detection efficiency for facilitating people' lives [1–6]. The IoT have uncommonly extended the proportion of information over the late years, which prepares abundant significant information in real-time applications [2]. Face detection technology as a computer technology applies the deep learning algorithm as its mathematical foundation theory to determine the location, size and color of a human face in a digital image by utilizing varieties of smart electronic products [7]. Convolutional Neural Network (CNN) model is often considered as a relatively basic network model to optimize the deep learning algorithm, which is commonly used in the field of face detection. Therefore, numerical researchers have paid more attention to optimize the methods of face detection for improving the detection accuracy.

© ICST Institute for Computer Sciences, Social Informatics and Telecommunications Engineering 2025
Published by Springer Nature Switzerland AG 2025. All Rights Reserved
X. Chen et al. (Eds.): IoTaaS 2023, LNICST 585, pp. 291–303, 2025.
https://doi.org/10.1007/978-3-031-70507-6_22

Inspired by the idea of cascade classification, early deep learning based models are based on the CNN architecture [9]. With the in-depth research on the CNN architecture, researchers have further proposed more detection models on its basis [1, 9]. The authors in [10] have cascaded the CNN structure on the basis of the waterfall idea of the Viola-Jones algorithm, which can operate at multiple resolutions and has stronger recognition ability than the single network structure. Chen in [11] have proposed Supervised Transformer Networks (STN) to improve the efficiency of face detection by combining Region Proposal Network (RPN) and R-CNN algorithm. However, how to further improve the detection accuracy is still a hotspot and sticking point for researchers.

Whale Optimization Algorithm (WOA) is a meta-heuristic optimization algorithm proposed by Mirjalili et al. in 2016, which has the advantages of simple mechanism, fast convergence and strong optimization ability [12]. The Whale Optimization Algorithm (WOA) has been widely researched and applied in various fields such as energy management [13], hydroelectric power generation prediction [14, 15], and the improvement of rumor refutation [16], owing to its inherent characteristics since its introduction. Abuntant researchers dedicate their studies to optimize the method of face detection and improve its detection accuray. The authors in [17] have proposed a framework uses data augmentation to refine the original dataset, transfer learning to fine-tune the pre-trained CNN model DenseNet201, and improved WOA for feature selection. The proposed framework achieves high classification accuracy and robustness on benchmark datasets. In [18], the authors have proposed a FER process using WOA-TLBO based MultiSVNN and demonstrate its effectiveness in terms of accuracy. The proposed FER arrangement comprises three phases: feature extraction, feature optimization, and emotion recognition. The authors in [19] have proposed a method for object detection based on the combination of Non-maximum Suppression (NMS) and the chaotic whale optimization algorithm and the proposed method can significantly improve the Average Precision (AP) of detectors compared with the most advanced methods.

However, these existing researches are limited in the following aspects.

i) In current research, CNN has shown stronger accuracy and generalization ability compared to traditional methods for face detection. However, CNN's detection performance is not optimal in the presence of different lighting, angles, facial expressions, or face occlusion.

ii) Parameter settings have a significant impact on the convergence speed and generalization ability of CNN. How to select appropriate parameters is a concern of many researchers.

iii) CNN requires significant computing resources and time to handle large-scale data, which may pose limitations in practical applications. How to improve CNN's ability to process large-scale data is an urgent problem to be solved.

To tackle these limitations, a hybrid WOA algorithm based Multi-Task Convolutional Neural Network (WOA-MTCNN) is proposed in this paper to further improve the detection accuracy for accurate face detection. The major contributions are summarized as follows:

i) We employed a cascaded CNN network structure which has shown to better detect faces in different environments, thus improving detection accuracy and generalization capability.

ii) We utilized an original heuristic optimization algorithm to optimize the parameters of CNN, in order to improve its detection accuracy.

iii) Combine the original heuristic optimization algorithm with MTCNN to optimize the training time of the model and improve its speed in processing large-scale data.

This paper studies the method of face detection, uses a MTCNN to build a detection model, which based on Python + Pytorch + PyQt and other technologies, and uses the WOA algorithm to optimize the model loss function weight and batch_size to improve the model. The purpose of face detection accuracy, and build a three-layer network structure to realize the face detection system.

The rest of this paper is organized as follows. Section 2 introduces the relevant theoretical knowledge of MTCNN. Section 3 introduces the WOA algorithm. Section 4 explains how to construct the WOA-MTCNN algorithm, and Sect. 5 presents the experimental results and practical applications of the algorithm.

2 MTCNN Model

The methodological principle of the MTCNN model can be summarized as: image pyramid + three-stage cascaded CNN. This chapter will briefly introduce the concept of CNN and image pyramid, and then detail the network structure and each loss function of the MTCNN model. The contents are as follows:

2.1 CNN

Convolutional Neural Network (CNN) model is a widely used feedforward neural network model. Inspired by the idea of cascaded classifiers, many early deep learning based models are based on cascaded CNN architectures [8]. In the past, the Full Con-nect Neural Network mainly had three obvious defects in the processing of large-size images, such as spatial information loss, training difficulties, and network overfitting, and the CNN model solved these problems very well [9].

A typical CNN model is mainly composed of the following three parts:

1. Convolutional layer: usually contains multiple learnable convolution kernels, which ex-tract image features by using "filters" (convolution kernels).
2. Pooling layer: reduce the number of parameters in the network and prevent overfitting.
3. Fully connected layer: implement classification and output results.

2.2 Image Pytamid

When discussing image pyramids, an important concept needs to be addressed first: scale. Scale is the size and resolution of an image. Before operating on an image, it is often necessary to pre-process the size of the image to adjust it to the target image needed for the study. And image pyramid refers to an important way of multi-scale image adjustment expression, which is mainly applied to image segmentation and fu-sion. Each layer of the image pyramid is derived from the same original image, only the scales of different layers are different. The number of generated layers of the image pyramid is mainly determined by two parameters, Minisize, which refers to the mini-mum face size in the input image as considered by the developer, and factor, which is the scaling factor of each layer to the edge length of the previous image. Figure 1 shows a schematic diagram of the image pyramid structure.

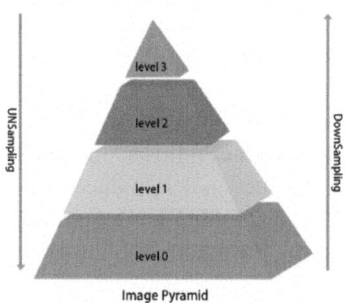

Fig. 1. Image pyramid

As from Fig. 1, the image pyramid can be divided into two generation methods by sampling direction.

1. Downward sampling: converting the image from level 0 to level 1, level 2, level 3, the image resolution keeps decreasing and the image becomes smaller.
2. Upward sampling: convert the image from level 3 to level 2, level 1, level 0, the image resolution continues to increase, and the image becomes larger.

In practical applications, the following two image pyramids are often used.

1. Gaussian pyramid: used for down-sampling, widely used in the field of image processing.
2. Laplacian pyramid: used to reconstruct an image by sampling up from the bottom of the pyramid.

2.3 MTCNN Net-Structure

MTCNN is an extension of the model proposed by Shenzhen Research Institute based on Li et al. [10] [16] for the two tasks of joint face detection and face keypoint localization. The model con-sists of Proposal Network (hereafter referred to as "P-Net"), Refine Network (hereafter referred to as "R-Net"), and Output Network (hereafter referred to as "The MTCNN Pipeline is shown in Fig. 2 [16].

P-Net is a fully convolutional neural network, similar to the idea of sliding window, which scans and detects whether each 12*12 region in each layer of the incoming image pyramid contains a face. If the region contains a face, the candidate frame of the face is returned, and after further obtaining the region of the candidate frame corresponding

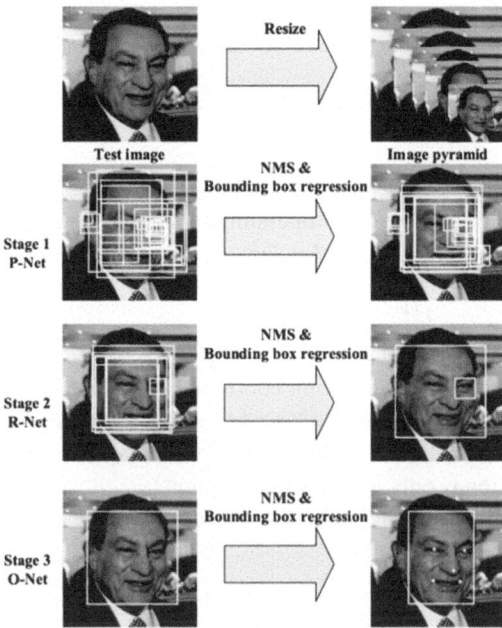

Fig. 2. MTCNN Pipeline

to the original image, the candidate frame with the highest score is retained and the candidate frame with too large overlapping area is removed by NMS.

R-Net is a simple convolutional neural network that bilinearly interpolates the candidate frames that P-Net thinks may contain faces to 24 × 24. In this layer of the network, we will further determine whether they contain faces, and if they do, we will also regress the candidate frames and their corresponding regions of the original image and filter them by NMS.

The O-Net is similar to the R-Net, it is a simple convolutional neural network, and the candidate frames that the R-Net in the previous layer thinks may contain faces are first bilinearly interpolated to 48 × 48 and used as the input of the O-Net. The final discrimination is performed on the image output from R-Net.

2.4 MTCNN Model Parameters

The most important metric for all convolutional neural network training is the loss function. In MTCNN, there are three tasks, which are: face and non-face classification, regression of face bounding box and face key point localization. In the following, the loss functions of the three tasks are explained in this paper.

1. Classification of faces and non-faces. It is actually a binary classification problem for faces, and for the input sample xi, a cross-entropy function is used, as follows.

$$L_i^{det} = -(y_i^{det}\log(pi) + (1 - y_i^{det})(1 - \log(pi)))$$

2. Face bounding box localization. For face target box regression, Euclidean distance is taken as.

$$L_i^{box} = \left|\left| \hat{y}_i^{box} - y_i^{box} \right|\right|$$

where $\hat{y}_i^{box}$ represents the coordinates of the bounding box corrected after the grid output, and y_i^{box} represents the real bounding box of the target face.

3. Face key point localization. Again Euclidean distance is taken to calculate.

$$L_i^{landmark} = \left|\left| \hat{y}_i^{landmark} - y_i^{landmark} \right|\right|$$

The $\hat{y}_i^{landmark}$ represents the keypoint coordinates obtained after the network calculation, and $y_i^{landmark}$ is the real coordinates of keypoints, which contains the horizontal and vertical coordinates of five keypoints. In this paper, we only focus on face detection, so keypoint localization is only used for introduction.

Combining the above three loss functions according to the different weights set, the total loss is:

$$min \sum_{i=1}^{N} \sum_{j \in \{det, box, landmark\}} \alpha_j \beta_i^j L_i^j$$

It should be noted that due to the differences in specific tasks of each layer of the net-work, the weights of each loss function are different for each layer of the network, and how to choose the appropriate weights for training to achieve the optimal training effect is a question worth exploring. In this paper, the joint whale optimization algorithm is chosen to optimize in order to find the optimal weight values.

Intersection-over-Union (IOU) is also a very important metric in model training. IOU is used to calculate the overlap of two overlapping images. The higher the overlap, the larger the value of the IOU. As shown in Fig. 3, the IOU is mainly used in applications related to target detec-tion. In this paper, a model is trained to output a regression frame that fits perfectly around an object. For example, in the image below, there is a green regression box and a blue regression box. The green box represents the true correct regression box and the blue box represents the regression box predicted by the model proposed in this paper. The goal of this model is to continuously improve its predicted values until it reaches the optimal situation where the blue box overlaps the green box completely, i.e., the IOU between the two boxes is equal to 1.

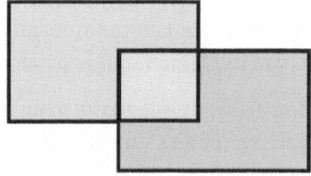

Fig. 3. IOU

The setting ratio for the model IOU is shown in Table 1. The three-layer model in the original MTCNN can achieve 94.6% accuracy in P-Net, 95.4% accuracy in R-Net, and 95.4% accuracy in O-Net.

Table 1. (IOU threshold definition).

Data Type	Negative	Positive	Part
IOU	< 0.3	> 0.65	0.4 ~ 0.65

3   Whale Optimization Algorithm

Whale Optimization Algorithm (WOA) is a meta-heuristic optimization algorithm proposed by Prof. Mirjalili in 2016 [7]. The algorithm seeks the optimal objective by simu-lating the behavioral pattern of humpback whale hunting.

3.1   Algorithm Fundamentals

Humpback whales have a special hunting method called bubble net foraging. In nature, humpback whales usually live in groups. During the feeding process, humpback whales will surround their prey in groups, spitting out bubbles during the spiral movement, forming a spiral "bubble net" and then forcing the prey tighter and tighter. WOA simulates this special feeding mechanism of humpback whales, which includes: encircling the prey, bubble net feeding mode (local search), searching for prey (global search).

4   Build WOA-MTCNN Algorithm

In this paper, the following comparisons and improvements are made to address the charac-teristics of the MTCNN model.

1. Minisize is dynamically set for the input image size to be detected to better adapt to the faces in different size images, so that the number of image pyramid layers to be de-tected by the incoming model is reasonable and the detection rate is improved.
2. The effects of different weight loss functions on the accuracy and recall of de-tection for the same batch_size in each layer of the network are compared.
3. Compare for different batch_size and study and analyze its effect on gradient descent direction.
4. Combine the whale optimization algorithm to find out the optimal loss function weights and batch_size.

The flow chart of the algorithm is as follows:
Step 1. Initialize the loss function weights and batch_size of MTCNN.
Step 2. Use the WOA algorithm to continuously update the individual whale positions until the abort criterion is satisfied.
Step 3. Output the optimal weights and batch_size parameters.
Step 4. Obtain the optimal parameters, train and simulate the prediction.
The specific flow chart is shown in Fig. 4.

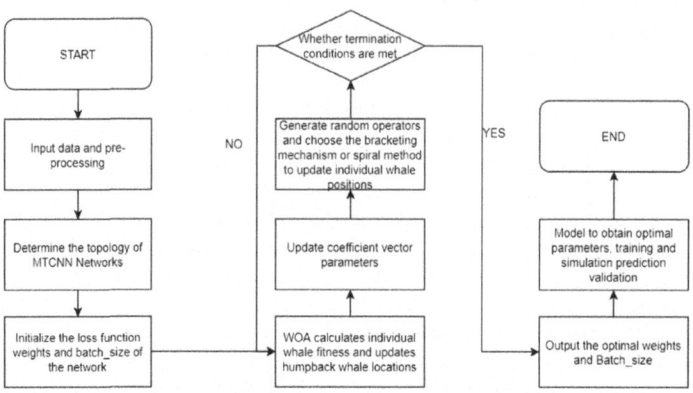

Fig. 4. Flow chart of the MTCNN algorithm

4.1 Experimental Design

In this paper, three sets of experiments are designed to compare and analyze the model accuracy and improve it.

Experiment 1.

Take the same loss function weights, modify the batch_size only, and compare the effect of different batch_size of 256 and 512 groups on the direction of gradient descent of the model.

Experiment 2.

Adopt the same batch _size, modify the loss function weights of the three-layer network, and compare the effect of different weights of each group on the accuracy of the model.

5   Evaluation Criteria

After training by modifying the individual variables, the accuracy of each layer of the network is compared to find the optimal combination for improving the accuracy of the model.

5.1   Experiment Result and Analysis

After training by modifying the individual variables, the accuracy of each layer of the network is compared to find the optimal combination for improving the accuracy of the model.

Experiment 1 results analysis

The loss function weights of 1:1 face classification and face frame regression are uniformly selected for this set of experimental three-layer network, and the batch_size is divided into two groups of 256 and 512 for training comparison analysis.

The experimental results are shown in Fig. 5 (orange Batch_size = 512, blue Batch_size = 256).

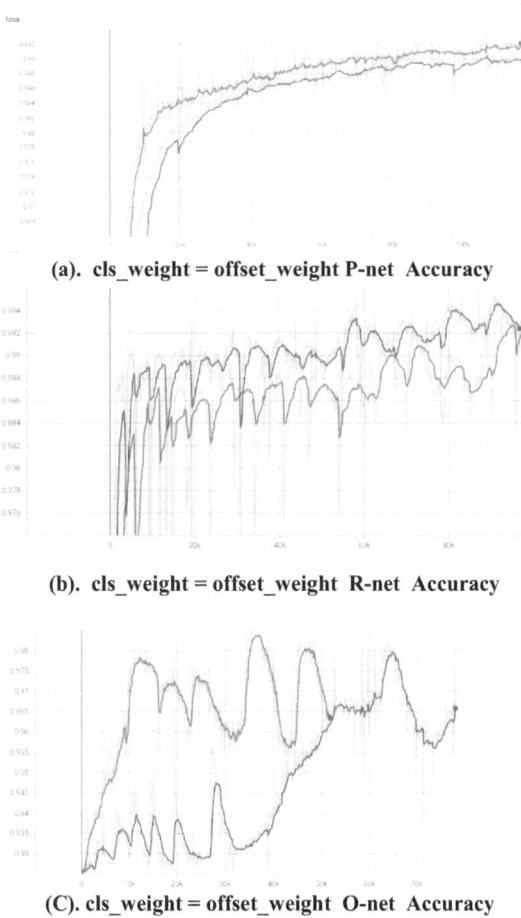

(a). cls_weight = offset_weight P-net Accuracy

(b). cls_weight = offset_weight R-net Accuracy

(C). cls_weight = offset_weight O-net Accuracy

Fig. 5. Different batch_size, same cls_weight

From Fig. 5(a), it can be concluded that in the P-layer network, both sets of data start to converge at 20k samples, and the accuracy increases with the increase of training data, and the training effect of Batch_size = 512 sets is better than that of Batch_size = 256 sets. However, the training effect is reversed for R-layer and O-layer networks, and the effect is better for Batch_size = 256 groups. Since the O-layer net-work is the final processing part of the whole network structure, which will get the final output results, and the accuracy rate of Batch_size = 512 groups fluctuates significantly by two factors, this paper believes that Batch_size = 256 can bring higher accuracy rate.

Experiment 2 Result Analysis

This group of experiments was uniformly selected with batch_size = 512, and the loss function of the three-layer network was divided into three groups for comparison training.

The experimental results are shown in Fig. 6 below (red cls_weight = 0.2, orange cls_weight = 0.5, blue cls_weight = 0.8).

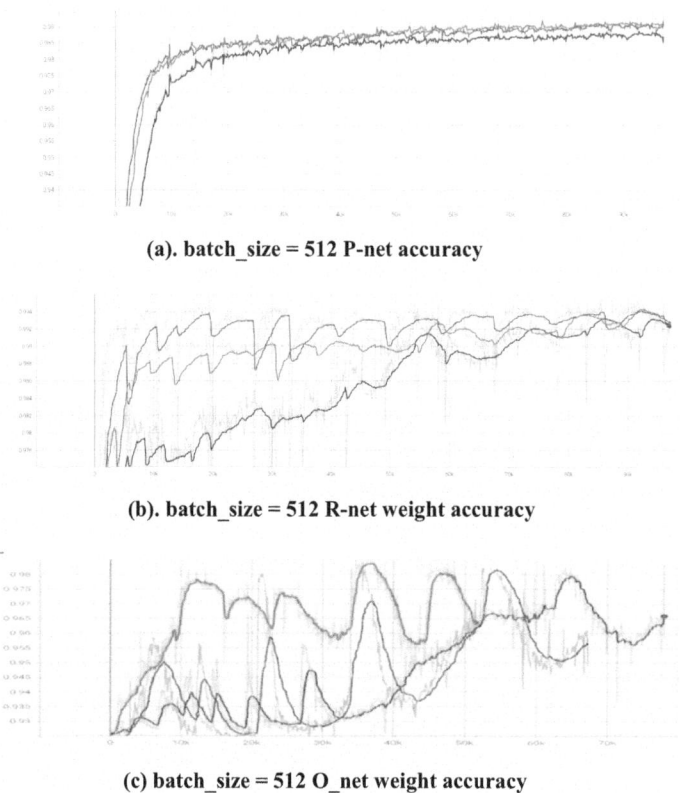

(a). batch_size = 512 P-net accuracy

(b). batch_size = 512 R-net weight accuracy

(c) batch_size = 512 O_net weight accuracy

Fig. 6. Same batch_size, different cls_weight

From Fig. 6(a), it can be concluded that all three groups converge well in the P-layer network, and the training effect is relatively poor for cls_weigh = 0.2. In the P-layer and O-layer networks, all three groups have large fluctuations, and cls_weight = 0.8 can converge faster and achieve higher accuracy in comparison. Therefore, the weight of classification loss function (cls) should be higher than the weight of regression loss function (offset) in order to obtain better training results.

5.2 Build and Demonstrate of the System

Our face detection system GUI interactive interface is used in Python PyQt5 framework to design and build, using Pyinstaller to package the system as a desktop application.

The main functions of the in-person face detection system are.

1. image uploading and rotating and saving.
2. detection of faces in the input static images.
3. Real-time detection of faces in the video stream captured by the camera.

The upper part of the software is the image box, and the lower part is the various function buttons. The left side of the upper half is the input box, the selected image will be displayed in the left image box, and the completed detected image will be displayed in the right output box. The buttons in the lower half are used to implement various functions. You can select the local image by Open File button or Ctrl + N, run the program by Run button, call the model to detect the image, then save the image with the face labeled after detection to local by Save File button or Ctrl + S, and finally exit the program by Exit button or Esc. If the direction of the input image is not positive, the image can be rotated by the Rotation button. If real-time face detection is required, you can switch the mode to real-time video detection mode by clicking the Change Mode button. You can switch between two modes of static image face detection and real-time face detection at any time by clicking the Change Mode button.

From Fig. 7, it can be seen that the system is able to adapt to different sizes of static and dynamic face detection, and can still accurately detect the face area even when part of the face is occluded.

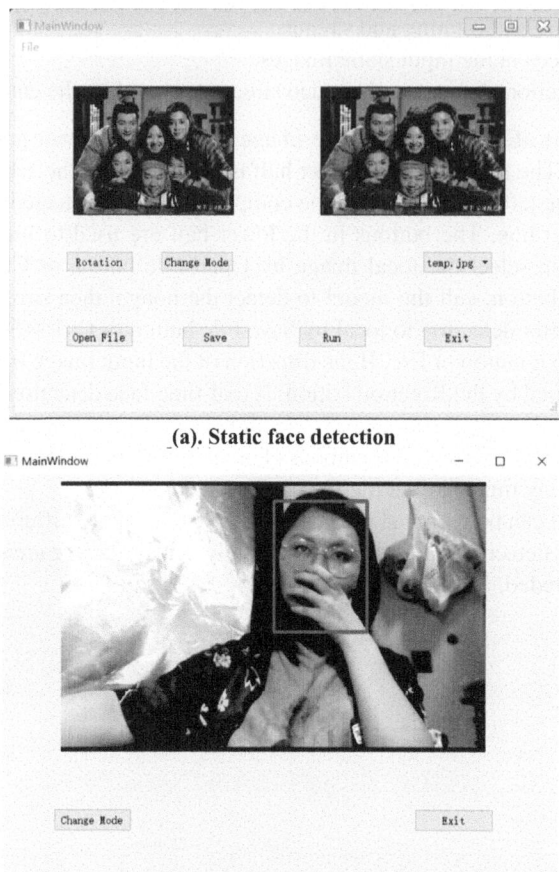

(a). Static face detection

(b). Real-time face detection

Fig. 7. Face detection system GUI

Acknowledgment. This work was supported in part by the National Natural Science Foundation of China under Grant 61901298, 71601085; in part by the Key Research and Development Project of Hubei Province, China under Grant 2020BCA084; in part by the Scientific Research Project of Education Department of Hubei Province under Grant B2022280; in part by the Young Talents Science and Technology Innovation Planning Program of Education Department of Hubei Province under Grant T2022045; in part by the Scientific Research Foundation of Jianghan University under Grant 2023KJZX18.

References

1. Cao, C., Cao, Z., Cui, Z.: LDGAN: a synthetic aperture radar image generation method for automatic target recognition. IEEE Trans. Geosci. Remote Sens. **58**(5), 3495–3508 (2020)
2. Chauhan, D., Kumar, A., Bedi, P., Athavale, V.A., Veeraiah, D., Pratap, B.R.: An effective face recognition system based on Cloud based IoT with a deep learning model. Microprocess. Microsyst. **81**, 103726 (2021)

3. Hu, P., Ning, H., Qiu, T., et al.: Security and privacy preservation scheme of face identification and resolution framework using fog computing in internet of things. IEEE Int. Things J. **4**(5), 1143–1155 (2017)

4. Firouzi, F., Farahani, B., Barzegari, M., Daneshmand, M.: AI-driven data monetization: the other face of data in IoT-based smart and connected health. IEEE Int. Things J. **9**(8), 5581–5599 (2020)

5. Aydin, I., Othman, N. A.: A new IoT combined face detection of people by using computer vision for security application. In 2017 IEEE International Artificial Intelligence and Data Processing Symposium (IDAP) pp. 1–6. (2017)

6. Chen D., G. Hua, F. Wen, and J. Sun, Supervised transformer network for efficient face detection. in European Conference on Computer Vision. Springer, pp. 122–138 (2016)

7. Kumar, A., Kaur, A., Kumar, M.: Face detection techniques: a review. Artif. Intell. Rev. **52**, 927–948 (2019)

8. Minaee, Shervin, et al. Going deeper into face detection: a survey. arXiv preprint arXiv:2103. 14983 (2021)

9. Alzubaidi, L., Zhang, J., Humaidi, A.J., et al.: Review of deep learning: concepts, CNN architectures, challenges, applications, future directions. J. Big Data **8**, 1–74 (2021)

10. Li, H., Lin, Z., Shen, X., Brandt, J., Hua, G.: A convolutional neural network cascade for face detection. In: Proceedings of the IEEE conference on computer vision and pattern recognition, pp.5325–5334 (2015)

11. Chen, D., Hua, G., Wen, F., et al.: Supervised transformer network for efficient face detection. Computer Vision–ECCV 2016: 14th European Conference, Amsterdam, The Netherlands, October 11-14, 2016, Proceedings, Part V 14. Springer International Publishing, pp. 122–138 (2016)

12. Mirjalili, S., Lewis, A.: The whale optimization algorithm. Adv. Eng. Softw. **95**, 51–67 (2016)

13. Xiong, X., Hu, X., Guo, H.: A hybrid optimized grey seasonal variation index model improved by whale optimization algorithm for forecasting the residential electricity consumption. Energy **234**, 121127 (2021)

14. Xiong, X., Hu, X., Tian, T., Guo, H., Liao, H.: A novel Optimized initial condition and Seasonal division based grey seasonal variation index model for hydropower generation. Appl. Energy **328**, 120180 (2022)

15. Li, Z.K., Hu, X., Guo, H., Xiong, X.: A novel weighted average weakening buffer operator based fractional order accumulation seasonal grouping grey model for predicting the hydropower generation. Energy **277**, 127568 (2023)

16. Hu, X., Xiong, X., Wu, Y., Shi, M.J., Wei, P., Ma, C.M.: A hybrid clustered SFLA-PSO algorithm for optimizing the timely and real-time rumor refutations in online social networks. Expert Syst. Appl. **212**, 118638 (2023)

17. Hussain, N., Khan, M.A., Kadry, S., et al.: Intelligent deep learning and improved whale optimization algorithm based framework for object recognition. Hum. Cent. Comput. Inf. Sci **11**(34), 1–17 (2021)

18. Lakshmi, A.V., Mohanaiah, P.: WOA-TLBO: Whale optimization algorithm with Teaching-learning-based optimization for global optimization and facial emotion recognition. Appl. Soft Comput. **110**, 107623 (2021)

19. Wu, G., Li, Y.: Non-maximum suppression for object detection based on the chaotic whale optimization algorithm. J. Vis. Commun. Image Represent. **74**, 102985 (2021)

20. Muthaiah, U., Chitra, S.: Mango pest detection using entropy-ELM with whale optimization algorithm. Intell. Autom. & Soft Comput. **35**(3) (2023)

Research on Big Data Information Big Model Processing System of IoT Under Computer Artificial Intelligence Technology

Ren Qiong⓪, Xi Hu⓪, and Junming Chang⁽✉⁾ ⓪

School of Artificial Intelligence, Jianghan University, Wuhan 430056, Hubei, China
qiongren@jhun.edu.cn, cjm72@163.com

Abstract. This paper intends to use cloud computing technology combined with multi-source heterogeneous data to study extensive data analysis and modeling methods for dense environments. This paper aims to improve the mining and detection of massive Internet of Things (IoT) big data in the cloud environment. Firstly, relevant statistical characteristics and correlation rules are extracted from massive IoT big data. Secondly, a multi-source heterogeneous network model based on block is proposed. This paper uses a multi-source isomer model to process the collected data, and it proposes a semantic ontology decomposition method for big data in dense IoT scenarios in a cloud environment, and establishes its association rule knowledge base. Meanwhile, the multi-source heterogeneous information transmission mechanism, and then the dense IoT in the cloud environment is analyzed and mined with big data. Experiments show the proposed algorithm performs better anti-jamming when applied in dense IoT environments. This method has better mining accuracy and less time cost.

Keywords: Cloud Computing · Internet of Things · Intensive Scene · Big Data Mining

1 Introduction

Due to the wide use of IoT technology in industry, agriculture and other fields, considerable data compression and anomaly detection have become the key technologies. Researchers use efficient data processing and analysis technology to make the real-time accuracy of IoT applications, reduce the system's consumption of resources and improve its application effect. it causes a lot of resource waste and data processing overhead [1–5]. It cannot solve the problem of effective and accurate analysis and processing of big data. In recent years, some researchers have used the idea of machine learning to propose an incremental data mining algorithm to obtain more profound knowledge. Some researchers use the information of GRNN-DBSCAN to establish the corresponding detection data analysis model to improve detection accuracy. Some researchers take the listed company of a blockchain in a particular region as a case, based on the principal component cluster analysis method, to carry out a specific analysis of the company's

© ICST Institute for Computer Sciences, Social Informatics and Telecommunications Engineering 2025
Published by Springer Nature Switzerland AG 2025. All Rights Reserved
X. Chen et al. (Eds.): IoTaaS 2023, LNICST 585, pp. 304–314, 2025.
https://doi.org/10.1007/978-3-031-70507-6_23

data. After all kinds of data are processed by clustering and classified, the required data can be quickly found from a large amount of data. This improves work efficiency. Studies have used blockchain technology to identify IoT devices and ensure that the devices are immutable [6]. It uses the hash table model based on "allowlist" to encrypt the device to achieve the security of the device. Previous studies have selected the privacy data of IoT with the most significant amount of information as the learning sample, then classified it by using differential privacy technology, and finally established the security protection model of the privacy data of IoT by using linear regression and other algorithms to achieve the security protection of IoT. Some researchers have studied large-scale data acquisition and analysis technology for large-scale IoT to improve system performance, but there are some problems, such as poor anti-multi-path interference performance. This paper will analyze big data and IoT-dense scenarios in cloud computing environments. It mainly includes.

(1) Extracting statistical feature quantity and association rule feature quantity from massive data;
(2) Establishing a knowledge base of association rules for massive data;
(3) Giving the correlation degree transmission and transmission mechanism of massive data;
(4) Carry of extensive data analysis and processing of data, the effectiveness of the proposed algorithm to improve the efficiency of dense IoT extensive data mining in the cloud environment is verified.

2 Design of an Data Processing Systems in IoT

As a service computing architecture for IoT, cloud computing has the characteristics of "quasi-virtual" between cloud and individual computing [7]. It dramatically improves computing speed by moving some of the cloud's work tasks to the cloud. A general IoT data processing architecture is shown in Fig. 1 (image cited in Data Flow: From the Edge to the Server/Cloud).

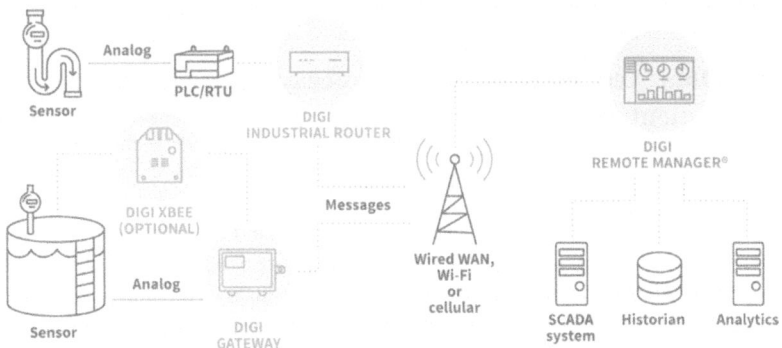

Fig.1. Basic data processing architecture of IoT.

As the amount of data increases, the data processing architecture in Fig. 1 causes the number of resources on the device to increase accordingly, which leads to lower data computation speed and higher resource consumption costs [8]. This paper intends to propose A Data analysis architecture combining offline and real-time analysis based on cloud Computing theory (Fig. 2 is quoted in A Novel Fog Computing Enabled Temporal Data Reduction Scheme in IoT Systems).

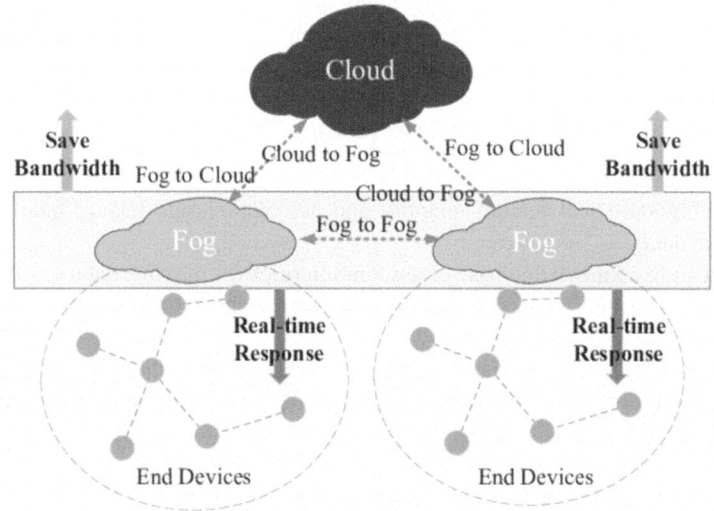

Fig. 2. Architecture of offline and real-time analysis based on fog computing.

As you can see from Fig. 2, this data analysis architecture is divided into two types: offline and just-in-time. The so-called offline analysis uses offline learning and correcting the obtained data [9]. After repeated learning, a revised model is finally obtained. Input the new model into the real-time analysis system to get the real-time data, and then the data comprehensive analysis and the final output results can be.

3   Mass Data Acquisition and Preprocessing in a Dense Environment

3.1   Extensive Data Sampling for Iot Intensive Scenarios

This paper takes multi-source heterogeneous information as the research object and wireless RFID and multi-source information fusion as the core to study the optimal sampling and feature classification of massive information for the large-scale IoT. Build a big data acquisition model in a dense environment. It uses WSN technology to construct RFID information collection tags. This paper intends to research statistics and large-scale IOT big data modeling based on the ZigBee network. The fusion scheduling method of considerable data feature extraction and data analysis for dense environments is studied. Firstly, $Y = \{y_1, y_2, \cdots, y_n\}$ two-valued semantic decision model for large-scale extensive data collection oriented to IoT is established, and its association map is established by taking the ZigBee network node as the networking network [10]. Secondly, the multi-source information transfer mechanism based on Fuzzy is established in the large-scale ample data distribution space, and finally, the multi-source information fusion mechanism of extensive data application oriented to cloud computing is obtained. The associated map will appear $\psi : P \rightarrow R^{2d+1}$. $\psi(c) = (g(c), g(v_1(c)), \cdots, g(v_{2d}(c)))^T$ is the node distribution group of a sample. For large-scale iot extensive data collection, its label distribution group is as follows:

$$y_i^{(t+1)} = (1 - \lambda)y_i^{(t)} + \frac{\lambda}{\delta_{ni}}(\zeta_i - \sum_{j=1}^{i-1} \delta_{ij}y_j^{(t+1)} - \sum_{j=i+1}^{n} \delta_{ij}y_j^{(t)}) \tag{1}$$

$$i = 1, 2, \cdots, n$$
$$t = 1, 2, \cdots, n$$

The feature classification is carried out based on the type attribute $\sigma_i (i = 1, 2, \cdots, n)$ of the big data in the dense scene of IoT, Hence $H = \{Y_1, Y_2, \cdots, Y_n\}$ is a vector distribution set on U. Extensive data collection in dense big data processing based on the node distribution model of extensive data sampling in dense scenarios. The networking model of its wireless sensing network nodes is shown in Fig. 3 below:

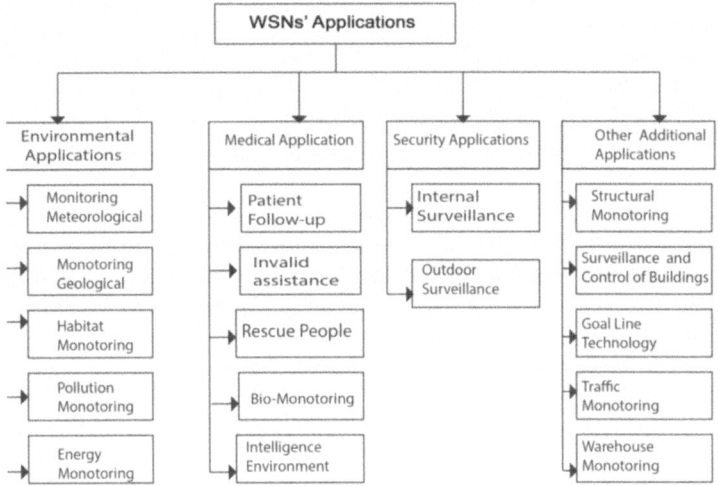

Fig. 3. Networking model of IoT WSN nodes for large-scale data collection.

The data is collected and extracted based on the wireless sensor network nodes for big data acquisition in the dense scene of IoT, as shown in Fig. 3.

3.2 Feature Extraction

This paper intends to study the multi-source heterogeneous information processing technology based on block, feature classification, and adaptive scheduling for the mass IoT [11]. In the process of using feature vectors to extract big data for analysis, this paper combines the use of IoT tools such as data mining, which plays a crucial role in processing a large amount of data.

$$s(t) = \sum_i \sum_{j=0}^{N_f-1} \sum_{k=0}^{K-1} \zeta_i \delta_k q(t - iT_s - jT_f - \sigma_j T_\sigma - \chi_k) +$$

$$\lambda(t) = \sum_i \sum_{j=0}^{N_f-1} \zeta_i q_n(t - iT_s - jT_f - \sigma_j T_\sigma - \chi_0) + \lambda(t) \tag{2}$$

Among them,

$$q_g(t) = \sum_{k=0}^{K-1} \delta_k q(t - \chi_{k,0}) \tag{3}$$

$\lambda(t)$ is a fuzzy weight extracted from the number of statistical features in the massive IoT big data. This paper intends to conduct distributed fusion research on the statistical feature quantity of large-scale iot big data based on fuzzy correlation degree constraints. This paper intends to study the adaptive fusion method. The regular statistical characteristics of mass data in IoT environment of large data sets are:

$$D(\lambda) = \frac{1}{T} \sum_{t=0}^{T-1} D_t(\lambda) \tag{4}$$

To establish a semantic similarity representation method for massive IoT big data in dense environments [12]. The finite data relation point is denoted as $[\delta_j, \zeta_j]$, and the relation point satisfies $y_j \in [\delta_j, \zeta_j]$. The objectives of routing and forwarding control of this integration node are:

$$y(n) = \frac{1}{\sqrt{N}} \Delta \sum_{t=0}^{N-1} Y(t) \exp(j2\pi kn/N), n = 0, 1 \cdots N - 1 \tag{5}$$

where, Δ is the extent of intelligent collection of massive information in a large-scale IoT environment; $\Delta = \{\delta_{i,j}, 0 < i, j < N\}$. $\delta_{i,j}$ is the transport node in the environment. This paper analyzes big data in IoT based on this model, and then conducts data processing on relevant feature vectors.

3.3 Association Rule Knowledge Base of Big Data in IoT Intensive Scenarios

This paper proposes an extensive data mining method for IoT-dense scenes based on cloud computing information fusion and fuzzy clustering and uses radio frequency tag identification technology to extract intelligent features from big data for IoT-dense scenes [13]. IoT dense scene big data multi-source distribution model is established:

$$E = [x_1, x_2, \cdots, x_d]$$ (6)

Dimensionality reduction uses multi-dimensional scaling characteristics to reduce dimension m to dimension d. The big data fusion mode in dense scenarios is obtained:

$$\max H(Y) = (H_1(Y), H_2(Y), \cdots, H_n(Y))$$
$$s.t. \, g_j(Y) \leq 0 (j = 1, 2, \cdots, q)$$ (7)
$$g_t(Y) = 0 (t = 1, 2, \cdots, q)$$

Realize multi-source heterogeneous information fusion in dense IoT environment. The expression of i in IoT is obtained:

$$Racall(Y, X) = \frac{Q(Y \cap X)}{Q(Y) + Q(X) - Q(Y \cap X)}$$ (8)

$$Overload(Y, X) = \frac{Q(Y \cap X)}{\min(Q(Y), Q(X))}$$ (9)

$$Time(Y, X) = \frac{2Q(Y \cap X)}{Q(Y) + Q(X)}$$ (10)

where, $Q(Y)$, $Q(X)$ represents the degree of correlation and integration between large-scale and high-density iot big data. Y, X is a jointly assigned feature vector set for large-scale iot big data. $Q(Y \cap X)$ is a cross-distributed collection of massive information in a dense environment [14]. It is assumed that the output parameter of the extensive data association knowledge base in IoT-intensive scenario in the cloud computing center is $param = \{G_1, G_2, e, g, g_2, g_3, h, H_1, H_2\}$, and the time interval of collection of the extensive data association rule base is T_f combined with the resource fusion scheduling method [15]. This paper presents a multi-objective optimization algorithm based on $T_s = N_f T_f$ function. The matching degree of large data mining in a dense iot environment is:

$$T_\sigma = ent(T_f / N_\sigma)$$ (11)

The feature distribution of the critical index of dense scene big data is set to $Y(y_1, y_2 \cdots y_D)$, and the distribution structure of knowledge of mining association rules of iot dense scene big data obtained in a restricted space makes it meet $\sigma_j T_\sigma < T_f, \forall j \in [0, N_f - 1]$.

3.4 Extensive Data Analysis in the Dense Environment of IoT Based on Cloud Technology

In this paper,a knowledge base of association rules for massive IoT data is established, and an association transmission control mechanism for massive IoT data is proposed based on the fusion analysis of association knowledge [16]. The calculation formula of the edge property distribution matrix $Z_{N \times 1}$ is as follows:

$$Z_{N \times 1} = D_{N \times K} \cdot T_{K \times 1} \tag{12}$$

The exact transfer probability of the ontology resource m is given to determine $e_t \geq 0, \sum\limits_{t=1}^{t} e_t = 1$. The discrete distribution model of extensive data mining in a dense environment is constructed by using fuzzy decision variables

$$s(t) = [s_1(t), s_2(t), \cdots, s_m(t)]^T \tag{13}$$

The feature mapping method of semantic ontology is applied to carry out adaptive mining of massive data in dense environments, and its spatial distribution matrix is as follows:

$$Y' = \begin{pmatrix} y_{11} & y_{12} & \cdots & y_{1n} \\ y_{21} & y_{22} & \cdots & y_{2n} \\ \vdots & \vdots & \ddots & \vdots \\ y_{(n-1)1} & y_{(n-1)2} & \cdots & y_{(n-1)n} \end{pmatrix} \tag{14}$$

The plaintext block feature quantity of big data in iot intensive scenarios is calculated [17]. In combination with the routing and forwarding control protocol of IoT, the association and fusion factor δ_{desira}^i of the big data model is obtained

$$\delta_{desira}^i = \delta_1 \cdot \frac{Den\ sit\ x_i}{\sum\limits_i Den\ sit\ x_i} + \delta_2 \frac{\Delta Q_i}{\Delta Q_{in\ it}} \tag{15}$$

Among them,

$$\begin{cases} \delta_1 + \delta_2 = 1, \delta_1, \delta_2 \in [0, 1] \\ \delta_2 = \dfrac{\max\limits_i(\Delta Q_i) - \min\limits_i(\Delta Q_i)}{\Delta Q_{in\ it}} \end{cases} \tag{16}$$

Considered the equivalent semantic mapping, the link set of extensive data distribution in IoT-dense scenarios satisfies $Q \in R^{n \times n}, R \in R^{m \times m}$ and $H \in R^{m \times m}$, and the feature distribution set satisfies $d \sim q(e, q)$.

Combined with the matching index set $E_t \in E(t = 1, 2, \cdots, t)$ of extensive data integration in IoT intensive scenarios, the optimized integrated graph model is $Q_i \in Q(i = 1, 2, \cdots, m)$. Correlation detection and mining of iot data are carried out according to the fusion results of correlation knowledge.

4 Experimental Results and Analysis

The correctness of IoT data privacy protection model in a heterogeneous cloud computing environment is tested by experiments on information loss degree, data availability, performance and security. The results of the experiment are shown below. The test compares the algorithm in literature [18] and literature [19] and the method in this paper.

4.1 Degree of Information Loss

In protecting private data,the papermust ensure the degree of information loss is shallow. Only in this way can the model have practical application value. For different IoT data, three ways are adopted to protect it from information loss. It is determined that the degree of information loss in this way is the smallest, and the optimal privacy data protection model is obtained. Figure 4 shows the five groups of experimental results. The algorithm can ensure the performance of privacy data protection. The information lost by the other two methods is much higher than that of the proposed methods, so the data protection model will likely become meaningless [20]. The low information loss of the proposed method is due to the preprocessing of the original data before establishing the protection model. At the same time, the algorithm can significantly ensure the integrity of the data, thus reducing the amount of information loss.

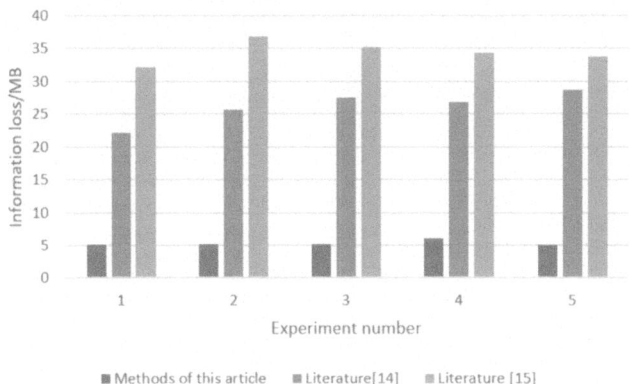

Fig. 4. Amount of information loss under the three algorithms.

4.2 Data Availability

In the privacy data protection model, the amount of data is a direct factor, and as the amount of data increases, data availability will also increase [21]. The comparison results are shown in Fig. 5. It can be seen that the method proposed here is the strongest under what kind of data volume, while the other two methods are not as good as the algorithm proposed here to some extent, so its correctness can be demonstrated.

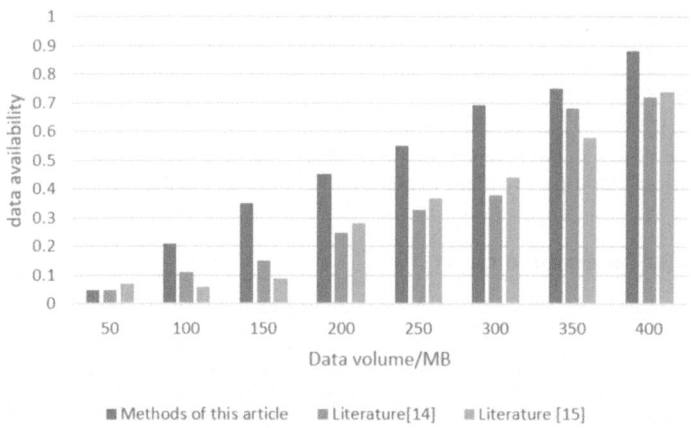

Fig. 5. Data availability for the three methods.

4.3 Model Protection Performance

By comparing the upload rate of the above three schemes with that of the unencrypted one, the scheme that is closest to the unencrypted one is obtained. The results are shown in Fig. 6. From Fig. 6, it can be seen that the method described in this paper has the closest upload speed to unencrypted data, indicating that it is the most effective of the three methods and confirming the overall efficiency of the method described in this paper.

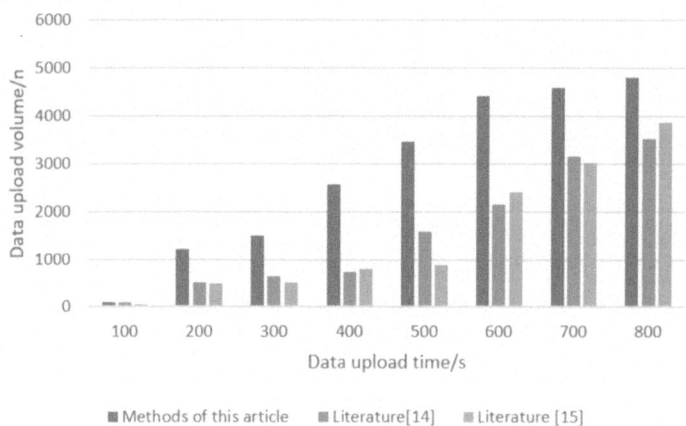

Fig. 6. Model protection performance of the three methods.

4.4 Security

The security problem in cryptography is evaluated by measuring the rate of change of ciphertext in cryptography. Assuming that the number of plaintexts is fixed in a cipher system, if any cipher system changes, the ciphertext change rate under the cipher system can be obtained, and then the propagation characteristics under the cipher system can be obtained. The security of the cryptosystem is judged. Table 1 lists the comparative data of the three experimental methods. The stronger the ciphertext change rate, the stronger the data diffusion.Table 1 can display the following data of the highest average ciphertext change rate, which further proves the security of the proposed method.

Table 1. Diffusivity of the three methods.

Experiment number	The ciphertext change rate of the proposed method	Reference [18] method ciphertext change rate	Reference [19] method ciphertext change rate
1	0.83	0.78	0.66
2	0.87	0.76	0.41
3	0.80	0.66	0.46
4	0.76	0.60	0.42
5	0.48	0.75	0.86
6	0.97	0.86	0.45
7	0.86	0.73	0.19
8	1.00	0.83	0.57
9	0.99	0.48	0.43
10	0.86	0.78	0.44
Mean value	*0.84*	*0.72*	0.49

5 Conclusion

This paper intends to use cloud computing technology combined with multi-source heterogeneous data to study extensive data analysis and modeling methods for dense environments. This paper intends to use WSN technology to build RFID data collection identification. At the same time, based on the ZigBee networking protocol, this paper conducts statistical analysis and fuzzy sampling research on massive IoT big data and studies the feature classification and adaptive scheduling of massive IoT big data through zoning fusion and fuzzy clustering technologies. At the same time, the high-density IoT extensive data mining method based on cloud services is studied. Through analysis, it is found that the algorithm has better accuracy, less time, and better overall performance in the dense, extensive data mining of IoT.

References

1. Liu, G., Rong, K., Tang, L., et al.: Research on technology integration and application of Shenzhen urban ecological Big Data intelligent management and service platform. Acta Ecol. Sin. **42**(4), 98–104 (2022)
2. Xiong, X., Xi, H., Guo, H.: A hybrid optimized grey seasonal variation index model improved by whale optimization algorithm for forecasting the residential electricity consumption. Energy **234**, 121127 (2021)
3. Xiong, X., Xi, H., Tian, T., Guo, H., Liao, H.: A novel Optimized initial condition and Seasonal division based Grey Seasonal Variation Index model for hydropower generation. Appl. Energy **328**, 120180 (2022)
4. Li, Z., Xi, H., Guo, H., Xiong, X.: A novel Weighted Average Weakening Buffer Operator based Fractional order accumulation Seasonal Grouping Grey Model for predicting the hydropower generation. Energy **277**, 127568 (2023)
5. Xi, H., Xiong, X., You, W., Shi, M., Wei, P., Ma, C.: A hybrid clustered SFLA-PSO algorithm for optimizing the timely and real-time rumor refutations in online social networks. Expert Syst. Appl. **212**, 118638 (2023)
6. Zheng, P.: Design of high precision ultrasonic gas flow monitoring system based on IoT. Instrum. Technol. Sens. **10**(2), 65–70 (2021)
7. He, S., He, X., Song, D., et al.: Multi-parameter integrated warning model of rock burst and intelligent identification cloud platform. J. China Univ. Min. Technol. **51**(5), 130–133 (2022)
8. Zhang, Y.-L., Wang, S., Ye, Z.: Industrial equipment based on IoT remote PLC control system design. Autom. Technol. Appl. **42**(3), 8–10 (2022)
9. Cheng, X., Lang, G.: Secure centralized storage of medical big data information based on IoT. Inf. Technol. **47**(1), 109–114 (2021)
10. Ding, G., Chen Qihang, X., Chen, et al.: Model sharing for GPU-accelerated DNN inference in big data processing systems. J. Tsinghua Univ.: Nat. Sci. Edit. **62**(9), 78–82 (2022)
11. Li, G.: Design of IoT Access identity security authentication system based on big data. Autom. Technol. Appl. **42**(4), 118–121 (2022)
12. An, Y., Zhu, Y., Wang, J.: Analysis of applicable conditions of distributed hash table in big data scenario of IoT. J. Comput. Sci. **44**(8), 170–177 (2021)
13. Li, Z., Geng, X., Kaiyong, X., et al.: Operation management practice of laboratory animal center based on IoT and big data technology. J. Exp. Anim. Sci. **38**(4), 22–29 (2022)
14. Liu, H.: Application analysis of embedded software based on big data in IoT technology. Microcomput. Appl. **39**(4), 195–198 (2021)
15. Luo, X., Pang, Z., Tan, S., et al.: Design and practice of water big data platform system based on cloud computing. Water Suppl. Drain. **48**(1), 17–26 (2022)
16. Yan, P., Zhou, L., Yan, H.: Research on IoT privacy data protection model under hybrid cloud storage. Comput. Simul. **40**(2), 530–534 (2022)
17. Weimin Guo, H., Zhao, J.Z., et al.: Big data analysis of Henan tobacco curing process based on IoT data acquisition technology. Tob. Sci. Technol. **54**(9), 92–99 (2021)
18. Huang, Z., Yang, J., Zhang, Y., Yin, Z.: Reputation evaluation model of iot data service based on blockchain. Comput. Eng. **48**(1), 33–42 (2022)
19. Rui, H., Rui, Z., Dong, X., et al.: Design and application of intelligent power system based on multi-sensor fusion. Mod. Electr. Technol. **44**(7), 4–8 (2021)
20. Li, Y., Wang, H., Fang, M.: Design and application of IoT electrical safety system in university laboratory. Mod. Electr. Technol. **46**(10), 66–70 (2022)
21. Chao, X., Guo, F., Chuankun, W.: MQTT-SE data encryption transmission algorithm. Appl. Comput. Syst. **31**(12), 169–177 (2022)

Design and Research of Intelligent Sorting Trash Bin Based on IoT

Yuxi Yang⑩, Yuanqiao Bi⑩, Fuxiang Jiang, Zhongying Hu, Weile Bai, Qifang Liu, and Xi Hu⁽⊠⁾

Jianghan University, Wuhan 430056, China
huxi027@163.com

Abstract. In view of the 'difficult' situation of trash front-end classification, this paper proposes a novel intelligent classification trash bin based on Internet of Things (IoT) technology. This trash bin uses both STM32C8T6 control module and K210 vision module to control the operation of the whole equipment. Firstly, the image of the trash bin is collected by the OV5642 camera. Secondly, the function of trash detection and classification can be realized by the K210 vision module. Finally, the recognition results are transmitted to the STM32C8T6 control module through the UART serial port in the form of data, which controls the motor module, ultrasonic module and buzzer module to achieve trash classification, compression crushing and other functions. The experimental results show that the average accuracy of trash recognition is more than 87%. Compared with the traditional smart trash bin, the hardware of our design is added with recyclable trash compression and kitchen waste crushing structure, and the software of our design is added with LCD display interface for providing a more reliable, efficient and low-cost solution for trash classification.

Keywords: Front-end processing · Intelligent sorting trash bin · K210 Visual module · STM32

1 Introduction

With population growth, urbanization, and changes in consumption patterns, China's trash production has continued to grow over the past few decades. China has become the world's largest generator of solid waste. If these wastes are not properly processed, it will have a negative impact on the environment [1]. In order to reduce the generation of trash and to improve the efficiency of trash recycling and processing, China has implemented a trash classification system nationwide since 2019 [2]. However, the trash classification system faces many challenges during the implementation process, such as insufficient public knowledge and awareness of trash classification, insufficient enforcement, and insufficient classification facilities.

Supported in part by the 2022 Ministry of Education Industry-Academia Collaboration Coordinated Education Project under Grant 220901576203216; in part by the 2023 Student Research Key Project of Jianghan University under Grant 2023zd142.

In order to solve various problems in the process of trash classification, re-searchers have developed smart trash bins that can autonomously identify and classify trash based on artificial intelligence technology [3–6] to reduce human burden and improve the accuracy and efficiency of trash classification. Kang zhuang et al. [7] used the Inception V3 model for trash identification and deployed it on Raspberry Pi 3B+. Shen Jian et al. [8] proposed an intelligent classification trash bin based on Jetson Nano. Zhou et al. [9] designed a smart trash bin based on the STM32F103ZET6 chip and the LD3320 speech recognition module, which facilitates trash classification and processing by manually speaking the name of the trash. Li et al. [10] proposed a smart trash bin based on Raspberry Pi and a 110-degree wide-angle camera, using the You Only Look Once vesion 5 (YOLO v5) model training data set to achieve a recognition ac-curacy of more than 90%.

The above-mentioned researches also have shortcomings in solving the problem of intelligent trash classification. Most of the results are not smart enough in functionality and cannot realize fully automatic trash identification and classification; some of the hardware is expensive and has no prospect of popularization and application. Therefore, it is very meaningful to design a trash classification system that is both fully automatic and low-cost. This article designs a smart trash bin based on STM32. The trash bin realizes automatic identification and classification of trash based on the STM32C8T6 micropro-cessor and the K210 module [11], achieving powerful performance while maintaining a low price. The smart trash bin model structure is as shown in Fig. 1.

The smart trash bin includes: 1. Trash storage port, 2. LCD display, 3. Steering gear, 4. Built-in trash bin, 5. Electric push rod, 6. Trash bin outer frame, 7. Trash temporary storage platform, 8. Camera. The outer frame of the model is constructed of aluminum profiles and edged with acrylic panels.

2   General Idea and Framework

The overall design idea is as follows: The smart trash bin use the K210 vision module for trash identification and classification, and uses STM32C8T6 to call ultrasonic waves, buzzers, and motors to achieve functions such as trash classification, full load detection, compression processing, and crushing processing. Meanwhile, it calls the LCD display module to display various parameters of the smart trash bin, which include whether the trash bin is full, the compression status of recyclable trash, and the completion of crushing kitchen waste. The frame of the smart trash bin is shown in Fig. 2. The device consists of five modules: STM32 control module, K210 vision module, ultrasonic and buzzer module, and motor module (mainly composed of three parts: trash classification module, compression module, and crushing module)), LCD display module. The STM32 control module can realize automatic detection and classification of trash by calling other modules and other functions.

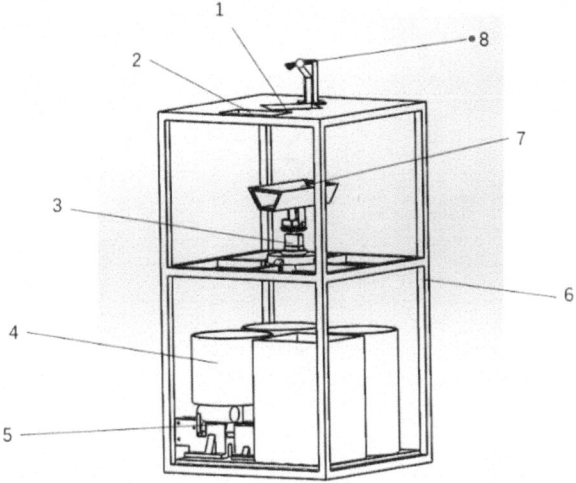

Fig. 1. Structure diagram of intelligent trash bin.

3 Hardware Structure

3.1 STM32 Control Module

The STM32 control module uses a 32-bit microcontroller STM32F103C8T6 developed based on the ARM Cortex-M core. The working frequency of these STM32 series 32-bit microcontrollers can reach up to 72MHz, and the internal use is 64K or 128K bytes flash program memory, with 20K bytes of SRAM data memory and built-in CRC cyclic redundancy check and 96-bit encoding (24-bit hexadecimal number) of the chip's unique serial number. Its main system consists of 4 control units [DCode bus (D-bus), system bus (S-bus), general DMA1, general DMA2] and 4 controlled units (internal SRAM, internal Flash, FSMC, AHB to APB bridge AHB2APBx), which are connected to each other through a multi-level AHB bus.

3.2 K210 Vision Module

This design uses the Maixpy development board equipped with the K210 chip, which is equipped with the RT-Thread operating system and uses the RISC-V 64-bit Dual Cores. Each core has a built-in independent floating point unit (FPU) with super computing power and a dedicated neural network processing unit (NPU) performing real-time video processing. At the base rate of 400MHz, the INT16 test has a performance of 300GMAC/s, and the entire machine consumes less than 1W.

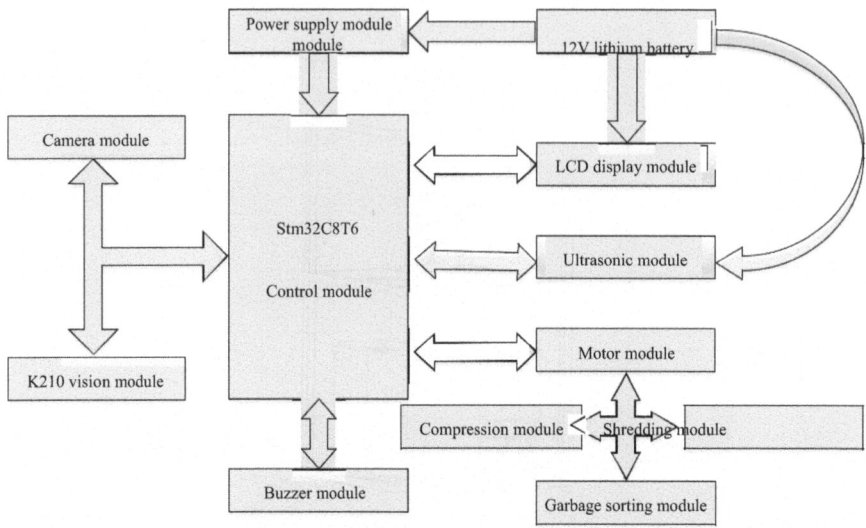

Fig. 2. Intelligent trash bin framework.

3.3 Camera Module

The camera sensor module uses OV5640 with 5 million pixels, supporting higher res-olutions. Meanwhile, the OV5640 photosensitive array reaches 2624x1964 resolution (physical size), supporting up to 2592x1944@15fps (QSXGA) or 90fps VGA (640480) image capture, with high acquisition rate and higher image pro-cessing performance, which can provide highly identifiable input values to the K210 vision module.

3.4 Ultrasonic and Buzzer Module

For full-load detection, it is essential to implement high-precision distance detection. We use the HC-SR04 ultrasonic module, which has the characteristics of high frequency, short wavelength, small diffraction phenomenon, good directionality, and becoming ray thus directional propagation. The detection distance ranges from 2cm to 450cm, and the accuracy can also reach 3mm. We use an active buzzer for the full load alarm, which contains an oscillation source inside and it will sound as soon as the power is turned on for easy operation.

3.5 Classification Platform Module

As shown in Fig. 3, the classification platform is composed of a placement plat-form 1, a connector 2, and a steering gear 3. The steering gear is a 20KG dual-axis steering gear of the RDS3218 model, while the connecting parts between the steering gears are printed using 3D printing technology. The placement platform is made of laser-cut acrylic sheets and is placed directly above the classified trash bin after assembly.

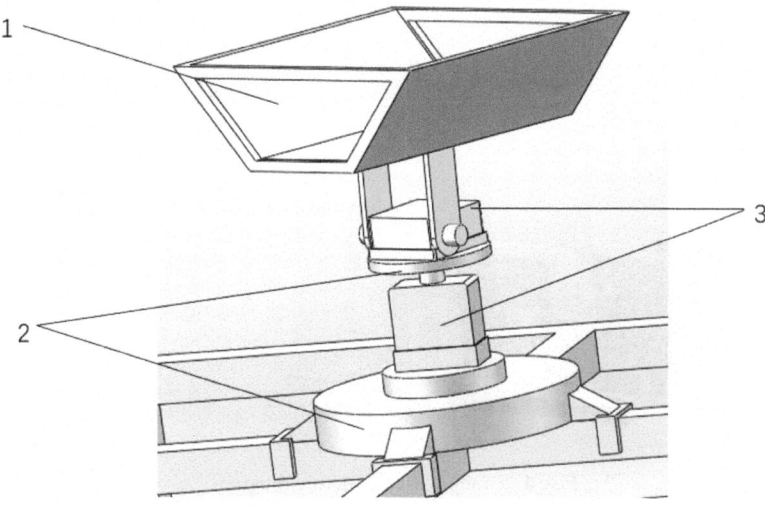

Fig. 3. Classification platform structure diagram.

3.6 Compression Module

As shown in Fig. 4, the compression module is composed of a rear-end fixed seat, an electric push rod, a guiding platform, a connecting piece of the push rod pressing plate, and a pressing plate. During the experiment, the rear-end fixed seat, the guiding platform, and the connecting piece were all independently designed with three-dimensional drawings through SolidWorks and printed with a 3D printer. The pressing plate was processed by sheet metal and all assembled together to form a compression module. The pressing plate and the trash bin form a certain wedge-shaped angle to compress the sorted recyclable garbage to achieve the purpose of improving the utilization rate of the space in the trash bin.

3.7 Shredding Module

As shown in Fig. 5, the crushing module is composed of a crushing blade 1, a crushing device bushing 2, and a motor module 3. The crushing blade is formed by laser cutting parts and sheet metal processing. The blade is installed on the rotating shaft. The rotating shaft and the bushing parts of the crushing device are made by turning aluminum bars. The assembled parts are installed on the stepping motor to form a crushing module. The sorted kitchen waste is subjected to a pulverized micro-treatment, which achieves the purpose of improving the utilization rate of the space in the trash bin.

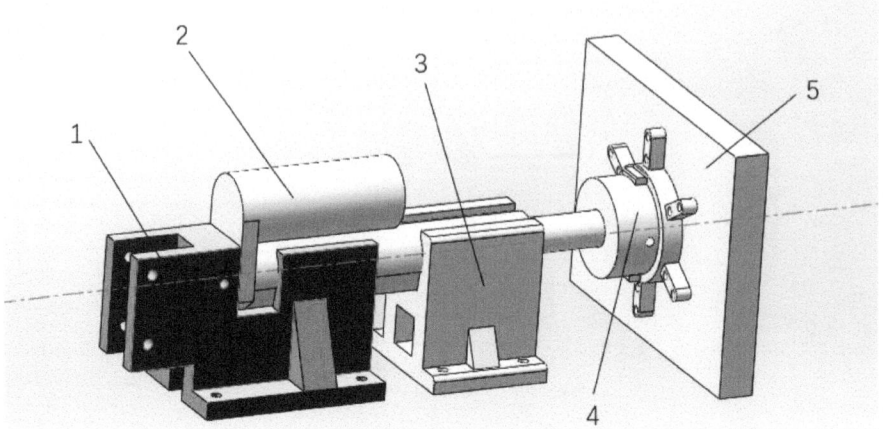

Fig. 4. Compression structure diagram.

3.8 Display Module

This module adopts the X5 series of Taojingchi (Shenzhen Taojingchi Electronics Co., Ltd.) serial screen, which is a kind of LCD screen with display function that can communicate through the serial port. It is generally composed of hardware equipment and operating software of the serial screen: the hardware part includes processors, LCD screens, touch panels, FLASH storage, RS232 or 485 serial port chips, audio and video decoding chips, SD card slots and other different units. The user needs to first use the USART HMI software of the serial screen to create the "project file" of its corresponding interface effect, and then download the prepared "project file" to the processor of the serial screen and FLASH to run through the PC and the serial port SD card of the serial screen.

4   Software System Design

The software structure of the smart trash bin is mainly composed of K210 and garbage classification algorithm design on STM32C8T6, camera control, ultra-sonic module and buzzer module control, steering gear control, and LCD display.

4.1   Trash Classification Algorithm Design

Image Preprocessing. In the process of image transmission and storage, due to various factors, such as sensor noise, signal interference, compression algorithm, the image may be affected by noise and damage, resulting in image quality degradation, which will directly affect the efficiency and accuracy of feature recognition [12]. In order to solve this problem, a series of image preprocessing techniques, such as denoising, image enhancement, sharpening, can be applied to eliminate or reduce the noise and damage to the image, for improving the success rate of feature recognition. By preprocessing the

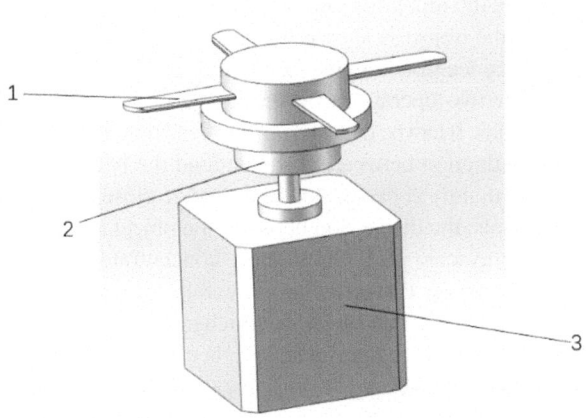

Fig. 5. Crushing structure diagram.

image, the influence of noise and damage can be effectively reduced, the success rate of feature recognition can be improved, and more accurate and reliable results can be obtained.

The light background is one of the important influencing factors in the image acquisition process, which can have a significant impact on the image data, in-cluding over-exposure, shadow effects, color distortion, which will seriously mask the characteristics of the object. To solve the problems caused by the light back-ground, it is necessary to use reasonable image preprocessing technology to reduce the influence of the light

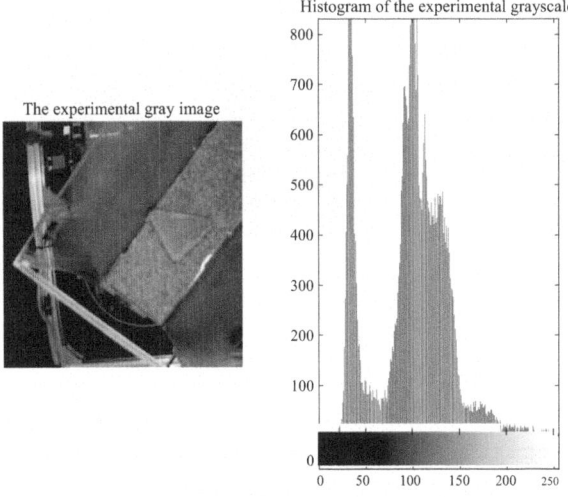

Fig. 6. Item grayscale.

background and improve the reliability and accuracy of object features. The experimental grayscale image of the object is shown in Fig. 6. It can be seen that the grayscale pixels of the object are concentrated in the range of 0–100.

This paper performs two operations on the image: reducing grayscale pixels and enhancing grayscale pixels. It can be observed from Fig. 7 that, in the image with reduced grayscale pixels, the distinction between the object and the background decreases, and the grayscale pixels are mainly concentrated in the range close to 0; while in the image with increased pixel pixels, the distinction between the object and the background contrast is enhanced, and grayscale pixels are mainly concentrated in the range of 100 to 200. Experimental results show that reducing grayscale pixels can make the difference between the object and the background smaller, which may make the object more difficult to identify or distinguish. Enhanced grayscale pixels can enhance the contrast between the object and the background, helping to improve the visibility and recognition of the object.

This paper performs a histogram equalization process on the enhanced grayscale image, and the experimental results are shown in Fig. 8. It can be observed that the contrast of the object is further enhanced, and the grayscale pixel distribution range of the image is expanded from 100 to 200 to 0 to 255. This means that the gray value range in the image is fully utilized, making the details in the image clearer. The three-dimensional feature map after histogram equalization processing of the garbage data set is shown in Fig. 9. It can be seen that different categories of trash bin be clearly distinguished.

Dataset The data set is independently completed by researchers through real-life photography. There are a total of 6,000 pictures of 12 items. Combined with the designed garbage classification hardware system, all garbage is divided into four categories, namely hazardous garbage, recyclable garbage, kitchen waste, and other garbage. The specific classification is shown in Table 1. Among them, the training samples account for 80%, and that is 4800; the number of verification samples accounts for 15%, and that is 900; the test samples account for 5%, and that is 300.

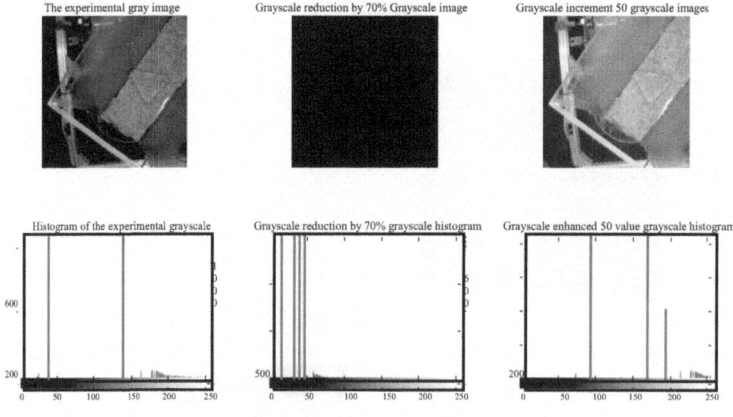

Fig. 7. Grey Processing.

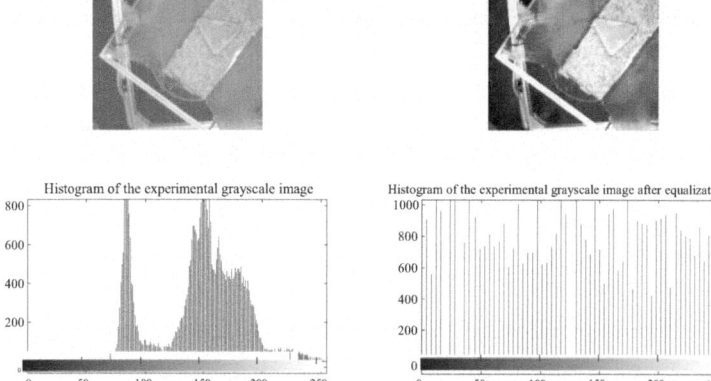

Fig. 8. Histogram equalization processing.

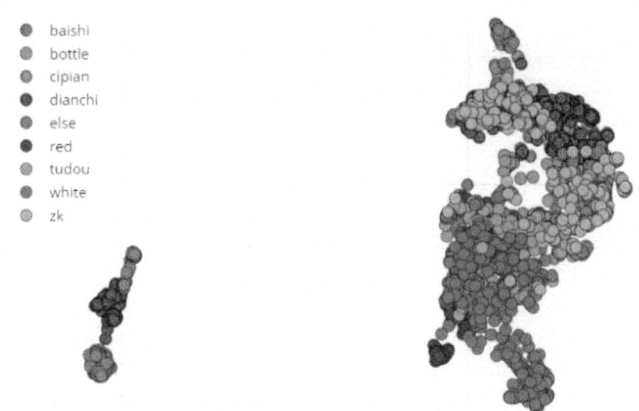

Fig. 9. 3D feature map.

Table 1. Trash dataset.

Hazardous trash		Recyclable trash		Kitchen trash		Other trash	
Battery	500	Can	500	Potato	500	Porcelain	500
Expired drugs	500	Small water bottle	500	White radish	500	Cobblestone	500
Thermometer	500	Carton	500	Carrot	500	Cigarette butt	500

Trash Classification Algorithm Design Due to the particularity of the K210 vision module used, we use the YOLOv2 target detection algorithm. YOLOv2 is a target detection algorithm based on deep learning. Its network structure mainly consists of two parts: feature extraction network and detection network.

Feature Extraction Network. YOLOv2 uses the Darknet-19 network [13] as the feature extraction network, as shown in Fig. 10. It consists of 19 convolutional layers and 5 pooling layers, similar to the VGG (Visual Geometry Group) net-work structure, but lighter than VGG. The input of this network is a 416×416 image, and the output is a 13×13×1024 feature map. After processing by the feature extraction network, YOLOv2 can convert the input image into a series of useful features for subsequent processing by the target detection network.

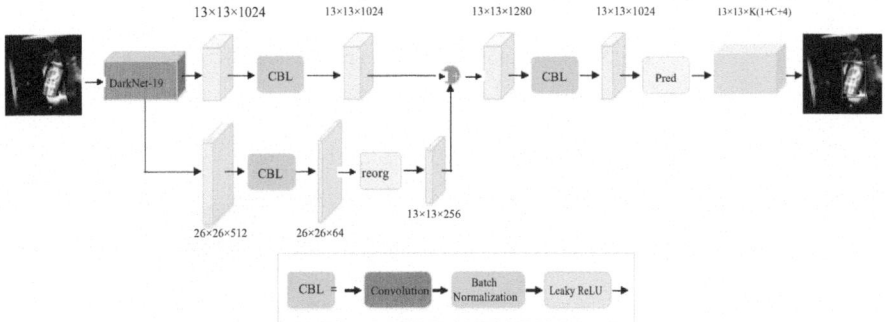

Fig. 10. Deep Learning Framework.

Detection Network The detection network in YOLOv2 includes three detection layers of different scales. Firstly, these three detection layers are respectively connected to the 13×13, 26×26, and 52×52 feature maps of the feature extraction network, and predict the positions and categories of all objects whose center points fall within each grid cell. Secondly, each detection layer consists of a convolutional layer and a fully connected layer to process the feature maps passed in from the feature extraction network and predict the output detection results. Finally, YOLOv2 uses the non-maximum suppression (NMS) algorithm to post-process the detection results, to remove overlapping candidate frames, and to output the final target detection results. The following is a detailed analysis of the working principle of YOLOv2.

When inputting a picture, YOLOv2 divides the input picture into S×S grid units. If the center of the target object falls into a certain mesh, this mesh is responsible for detecting the object. Each grid unit predicts B border positions, including 5 normalized prediction parameters: the offset of the center point of the target border position relative to the upper left corner of the grid, and the width and height of the border relative to the width and height of the entire image ratio, and give the corresponding confidence [14].The expression is as follows

$$Confidence = \Pr(Object) \times IOU_{pred}^{truth} \tag{1}$$

where Pr(*Object*) is the probability of the pure target in the grid, if it exists, the target takes 1, otherwise it takes 0. *IOU* (intersection over union) is the coincidence degree of the target frame predicted by the network with the target frame marked in the original input image, which can be expressed as

$$IOU_{pred}^{truth} = \frac{box_{pred} \cap box_{truth}}{box_{pred} \cup box_{truth}} \tag{2}$$

where box_{pred} is the marked target bounding box and box_{truth} is the predicted target bounding box.

The class-specific confidence score for each candidate box is:

$$Conf_i = \Pr(Class_i|Object) \times \Pr(Object) \times IOU_{pred}^{truth} \tag{3}$$

Where Pr(*Class_i|Object*) is the conditional probability of the target category. For each candidate box, predict the probability of the target and the position of the bounding box, then the predicted value of each candidate box output is:

$$[x, y, w, h, Confidence, Conf_i] \tag{4}$$

where $(x, y)$is the offset of the center point of the target frame position relative to the upper left corner of the grid, $(w, h)$is the ratio of the width and height of the frame to the width and height of the entire image, *Conf idence* is the confidence, and $Conf_i$ is the probability of the target category. For each image input, the final network output is a vector [15], which can be expressed as

$$S \times S \times B \times [x, y, w, h, Confidence, Conf_i] \tag{5}$$

In general, the network structure of YOLOv2 is an end-to-end fully convolutional neural network [16], which can efficiently detect objects in the input image and achieve relatively high detection accuracy.

Model Usage. The first step: training the model and propagate forward through the network: inputting the pre-processed image into the YOLOv2 network, and extracting the feature information of the image through a series of operations such as convolution layer, pooling layer and fully connected layer. Candidate box generation: Converting predictions to a sequence of bounding boxes, including coordinates and target probabilities for each box. Sorted by probability from large to small, retaining the box with the highest probability, and suppressing other boxes that intersect with it to reduce repeated detection. Object category recognition: Inputting the bounding box and the image into the classification network together, and outputting the probability distribution of the objects in each box through the classification network. Threshold processing: retaining the candidate boxes whose probability values are greater than the preset threshold, and removing the candidate boxes whose probability values are too low. Bounding box decoding: According to the coordinates of the candidate box and the information of the image, the actual position of the bounding box is decoded. Non-maximum value suppression (NMS): Through the non-maximum value suppression algorithm, bounding boxes with excessive overlap are removed, and the trained model is finally output. The training process is shown in Fig. 11.

The second step: import the trained model file into the K210 vision module, and call the built-in neural network processor KPU of the K210 vision module, by loading and running the program file and model file written in Maixpy IDE [17] to achieve the target detection. The classification process is shown in Fig. 12.

4.2 Camera Control

The camera is connected with K210 through DVP parallel interface. In the experiment, by writing a program on Maixpy IDE, the camera recognizes the image and transmits the image to the interface specified by the K210 vision module recognition program. The recognition program performs frame-by-frame target detection on the images sent back by the camera module in the interface. When the target is recognized, the data is sent to the STM32C8T6 main control chip to control the corresponding steering gear and display module. The capture process is shown in Fig. 13.

4.3 Ultrasonic Module and Buzzer Module Control

As shown in Fig. 14, the trash bin uses an ultrasonic module and a buzzer module to realize full load detection and early warning functions. The ultrasonic module uses HC-SR04 ultrasonic to calculate the distance to obstacles by obtaining the time between ultrasonic transmission and reception. The buzzer module uses an active buzzer, which is connected to the STM32C8T6 main control module through the IO port. In our design,

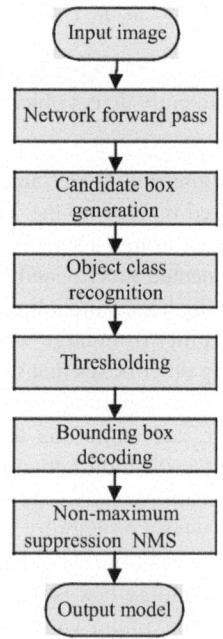

Fig. 11. Training model process.

the ultrasonic module is placed above the smart trash bin, and it is used to calculate the height of the garbage in the smart trash bin and feed back the storage height of the garbage in the bucket to the STM32C8T6 main control module to realize full load detection. When the STM32C8T6 module sends data to the buzzer module through the IO port when the distance transmitted by the ultrasonic module is lower than the set full-load threshold, it will issue a full-load alarm.

4.4 Servo Control

In our study, the steering gear is mainly used to handle the parts that require mechanized control to realize functions such as garbage placement, recyclable garbage compression, and kitchen waste crushing. The overall process is completed through the PID control algorithm. The specific implementation is to write the PWM wave function of the steering gear in the STM32C8T6 main control chip, process the different class parameters returned by K210, compress the recyclable garbage, and crush the kitchen waste. When a PWM signal is generated from the GPIO port of the STM32C8T6 main control chip, it is connected to the steering gear, which drives the mechanical structure to release garbage, compress garbage, and crush garbage to realize the automatic classification, compression, and crushing functions of garbage. The steering gear control process is shown in Fig. 15.

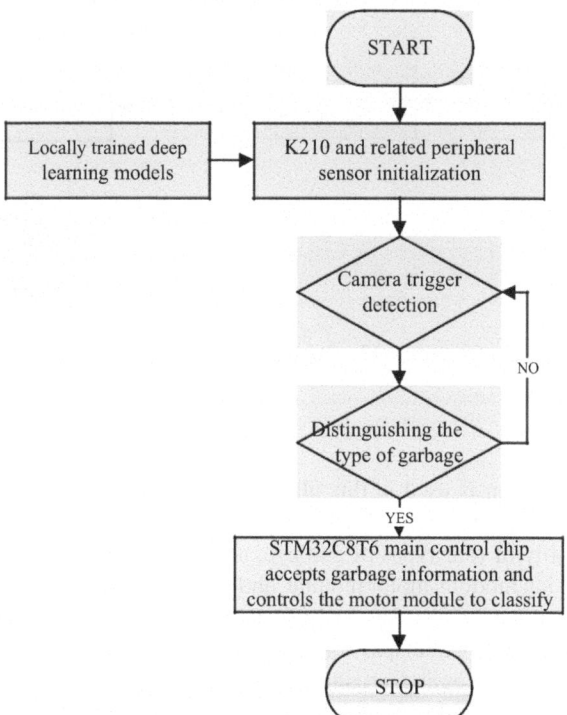

Fig. 12. Trash sorting process.

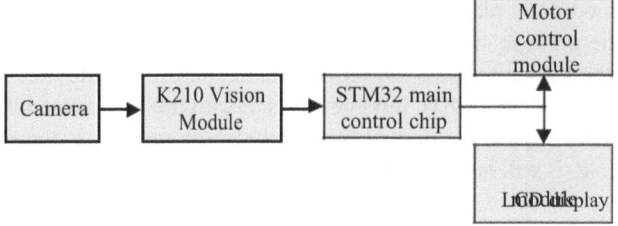

Fig. 13. Camera capture process.

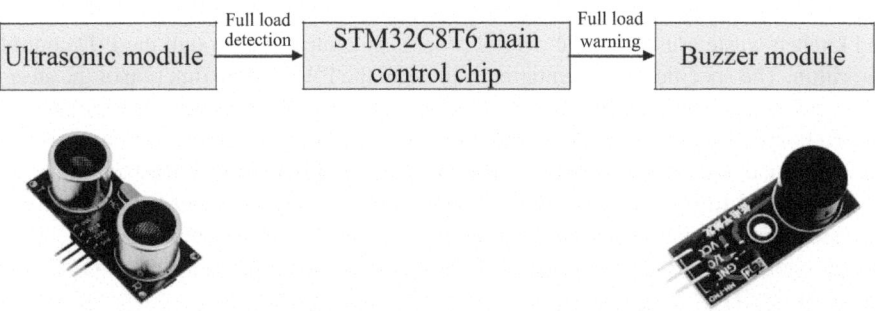

Fig. 14. Full load detection and early warning.

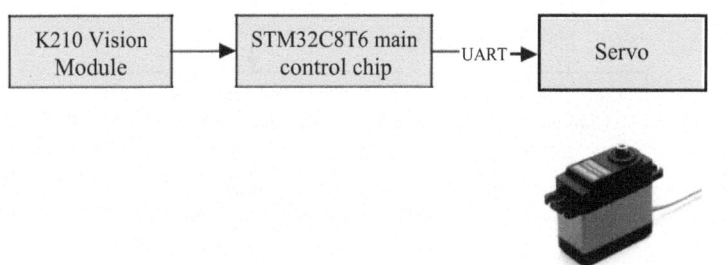

Fig. 15. Servo control flow.

4.5 LCD Display

The LCD display screen is used in this platform to display various parameters of the intelligent garbage classification system, including the order of delivery, the type of delivery, the quantity of four types of garbage, and whether the delivery is successful. After the K210 vision module, motor module, and ultrasonic module process the garbage in real time, the data is transmitted to the LCD display module through the STM32C8T6 module. The LCD module will display the garbage type, the amount of garbage, whether it is full, compression processing, crushing processing, etc. The operating environment of the system is shown in Table 2, and the interface designed in this paper is shown in Fig. 16.

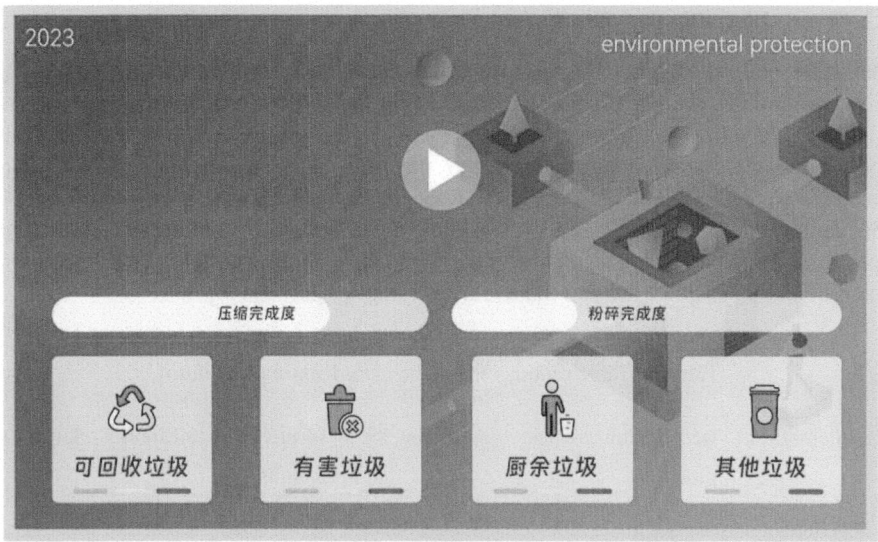

Fig. 16. Servo control flow.

Table 2. Operating environment.

Hardware Environment		Software Environment	
	Intel(R) Core(TM)		Windows10 Home
Processor	i5-10200H	Operating System	Edition
	CPU @2.40GHz		
Memory	8GB	Development Tools	USART HMI IDE

5 System Test

5.1 Specific Debugging

During debugging, import the iterative weight model and Python program from the garbage classification algorithm design into an SD card, place it into the testing Sipeed Maix Bit K210 development board, and put the C language program into the STM32C8T6 development board. The 12 kinds of garbage are put on the classification platform in turn, the camera module collects and acquires the garbage images, puts the collected image data into the K210 vision module, and the K210 vision module sends the processed data to the STM32C8T6 main control chip through the serial port, STM32C8T6 The main control chip conducts data analysis, controls the steering gear to perform garbage delivery, recyclable garbage compression, and kitchen waste crushing, and sends the information to the LCD display module through the serial port.

5.2 Trash Identification Results

Through specific debugging, the various garbage recognition results are shown in Table 3. It can be observed that the recognition accuracy of the system for all kinds of garbage is above 87%, and the recognition time is less than 50ms. Com-pared with he raspberry pie and jetson nano modules in the literature [7, 18], this module has a shorter recognition time while maintaining a high recognition rate, and the detailed time is shown in Table 4. The trash bin can accurately identify the types of garbage, and the mechanical structure operates normally, which can well meet the working requirements of the smart trash bin and efficiently complete the automatic classification of garbage types.

Table 3. Table captions should be placed above the tables.

Test items	Recognition average time(ms)	Accuracy(%)	Identify Classification Results	Servo
Battery	29	93.4	hazardous trash	action
Expired drugs	37	90.2	hazardous trash	action
Thermometer	34	91.1	hazardous trash	action
Cans	29	92	recyclable trash	action
Water bottle	32	91.3	recyclable trash	action
Carton	30	92.5	recyclable trash	action
Porcelain	31	89.9	other trash	action
Cobblestone	33	88.4	other trash	action
Cigarette butt	41	90.3	other trash	action
Potato	37	87.2	kitchen trash	action
White radish	32	91.2	kitchen trash	action
Carrot	33	89.5	kitchen trash	action

Table 4. Recognition time.

Module name	Single frame recognition average speed(ms)
Maixbit	37
Jetson nano	550
Raspberry pie	910

5.3 Innovation Advantages

Compared with the traditional smart garbage can in literature [7, 8, 11], this pa-per adds recyclable garbage compression and kitchen waste crushing mechanical structure in the hardware structure, which can accommodate more recyclable garbage and kitchen waste. To a certain extent, the volume of the trash bin remains unchanged but its capacity increases. In terms of software structure, an LCD interface that can display the status of the trash bin in real time is added, which can display the current capacity of the smart trash bin, whether it is full, and the degree of compression and crushing in real time.

In terms of cost, compared with the mainstream Raspberry Pi, OpenMV, and Jetson Nano modules on the market, the prices of the modules used in this product are only half of them. The prices of the above modules are shown in Table 5. The prices of Raspberry Pi 4th generation 4G single board and Xingtong OpenMV H7 have reached more than 400, and the price of JETSON NANO B01 4GB single board is as high as 1199. The MAIX Bit board used in this paper only costs 148 and can achieve much faster recognition speed than them.

Table 5. Price of each module.

Module name	Price(¥)
MAIX Bit single board	148
Raspberry Pi 4th Generation 4G Single Board	462
OpenMV4 H7	429
JETSON NANO B01 4GB single board	1199

6 Conclusion

For the front-end garbage sorting, this project designs an intelligent sorting trash bin based on the STM32 microcontroller. The intelligent sorting trash bin can classify garbage with an accuracy rate of over 87%, and can display various parameters of the trash bin through the LCD display. In addition, the smart trash bin is also equipped with early warning, compression and crushing functions, which can realize the alarm of full load garbage, compress recyclable garbage and crush kitchen waste. The designed intelligent sorting trash bin satisfies people's intelligent treatment of front-end garbage sorting to a certain extent, and can effectively improve users' environmental protection awareness and quality of life.

In the future research, the function of human-computer interaction and more types of garbage will be added. It is planned to realize the function of human-computer interaction by adding a voice broadcast module and a wireless network module on the trash bin, and further improve the intelligence level of the intelligent garbage classification system. The types of data sets will be added to achieve accurate identification of more types of garbage, highlighting the humanized characteristics of the intelligent garbage classification system.

References

1. Ruyi, L.: Status quo and reflection of "Duality"of solid waste in china——case study of domestic garbage Impacts on ecological environment. Environ. Sci. Manag. **46**(04), 14–18 (2021)
2. Junze, L., Zhongmei, L.: The current situation of China's urban household waste separation system and legal countermeasures. Sci. Dev. **11**, 92–97 (2022)
3. Xiong, X., Hu, X., Guo, H.: A hybrid optimized grey seasonal variation index model improved by whale optimization algorithm for forecasting the residential electricity consumption. Energy. **234**, 121127 (2021)
4. Xiong, X., Hu, X., Tian, T., Guo, H., Liao, H.: A novel optimized initial condition and seasonal division based grey seasonal variation index model for hydropower generation. Appl. Energy. **328**, 120180 (2022)
5. Li, Z.K., Hu, X., Guo, H., Xiong, X: A novel weighted average weakening buffer operator based fractional order accumulation seasonal grouping grey model for predicting the hydropower generation. Energy. **277**, 127568 (2023)
6. Hu, X., Xiong, X., Wu, Y., Shi, M. J., Wei, P., Ma, C. M.: A hybrid clustered SFLA-PSO algorithm for optimizing the timely and real-time rumor refutations in online social networks. Expert Syst. Appl. **212**, 118638 (2023)
7. Kang, Z., Yang, J., Guo, H.: Automatic garbage classification system based on machine vision. J. Zhejiang University (Engineering Science) **54**(07), 1272–1280+1307 (2020)
8. Jian, S., Mingxing, W., Zhou Xin, W., Yang,: Design of intelligent sorting garbage bin based on jetson nano. Sci. Technol. Innov. **03**, 61–63 (2023)
9. Zhou, C., Chen, Z., Lv, X., et al.: Design of intelligent sorting trash dustbin based on STM32. In: E3S Web of Conferences. EDP Sciences, vol. 198 (2020)
10. Li, G., Ren, Y., Chu, N., et al.: Intelligent classification trash bin based on deep learning. In: International Conference on Sustainable Technology and Management (ICSTM 2022). SPIE, vol. 12299, pp. 208–218 (2022)
11. Zifeng, F., Feng, Z.: Design of intelligent garbage classification platform based on kendryte K210 and YOLOv2. Autom. Instr. **36**(08), 102–106 (2021)
12. Xueming, Z., Yanyue, P., Fenghua, W., et al.: Automatic classification bin based on artificial intelligence technology. In: 2022 IEEE 6th Information Technology and Mechatronics Engineering Conference (ITOEC). IEEE, vol. 6, pp. 408–413 (2022)
13. Sharif, M., Amin, J., Siddiqa, A., et al.: Recognition of different types of leuko-cytes using YOLOv2 and optimized bag-of-features. IEEE Access **8**, 167448–167459 (2020)
14. Lai, Q., Yang, J., Tan, B.: A model for automatic identification and defect diagnosis of insulators based on YOLOv2 network. Electr. Power. **52**(7), 31–39 (2019)
15. Gao, Z., Li, S., Chen, J.: Pedestrian detection method based on YOLO network. Comput. Eng. **44**(5), 215–219,226 (2018)
16. Lei, W.: Object detection of suckling piglets based on jetson nano and YOLO v5. Chongqing University (2018)
17. Torres-Sánchez E., Alastruey-Benedé, J., Torres-Moreno, E.: Developing an AI IoT application with open software on a RISC-V SoC. In: 2020 XXXV Conference on Design of Circuits and Integrated Systems (DCIS). IEEE, pp. 1–6 (2020)
18. Ding, Q., Liu, L., Chen, J.: Object detection of suckling piglets based on Jetson Nano and YOLO v5. Trans. Chin. Soc. Agric. Mach. **53**(3), 277–284 (2022)

The Intelligent Application of IoT and 3D Visualization Technology in a Road Maintenance Base

Ronghua Huang[1], Lu Guan[1,2], Yongcheng Bao[1], Jinlei Yang[1], and Leilei Chen[3(✉)]

[1] Jiangsu Integrity Transport Technology Co., Ltd., NanJing 211100, China
[2] Wu Han Polytechnic University, WuHan 430048, China
[3] Key Laboratory of Safety and Risk Management on Transport Infrastructures, Southeast University, NanJing 210018, China
Chenleilei@seu.edu.cn

Abstract. In the field of "new infrastructure" intelligent management and control, the Internet of Things and 3D visualization of these two technologies are developing more and more rapidly, and complement each other, which has also aroused the keen attention of road maintenance base managers. This paper will take a road maintenance base as the research object, to explore the practical application of Internet of Things 3D visualization technology in this particular scene. According to the needs of the whole project, through real-time monitoring and data collection of each business data in the intelligent road maintenance base, we analyze the different operational efficiency, energy consumption and output analysis under the traditional mode and the new mode of applying IoT 3D visualization technology, so as to provide a new solution for the intelligent operation and control of the road maintenance base in the future by using IoT 3D visualization technology.

Keywords: IoT and 3D Visualization · Road maintenance base · Intelligent application

1 Introduction

Internet of Things 3D Visualization is a technology that combines Internet of Things (IoT) and 3D Visualization (3D Visualization). The former collects, transmits and shares information in real time through a variety of devices connected to the Internet; the latter presents data in graphical form through BIM (Building Information Modeling) modeling technology and 3D graphic technology, enabling people to understand and analyze the data more intuitively and clearly. IoT 3D visualization technology, it is the integration of the advantages of the above two, the data collected by the Internet of Things, attached to the structure of the main body of the three-dimensional graphic display, so that users can better understand the meaning and relevance of the data represented by the application is very broad, in architectural design, transportation, urban planning, industrial manufacturing and other fields play a role. This technology can integrate real-time data from

X. Chen et al. (Eds.): IoTaaS 2023, LNICST 585, pp. 333–346, 2025.
https://doi.org/10.1007/978-3-031-70507-6_25

sensors, equipment, people, etc. with 3D models to form an interactive visualization interface that achieves a sense of realism in the observation and simulation of objects, scenes, and processes, which can help users better plan and make decisions, improve efficiency, reduce errors, and provide a better user experience.

With the rapid development of transportation roads and the growth of demand, how to improve the efficiency of road material production and provide road safety and stable quality has become an urgent issue. The central control room of the road maintenance base, as the core of the base production system, plays an important role in monitoring, controlling and managing the whole process of road material production. The central control room of the base is an information-intensive environment that involves the monitoring and control of many parameters, such as temperature, humidity and light.

However, there are some problems in the traditional control of road maintenance bases, such as the difficulty of data acquisition, inconvenient control operation, and untimely fault detection in hardware, while in the software platform, most of the 2.5D oblique view + dynamic picture display technology is used to realize low-cost pseudo three-dimensional stereoscopic graphic interface, which is not intuitive enough for easy use as a whole.The 2.5D technology adopts a multi-level superposition of planar images and transformations in order to create a visual effect that approximates a three-dimensional effect[1]. Unlike traditional flat images, 2.5D technology makes flat images look more three-dimensional and deep by processing the perspective, shadow and lighting of the image, but actually still consists of flat images. This technology can be used to create a more realistic sense of space and dynamics by adding layers, projection effects, motion effects and other means.

In order to solve these problems, IoT 3D visualization technology has emerged, bringing new applications and improvement possibilities to the road maintenance base [2].

IoT technology, as a derivative of Internet technology, through data collection, information processing and finally big data analysis can make things and objects further extend under the connection of Internet platform [3]. Its main features include extensive connectivity, real-time, intelligence and automation, etc. [4]. 3D technology refers to a technology based on three-dimensional spatial modeling and image processing technology for creating, displaying, manipulating and interacting with three-dimensional images and scenes. It uses advanced graphics rendering techniques by simulating real-world objects and environments so that observers can feel a realistic sense of three-dimensionality in virtual environments and be able to interact with them [5].

IoT 3D visualization technology enables the road maintenance base to realize real-time monitoring and management, automated operation and maintenance, data analysis and optimization, environmental protection and energy saving, as well as providing intelligent services and decision support. With the support of IoT 3D visualization technology, the whole of the maintenance base can present the real operation and control situation in multiple dimensions, and it is more conducive to the subsequent access of other contents.

In this paper, we will analyze the issues around how to select the IoT 3D visualization technology, the advantages and disadvantages in the application of the case study and the challenges and opportunities that the technology will face, and the research can play a certain role in guiding similar projects in the future.

Literature [6] in the previous summary predicted that the development of the Internet of Things will go through four stages, through the development of these years at present the Internet of Things has entered the stage of full intelligence, the Internet of Things technology will also face many serious challenges. Literature [7] applies IoT technology to building construction from attendance, alarms, hazard monitoring and other aspects of the systematic elaboration of the role of building safety management. Literature [8] analyzes the necessity of intelligent transportation construction based on IoT technology, describes the key technology of IoT application in intelligent transportation, and discusses the specific application of IoT technology in intelligent transportation from the aspects of vehicle speed, traffic flow, and urban public transportation. Literature [9] realized the IoT interoperability of vehicles by applying intelligent technology to the monitoring of railroads. Literature [10] applies IoT technology to the management automation of agriculture, and investigates in detail the control model of the measurement components related to the control algorithm of IoT technology and the processing algorithm of sensor indication. The application and promotion of the above technology provides technical support for the application of IoT technology in the intelligent road maintenance base, but at present the application of IoT technology in the intelligent road maintenance base is still imperfect, and there are still many difficulties, this paper aims to provide technical support for the future when there are similar projects.

2   Application Case Analysis

This paper analyzes and discusses the practical application of 3D visualization technology of Internet of Things based on a road maintenance base construction intelligence engineering project in Jiangsu Province. The base is located in Yancheng City, Jiangsu Province, and undertakes the maintenance and protection work of part of the highway network in Jiangsu Province. This project will weighbridge area, production area, mixing area, tank area, material area, relay warehouse and other monitoring data of each plant area through the wisdom of the base center control room large screen system display, and provide alarm information on this.

2.1   Engineering Requirements Analysis

The original user requirements collected for this engineering project are as follows:

(1) Display real-time animation of work in various factory areas through 2.5D technology;
(2) Monitor the real-time production situation of each factory area and achieve timely reporting;
(3) Connect the data monitored by various sub business systems;
(4) Enter each subsystem to query detailed data through unified permissions.

Now based on customer demand, the project site visits, found that when using 2.5D technology output of the animation model as well as the screen can only show the object in a single angle of the model rendering effect, to see the full range of civil structures, the distribution of Internet of Things equipment, and not conducive to the reading and comparison of the various plants of the multiple sets of data, the overall intuition is poor. Compared to the effect of 2.5D picture rendering, 3D model can not only more intuitively express the full picture of the object in all angles, but also in the performance of graphic dynamics is very advantageous [11].

The use of Internet of Things 3D visualization technology, can be more intelligent and scientific management of the maintenance base, so as to enhance the production of raw materials out of the quality. For example: the use of RFID equipment, the realization of the stone into the field without personnel guarding, different specifications of the stone transported to the maintenance base by dump trucks, dump trucks with cargo specification information of the radio frequency card, unattended weighbridge is equipped with vehicle number identification and card reading equipment, can automatically save the vehicle information and weighing information to the system. Dust concentration monitoring and automatic spraying system are established in the stockpile area, and the spraying system is automatically turned on when the dust concentration exceeds the set value. Temperature, humidity and environmental data are collected in the lab through DTU devices. Using AI edge boxes with algorithms, behaviors of not wearing safety

Fig. 1. Comparison of 2.5D and 3D model images

helmets and safety suits are identified and detected and warned. All of the above IoT devices can - in combination with 3D visualization technology - present location and data, while at the same time providing over-limit warnings through intuitive material changes.

Various equipment status, material management, production settings, and personnel flow information of the maintenance base are also synchronized and uploaded to the large screen platform in the control room of the base, which facilitates the overall management of the maintenance base. The 3D model of the road maintenance base can help decision makers make quick and accurate decisions in case of emergency. The following figure shows the difference between 2.5D and 3D in presentation (Fig. 1).

By clicking on the left side of the platform, you can quickly switch to the corresponding regional perspective, and then by clicking on the equipment in the model, you can get the current production and operation of the equipment. On the right hand side, you can visualize statistical information. In case of overrun or danger (e.g. edge box recognizes the phenomenon of not wearing a helmet), an alarm message will be popped up to remind the user to deal with it in time.

2.2   Engineering IoT Connection Implementation Requirements Change

In order to upgrade the 2.5D model display to 3D model display, we have to realize it through modeling technology and front-end WebGL programming technology. Firstly, we use conventional 3D modeling software (3dsMax software is used in this project) to establish 3D models and model animations that match the real structure and equipment, and at the same time, in the process of modeling, we carry out UV mapping and reduce the surface of some unnecessary surface positions; secondly, we bind the IoT devices (e.g., cameras) with the structure of the main body for the subordination of multiple information, and introduce dynamic data of the parsing interface from the background; then, we partition and cut the model file and sequentially implement it with front-end WebGL programming technology. Secondly, the model files are partitioned and cut into multiple files sequentially exported from the modeling software, and unified lightweight processing and compression is carried out to generate suitable loadable formats such as glb/fbx for loading on web pages.

At the software development level, the project interface is based on the VUE framework as a whole, while the open-source Three.js 3D engine library is introduced. The official raw script is used to load the 3D file format of glb/fbx, and the appropriate scene and camera viewpoints and lighting are created, which are rendered on the web page using the WebGL renderer. Subsequently, loop functions are created and local animation effects are realized by modifying parameters such as the rotation angle and position of the mesh, playing keyframes, and calling the renderer's render() method to render the scene and camera to achieve the effect of displaying 3D (Fig. 2).

Through this approach, on the one hand, the platform can make the Internet of Things to realize the intelligent equipment to find and locate, on the other hand, also can make the Internet of Things platform real-time record of the dynamic information of the production of equipment, so that the whole project can achieve the refinement of the management. The combination of BIM model and Internet of Things equipment data can largely meet the needs after the change, not only realize the rendering effect

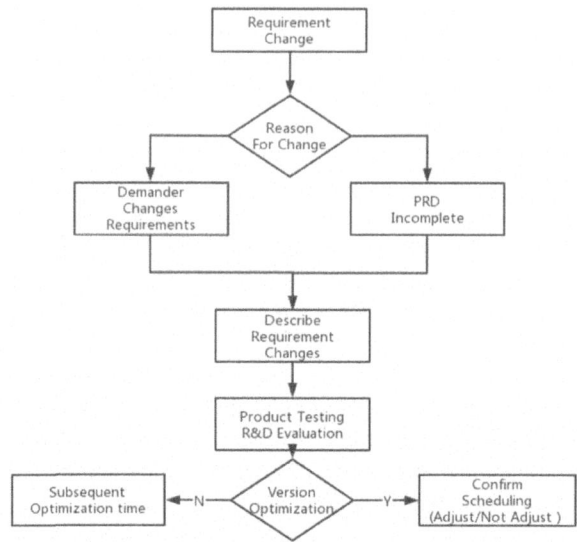

Fig. 2. Task flowchart for implementing requirement changes

of 3D stereo graphics, but also provide a very feasible solution for the overall project operation control and future development.

2.3   Application of IoT and 3D Visualization Technology

The application of Internet of Things (IoT) technology in the construction of road maintenance bases includes sensor-monitored data collection, remote control and operation, and fault detection and early warning. By installing suitable sensors and utilizing wireless networks to transmit data, base managers can monitor the operating status of equipment in real time and control it remotely. At the same time, based on sensor data analysis, the system can timely detect equipment failure and send early warning information to improve equipment reliability and operational efficiency.

Various types of sensors applied in the road maintenance base, including: temperature sensors, humidity sensors, smoke sensors, speed sensors, infrared sensors, weighbridge collection equipment and so on. Through the application of IoT technology, the air temperature, humidity, light intensity and other production-related information data and equipment operating speed can be collected in real time from each plant, and the data collected by the sensors are transmitted to the central entity server or cloud platform through wired and wireless networks for further background analysis.

Based on IoT technology, base managers can control and operate base equipment remotely from anywhere via the network. First, using wired and wireless communication networking technology, IoT devices can be seamlessly connected to the central server or cloud platform. Secondly, the cloud platform has the function of data storage and analysis, which provides users with an interface for remote management and control. Further, the remote control process should be parsed using specific protocols with corresponding message rules, such as HTTP(S), MQTT, Socket, etc., to ensure the safety and reliability of remote operation. Finally, user-friendly remote operation interfaces, such as Web interfaces and cell phone applications, provide an intuitive and convenient remote management and control experience.

The IoT technology detects the failure of equipment in the base in time based on data analysis and pattern recognition from sensors and sends early warning information to relevant personnel via SMS and email for timely handling. The technology utilizes sensors to collect the operating data of the equipment and analyze it in comparison with the pre-set indicator thresholds to detect the presence of anomalies. Once an abnormal state is detected, the system quickly sends out an early warning notification via a cloud platform or other forms so that appropriate maintenance and treatment measures can be taken in a timely manner. Such a fault detection and early warning system can improve the reliability and operational efficiency of the equipment, reduce the losses caused by failures, and has an important application value for road maintenance management and other intelligent emerging fields (Fig. 3).

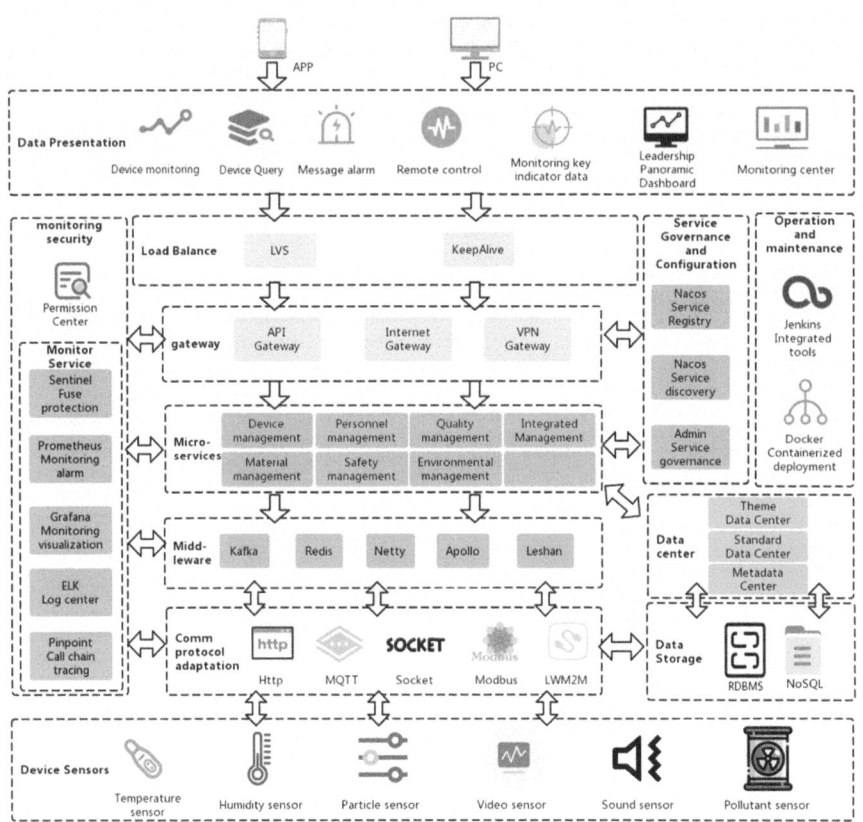

Fig. 3. Application Architecture of this Technology for Road Maintenance Base

3 Analysis and Evaluation of Application Effects

Through the application of IoT technology, the operational efficiency of the central control room of the intelligent road maintenance base can be improved, realizing the reduction of human input and the effective use of resources. In addition, through the Internet of Things technology to realize the early warning of failure and remote operation, can reduce the maintenance cost to a certain extent. At the same time, IoT technology can also enhance the security and monitoring reliability of the base center control room, and guarantee the stability and quality of road maintenance base production.

3.1 Efficiency Analysis

Evaluating the effectiveness of the IoT system in managing the road maintenance base provides a clear picture of the operational efficiency of the entire base. The figure below shows a flow chart of the value of operational efficiency between using the IoT system and traditional methods. The flowchart analyzes the work time spent, resource efficiency utilization, etc., which greatly improves the productivity of the entire base. A brief description and explanation of the IoT road maintenance base value flowchart is provided below (Fig. 4).

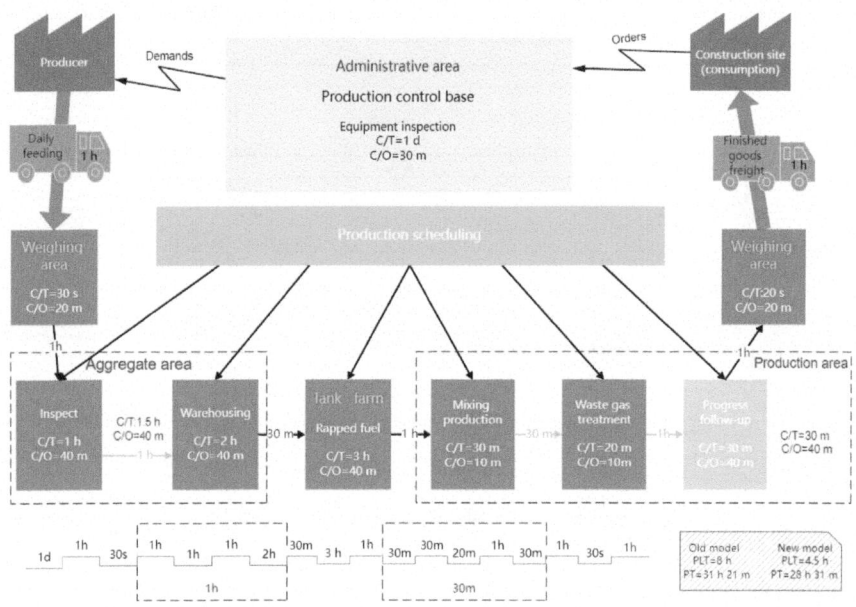

Fig. 4. Business Flow Value Transfer Process of Road Maintenance Base. **Note:** C/T (Cycle time): The time when the machine completes the task; C/O (Change time): Component change time; PLT (Product lead time): The delivery cycle time of a single product; PT (Process time): Production process time. Where 'h', 'm', and 's' represent time units of hours, minutes, and seconds.

As shown in the figure above demonstrates the operation of the entire base business. In the process can be seen from the construction side to provide orders to the production base as well as the production base and then through the supply side of the material transported to the base processing. The small rectangle in the figure shows the whole construction process of the traditional road maintenance base, and each link shows the machine completion time and part mold time, and the red dotted line shows the production link of the new model machine under the Internet of Things, and its completion time and part mold time. The stepped timeline at the bottom shows and counts the time needed in the whole processsualization, with the machine completion time at the bottom of the steps and the time between machines at the top of the steps.

The time statistics in the graph show that the traditional model requires a total of 39 h and 21 min per production run, while the new model with IoT requires a total of 33 h and 1 min per production run, which is a reduction of 6 h of working time. The main reductions in time are the extra labor time and the time spent switching machines between sites before the IoT was used. The new model under IoT reduces the delivery cycle time by 3.5 h and the production process time by 3 h.

The value process map clearly shows the entire process chain, identifying and eliminating unnecessary links and wasted time in the original program using IoT technology. It helps managers better understand and grasp the entire production process, and improves the utilization of production resources and production efficiency.

3.2 Energy Consumption Management of IoT and 3D Visualization Devices

The widespread use of IoT technology in areas such as smart road maintenance bases gives us more opportunities to manage and optimize energy consumption. However, the energy consumption of IoT devices themselves has become one of the challenges that need to be addressed. Therefore, how to effectively manage and control the energy consumption of IoT devices, extend battery life, reduce energy consumption and minimize the impact on the environment has become one of the important issues we are facing. Next, we will have an in-depth discussion on the management of energy consumption of IoT technology in smart road maintenance bases, and analyze the advantages, challenges and related solutions. The following is a comparative analysis of the power and water energy consumption of the road maintenance base in two years under the old model and the new model in half a year each (Fig. 5).

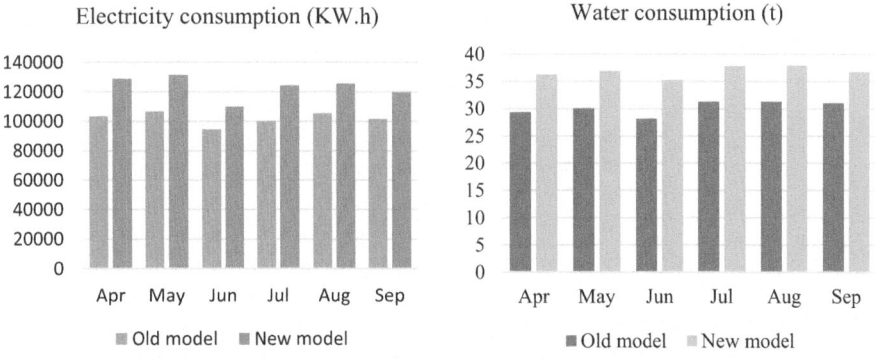

Fig. 5. Comparison and Analysis of Energy Sources between Electricity and Water Modes

The above figure shows that the energy consumption in the old model is lower than that in the new model, so the IoT technology increases the percentage of energy consumption when applied to the road maintenance base project. In road maintenance bases, the use of high-efficiency sensors, the selection of low-power communication methods and the adoption of intelligent energy management systems can improve the efficiency of system operation. However, large-scale deployments need to handle a large amount of data streams, and frequent device communication and data transmission may increase energy consumption. At the same time, keeping certain devices always on can further increase energy consumption. Therefore, overall energy management requires comprehensive consideration of the relationship between different devices and systems, and appropriate strategies, such as configuring device sleep/wake mechanisms, optimizing sensor operating modes, using energy-efficient devices, and optimizing data transmission methods. Effective energy management can only be achieved by comprehensively considering the relationship between balancing energy consumption and system requirements.

However, whether the application of IoT technology in smart road maintenance bases is reasonable or not also requires a comparison of the efficacy of the outputs in order to arrive at a rationalization, and the capacity of the road maintenance bases in these two modes will be further analyzed in the following.

3.3 Capacity Analysis

As one of the important fields of the application of Internet of Things (IoT) technology, the intelligent road maintenance base realizes the intelligent management and control of road maintenance equipment and infrastructure through the integration of sensors, communication networks and data analysis and other technical means. However, while promoting the development of intelligent road maintenance base, we need to pay attention not only to its energy consumption but also to the effect of its output. Therefore,

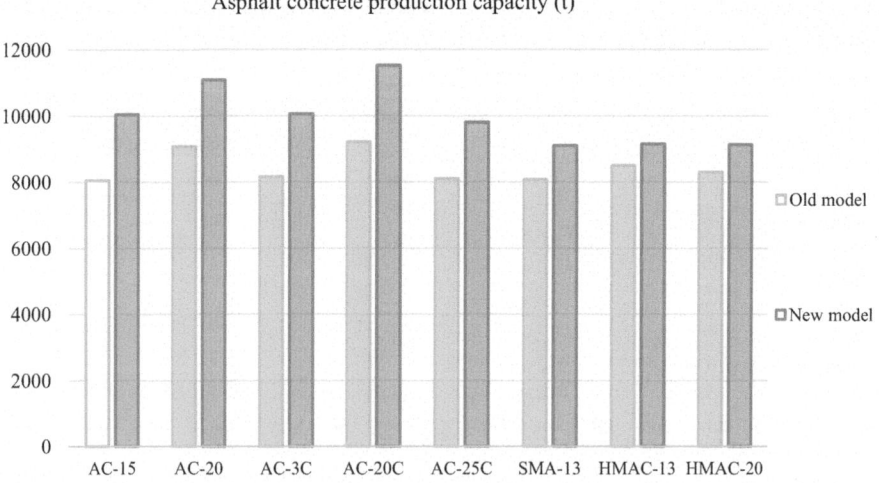

Fig. 6. Comparison of Asphalt concrete Production

the following will be targeted to analyze the capacity. A comprehensive assessment of the output effect of IoT technology in smart road maintenance bases can provide strong support and guidance for improving energy efficiency, optimizing operation and management, and promoting application. The following figure compares the output of different types of concrete for one month in the road maintenance base under the old model with the output of different types of concrete for one month under the application of IoT technology (Fig. 6).

The above figure shows that the output of concrete in the intelligent road maintenance base with the application of IoT technology is more than the output of concrete in the road base of the traditional model, and it can also be seen from the value flow chart that the intelligent road maintenance base with the application of IoT technology has a lower mold change time than the traditional one, so it can also produce more different types of soil mixing materials in the same time. The results of capacity analysis show that it can significantly improve the production efficiency and product quality. Not only that, the intelligent road maintenance base applying IoT technology is also able to realize the base's highly automated and precisely regulated production process through real-time monitoring of the raw material supply status, intelligent proportioning and process control, as well as remote monitoring of the equipment operation status and failure warning. This helps to increase production and reduce downtime, as well as ensure product consistency and stability, meet customer demand and enhance competitiveness.

Through the above evaluation of efficiency analysis, energy consumption management, capacity analysis and other indicators, we can get a comprehensive understanding of the effect of the engineering application of IOT technology in the intelligent road maintenance base. In terms of efficiency, it improves the utilization of production resources and productivity, in terms of energy consumption, it can achieve the balance of energy consumption through the formulation of appropriate strategies, and in terms of capacity analysis, it improves the output of products, improves the management ability and reduces the input of human resources. This will help to improve the management efficiency, resource utilization and safety of the road maintenance base, thus realizing higher economic and social benefits.

4 Challenges Faced and Future Development Direction

The application of IoT technologies in smart road maintenance bases is still facing a number of challenges, such as security and privacy protection, technical standards and interoperability, cost and sustainability. To address these issues, future directions include enhancing data protection and privacy protection, establishing unified IoT standards and protocols, reducing the cost of IoT devices, and optimizing the energy consumption of IoT technologies. Meanwhile, the combination of IoT technology with artificial intelligence, big data and other technologies can be further explored to realize smarter and more efficient production of intelligent road maintenance bases.

4.1 Challenges Faced

(1) There is still a disconnect between the requirements and perception layers.When the IoT and 3D visualization technology is applied to the construction of smart road

maintenance bases, we need to carry out perceptual layer technology innovation work based on specific functional requirements. Due to the current perception layer technology not being fully applicable to the field of smart road maintenance.Therefore, there are high requirements for optimizing the distribution of sensing devices, miniaturizing technology, making it multifunctional, and reducing power consumption. So we need to innovate application of IoT and 3D visualization technology to meet the specific needs of the smart road maintenance field.

(2) The complexity and scale of data are increasing.In the context of the closer connection between the Internet of Things and 3D scenes, a large amount of data will be generated, including geometric models, sensors, devices, personnel, and other aspects of data.Processing and analyzing these massive amounts of data is a challenge that requires efficient data storage, computation, rendering, and processing capabilities.Data quality is crucial for accurate 3D visualization. However, data in the Internet of Things environment may be affected by sensor failures, noise interference, data loss, and other issues, which may lead to inaccurate visualization results.

(3) The research on underlying models and algorithms is weak.The road maintenance base can collect a large amount of road maintenance related data through Internet of Things technology. At the application layer, theoretical algorithms such as data cleaning and analysis, deep learning, etc. based on a large amount of historical data can provide more accurate safety production and consulting services at the current stage. However, there is still a lag in the application layer in this regard, and it is necessary to strengthen the research on the underlying models and algorithms. Consider improving the application layer level from multiple factors.

(4) The quality of grassroots talents is not high.Due to the limited exposure of grassroots practitioners to IoT knowledge, the reconstruction of IoT infrastructure is severely hindered [11].Therefore, it is necessary to strengthen the training of relevant personnel, optimize talent introduction plans, and create a high-quality and high-level team of grassroots practitioners in the IoT. Moreover, the government should strengthen the construction of relevant laws and regulations to create a good atmosphere for the IoT and 3D visualization technology in the field of smart road maintenance bases.

The IoT and 3D visualization technology faces many challenges in the intelligent management and control of road maintenance bases. Therefore, it is necessary to guide innovation in the perception layer through demand guidance, research on bottom strengthening layer models and algorithms, and vigorously cultivate grassroots talents. Completing these tasks can promote the construction of smart road maintenance bases and the application of IoT and 3D visualization technology. This will further improve the quality and efficiency of maintenance work, and bring significant improvements to road maintenance management.

4.2 Future Development Direction

One of the future directions of IoT technology in smart road maintenance bases is data intelligence. With the wide application of IoT devices, the maintenance base will be able to collect and analyze a variety of data in real time, including road condition information, equipment operation status, traffic flow and so on. By integrating big data technology and artificial intelligence algorithms, these data can be intelligently processed and analyzed to extract valuable information and make predictions. For example, by analyzing road cameras and mining traffic flow data, changes in road conditions can be predicted in advance, providing maintenance personnel with timely maintenance plans.

Another development of IoT technology in the smart road maintenance base is automated monitoring and control. Real-time monitoring of maintenance equipment, road conditions and environmental parameters can be realized by installing sensors and collection devices on the equipment. These monitoring data can be transmitted to the center console through wireless communication technology to provide administrators with timely alarms on work status and abnormalities. In addition, IoT technology can also realize remote control of equipment, allowing managers to operate equipment remotely through intelligent terminal devices, thus improving operation and maintenance efficiency and response speed.

Another important development direction of IoT technology in the smart road maintenance base is predictive maintenance and optimization. With the monitoring and data analysis capabilities of IoT technology, real-time monitoring and prediction of the health status of maintenance equipment can be realized. By obtaining the vibration, temperature, current and other parameters of the equipment, combined with advanced algorithmic analysis and modeling, it is possible to predict the possible failure of the equipment in advance and carry out reasonable maintenance planning and optimization scheduling according to the prediction results. This can avoid stoppages and delays caused by equipment failures and improve the reliability and operational efficiency of the equipment, thus reducing maintenance costs and improving work efficiency.

The future development direction of IoT technology in smart road maintenance base mainly includes data intelligence, automated monitoring and control, predictive maintenance and optimization. These development directions will provide smarter and more efficient management and services for the work of smart road maintenance bases, and improve the quality and efficiency of roads in the maintenance process.

5   Conclusion

By analyzing the application case of IoT technology in base central control room, this paper shows that IoT technology plays an important role in improving the management and operation efficiency of base central control room.

(1) The road maintenance base applying IoT technology improves the efficiency of the whole production as well as improves the production system by removing the time of material conversion and reducing the redundant operation links.

(2) Comparison of the energy consumption of the road maintenance base using IOT technology and the traditional road maintenance base shows that although the energy consumption is higher in the new model, it can be balanced by optimization strategies.

(3) Comparison of the production capacity of road maintenance bases applying IOT technology and traditional road maintenance bases shows that the production capacity of the new model has a greater increase and the conversion between the production of different types of products is also faster.

At present, the application of Internet of Things technology in intelligent road maintenance base is not particularly mature, but the impact is very far-reaching, with the rapid development of Internet of Things technology, through further research and innovation, the application of Internet of Things technology in the field of intelligent road maintenance base will be more extensive and in-depth, for road maintenance to bring greater benefits and improvements.

References

1. Dong, Z., Li, B., Wan, J., Suo, H., Zhang, D.: An intelligent IoT-based traffic management framework for the transportation system. Mob. Netw. Appl. **24**(5), 1566–1579 (2019)
2. Hu, Y.: Internet of things technology and applications. Electron. Technol. Softw. Eng. **4**, 20–22 (2018). China
3. Wang, W., Mi, H., Ri, A., Abuli, K., Peng, B.: The application of internet of things technology in agriculture. Mod. Agric. Technol. **49**(22), 245–246 (2020). China
4. Zhang, Z.: Research on the application of internet of things technology in safety management of construction projects. Metall. Manag. **09**, 15–17 (2023). China
5. Yu, X., Zheng, W., Zhang, Y.: The integrated application of internet of things technology in smart city construction. China New Commun. **25**(10), 72–74 (2023). China
6. Balog, M., Knapčíková, L.: Smart techniques for technical conditions monitoring of railway wagons. In: 3rd EAI International Conference on Management of Manufacturing Systems (2018)
7. Romanova, A.M., Galin, R.R., Trefilov, M.P.: Application of IoT technologies for automation of management in agriculture. IOP Conf. Ser. Earth Environ. Sci. **315**(3), 032032 (2019)
8. Song, Y., Cheng, C., Fei, Y., et al.: 2.5D Image based Robotic Grasping. CoRR (2019). https://arxiv.org/abs/1905.13675
9. Yuting, L.: Design of 3D image visual communication system for automatic reconstruction of digital images. Adv. Multimed. **2022**, 1 (2022)
10. Xuezhao, Z., Hang, G.: Research on subway construction monitoring and warning system based on internet of things technology. J. Phys. Conf. Ser. **1885**(2), 022052 (2021)
11. Yan, W., Zhang, L.: Exploring the application of 3D GIS in smart cities. Netw. Secur. Technol. Appl. **06**, 136–137 (2020). China

A New Method of Integrated Radar-Communication System Waveform Design and Signal Processing Based on OFDM Block Subcarrier Allocation

Zhan Xu[1]([✉]), Cong Quan[1], Weige Zhu[2], and Xiaolong Yang[1]

[1] School of Information and Communication Engineering, Beijing Information Science and Technology University, Beijing 100071, China
{xuzhan,2021020546,xiaolongyang}@bistu.edu.cn
[2] Shanghai Institute of Satellite Engineering, Shanghai, China

Abstract. In the context of the Internet of Vehicles (IoV) and sixth-generation (6G) wireless communication, wireless radar and communication (RadCom) systems face the dual challenges of improving spectrum utilization efficiency and lowering interference levels. The use of orthogonal frequency division multiplexing (OFDM) signals in a shared waveform system has the potential to mitigate mutual interference between communication and radar while also meeting the need for improved range resolution. Some researchers have proposed using the odd and even carriers of OFDM signals to modulate radar and communication functions, intending to achieve integration. Nevertheless, this methodology presents several concerns, such as the potential for interference between radar carriers and communication carriers and the negative impact caused by the cyclic prefix (CP) on radar performance. This study presents a new method that leverages OFDM and block subcarrier allocation techniques to enhance the integration of radar and communication system performance. The primary objective is to mitigate interference by consolidating radar and communication subcarriers while minimizing the detrimental effects of CP on radar performance by utilizing zero padding (ZP) as a replacement for CP. Furthermore, this method reduces pilot tone costs by utilizing radar data to estimate Doppler frequency offsets. It can dynamically adjust the number of radar and communication subcarriers to accommodate evolving performance demands. Simulation results indicate that in the presence of residual frequency offset, this solution enhances communication performance while slightly degrading radar performance.

Keywords: RadCom · OFDM · Block Subcarrier Allocation

This work was supported in part by the National Key Research and Development Program(308), in part by the R&D Program of Beijing Municipal Education Commission (KM202211232006) and in part by the Major Research Fostering Project to Promote the Colleges Classified Development of Beijing Information Science & Technology University(No. 2121YJPY222).

X. Chen et al. (Eds.): IoTaaS 2023, LNICST 585, pp. 347–357, 2025.
https://doi.org/10.1007/978-3-031-70507-6_26

1   Introduction

Due to the rapid advancement of electronic information technology, the utilization of frequency bands, hardware/system design, and signal processing in wireless communications and radar detection exhibit similar development trends [1]. In contemporary and more intricate tasks and situations, conventional radar and communication systems face various obstacles, such as constrained spectrum resources, intensified electromagnetic interference, and heightened system complexity [2]. In order to tackle these concerns, much focus is devoted to investigating radar-communication integration [3,4]. The integration of radar communication holds significant potential in several fields, encompassing but not restricted to earthquake response, vehicle networking, and terrain surveying and mapping.

OFDM is advantageous for applications that need fast transmission and accurate distance resolution because of its exceptional spectral efficiency, robust resistance to multipath effects, flexible subcarrier modulation, and straightforward implementation. As a result, OFDM has emerged as a highly favorable option for integrating radar communication systems [5,6]. Several academics have studied the integrated design of radar communication utilizing OFDM waveform sharing [7,8]. The analysis conducted in reference [9] examined the effects of several carrier allocation techniques on radar mutual information and transmission data rate. The researcher conducted that analysis using conventional cyclic prefix orthogonal frequency division multiplexing (CP OFDM). However, using CP can reduce energy consumption and produce misleading objectives, thus influencing the efficacy of radar systems. In the study conducted by the authors in reference [10], a blank guard interval was utilized as a substitute for the cyclic prefix. The researcher proposed this method in traditional odd-even carrier allocation OFDM technology. Although this methodology improves the performance of radar systems, it concurrently introduces heightened interference between the radar subcarriers and communication subcarriers. Researchers introduced a Chirp signal-based multi-carrier radar communication system in a prior investigation [11] to facilitate signal sharing. However, residual frequency offset compromises the integrity of the signals' orthogonality, leading to the system's overall performance deterioration. Several researchers [12,13] have performed channel estimation and Doppler frequency offset correction by employing training sequences and repeated symbols. It is worth mentioning that these training sequences and repeated symbols also use a portion of the available spectrum resources.

The main contributions of this paper are as follows:

(1) This paper proposes a radar communication system scheme based on block subcarrier allocation of OFDM. By employing block subcarrier allocation, the radar and communication subcarriers are organized into groups, thereby minimizing interference from the radar carrier to the communication carrier and enhancing overall communication performance.
(2) The proposed scheme uses ZP as a substitute for CP. ZP performs a comparable function to CP by reducing Inter-Carrier Interference (ICI) and

Inter-Symbol Interference (ISI). This simultaneous adoption of ZP enhances energy efficiency and mitigates the adverse effects of CP on radar performance.

(3) The scheme presented in this paper employs radar signals to estimate frequency offsets to facilitate cooperative work between radar and communication functionalities.

The primary structure of this paper is organized as follows: In Sect. 2, we present a signal model that utilizes block subcarrier allocation within the framework of OFDM. Moving forward, Sect. 3 offers a comprehensive exposition of the integrated signal design and waveform processing methodology proposed in this study. Section 4 presents detailed simulation experiments that validate the efficacy of the proposed approach. Finally, Sect. 5 provides a succinct summary of the entire body of work.

2   RadCom Integrated Signal Model

OFDM subcarriers exhibit equidistant frequency spacing. As a subcarrier attains its peak value in the frequency domain, the remaining subcarriers assume zero amplitude, thereby ensuring inherent orthogonality among them [14]. As shown in Fig. 1, predefined subcarrier assignment rules determine the allocation of subcarriers for radar signals or communication signals [15]. The orthogonal nature of subcarriers allows for effective concurrent radar detection and communication transmission without reciprocal interference.

The methodology described in this study enables the allocation of extra subcarriers or the increase in energy allocation to subcarriers dedicated to information transmission in situations that need improved communication transmission speeds. Similarly, when faced with situations that need enhanced radar detection capabilities, the approach outlined in this research article facilitates the allocation of additional subcarriers for detection purposes or a higher allocation of energy to subcarriers specifically designated for radar detection.

In this scheme, we denote the total OFDM subcarriers as N_s and categorize them into subcarrier blocks, which we represent as G_B. Specifically, radar detection allocates N subcarriers, while communication transmission allocates $N_s - N$ subcarriers. Within this framework, precisely $\frac{G_B}{2}$ subcarrier chunks serve the purpose of radar detection, leaving the complementary $\frac{G_B}{2}$ subcarrier chunks assigned to the realm of communication transmission. The discrete subcarrier data sequence employed for Inverse Fast Fourier Transform (IFFT) is:

$$\mathbf{Y} = \mathbf{M_r X_r} + \mathbf{M_c X_c} \tag{1}$$

where in $\mathbf{X_r} \in \mathbf{C}^{N_s \times 1}$ and $\mathbf{X_c} \in \mathbf{C}^{N_s \times 1}$ represent signals in the radar frequency domain and the communication domain, respectively. The matrices $\mathbf{M_r}$ and $\mathbf{M_c}$ correspond to the subcarrier configurations for radar and communication systems, while matrices $\mathbf{D_{r_{-i}}}$ and $\mathbf{D_{c_{-i}}}$ pertain to the subcarrier block configurations specific to radar and communication.

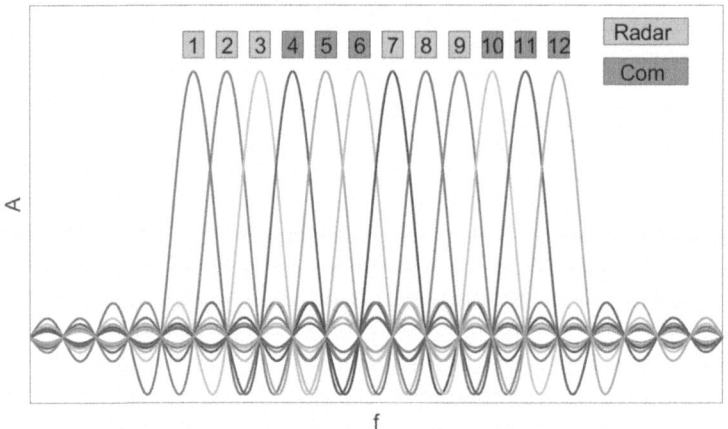

Fig. 1. Block Subcarrier Allocation.

$$\mathbf{M_r} = \text{diag} \left\{ \mathbf{M_r}(1), \cdots, \mathbf{M_r}(k), \cdots, \mathbf{M_r}(N_s) \right\} \tag{2}$$

$$\mathbf{M_c} = \text{diag} \left\{ \mathbf{M_c}(1), \cdots, \mathbf{M_c}(k), \cdots, \mathbf{M_c}(N_s) \right\} \tag{3}$$

$$\mathbf{D_{r_{-i}}} = [\mathbf{M_r}((i-1)\frac{N_s}{G_B} + 1), \ldots, \mathbf{M_r}(i\frac{N}{G_B})] \tag{4}$$

$$\mathbf{D_{c_{-i}}} = [\mathbf{M_c}((i-1)\frac{N_s}{G_B} + 1), \ldots, \mathbf{M_c}(i\frac{N}{G_B})] \tag{5}$$

The variables $\mathbf{M_r}(k)$ and $\mathbf{M_c}(k)$ take binary values of 0 or 1, subject to the constraint $\mathbf{M_r}(k) + \mathbf{M_c}(k) = \mathbf{I}$, where $\mathbf{I} \in \mathbf{C}^{\frac{N_s}{G_B} \times 1}$ represents the unity array. When $\mathbf{M_r}(k) = 1$ and $\mathbf{M_c}(k) = 0$, the status quo is maintained, indicating the assignment of the kth subcarrier to the radar signal. Similarly, when $\mathbf{M_r}(k) = 0$ and $\mathbf{M_c}(k) = 1$, the status quo is upheld, signifying the assignment of the kth subcarrier to the communication signal. Here, $i = 1, 2, \cdots, \frac{N_s}{G_B}$ represents the subcarrier block sequence. The subcarrier data sequence employed for OFDM modulation can also be represented as

$$\mathbf{Y} = [\mathbf{D_{r_{-1}}}, \mathbf{D_{c_{-1}}}, \ldots, \mathbf{D_{r_{-i}}}, \mathbf{D_{c_{-i}}}] \tag{6}$$

The radar employs a Chirp signal as its transmission waveform. Given the utilization of N subcarriers for radar detection, the frequency-domain radar signal r exhibits N non-zero spectral components. These spectral components correspond to the discrete spectrum samples of the Chirp signal. $r(n)$ can be expressed as

$$r(n) = \text{DFT} \left[\exp \left(j\pi k_r \left(\frac{n-1}{F_s} \right)^2 \right) \right] \tag{7}$$

where in $n = 1, 2, \cdots, N$, k_r represents the frequency modulation slope, F_s denotes the sampling frequency, which adheres to the condition $N = F_s T$; here, T signifies the period of the Chirp signal.

3 Integrated Signal Design and Processing Method for RadCom

3.1 Integrated Signal Design Method

The multipath effect can give rise to ICI and ISI in conventional multi-carrier communication systems like OFDM, disrupting the orthogonal relationship among subcarriers. Traditional strategies frequently use the CP as a protective interval to address these issues. This methodology ensures that the receiver's window encompasses only a single OFDM symbol, enhancing the system's resistance to interference and the overall transmission quality. However, it is essential to recognize that while using CP improves communication effectiveness, it can potentially lead to reduced energy efficiency and have implications for radar detection.

As seen in Fig. 2, the methodology proposed in this research replaces CP with ZP. Upon reception, the received signal is divided into partitions, ensuring that only the current OFDM symbol is present within the receiving window, which partitioning aids in mitigating ISI. Additionally, the guard interval is obtained from the following OFDM symbols and appended to the beginning of the current signal. This approach ensures the integrity of every character, thereby reducing the impact of ICI.

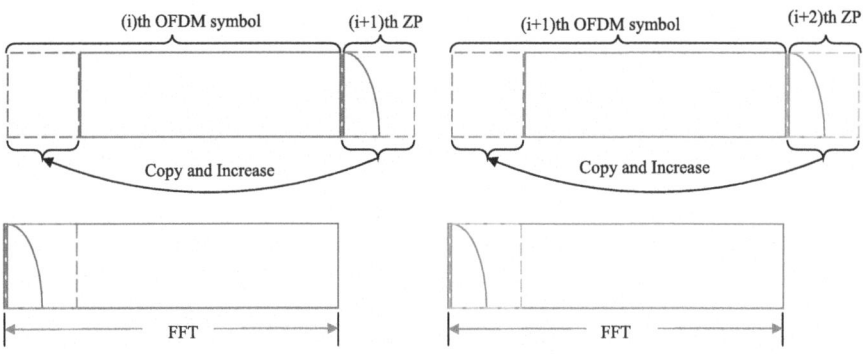

Fig. 2. The replication and addition of ZP.

3.2 Flow of Integrated Signal Processing

As shown in Fig. 3, this paper presents the formation and processing flow of the integrated radar communication signal. The transmitting end combines radar and communication signals to create a subcarrier data sequence. We then transform this sequence into time-domain data using IFFT modulation and insert a guard interval, in the form of ZP, between adjacent OFDM symbols. At the receiving end, the preamble serves the purpose of preliminary frequency offset estimation. Following this, frequency offset correction and guard interval removal are performed separately for each symbol. Later, the Fast Fourier Transform (FFT) is used, facilitating the subsequent segregation of radar and communication carriers. Subsequently, communication information is being recovered via demodulation. Simultaneously, target information is extracted from the radar echo signal through IFFT modulation and pulse compression.

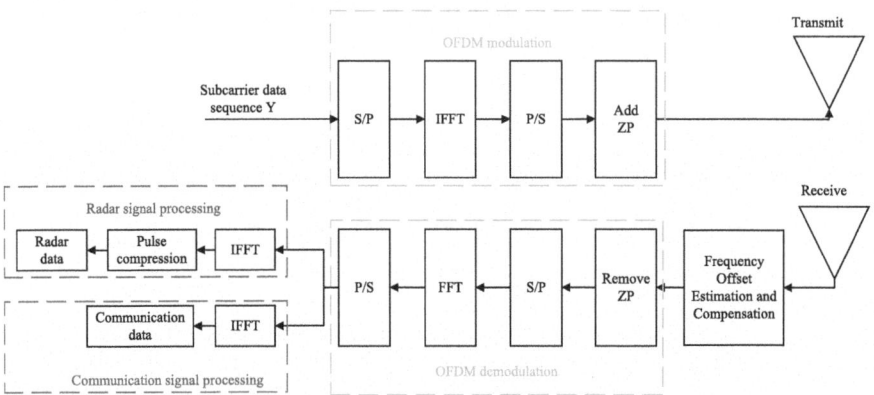

Fig. 3. Process flow of integrated radar communication system.

3.3   Method for Estimation and Compensation of Frequency Offset

In an OFDM system, Doppler frequency shifts can introduce interference, disrupting the orthogonality among subcarriers and causing changes and degradation in the constellation diagram. These changes and degradation detrimentally affect the overall system functioning. The methodology proposed in this study uses radar data to estimate frequency offsets, differing from traditional techniques. Adopting this methodology reduces the need for training sequences and pilot frequencies, preserving system resources.

Within the framework of radar communication integration, a Doppler frequency offset engenders the emergence of two discernible categories of impacts. The first issue is the reciprocal interference between radar and communication subcarriers. The second aspect pertains to self-interference between radar subcarriers and communication subcarriers. The methodology proposed in this research article involves segmenting OFDM subcarriers into distinct blocks. We assign subcarrier blocks of even order for radar detection purposes and designate subcarrier blocks of odd order for communication transmission. This strategy reduces the interference caused by radar signal subcarriers on communication signal subcarriers, improving communication performance.

The process of frequency offset estimation and compensation using radar information is depicted in Fig. 4. In this process, two consecutive OFDM symbols, namely $yi + 1$ and yi, are initially stored in a buffer. Subsequently, the time-domain signal undergoes transformation into a frequency-domain signal through FFT, enabling the extraction of radar-related information. This information includes Y_{i+1} and Y_i, which are calculated to obtain ε.

$$\varepsilon = \arg\left(Y_{i+1} \cdot X_{i+1} \cdot (Y_i \cdot X_i)^*\right) \frac{1}{2\pi} \cdot \frac{N_{fft}}{N_{fft} + N_{zp}} \tag{8}$$

where in ε represents the estimated frequency offset value used to compensate for the frequency offset within the received signal in the time domain. X_{i+1} and X_i denote separate known radar information from different symbols. N_{fft} corresponds to the number of FFT points within a single OFDM symbol, while N_{zp} represents the length of the guard interval.

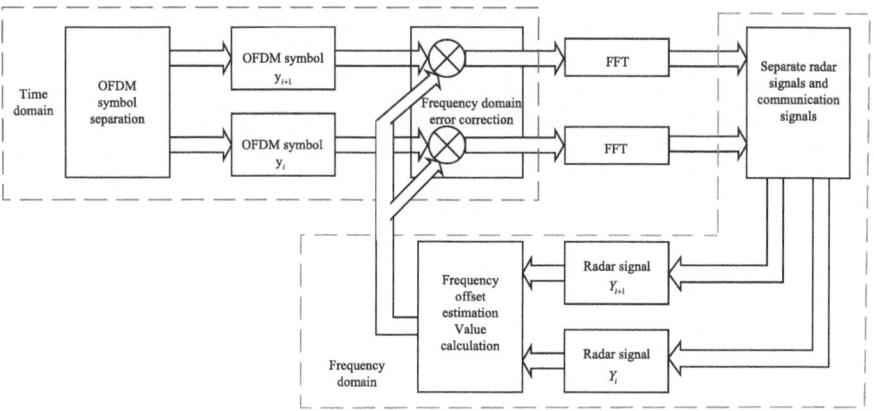

Fig. 4. Frequency offset estimation and compensation process.

4   Simulation

The simulation experiment validated the effectiveness of the radar communication integrated waveform design scheme and processing approach described in this research. The radar signal employs the Chirp signal and modulates the communication information using Quadrature Phase Shift Keying (QPSK) modulation. As seen in Fig. 5, it became apparent that an escalation in residual frequency offset resulted in a progressive displacement of the constellation diagram from its original form. As a result, these changes resulted in a gradual decline in the system's overall effectiveness.

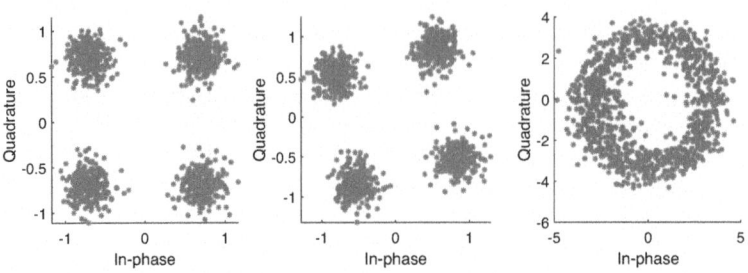

Fig. 5. Influence of Frequency Offset on Signal Constellation Diagram.

The simulation results illustrating the pulse are presented in Fig. 6. Upon reception, the radar echo signals underwent the process of pulse compression. As the residual frequency deviation increased, it led to fluctuations in the pulse compression's location and amplitude. These changes had a detrimental influence on the performance of radar detection performance.

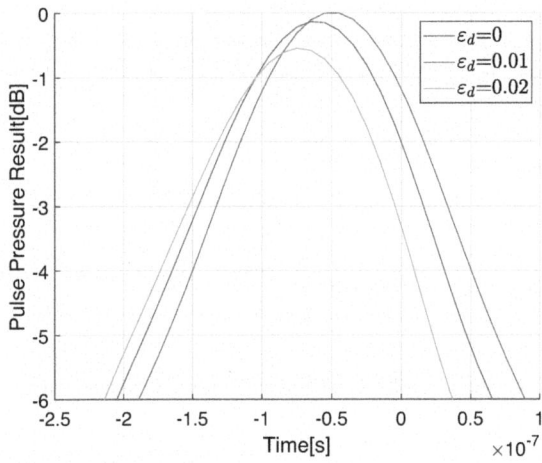

Fig. 6. The Influence of Residual Frequency Deviation on the Peak Amplitude and Position of Radar Pulse Compression.

As seen in Fig. 7, a comparative analysis was conducted between the conventional method employing the odd-even carrier allocation strategy and the new approach introduced in this research, assuming the presence of a residual frequency offset. References [9,10] outlined a methodology that employed OFDM sub-carrier allocation, where in they assigned radar modulation to odd-numbered carriers and communication modulation to even-numbered carriers, successfully integrating radar and communication functionalities. Building upon this foundation, this study proposes a new methodology for enhancing the allocation of subcarriers. The categorization of OFDM subcarriers into different groups assigns some for communication and others for radar. This new methodology facilitates the integration of radar and communication systems and improves overall communication performance.

The residual frequency offset included in radar transmissions has two primary impacts. Firstly, self-interference within the radar carrier results in energy dispersion towards neighboring sub-carriers, thus diminishing the integrated side lobe ratio (ISLR). Secondly, the presence of communication carriers interferes with the radar carrier, leading to altered properties and peak position of radar pulses.

This new methodology aims to mitigate the mutual interference between radar subcarriers and communications subcarriers. Nevertheless, this increased self-interference among radar subcarriers has led to a slight decline in radar performance parameters. For example, the paper's radar signal design yielded a measured peak side lobe ratio (PSLR) of −20.52 dB at a signal-to-noise ratio (SNR) of 3 dB. The result was inferior to the −20.82 dB acquired using the conventional approach. Similarly, ISLR was −10.83 dB for the proposed method, showing a minor decrement compared with the −11.07 dB of the conventional approach.

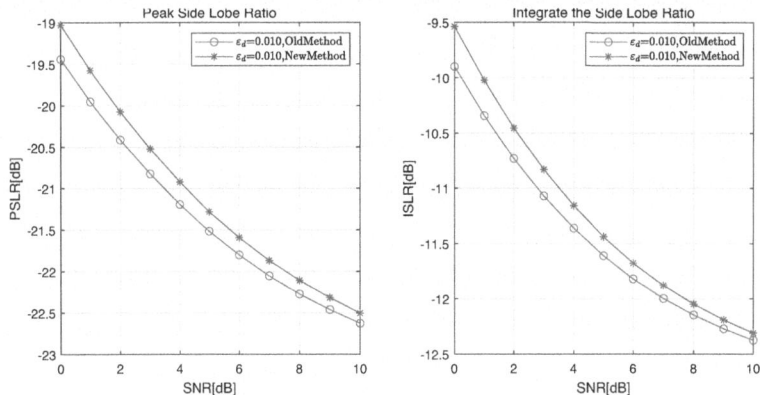

Fig. 7. Influence of Residual Frequency Offset on Radar Peak Sidelobe Ratio and Radar Integral Sidelobe Ratio. The conventional approach(OldMethod). The new approach proposed in this study (NewMethod).

As seen in Fig. 8, an augmentation in the SNR led to a progressive decrease in the communication system's bit error rate (BER). The residual frequency offset has two primary impacts on communication signals. Firstly, this phenomenon induces self-interference within communication carriers, leading to elevated bit error rates due to energy leakage towards neighboring sub-carriers. Secondly, it gives rise to interference between radar carriers and communication carriers, resulting in the distortion of the communication constellation diagram and compromising the overall performance of communication systems. The new approach presented in this research demonstrates superior performance in transmission bit error rate compared to the conventional method, given an equivalent residual frequency offset. This new methodology exhibited enhanced performance during the experiment compared to the conventional approach when the residual frequency offset was set at $\varepsilon_d = 0.025$, and the BER was $1 \cdot 10^{-5}$. This improvement manifested as a gain of 0.75 dB.

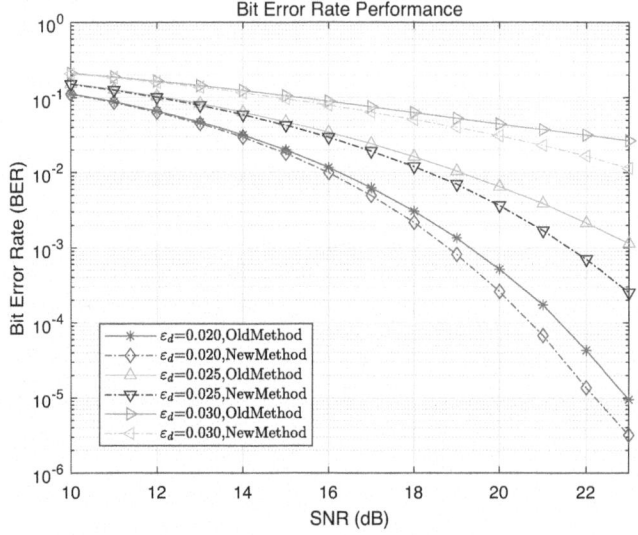

Fig. 8. Communication Bit Error Rate Comparison.

5   Conclusion

This paper delves into waveform design and processing methods for integrating radar and communication systems. It analyzes the limitations of conventional approaches in scenarios involving residual frequency offset and presents a novel integrated waveform design scheme based on OFDM block subcarrier allocation. This paper analyzes the effects of Doppler frequency offset on the radar communication integration signal and presents a corresponding approach for estimating and compensating for the frequency offset. Simulation trials confirmed the efficacy of this methodology. Compared with the traditional OFDM waveform design method, the methodology proposed in this research study utilizes block subcarrier allocation instead of alternating subcarrier allocation. Block subcarrier allocation reduces the interference of radar subcarriers with communication subcarriers. Simulation results indicate that when a residual frequency offset is present, the proposed strategy slightly decreases radar performance but improves communication reliability.

References

1. Bo, X., Kai, H., Yongxiang, L.: Development and prospect of radar and communication integration. J. Electron. Inf. Technol. **41**(3), 739–750 (2019)
2. Zhang, J.A., Liu, F., Masouros, C., et al.: An overview of signal processing techniques for joint communication and radar sensing. IEEE J. Sel. Top. Signal Process. **15**(6), 1295–1315 (2021)
3. Ma, D., Liu, X., Tianyao, H., et al.: Joint radar and communications: shared waveform designs and performance bounds. J. Radars **11**(2), 198–212 (2022)
4. Wild, T., Braun, V., Viswanathan, H.: Joint design of communication and sensing for beyond 5G and 6G systems. IEEE Access **2**, 30845–30857 (2021)
5. Wang Z, Han K, Jiang J, et al.: Symbiotic sensing and communications towards 6G: vision, applications, and technology trends. In: 2021 IEEE 94th Vehicular Technology Conference (VTC2021-Fall), pp. 1–5 (2021)
6. de Oliveira, L.G., Nuss, B., Alabd, M.B., et al.: Joint radar-communication systems: modulation schemes and system design. IEEE Trans. Microw. Theory Tech. **70**(3), 1521–1551 (2021)
7. Chen, Y., Liao, G., Liu, Y., et al.: Joint subcarrier and power allocation for integrated OFDM waveform in RadCom systems. IEEE Commun. Lett. **27**(1), 253–257 (2022)
8. Huang, Y., Hu, S., Ma, S., et al.: Designing low-PAPR waveform for OFDM-based RadCom systems. IEEE Trans. Wireless Commun. **21**(9), 6979–6993 (2022)
9. Yang B, Zhao S, Yi M.: Subcarrier multiplexing OFDM-based radar communication integration. In: 2021 13th International Conference on Wireless Communications and Signal Processing (WCSP), pp. 1–5 (2021)
10. Yuzhen, Z., Longyong, C., Fubo, Z., et al.: A new method of joint radar and communication waveform design and signal processing based on OFDM-chirp. J. Radars **10**(3), 453–466 (2021)
11. Huiting, Y., Yu, Z., Yabin, G.U., et al.: Design of integrated radar and communication signal based on multicarrier parameter modulation signal. J. Radars **8**(1), 54–63 (2019)
12. Zuo, J., Yang, R., Luo, S., et al.: Waveform design of integrated radar and communication signals based on TDS-OFDM. J. Natl. Univ. Defense Technol. **42**(5) (2020)
13. Zhou Q, Tian X, Zhang T.: Low complexity ICI mitigation in OFDM based RadCom systems. In: 2020 International Conference on Wireless Communications and Signal Processing (WCSP), pp. 1022–1027 (2020)
14. Norrie G, Paine S.: Design and demonstration of an OFDM based RadCom system. In: 2023 IEEE Radar Conference (RadarConf23), pp. 1–6 (2023)
15. Nguyen, N.T., Shlezinger, N., Eldar, Y.C., Juntti, M.: Multiuser MIMO Wideband Joint Communications and Sensing System with Subcarrier Allocation. IEEE Trans. Signal Process. (2023)

A Q-Learning Approach to Energy-Efficient Routing in BLE Mesh Network Based on Duty Cycle Scanning

Longrong Jiang[1,2,3], Jing Liu[1(✉)], and Lan Wang[1]

[1] College of Electronics and Information Engineering, Shenzhen University, Shenzhen, China
liujing@szu.edu.cn
[2] Research Institute of Tsinghua University in Shenzhen (RITS), Shenzhen, China
[3] Guangxi Key Laboratory of Wireless Wideband Communication and Signal Processing,
Guilin, China

Abstract. The Bluetooth Special Interest Group (SIG) introduced the Bluetooth Low Energy Mesh (BLE Mesh) network specification in 2017, enabling multi-to-multi communication capability for devices operating on the Bluetooth Low Energy protocol. This specification has made BLE mesh network versatile for a range of Internet of Things (IoT) applications, particularly in building lighting and smart home systems. However, the existing BLE mesh network specification employs a managed-flood-based mechanism at the network layer for message dissemination, resulting in both message redundancy and unnecessary energy expenditure. This paper makes two innovative contributions to address these shortcomings: 1) Introduction of a broadcast routing protocol based on Q-learning algorithms. This approach enables network nodes to optimally select the next-hop relay node utilizing localized Q-value tables, thereby substantially mitigating data packet redundancy within the network. 2) Formulation of a comprehensive set of scanning-broadcasting strategies. These strategies not only ensure the reliable transmission of data packets but also facilitate a low-power standby mode for the majority of the network nodes' operational time, thereby enhancing the overall energy efficiency of the network. Based on the results of our simulation experiments, the proposed methodology significantly enhances the longevity of nodes while concurrently minimizing message redundancy within BLE mesh network.

Keywords: Bluetooth Low Energy mesh · Q-learning · energy consumption

1 Introduction

The architecture of the BLE mesh network is hierarchically designed, based on the core specifications of Bluetooth Low Energy (BLE). It consists of multiple layers, organized from top to bottom as follows: model layer, foundation model layer, access layer, upper

The Work Is Supported Partly By the Shenzhen Natural Science Foundation Under Grant JCYJ20200109143016563, and the Opening Project of Guangxi Key Laboratory of Wireless Wideband Communication and Signal Processing and Key Laboratory of Cognitive Radio and Information Processing, Ministry of Education Under Grant GXKL06220201.

X. Chen et al. (Eds.): IoTaaS 2023, LNICST 585, pp. 358–370, 2025.
https://doi.org/10.1007/978-3-031-70507-6_27

transport layer, lower transport layer, network layer, bearer layer, and the BLE core specification layer. In the bearer layer of the BLE mesh network, two types of communication methods are defined: advertising bearer (ADV bearer) and generic attribute profile bearer (GATT bearer) [1]. In the ADV bearer-based communication, three out of the 40 channels defined in the BLE core specification are used for message transmission. For devices that do not use broadcasting channels for data transmission, such as smartphones, communication is facilitated through GATT connections, enabling interaction with broadcast-based BLE mesh devices via a proxy. At the Network layer, the BLE mesh Profile mandates the use of a managed-flood-based routing mechanism. To prevent broadcast storms, network message cache and time to live (TTL) are employed to limit the number of times a message is forwarded within the network. The network message cache stores processed messages for a certain period or number of messages, preventing further processing of the same message. The TTL field is added to the message, decrementing by one each time the message is relayed. When the TTL value falls below 2, the message is no longer forwarded by the relay nodes. The BLE mesh network model and different communication methods within the network are illustrated in Fig. 1.

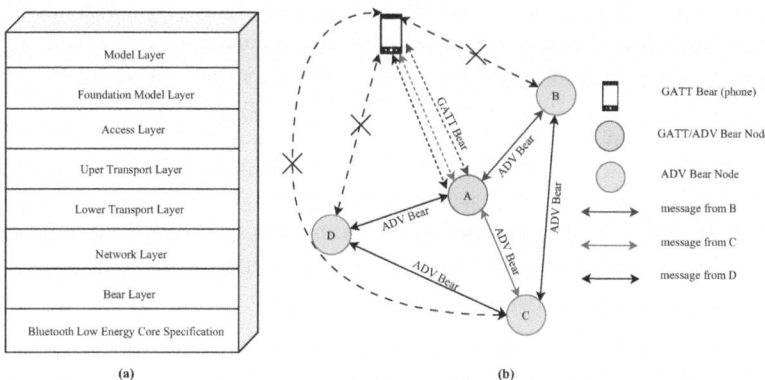

Fig. 1. (a) BLE mesh network architecture. (b) Illustration of communication mechanisms between ADV bearer and GATT bearer nodes in the BLE mesh network.

Despite the constraints introduced by TTL and message caching in the managed flooding mechanism, nodes still engage in superfluous broadcasts, leading to a significant prevalence of duplicate messages in the network. Moreover, the absence of a synchronization mechanism among nodes necessitates that relay nodes maintain a 100% scanning duty cycle, exacerbating the energy consumption issue [2]. In forthcoming iterations of the BLE mesh specification, it is anticipated that the integration of advanced energy-efficient routing algorithms will significantly contribute to extending the overall lifespan of the network.

Research by Pai-Chet Ng and colleagues has proposed a method called BOM [3], which incorporates mesh functionality into Beacon networks. This method employs a bounded flooding algorithm based on the Received Signal Strength Indicator (RSSI) to mitigate broadcast redundancy. By determining the message forwarding probability through the received signal strength, the introduction of Beacon technology into BLE mesh network reduces the frequency of message forwarding based on the managed-flood-mechanism [4]. Furthermore, Emil and others [5], have introduced a relay node selection mechanism in BLE mesh network to reduce message redundancy. They conducted performance evaluations of BLE mesh network employing various relay node selection algorithms, such as K2 Pruning [6], Greedy Connect [7], and Dominator [8], tailoring the choice of algorithm to the network's dynamic nature and scale. Given the dynamic characteristics, energy constraints, and connectionless features of BLE mesh network, a routing mechanism based on Q-learning may offer a more suitable solution to the challenges of message redundancy and high energy consumption.

In fact, routing mechanisms based on Q-learning were initially proposed in telephone networks in the last century [9], taking into account network congestion and hop count to the destination to find the optimal routing path. In Q-learning-based routing algorithms, each node relies solely on local information and operates in a fully distributed manner. Due to its decentralized and adaptive nature, this routing algorithm has been widely applied in wireless sensor networks to optimize metrics such as network latency and energy consumption. A high-energy-efficient underwater sensor network routing algorithm (QELAR) [10] has been introduced, incorporating Q-learning to balance node energy consumption and extend network lifespan. To consider energy consumption more comprehensively, Xing Su and colleagues [11] have included node orientation, transmission distance, energy consumption for data transmission, and remaining node energy into the Q-learning reward function to achieve high-energy-efficient routing.

In summary, given that the existing routing mechanisms in BLE mesh network require further refinement, a Q-learning-based approach aligns well with the network's dynamic, distributed, and energy-constrained nature. This paper, therefore, concentrates on implementing next-hop relay node selection through Q-learning and introduces a set of scanning-broadcasting strategies aimed at minimizing energy consumption. The primary contributions of this paper are:

- The introduction of a Q-learning-based routing algorithm for BLE mesh network. This algorithm, grounded in managed-flood mechanisms, integrates both the hop count to the destination node and the residual energy of neighboring nodes into its reward function. The objective is to balance energy consumption across nodes while minimizing routing overhead, thereby selecting the most efficient node for packet forwarding.
- The proposal of a scanning-broadcasting strategy that enables nodes in asynchronous BLE mesh network to reduce scanning time and increase the duration spent in low-power standby mode, thereby enhancing energy efficiency and extending network longevity.

The remainder of this paper is structured as follows: Sect. 2 elucidates the mathematical model underlying routing in BLE mesh network. Section 3 introduces the basic principle of the proposed approach in detail. Section 4 analyzes simulation results; and Sect. 5 offers concluding remarks.

2   Mathematical Modeling of BLE Mesh Network Routing

To offer a more precise depiction of the interrelationships among relay nodes within BLE mesh network, we model the network as an undirected graph $G(R, E)$. In this graph, the vertices correspond to the relay nodes in the network and are denoted by the set $R = \{r_1, r_2, ..., r_m\}$. For each relay node r_i, its set of neighboring nodes is represented as $N_{r_i} = \{n_1, n_2, ...n_k, \forall n_i \in R\}$. The edges of the graph, which encapsulate the links between relay nodes and their neighbors, are captured by the set $E = \{e(r_i, n_j) | r_i \in R, n_j \in N_{r_i}\}$.

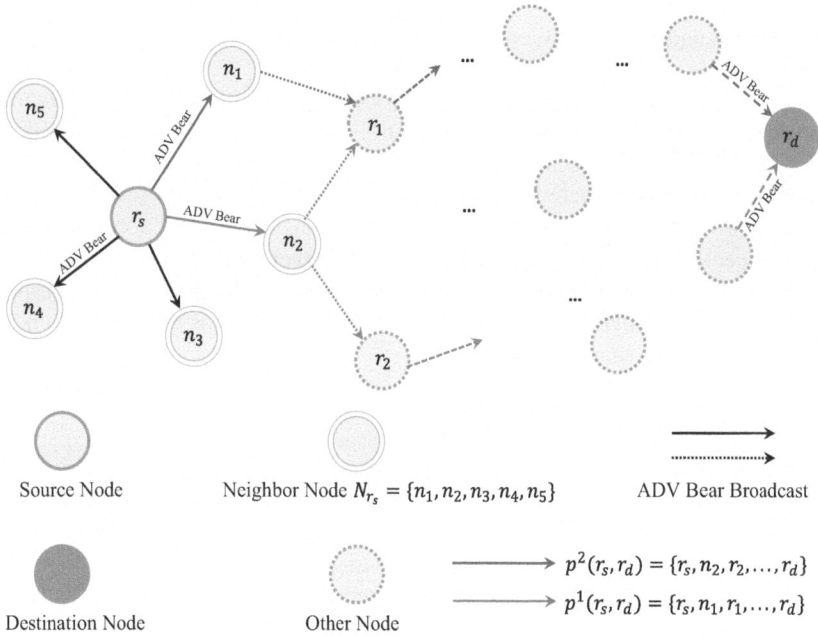

Fig. 2. Model of BLE mesh network routing.

The collection of all possible paths from a source node r_s to a destination node r_d is denoted as $P(r_s, r_d) = \{p^1(r_s, r_d), p^2(r_s, r_d), ..., p^q(r_s, r_d)\}$. Each specific path $p^i_{r_s, r_d}$ can be conceptualized as a sequence of relay nodes $p^i(r_s, r_d) = \{r_{s0}, r_{s1}, ..., r_{sk}, r_{s0} = r_s, r_{sk} = r_d, e(r_{si}, r_{s(i+1)}) \in E\}$ as illustrated in Fig. 2. Associated with each edge $e(r_{si}, r_{s(i+1)})$ are an energy cost $c(e(r_i, r_j))$ and a delay $d(e(r_i, r_j))$. Given a maximum permissible delay Δ_{delay} for the packet transmission from the source to the destination, we formulate the following constrained optimization problem:

$$\min_{p(r_s, r_d) \in P} \sum_{e \in p(r_s, r_d)} c(e)$$
$$\text{s.t} \sum_{e \in p(r_s, r_d)} d(e) \leq \Delta_{delay} \tag{1}$$

3 Proposed Approaches

3.1 Q-Learning-Based Routing Algorithm in BLE Mesh Network

The optimization problem under consideration exhibits considerable complexity, attributable to the exponential proliferation of path combinations as a function of network scale. This complexity is further exacerbated by the imposition of multiple constraints on the optimization objectives, such as energy efficiency and latency, as well as the inherently dynamic and stochastic nature of the network state. Moreover, the problem may manifest non-linear and potentially non-convex characteristics, rendering traditional optimization algorithms suboptimal for identifying globally optimal solutions. In light of these challenges, the Q-learning algorithm, renowned for its robust online learning capabilities and adaptability, emerges as an efficacious strategy for routing decisions within nodes.

First, the computational simplicity of the Q-learning algorithm renders it particularly amenable to implementation on resource-constrained devices, such as those prevalent in wireless sensor networks. Second, Q-learning, being a model-free reinforcement learning algorithm, possesses inherent adaptability. It learns an action-value function, denoted as $Q(s, a)$, through direct interactions with the environment. This function serves to estimate the expected long-term reward associated with executing a specific action a under a given state s. In light of the unique characteristics and constraints of BLE mesh network, the Q-learning algorithm's action-value function $Q(s, a)$ is adapted and updated according to the following equation:

$$Q(s, a) \leftarrow (1 - \alpha) \cdot Q(s, a) + \alpha \cdot [f_r + \gamma \cdot \max_{a'} Q(s', a')] \tag{2}$$

In the Q-learning paradigm, two critical parameters are defined: α and γ, both of which are confined to the interval (0,1]. The learning rate, denoted by α, quantifies the proportion by which the newly acquired Q-value should influence the existing Q-value. Concurrently, the discount factor γ serves to weigh the significance of prospective rewards in the decision-making process. In the specialized context of BLE mesh network augmented with Q-learning algorithms, the network architecture can be abstracted as a dynamic environment. Within this environment, the state-space of a node is intricately linked to individual data packets. Specifically, when a node r_i is tasked with processing a data packet originating from a source node r_s and destined for r_d the state of r_i is explicitly defined as r_d, signifying its current engagement in routing a packet towards r_d. In this scenario, the action set A for r_i is constituted by its neighboring nodes, formally represented as $A = N_{r_i}$. Upon successful transmission of the data packet to a neighboring node n_j, the node r_i evaluates the reward associated with this particular action using a predefined reward function $f(r_i, n_j)$. Subsequently, the Q-value for r_i is updated in accordance with the Q-learning update formula, which, when tailored to address the nuances of this routing problem, is articulated as follows:

$$Q(r_d, n_j) \leftarrow (1 - \alpha) \cdot Q(r_d, n_j) + \alpha \cdot [f(r_i, n_j) + \gamma \cdot \max_{a \in N_{n_j}} Q(n_j, a)] \tag{3}$$

In this equation $f(r_i, n_j)$ represents the reward function for the action of transmitting a packet from node r_i to n_j. This reward function incorporates both the hop count to the destination and the residual energy of the node, and is formulated as:

$$f(r_i, n_j) = -\beta \cdot h + (1 - \beta) \cdot c(n_j) \tag{4}$$

$$h = \begin{cases} 0, & n_j = r_d \\ 1, & n_j \neq r_d \end{cases} \tag{5}$$

$$c(n_j) = \frac{E_{n_j}}{\overline{E}_{N_{r_i}}} \tag{6}$$

Here, h serves as a constant penalty, incentivizing nodes to minimize the hop count, thereby reducing latency. However, focusing solely on the shortest path may compromise network longevity. To address this, the reward function also incorporates the residual energy of nodes, normalized by the average energy of their neighbors $\overline{E}_{N_{r_i}}$, to achieve a balanced network load. The parameter β, where $\beta \in (0,1]$, is introduced to fine-tune the trade-off between energy efficiency and latency.

The proposed Q-learning-based routing algorithm retains the managed-flood's message caching and TTL mechanisms. It operates in two distinct phases, as delineated in the subsequent Fig. 3.

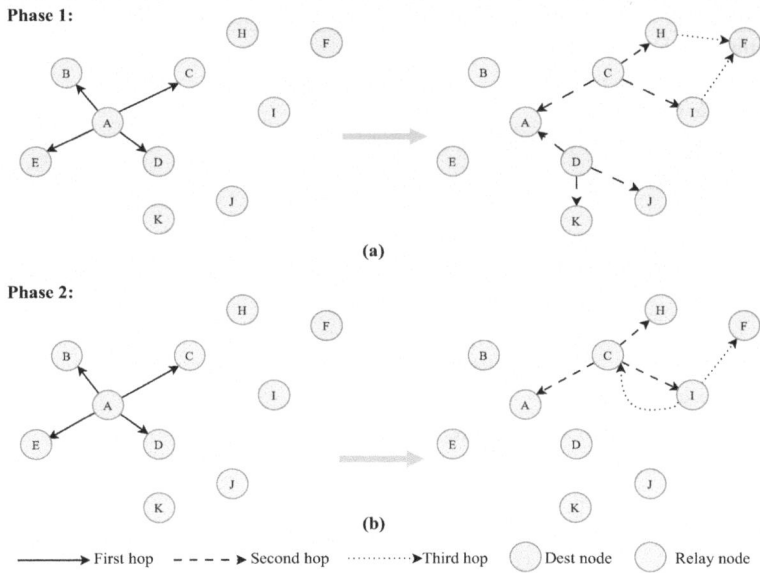

Fig. 3. (a) The initial broadcast-based Q-learning for rapid Q-value convergence among neighboring nodes. (b) The targeted packet forwarding based on the updated Q-table, facilitated by a caching mechanism to prevent redundant re-broadcasts.

Phase 1: The initial stage of the algorithm, termed as the preliminary phase, is characterized by a broadcast-oriented approach to data dissemination, particularly when a node is tasked with managing the initial set of data packets directed towards a specific destination node n_{r_d}. This phase is regulated by a threshold parameter, M_{r_d}, which determines the number of packets, m, a node handles before transitioning to the subsequent phase. Specifically, when $m < M_{r_d}$ the node employs a broadcast bearer, ensuring that all neighboring nodes within its vicinity receive the packet by scanning the designated broadcast channels. This mechanism, which essentially constitutes an exhaustive execution of the available action set, instigates an immediate update of all pertinent $Q(r_d, n_j)$, where $n_j \in N_{r_i}$ This broadcast-based Q-learning mechanism serves a dual purpose: it not only guarantees the reliable transmission of packets to the intended destination but also expedites the convergence of Q-values across the neighboring nodes by leveraging the widespread dissemination of packet information during the initial learning phase.

Phase 2: Upon concluding the swift learning phase, nodes refer to their Q-table to designate the next-hop neighbor for packet forwarding. This targeted forwarding ensures that even if other neighbors receive the packet, they will not re-broadcast it due to the existing caching mechanism. Concurrently, throughout the routing procedure, the Q-value table of nodes is adaptively updated utilizing a designated reward function, which strategically balances energy expenditure amongst neighboring nodes, ensuring an equitable distribution of energy consumption and mitigating premature node depletion within the network. The detailed procedure of the proposed algorithm is outlined in Algorithm 1.

Algorithm 1 The proposed Q-learning-Based routing approach

Input: neighbor nodes N_{r_i}

Output: next hop node

1: **While** $E_{r_i} > 0$ **do**
2:      **if** packet already cached or TTL < 2 **do**
3:          Drop packet
4:      **else**
5:          **if** the count of handle packet to destination node $m < M_{r_d}$ **do**
6:              **for each** $n_j \in N_{r_i}$ **do**
7:                  Calculate $c(n_j)$ based on $E_{n_j}, \overline{E}_{N_{r_i}}$
8:                  Calculate $f(r_i, n_j)$
9:                  Node r_i update $Q(r_d, n_j)$
10:             **end**
11:             return action $a = N_{r_i}$
12:         **else**
13:             Select n_j with $max\ Q(r_d, n_j)$
14:             Calculate $c(n_j)$ based on $E_{n_j}, \overline{E}_{N_{r_i}}$
15:             Calculate $f(r_i, n_j)$
16:             Update $Q(r_d, n_j)$
17:             return action $a = n_j$
18:         **end if**
19:     **end if**
20: **end**

3.2   Duty Cycle Scanning Mechanism in BLE Mesh Network

BLE devices function within the 40 channels of the 2.4 GHz ISM frequency band. Specifically, nodes utilizing the broadcast bearer layer for communication employ three dedicated BLE broadcast channels—namely, channels 37, 38, and 39. According to BLE specifications [12], the operational states of BLE devices can be classified into initialization, standby, scanning, broadcasting, and connection. In BLE mesh network, relay devices operating on the broadcast bearer layer are perpetually in a connectionless state. This study is primarily concerned with the scanning, broadcasting, and standby states, which are most pertinent to the functioning of BLE mesh network.

When a node in the BLE mesh network necessitates data transmission, it disseminates the data via the broadcast channel. The managed-flood transmission mechanism in the BLE mesh Profile stipulates a 100% scanning duty cycle for relay nodes to ensure that devices exclusively supporting broadcast bearers can receive data in a connectionless milieu. This continuous scanning significantly escalates the energy expenditure of the nodes. To ameliorate this, we introduce a duty cycle scanning and repetitive broadcasting communication mechanism. This mechanism aims to optimize the time nodes spend in the Standby state, thereby prolonging their operational lifespan, while concurrently ensuring the reliable transmission of messages.

In the proposed mechanism, when a node has a message to transmit, it repetitively broadcasts the data packet thrice, transitioning to a Standby state for a duration t_{st} after each broadcast cycle. Adjacent nodes, to ensure the successful reception of at least one of the three broadcast messages, oscillate between Scanning and Standby states. The duration of the Scanning state is t_{sc} and the Standby duration t_{st} is synchronized with that of the broadcasting node. This ensures the reliable inter-node transmission of data packets in asynchronous scenarios, as illustrated in Fig. 4.

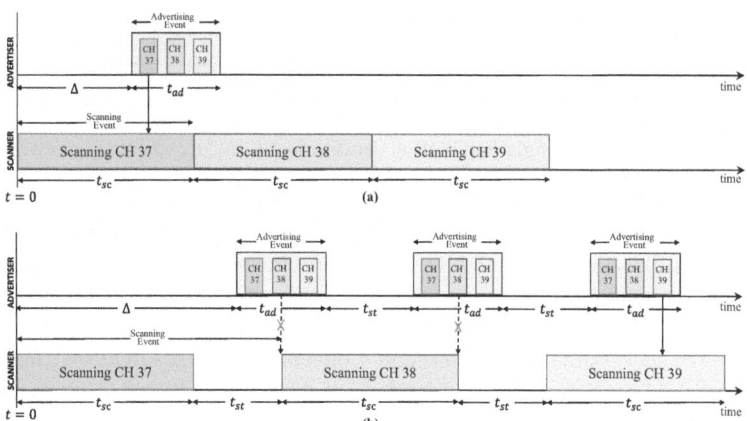

Fig. 4. Comparison of packet transmission mechanisms in BLE mesh network. (a) Managed-flood with 100% duty cycle scanning. (b) Proposed approach employing three broadcasts and sub-100% duty cycle scanning for enhanced packet reception.

To explore the optimal relationship between the scanning time t_{sc} and the standby time t_{st} this study employs the Monte Carlo simulation method. In the simulation, we assume $t_{sc} = k \cdot t_{st}$, where k is an adjustable coefficient. We further assume that the broadcasting node initiates the broadcasting of data packets at an arbitrary moment. The single-hop Packet Delivery Rate (PDR) is an instrumental metric, meticulously quantifying the efficacy of data packet transmissions over an immediate link, signifying the successful conveyance between nodes without intermediary interpositions. Our simulations revealed discernible fluctuations in the single-hop PDR across varied k coefficients. Preliminary findings suggest that, predicated on the scanning-broadcasting paradigm introduced herein, a scanning apparatus can adeptly intercept data packets dispatched by its broadcasting counterpart, given the condition that k exceeds 1, or equivalently, $t_{sc} > t_{st}$. The results are illustrated in the Fig. 5.

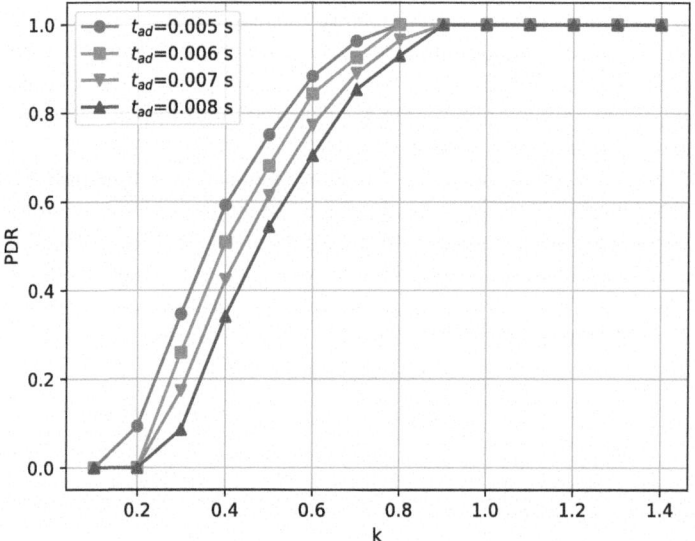

Fig. 5. Variations in single-hop PDR under different k values, where $t_{st} = 0.03$ s.

Taking into account channel congestion, unstable wireless environments, and potential channel conflicts that could inhibit successful packet reception, relay node r_i enters a backoff period t_b post-broadcast to monitor the broadcast channel. If a neighboring node n_j successfully receives and rebroadcasts the packet, r_i interprets this as an Acknowledgment (ACK) of successful data transmission. Conversely, if n_j fails to receive the packet, r_i reinitiates the broadcast cycle post-backoff. If the retransmission attempts exceed a predefined threshold, r_i designates an alternative neighboring node for packet forwarding and minimizes the Q-value for broadcasting to n_j. The retransmission mechanism is elucidated in Fig. 6.

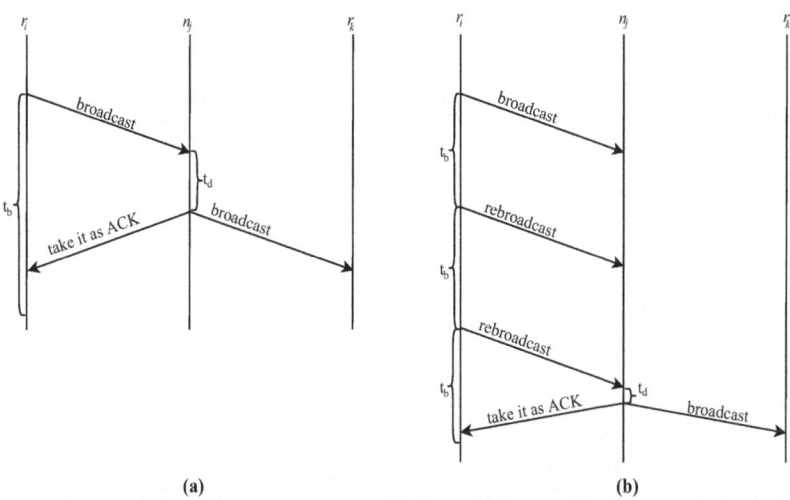

Fig. 6. (a) Successfully transfer packet. (b) Case of failure and retransmission.

4   The Result and Discussion

This section presents a comparative analysis of the simulation results for the proposed Q-learning-based BLE mesh network routing algorithm and the managed flooding mechanism. The simulations are conducted on the OMNeT++ platform, focusing on path overhead and average node lifetime.

4.1   Simulation Parameters

The parameters for network simulation are detailed in Table 1. Energy consumption data is sourced from [13]. To facilitate simulation, all intermediate physical-layer states during transitions between broadcasting, scanning, and standby modes are treated as standby states, and their energy consumption is averaged.

Table 1. Simulation parameters

Parameters	Value
t_{sc} Scanning duration	0.05 s
t_{st} Standby duration	0.03 s
t_{ad} Broadcasting duration	0.006 s
I_{sc} Current consumption on scanning	6.3 mA
I_{st} Current consumption on standby	1.9 mA

(*continued*)

Table 1. (*continued*)

Parameters	Value
I_{ad} Current consumption on broadcasting at 0 dBm	6.2 mA
N Numbers of BLE node	40
α, γ, β	0.8, 0.9, 0.7

4.2   Simulation Results

Average Path Overhead. Defined as the average number of times a data packet is forwarded from the source node to the destination node. Let M_i represent the number of times the ith data packet is forwarded in the network, and m represent the number of data packets reaching the destination node. The formula is:

$$M = \frac{\sum_i M_i}{m} \tag{7}$$

In managed-flooding-based BLE mesh network, when a source node sends a data packet to a destination node, it broadcasts the packet to its neighboring nodes. These neighboring nodes, upon receiving the packet, further rebroadcast it. With a sufficiently large TTL, this ensures that all nodes in the network, including the destination node, receive the packet. The frequency of packet broadcasting is directly proportional to the number of nodes in the network. The current study introduces a Q-learning-based routing algorithm that takes full advantage of this broadcasting characteristic to implement a multi-action Q-learning process. This facilitates the rapid convergence of Q-values. During the packet forwarding phase, the algorithm employs these Q-values to designate, within the broadcast packet, which neighboring nodes should rebroadcast the packet. This targeted forwarding mechanism effectively minimizes packet redundancy within the network. The relationship between the number of packets generated in the network and the number of packets sent by the source node is depicted in the corresponding Fig. 7.

Node Lifetime. Correlated with the node's battery capacity $E_{battery}$ and average current $\bar{I}$. The average current can be calculated as the ratio of the total energy consumed during the simulation to the simulation time. The formula is:

$$\begin{aligned} T_{lifetime} &= \frac{E_{battery}}{\bar{I}} \\ \bar{I} &= \frac{I_{st} \cdot T_{st} + I_{sc} \cdot T_{sc} + I_{ad} \cdot T_{ad}}{T_{sc} + T_{sc} + T_{ad}} \end{aligned} \tag{8}$$

In addition to reducing packet redundancy and balancing energy consumption, the proposed broadcasting-scanning mechanism allows nodes to enter standby mode more frequently, thereby reducing energy consumption and extending node lifetime by at least 30%, as shown in Fig. 8.

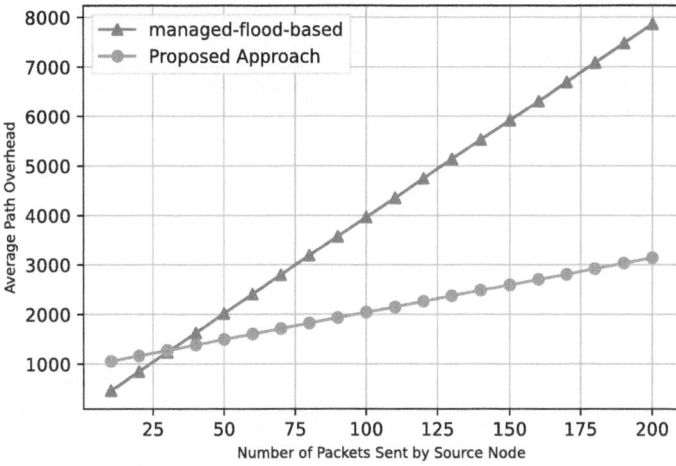

Fig. 7. The relationship between the number of data packets sent by the source node and the average path overhead in the network.

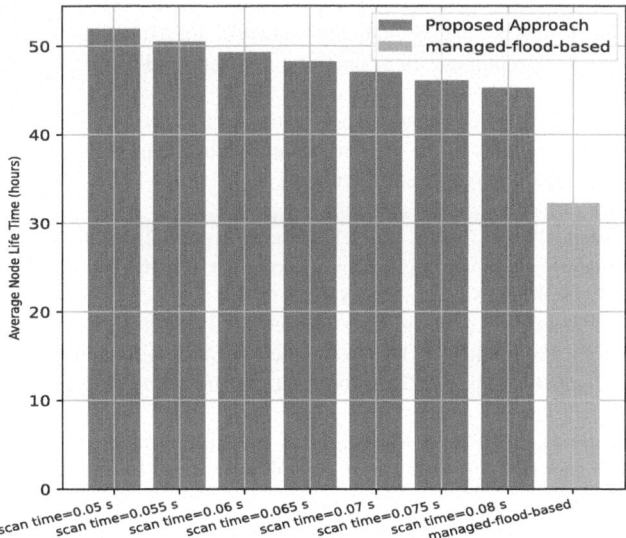

Fig. 8. Comparison of node average lifetime: the proposed approach with variable scanning durations vs. managed-flood-based.

5 Conclusion

This paper proposes a novel routing approach for BLE mesh network. The approach combines Q-learning algorithms with a duty cycle scanning mechanism and builds upon the existing managed flooding techniques. The algorithm incorporates both the hop count to the destination node and the residual energy of nodes into the reward function. This enables nodes to determine the next relay node based on their Q-values, thereby achieving a more balanced energy consumption across the network. To maximize node lifetime, we introduce a scanning-broadcasting mechanism that not only ensures reliable data packet transmission in asynchronous states but also allows nodes to enter a low-power standby mode as much as possible, thereby reducing their energy consumption. Simulation results indicate that our proposed method outperforms managed flooding in terms of path overhead and extends the lifetime of network nodes.

References

1. Mesh   Profile.   https://www.bluetooth.com/specifications/specs/mesh-profile-1-0-1/. Accessed 29 Aug 2023
2. Perez-Diaz-de-Cerio, D., Valenzuela, J.L., Garcia-Lozano, M., Hernández-Solana, Á., Valdovinos, A.: BMADS: BLE mesh asynchronous dynamic scanning. IEEE Internet Things J. **8**, 2558–2573 (2021)
3. Ng, P.C., She, J.: a novel overlay mesh with Bluetooth low energy network. In: 2019 IEEE Wireless Communications and Networking Conference (WCNC), pp. 1–6 (2019)
4. Ng, P.C., She, J., Spachos, P.: Energy-efficient overlay protocol for BLE beacon-based mesh network. IEEE Trans. Mob. Comput. **22**, 1 (2021)
5. Hansen, E.A.J., Nielsen, M.H., Serup, D.E., Williams, R.J., Madsen, T.K., Abildgren, R.: On relay selection approaches in Bluetooth mesh networks. In: 2018 10th International Congress on Ultra Modern Telecommunications and Control Systems and Workshops (ICUMT), pp. 1–5 (2018)
6. Wu, J., Li, H.: On calculating connected dominating set for efficient routing in ad hoc wireless networks. In: Proceedings of the 3rd International Workshop on Discrete Algorithms and Methods for Mobile Computing and Communications, pp. 7–14. ACM, Seattle Washington USA (1999)
7. Dhawan, A., Scoville, N., Tanco, M.: A Distributed greedy algorithm for constructing connected dominating sets in wireless sensor networks. In: International Conference on Sensor Networks (SENSORNETS 2014), pp. 181–187 (2014)
8. Kuhn, F., Wattenhofer, R., Zhang, Y., Zollinger, A.: Geometric ad-hoc routing: of theory and practice. In: Proceedings of the Twenty-Second Annual Symposium on Principles of Distributed Computing, pp. 63–72. Association for Computing Machinery, New York, NY, USA (2003)
9. Boyan, J., Littman, M.: Packet Routing in dynamically changing networks: a reinforcement learning approach. In: Advances in Neural Information Processing Systems. Morgan-Kaufmann (1993)
10. Hu, T., Fei, Y.: QELAR: A machine-learning-based adaptive routing protocol for energy-efficient and lifetime-extended underwater sensor networks. IEEE Trans. Mob. Comput. **9**, 796–809 (2010)
11. Su, X., Ren, Y., Cai, Z., Liang, Y., Guo, L.: A Q-learning based routing approach for energy efficient information transmission in wireless sensor network. IEEE Trans. Netw. Serv. Manag. **20**, 1 (2022)
12. Core Specification. Bluetooth® Technology Website. https://www.bluetooth.com/specifications/specs/core-specification-5-0/. Accessed 30 Aug 2023
13. Online Power Profiler for Bluetooth LE - opp - Online Power Profiler - Nordic DevZone. https://devzone.nordicsemi.com/power/w/opp/2/online-power-profiler-for-bluetooth-le. Accessed 31 Aug 2023

Improved Plate Defect Detection Algorithm Based on YOLOv5

Zijie Wang[1,2], Lan Wang[1(✉)], and Sihui Zheng[3]

[1] College of Electronics and Information Engineering, Shenzhen University, Shenzhen, China
wanglan@szu.edu.cn
[2] Research Institute of Tsinghua University in Shenzhen (RITS), Shenzhen, China
[3] Shenzhen International Graduate School, Tsinghua University, Shenzhen, China

Abstract. Furniture plates, being a crucial raw material in furniture manufacturing, often exhibit various defects during their production. These defects potentially compromise the quality of the finished furniture products and inflate production costs. Traditional methods for detecting plate defects face challenges, particularly in identifying less distinct features and handling surface noise, leading to suboptimal detection results. To address these limitations, this study introduces a specialized dataset named the "Furniture Plate Defect Dataset" for evaluating and improving defect detection algorithms more comprehensively. Furthermore, the study employs an enhanced version of the YOLOv5 algorithm, augmented with a small object detection head and incorporated with a Convolutional Block Attention Module (CBAM) to specifically optimize for plate defects. Experimental results demonstrate that with extensive training and fine-tuning on the newly constructed dataset, the enhanced YOLOv5 algorithm exhibits significant improvements in defect detection in furniture plates. The upgraded algorithm is adept at accurately identifying both texture-related and shape-related defects thereby substantially improving the detection's accuracy and robustness. In summary, the refined YOLOv5 algorithm excels in defect detection, reaching an mAP50 of 81.6%, indicating its considerable potential for application.

Keywords: Defect detection · YOLOv5 · CBAM · Small object detection

1 Introduction

Furniture sheets, as one of the essential raw materials in the furniture manufacturing industry, have a significant demand and broad application prospects in the market. However, during the manufacturing process, various defects often appear on the surface of the sheets, such as textural and shape defects. These issues directly affect the quality and lifespan of the furniture products. To ensure product quality, there is an urgent need for sheet defect detection technology in industrial production lines. However, the complexity of furniture sheet surface defects makes their definition ambiguous, and defect

The work is supported by the Shenzhen Natural Science Foundation under Grant JCYJ20200109143016563.

X. Chen et al. (Eds.): IoTaaS 2023, LNICST 585, pp. 371–384, 2025.
https://doi.org/10.1007/978-3-031-70507-6_28

features are hard to unify. Currently, there are two primary defect detection methods applied to furniture sheets: supervised and unsupervised methods. Supervised methods [1] typically use neural networks to learn defect features, achieving high-accuracy defect detection. However, this approach requires a substantial amount of defect sample data for training, and obtaining sufficient defect data is often a challenging task in real-world scenarios. Another method is unsupervised defect detection [2], which detects differences between generated fake images and defect images through generative networks. Although unsupervised methods avoid the need for vast sample data, its image segmentation process makes it challenging to apply on ultra-high-resolution and non-uniformly sized sheet images. Moreover, its extended processing time limits its application in actual production environments.

In recent years, the application of deep learning convolutional neural networks (CNN) in defect detection has made remarkable progress. CNN is a deep learning model used for image classification and object detection, which can automatically learn image features and perform classification and detection. In the field of defect detection, CNN have been widely applied to surface defects [3], welding defects [4], crack defects [5], and various other types of defect detection tasks. This method can directly extract features from raw images and perform classification and detection without the need for manual feature extraction and classifier design.

Moreover, object detection methods could be broadly categorized based on the requirement of region proposals into two classes: two-stage algorithms [6–8] and one-stage algorithms [9–11].

Two-stage detectors, exemplified by algorithms like R-CNN [12], Fast R-CNN [13], and Faster R-CNN [14], typically comprise two steps: proposing object regions and then classifying these regions. This methodology initially generates a set of region proposals that might contain objects and then classifies these regions to specific object categories. Though these methods often deliver high accuracy, they can be computationally demanding due to the two-stage nature of the approach.

In contrast, one-stage detectors, such as YOLO [15] and SSD [16], eliminate the preliminary step of proposing object regions. Instead, they predict bounding boxes and class probabilities directly from the input images in one go. This streamlined approach not only improves efficiency, making it apt for real-time applications, but also maintains competitive accuracy. Among these, YOLO is particularly noteworthy. Over time, several iterations of YOLO have been released, each optimizing and refining the model, resulting in a detector known for its speed and accuracy.

While advancements in CNN for defect detection have been rapid, each industry's defect datasets typically possess their unique features and patterns. Therefore, when applying CNN to defect datasets from different industries, it is crucial to consider the specificities of each dataset and make the necessary modifications and optimizations to achieve optimal performance.

The defect dataset in this study pertains to defects in manufactured boards. Manufacturing defect datasets often include flaws found on various mechanical parts and workpieces, such as surface cracks and damages. These defects vary in shapes and sizes and usually appear against intricate backgrounds, necessitating specialized image enhancement techniques. Given the distinctiveness of defect datasets across industries,

CNN can't be directly replicated. When applying CNN to defect datasets of different industries, adjustments in network architecture, training strategies, image enhancement, and segmentation techniques are imperative for desired outcomes.

Addressing these challenges, this paper introduces an innovative algorithm for furniture plate defect detection, aiming to achieve efficient and accurate defect detection with a limited number of defect samples, even in complex plate image scenarios. To counteract the imbalance in defect sample data, we've integrated effective data balancing strategies. By leveraging transfer learning [17] and data augmentation techniques [18], we make the most out of the available defect samples, enhancing the algorithm's accuracy and robustness.

To bolster the research and evaluation of our algorithm, we've curated a comprehensive plate defect database that encapsulates various types and severities of defect samples. This serves as a robust foundation for future research and algorithm comparisons. The presented research, with its limited sample data training, manifests effective applications in defect detection.

In this paper, we'll primarily discuss the proposed algorithm and validate its effectiveness in furniture plate defect detection through comparative experimental results. Our research will substantially support the quality control and production efficiency of the furniture manufacturing industry. Furthermore, it will serve as a significant reference in addressing the limited sample challenges across various domains. Looking ahead, we aim to further optimize the algorithm's performance, explore more real-world applications, and continuously refine our defect database, driving the evolution and application of furniture plate defect detection technology.

The rest of the paper is structured as follows: Sect. 2 discusses related work. Section 3 delves into dataset collection and processing. Section 4 presents the research methodology. Section 5 presents the training process and results. Finally, Sect. 6 summarizes the conclusions of this paper.

2 Related Work

In the domain of defect detection, early methodologies relied heavily on image processing algorithms. These algorithms worked by extracting surface features like textures and shapes from the plates and subsequently used combined rules and thresholds to detect defects. Commonly adopted methods included edge detection, texture analysis, and morphological processing.

Luo et al. [19] proposed an image binarization optimization algorithm based on a local thresholding method, specifically targeting the non-uniform background issues in wood defect images. Experimental results demonstrated that their method substantially improved wood defect image segmentation under complex backgrounds, achieving an impressive 92.6% accuracy rate. Pahlberg et al. [20] and colleagues explored the fusion of two feature detection methods to automatically match and identify individual Scots pine boards. The first approach involved a block matching method utilizing normalized sum of squared differences to detect corners and subsequently match the surrounding square regions. The second approach was anchored on the Accelerated Robust Feature (SURF) matching method. The fusion of these two detection techniques significantly boosted the recognition rate of wooden boards, pushing the matching accuracy beyond 90%.

As the wave of CNN took over, defect detection methods founded on machine learning began to gain traction. Such techniques revolved around algorithms that learned defect characteristics from a plethora of samples, facilitating automated defect detection. Compared to traditional image processing methods, machine-learning-oriented defect detection approaches augmented both detection accuracy and robustness. However, these methods are often contingent on having an extensive defect dataset for training.

Building upon VGG16, HE et al. [21] introduced the Mix-FCN, a hybrid fully convolutional neural network. While ensuring automated defect classification, this model also accelerated the detection speed, processing 50 images in just 0.368 s. Yang et al. [22] and team presented a deep extreme learning machine model that married deep learning feature extraction techniques with an extreme learning machine classification method, achieving an outstanding 96.72% accuracy rate on a wood defect dataset.

Shi et al. [23] proposed the glance multiple channel mask region convolution neural network (R-CNN). By employing neural network architecture search techniques and genetic algorithm optimization, they achieved a commendable 98.70% overall classification accuracy and 95.31% mean average precision. Xu et al. [24] modified the YOLOv5n and YOLOv5m models by incorporating the SimAM attention model and utilizing Ghost convolution to reduce model parameters. This enhancement led to a 1.5% uplift in map0.5 while concurrently slashing the parameters by over 50%.

Another frontier in defect detection is the use of reconstruction network methods. The hallmark of these methods is that they don't rely on a vast defect dataset. Instead, they necessitate training on normal data to develop a network adept at reconstructing data. Schlegl [25] was a trailblazer in utilizing deep convolutional Generative Adversarial Networks (GAN) for medical image defect detection, primarily focusing on disease prediction. The approach involved learning the features of normal images and eventually detecting defects. Building on AnoGAN, Han et al. [26] introduced enhancements by incorporating an encoder to generate latent variables, eliminating the need for extensive time-consuming prefix variable generation. Zavrtanik [27] adopted autoencoders to reconstruct images and, to address the limitations associated with autoencoders' inability to fully reconstruct anomalous regions, employed random deletion of parts of the image area.

In summary, from the rudiments of image processing to the sophistication of neural networks and reconstruction methods, the landscape of defect detection has witnessed a remarkable transformation over the years.

3   Sheet Defect Dataset

This section provides an overview of the sheet defect database composition and the associated preprocessing steps.

3.1   Image Collection

In actual furniture sheet production lines, defective sheets are rare. They can only be collected over extended periods and through active manual inspection. For this project, an industrial digital camera, LA-CM-08K-08A-00-R, was employed for image acquisition. A collection of 313 defect data images was acquired from the production line of a certain Company's wood plate manufacturing facility. These images were categorized into three classes: edge breakage, scratches, and damaged holes. Due to the wide range of surface patterns found on furniture boards, which often include intricate textures and patterns resembling board defects, our plate defect detection model faces significant challenges. In particular, certain plate patterns and surface markings bear a striking resemblance to actual defects, making it difficult for our model to accurately distinguish between them. This presents a major obstacle in achieving reliable plate defect detection, and part of the defect pictures in the dataset are shown in Fig. 1.

Fig. 1. Part of the sheet defect dataset image.

3.2 Dataset Processing

To streamline the training process and facilitate accurate labeling, the original sheet images collected exhibited high pixel values and were resized to a length of 1280 pixels. The Lanczos interpolation method was employed for resizing, with the shorter side downscaled proportionally. The annotation process involved utilizing the labelimg tool to obtain precise annotation data.

The resulting dataset consisted of 567 instances of edge breakages, 456 instances of scratches, and 324 instances of damaged holes. While the number of hole defects was relatively lower compared to the other two categories, the unique characteristics of hole defects rendered them more distinguishable. Conversely, edge breakages and scratches were more susceptible to the interference of sheet patterns, making the identification of holes comparatively easier to identify. The distribution of defects on the training dataset and the height and width of the defects accounted for in the image are shown in Fig. 2.

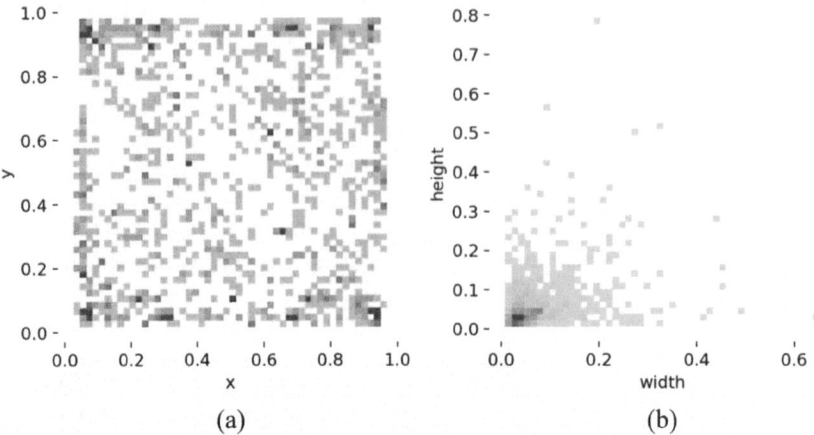

Fig. 2. (a) The distribution of defects' center point coordinates on the training dataset. (b) The distributions of the defects' width and length on the training dataset.

3.3 Incorporating Negative Samples

Owing to the scarcity of defect data, the trained network had difficulty discerning actual defects. The missed detection rate for holes stood at 0.39, and the false positive rate for scratches was as high as 0.45. Observing the excessive false positive rates for defects like holes, 210 non-defective sheet samples were added to the dataset. This intervention reduced the missed detection rate for holes to 0.24 and the false positive rate for scratches to 0.22. This shows that when training, the model learns to distinguish objects of interest from the background and assign them appropriate class labels. In the inference stage, the model can better distinguish the detected target objects from the background and provide corresponding detection boxes and category labels.

4   Network Method

4.1   Improved YOLOv5 Structure

The primary goal of this work is to develop a network that offers enhanced identification capabilities for our plate defect dataset.

Although YOLOv7 [28] has demonstrated better performance than YOLOv5 on the COCO dataset, YOLOv5 presents stronger potential for improvement while maintaining similar detection results. Therefore, we have opted to use YOLOv5 as the baseline model for our enhancements. Addressing the stated objective, we have crafted a deep learning network based on YOLOv5, striving to elevate the recognition capabilities for the plate defect dataset. YOLOv5 is considered among the advanced object detection algorithms and is lauded for its efficiency, precision, and user-friendly training approach. Building on the YOLOv5 foundation, we have introduced CBAM [29], an attention mechanism, aiming to augment the network's feature extraction prowess and target recognition accuracy. Also, bearing in mind the presence of tiny objects within the plate defect dataset, a small object detection head was added to the original YOLOv5, ensuring enhanced recognition and precise localization of minute defects [30]. Such refinements enable our network to aptly cater to the plate defect dataset, offering more precise and trustworthy defect identification outcomes, the overall structure of the proposed network is shown in Fig. 3.

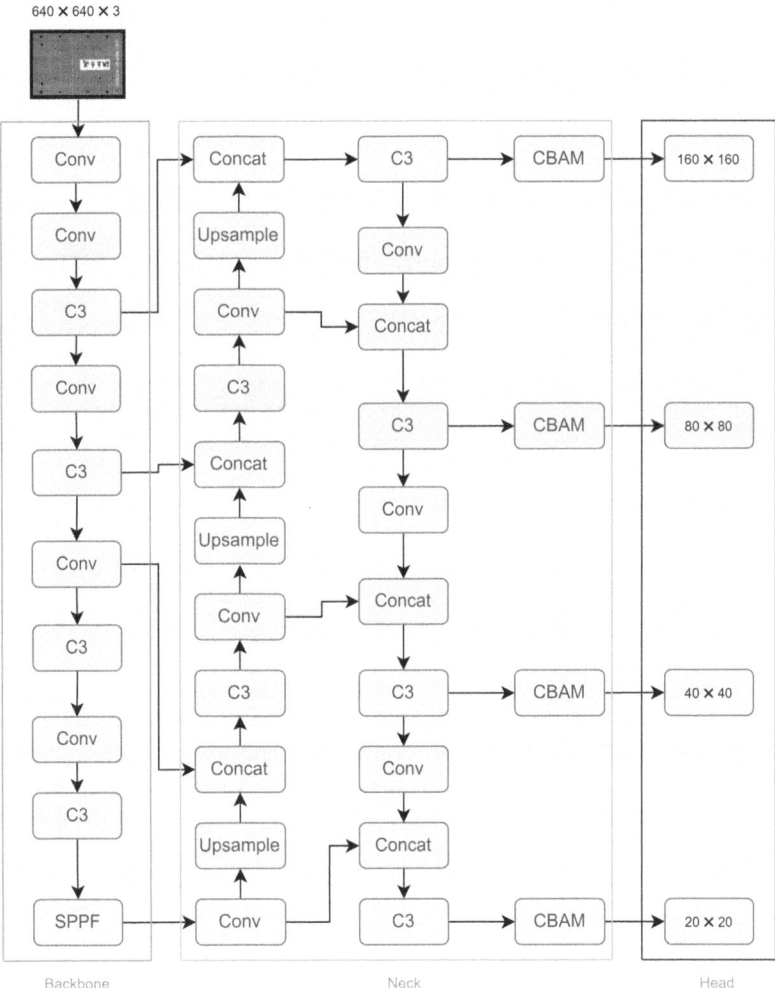

Fig. 3. The overall structure of the proposed network.

4.2   Add CBAM Module

CBAM is a lightweight attention module capable of deploying Attention both in channel and spatial dimensions. The backbone of YOLOv5 is already adept at feature extraction, reducing its modifications aids in our transfer learning. Defects often have small sizes and subtle texture changes, requiring models that can accurately focus on and capture these detailed features. The integration of CBAM into YOLOv5 is designed to amplify the influence of limited features on detection outcomes. The schematic diagram of the CBAM structure is shown in Fig. 4.

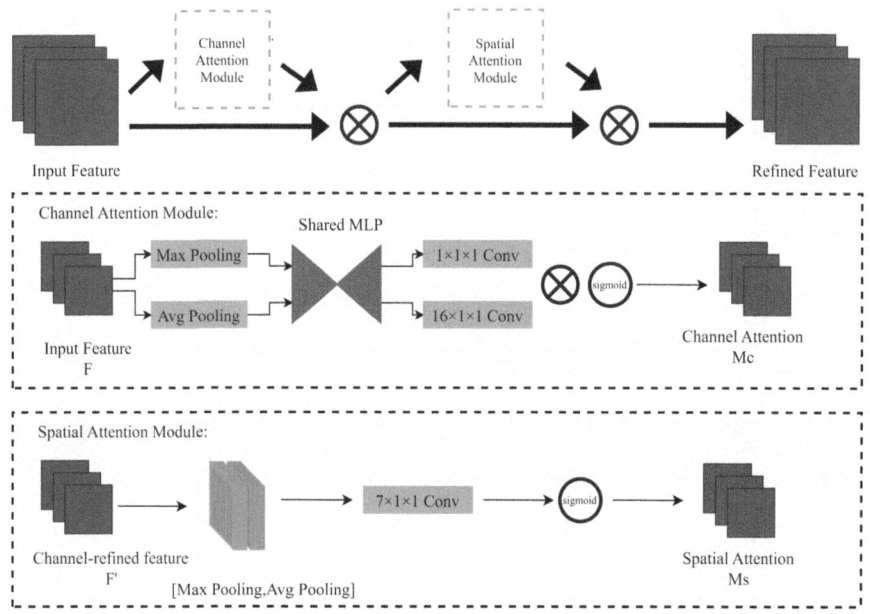

Fig. 4. CBAM attention module.

The CBAM consists of two independent sub-modules: Channel Attention Module and Spatial Attention Module. They perform channel and spatial attention operations, respectively. In the Channel Attention Module, the input feature map undergoes global average pooling and global max pooling in width and height. These pooled features are passed through Multi-Layer Perceptrons (MLP) and summed element-wise. Subsequently, a sigmoid activation function generates the final channel attention feature map. The mathematical representation of the Channel Attention Module is expressed as:

$$Mc(F) = \sigma(MLP(AvgPool(F)) + MLP(MaxPool(F))) \qquad (1)$$

The output feature map from the Channel Attention Module serves as the input for the Spatial Attention Module. Initially, global average and max pooling operations are executed across channels to produce two distinct feature maps. These maps are then concatenated channel-wise, followed by a convolutional operation to reduce the dimensions to a single channel. Finally, a sigmoid activation function generates the spatial attention feature. The output features of the Spatial Attention Module are element-wise multiplied by the input features, generating the final output feature map of the

CBAM. The formulation of the Spatial Attention Module is as follows:

$$Ms(F) = \sigma(f^{7 \times 7}([AvgPool(F); MaxPool(F)])) \tag{2}$$

Incorporating CBAM at the end of the neck region in the YOLOv5 architecture substantially enriches the model's feature representation capabilities during the final stage of feature fusion. It adaptively selects important channels and spatial locations, thereby bolstering feature expressiveness and perceptual abilities. By integrating CBAM, the YOLOv5 model shows better in its performance for defect detection tasks.

4.3 Small Object Detection Head

As can be inferred from the Fig. 2, The overall structure of the proposed net-work, small objects are a significant part of the training data. The fundamental YOLOv5 has three detection heads, performing detections on feature maps sized 20×20, 40×40, and 80×80. Assuming that a defect target, when resized to 640 pixels in the input image, has a pixel value of 8, it would vanish post-convolution on an 80×80 feature map. Our dataset has a high proportion of small targets, and there are many defects with pixel values less than 8. Therefore, it is necessary to add a small Object detection head.

In our revised approach, we continued from the 80×80 feature map concatenation point of the original YOLOv5. It undergoes a C3 structure, convolution, up-sampling, and concatenation with the backbone's first C3. This sequence is followed by another C3 and CBAM to yield a 160×160 feature map.

5   Experimental Process and Analysis of Results

YOLOv5 offers four different variants, differentiated by their level of complexity: YOLOv5s, YOLOv5m, YOLOv5l, and YOLOv5x. After careful consideration, YOLOv5l was selected for modification due to its balanced trade-off between detection accuracy and training difficulty.

The training dataset consists of 264 images, and the testing dataset comprises 50 images. Given the relatively small size of the training set and the absence of pre-trained weights for the modified architecture, the model was trained for an extended duration of 600 epochs. The batch size was set to 32, and all training images were resized to a uniform dimension of 640×640.The hardware and software environment configuration used for all experiments in this article is shown in Table 1.

In the domain of object detection, commonly used evaluation metrics include Average Precision (AP), Mean Average Precision (mAP), Precision (P), and Recall (R). These metrics provide a comprehensive assessment of a model's effectiveness in terms of both its discriminatory power and its ability to correctly identify positive samples. True Positive (TP): The number of actual positive samples correctly predicted as positive. False Negative (FN): The number of actual positive samples incorrectly predicted as negative. False Positive (FP): The number of actual negative samples incorrectly predicted as positive. True Negative (TN): The number of actual negative samples correctly predicted

Table 1. Experimental environment configuration.

Operating system	Centos 7
CPU	Intel(R) Xeon(R) CPU E5-2680 v3 @ 2.50 GHz
GPU	NVIDIA GTX 1080Ti 11G
Memory	125 G
Programing language	Python 3.7
AIgorithm framework	Pytorch 1.7.0
Development environment	Anaconda

as negative. The metrics Precision (P), Recall (R), Average Precision (AP), and Mean Average Precision (mAP) can be defined as follows:

$$P = \frac{TP}{TP + FP} \tag{3}$$

$$R = \frac{TP}{TP + FN} \tag{4}$$

$$AP = \frac{P_1 + P_2 + \cdots + P_n}{n} \tag{5}$$

$$mAP = \frac{AP_1 + AP_2 + \cdots + AP_n}{n} \tag{6}$$

In the experimental process, four CBAM modules were appended to the end of the Neck, along with the inclusion of a small object detection head, aiming to enhance the model's capability in detecting plate defects. In order to validate the effectiveness of the attention modules and the small object detection head within the plate defect detection model, comparative experiments were conducted. The detection performance of the model with the integration of CBAM positions and the small object detection head in YOLOv5 was compared, and the comparative results are presented in Table 2.

Table 2. The comparison of models.

Model	CBAM	Little Head	P/%	R/%	mAP@0.5/%
YOLOv5l	×	×	82.1	76.4	80.1
Improve1	3	×	80.8	75.1	80.4
Improve2	4	×	82.0	71.4	78.9
Improve3	×	√	80.2	71.8	79.7
Improve4	5	√	78.4	76.5	81.3
YOLOv5l-ours	4	√	83.3	71.2	**81.6**

From the experimental data in Table 2, it can be seen that compared with Improve1 where CBAM was not added at the end of the backbone, adding CBAM to the backbone in Improve 4 that did not lead to an increase in detection performance, but a drop in map50 from 80.4% to 78.9%. This outcome can be attributed to the fact that the original main feature extraction network of YOLOv5 is already proficient, and the relatively small size of our dataset is insufficient to effectively train the newly introduced CBAM-enhanced main network. However, the introduction of CBAM to the Neck of YOLOv5 has shown beneficial effects in terms of fusing features of various scales more effectively, thereby enhancing the model's perceptual capability and accuracy.

We selected Faster R-CNN, SSD, and YOLOv8 as comparative experiments in the context of object detection. All these algorithms were trained on pre-trained base models. This approach not only significantly reduces training time but also enhances the detection performance of the networks. The final training outcomes and evaluations of each algorithm are summarized in Table 3.

Table 3. The comparison of different algorithms.

Model	Backbone	P/%	R/%	mAP@0.5/%
Faster R-CNN	ResNet-50	39.4	78.5	62.6
SSD	ResNet-50	88.9	39.0	71.5
YOLOv8	CSPDarkNet-53	71.34	73.9	77.2
YOLOv5s	CSPDarkNet-53	79.0	70.8	78.9
YOLOv5l	CSPDarkNet-53	82.1	76.4	80.1
YOLOv5x	CSPDarkNet-53	83.1	73.9	80.3
YOLOv5l-ours	CSPDarkNet-53	83.3	71.2	**81.6**

Compared to the original YOLOv5l model, our proposed method achieved an approximately 1.5% improvement in mAP. Furthermore, when compared to other algorithms, our method demonstrated superior performance on the test dataset. This leads to the conclusion that the detection approach proposed by the author, involving the incorporation of a small object detection head and CBAM attention modules, significantly enhances the efficacy of plate defect detection. Figure 5 shows the different sheet defects predicted by our algorithm model.

In order to verify the effectiveness of this algorithm, we introduced the NEU steel defect dataset, which is similar to our plate defect dataset, for comparative experiments. The results and evaluations before and after improvement for each defect dataset are summarized in Table 4.

Judging from the results of the NEU steel defect dataset, our algorithm has improved defect detection.

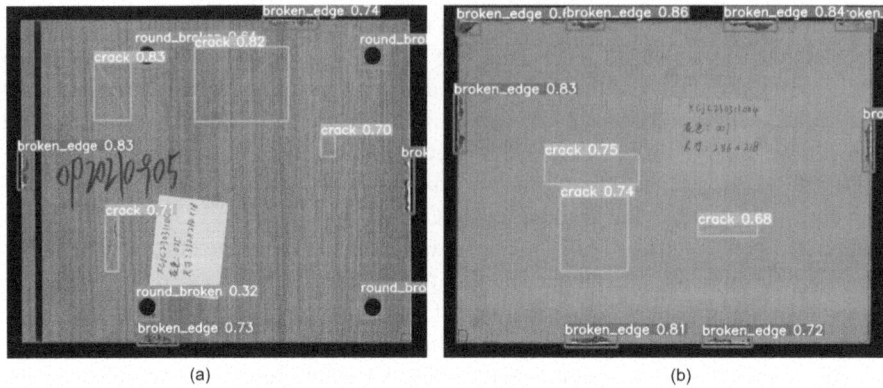

(a)   (b)

Fig. 5. Predicted plate defect images.

Table 4. The comparison of different datasets.

Model	Improve	P/%	R/%	mAP@0.5/%
NEU-DET	×	73.4	77.6	80.3
	√	73.4	82.7	**85.7**
Our dataset	×	82.1	76.4	80.1
	√	83.3	71.2	**81.6**

6 Conclusion

Based on the plate defect dataset provided by a certain intelligence company, this paper addresses challenges related to defect feature complexity and the small size of defect targets. By enhancing the YOLOv5 object detection algorithm, notable improvements have been achieved in its detection performance on this dataset.

Experimental results underscore the effectiveness of this approach in enhancing plate defect detection. The proposed model demonstrates an approximate 1.5% increase in AP compared to the original YOLOv5l model.

To simulate a real-life scenario in plate production, we have curated a novel wood plate defect dataset characterized by a high proportion of small-sized targets, effectively reflecting the actual defects found in production. This dataset provides valuable material for an objective evaluation of the model's performance.

References

1. Cai, J., Zhang, L.-B.: Apple surface defect detection based on deep learning. In: 2021 International Conference on Electronic Information Technology and Smart Agriculture (ICEITSA), pp. 491–495 (2021)

2. Gao, Y., Gao, L., Li, X.: A generative adversarial network based deep learning method for low-quality defect image reconstruction and recognition. IEEE Trans. Ind. Inf. **17**, 3231–3240 (2021). https://doi.org/10.1109/TII.2020.3008703

3. Xie, Q., Zhou, W., Tan, H., Wang, X.: Surface defect recognition in steel plates based on impoved faster R-CNN. In: 2022 41st Chinese Control Conference (CCC), pp. 6759–6764 (2022)

4. Melakhsou, A.A., Baton-Hubert, M., Casoetto, N.: Computer vision based welding defect detection using YOLOv3. In: 2022 IEEE 27th International Conference on Emerging Technologies and Factory Automation (ETFA), pp. 1–6 (2022)

5. Rehana, K.C., Remya, G.: Road damage detection and classification using YOLOv5. In: 2022 Third International Conference on Intelligent Computing Instrumentation and Control Technologies (ICICICT), pp. 489–494 (2022)

6. Lin, C.-H., Ho, C.-W., Hu, G.-H., Kuo, P.-C., Hu, C.-Y.: Alloy cast product defect detection based on object detection. In: 2021 International Symposium on Intelligent Signal Processing and Communication Systems (ISPACS), pp. 1–2 (2021)

7. Li, L., Jiang, Z., Li, Y.: Surface defect detection algorithm of aluminum based on improved faster RCNN. In: 2021 IEEE 9th International Conference on Information, Communication and Networks (ICICN), pp. 527–531 (2021)

8. Luo, L., Deng, C., Wu, Z., Wang, S., Ye, T.: Automobile airbag defect detection algorithm based on improved faster RCNN. In: 2021 International Conference on Computer Engineering and Artificial Intelligence (ICCEAI), pp. 281–285 (2021)

9. Liu, Y., Wang, J., Yu, H., Li, F., Yu, L., Zhang, C.: Surface defect detection of steel products based on improved YOLOv5. In: 2022 41st Chinese Control Conference (CCC), pp. 5794–5799 (2022)

10. Kuan-Ying, S., Ming-Fei, C., Po-Cheng, T., Cheng-Han, T.: Establish a dynamic detection system for metal bicycle frame defects based on YOLO object detection. In: 2022 IET International Conference on Engineering Technologies and Applications (IET-ICETA), pp. 1–2 (2022)

11. Guan, S., Wang, X., Wang, J., Yu, Z., Wang, X., Zhang, C., Liu, T., Liu, D., Wang, J., Zhang, L.: Ceramic ring defect detection based on improved YOLOv5. In: 2022 3rd International Conference on Computer Vision, Image and Deep Learning & International Conference on Computer Engineering and Applications (CVIDL & ICCEA), pp. 115–118 (2022)

12. Girshick, R., Donahue, J., Darrell, T., Malik, J.: Rich feature hierarchies for accurate object detection and semantic segmentation. In: 2014 IEEE Conference on Computer Vision and Pattern Recognition, pp. 580–587 (2014)

13. Girshick, R.: Fast R-CNN (2015). http://arxiv.org/abs/1504.08083

14. Ren, S., He, K., Girshick, R., Sun, J.: Faster R-CNN: Towards Real-Time Object Detection with Region Proposal Networks (2016). http://arxiv.org/abs/1506.01497

15. Redmon, J., Divvala, S., Girshick, R., Farhadi, A.: You only look once: unified, real-time object detection. In: 2016 IEEE Conference on Computer Vision and Pattern Recognition (CVPR), pp. 779–788 (2016)

16. Liu, W., Anguelov, D., Erhan, D., Szegedy, C., Reed, S.E., Fu, C.-Y., Berg, A.C.: SSD: single shot multibox detector. In: Leibe, B., Matas, J., Sebe, N., Welling, M. (eds.) Computer Vision - ECCV 2016 - 14th European Conference, Amsterdam, The Netherlands, October 11–14, 2016, Proceedings, Part I, pp. 21–37. Springer, Cham (2016). https://doi.org/10.1007/978-3-319-46448-0_2

17. Li, B., Ren, F., Ni, H., Kang, X., Lv, S., Hao, Z.: Classification method of surface defects of aluminum profile based on transfer learning. In: 2022 International Conference on Machine Learning and Intelligent Systems Engineering (MLISE), pp. 1–5 (2022)

18. Kaur, P., Khehra, B.S., Mavi, Er.B.S.: Data augmentation for object detection: a review. In: 2021 IEEE International Midwest Symposium on Circuits and Systems (MWSCAS), pp. 537–543 (2021)
19. Luo, W., Sun, L.: An improved binarization algorithm of wood image defect segmentation based on non-uniform background. J. For. Res. **30**, 1527–1533 (2019)
20. Pahlberg, T., Hagman, O., Thurley, M.: Recognition of boards using wood fingerprints based on a fusion of feature detection methods. Comput. Electron. Agric. **111**, 164–173 (2015)
21. He, T., Liu, Y., Xu, C., Zhou, X., Hu, Z., Fan, J.: A fully convolutional neural network for wood defect location and identification. IEEE Access. **7**, 123453–123462 (2019)
22. Yang, Y., Zhou, X., Liu, Y., Hu, Z., Ding, F.: Wood defect detection based on depth extreme learning machine. Appl. Sci. **10**, 7488 (2020)
23. Shi, J., Li, Z., Zhu, T., Wang, D., Ni, C.: Defect detection of industry wood veneer based on NAS and multi-channel mask R-CNN. Sensors **20**, 4398 (2020)
24. Xu, J., Yang, H., Wan, Z., Mu, H., Qi, D., Han, S.: Wood surface defects detection based on the improved YOLOv5-C3Ghost with SimAm module. IEEE Access **11**, 105281 (2023)
25. Schlegl, T., Seeböck, P., Waldstein, S.M., Schmidt-Erfurth, U., Langs, G.: Unsupervised anomaly detection with generative adversarial networks to guide marker discovery. In: Niethammer, M., et al. (eds.) Information Processing in Medical Imaging, pp. 146–157. Springer International Publishing, Cham (2017). https://doi.org/10.1007/b137723
26. Han, X., Chen, X., Liu, L.-P.: GAN ensemble for anomaly detection. Proc. AAAI Conf. Artif. Intell. **35**, 4090–4097 (2021)
27. Zavrtanik, V., Kristan, M., Skočaj, D.: Reconstruction by inpainting for visual anomaly detection. Pattern Recogn. **112**, 107706 (2021)
28. Wang, C.-Y., Bochkovskiy, A., Liao, H.-Y.M.: YOLOv7: Trainable Bag-of-Freebies Sets New State-of-the-Art for Real-Time Object Detectors (2022). http://arxiv.org/abs/2207.02696
29. Woo, S., Park, J., Lee, J.-Y., Kweon, I.S.: CBAM: convolutional block attention module. In: Proceedings of the European Conference on Computer Vision (ECCV), pp. 3–19 (2018)
30. Benjumea, A., Teeti, I., Cuzzolin, F., Bradley, A.: YOLO-Z: Improving Small Object Detection in YOLOv5 for Autonomous Vehicles. https://arxiv.org/abs/2112.11798v4. Accessed 28 July 2023

HPSO-WOA-SFO: A Novel Hybrid Swarm Intelligence Approach for Enhancing Discrete Road Path Planning

You Wu[1]📧, Xi Hu[2]📧, and Guosheng Zhu[1(✉)]

[1] School of Cyber Science and Technology, Hubei University, Wuhan 430062, China
zhuguosheng@hubu.edu.cn
[2] School of Artificial Intelligence, Jianghan University, Wuhan 430056, China

Abstract. The Hybrid Particle Swarm Optimization-Whale Optimization Algorithm-Sailfish Optimizer (HPSO-WOA-SFO) is proposed for solving multi-obstacle discrete road path planning. This paper proposes to utilize the advantage of the two-population update iteration of the sailfish algorithm to integrate the PSO and WOA into the SFO to enhance its exploitation ability and exploration ability, respectively. Meanwhile, the two communication mechanisms between the two populations of the SFO are studied in depth, and their algorithmic advantages and application scenarios are analyzed. Comparative experiments with four representative path planning algorithms and ablative experiments involving HPSO-WOA-SFO are conducted. The results demonstrate that, on average, HPSO-WOA-SFO outperforms the comparative algorithms by 21.40% in terms of global optimal convergence accuracy and is 10.71% faster in terms of convergence speed. Moreover, the proposed algorithm rapidly escapes local optima and enhances global optimality by 17.47% when trapped in local optima during the optimization process.

Keywords: Evolutionary Algorithm · Discrete Space Optimization Problem · Sailfish Optimization Algorithm · UAV Path Planning

1 Introduction

Today, the civilian application areas of UAVs are rapidly expanding, including real-time surveillance, providing wireless coverage, remote sensing, search and rescue, cargo transportation, security and surveillance, precision agriculture, and

This work was supported in part by the National Natural Science Foundation of China under Grant 61901298; in part by the Young Talents Science and Technology Innovation Planning Program of Education Department of Hubei Province under Grant T2022045; in part by the Scientific Research Project of Education Department of Hubei Province under Grant B2022280; in part by the Scientific Research Foundation of Jianghan University under Grant 2023KJZX18.

X. Chen et al. (Eds.): IoTaaS 2023, LNICST 585, pp. 385–395, 2025.
https://doi.org/10.1007/978-3-031-70507-6_29

civil infrastructure inspection [1]. One of the most important problems that need to be explored is the UAV path planning problem, which aims to find the optimal path between the source and the destination [2]. The unmanned aerial vehicle path planning problem is regarded as a highly complex global optimization problem with NP-hard characteristics [3], Therefore, employing metaheuristic algorithms to thoroughly search the discrete road space, aiming to discover the optimal and fastest paths, has become one of the predominant approaches for addressing this issue.

The key to utilizing metaheuristic algorithms for solving the discrete road path planning problem lies in their ability to efficiently search for optimal paths. Among the mainstream optimization algorithms are several noteworthy ones, including Genetic Algorithm [4], Particle Swarm Optimization (PSO) [5], Whale Optimization Algorithm (WOA) [6], and Grey Wolf Optimizer (GWO) [7]. The Sailfish Optimizer (SFO) [8] is also among these algorithms. Notably, the Sailfish Optimizer is considered a highly promising optimization algorithm and has garnered significant attention from researchers. This algorithm features the dual-population search characteristic, enabling it to simultaneously perform exploration and exploitation during iterations. It also incorporates an effective population communication mechanism. As a result, when compared to traditional single-meta heuristic algorithms, the Sailfish Optimizer exhibits various advantages, including high iteration efficiency, strong flexibility, and remarkable scalability.

In addition to its applications in road path planning, metaheuristic algorithms have been employed in various other domains, such as forecasting residential electricity consumption. One such example is the hybrid optimized grey seasonal variation index model [9]. This model has demonstrated enhanced accuracy in predicting residential electricity consumption. Furthermore, in the context of hydropower generation prediction, metaheuristic algorithms have played a crucial role. A novel Optimized Grey Seasonal Variation Index model [10] has been proposed, leveraging the power of metaheuristic optimization to improve forecasting accuracy. Additionally, for the prediction of hydropower generation, a novel Weighted Average Weakening Buffer Operator [11] has been developed, incorporating metaheuristic techniques for improved performance. In the realm of online social networks, a hybrid clustered SFLA-PSO algorithm [12]has been introduced, showcasing the versatility of metaheuristic algorithms in tackling real-world problems".

Recently, various enhanced applications of SFO have been published in journals across different fields. The scalability of the Sailfish Optimizer has been fully realized. For instance, researchers have proposed improved SFO algorithm models with three distinct characteristics dynamic discrete, dynamic continuous, and static continuous based on the varying nature of berth allocation problems for ships, in order to compare their advantages and disadvantages [13]. Moreover, the Sailfish Optimizer has been hybridized with the Grey Wolf Optimizer and applied to the electric vehicle charging station scheduling problem in urban settings, yielding significant optimization outcomes for a substantial number of vehicles [14]. As well, in the feature selection area some researchers proposed to map the continuous solution space of the SFO algorithm to the BSFO in binary space using the Sigmoid transformation function, and also mixed it with the AβHC algorithm to become the ASF algorithm to enhance its development capability [15].

This paper proposes a Hybrid Particle Swarm Optimization - Whale Optimization Algorithm - Sailfish Optimizer (HPSO-WOA-SFO) to solve UAV discrete road path planning. By integrating PSO and WOA with two populations, the SFO algorithm's exploitation and exploration capabilities are effectively enhanced. Moreover, in order to improve the population communication efficiency, this study analyzes the update and exchange process of the two populations in the SFO algorithm, adapting it to the path planning problem addressed. Then, the experimental results of HPSO-WOA-SFO in this paper show that HPSO-WOA-SFO is 21.40% better than the comparison algorithm in the global optimal convergence accuracy on average.

The remaining sections of this paper are organized as follows. Section 2 describes a hybrid PSO-SFO and analyze its principles. Section 3 describes and analyzes the hybrid WOA-SFO formulation and principles. Section 4 describes the application process of the above two hybrid algorithms in the dual population and discusses the characteristics of node update mechanism. Section 5 summarizes the algorithm design of HPSO-WOA-SFO and the corresponding experimental results.

2 Enhancing Population Exploitation with Hybrid PSO-SFO Algorithm

The sailfish optimization algorithm uses a sailfish population and a sardine population for exploitation iterations and exploration iterations [8] respectively. Where the purpose of the sailfish population is to find better values around the elite sailfish nodes to replace the elite sailfish nodes, thus acting as a exploitation population. Therefore, this paper applies the PSO's historical optimal node and current optimal node's to the current node iteration of the sailfish swarm. The node iteration of the sailfish population is extended from iterating with the current 'elite sailfish' (the best node in the sailfish population) and 'injured sardine' (the best node in the sardine) as parameters to iterating with its own historical optimum, 'elite sailfish', 'injured sardine' as parameters for iteration, which can maximize the use of each iteration of each node has an advantage in the path information, The iterative process is shown in Eq. (1) below:

$$N^i_{new_{SF}} = r_1 \times \left(X_{best} - \lambda_i \times r_2 \times \left(X_{best} - X^i_{old_{SF}} \right) \right)$$
$$+ (1 - r_1) \times \left(X^i_{elite_{SF}} - \lambda \times r_3 \times \left(\frac{X^i_{elite_{SF}} + X^i_{injured_S}}{2} \right) - X^i_{old_{SF}} \right)$$
$$\tag{1}$$

where X_{best} is the historical optimal value of the individual of this sailfish node, $X^i_{elite_{SF}}$ is the location of the optimal individual of the sailfish node in the i-th iteration, $X^i_{injured_S}$ is the location of the optimal individual of the sardine in the i-th iteration, $X^i_{old_{SF}}$ is the location of the current primary UAV node in the i-th iteration, r_1, r_2 and r_3 are uniformly distributed random numbers ranging from 0 to 1, and λ_i is the coefficients generated in the i-th iteration, as shown in Eq. (2):

$$\lambda_i = 2 \times rand(0,1) \times PD - PD \tag{2}$$

where PD is the sardine distribution density, which represents the proportion of sardine population in the whole population at each iteration. The number of sardine nodes decreases as the sardines run out of energy and are captured by sailfish nodes, which is calculated as shown in (3):

$$PD = 1 - \left(\frac{N_{SF}}{N_{SF} + N_S} \right) \tag{3}$$

where N_{SF} and N_S represent the number of sailfish population and the number of sardine population at each iteration, respectively. Since the sardine population will be removed from the sardine population and replaced by the elite sailfish when a better node than the elite sailfish appears in the sardine population, so the number of sardine population should be more than the sailfish population as much as possible. So the number of sardine population should be as much as possible than the sailfish population to ensure the iterative efficiency of sardine diversity. As shown in Eq. (1), this paper uses a random number to adjust the proportion of the influence of the traditional sailfish algorithm and the PSO algorithm in the iteration of sailfish nodes, which can prevent the algorithm from falling into the local optimum to some extent. This value can also be replaced by a fixed value to find the most suitable coefficient for the current problem.

3   Enhancing Population Exploration with Hybrid WOA-SFO Algorithm

In the sailfish algorithm, the sardine population is iterated by exploring the local optimum of the neighborhood of its non-sardine nodes by fleeing in the opposite direction according to the position of the sailfish selected when this iteration is made. In this paper, we propose to combine the exploration method of node spiral movement of WOA into the single vector movement of sardines, which makes the iteration results of sardines more diversified and thus improves the exploration efficiency of each sardine node.

In the sardine iterative algorithm, when $AP \geq 0.5$ the sardine node randomly selects any sailfish node to escape so that the algorithm explores as much as possible the unknown domain in the early stage, while when $AP < 0.5$ the sardine turns to select the position of the elite sailfish iteratively to assist the algorithm to break through the local optimum as the premise of exploration. In this paper, we propose to add a random factor p to let the sardine node choose the modified spiral iteration formula of WOA to iterate in the direction of the tangent of the spiral in each round of iteration, which uses the global optimum of the current iteration (the elite sailfish node) as a parameter as shown in Eq. (4):

$$
X^i_{news} = \begin{cases} \begin{cases} \vec{A} \times \vec{D} + AP & \text{if } AP \geq 0.5 \\ \vec{A} \times \vec{D}' + AP & \text{if } AP < 0.5 \end{cases} & \text{if } p < 0.5 \\ \vec{D}'' \times \ell^{bl} \times cos(2\pi l) + AP & \text{if } p \geq 0.5 \end{cases} \tag{4}
$$

$$
\vec{D} = \left| \vec{C} * X^i_{rand_{SF}} - X^i_{old_S} \right| \tag{5}
$$

$$
\vec{D}' = \left| \vec{C} * X^i_{elite_{SF}} - X^i_{old_S} \right| \tag{6}
$$

$$
\vec{D}'' = \left| X^i_{elite_{SF}} - X^i_{old_S} \right| \tag{7}
$$

where i represents the current iteration number, $\vec{D}$, $\vec{D}'$ and $\vec{D}''$ represent the relative distance between the current sardine node and the selected individual sailfish node in the ith iteration. b is a constant defining the shape of the helix, l is a random number in the range $[-1, 1]$. AP is the value representing the average energy consumption of the sardine population when this iteration, as shown in Eq. (8):

$$
AP = a \times (1 - (2 \times Itr \times \varepsilon)) \tag{8}
$$

a controls the range of AP, ε is the reciprocal of the two times maximum iteration number, when AP decreases from a to 0, the population iteration ends. By the parameter AP control sardine nodes can have the ability to effectively break through the local optimum in both the early and late stages of the algorithm iteration, to ensure that the algorithm can stably find the near-optimal solution.

$\vec{A}$ and $\vec{C}$ are coefficient vectors, as shown in Eq. (9) and (10):

$$
\vec{A} = 2 \times \vec{\alpha} \times \vec{r} - \vec{\alpha} \tag{9}
$$

$$
\vec{C} = 2 \times \vec{r} \tag{10}
$$

where $\vec{\alpha}$ is used to denote the hunting density of the sailfish nodes whose value decreases linearly from 2 to 0 with iterations, $\vec{A}$ is a random value in the range $[-\alpha, \alpha]$, and $\vec{r}$ is a uniformly distributed random vector from 0 to 1.

The main purpose of the sardine population is to obtain as many better candidate solutions from the current path solution space as possible in the limited iteration period, and deliver them to the sailfish nodes for iteration. Unlike the iterative approach of the sailfish population, this paper argues that the iterative approach of the sardine focuses more on operative stochastic exploration rather than structural learning with other locally optimal nodes as the algorithm in Sect. 2, which also makes the algorithm more efficient.

4   Application and Analysis of the Dual-Population Mechanism

The interaction between the sailfish and sardine populations occurs when a candidate solution in the sardine population outperforms the elite sailfish. At this point, the elite sailfish removes the sardine and replaces its own candidate solution. Throughout the algorithm's iterations, the sailfish continuously extracts new local optima from the sardine population, repeatedly breaking through the current iteration's local optima. During this process, the number of sardines gradually decreases as the sailfish captures them. Since the sardines' iteration process is independent of the sardine population as a whole and only depends on the sailfish nodes, the number of sardine nodes is linearly related to the diversity of randomly generated candidate solutions in the current iteration. Therefore, the sardine capture mechanism during the interaction between the sailfish and sardine populations influences the diversity of the entire algorithm.

After a certain number of iterations, the entire algorithm tends to stabilize at an approximate optimal value. This is because it becomes challenging for the sailfish iteration algorithm to develop solutions better than the current ones. On the other hand, the sardine population's iteration process, which essentially involves random exploration radiating from a starting point towards sailfish nodes, can easily lead to incorrect exploration directions. Thus, when a sardine is captured by a sailfish, the behavior of reiterating with a new random starting point is a key mechanism for the sailfish optimization algorithm to achieve local optima.

Through experimental analysis, this paper concludes that generating a new random sardine node immediately after capturing one can maintain the sardine population's diversity exploration efficiency. Conversely, retaining captured sardine nodes and generating a batch of new sardine nodes after reaching a certain quantity can make the algorithm's iterations more breakthrough-oriented. However, since the sardine node capture behavior is not frequent, the number of sardines generated at once significantly affects the sardine population's iteration progress. It may result in only a few replenishments occurring even after 500 iterations. Therefore, the value should be adjusted according to the actual situation during the formal algorithm iterations.

5   Experiments

5.1   Experimental Environment

In this paper, the specified global terrain model is obtained from the GEBCO_2022 dataset released by the Global Bathymetric Chart of the Oceans (GEBCO): the coordinates are LNG:40.0500, LAT:154.0000; the size of the sampling matrix is $20\,km * 20\,km * 20\,km$; the size of the 3D grid model is $200 * 200 * 200$; the hardware environment of the experiment is M2 chip, 8G memory; the operating system is MAC, and the algorithm is realized by MATLABr2022b software.

In the HPSO-WOA-SFO algorithm, 200 nodes are used for iteration, in which the number of sailfish nodes is 100 nodes and the number of sardine nodes is 100 nodes, the upper bound of each dimension value of the node is 1, and the lower bound is 0, with a total of 3,395 dimensions, and the maximum number of iterations is 400 iterations, and the initial value of the node is randomly generated by the initialization of the algorithm, and the ε is 0.00125 and the AP behavior threshold is 0.5.

5.2   Results and Analysis

Comparison Experiment. In the unified experimental environment, HPSO-WOA-SFO with PSO, SFO, GWO, and WOA performs path planning optimization experiments in the path planning solution space, and the simulation results are shown in Figs. 1 and 2:

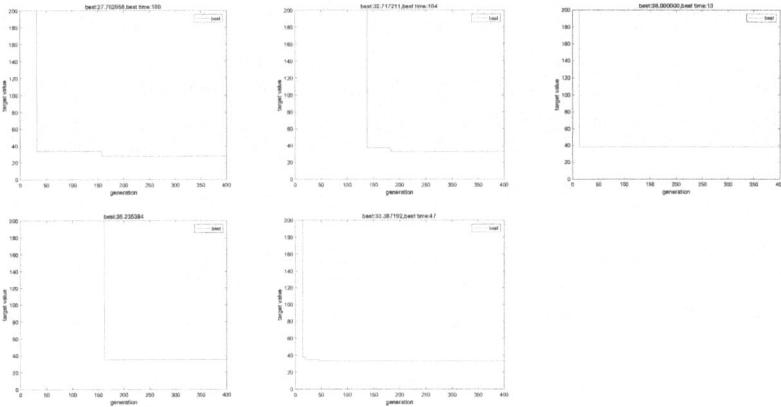

Fig. 1. (a) Iterative plot of optimal values of HPSO-WOA-SFO (b) Iterative map of optimal values of SFO (c) Iterative map of GWO optima (d) Iterative map of WOA optima (e) Iterative map of PSO optima.

Figure 1 shows the convergence optimal solution of each iteration of each path planning algorithm in the path planning solution space, and Fig. 2 shows the visualization path of the optimal solution at the end of the iteration in the 3D map of seabed topography and geomorphology. As shown in the bold part of Table 1, the experiments show that HPSO-WOA-SFO has obvious advantages in both convergence speed and convergence optimal value, as shown in Fig. 1(a), a better local optimal solution is found at the 32nd iteration and 161st iteration, and the global optimal value of 27.76 is finally found after the 199th iteration. Comparison with the SFO shown in Fig. 1(b) shows that, when improving the SFO Comparing with the SFO shown in Fig. 1(b), it can be seen that after improving the sailfish iteration process and the sardine iteration process in the

Table 1. Iterative Optimization Comparison Table of HPSO-WOA-SFO with Other Algorithms.

Algorithm	Global optimum/iter	First local optimum/iter
HPSO-WOA-SFO	**27.76**/199	**33.64**/32
SFO	32.71/186	37.08/140
GWO	38.00/13	38.00/13
WOA	35.23/162	35.23/162
PSO	33.38/47	38.05/16

SFO, the local optimal solution searching speed and the convergence accuracy of the local optimal solution of the HPSO-WOA-SFO algorithm are both improved. For the path planning problem with decentralized roads, each search for a better local optimal solution represents a breakthrough in the optimization result, as shown in Figs. 1(c) and (d), GWO and WOA are trapped in the local optimum in the solution space and cannot break through although they have found the local optimal solution. GWO, as shown in Fig. 1(c), finds the optimal value after the 13th iteration, and fails to find a more efficient path after the next 387 iterations, indicating that GWO still needs to be improved when exploring the data in the discrete solution space. PSO algorithm, as shown in Fig. 1(e), finds the local optimal solution and successfully improves the convergence accuracy at the 16th iteration, indicating that PSO algorithm is very efficient in this path The PSO algorithm is effective in this path planning problem, but it is unable to find other local optimal solutions, and the subsequent iterations also fall into the local optimum.

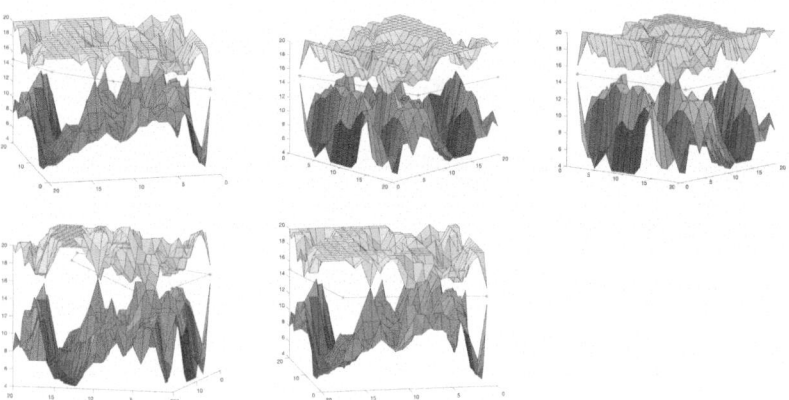

Fig. 2. (a) Iterative plot of optimal values of HPSO-WOA-SFO(b) Iterative map of optimal values of SFO (c) Iterative map of optima (d) Iterative map of WOA optima (e) Iterative map of PSO optima.

HPSO-WOA-SFO Ablation Experiment. The HPSO-WOA-SFO ablation experiment is divided into two groups of comparison experiments, HPSO-SFO and HWOA-SFO. The HPSO-SFO ablation experiment combines the iterative process of the sardine school in the original SFO with the HPSO-SFO; and the HWOA-SFO ablation experiment uses the iterative process of the sailfish school in the original SFO in combination with the HWOA-SFO and compares the two groups of ablation experimental subjects with the HPSO-WOA-SFO for a control. The HPSO-WOA-SFO ablation experiments of HPSO-SFO and HWOA-SFO were conducted to compare the experimental data as shown in Fig. 3:

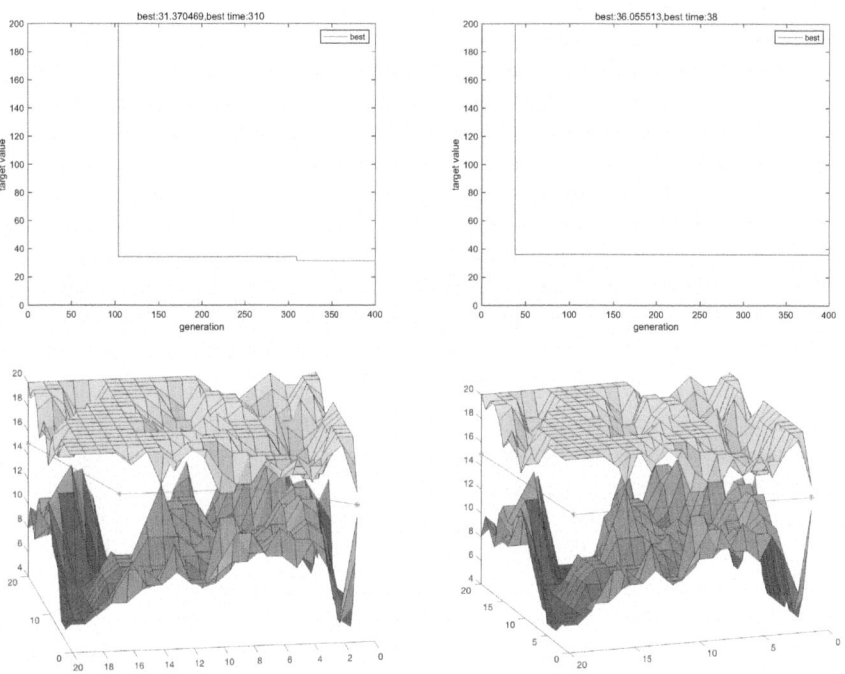

Fig. 3. (a) Iterative map of optimal values of HPSO-SFO (b) HWOA-SFO optimal value iterative map (c) Optimal roadmap for HPSO-SFO (d) HWOA-SFO optimal roadmap.

HPSO-SFO, as shown in Fig. 3(a), searches the local optimum value at the 104th iteration indicating its weak searching ability, but breaks through the optimum value to 34.27 at the 310th iteration. The fact that HPSO-SFO can break through the convergence accuracy of the difference of 2 in spite of its weak global optimization searching ability indicates the validity of its ability of convergence accuracy. IEFM, as shown in Fig. 3(b), searches the local optimum value to 36 at the 38th iteration, and has an advantage in the value of local optimum solution compared with the data in Table 1, showing the characteristics

Table 2. Comparison table of iterative optimization search for HPSO-WOA-SFO ablation experiments.

Algorithm	Global optimum/iter	First local optimum/iter
HPSO-WOA-SFO	**27.76**/199	**33.64**/32
HPSO-SFO	31.37/310	34.27/104
HWOA-SFO	36.00/38	36.00/38

of HWOA-SFO in terms of its optimization searching ability. HWOA-SFO, as shown in Fig. 3(b), searches for the local optimal solution value of 36 at the 38th iteration, which is advantageous in the value of the local optimal solution compared with the data in Table 1, showing the characteristics of HWOA-SFO in the optimization ability, and falls into the local optimum after that showing the limitation of the original SFO algorithm (Table 2).

6   Conclusion

This paper aims to address the issue of relatively strong discreteness in unmanned aerial vehicle path planning. It combines the scalability of the sailfish optimization algorithm with the improvement in exploitation and exploration capabilities through the integration of the Particle Swarm Optimization and Whale Optimization Algorithm. This enhancement allows the sailfish iterative algorithm to fully absorb the path structures of other excellent nodes in the population, thereby developing better solutions. Simultaneously, the sardine iterative algorithm efficiently explores the solution space, fully harnessing the advantages of the algorithm. Furthermore, this paper analyzes the strengths and weaknesses of the dual-population exchange mechanism implementation and demonstrates that within the sailfish optimization algorithm, the dual-population exchange mechanism plays a crucial role in determining the algorithm's diversity and optimization capability.

The experimental results show that HPSO-WOA-SFO can improve the global optimal convergence accuracy by 21.40% and the convergence speed by 10.71% compared with various path planning algorithms, and can quickly break through the local optimal when the algorithm is stuck in the local optimal, which makes the algorithm's global optimal value improve by 17.47%.

References

1. Hazim, S., et al.: Unmanned aerial vehicles (UAVs): a survey on civil applications and key research challenges. IEEE Access **7**, 48572–48634 (2019)
2. Shubhani, A., Neeraj, K.: Path planning techniques for unmanned aerial vehicles: a review, solutions, and challenges. Comput. Commun. **149**, 270–299 (2020)
3. Faiza, G., et al.: Implementation of bio-inspired hybrid algorithm with mutation operator for robotic path planning. J. Parallel Distrib. Comput. **169**, 171–184 (2022)

4. John, H.H.: Genetic algorithms. Sci. Am. **267**(1), 66–73 (1992)
5. James, K., Russell, E.: Particle swarm optimization. In: Proceedings of ICNN 1995 - International Conference on Neural Networks, pp. 1942–1948. IEEE, Perth (2010)
6. Seyedali, M., Andrew, L.: The whale optimization algorithm. Adv. Eng. Softw. **95**, 51–67 (2016)
7. Seyedali, M., Lewus, A.: Grey wolf optimizer. Adv. Eng. Softw. **69**, 46–61 (2014)
8. Shadravan, S., et al.: The sailfish optimizer: a novel nature-inspired metaheuristic algorithm for solving constrained engineering optimization problems. Eng. Appl. Artif. Intell. **80**, 20–34 (2019)
9. Xiong, X., Hu, X., Guo, H.: A hybrid optimized grey seasonal variation index model improved by whale optimization algorithm for forecasting the residential electricity consumption. Energy **234**, 121127 (2021)
10. Xiong, X., et al.: A novel Optimized initial condition and Seasonal division based grey Seasonal Variation Index model for hydropower generation. Energy **328**, 120180 (2022)
11. Li, Z.K., et al.: A novel weighted average weakening buffer operator based fractional order accumulation seasonal grouping grey model for predicting the hydropower generation. Energy **277**, 127568 (2023)
12. Hu, X., et al.: A hybrid clustered SFLA-PSO algorithm for optimizing the timely and real-time rumor refutations in online social networks. Expert Syst. Appl. **212**, 118638 (2023)
13. Issam, E.H., et al.: Comparison of planning models for dynamic berth allocation problem using a sailfish-based algorithm. In: Proceedings of the 24th International Conference KES2020, pp. 3112–3120. Elsevier Procedia, Online (2020)
14. Rajasekaran, R., et al.: A novel intelligent transport system charging scheduling for electric vehicles using grey wolf optimizer and sailfish optimization algorithms. Part A: Recov. Utiliz. Environ. Effects **44**(2), 3555–3575 (2022)
15. Ghosh, K.K., et al.: Improved binary sailfish optimizer based on adaptive-hill climbing for feature selection. IEEE Access **8**, 83548–83560 (2020)

Cooperative Coded Caching in Internet of Vehicles Based on Coded Prefetching

Yifan Lin and Congduan Li[✉]

School of Electronics and Communication Enginerring,
Sun Yat-sen University, Shenzhen 518107, China
linyf28@mail2.sysu.edu.cn, licongd@mail.sysu.edu.cn

Abstract. A lot of networks have high temporal variability, which means in the peak hours, the users' requests may exceed the loading capacity, cause congestion. During the off-peak hours, the network resources is underutilized. Caching is a technique to shift the traffic from peak to off-peak hours, by prefetching some content at or near the end users. Coded caching can reduce the peak rate further by jointly optimizing the placement and delivery. In this paper, we consider a novel coded caching model with allowing interaction between cooperative users, and propose a centralized scheme. We use Greedy Constrained Coloring to exploit the multicasting opportunities, and coded prefetching to reduce the redundancy in the cache due to the interaction between users.

Keywords: Network coding · Coded caching · Internet of Vehicles

1 Introduction

Caching is a technique to reduce the traffic rate during the peak hours by placing some contents at or near the end users in advance. Based on it, coded caching, first proposed by Maddah-Ali and Niesen in 2014 [7], achieves a much better performance than the uncoded caching by jointly optimizing the delivery and placement phase, where the multicasting opportunities can be created so we can serve different demands by a single coded message. The well-known Maddah-Ali-Niesen (MAN) scheme was proposed in [7]. After that, various branches of coded caching problems have been studied. The decentralized system model was studied by Maddah-Ali and Niesen [8], in which users pick the contents to cache independently at the placement phase. They also studied the model with nonuniform user demands [10], creating the multicasting opportunities by grouping the users. Ji et al. give the order-optimal delivery rate on the nonuniform demands model [6], by proposing the Random Least Frequently Used placement with Greedy Constrained Coloring delivery (RLFU-GCC) scheme.

Shared caching problem, which allows multiple users to share a single cache memory, is also studied by lots of researchers. Parrinello et al. proposed the optimum caching scheme with uncoded prefetching for a shared caches system [11].

X. Chen et al. (Eds.): IoTaaS 2023, LNICST 585, pp. 396–413, 2025.
https://doi.org/10.1007/978-3-031-70507-6_30

Asadi et al. studied the centralized caching with shared caches in heterogeneous cellular networks [1]. Decentralized coded caching for shared caching is studied by Dutta et al. [2]. Ibrahim et al. studied a D2D model with distinct cache size [4]. These works focus the model that users can be divided into several groups that users in a same group can communicate or share the cache with each other, or the model that all the users can communicate with each other. Ji et al. studied the coded caching system in wireless D2D network [5], where users in a grid network can communicate with other users within a certain distance, and at the delivery phase, the users will be completely served by other users, without the base station. Then based on this model, Çağkan Yapar et al. proposed a optimal scheme with uncoded cache placement and one-shot delivery.

In order to minimize efficiency loss, wireless communication is typically utilized only for the final leg in large scale communication networks. This unique structure allows for improvement of the interface between the physical and data link layers as a means of mitigating architectural inefficiencies within the wireless portion of the network [13].

Multi-access coded caching (MACC) system, which allows single user to access multiple caches, is first studied by Hachem et al. in 2017 [3]. A (K, N, L, M)-MACC system refer to a coded caching system with N files, K users and caches and each user has the access to L caches with a cyclic wraparound. Actually, our proposed system model is a limited MACC system(see Sect. 2 and Sect. 5) Hachem et al. proposed the MACC system model in [3] with multi-level files popularity settings and a coloring-based scheme. MACC system with uncoded prefetching was studied by Reddy et al. [12]. In [12], the authors proposed a new upper bound of the rate sometimes lower than the rate in [3], an order-optimal rate for MACC system with $L > K/2$, and the exact optimal rate for some special cases. Namboodiri et al. derived a tighter lower bound by adopting the sliding-window subset entropy inequality in the proof [9].

The above MACC systems are symmetric in both user indexing and file indexing [14]. The system model we propose in this paper shares similarities with MACC system but deviates in symmetry in file indexing, constituting a significant divergence from existing system models.

On the other hand, along with the development of 5G, the researches on Internet of Vehicles (IoV) develop rapidly. IoV contains vehicle-to-vehicle (V2V) communication, vehicle-to-RSU (Road side unit) communication and so on. In this paper, we apply the coded caching to the IoV scene, modeling it as a coded caching system with constrained D2D communication. In our model, all the users line up in a row geometrically, corresponding to the single lane model in IoV field. The RSU will act as the base station.

In this paper, we study a MACC-like model and make the following contributions:

- A delivery scheme based on greedy constrained coloring is introduced for our proposed model, which can reduce the rate over the shared link by merging the user cooperation sets to reduce the transmissions times.

- A coded placement technique based on MAN placement in [7] is introduced for our proposed model, which can reduce the memory size requirement with keeping the cache content accessible to users unchanged.
- A new achievable rate is derived based on a scheme with coded placement and graph coloring.

The rest of the paper is organized as follows. Section 2 briefly describes the system model. Section 3 describes our delivery scheme. Section 4 describes our coded placement scheme. Section 5 describes a cut-set type lower bound and shows the performance of our proposed scheme.

2   System Model

As shown in Fig. 1, we consider a centralized model based on the model in [7], K users are connected to a server through a error-free, shared link. The server contains N files of equal size F bits, labeled as $W_1, W_2, \cdots, W_N$. Each user k is equipped with a cache memory Z_k of size MF bits. Each user can access not only its own cache, but also its adjacent users' cache(s), assuming that all the users line up in a row by its label. In the following discussion, we refer a user's adjacent users as its cooperative users. For example, in Fig. 1, user 2 have the access of the caches Z_1 and Z_3, and its own cache Z_2, means that it can access a total of three users' caches.

In particular, the first user and the last user in the row can only access a total of two users' caches. For example, user 1 only have the access of Z_1 and Z_2 due to the fact that there is no user on its left side. Similarly, user 5 only have the access of Z_4 and Z_5. Fig. 2 shows the corresponding IoV model.

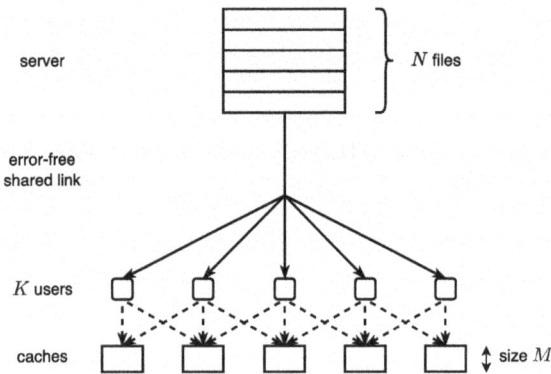

Fig. 1. Caching system considered in this paper. A server containing N files is connected to K users through a shared error-free link. Each user is equipped with a cache of size MF bits, and have the access of its own and its cooperative users' caches. In this figure, $K = N = 5$. User 1 and K only have the access of two caches because they are the "edge" users.

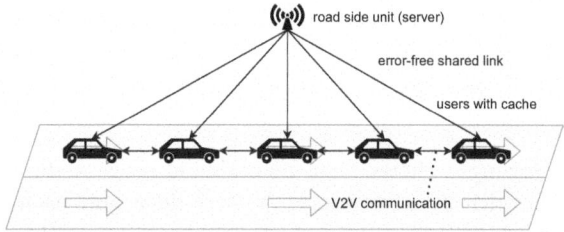

Fig. 2. The IoV model corresponding to the coded caching system model. The road side unit act as the central server and the vehicles act as the users with cache.

To simplify the problem, we assume that users can get contents from its cooperative users' cache *at no cost*.

The operation of a coded caching system will be divided into two phases. In the placement phase, all the caches will be filled without the knowledge of the user demands. In the delivery phase, each user requests exactly one file W_{d_i} from the server. Then the server transmits a series of multicast message through the error-free shared link according to all user demands $\mathbf{d} = (d_1, \cdots, d_K)$. Each user can recover the file required with the transmitted messages and the cached contents it can access. The goal is to design the placement phase and the delivery phase to minimize the peak rate on the shared link.

For ease of reading, the following notations and rules are adopted.

– $W_{i,\mathcal{U}}$: subfile of file W_i, which stored in the caches of all the users in $\mathcal{U}$.
– For any positive integer K and integer $q < K$, let $[K] = \{1, 2, \ldots, K\}$ and $\binom{[K]}{q} = \{\mathcal{D} | \mathcal{D} \subseteq [K], |\mathcal{D}| = q\}$. When $q \leq 0$, $\binom{[K]}{q} = \emptyset$.
– $\mathcal{W}$: set of subfiles.
– Let $\mathcal{W}_1, \mathcal{W}_2$ be two sets of subfiles, $|\mathcal{W}_1| = |\mathcal{W}_2| = n$, $w_{i,j}$ be the j-th subfile in $\mathcal{W}_i$, $\mathcal{W}_1 \oplus \mathcal{W}_2$ donates a set of coded subfiles i.e. $\mathcal{W}_1 \oplus \mathcal{W}_2 = \{w_{1,1} \oplus w_{2,1}, w_{1,2} \oplus w_{2,2}, \ldots, w_{1,n} \oplus w_{2,n}\}$.
– For the calculation of user index in the following discuss, we follow a cyclic wrap-around rule, i.e. user -1, 0 refer to user $K - 1$, K, and user $K + 1$, $K + 2$ refer to user 1, 2, etc.

3   Delivery Phase Design

Our research base on the scheme proposed by Maddah Ali and Niesen in [7], which will be called as the MAN scheme.

In the MAN scheme, we select s users in $[K]$ to form a user cooperation set $\mathcal{S}$. For each user cooperation set, a message

$$X_{\mathcal{S}} = \oplus_{k \in \mathcal{S}} W_{d_u, \mathcal{S} \setminus k}, \tag{1}$$

is generated based on the users' demand and caches, and sent to all users in the set. This ensures that each user in S can decode a subfile of the file it requested upon receiving the message. After generating and sending the messages to all possible user cooperation sets, all users should be able to obtain the file they requested. In our settings, the delivery phase needs to be redesign to aviod the message redundancy.

Example 1. This example shows that how the message redundancy appears. Consider a system with $K = 8$ users, $N = 8$ files and each user equipped with a cache size of $M = 3$. According to the MAN scheme, the size of the user cooperation set $s = MK/N + 1 = 4$.

Taking the user cooperation set $\mathcal{S} = \{1, 2, 4, 6\}$ as an example, assuming $d_i = W_i$, the message

$$X_{\mathcal{S}} = W_{d_1, \{2,4,6\}} \oplus W_{d_2, \{1,4,6\}} \oplus W_{d_4, \{1,2,6\}} \oplus W_{d_6, \{1,2,4\}},$$

is generated then multicasted to all users in $\mathcal{S}$.

For user 1, it have the access of Z_2, meanwhile the subfile $W_{d_1, \{2,4,6\}}$ is stored in Z_2. Therefore this transmitted message makes no contribution to user 1.

However, for user 4, it still needs $X_{\mathcal{S}}$ to recover the subfile it requested, due to the fact that the subfile $W_{d_4, \{1,2,6\}}$ does not exist in any cache it have the access, i.e. Z_3, Z_4 and Z_5.   □

Here we give some definitions.

Definition 1. *For a user* $u \in [K]$, *let*

$$A(u) = \begin{cases} \{u+1\} & ,u = 1, \\ \{u-1, u+1\} & ,1 < u < K, \\ \{u-1\} & ,u = K, \end{cases} \tag{2}$$

$$\mathcal{Z}(u) = \mathcal{A}(u) \cup \{u\}, \tag{3}$$

refer to the adjacent user(s) of u *and the caches that* u *can access, respectively. For a user cooperation set* $\mathcal{S}$, *let*

$$\mathcal{T}_{\mathcal{S}} = \{u \in \mathcal{S} | \mathcal{A}(u) \cap \mathcal{S} = \emptyset\}, \tag{4}$$

$$\mathcal{N}_{\mathcal{S}} = \{u \in \mathcal{S} | \mathcal{A}(u) \cap \mathcal{S} \neq \emptyset\}, \tag{5}$$

refer to its target users set and non-target users set, respectively

For a user $k \in \mathcal{S}$, *if none of its adjacent user(s) is the member of* $\mathcal{S}$, *we say user* k *is a target user of* $\mathcal{S}$, *which means it needs the message* $X_{\mathcal{S}}$ *to recover the file it requested; If any of its adjacent user(s) is the member of* $\mathcal{S}$, *we say user* k *is a non-target user of* $\mathcal{S}$, *which means the message* $X_{\mathcal{S}}$ *makes no contribution to it.*

With the definitions above, we have $\mathcal{T}_{\mathcal{S}} = \{4, 6\}, \mathcal{N}_{\mathcal{S}} = \{1, 2\}$ in Example 1.

For each user cooperation set $\mathcal{S}$, due to the fact that the message $X_{\mathcal{S}}$ makes no contribution to the users in $\mathcal{N}_{\mathcal{S}}$, the message generated only for the users in $\mathcal{T}_{\mathcal{S}}$, i.e.

$$X_{\mathcal{S}} = \oplus_{u \in \mathcal{T}_{\mathcal{S}}} W_{d_u, S \setminus \{u\}} \tag{6}$$

Based on the number of target users, the user cooperation sets can be classified into three categories.

1. For the user cooperation sets with $\mathcal{T}_\mathcal{S} = \emptyset$, they will be omitted since they make no contribution to any users.
2. For the user cooperation sets with $\mathcal{T}_\mathcal{S} = \mathcal{S}$, the corresponding generated messages $X_\mathcal{S}$ will be multicasted to their respective target users.
3. For the user cooperation sets with $\mathcal{T}_\mathcal{S} \subset \mathcal{S}, \mathcal{T}_\mathcal{S} \neq \emptyset$, some messages will be merged into a single one to exploit the multicasting opportunities and reduce the transmission rate on the shared link. The following part in this section describes the specific merging approach.

Our scheme is based on the conflict graph and Greedy Constrained Coloring(GCC). Given

$$\mathbf{S} = \{\mathcal{S}|\mathcal{T}_\mathcal{S} \subset \mathcal{S}, \mathcal{T}_\mathcal{S} \neq \emptyset\},$$

the conflict graph is defined as follows:

Definition 2. *The conflict graph $\mathcal{H}_\mathbf{S}$ is formed by:*

- **Vertex set:** *The set of vertices in $\mathcal{H}_\mathbf{S}$ is the set of all user cooperation sets in $\mathbf{S}$. The vertex corresponding to the user cooperation set $\mathcal{S}_i$ is represented by v_i.*
- **Edge set:** *There exists an edge (v_i, v_j) connecting vertices v_i and v_j in $\mathcal{H}_\mathbf{S}$ if and only if the following merge condition is NOT satisfied:*

$$
\begin{aligned}
&\bigwedge_{u \in \mathcal{T}_{\mathcal{S}_i}} (\mathcal{Z}(u) \cap \mathcal{N}_{\mathcal{S}_j} \neq \emptyset) \\
&\wedge \bigwedge_{u \in \mathcal{T}_{\mathcal{S}_j}} (\mathcal{Z}(u) \cap \mathcal{N}_{\mathcal{S}_i} \neq \emptyset),
\end{aligned}
\tag{7}
$$

$\square$

We utilize the GCC algorithm, as presented in Algorithm 1, to assign colors to all the vertices in $\mathcal{H}_\mathbf{S}$.

Algorithm 1. Greedy Constrained Coloring

1: Initialize $\mathcal{V} = $ Vertex-set$(\mathcal{H}_\mathbf{S})$.
2: **while** $\mathcal{V} \neq \emptyset$ **do**
3:     Pick any $v \in \mathcal{V}$, and let $\mathcal{I} = \{v\}$
4:     **for all** $v' \in \mathcal{V} \backslash \mathcal{I}$ **do**
5:         **if** There is no edge between v' and $\mathcal{I}$ **then**
6:             $\mathcal{I} \leftarrow \mathcal{I} \cup v'$
7:         **end if**
8:     **end for**
9:     Color all the vertices of resulting set $\mathcal{I}$ by an unused color.
10:    Let $\mathcal{V} \leftarrow \mathcal{V} \backslash \mathcal{I}$
11: **end while**

Next, the user cooperation sets of the same color will jointly generate a single message

$$X_\Sigma = \oplus_{S \in \Sigma} \left[\oplus_{u \in \mathcal{T}_S} W_{d_u, S \setminus \{u\}} \right]$$

where Σ is the collection of user cooperation sets S of the same color. By multi-casting this message to all users in $\bigcup_{S \in \Sigma} \mathcal{T}_S$, we effectively decrease the amount of message that needs to be transmitted from $|\Sigma|$ to just one.

Theorem 1. *Letting* $\chi(\mathcal{H}_\mathbf{S})$ *donate the chromatic number of* $\mathcal{H}_\mathbf{S}$, $M \in \{0, N/K, 2N/K, \ldots, N\}$, $t = MK/N$, *an upper bound of the delivery rate on the shared link*

$$R_{GCC}(M) = \left(\binom{K-t}{t+1} + \chi(\mathcal{H}_\mathbf{S}) \right) \frac{1}{\binom{K}{t}}. \tag{8}$$

The first factor is the total number of coded messages we should send over the shared link, each size of $1/\binom{K}{t}$, which is the second factor in $R_{GCC}(M)$. $\binom{K-t}{t+1}$ is the number of user cooperation sets with $\mathcal{T}_S = S$. Note that the size of each coded message is also the size of each subfile, normalized by the file size.

The rate $R_{GCC}(M)$ is achieved by our proposed scheme. We formally describe its delivery phase in Algorithm 2. Its placement phase is the same as MAN scheme, described in Algorithm 1 in [7].

Algorithm 2. Coded Caching Delivery

Require: $N, K, M \in \{0, N/K, 2N/K, \ldots, N\}$
1: $s \leftarrow MK/N + 1$
2: $\mathfrak{S} \leftarrow \{S \subseteq \{1, \ldots, K\} : |S| = s\}$
3: $X_1 \leftarrow (\oplus_{u \in S} W_{d_u, S \setminus \{u\}} : S \in \mathfrak{S}, l_S = 0)$
4: $\mathbf{S} \leftarrow \{S \in \mathfrak{S} : 2 \leq l_S < s\}$
5: Generate the conflict graph $\mathcal{H}_\mathbf{S}$ and color it with GCC.
6: $\mathfrak{E} \leftarrow \{\Sigma : \text{collection of user cooperation sets with same color.}\}$
7: $X_2 \leftarrow (\oplus_{S \in \Sigma} (\oplus_{u \in \mathcal{T}_S} W_{d_u, S \setminus \{u\}}) : \Sigma \in \mathfrak{E})$
8: Send X_1 and X_2 to users.

Remark 1. The merge condition (7) consists of two symmetric subconditions. Focus on the first one, it means for each user u in the target users set of S_i, at least one user in $\mathcal{Z}(u)$ should be the member of $\mathcal{N}_{S_j}$, the non-target users set of S_j.

Focus on a subset S', for a user $k \in S', S' \in \Sigma$, the coded message it received can be rewritten in

$$\begin{aligned} X_\Sigma = &W_{d_k, S' \setminus \{k\}} \\ &\oplus \bigoplus_{u \in \mathcal{T}_{S'} \setminus \{k\}} W_{d_u, S' \setminus \{u\}} \\ &\oplus \bigoplus_{S \in \Sigma \setminus \{S'\}} \left(\bigoplus_{u \in \mathcal{T}_S} W_{d_u, S \setminus \{u\}} \right) \end{aligned} \tag{9}$$

The first term is the subfile user k requests. The second term is the subfiles that the other target users in $\mathcal{S}'$ request, which are cached in the cache of user k. The third term is the subfiles that the target users in $\mathcal{S} \in \Sigma \backslash \{\mathcal{S}'\}$ request, which are cached in at least one cache of users in $\mathcal{Z}(k)$ due to

$$\mathcal{N}_\mathcal{S} \subseteq \mathcal{S} \backslash \{u\} \wedge \mathcal{Z}(k) \cap \mathcal{N}_\mathcal{S} \neq \emptyset \Rightarrow \mathcal{Z}(k) \cap \mathcal{S} \backslash \{u\} \neq \emptyset$$

Example 2. Consider a network with $K = N = 5, M = 2$, then $t = 2, s = 3$. Assume that $d_i = W_i$, we have a total of $\binom{K}{s} = 10$ user cooperation sets. For $\mathcal{S}_1 = \{1, 2, 3\}, \mathcal{S}_7 = \{2, 3, 4\}, \mathcal{S}_{10} = \{3, 4, 5\}$, they are omitted due to $\mathcal{T}_{\mathcal{S}_i} = \emptyset, i = 1, 7, 10$. For $\mathcal{S}_5 = \{1, 3, 5\}$ with $\mathcal{T}_{\mathcal{S}_5} = \mathcal{S}_5$, the signal

$$X_{\mathcal{S}_5} = W_{1, \{3,5\}} \oplus W_{3, \{1,5\}} \oplus W_{5, \{1,3\}},$$

is generated and multicasted to user $1, 3$ and 5.

Then for the left six sets, let $\mathbf{S} = \{\mathcal{S}_2, \mathcal{S}_3, \mathcal{S}_4, \mathcal{S}_6, \mathcal{S}_8, \mathcal{S}_9\}$, generate the conflict graph $\mathcal{H}_\mathbf{S}$ and color it by GCC. The conflict graph and coloring result are shown in Fig. 3.

Hence, the messages of $\mathcal{S}_2 =$ and $\mathcal{S}_4$ will be merged, resulting in $\Sigma_1 = \{\mathcal{S}_2, \mathcal{S}_4\}$ and the corresponding message

$$X_{\Sigma_1} = W_{4, \{1,2\}} \oplus W_{1, \{3,4\}}.$$

By multicasting X_{Σ_1} to user 1 and 4, user 1 can recover the subfile $W_{1, \{3,4\}}$ and user 4 can recover the subfile $W_{4, \{1,2\}}$.

Similarly, for $\Sigma_2 = \{\mathcal{S}_3, \mathcal{S}_6\}$ and $\Sigma_3 = \{\mathcal{S}_8, \mathcal{S}_9\}$, the messages

$$X_{\Sigma_2} = W_{5, \{1,2\}} \oplus W_{1, \{4,5\}}$$

$$X_{\Sigma_3} = W_{2, \{4,5\}} \oplus W_{5, \{2,3\}}$$

are generated and multicasted to the corresponding users, respectively.

After all the messages sent over the shared link, user 1 has access to 4 subfiles of W_1 in its own cache:

$$W_{1, \{1,2\}}, W_{1, \{1,3\}}, W_{1, \{1,4\}}, W_{1, \{1,4\}},$$

has access to 3 subfiles of W_1 in user 2's cache:

$$W_{1, \{2,3\}}, W_{1, \{2,4\}}, W_{1, \{2,5\}},$$

can solve $W_{1, \{3,5\}}$ from $X_{\mathcal{S}_5}$, solve $W_{1, \{3,4\}}$ from X_{Σ_1}, solve $W_{1, \{4,5\}}$ from X_{Σ_2}. Therefore user 1 can recover its required file W_1 because it has access to all the subfiles of W_1. Similarly for other users.

Hence all users can recover its required file after four coded messages sent, each size of $1/\binom{K}{t}$. $\qquad\qquad\qquad\qquad\qquad\qquad\qquad\qquad\qquad\qquad\qquad\square$

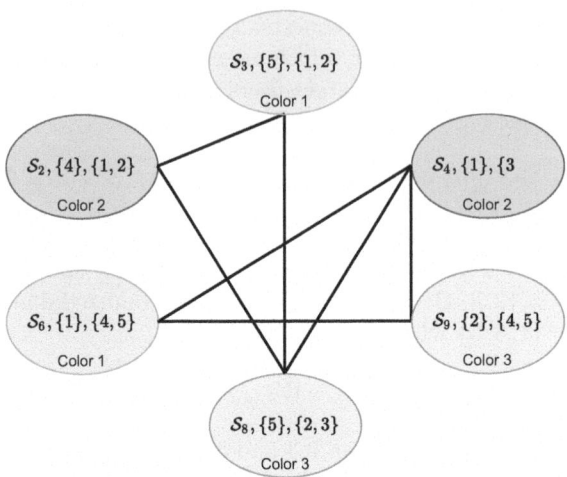

Fig. 3. Conflict graph of Example 2 with coloring by GCC, the vertices are labeled by { the user cooperation set, its target users set, its non-target users set }.

4   Placement Phase Design

In this section we focus on the design of the placement phase and a scheme base on the MAN placement is proposed. In the MAN scheme, each file is devided into $\binom{K}{t}$ subfiles of equal size, where $t = MK/N$. Each subfile will be stored in t users' caches to create more multicast opportunities. In our system model, there is some redundancy in the cache space that each user can access, due to the cache sharing between cooperative users, shown in Example 3.

Example 3. Consider a system with $K = 6$ users, $N = 6$ files, each user equipped with a cache of size $M = 2$, the MAN scheme gives the placement of Table 1, where $n \in \{1, \dots, 6\}$, each column refer to a user's cache. For the conciseness, when there is no ambiguity, the brackets and commas in the labels of subfiles are omitted, e.g. $W_{n,12}$ means $W_{n,\{1,2\}}$.

For user 2, $W_{n,12}, W_{n,23}, W_{n,13}$ appear twice in the caches it can access, respectively.

Table 1. Placement under MAN scheme in Example 3

User 1	User 2	User 3	User 4	User 5	User 6
$W_{n,12}$	$W_{n,23}$	$W_{n,34}$	$W_{n,45}$	$W_{n,56}$	$W_{n,16}$
$W_{n,13}$	$W_{n,24}$	$W_{n,35}$	$W_{n,46}$	$W_{n,15}$	$W_{n,26}$
$W_{n,14}$	$W_{n,25}$	$W_{n,36}$	$W_{n,14}$	$W_{n,25}$	$W_{n,36}$
$W_{n,15}$	$W_{n,26}$	$W_{n,13}$	$W_{n,24}$	$W_{n,35}$	$W_{n,46}$
$W_{n,16}$	$W_{n,12}$	$W_{n,23}$	$W_{n,34}$	$W_{n,45}$	$W_{n,56}$

Based on the MAN placement scheme, we use **coded prefetching** to reduce the cache size M, on the premise that the contents that each user can access remain unchanged. We propose two schemes for different case.

Let $t = MK/N$, we consider the system that t is an integer, i.e. $M \in 0, N/K, 2N/K, \ldots, N$. Besides, there is no redundancy at the case that $t = 1$, so the following two schemes only consider the case that $t \geq 2$.

4.1   Coded Prefetching Scheme A

Scheme A is suitable for the case where t is small, we first give the result:

$$t'_A = t * \left(1 - \frac{\binom{K-4}{t-2} + \binom{K-4}{t-3}}{\binom{K-1}{t-1}}\right) \tag{10}$$

i.e. we can almost achieve the rate $R_{GCC}(M), M = tN/K$ at $M' = t'_A N/K$. In this scheme, we need to send some extra packets in delivery phase. The rate-memory tradeoff

$$R_A(M') = R_{GCC}(M) + \frac{\binom{K-4}{t-2}}{\binom{K}{t}}. \tag{11}$$

Here is the describe of the scheme A. After placing the subfiles according to the MAN scheme, we proceed to modify the cache contents through two steps:

– **Step 1**: For each user i, delete the subfiles $\mathcal{W}_1(i) = (W_{n,\{i-2,i,i+1\}\cup\mathcal{X}})$ and $\mathcal{W}_2(i) = (W_{n,\{i-2,i-1,i\}\cup\mathcal{X}})$, then place the coded subfiles

$$\mathcal{W}_1(i) \oplus \mathcal{W}_2(i) = (W_{n,\{i-2,i,i+1\}\cup\mathcal{X}} \oplus W_{n,\{i-2,i-1,i\}\cup\mathcal{X}}),$$

where $\mathcal{X} \in \binom{[K]\setminus\{i-2,i-1,i,i+1\}}{t-3}$. For the case where $t = 2$, Step 1 is omitted.

In Step 1, we delete $2\binom{K-4}{t-3}$ subfiles, then place $\binom{K-4}{t-3}$ coded subfiles.

– **Step 2**: For each user i, delete the subfiles $\mathcal{W}_3(i) = (W_{n,\{i,i+1\}\cup\mathcal{X}})$ and $\mathcal{W}_4(i) = (W_{n,\{i-2,i\}\cup\mathcal{X}})$, then place the coded subfiles

$$\mathcal{W}_3(i) \oplus \mathcal{W}_4(i) = (W_{n,\{i,i+1\}\cup\mathcal{X}} \oplus W_{n,\{i-2,i\}\cup\mathcal{X}}),$$

where $\mathcal{X} \in \binom{[K]\setminus\{i-2,i-1,i,i+1\}}{t-2}$.

In Step 2, we delete $2\binom{K-4}{t-2}$ subfiles, then place $\binom{K-4}{t-2}$ subfiles. In delivery phase, we should send $\mathcal{W}_4(2)_{d_1} \oplus \mathcal{W}_3(K)_{d_K}$ to the "edge" user i.e. user 1 and user K.

The proof of the fact that the contents that each user can access remain unchanged after these two steps is shown in Appendix A.

Note that in MAN scheme we place $\binom{K-1}{t-1}$ subfiles in each cache, and the extra messages we send in delivery phase is of size $\binom{K-4}{t-2}/\binom{K}{t}$, we have (10) and (11).

4.2   Coded Prefetching Scheme B

Scheme B is suitable for bigger t, we first give the result:

$$t'_B = t * \left(1 - \frac{\binom{K-2}{t-2}}{2\binom{K-1}{t-1}}\right) \tag{12}$$

i.e. we can achieve the rate $R_{GCC}(M), M = tN/K$ at $M' = t'_B N/K$. The rate-memory tradeoff

$$R_B(M') = R_{GCC}(M). \tag{13}$$

Here is the describe of the scheme B. In Scheme B, we first divide each file W_n into two parts of equal size W_n^1, W_n^2 and place them in two steps.

- **Step 1**: Place all the files W_n^1 in MAN scheme, which fills half of the cache. For each user i numbered even, $i \neq K$, delete the subfiles $\mathcal{W}_5(i) = (W_{n,\{i-1,i,i+1\}\cup\mathcal{X}}^1), \mathcal{W}_6(i) = (W_{n,\{i-1,i\}\cup\mathcal{Y}}^1), \mathcal{W}_7(i) = (W_{n,\{i,i+1\}\cup\mathcal{Y}}^1)$, then place the coded subfiles

$$\mathcal{W}_6(i) \oplus \mathcal{W}_7(i) = (W_{n,\{i-1,i\}\cup\mathcal{Y}}^1 \oplus W_{n,\{i,i+1\}\cup\mathcal{Y}}^1),$$

  where $\mathcal{X} \in \binom{[K]\setminus\{i-1,i,i+1\}}{t-3}, \mathcal{Y} \in \binom{[K]\setminus\{i-1,i,i+1\}}{t-2}$. If K is even, then for user K, delete the subfiles $W_{n,\{K-1,K\}\cup\mathcal{Q}}^1$, where $\mathcal{Q} \in \binom{[K]\setminus\{K-1,K\}}{t-2}$.

In Step 1, each user numbered even can still access the subfiles deleted from adjacent users' caches. Each user j numbered odd can access $\mathcal{W}_6(j+1)$ and $\mathcal{W}_7(j-1)$ so it can recover $\mathcal{W}_7(j+1)$ and $\mathcal{W}_6(j-1)$. Therefore after Step 1, the contents(W_n^1) that each user can access remain unchanged for each user.

- **Step 2**: Place all the files W_n^2 in MAN scheme, which fills rest half of the cache. For each user i numbered odd, $i \neq 1, K$, delete the subfiles $\mathcal{W}_5(i) = (W_{n,\{i-1,i,i+1\}\cup\mathcal{X}}^2), \mathcal{W}_6(i) = (W_{n,\{i-1,i\}\cup\mathcal{Y}}^2), \mathcal{W}_7(i) = (W_{n,\{i,i+1\}\cup\mathcal{Y}}^2)$, then place the coded subfiles

$$\mathcal{W}_6(i) \oplus \mathcal{W}_7(i) = (W_{n,\{i-1,i\}\cup\mathcal{Y}}^2 \oplus W_{n,\{i,i+1\}\cup\mathcal{Y}}^2),$$

  where $\mathcal{X} \in \binom{[K]\setminus\{i-1,i,i+1\}}{t-3}, \mathcal{Y} \in \binom{[K]\setminus\{i-1,i,i+1\}}{t-2}$. For user 1, delete the subfiles $W_{n,\{1,2\}\cup\mathcal{Q}}^2$, where $\mathcal{Q} \in \binom{[K]\setminus\{1,2\}}{t-2}$. If K is odd, then for user K, delete the subfiles $W_{n,\{K-1,K\}\cup\mathcal{P}}^2$, where $\mathcal{P} \in \binom{[K]\setminus\{K-1,K\}}{t-2}$.

Step 2 is a repetition of Step 1 for each user numbered odd and W_n^2. Therefore after Step 2, the contents(W_n^2) that each user can access remain unchanged for each user.

$\binom{K-2}{t-2}/2$ subfiles are deleted for each user, so we have (12) and (13) proved.

Table 2. Placement under Scheme A in Example 3

User 1	User 2	User 3	User 4	User 5	User 6
$W_{n,13}$	$W_{n,24}$	$W_{n,35}$	$W_{n,46}$	$W_{n,15}$	$W_{n,26}$
$W_{n,14}$	$W_{n,25}$	$W_{n,36}$	$W_{n,14}$	$W_{n,25}$	$W_{n,36}$
$W_{n,15} \oplus W_{n,12}$	$W_{n,26} \oplus W_{n,23}$	$W_{n,13} \oplus W_{n,34}$	$W_{n,24} \oplus W_{n,45}$	$W_{n,35} \oplus W_{n,56}$	$W_{n,46} \oplus W_{n,16}$
$W_{n,16}$	$W_{n,12}$	$W_{n,23}$	$W_{n,34}$	$W_{n,45}$	$W_{n,56}$

Table 3. Placement under Scheme B in Example 3

User 1	User 2	User 3	User 4	User 5	User 6
$W^1_{n,12}$		$W^1_{n,34}$		$W^1_{n,56}$	$W^1_{n,16}$
$W^1_{n,13}$	$W^1_{n,24}$	$W^1_{n,35}$	$W^1_{n,46}$	$W^1_{n,15}$	$W^1_{n,26}$
$W^1_{n,14}$	$W^1_{n,25}$	$W^1_{n,36}$	$W^1_{n,14}$	$W^1_{n,25}$	$W^1_{n,36}$
$W^1_{n,15}$	$W^1_{n,26}$	$W^1_{n,13}$	$W^1_{n,24}$	$W^1_{n,35}$	$W^1_{n,46}$
$W^1_{n,16}$	$W^1_{n,12} \oplus W^1_{n,23}$	$W^1_{n,23}$	$W^1_{n,34} \oplus W^1_{n,45}$	$W^1_{n,45}$	
	$W^2_{n,23}$		$W^2_{n,45}$		$W^2_{n,16}$
$W^2_{n,13}$	$W^2_{n,24}$	$W^2_{n,35}$	$W^2_{n,46}$	$W^2_{n,15}$	$W^2_{n,26}$
$W^2_{n,14}$	$W^2_{n,25}$	$W^2_{n,36}$	$W^2_{n,14}$	$W^2_{n,25}$	$W^2_{n,36}$
$W^2_{n,15}$	$W^2_{n,26}$	$W^2_{n,13}$	$W^2_{n,24}$	$W^2_{n,35}$	$W^2_{n,46}$
$W^2_{n,16}$	$W^2_{n,12}$	$W^2_{n,23} \oplus W^2_{n,34}$	$W^2_{n,34}$	$W^2_{n,45} \oplus W^2_{n,56}$	$W^2_{n,56}$

Table 2 and Table 3 shows the placement under scheme A and B in Example 3, respectively. In scheme A, we should send $W_{d_1,26} \oplus W_{d_6,16}$ to user 1 and 6 in delivery phase.

Finally we choose the scheme with lower rate, i.e.

$$R_{final}(M) = \min\{R_A(M), R_B(M)\}.$$

5   Performance Analysis

In this section, we show the performance of our proposed scheme.

As mentioned earlier, our proposed system model can be considered a MACC system with L values between 2 and 3. The key differentiation from existing MACC systems is the asymmetrical network topology.

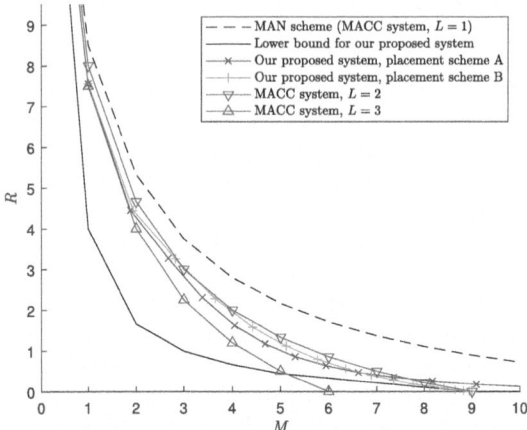

Fig. 4. Rate R on the shared link in the delivery phase as a function of memory size M for $N = K = 18$. Scheme A performs better at lower M. Scheme B performs better at bigger M and reaches zero at $t = N/2 = 9$.

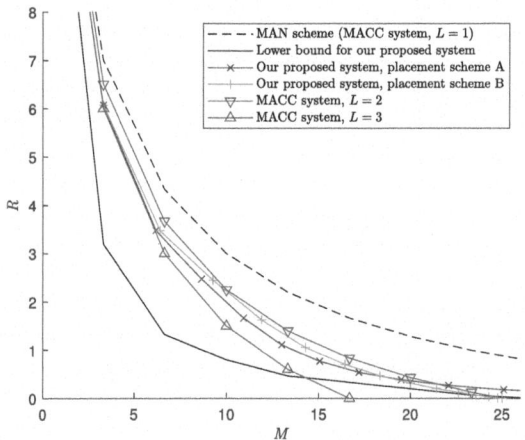

Fig. 5. Rate R on the shared link in the delivery phase as a function of memory size M for $N = 50, K = 15$. Scheme A performs better at lower M. Scheme B performs better at bigger M and reaches zero at $t = N/2 = 25$.

As shown in Fig. 4, the delivery rate of our scheme (system) is between the rate of MACC system with $L = 2$ and $L = 3$ in [3], which matches the system settings: most of users have the access to three caches as the MACC system with $L = 3$, but the bottleneck of the system is the edge users, who only have the access to two caches as the MACC system with $L = 2$. The placement scheme A performs better at small M. With the increase of M, the rate of placement scheme B decreases faster than scheme A and achieves 0 rate at $M = N/2$. Fig. 5 shows the case of $N = 50, K = 15$.

The lower bound is

$$R(M) \geq \max_{s \in \{1,\ldots,\min\{N,K\}\}} \left(s - \frac{\min(s+1, K)}{\lfloor N/s \rfloor} M \right). \tag{14}$$

The proof of the lower bound is shown in Appendix B

6   Conclusion

In this paper, we proposed a novel model of coded caching inspired by the V2V scene, allowing communication between cooperative users. Based on this model, we designed a scheme with coded prefetching to reduce the redundancy in the cache contents and Greedy Constrained Coloring to exploit the multicasting opportunities. We showed its performance, comparing to the Multi-access Coded Caching system.

Acknowledgement. This work was supported by the National Science Foundation of China (NSFC) with grant no. 62271514 and the Science, Technology and Innovation Commission of Shenzhen Municipality with grant no. JCYJ20210324120002007, and ZDSYS20210623091807023.

A   Proof of Placement Scheme A

A.1   Proof of Step 1

Here we show the proof of the fact that after step 1, the contents that each user can access remain unchanged.

Table 4. Subfiles placed in two users after Step 1 in Scheme A.

User i	User $i+1$
$\mathcal{W}_1(i) \oplus \mathcal{W}_2(i)$	$\mathcal{W}_1(i+1) \oplus \mathcal{W}_2(i+1)$
$\mathcal{W}_n 2(i+1)$	$\mathcal{W}_1(i)$

For two users $i, i+1$, shown in Table 4, $\mathcal{W}_1(i)$ is cached in the cache of user $i+1$, $\mathcal{W}_2(i+1)$ is cached in the cache of user i. Table 5 shows which users will be and will not be included in the labels of the subfiles in these sets. Due to the fact

$$\mathcal{W}_1(i) \cap \mathcal{W}_1(i+1) = \emptyset, \tag{15a}$$
$$\mathcal{W}_1(i) \cap \mathcal{W}_2(i+1) = \emptyset, \tag{15b}$$
$$\mathcal{W}_2(i) \cap \mathcal{W}_2(i+1) = \emptyset, \tag{15c}$$

both of them can recover $\mathcal{W}_2(i)$ and $\mathcal{W}_1(i+1)$.

Table 5. Labels in the subfiles sets in Step 1, Scheme A.

set	contains	not contains
$\mathcal{W}_1(i)$	$i-2, i, i+1$	i
$\mathcal{W}_2(i)$	$i-2, i-1, i$	$i+1$
$\mathcal{W}_1(i+1)$	$i-1, i, i+1$	i
$\mathcal{W}_2(i+1)$	$i-1, i, i+1$	$i+2$

The label of subfile in $W_1(i)$ must contains i, and the label of subfile in $W_1(i+1)$ must not contains i, therefore we have (15a). The label of subfile in $W_2(i+1)$ must contains $i-1$, and the label of subfile in $W_1(i)$ must not contains $i-1$, therefore we have (15b). The label of subfile in $W_2(i+1)$ must contains $i+1$, and the label of subfile in $W_2(i)$ must not contains $i+1$, therefore we have (15c).

Therefore after step 1, the contents that each user can access remain unchanged.

A.2   Proof of Step 2

Table 6. Subfiles placed in three users after Step 2 in Scheme A.

User $i-1$	User i	User $i+1$
$\mathcal{W}_3(i-1) \oplus \mathcal{W}_4(i-1)$	$\mathcal{W}_3(i) \oplus \mathcal{W}_4(i)$	$\mathcal{W}_3(i+1) \oplus \mathcal{W}_4(i+1)$
part of $\mathcal{W}_4(i+1)$	$\mathcal{W}_3(i-1)$	$\mathcal{W}_3(i)$

For user $i, i \neq 1, K$, shown in Table 6 it can access $W_3(i)$ in the cache of user $i+1$, then recover $W_4(i)$ from the coded subfiles. It can access $W_3(i-1)$ in its own cache, then recover $W_4(i-1)$ from the coded subfiles in the cache of user $i-1$. Then it can access $W_4(i+1)$ in the cache of user $i-1$, and recover

Table 7. Labels in the subfiles sets in Step 2, Scheme A.

set	contains	not contains
$\mathcal{W}_3(i-1)$	$i-i, i$	$i-3, i-2$
$\mathcal{W}_3(i)$	$i, i+1$	$i-2, i-1$
$\mathcal{W}_3(i+1)$	$i+1, i+2$	$i-1, i$
$\mathcal{W}_4(i-1)$	$i-3, i-1$	$i-2, i$
$\mathcal{W}_4(i)$	$i-2, i$	$i-1, i+1$
$\mathcal{W}_4(i+1)$	$i-1, i+1$	$i, i+2$

$\mathcal{W}_3(i+1)$ from the coded subfiles in the cache of user $i+1$. Table 7 shows which users will be and will not be included in the labels of the subfiles in these sets.

We should prove the fact

$$\mathcal{W}_3(i) \cap \mathcal{W}_3(i+1) = \emptyset, \tag{16a}$$

$$\mathcal{W}_3(i) \cap \mathcal{W}_4(i+1) = \emptyset, \tag{16b}$$

$$\mathcal{W}_4(i+1) \cap \mathcal{W}_3(i-1) = \emptyset, \tag{16c}$$

The label of subfile in $\mathcal{W}_3(i)$ must contains i, and the label of subfile in $\mathcal{W}_3(i+1)$ must not contains i, therefore we have (16a). The label of subfile in $\mathcal{W}_3(i)$ must contains i, and the label of subfile in $\mathcal{W}_4(i+1)$ must not contains i, therefore we have (16b). The label of subfile in $\mathcal{W}_3(i-1)$ must contains i, and the label of subfile in $\mathcal{W}_4(i+1)$ must not contains i, therefore we have (16c). Besides, althrough $\mathcal{W}_4(i+1) \cap \mathcal{W}_4(i-1) \neq \emptyset$, user i can first recover $\mathcal{W}_4(i-1)$ then it can access all subfiles in $\mathcal{W}_4(i+1)$.

For user 1, it does not have the access of $\mathcal{W}_4(2)$ because user 0 does not exist. For user K, it does not have the access of $\mathcal{W}_3(K)$ because user $K+1$ does not exist. We send

$$X = \mathcal{W}_4(2)_{d_1} \oplus \mathcal{W}_3(K)_{d_K}$$

to user 1 and K in delivery phase, with some reordering of the subfiles.

User 1 can access $\mathcal{W}_3(K)_{d_1}$ in its own cache so it can solve $\mathcal{W}_4(2)_{d_1}$. User K can access $\mathcal{W}_4(2)_{d_K}$ except the subfiles in

$$\mathcal{W}_8 = \mathcal{W}_4(2)_{d_K} \cap \mathcal{W}_4(K)_{d_K} = W_{d_K, \{2, K-2, K\} \cup \mathcal{X}}$$

where $\mathcal{X} \in \binom{[K] \backslash \{K-2, K-1, K, 1, 2, 3\}}{t-3}$.

Let

$$\mathcal{W}_9 = W_{d_K, \{1, 2, K\} \cup \mathcal{X}}$$

, note that $\mathcal{W}_9 \subset \mathcal{W}_3(K)_{d_K}$. Here $\mathcal{W}_9$ contains the subfiles coded with the subfiles in $\mathcal{W}_8$ stored in the cache of user K. When constructing message X, we should aviod the subfiles in $\mathcal{W}_8 \oplus \mathcal{W}_9$ appear in X by reordering the subfiles in $\mathcal{W}_4(2)_{d_1}$ and $\mathcal{W}_3(K)_{d_K}$, to make sure that user K can solve $\mathcal{W}_9$, then solve $\mathcal{W}_8$.

We should prove that the number of subfiles in $\mathcal{W}_9$ does not exceed half of the number of subfiles in $\mathcal{W}_3(K)_{d_K}$, i.e.

$$\binom{K-6}{t-3} \leq \binom{K-4}{t-2} \Big/ 2 \tag{17}$$

where $0 < t < K$, t and K are integer. Expand (17) we have

$$K^2 - 5K + 2t^2 - 2Kt + 12 \geq 0 \tag{18}$$

Let $g(K, t)$ be the left-hand side of (18), $g(K, t)$ reaches its minimum value at $K = 5, t = 2.5$. It can be easily proved that $g(K, t) \geq 0$ when $4 \leq K \leq 6, 2 \leq t \leq 4$. Therefore we have (17) proved.

A.3   Proof of the Independence of Step 1 and Step 2

In the last part of the proof, we show that we modify the different subfiles in Step 1 and Step 2. We proof the fact

$$W_1(i) \cap W_3(i) = \emptyset, \tag{19a}$$
$$W_1(i) \cap W_4(i) = \emptyset, \tag{19b}$$
$$W_2(i) \cap W_3(i) = \emptyset, \tag{19c}$$
$$W_2(i) \cap W_4(i) = \emptyset, \tag{19d}$$

The users will be and will not be included in the labels of the subfiles in these sets are shown in Table 5 and Table 7. The label of subfile in $W_1(i)$ must contains $i-2$, and the label of subfile in $W_3(i)$ must not contains $i-2$, therefore we have (19a). The label of subfile in $W_1(i)$ must contains $i+1$, and the label of subfile in $W_4(i)$ must not contains $i+1$, therefore we have (19b). The label of subfile in $W_2(i)$ must contains $i-2$, and the label of subfile in $W_3(i)$ must not contains $i-2$, therefore we have (19c). The label of subfile in $W_2(i)$ must contains $i-1$, and the label of subfile in $W_4(i)$ must not contains $i-1$, therefore we have (19d).

B   Proof of the Lower Bound

Let $s \in \{1, \ldots, \min\{N, K\}\}$ and select arbitrary s users, called $\mathcal{U}_s$. Let $\mathcal{L}(\mathcal{U}_s)$ be the caches that users in $\mathcal{U}_s$ can access and $L(\mathcal{U}_s) = |\mathcal{L}(\mathcal{U}_s)|$, i.e. the number of the caches that users in $\mathcal{U}_s$ can access, we have

$$L(\mathcal{U}_s) \geq s + 1. \tag{20}$$

Note that $L(\mathcal{U}_s) = s + 1$ only when $\mathcal{U}_s = [s]$ or $\mathcal{U}_s = [K] \backslash [K - s]$. For any other case, $L(\mathcal{U}_s) > s + 1$.

For the users in $\mathcal{U}_s$, there exist a user demand and a corresponding input to the shared link, say X_1, such that X_1 and $\mathcal{L}(\mathcal{U}_s)$ determine the file $W_1, \ldots, W_s$. Similarly, there exist a user demand and a corresponding input to the shared link, say X_2, such that X_2 and $\mathcal{L}(\mathcal{U}_s)$ determine the file $W_{s+1}, \ldots, W_{2s}$. Continue in the same manner selecting $X_3, \ldots, X_{\lfloor N/s \rfloor}$, we have $X_1, \ldots, X_{\lfloor N/s \rfloor}$ and $\mathcal{L}(\mathcal{U}_s)$ determine the files $W_1, \ldots, W_{s\lfloor N/s \rfloor}$.

Consider the cut separating $X_1, \ldots, X_{\lfloor N/s \rfloor}$ and $\mathcal{L}(\mathcal{U}_s)$ from the corresponding users. By the cut-set bound,

$$\lfloor N/s \rfloor R(M) + L(\mathcal{U}_s)M \geq s \lfloor N/s \rfloor.$$

Solving for R and optimizing over all possible s and $\mathcal{U}_s$, we have (14) proofed.

References

1. Asadi, B., Ong, L.: Centralized caching with shared caches in heterogeneous cellular networks. In: 2019 IEEE 20th International Workshop on Signal Processing Advances in Wireless Communications (SPAWC), pp. 1–5 (2019). https://doi.org/10.1109/SPAWC.2019.8815401

2. Dutta, M., Thomas, A.: Decentralized coded caching for shared caches. IEEE Commun. Lett. **25**(5), 1458–1462 (2021). https://doi.org/10.1109/LCOMM.2021.3052237

3. Hachem, J., Karamchandani, N., Diggavi, S.N.: Coded caching for multi-level popularity and access. IEEE Trans. Inf. Theory **63**(5), 3108–3141 (2017). https://doi.org/10.1109/TIT.2017.2664817

4. Ibrahim, A.M., Zewail, A.A., Yener, A.: Device-to-device coded-caching with distinct cache sizes. IEEE Trans. Commun. **68**(5), 2748–2762 (2020). https://doi.org/10.1109/TCOMM.2020.2970950

5. Ji, M., Caire, G., Molisch, A.F.: Fundamental limits of caching in wireless D2D networks. IEEE Trans. Inf. Theory **62**(2), 849–869 (2016). https://doi.org/10.1109/TIT.2015.2504556

6. Ji, M., Tulino, A.M., Llorca, J., Caire, G.: Order-optimal rate of caching and coded multicasting with random demands. IEEE Trans. Inf. Theory **63**(6), 3923–3949 (2017). https://doi.org/10.1109/TIT.2017.2695611

7. Maddah-Ali, M.A., Niesen, U.: Fundamental limits of caching. IEEE Trans. Inf. Theory **60**(5), 2856–2867 (2014). https://doi.org/10.1109/TIT.2014.2306938

8. Maddah-Ali, M.A., Niesen, U.: Decentralized coded caching attains order-optimal memory-rate tradeoff. IEEE/ACM Trans. Networking **23**(4), 1029–1040 (2015). https://doi.org/10.1109/TNET.2014.2317316

9. Namboodiri, K.K.K., Rajan, B.S.: Improved lower bounds for multi-access coded caching. IEEE Trans. Commun. **70**(7), 4454–4468 (2022). https://doi.org/10.1109/TCOMM.2022.3174890

10. Niesen, U., Maddah-Ali, M.A.: Coded caching with nonuniform demands. IEEE Trans. Inf. Theory **63**(2), 1146–1158 (2017). https://doi.org/10.1109/TIT.2016.2639522

11. Parrinello, E., Ünsal, A., Elia, P.: Fundamental limits of coded caching with multiple antennas, shared caches and uncoded prefetching. IEEE Trans. Inf. Theory **66**(4), 2252–2268 (2020). https://doi.org/10.1109/TIT.2019.2955384

12. Reddy, K.S., Karamchandani, N.: Rate-memory trade-off for multi-access coded caching with uncoded placement. IEEE Trans. Commun. **68**(6), 3261–3274 (2020). https://doi.org/10.1109/TCOMM.2020.2980817

13. Tang, Y., Heydaryan, F., Luo, J.: Distributed coding in a multiple access environment. Found. Trends. Netw. **12**(4), 260–412 (2018). https://doi.org/10.1561/1300000063

14. Tian, C.: Symmetry, demand types and outer bounds in caching systems. In: 2016 IEEE International Symposium on Information Theory (ISIT), pp. 825–829 (2016). https://doi.org/10.1109/ISIT.2016.7541414

Study on Demand Forecasting and Scheduling Routes of Shared Bicycles

He Wang[1]([✉]), Haoyang Zhou[1], Wenbing Yang[2], Xiangkai Qiu[2], and Shangjing Lin[1]

[1] Institute of Electronic Engineering, Beijing University of Posts and Telecommunications,
Beijing, China
2206574108@qq.com, {zhouhaoyang,linshangjing}@bupt.edu.cn
[2] Institute of Artificial Intelligence, Beijing University of Posts and Telecommunications,
Beijing, China

Abstract. This paper endeavors to address the pressing issue of resource wastage in shared bicycles by proposing an innovative approach to optimize their utilization and cater to the demands of urban residents. The proposed solution involves devising an efficient vehicle dispatch roadmap based on predictive demand modeling. Leveraging the open-source Beijing shared bicycle dataset, the research analyzes the spatio-temporal correlations within order data. The Temporal Graph Convolutional Network (T-GCN) is selected as the predictive model to forecast shared bicycle demand. Subsequently, the Genetic Algorithm (GA) is employed to determine an optimal dispatch route, thereby significantly improving the overall utilization rate of shared bicycles.

Keywords: shared bicycle · spatio-temporal prediction · centralized dispatching

Foreword

In recent years, shared bicycles have become popular. However, there are several problems associated with them. The most significant problem that affects the user experience is the imbalance between supply and demand, leading to low turnover. While scheduling shared bicycles can alleviate this issue, there may still be instances where users have to wait for a long time due to scheduling delays. Therefore, the key to addressing this problem is to effectively use the scheduling method.

Many current algorithms rely on static scheduling methods, which schedule bicycles overnight based on the usage from the previous day in order to meet the needs of users for the following day. However, this method requires data from the previous day and since the flow of bicycles can vary from day to day, the scheduling outcome may not be optimal and there may still be a shortage of bicycles.

The flow of shared bicycles has a certain regularity in time and space. For instance, when it comes to time, the need for bicycles on weekdays remains consistent across most areas. In terms of location, areas with a higher demand for shared bicycles tend to

Fund project: This work is supported by Research Innovation Fund for College Students of Beijing University of Posts and Telecommunications funding under grant 202302018.

X. Chen et al. (Eds.): IoTaaS 2023, LNICST 585, pp. 414–424, 2025.
https://doi.org/10.1007/978-3-031-70507-6_31

have specific amenities such as homes, subway stations, and entertainment areas. While it is not possible to directly compare data from the first day to the second day, a deep learning algorithm can be utilized to make predictions. This algorithm takes into account the spatio-temporal characteristics of the data, resulting in more accurate predictions. These predictions are then fed into a scheduling algorithm, which produces a scheduling map. This map can be used to schedule cars in a way that meets the needs of users during various time periods.

At present, most of the solutions for traffic prediction are based on neural networks. Songjiang Li et al. [1] proposed an accurate multi-task learning recurrent neural network model (MTL-RNN) for short-term traffic prediction on highway networks, but it is limited to short-term changes. Shuyun Qian [2] integrated multi-graph convolution and attention mechanisms into the Seq2Seq framework for long-time traffic prediction, yet disregarded the spatial correlation of data. Jiansong Liu [3] introduced the Spatio-Temporal Graph-CoordAttention network (STGCA), which considers both temporal and spatial dimensions, but its prediction range is small, limiting its applicability on a large scale. Qiwen Yang [4] developed an Adaptive Parallel Structured Neural Network (APSNN) to address consistency problems in neural network training, but it struggles to adapt to the number of hidden nodes, affecting the neural network structure. Ming Wang [5] proposed a multi-timescale spatio-temporal graph network model, but it lacks stability.

Outside the realm of neural networks, Yusen Chen [6] designed a dynamic prediction system focused on highway networks, but its migration to shared bicycle prediction poses challenges.

In the realm of scheduling algorithms, the main focus has been on static scheduling. Hui Liu et al. [7] employed a modified hybrid taboo-particle swarm algorithm to address the problem. Zhiyong Zhang et al. [8] proposed an ant colony algorithm-based approach to optimize the model. Jiantong Zhang et al. [9] explored the use of Variable Neighborhood Search (VNS) algorithm to find local optimal solutions. Jun Zhou et al. [10] presented an equilibrium strategy for integrated bicycle scheduling around subway stations using multi-model technology, combining the home range method of animals in ecology and mean-shift clustering analysis. Ruochen Kong [11] opted for the genetic algorithm to satisfy the demand for bicycles on campus. Zichun Hu [12] performed scheduling area division through K-means clustering analysis and further improved the genetic algorithm to handle peak period scheduling.

All the above algorithms can schedule shared bicycles, but their scheduling is not predicted in advance, and has a large lag, which can hardly meet the needs of peak users.

To address the aforementioned issues, this paper presents strategies to tackle shared bicycle demand prediction and scheduling challenges. The aim of this paper is to maximize bicycle utilization, enhance user experience, and minimize operational costs for enterprises.

1 Spatial and Temporal Characterization of Demand for Shared Bicycles

In this paper, we utilize the 2017 bike-sharing dataset of Haidian District, Beijing for analysis. The dataset comprises bike-sharing order data spanning 14 days, from 27th June to 10th July. The data information includes various attributes such as orderid, userid, bikeid, biketype, starttime, start_loc, and end_loc, as displayed in Table 1.

Table 1. Labels of the data set

label	data type	typology
orderid	int	1893973
userid	int	451147
bikeid	int	210617
biketype	int	1
starttime	datetime	2017/5/20 23:35
geohashed_start_loc	char	wx4snhx
geohashed_end_loc	char	wx4s nhj

The start and end positions are encrypted by Geohash and decoded to get the approximate latitude and longitude ranges.

The dataset was organized based on time, and the 14-day data was segmented into 355 hourly time periods. Subsequently, the location information from the data was extracted and subjected to clustering using the OPTICS algorithm to eliminate outliers. As a result, the primary bicycle usage area, representing the urban region, was identified. This area was further divided into grids of size 50 * 50 for subsequent data analysis and processing.

1.1 Time Dimension Correlation Analysis

Figure 1 illustrates the weekly change in shared bicycle orders within a grid. It shows that shared bicycle orders have a strong temporal correlation. The trend and number of daily order changes are nearly identical. Although there is a deviation in quantity on Saturdays and Sundays, the trend remains roughly the same.

1.2 Spatial Dimension Correlation Analysis

In order to analyze the spatial dimensions, the spatial distribution of all grid data at a specific time is shown in Fig. 2. Most orders are concentrated in the downtown area with few in the outskirts. At the same time, a small variation in order volume was noted in neighboring grids, indicating a strong correlation between bike flow and the surrounding environment.

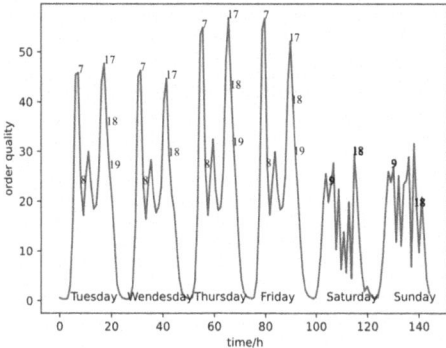

Fig. 1. The weekly change in shared bicycle orders within a grid

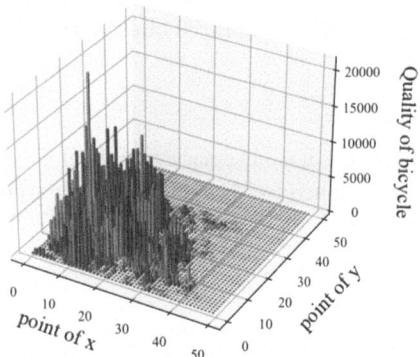

Fig. 2. Demand for bicycles in the whole grid at a specific time

2 Algorithm Design

In this paper, the following assumptions were made.

① The sum of the number of bicycles in all raster areas is constant without introducing additional bicycles.

② It is necessary to utilize the bicycles parked in the area as much as possible to meet the needs of users without introducing additional bicycles.

③ After scheduling, if the number of bicycles parked in a certain grid still cannot meet the demand of users, additional bicycles can be introduced in advance at this location, but the number of bicycles introduced must be minimal.

In predicting bicycle mobility, this paper utilizes the T-GCN algorithm which treats input data as spatio-temporal data resulting in more precise prediction outcomes. The T-GCN algorithm takes into account both spatial and temporal aspects of the data, making it very effective in boosting the accuracy of predictions.

To process the predicted data, the following variables are defined.

$Store_{t,x,y}$: At the beginning of the time period t, the number of bicycles parked at raster coordinates (x, y).

Out$_{t,x,y}$: During the time periodt, the number of bicycles ridden out from the raster coordinates(x, y).

In$_{t,x,y}$: During the time periodt, the number of bicycles ridden in to the taster coordinates(x, y).

Initially Store$_{0,x,y}$ is known data, and with the flow of time, the Store$_{t,x,y}$ is updated according to the Eq. (1).

$$Store_{t+1,x,y} = Store_{t,x,y} - Out_{t,x,y} + In_{t,x,y} \tag{1}$$

Therefore, the goal of this paper is to calculate the amount of scheduling needed Scheduled$_{t,x,y}$ at each moment by scheduling algorithm to make sure that Store$_{t+1,x,y}$ satisfies the Eq. (2).

$$Store_{t+1,x,y} = Store_{t,x,y} - Out_{t,x,y} + In_{t,x,y} + Scheduled_{t,x,y} \tag{2}$$

Therefore, the Store$_{t+1,x,y}$ can be stabilized after scheduling.

2.1 Objective Function

Based on the above assumptions, it is necessary to make the bicycles used in each time period come from the storage capacity of the region as much as possible, so the following indicator is proposed in Eq. (3).

$$DemandRate_t = \frac{\sum_{x,y} Min(Store_{t,x,y}, Out_{t,x,y})}{\sum_{x,y} Out_{t,x,y}} \tag{3}$$

It indicates the proportion of bicycles used that come from regional storage.

2.2 Algorithmic Ideas

Genetic Algorithm (GA) originated from the computer simulation research on biological systems, is a stochastic global search optimization method, which simulates the phenomena of replication, crossover and mutation occurring in natural selection and heredity, starting from any initial population, through random selection, crossover and mutation operations, to produce a group of individuals better suited to the environment, making the group evolve to better and better regions in the search space, so that generation after generation, it keeps reproducing and evolving, and finally converges to a group of individuals that are best adapted to the environment, so as to find a high-quality solution to the problem.

Specify the transportation path of the transporter as a series of sequential rasters, for example:

$$Routine = (x_1, y_1)(x_2, y_2)\ldots\ldots(x_n, y_n) \tag{4}$$

It can be assumed that the number of bicycles in reserve on the grid will match the demand for the next moment once the transportation vehicles have completed their scheduling and passed through each point. All bicycles on the route will be distributed based on the proportion of demand for each grid to the total demand. The number of bicycles on each grid will be balanced according to the Eq. (5). The total number of bicycles on the grids will be added up and then allocated accordingly.

$$\text{Store}_{t+1,x,y} = \frac{\sum_{i=1}^{\text{Routine}} \text{Store}_{t,x,y}}{n} \tag{5}$$

Now it is necessary to consider how to choose a suitable route so that at the end of the time period t, the reserves of bicycles can meet the demand of the next time period (so that the DemandRate of bicycles in the area of the next time period is as large as possible), which needs to have predicted the demand distribution of the next time period. In order to select the optimal scheduling points and routes, this paper needs to use genetic algorithm optimization twice.

Each raster is coded and expressed as an integer, and this integer is used as a gene on the chromosome as shown in the equation.

$$\text{Gene}_i = y_i \times 50 + x_i \tag{6}$$

The selected path is then represented as a chromosome as:

$$\text{Routine}_i = \text{Chorm}_i = (\text{Gene}_1, \text{Gene}_2 \ldots \ldots \text{Gene}_n) \tag{7}$$

Next set up the crossover and mutation operations in the genetic algorithm.

Crossover: Select a series of position genes from the chromosome, and exchange these genes in the two chromosomes, which is equivalent to exchanging the selection points on the path, so as to obtain two new scheduling paths. The specific operation is as follows: First, a random sequence of 01 with a length equal to the number of selected chromosome genes, such as 00100, is generated, and then the two selected crossover position genes at the corresponding position (that is, the gene with the number of 1 in the corresponding random sequence) are numerically exchanged, as shown in Fig. 3.

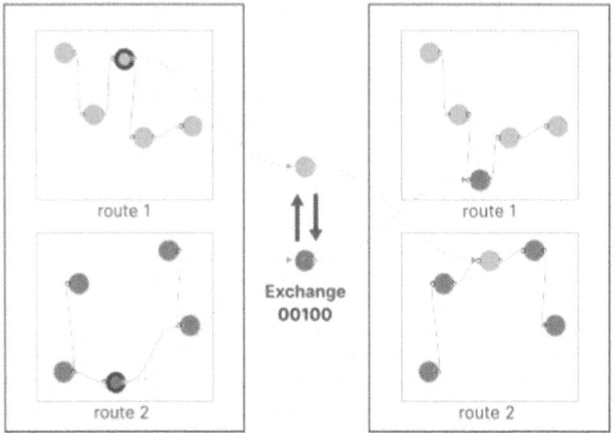

Fig. 3. Schematic diagram of cross operation

Mutation: To introduce mutation in the chromosome, a fixed probability p_i is assigned to each gene selected as a target. For a chromosome of length n, approximately $\sum_{i=0}^{n} p_i$ genes will be mutated. These selected genes are randomly displaced within the threshold value to obtain the path after mutation, as shown in Fig. 4.

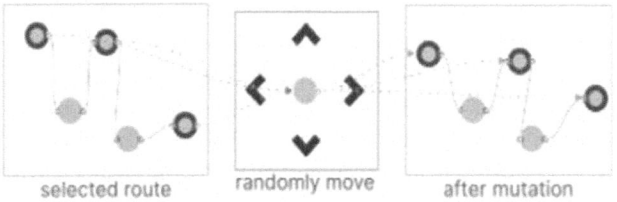

selected route   randomly move   after mutation

Fig. 4. Schematic diagram of mutation operation

Finally, the objective function for optimization is set, which calculates DemandRate after scheduling. This data employs a function to compute DemandRate after scheduling each grid based on the scheme.

3 Experiment

Based on the existing data, the prediction of the change in the number of bicycles is obtained by forecasting their demand and further using genetic algorithms, scheduling routes are given to improve the utilization of bicycles.

3.1 Demand Projections

Considering the number of shared bicycle orders as a set of time series data, after the corresponding preprocessing of the data, the obtained adjacency matrix and feature matrix are regarded as spatial data input into the T-GCN model, and the following prediction results can be obtained:

In the Fig. 5, the orange curve is the actual data and the blue is the forecast data. The forecast curve basically coincides with the actual curve, and the trend of the forecast curve still matches the actual in the time period where there is a large difference. Therefore, the prediction results have strong accuracy. In the subsequent scheduling program, the above data prediction results are utilized for scheduling.

3.2 Experimental Steps

No intervention Experiments

The changes in DemandRate without introducing bicycles are shown in the Fig. 6. As can be seen from the graph, DemandRate intermittently drops to around 0.8, indicating the continuous need to introduce new bicycles during this time period to meet the users' demand for bicycles.

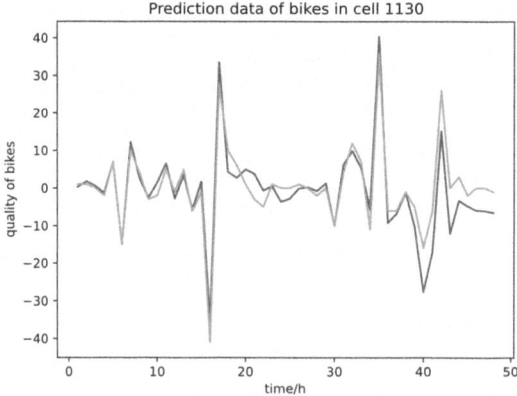

Fig. 5. Comparison of predicted and actual results of changes in the number of bicycles in a grid

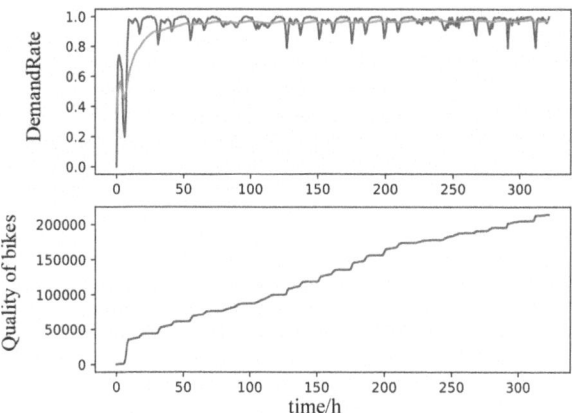

Fig. 6. Changes in the rate of demand for bicycles and changes in the number of bicycles under unmanned intervention

Demand Scheduling of Shared Bicycles Based on Genetic Algorithm

In order to accelerate the convergence of the genetic algorithm, the greedy algorithm was used once first, and the rasters with more remaining bicycles and more lack of bicycles were selected as the genes of the initial population, which enabled the algorithmic process to enter into a better population state in advance.

After the optimization is completed, the genetic algorithm is used to calculate the model of the TSP problem and the shortest path to the optimal scheduling point. This process also uses the greedy algorithm to calculate the better initial population, thus accelerating the convergence of the genetic algorithm.

After two optimization choices of genetic algorithm, we can get the scheduling route map of the dispatching vehicle in each time period (Figs. 7 and 8).

After receiving the scheduling plan, the dispatching vehicle can real-time schedule the available bicycles to the grids with a shortage of bicycles, thus accomplishing the scheduling task efficiently.

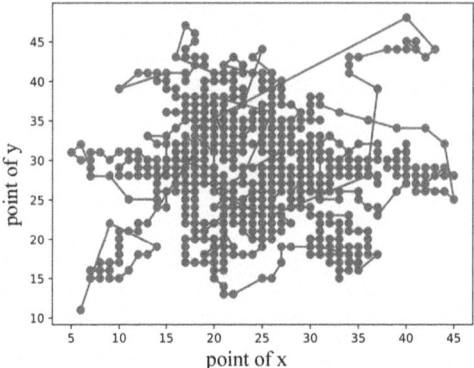

Fig. 7. Peak Dispatch Road map

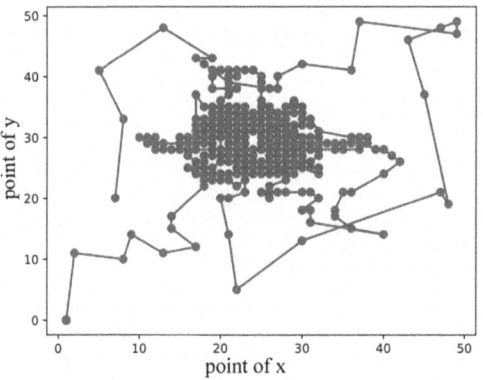

Fig. 8. Low-peak dispatch road map

The following results are obtained after implementing the scheduling scheme described above (Figs. 9 and 10):

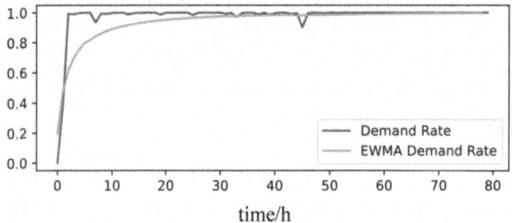

Fig. 9. Demand curve after genetic algorithm scheduling

Over time, the DemandRate gradually converges to 1 and does not suddenly decrease significantly most of the time, stabilizing the bicycle utilization rate at a high level. At the same time, the number of bicycles required drops to about 150,000 and approaches

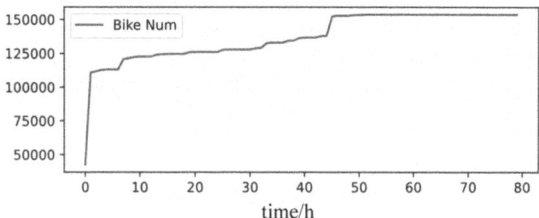

Fig. 10. Change in the number of bicycles after genetic algorithm scheduling

equilibrium in a short period of time, thus eliminating the need to continuously introduce new bicycles and achieving efficient bicycle utilization.

4 Conclusion

This paper examines the correlation between shared bicycle orders and time and location through spatio-temporal analysis to better cater to the needs of urban shared bicycles. The T-GCN algorithm is utilized to predict bicycle flow and generate prediction results. To improve the utilization and environment of shared bicycles, dispatching vehicles are introduced using a genetic algorithm to dispatch bicycles according to a designated route.

References

1. Songjiang, L., Shaojing, Z., Huamin, Y., et al.: Traffic prediction based on spatio-temporal correlation multitask neural network. Comput. Appl. Softw. **38**(09), 286–292 (2021)
2. Qian, S.: Research on long-time traffic prediction based on multi-graph convolution and attention. Mod. Comput. **29**(03), 34–38 (2023)
3. Liu, J.S., Kang, Y., Li, H., et al.: A spatio-temporal Graph-CoordAttention network for traffic flow prediction. Comput. Sci. **50**(S1), 568–574 (2023)
4. Qi-Wen, Y.A.N.G., Yue, L.I., Jun-Na, W.U., et al.: Traffic flow prediction based on adaptive parallel structure neural network. Comput. Meas. Control **31**(04), 42–48 (2023). https://doi.org/10.16526/j.cnki.11-4762/tp.2023.04.007
5. Wang, M., Peng, S., Huang, F.: A traffic flow prediction model based on multi-timescale spatio-temporal graph networks. Comput. Sci. **49**(08), 40–48 (2022)
6. Yusen, C.: Dynamic traffic prediction of highway networks. Highw. Transp. Sci. Technol. **04**, 1–8 (1995)
7. Liu, H., Zhong, J.: A particle swarm algorithm-based optimization method for interstation scheduling of shared bikes. J. Xichang Coll. (Nat. Sci. Ed.) **33**(02), 67–69 (2019). https://doi.org/10.16104/j.issn.1673-1891.2019.02.015
8. Zhang, Z.-Y., Zhang, X.: Shared bikes scheduling under users' travel uncertainty. IEEE Access **8**, 3123–3143 (2020). https://doi.org/10.1109/ACCESS.2019.2961628
9. Zhang, J., Dai, Q., Ding, Y.: Optimization study of shared bicycle scheduling considering demand splittable. Shanghai Manag. Sci. **45**(01), 119–125 (2023)
10. Zhou, J., Zhou, Q., Lin, Y.: The active home domain of shared bicycles around subway stations and its scheduling strategy. In: Academic Committee on Urban Transportation Planning, China Society of Urban Planning. Green-Wisdom-Integration-Proceedings of the 2021/2022 Annual Conference on Urban Transportation Planning in China. [Publisher unknown], pp. 19 (2022). https://doi.org/10.26914/c.cnkihy.2022.059197

11. Kong, R., He, S., Sheng, Y., et al.: A genetic algorithm-based scheduling method for shared bicycles on university campuses. Transp. Sci. Technol. **311**(02), 132–135 (2022)
12. Huizhi, C.: Optimization research on peak period shared bicycle scheduling based on improved genetic algorithm. Nanjing University of Finance and Economics (2021). https://doi.org/10.27705/d.cnki.gnjcj.2021.000298

Dynamic Scheduling Strategy Based on Demand Prediction of Shared Bike

Xiangkai Qiu[1]([✉]), Wenbing Yang[1], Haoyang Zhou[2], He Wang[2], and Shangjing Lin[2]

[1] Institute of Artificial Intelligence, Beijing University of Posts and Telecommunications,
Beijing, China
dnull123p@gmail.com
[2] Institute of Electronic Engineering, Beijing University of Posts and Telecommunications,
Beijing, China
{zhouhaoyang,linshangjing}@bupt.edu.cn

Abstract. This paper aims to address the issue of imbalanced supply and demand in shared bikes by proposing the concept of 'red packet bike', utilizing the open-source Beijing Shared Bike Dataset. The Temporal Graph Convolutional Network (T-GCN) is selected to predict the demand for shared bikes based on the analysis of spatio-temporal correlations in the order data. Additionally, a user incentive scheduling algorithm is designed using the breadth-first algorithm (BFS) and presented in the form of distributing the red packet bikes, thereby delegating the scheduling problem to the users to solve.

Keywords: Shared bike · Spatio-temporal analysis · User incentive scheduling

Foreword

Shared bike has become a popular mode of transportation for many people. However, it faces several challenges in daily life, such as low usage rates, imbalances in supply and demand, and increased costs for companies. These issues have led to a decrease in user satisfaction. Merely investing in more bikes will not solve these problems, as it can lead to road congestion and damage to existing bikes. A better solution is to schedule the bikes effectively. However, this is a challenging task, as the flow of shared bikes depends heavily on time and location. Finding the right scheduling method that meets users' needs is a difficult balance to achieve.

Most current strategies for managing shared bike systems rely on static rebalancing algorithms that schedule bikes at night to accommodate demand the next day. However, this approach has a delay and does not address the underlying issue of long-term imbalances between supply and demand for bicycles.

The use of shared bikes follows a certain pattern. Analyzing the relationship between bicycle usage and time and location reveals a strong correlation. This data can be treated as spatio-temporal data and used in deep learning algorithms to predict bicycle traffic.

Fund project: This work is supported by Research Innovation Fund for College Students of Beijing University of Posts and Telecommunications funding under grant 202302018.

X. Chen et al. (Eds.): IoTaaS 2023, LNICST 585, pp. 425–435, 2025.
https://doi.org/10.1007/978-3-031-70507-6_32

By adjusting for influencing factors, accurate predictions can be made. Platform can then use these predictions in real-time to deploy a user incentive system, encouraging users to schedule rides independently. By offering certain rewards, such as red envelopes, the platform can address the issue of supply and demand imbalance for shared bikes.

1 Related Work

1.1 Estimated Demand and Parking for Shared Bike

In the past, studies about predicting demand and parking for shared bikes relied on statistical models. Zou et al. [1] used a time series model to predict travel issues for users within an hour based on their usage information. Kamarianakis et al. [2] created a nonlinear traffic flow model using the time series model to analyze real-time traffic flow. However, statistical models struggle with processing large amounts of data and are better suited for making small-scale predictions.

Most studies on predicting shared bikes demand and parking patterns are based on deep learning techniques. Jia Xianguang et al.'s [3] Bi-LSTM model resulted in low accuracy when predicting e-hailing car trajectories. Lin et al. [4] used GNN to predict the hour-level demand of a single station in the station-based public bike network and employed the long and short term memory neural network to capture the temporal correlation of demand sequence. While they talked about the temporal correlation of shared bike data, their discussion on spatial correlation was limited. Qian Xingjian's [5] MGCN-TCN model, on the other hand, considered both the temporal correlation and spatial relationship between shared bike stations, resulting in more accurate predictions. Additionally, Miao Xiaofeng et al. [6] accounted for the impact of weather on the data and used the LSTM model to train separately through various feature inputs. Their findings showed that the addition of spatio-temporal features improved prediction accuracy.

It can be seen that considering only the time correlation does not produce ideal prediction results. Inputting shared bike data as spatio-temporal data can effectively improve prediction accuracy.

1.2 Recommended Routes for Dispatch Vehicles

Currently, academic research on the scheduling of shared bikes primarily concentrates on addressing the Vehicle Routing Problem (VRP). Shi Bing et al. [7] have attempted to delegate scheduling tasks to users through incentive strategies and multiple algorithms to reduce costs. Liu Xinyu et al. [8] have utilized a genetic algorithm and several rounds of algorithm iteration to establish static scheduling for bikes. HaiTao Xu et al. [9] have implemented the K-means and random forest algorithm to forecast bike flow and further used the enhanced genetic algorithm (E-GA) for scheduling to obtain a more precise scheduling strategy. Zeng Qiongyan [10] has developed a scheduling model for shared bikes that aims to maximize total profit by using the simulated annealing algorithm. Kadri [11] transformed the problem into an optimization issue of site balance and scheduling, proposed algorithms like the greedy algorithm, and gave examples to prove its practicality. Caggiani et al. [12] have focused on free-floating systems that allow bikes to be scheduled anywhere and utilized dynamic redistribution to enhance user satisfaction.

Many algorithms have been developed to optimize shared bike systems, but most rely on static scheduling algorithms which cannot keep up with the needs of today's society. Therefore, a new dynamic algorithm is necessary to solve the problem in real-time.

2 Definition of Concepts

In predicting the bike flow data, this paper adopts the T-GCN algorithm to make accurate predictions. To streamline the process, the paper simplifies the data representation by rasterizing the latitude and longitude coordinate information from the bike dataset, see 4.1.

The following assumptions are made:

① Without introducing additional bikes, the total number of bikes in all grid areas is constant.

② Without introducing additional bikes, it is necessary to maximise the use of bikes parking in the area to meet the needs of the users.

③ After scheduling, if the number of bikes parked in a grid still does not satisfy the user's demand, additional bikes can be brought forward to that location, but the number of bikes brought forward must be minimal.

For the purpose of processing the predicted data, some variables are declared in Table 1.

Table 1. Used variable declaration

Variable	Meaning
$Out_{t,x,y}$	the number of bikes ridden out at the time period t with raster coordinates (x, y)
$In_{t,x,y}$	the number of bikes ridden in at the time period t with raster coordinates (x, y)
$Scheduled_{t,x,y}$	The total number of bikes artificially introduced or dispatched to a grid with grid coordinates (x, y) in the t time period
$ScheduledIn_{t,x,y}$	The number of bikes introduced to a grid with grid coordinates (x, y) in the t time period
$ScheduledOut_{t,x,y}$	The number of bikes dispatched to a grid with grid coordinates (x, y) in the t time period
$Store_{t,x,y}$	the number of bikes parked at the time period t with raster coordinates (x, y)

$Store_{0,x,y}$ is known, and as time flows, $Store_{t,x,y}$ is updated according to the Eq. (1):

$$Store_{t+1,x,y} = Store_{t,x,y} - Out_{t,x,y} + In_{t,x,y} \qquad (1)$$

The goal of this paper is to compute, by means of a scheduling algorithm, the amount of $Scheduled_{t,x,y}$ required at each moment such that $Store_{t,x,y}$ satisfies the Eq. (2).

$$Store_{t+1,x,y} = Store_{t,x,y} - Out_{t,x,y} + In_{t,x,y} + Scheduled_{t,x,y} \tag{2}$$

The number of schedules in each raster at each moment in time is:

$$Scheduled_{t,x,y} = ScheduledIn_{t,x,y} - ScheduledOut_{t,x,y} \tag{3}$$

Besides, define the following variables:

Definition 1. *DemandRate$_t$* In order to improve the bike utilization rate, based on the assumption that the bikes used per unit of time will be derived as much as possible from the storage capacity in the area, the Eq. (4) are proposed.

$$DemandRate_t = \frac{\sum_{x,y} Min\left(Store_{t,x,y}, Out_{t,x,y}\right)}{\sum_{x,y} Out_{t,x,y}} \tag{4}$$

It indicates the proportion of bikes used that come from regional storage.

Definition 2 *DemandDegree* To issue red packets to users, the user's eligibility must first be determined based on scheduling conditions. The *DemandDegree* is then used to evaluate the user. It can be expressed as:

$$\begin{aligned}
DemandDegree = \max_{1 \le i \le 6} Out_{endtime+i,end_x,end_y} \times (7 - i) \\
- \max_{1 \le i \le 4} Out_{starttime+i,start_x,start_y} \times (5 - i)
\end{aligned} \tag{5}$$

DemandDegree is determined by two factors: the forecast demand for bicycles at the starting and ending locations, and the length of the forecast time from now. It represents how beneficial a user's bike route is to the scheduling strategy. The higher the *DemandDegree*, the more the user's cycling direction helps with bike scheduling and the more likely the user is to receive a red packet reward.

Definition 3 *redPacket* *redPacket* in this paper refers to the sum of red packets that users issue. To ensure normal scheduling and sufficient user participation, we inform users of nearby scheduling points when they scan the car. This encourages users to actively move to high-demand areas, helping to solve scheduling problems. The red packet amount can be adjusted based on the *DemandDegree*. Therefore, the red packet amounts are as follows:

$$redPacket = max\left(0, RidingCost - 1 + \frac{\ln(DemandDegree)}{6}\right) \tag{6}$$

3   Scheduling Frameworks

Red packet bike is by sending red packets to the user, inducing them to change the destination, so as to achieve the purpose of scheduling. On the definition of scheduling, that is, make $In_{t,x_1,y_1} - 1$, and make $In_{t,x_2,y_2} + 1$, and produce a certain cost of spending, which (x_1, y_1) is the user was intended to arrive at the grid, (x_2, y_2) is the scheduling of the user's actual arrival after the grid. The scheduling scheme can be expressed as a series of pairs of numbers such as $[(x_1, y_1), (x_2, y_2)]$. The scheduling algorithm needs to produce a scheme that minimizes the scheduling cost while making the DemandRate curve smooth at 1.

In this paper, red packet bike scheduling is divided into two solutions:

① Inducing the user to change the borrowing point: while recommending to the user the endpoints with a large red packet value.
② Inducing the user to change the point of return: when the user is ready to park the bike, he or she is guided to park the bike in a parking spot with a red packet.

The optimization objective is DemandRate. Let Δ DemandRate be the amount of DemandRate change before and after scheduling. Since redPacket ≥ 0 although Δ DemandRate can be positive or negative, it is necessary to ensure that each scheduling in the scheduling scheme can make Δ DemandRate > 0. It is easy to know that Δ DemandRate > 0 can only be made if a bike parked in a region with an overflow of bikes is moved to a region with an insufficient number of bikes. When a user intends to park the bike in an area with an overflow of bikes, the system initiates a search in the nearby grid areas to identify potential regions that require bike dispatching. The system then calculates the red packet value based on the nearest zone and sends this value as an incentive to the user. By doing so, the user is encouraged to change their bike's end position, thus actively participating in the bike redistribution process. This approach effectively induces users to contribute to the optimization of bike scheduling by moving bikes to areas where demand is higher, ultimately improving the overall bike-sharing system's efficiency.

4   Example Analyses

4.1   Dataset Introduction

This paper has chosen the Beijing shared bike data set from Kaggle platform, which has a vast amount of data (over 3.2 million) covering the period between May 10, 2017 and May 24, 2017. This data set records the order of shared bikes in Beijing, the capital of China, which is a super first-tier city. The selected data set of Beijing can effectively reflect some characteristics of shared bicycle orders, and it is also easy to analyze and process due to its large size. The data set includes fields such as orderid, userid, bikeid, biketype, starttime, start_loc, and end_loc, as shown in Table 2.

The starting and ending positions within this data are encoded using Geohash. Decoding these Geohashes yields the approximate latitude and longitude data.

To facilitate analysis and observation, the dataset is segmented according to time, resulting in 355 distinct hourly intervals over the course of the 14-day period. Location

Table 2. Labels of the data set

label	type	example
orderid	int	3454200
userid	int	81375
bikeid	int	356681
biketype	int	1
starttime	datetime	2017/5/14 22:17
geohashed_start_loc	String	wx4g15x
geohashed_end_loc	String	wx4g1ej

information is then extracted from the data. The OPTICS algorithm is applied to cluster the points and remove outliers, thereby revealing the primary usage areas for the bicycles.

The area under consideration was classified as urban and partitioned into a 50*50 raster grid to facilitate subsequent data analysis and processing.

4.2 Spatio-Temporal Characterisation of Demand for Shared Bike

Time Dimension Correlation Analysis
In order to analyze the data, one grid is randomly selected out of 2500 for visualization. This process obtains the weekly order situation of shared bikes, as shown in Fig. 1.

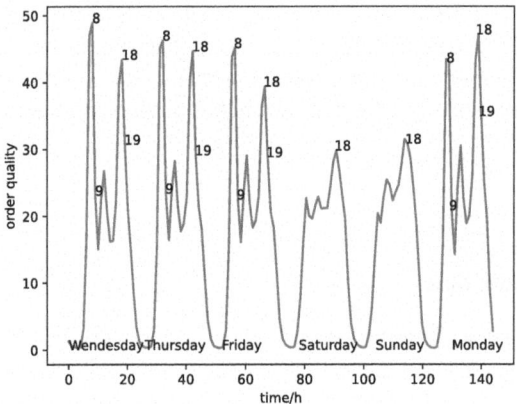

Fig. 1. One-week change in shared bike orders

Based on the time distribution, it is evident that the collected data exhibits a notable periodicity with a double hump trend, particularly at 8 am and 6 pm. However, it should be noted that the trend of the selected data is affected by rain interference on Saturdays and Sundays, resulting in a different pattern.

Spatial Dimension Correlation Analysis

During a certain period of time, the order data of all grids was randomly selected to create a thermal distribution diagram and perform spatial feature analysis, as seen in Fig. 2. The blue color represents bikes heading out while the red color represents bikes coming in. It is evident that the majority of orders were placed in the downtown area, while there were few orders in the outskirts. Additionally, it can be observed that the increase and decrease of bikes are adjacent and staggered, this means that bike flow is closely tied to the surrounding area.

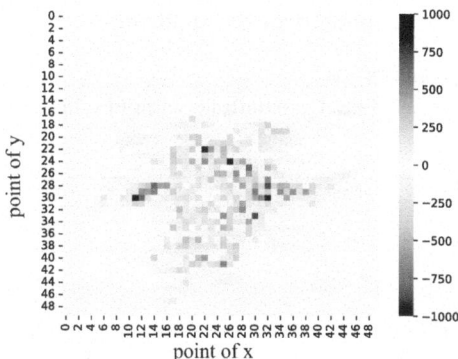

Fig. 2. Heat distribution of shared bike orders

T-GCN Model Predictions

We utilize the time series data in conjunction with the spatial adjacency matrix as our input data. Through the application of the Temporal Graph Convolutional Network (T-GCN) algorithm, we can derive more accurate predictions. After the appropriate.

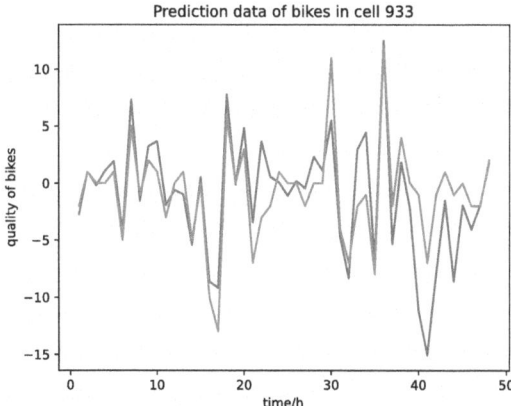

Fig. 3. Predicted results of changes in the number of bicycles in a given grid

preprocessing of the data, the resulting adjacency matrix and feature matrix are separately input into the model, producing the following predictive outcomes:

In Fig. 3, the orange curve represents the actual data while the blue curve depicts the predicted data. Observing the graph, we can deduce that the predicted data will also exhibit morning and evening demand peaks for one of the rasters in the selected area. The prediction results align reasonably well with the original data, suggesting a degree of reliability for both the chosen area and the predictions. The data predicted by this algorithm can be utilized in subsequent scheduling programs.

4.3   Red Packet Bike Scheduling Strategy Application

No Intervention Experiments
Calculate the image changes of the DemandRate without scheduling as follows (Fig. 4):

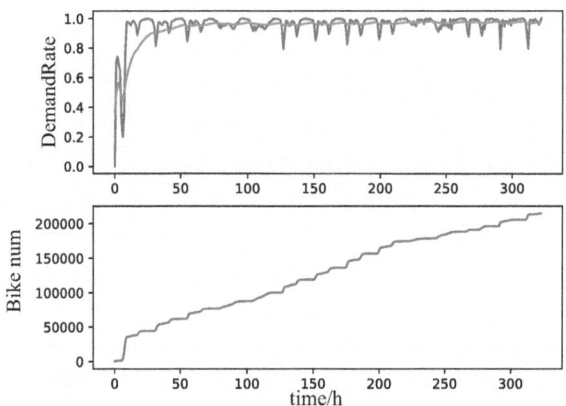

Fig. 4. Changes in DemandRate and number of bikes during natural migration

DemandRate intermittently plummeted to around 0.8, making it necessary to continuously introduce new bikes to meet user demand over this time period.

Simulation of Red Packet Bike Allocation Based on BFS

Programme Implemention
Considering the user's starting point as the center, and using demand and distance as measures, we recommend to the user both the starting and ending points where the value of the red packet can be maximized, as illustrated in Fig. 5.

In the Fig. 5, the green dot is the user's starting point, the darker the green means the more recommended this place is as the starting point, and the darker the red means the more recommended this place is as the end point. In this way, the user is provided with a variety of options to dispatch the bike and get the red packet, the user can view the red packet map when they want to use the shared bike and accordingly drive the car from the area with too many bikes to the area with too few bikes as much as possible. This allows the user to dispatch their own bikes.

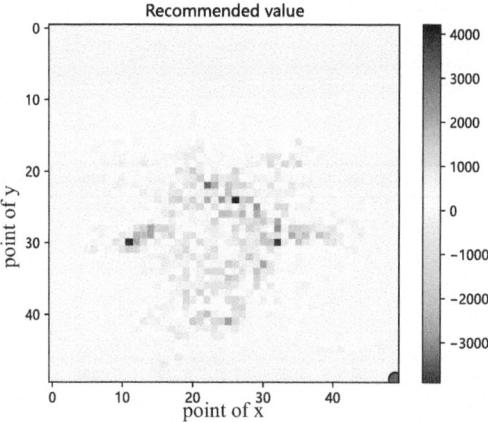

Fig. 5. Recommendation map of bike using by users of a certain grid

Results-Based Assessment

By employing the Manhattan distance as the distance metric for calculating the redPacket, , we obtain the following results after executing the above-described scheduling scheme (Figs. 6 and 7).

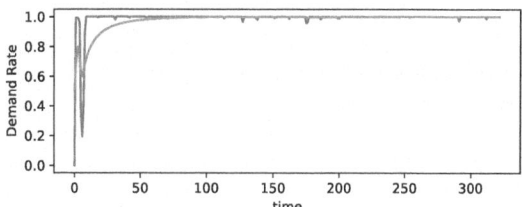

Fig. 6. *DemandRate* change curve after scheduling

After a certain period of time, the total demand for bikes decreases to approximately 40,000 and then stabilizes, all the while incurring continuous dispatch costs. Concurrently, the curve of DemandRate at 1 becomes smoother, resulting in a relatively high level of bike usage.

In practical applications, users can utilize the red packet car by receiving a discount on cycling or a direct red packet reward after successfully scheduling the bike. However, there are potential issues with this approach. For instance, some users may not want to use the red packet car method of scheduling and may choose unsuitable routes instead. Additionally, if the red packet is too large, some people may use it as a way to make money by riding the red packet car, which can be more expensive for the company than group scheduling of dispatch cars. If the red packet is too small, users may not find it worthwhile to use the red packet car. These practical concerns have yet to be addressed.

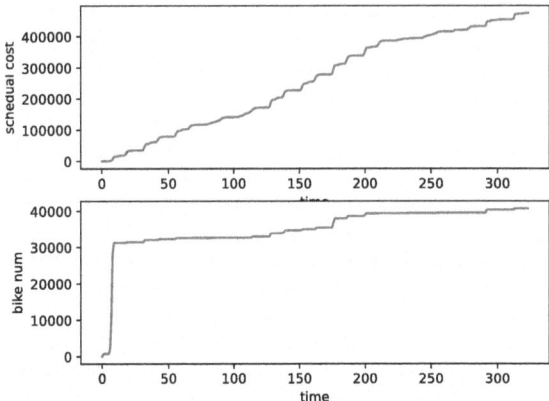

Fig. 7. Dispatch generation costs and changes in number of bikes

5 Conclusion

This paper focuses on the forecasting and scheduling of shared bicycles. The study uses a dataset from the Haidian District in Beijing, which is input as spatio-temporal data and analyzed using the T-GCN algorithm. The results are relatively accurate and effective. Additionally, the BFS algorithm is introduced to improve the utilization rate of bikes through the use of red packet cars for active scheduling of users. This helps to create a better environment for the use of shared bikes. However, there may be potential problems with this approach that require further investigation and analysis.

References

1. Zou, Y., Zhu, X., Zhang, Y., et al.: A space–time diurnal method for short-term freeway travel time prediction. Transp. Res. Part C Emerg. Technol. **43**, 33–49 (2014)
2. Kamarianakis, Y., Shen, W., Wynter, L.: Real-time road traffic forecasting using regime-switching space-time models and adaptive LASSO. Appl. Stoch. Model. Bus. Ind. **28**(4), 297–315 (2012)
3. Jia, X., Feng, C., Su, Z., et al.: Traffic prediction by Bi-LSTM for urban traffic grid clustering. J. Chongqing Univ., 1–14 (2023). http://kns.cnki.net/kcms/detail/50.1044.N.20230706.0952.002.html
4. Lin, L., He, Z., Peeta, S.: Predicting station-level hourly demand in a large-scale bikesharing network: a graph convolutional neural network approach. Transp. Res. Part C Emerg. Technol. **97**, 258–276 (2018)
5. Xingjian, Q.: Research on demand prediction of shared bicycle based on spatio-temporal dependence. East China Normal Univ. (2021). https://doi.org/10.27149/d.cnki.ghdsu.2021.000710
6. MIAO Xiaofeng,FAN Shurui,CAO Dandan et al. Demand prediction of shared bicycle stations based on LSTM and spatio-temporal combination[J]. Journal of Inner Mongolia University of Technology(Natural Science Edition), 2020,39(03):24–31.https://doi.org/10.13785/j.cnki.nmggydxxbzrkxb.2020.03.004
7. Shi, B., Huang, X., Song, Z., Xu, J.: User incentive based bike-sharing dispatching strategy. J. Comput. Appl. **42**(11), 3395–3403 (2022)

8. Xin-yu, L.I.U., Qun, C.H.E.N.: An optimization model for bike repositioning in bike-sharing systems considering both demands for borrowing or returning bikes and costs of repositioning operations. China J. Highw. Transp. **32**(7), 146–157 (2019)

9. Xu, H., Duan, F., Pu, P.: Dynamic bicycle scheduling problem based on short-term demand prediction. Appl. Intell. **49**, 1968–1981 (2019). https://doi.org/10.1007/s10489-018-1360-6

10. Zen, Q., Yang, S.: Research on dynamic scheduling of shared bicycles based on simulated annealing algorithm. J. Compr. Transp. **45**(02), 75–79 (2023)

11. Kadri, A.A.: Simulation and optimization models for scheduling and balancing the public bicycle-sharing systems. Other [cs.OH]. Université de Lorraine (2015). English. ⟨NNT : 2015LORR0268⟩. ⟨tel-01754554⟩

12. Caggiani, L., Camporeale, R., Ottomanelli, M., Szeto, W.Y.: A modeling framework for the dynamic management of free-floating bike-sharing systems. Transp. Res. Part C Emerg. Technol. **87**, 159–182 (2018). https://doi.org/10.1016/j.trc.2018.01.001

Peak Age of Information Optimization: CSMA Versus Aloha

Dewei Wu$^{(\boxtimes)}$, Wen Zhan, Xinghua Sun, and Jiyun Qiu

Shenzhen Campus of Sun Yat-sen University, Shenzhen, China
wudw5@mail2.sysu.edu.cn, {zhanw6,sunxinghua,qiujy8}@mail.sysu.edu.cn

Abstract. In this paper, we focus on the Peak Age-of-Information (PAoI) performance in Carrier Sense Multiple Access (CSMA) networks. Specifically, by assuming that sensors are equipped with unit-size buffers and the Bernoulli update process, the PAoI expression and the optimal access probability for minimizing PAoI are derived. A comparison between the optimal PAoI in CSMA and that in Aloha is presented, identifying the age performance in CSMA could be inferior to that in Aloha if the ratio of sensing time to packet length is high. The critical threshold in terms of this ratio is characterized, which is shown as a decreasing function of traffic arrival rate. It reveals that compared to CSMA, Aloha is a better choice in scenarios with large propagation delay and light traffic, such as low earth orbit mobile-satellite communications for Internet-of-Things services.

Keywords: Age of information · CSMA · Aloha

1 Introduction

With the rapid advancement of the Internet of Things (IoT), emerging IoT applications necessitate more stringent information timeliness requirements. In domains such as environmental monitoring, vehicular networking and intelligent healthcare, swift and accurate system responses are essential for enabling effective decision-making by servers [1]. In order to characterize information timeliness in wireless networks, the concept of Age-of-Information (AoI) was initially introduced in [2], which measures the time elapsed since the generation of the most recent successfully transmitted update. How to optimize AoI performance is vital for propelling networks towards heightened productivity.

As an elegant solution for multiple sensors to access a shared channel, Carrier Sense Multiple Access (CSMA), has been widely applied such as wireless ad-hoc networks and WiFi [3]. For the existing works of optimizing throughput or delay performance of CSMA, the design of optimal parameters has long been considered a challenging issue, since CSMA has the notorious bi-stability property similar to which in Aloha [4], i.e., the network may have two distinct steady operating points.

© ICST Institute for Computer Sciences, Social Informatics and Telecommunications Engineering 2025
Published by Springer Nature Switzerland AG 2025. All Rights Reserved
X. Chen et al. (Eds.): IoTaaS 2023, LNICST 585, pp. 436–450, 2025.
https://doi.org/10.1007/978-3-031-70507-6_33

In recent years, the AoI characterization and optimization of CSMA networks have garnered considerable attention [5–10]. The studies [5,6] focused on characterizing the average AoI performance in vehicular network scenarios under different assumptions. The paper [7] derived the closed form expression of the average AoI of a ultra dense IoT system in the presence of noisy channels by using the stochastic hybrid systems approach. The work [8] characterized the worst AoI of wireless sensor networks, revealing the necessity of tuning the contention window size to minimize AoI via numerical results. The work [9] minimized the AoI of CSMA-based ad-hoc networks by optimizing the back-off timer, while the study [10] focused on how to tune the channel attempt probability to optimize AoI performance. Note that studies [8–10] are based on the assumption that each node is always saturated by allowing dummy packets to be sent when the buffer is empty. Although this assumption simplifies the mathematical complexity, it inadvertently lowers the network performance ceiling, as dummy packets also compete for channel resources without contributing to AoI. Thus, how to exactly characterize and optimize the information timeliness in CSMA networks remains a worthwhile and critical issue.

Another representative random access protocol, Aloha permits sensors with non-empty buffers to access the channel with a specific probability at the beginning of each time slot without channel sensing [11]. In contrast, CSMA requires each sensor to sense the channel and transmit only if the channel is detected as idle. The analysis in [12] reveals that when packet length is small, the benefits of sensing may not necessarily outweigh the costs, and CSMA's access efficiency could be inferior to that of Aloha in terms of sum rate performance. In this paper, we are interested in the following issues: Does such a threshold exist in terms of age performance? If it exists, then how does this threshold vary with system parameters? We aim to address these open issues in CSMA networks by considering the metric termed Peak Age of Information (PAoI)[1] , which is defined as the maximum AoI achieved before a packet is received.

Our contributions can be summarized as follows:

- *PAoI characterization and optimization*: By leveraging the embedded Markov chain in [4], the explicit expression of PAoI in CSMA networks is derived, based on which PAoI is further minimized by properly tuning the access probability. Our analysis demonstrates that the minimum PAoI decreases with the mini-slot length and linearly increases with the number of sources when the network size is large.
- *Random access protocol comparison*: Based on our previous work [14] on Aloha protocol, we compare CSMA and Aloha regarding the optimal PAoI. It is found that CSMA outperforms Aloha only when the mini-slot length of CSMA falls below a critical threshold. This critical threshold decreases lin-

---

[1] The adoption of PAoI as an age metric stems from its stationary distribution, which can be conveniently characterized through established queueing theory techniques [13]. The insights gained from this analysis can also be leveraged to incorporate different age metrics, including the mean AoI.

early with the traffic arrival rate λ when the aggregate input rate $\hat{\lambda} < 0.48$; otherwise, it remains constant at 0.44.

The remaining parts of this paper are arranged as follows. The system model and preliminary analysis of bi-stable behavior are provided in Sect. 2. In Sect. 3.3, we derive PAoI and further minimize it by optimally tuning the channel access probability of each sensor. In Sect. 4, insights regarding the PAoI performance between CSMA and Aloha networks are provided. Summarizing findings are concluded in Sect. 5.

2   System Model and Problem Formulation

Consider a CSMA network consisting of n sensors and a public server. Each sensor has a unit-sized buffer and all the sensors are synchronized and can sense the channel to determine its availability. The packet arrivals obey the Bernoulli distribution with parameter λ the newly arrived packet may be dropped out when the buffer is full. With a non-empty buffer, the sensors will access the channel with probability q if the channel is idle. The packet is successfully transmitted only if there is no other concurrent transmission [15], and the packet in the buffer will keep being served until it is successfully transmitted.

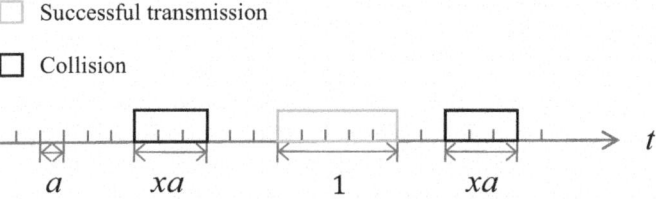

Fig. 1. Time slots in CSMA networks.

An illustration of the time slots in CSMA networks is presented in Fig. 1. Specifically, the time is divided into smaller mini-slots a, where the length a is the ratio of the propagation delay needed by each sensor for sensing the channel to the time required for packet transmission. Packets are transmitted over a noiseless channel and we assume each packet has the same size and that the transmission time required is one time slot. Suppose that the sensors can only start transmission at the start of the mini-slot, and it takes each sensor $0 \leq x \leq 1/a$ mini-slots to detect the collision and further abort the ongoing update transmission. In this paper, we assume $x = 1/a$, which indicates that the sensors are operating in the half-duplex mode and remain unaware of any collisions until the packet transmission is finished.

Let p denote the successful probability of each access. Note that a discrete-time Markov model for characterizing the Head-of-Line packets behavior in CSMA network has been established in [4]. By substituting the offered load given in Eq. (3) of [16] into the steady-state point equation given in Eq. (31) of [4], the successful transmission probability is obtained as

$$p = \exp\left(\frac{n\lambda q(1+a-p)}{\lambda(1+a-p+q)+qp}\right). \tag{1}$$

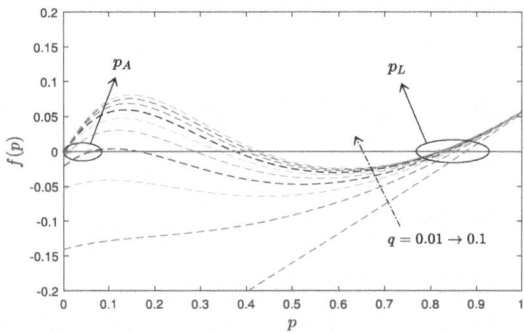

Fig. 2. Roots of (1). The intersection points of the solid line and the dashed line represent the steady-state points p_L and p_A. $n = 100$, $\lambda = 0.006$, $a = 0.1$, q is from 0.01 to 0.1 with step length 0.01.

It is clear that p is determined by the number of sensors n, the access probability q, the mini-slot length a and the traffic arrival rate λ. For illustration, we construct $f(p) = p - \exp\left(\frac{n\lambda q(1+a-p)}{\lambda(1+a-p+q)+qp}\right)$, and $f(p) = 0$ has the same roots as (1). The numerical results are presented in Fig. 2. It reveals that (1) has either one root p_L or three roots $0 < p_A < p_S < p_L < 1$, where p_A is the undesired steady-state point, p_L is the desired steady-state point and p_S is the unstable point [4]. Depending on the number of steady-state points, we can define the stable region as below:

– **Bi-stable region** $\mathcal{B} = \{(n, q, \lambda, a) |$ The CSMA network has two steady-state points, p_A and $p_L\}$.
– **Mono-stable region** $\mathcal{M} = \{(n, q, \lambda, a) |$ The CSMA network has one steady-state point $p_L\}$.

The network stays either at the mono-stable region $\mathcal{M}$ or the bi-stable region $\mathcal{B}$. It has long been observed that in $\mathcal{B}$, the network may drop from p_L to the undesired point p_A in an unpredictable way, leading to intolerable poor performance since $p_A \ll p_L$ [4]. Therefore, the network should stay in $\mathcal{M}$ for avoiding the dropping risk. Under this consideration, our target is minimizing the PAoI

A by the optimal configuration of access probability q given the network scale n, the input rate λ and the mini-slot length a, i.e.,

$$A^* = \min_{0 < q \leq 1} A,$$
$$\text{s. t. } \{n, q, \lambda, a\} \in \mathcal{M}. \tag{2}$$

3 Peak Age of Information Optimization

This section aims to optimize the PAoI in CSMA networks. We will start by deriving the explicit expression of the PAoI in CSMA networks.

3.1 PAoI Analysis

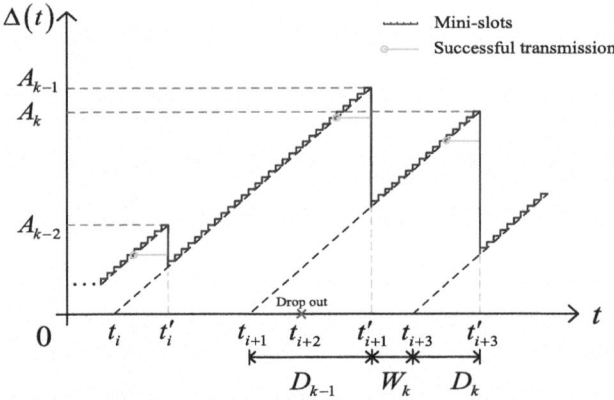

Fig. 3. AoI trace in a CSMA network with the mini-slot length $a = 0.2$.

A graphical illustration of the AoI evolution over time is presented in Fig. 3. The time instances at which each packet arrives and is successfully transmitted are denoted by t_i and t'_i respectively, $i \in \{1, 2, \ldots\}$. Only successfully transmitted packets are marked in the figure. Each transmission takes 5 mini-slots, as determined by $a = 0.2$. It can be seen from Fig. 3 that the AoI $\Delta(t)$ increases over time, and $\Delta(t)$ decreases to $t - u(t)$ if and only if an update has been received by the server, where $u(t) = \max\{t_i | 0 < t'_i < t\}$ and $t \in \{1, 2, \cdots\}$. Note that some packets are discarded because of the limited size of the buffer, such as the packet arrived at t_{i+2}. To avoid ambiguity, we take k to denote the index of informative packets that determine the PAoI [17, 18].

The PAoI A_k, which is defined as the AoI achieved immediately before receiving the kth packet, is shown in Fig. 3. The average PAoI can be expressed as $A \triangleq \lim_{T \to \infty} \sup \frac{\sum_{t=1}^{T} \Delta(t) \mathbf{1}\{\Delta(t+1) \leq \Delta(t)\}}{\sum_{t=1}^{T} \mathbf{1}\{\Delta(t+1) \leq \Delta(t)\}}$ [19]. The informative packets are those that arrive when the buffer is empty such as the ith, $i+1^{th}$, and $i+3^{th}$ packets illustrated in Fig. 3. Accordingly, following the kth packet reception, the PAoI A_k can be expressed as

$$A_k = D_{k-1} + W_k + D_k, \tag{3}$$

where

- D_k represents the access delay, which is the duration from the first packet to arrive after the successful transmission of the $k-1^{th}$ packet until to the kth packet. The mean access delay is given by [4]

$$E[D_k] = \frac{1}{p} + \frac{1+a-p}{qp}. \tag{4}$$

- W_k represents the idle period, the duration from the successful transmission of $k-1^{th}$ packet to the arrival of a new one. Note that the packet arrival rate in each mini-slot a is given by $a\lambda$, so that the idle period is obtained by

$$E[W_k] = \frac{1}{a\lambda} \cdot a = \frac{1}{\lambda}. \tag{5}$$

As W_k and D_k are independent and identically distributed random variables, we have $E[D_{k-1}] = E[D_k]$. By further combining (3)–(5), the average PAoI in CSMA networks can be expressed as

$$A = \frac{1}{\lambda} + \frac{2}{p} - \frac{2}{q} + \frac{2(1+a)}{qp}. \tag{6}$$

3.2   PAoI Optimization

The following lemma shows the optimal configuration of access probability for PAoI minimization on the condition of network state $p = p_L$.

Lemma 1. *With $p = p_L$, the optimal channel access probability for PAoI minimization is given by*

$$q_M = \begin{cases} \dfrac{\lambda(1+a)\left(1+\mathbb{W}_0\left(\frac{-e^{-1}}{1+a}\right)\right)}{(1+a)\left(n\lambda+\mathbb{W}_0\left(\frac{-e^{-1}}{1+a}\right)\right)-\lambda}, & \text{if } n > \frac{\lambda(2+a-p')+p'}{\lambda(1+a)}, \\ 1, & \text{otherwise,} \end{cases} \tag{7}$$

where $\mathbb{W}_0(\cdot)$ is the principal branch of the Lambert W function and p' is the steady-state point in (1) with $q = 1$.

Proof. See Appendix A.

Lemma 1 presents the optimal access probability when the network operates at the desired steady-state point p_L. As discussed in Sect. 2, if the network stays in the bi-stable region, then it may not stay at p_L and drop to the undesired steady-state point p_A. To avoid this risk, the optimal access probability for minimizing PAoI with $\{n, q, \lambda, a\} \in \mathcal{M}$ is given by Theorem 1.

Theorem 1. *For minimizing the PAoI of CSMA networks, the optimal channel access probability is given by*

$$q^* = \begin{cases} \dfrac{\lambda(1+a)\left(1+W_0\left(\frac{-e^{-1}}{1+a}\right)\right)}{(1+a)\left(n\lambda+W_0\left(\frac{-e^{-1}}{1+a}\right)\right)-\lambda}, & \lambda > \lambda_0, \\[2em] q_B, & otherwise, \end{cases} \tag{8}$$

where q_B is the non-zero root of the equation (9) and λ_0 is the non-zero root of equation $q_B = \dfrac{\lambda(1+a)\left(1+W_0\left(\frac{-e^{-1}}{1+a}\right)\right)}{(1+a)\left(n\lambda+W_0\left(\frac{-e^{-1}}{1+a}\right)\right)-\lambda}$,

$$\ln\left(\frac{n\lambda q_B^2(1+a+\lambda)}{(q_B-\lambda)^2}\left(\frac{1}{2}-\mu-\sqrt{\frac{1}{4}-\mu}\right)\right) = \frac{n\lambda q_B}{q_B-\lambda} - \frac{1}{\frac{1}{2}-\sqrt{\frac{1}{4}-\mu}}, \tag{9}$$

where $\mu = \frac{(q_B-\lambda)(1+a+q_B)}{nq_B^2(1+a+\lambda)}$.

Proof. See Appendix B.

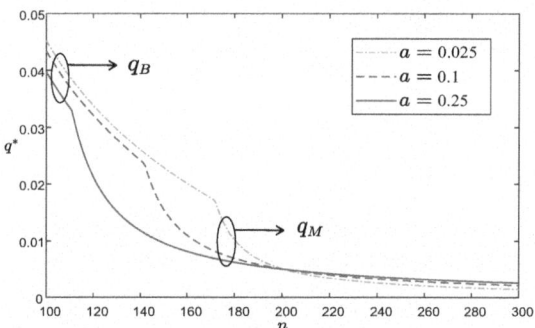

Fig. 4. Optimal channel access probability q^* versus the number of sensors n, $\lambda = 0.005$, $a = 0.025, 0.1$ or 0.25.

By comparing Lemma 1 and Theorem 1, we see that when the packet arrival rate λ is large, the network operates at $p = p_L$ and the optimal solution is obtained according to Lemma 1. Otherwise, the network may fall into the bistable region $\mathcal{B}$ and operate at $p = p_A$. In such case, Theorem 1 points out that the access probability should be set to the region boundary given by (9), with which the CSMA network can minimize PAoI while operating at $p = p_L$. Fig. 4 depicts how the optimal access probability q^* varies with the network scale with the mini-slot length $a = 0.025, 0.1$ or 0.25. We can see that q^* decreases with the network size n. By virtue of a stronger capability of detecting channel collision, i.e., a smaller a, each sensor can take an aggressive transmission strategy with a larger q if the network size is small. When n is large, we have $n\lambda > 1$, i.e., almost all sensors in the network have a non-empty buffer and are always listening to the channel to prepare for packet transmission. In this case, a smaller a for a certain channel idle time means more chances for making transmission decisions, therefore q^* for each mini-slot decreases slightly as a decreases to improve the successful transmission probability.

3.3   Simulation Results

Simulations are conducted to verify the above analysis. The simulation settings are identical to the system model and therefore, the details are omitted here.

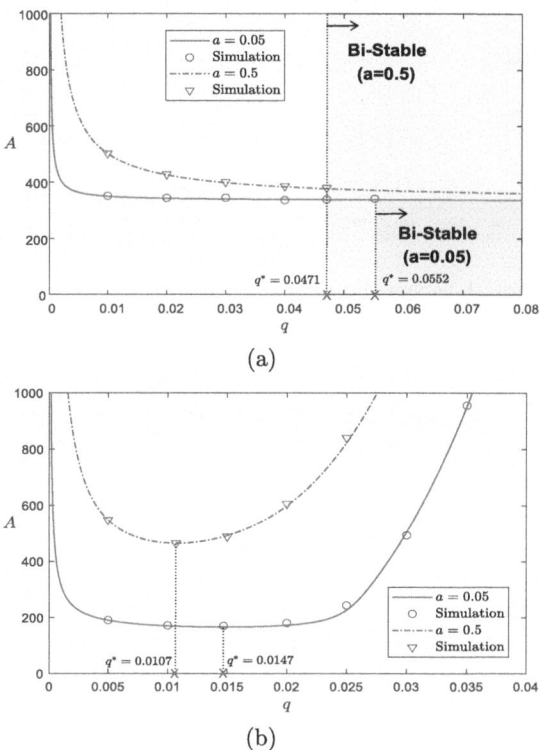

(a)

(b)

Fig. 5. PAoI A versus the channel access probability q, $n = 100$, $a = 0.05$ or 0.5. (a) $\lambda = 0.003$. (b) $\lambda = 0.009$.

Fig. 5 illustrates how the PAoI A varies with the access probability with the mini-slot length $a \in \{0.05, 0.5\}$. The packet arrival rate is set to $\lambda = 0.003$ in Fig. 5a and $\lambda = 0.009$ in Fig. 5b. It can be observed from Fig. 5a that the PAoI A decreases as the channel access probability increase before the network falls into $\mathcal{B}$. However, the channel access probability should not exceed a certain threshold to prevent the network from falling into the bi-stable region, where the network performance is unacceptable as we have discussed in Sect. 2. In addition, it can be seen that with a smaller mini-slot length a, the optimal channel access probability is higher and the corresponding minimum PAoI is also lower. A similar trend can also be observed in Fig. 5b. With $\lambda = 0.009$, the network stays in $\mathcal{M}$ and the PAoI is minimized with $q = q^*$. The minimum PAoI can further be reduced with a smaller mini-slot length a since the source can quickly sense the channel state and make transmission decisions accordingly.

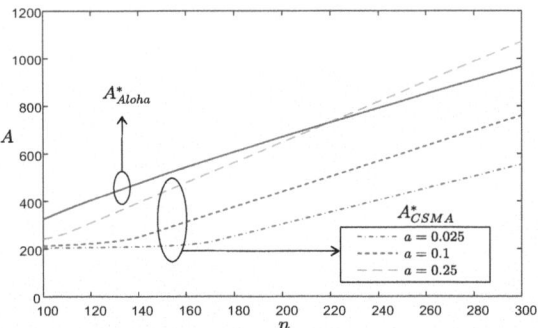

Fig. 6. Optimal PAoI A versus the number of sensors n, $q = q^*$, $\lambda = 0.005$, $a = 0.025, 0.1$ or 0.25.

4   Minimum PAoI Comparison: CSMA Versus Aloha

So far, we have demonstrated how to tune the channel access probability for minimizing the PAoI in CSMA network. Note that another representative random access scheme, Aloha, also has drawn wide attention on age performance evaluation [20]. In contrast to CSMA, where each sensor senses the channel first and transmission happens only when the channel is idle, with Aloha, each sensor transmits if there is a request. In this section, we compare CSMA and Aloha from the view of minimum PAoI.

In our previous study [14], we evaluated and optimized PAoI of Aloha networks, where the following theorem was obtained on the optimal tuning of backoff parameters.

Theorem 2. *For minimizing the PAoI of Aloha networks, the optimal channel access probability is given by*

$$q^*_{Aloha} = \begin{cases} \dfrac{\lambda}{n\lambda - e^{-1}} & \lambda > \dfrac{\hat{\lambda}_0}{n}, \\[3mm] \dfrac{4\mathbb{W}^2_{-1}(-\frac{\sqrt{n\lambda}}{2})}{n(-2\mathbb{W}_{-1}(-\frac{\sqrt{n\lambda}}{2})-1)} & otherwise, \end{cases} \tag{10}$$

where $\hat{\lambda}_0 \approx 0.48$ and $\mathbb{W}_{-1}(\cdot)$ is the secondary branch of Lambert W function.

Proof. The proof is presented in [14].

To avoid ambiguity, let us denote the minimum PAoI of CSMA as A^*_{CSMA} and that of Aloha as A^*_{Aloha}. Fig. 6 shows how the minimum PAoI varies with n with the mini-slot length $a \in \{0.025, 0.1, 0.25\}$. It can be seen that a smaller mini-slot length a results in a lower A^*_{CSMA}. While both A^*_{CSMA} and A^*_{Aloha} increases with the network size n, especially when n is large. The use of carrier sensing has long been believed to greatly improve access efficiency. Yet, a closer look at A^*_{CSMA} with $a = 0.25$ suggests that when the network scale is large, the age performance of CSMA is inferior to that of Aloha, i.e., $A^*_{CSMA} > A^*_{Aloha}$.

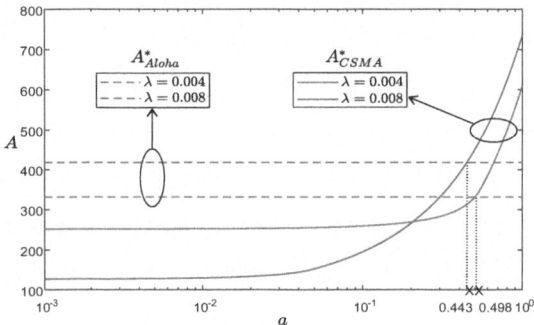

Fig. 7. PAoI A versus the mini-slot length a, $q = q^*$, $n = 100$, $\lambda = 0.004$ or 0.008.

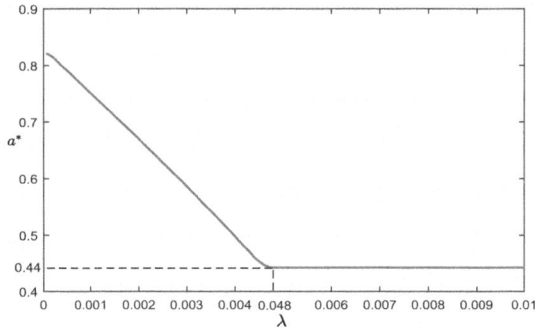

Fig. 8. Mini-slot threshold of PAoI a^* versus the packet arrival rate λ, $q = q^*$, $n = 100$.

Similar observations can also be found in Fig. 7, which illustrates how the minimum PAoI varies with the mini-slot length a and $\lambda = 0.004$ or 0.008. The PAoI in Aloha A^*_{Aloha} remains constant since there is no carrier sensing before transmission. The PAoI in CSMA A^*_{CSMA} is lower for larger arrival rate λ when mini-slot length a is small. It is because more sources have packets to be sent instead of waiting for fresh ones passively. It is clear that with a smaller mini-slot length a, the sensors sense the channel more frequently, which can help to avoid collision and improve the PAoI performance in CSMA networks. Yet, once more, we observe that as a increases, $A^*_{CSMA}|_{\lambda=0.004}$ outperforms $A^*_{CSMA}|_{\lambda=0.008}$ due to the negative impact of excessive channel listening overhead on network performance when a majority of sources with packets participating in contention. Furthermore, A^*_{CSMA} grows as well and finally $A^*_{CSMA} > A^*_{Aloha}$. It indicates that when the mini-slot length is large, CSMA is inferior to Aloha because the sources will experience excessive overhead in terms of channel sensing.

Let us define a critical threshold in terms of the mini-slot length a as a^*, above which $A^*_{CSMA} > A^*_{Aloha}$. Via numerical calculation according to (6) and (8) in this paper, and (10) in [14], Fig. 8 depicts how this critical threshold a^* varies with the input rate λ. It can be observed that when $\lambda > 0.048$, the critical threshold a^* is constant at 0.44 because each sensor usually has a non-empty buffer, with which the effect of λ is trivial. While, if $\lambda < 0.048$, we have $\lambda < \frac{\lambda_0}{n}$, and the optimal access probability in Theorem 2 should be adaptively tuned according to λ, with which the critical threshold a^* decreases as the input rate λ grows.

The above discussion sheds important light on practical system design. Specifically, the length of mini slots is determined by the ratio of the sensing time to the packet length, which is often limited by the propagation delay. Our analysis indicates that the benefit of sensing in CSMA is significant only for the wireless network with sufficiently small propagation delays. Yet, for non-terrestrial networks, such as low earth orbit mobile-satellite communications, where the propagation delay is expected to be large, Aloha may be a more suitable multiple access protocol than CSMA in terms of PAoI performance.

5   Conclusion

This paper presents the PAoI analysis in CSMA networks. By characterizing the steady-state points and PAoI, we derive the optimal access probability for minimizing PAoI, taking into account the bi-stability of CSMA. Furthermore, we compare the minimum PAoI in Aloha and CSMA, demonstrating that the advantage of CSMA networks is more pronounced with a smaller mini-slot length a. Specifically, there exists a critical threshold for a, where Aloha and CSMA networks exhibit the same optimal PAoI performance. Our analysis reveals that the benefit of carrier sensing for PAoI exists only when the propagation delay is small, whereas in applications with high propagation delay, such as non-terrestrial communication, Aloha may be a more suitable protocol.

It should be noted that this paper focuses on the PAoI optimization of CSMA networks based on Bernoulli packet arrival. Future work may explore optimizing PAoI with different traffic models and packet management, and explore how jointly tuning traffic rate and channel access probability to achieve better PAoI performance.

Acknowledgement. The work of W. Zhan was supported in part by The Shenzhen Science and Technology Program (No. RCBS20210706092408010), in part by National

Natural Science Foundation of China under Grant 62001524. The work of X. Sun was supported by Guangdong Basic and Applied Basic Research Foundation under Grant 2024A1515012015.

A   Proof of Lemma 1

According to (1) and (6), we have

$$
\frac{\partial A}{\partial q} = \frac{-2}{q^2 p^2} \left(\frac{-n\lambda^2 pq(1 + a + q)\zeta^2}{(pq + \lambda(\zeta + q))^2 - n\lambda pq^2(1 + a + \lambda)} + p\zeta \right). \tag{11}
$$

where $\zeta = 1 + a - p$. It can be further obtained that $\lim_{q \to 0^+} \frac{\partial A}{\partial q} < 0$. When $n > \frac{\lambda(2 + a - p') + p'}{\lambda(1 + a)}$, we have $\lim_{q \to 1} \frac{\partial A}{\partial q} > 0$ and the PAoI can be optimized by $q_M \in (0, 1)$, where p' is the steady-state point obtained by substituting $q = 1$ in (1) and the optimal access probability q_M can be derived by solving $\frac{\partial A}{\partial q} = 0$ that

$$
q_M = \frac{\lambda(1 + a - p_t)}{n\lambda(1 + a) - \lambda - p_t}, \tag{12}
$$

where $p_t = \exp\left(\frac{p_t}{1+a} - 1\right)$. Otherwise, we have $\frac{\partial A}{\partial q} < 0$ for $q \in (0, 1]$, and the channel access probability is given by $q = 1$. Finally, (7) is obtained by levering the Lambert W function and combing the above analysis.

B   Proof of Theorem 1

The CSMA network region is illustrated in Fig. 9, which shares the bi-stable property in Aloha [4,21]. It is clear that the optimal access probability q_M of (7), is included in the mono-stable region if and only if the packet arrival rate is high enough that $\lambda > \lambda_0$, where λ_0 is the intersection point of q_M and the bi-stable region boundary. Otherwise, the condition of $p = p_L$ does not hold. According to (7), we have

$$
\arg\min_q A|_{\lambda > \lambda_0} = \frac{\lambda(1 + a)\left(1 + \mathbb{W}_0\left(\frac{-e^{-1}}{1+a}\right)\right)}{(1 + a)\left(n\lambda + \mathbb{W}_0\left(\frac{-e^{-1}}{1+a}\right)\right) - \lambda}. \tag{13}
$$

When $\lambda < \lambda_0$, the access probability q_M will cause the network to fall into $\mathcal{B}$ and the network performance may degenerate sharply over time [4]. Fig. 10 illustrates the PAoI in different regions, which can be observed that the PAoI with the undesired point p_A is intolerable high since the successful transmission probability $p = p_A$ is far lower than that with $p = p_L$ as Fig. 2 illustrated. The PAoI decreases with q before the network shifts to bi-stable region $\mathcal{B}$. In such case, q^* is the critical value before the network falls in $\mathcal{B}$, which we mark as q_B and we have

$$\arg\min_{q} A|_{\lambda \leq \lambda_0} = q_B. \tag{14}$$

The following analysis we focus on how to solve this critical value q_B. Based on (1), let

$$f_1(p) = -ln(p) - \frac{M}{N+p}, \tag{15}$$

where

$$M = \frac{n\lambda q^2(1+a+\lambda)}{(q-\lambda)^2}, N = \frac{\lambda(1+a+q)}{q-\lambda}. \tag{16}$$

Since $f_1(p) = 0$ is equivalent to (1), it can be utilized to analyze the number of roots. We can obtain the first derivative of $f_1(p)$ about p with respect to p as

$$f_1'(p) = \frac{g(p)}{p(N+p)^2}, \tag{17}$$

where $g(p) = -(p+N-\frac{M}{2})^2 + \frac{M^2}{4} - MN$.

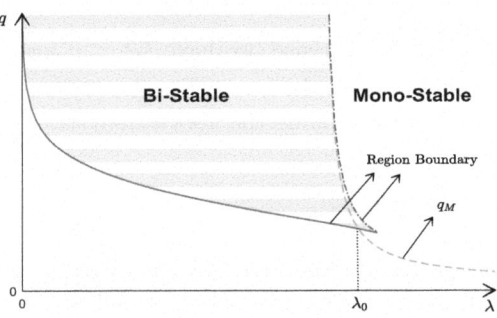

Fig. 9. The CSMA network region illustration.

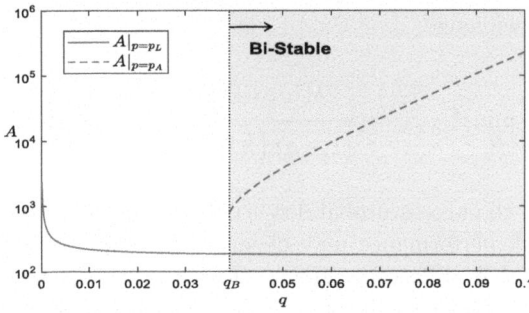

Fig. 10. PAoI performance at two distinct points p_L and p_A.

Note that $g(p)$ has the same form as Eq. (27) in [19] so we omit the root analysis in Appendix B of [19] due to the limited page. Another branch of the optimal access probability q_B, which is the boundary between the regions $\mathcal{M}$ and $\mathcal{B}$, can be expressed as $f_1(p_1') = 0$, where p_1' is given by Eq. (29) in [19]. By combing (15), (16), q_B can be simplified as (9). Finally, the optimal channel access probability can be obtained by combining (7), (9) , (13) and (14).

References

1. Guo, C., Wang, X., Liang, L., Li, G.Y.: Age of information, latency, and reliability in intelligent vehicular networks. IEEE Net., Early Access. (2022). https://doi.org/10.1109/MNET.124.2200132
2. Kaul, S., Yates, R., Gruteser, M.: Real-time status: how often should one update? In: Proc. IEEE INFOCOM (2012)
3. Part 11: Wireless LAN Medium Access Control (MAC) Physics Layer 1033 (PHY) Specifications, Standard 802.11–2012 (2012)
4. Dai, L.: Toward a coherent theory of csma and aloha. IEEE Trans. Wirel. Commun. **12**(7), 3428–3444 (2013)
5. Kaul, S., Gruteser, M., Rai, V., Kenney, J.: Minimizing age of information in vehicular networks. In: Proc. 8th Annu. IEEE Commun. Soc. Conf. Sensor, Mesh Ad Hoc Commun. Netw, pp. 350–358 (2011)
6. Baiocchi, A., Turcanu, I.: Age of information of one-hop broadcast communications in a CSMA network. IEEE Commun. Lett. **25**(1), 294–298 (2021)
7. Zhou, B., Saad, W.: Performance analysis of age of information in ultra-dense internet of things systems with noisy channels. IEEE Trans. Wirel. Commun. **21**(5), 3493–3507 (2022)
8. Moltafet, M., Leinonen, M., Codreanu, M.: Worst case age of information in wireless sensor networks: a multi-access channel. IEEE Wirel. Commun. Lett. **9**(3), 321–325 (2020)
9. Maatouk, A., Assaad, M., Ephremides, A.: On the age of information in a CSMA environment. IEEE/ACM Trans. Netw. **28**(2), 818–831 (2020)
10. Wu, Y., Wu, S., Zhang, L., Jiao, J., Zhang, N., Zhang, Q.: Random access with and without sensing in non-terrestrial networks for timely updates. In: Proc. IEEE Int. Conf. Commun. (ICC), pp. 1–6 (2021)
11. Sun, X., Zhan, W., Liu, W., Li, Y., Liu, Q.: Sum rate and access delay optimization of short-packet aloha. IEEE Open J. Commun. Soc. **3**, 1501–1514 (2022)
12. Sun, X., Dai, L.: To sense or not to sense: a comparative study of CSMA with Aloha. IEEE Trans. Commun. **67**(11), 7587–7603 (2019)
13. Inoue, Y., Masuyama, H., Takine, T., Tanaka, T.: A general formula for the stationary distribution of the age of information and its application to single-server queues. IEEE Trans. Inf. Theory **65**(12), 8305–8324 (2019)
14. Wu, D., Zhan, W., Sun, X., Zhou, B., Liu, J.: Peak age of information optimization of slotted Aloha. In: Proc. IEEE 96th Veh. Technol. Conf. (VTC-Fall), pp. 1–7 (2022)
15. Chen, X., Gatsis, K., Hassani, H., Bidokhti, S.S.: Age of information in random access channels. IEEE Trans. Inf. Theory **68**(10), 6548–6568 (2022)
16. Zhan, W., Dai, L.: Massive random access of machine-to-machine communications in LTE networks: modeling and throughput optimization. IEEE Trans. Wirel. Commun. **17**(4), 2771–2785 (2018)

17. Maatouk, A., Kriouile, S., Assaad, M., Ephremides, A.: The age of incorrect information: a new performance metric for status updates. IEEE/ACM Trans. Netw. **28**(5), 2215–2228 (2020)
18. Yatesp, R.D., Sun, Y., Brown, D.R., III., Kaul, S.K., Modiano, E., Ulukus, S.: Age of information: an introduction and survey. IEEE J. Sel. Area Comm. **39**(5), 1183–1210 (2021)
19. Sun, X., Zhao, F., Yang, H.H., Zhan, W., Wang, X., Quek, T.Q.S.: Optimizing age of information in random-access poisson networks. IEEE Internet Things J. **9**(9), 6816–6829 (2022)
20. Zhan, W., Wu, D., Sun, X., Guo, Z., Liu, P., Liu, J.: Peak age of information optimization of slotted aloha: FCFS versus LCFS. IEEE Trans. Netw. Sci. Eng., Early Access (2023). https://doi.org/10.1109/TNSE.2023.3272360
21. Zhan, W., Dai, L.: Access delay optimization of M2M communications in LTE networks. IEEE Wireless Commun. Lett. **8**(6), 1675–1678 (2019)

Author Index

SPRINGER NATURE

GPSR Compliance

The European Union's (EU) General Product Safety Regulation (GPSR) is a set of rules that requires consumer products to be safe and our obligations to ensure this.

If you have any concerns about our products, you can contact us on ProductSafety@springernature.com

In case Publisher is established outside the EU, the EU authorized representative is:

Springer Nature Customer Service Center GmbH
Europaplatz 3
69115 Heidelberg, Germany

The manufacturer's authorised representative in the EU is Springer
Nature Customer Service Centre GmbH, Europaplatz 3, 69115 Heidelberg,
Germany. If you have any concerns regarding our products, please
contact ProductSafety@springernature.com

Printed and bound by CPI Group (UK) Ltd, Croydon, CR0 4YY
27/04/2026
02097845-0009